William Gilmore Simms

Vasconselos

a Romance of the New World

William Gilmore Simms

Vasconselos
a Romance of the New World

ISBN/EAN: 9783743305427

Manufactured in Europe, USA, Canada, Australia, Japa

Cover: Foto ©Thomas Meinert / pixelio.de

Manufactured and distributed by brebook publishing software (www.brebook.com)

William Gilmore Simms

Vasconselos

VASCONSELOS.

CHAPTER I.

> "Nature did Design us to be warriors, and to break through our ring, the sea, by which we are environed; and we, by force, must fetch in what is wanting, or precious to us."
>
> MASSINGER.

It is the province of romance, even more decidedly than history, to recall the deeds and adventures of the past. It is to fiction that we must chiefly look for those living and breathing creations which history quite too unfrequently deigns to summon to her service. The warm atmosphere of present emotions, and present purposes, belongs to the *dramatis personæ* of art; and she is never so well satisfied in showing us human performances, as when she betrays the passions and affections by which they were dictated and endured. It is in spells and possessions of this character, that she so commonly supersedes the sterner muse whose province she so frequently invades; and her offices are not the less legitimate, as regards the truthfulness of things in general, than are those of history, because she supplies those details which the latter, unwisely as we think, but too commonly, holds beneath her regard. In the work before us, however, it is our purpose to slight neither agency. We shall defer to each of them, in turn, as they may be made to serve a common purpose. They both appeal to our assistance, and equally spread their possessions beneath our eyes. We shall employ, without violating, the *material resources* of the Historian, while seeking to endow

them with a vitality which fiction only can confer. [...]
suit of this object that we entreat the reader to suppo[se...]
ward curtain withdrawn, unveiling, if only for a m[...]
aspects of a period not so remote as to lie wholly b[eyond our]
sympathies. We propose to look back to that dawn o[f the six-]
teenth century; at all events, to such a portion of the [...]
landscape of that period, as to show us some of the f[irst ...]
gleams of European light upon the savage dominio[ns of the]
Western Continent. To review this epoch is, in fact, [...]
the small but impressive beginnings of a wondrous [drama in]
which we, ourselves, are still living actors. The scene [...]
within our grasp. The names of the persons of our [...]
have not yet ceased from sounding in our ears; and t[he ...]
of performance is one, the boards of which, even at thi[s ...]
are echoing beneath their mighty footsteps. Our cu[rious]
interest may well be awakened for awhile, to an action[s...]
of which, in some degree, are inuring to our present b[...]

It is just three hundred years, since, in the spring s[eason of the]
year of Grace, one thousand five hundred and thirty[...]
infant city of Havana resounded with the tread of [the]
noblest bodies of Spanish chivalry that ever set foot in [the west-]
ern hemisphere. That gay and gallant cavalier, He[rnan de]
Soto—equally the courtier and the soldier—having w[on]
no less than fame, under Francis Pizarro in Peru, h[ad re-]
solved upon an independent enterprise, in another reg[ion of ...]
self. This enterprise, in the extravagant expectatio[ns of the]
period, promised to be of even more magnificent r[esults than]
those of his great predecessor and companion, al[ready distin-]
guished by his sovereign as the Adelantado of Florid[a.]

Florida—that wondrous *terra incognita*, which, f[or a long]
time, led the European imagination astray—our amb[itious cava-]
lier was now busied in making the grandest prepa[rations for its]
conquest. A thousand soldiers, many of whom [were of the]
noblest blood of Spain and Portugal, had assemble[d ...]
for this enterprise, swelling his train with a strengt[h ...]
ised to make certain all his anticipations. More [...]

of this brilliant force—for such it was, if we compare it with the small and ill-organized bands which were usually deemed sufficient for the conflict with the Indian races of America—consisted of cavalry;—belted knights, brave soldiers, already practised in the wars of Mexico and Peru, and young, hopeful gallants, of high blood, who had their fortunes to make, and who had expended the last remains of their patrimony in the decorations, for this enterprise, of their steeds and persons. The rest were stout bowmen and arquebusiers,—men of tough sinews, and morals quite as tough—rude, sturdy, desperate, in doublets of quilted cotton, which were only not quite impenetrable to an Indian arrow. Well might the ambitious spirit of Hernando de Soto become confident of success as he reviewed his squadrons. Their numbers, their manly vigor, their ardent enthusiasm, the splendor of their armor, the admirable horsemanship of his cavaliers—all tended to assure him of his future triumphs; neither Cortez nor Pizarro had been half so fortunate in such an equipment; and our adelantado, as he surveyed his forces, became impatient of the hour when he should dart upon the conquest which he already regarded as secure. Compelled, however, to await the tardy process of getting ships and stores in readiness, he enlivened the interval of delay, by exercising his gallants in all the military and social amusements in which they took delight. While in Cuba, moved by the policy of winning to his banner the wealth and enterprise of the island, he cheerfully encouraged his knights and captains to engage in all those exercises of chivalry which could possibly beguile the affections of the people. The days were accordingly consumed in tilts and tournaments, bull-fights, and other manly sports. The nights were yielded to balls and masquerades, in which the victor of the morning but too commonly found himself vanquished by the feeblest as well as fairest of his foes. The Spaniard, naturally a person of parade and pomp, but too frequently sacrificed the substance of a life to the shadow which his fancy loved. The resources of an entire household were sometimes exhausted in making gay the greener hours of its young cadet. Beauty necessarily strove, with equal fervor, to render her taste and treasure appropriate auxiliaries to her natural charms; and thus it was that the brief interval during which our adventurers lingered in the island, after reaching it from Spain, passed like a dream of enchantment—one of those fairy tales of pleasure that we read of in the romances of Arabia. But the time was fast approaching when these gay scenes of pleasure—the relaxations and the mimicry of war—were to give place to its absolute and hard realities. The arrangements of our adelantado were at length nearly completed. The ships had taken in most of their stores, and two of them had been already dispatched with the view to a better exploration of the coast of Florida, and in search of a fitting harbor for the descent of the armament. But a few weeks—perhaps days—would elapse, and the little city would sink into its ancient dullness and repose. The sad thought of separation from such delights as had been enjoyed by all parties, could only be dissipated by renewed efforts at enjoyment. Gloomy reflections were only to be banished by fresh indulgences; and, duly, as the time lessened for delay, the plans and schemes for pleasure were hurriedly increased. The young damsels of Cuba put forth all their attractions to arrest the fugitive hearts whose heroic influences had but too much touched their own; and more than one brave cavalier was found to hesitate as the time drew nigh for his departure. His imagination painfully contrasted the pleasures which he enjoyed, with the toils and perils which were in prospect. Care and anxiety naturally followed such comparisons; and, though the sports of the island were not forborne until the armament had fairly taken its departure, yet were they felt to be more or less deeply shadowed by the consciousness of the change which was at hand. The song was growing much less lively than at first—the tinkle of the guitar less frequent and merry—the voice of the singer more subdued, while the tremulous sighs that mingled with its strain, and formed its tender echo and fitting accompaniment, bore evidence quite as frequently of the really saddened fancy, as of the beguiling artifice of the fair musician.

The cares of Hernando de Soto were of a different character

Though wedded to one of the most lovely of all the beauties of Spain,—a princely dame, of family quite as distinguished as her charms,—it was not the tender passion which disturbed his fancies. Love satisfied—the early gush of youthful ardor lulled to rest by gratification—and ambition, that sterner passion which more particularly inspires the bosom of the matured man, superseding all others, except avarice, took possession of his soul, swaying it with little interruption or interval. He was only anxious to be gone on his path of triumph; and every event which was calculated to delay his departure was an additional source of anxiety, and even bitterness. Of these delays, the causes were frequent. The very sports and pleasures which he encouraged sometimes embarrassed the toils of his subordinates while diminishing his own resources, and the shows of reluctance and hesitation on the part of some of his favorite officers, together with certain awkward domestic occurrences, at which it is only necessary that we should glance in passing, rendered active all that was irritable and unamiable in his temper and deportment. It is our fortune to place him before our readers at a moment which found him particularly ruffled by the misconduct of one favorite cavalier, and the expected falling off of another. In a private chamber of the Governor's palace,—for he was Governor-General of Cuba, as well as Adelantado of Florida,—he holds in close conference one of his chief advisers. Hernando de Soto was at this time about thirty-six years of age, in the very prime of manhood, healthy, vigorous, accomplished, graceful in carriage, commanding in deportment; above the middle height, of a countenance dark and animated, and with a large and fiery eye. Of noble family, a gentleman "by all four descents," as was the phrase, he had yet gone forth as a mere adventurer on the conquest of Peru. There he had proved his personal merits to be superior to those of birth; ranking next to Pizarro himself in the use of lance and sword, and particularly distinguished by wonderful excellence in horsemanship. He might have retired in ease and affluence on the wealth and reputation which he acquired in Peru, but that the master passion of his soul forbade the early of endowments, of strength, skill and courage, which were too precious and too conspicuous to be consigned to inactivity. It was a fate that brought him once more from his native country in search of greater distinctions than he had yet acquired, in a perilous strife with the fierce natives that occupied the melancholy wastes of Florida.

His companion, at the moment when we seek to present him to the reader, was a person of a very different mood and character. Don Balthazar de Alvaro was a cold, dark, and somewhat ostentatious hidalgo,—a man of passions rather more intense than fierce,—subtle, yet tenacious,—capable of secret vices, yet equally capable of concealing them,—a prudent man, in the worldly signification of the term, yet a profligate in every better sense. But he outraged few external proprieties. He had the cunning of the serpent, without the dove's innocence, and possessed the art of hiding the fang and venom from discovery, even at the moment when he most harbored and prepared both faculties for use. He had been for ten years a resident of the island, was a man of large estates, and larger enterprises, with involvements more than corresponding with the former, and such as might well be supposed to follow from a somewhat reckless indulgence of the latter. He was now forty-five years of age, and remarkably erect and vigorous, had frequently distinguished himself in war with the Indians, and it surprised nobody in that day that he should eagerly prepare to embark his fortunes with those of Hernando de Soto. The public voice imputed to him and other cavaliers no higher ambition in undertaking this enterprise than the capture of such a number of red-men of the continent as would enable them to stock with slaves their vast landed estates in Cuba. Don Balthazar was a widower, without family, save in the person of a single niece, the only child of a brother, who, with his wife, had been dead for several years. The child had been thrown upon the care of her uncle from an early period. She was now seventeen, with considerable estates of her own, upon which it was shrewdly conjectured that her uncle had trespassed frequently, and with no light hand. She was as beautiful as young,—a tall, majestic woman, with pale but highly expressive features, a deep, dark eye, full of tenderness and thought, with an expression of melancholy in her countenance, which seemed rather to heighten than disparage the eminent beauty of her face. We shall see and hear more of her hereafter.

While the two cavaliers conferred together, De Soto paced the apartment with an air of much vexation and anxiety. He showed himself deeply chafed with matters, the discussion of which had evidently occupied for some time before the thoughts and feelings of the two. Don Balthazar kept in a sitting posture; he watched the movements of his superior with eyes that sometimes gleamed with a sinister expression. This seemed to show him not wholly dissatisfied with the annoyances of the other; a slight smile at moments played about his mouth,—but these were not allowed to attract the notice of De Soto, who broke into speech occasionally in regard to the subject of his vexation.

"Methinks, Don Balthazar, you make too light of this mischief! You forget that it was to the particular care of my wife that the Count de Gomera confided his daughter. What if she were a natural child?—did he love her the less? Was she the less honored by the people under her father's government? You say that she had the mother's weakness! All women are weak; and that she should yield when man persuades, is due rather to her nature than to the vices in her heart. Her security is in our justice, and if that fails, she fails also. But Leonora de Bovadilla should have had additional securities in my household; and I hold it as an outrage on myself, scarcely to be forgiven, with any atonement made, that one of my own trusted Lieutenants should have been the first to abuse these securities. It is a wrong done to my wife's honor and mine own, which; but for the responsibilities of this expedition, would impel me to punish the transgressor with lance and sword, and compel him to make the last atonement with his blood!"

"It is better that he should make atonement by marrying the girl," was the reply of the other. "I trow, it shall better please one of the parties at least."

"It shall please them both! He shall marry her, or he makes of me such an enemy as shall make death itself a desirable release to him from punishment."

"He is prepared for this," said the other. "Let your anger cool. Saving the offence to yourself and your honorable lady, there will be no wrong done to the damsel. He will repair the breach in her condition, and make an honest woman of her; so that no one shall have reason to complain. Nuno de Tobar is a free gallant. What he hath done hath not been of purpose, but in the warmth of a passion, that has rather found its countenance in the easy nature of the damsel herself,—perhaps in her own willingness,——"

"Nay, nay; I will not have it so, Don Balthazar," was the impetuous response of De Soto;—"this is too much thy irreverent way of speaking where woman is concerned. The virtue and modesty of the Lady Leonora were above reproach."

"Well, I mean not harm, your Excellency; we speak of women as we have found them. It has been your fortune to meet only with such as are pure; but I——"

"Let it pass, Señor," was the interruption. "Thou wilt see Nuno de Tobar, and teach him my desires—my demands. Let him marry the Lady Leonora without delay. Myself and the Lady Isabella shall grace the nuptials, which shall not be slighted. There shall be state in the arrangements, such as becomes the daughter of the Count de Gomera; such as becomes a lady in the guardianship of my wife. I will give him no countenance till this be done! I will not see him till the moment when he unites his hand with the maiden he hath wronged, under the sanction of the Holy Church."

The speaker was suddenly answered from another quarter,—

"Alas! your Excellency, but the offender must again trespass, and again rely upon your generous nature in the hope for pardon," said the voice of a third person, who entered the door of the chamber at this moment.

"How now, Señor! wast thou not forbidden this presence?" demanded De Soto, angrily. The intruder was the offending cavalier, Nuno de Tobar, whose *liaison* with the fair charge of the adelantado had formed the subject of the preceding conference. No more graceful or superb cavalier had ever found favor in the eyes of woman; and, as now, with a softened demeanor, with the air of a man conscious of offence, and sincerely regretting it, he entered the presence of his superior, his frank and ingenuous countenance, his noble though modest carriage, insensibly won upon the mood of De Soto, and prepared him to listen patiently to the apologies of the offender.

"I have erred," he continued, "and I crave pardon for my offence. I will make all the amendment in my power. Unhappily, I can make but little ——"

"Thou wilt wed with the Lady Leonora?"

"That were no atonement, your highness, since I shall esteem it rather a reward for services yet to be performed, that you confer upon me a prize the most precious to my fancy. That the Lady Leonora has suffered me to know what is the power which my heart exercises upon hers, rather commends her to my love, than lessens the value which I set upon her. Believe me, Señor, that, in giving me this lady, you offer the most powerful motives to my courage and fidelity, in the progress which lies before us, in the deep forests of the Floridian."

This was so gracefully said that De Soto was disarmed. He was only too glad of the opportunity, thus afforded him, by the readiness of the offender to repair his misconduct, to take once more into favor one of the most accomplished gallants in his train.

"I have been angry with thee, Nuno de Tobar, but thy heart has not meant to offend. Away with thee, then; I forgive thee! See, if thy lady-love shall so readily forgive thee, in making her ready to attend thee to the altar. Thou shalt be duly warned of the time when it shall please my wife to see thee wedded to thine. Meanwhile, prepare thee with all dispatch, for there must be no needless delays in our expedition. Our departure is at hand."

Some further conference ensued between the parties, and

1*

when the young cavalier had left the presence, which he did without rendering necessary the commands of his superior, De Soto resumed as follows:

"This passeth my hope! I had feared a struggle with the hot passions of this youth. Few men tolerate compulsion in affairs of love; still fewer the necessity of an alliance with the thing they have dishonored. Strange that we should be so heedful of a stain which is of our own making: but verily such is man's nature. That Nuno de Tobar is so easy in this matter,—though it likes me as repairing the shame of the Lady Leonora, and relieving me of some of the trouble in my path,—yet somewhat lessens him in my favor. He seemeth to me rather heedless on the point of honor."

"Nay, your excellency is now unreasonable," was the answer of Don Balthazar; "Nuno de Tobar is a philosopher somewhat after my own fashion. He hath made no large calculation upon the sex; therefore he shall not suffer greatly from experience hereafter. Thou wilt do well to suffer him to see no diminution of thy favor. Hast thou not declared him thy lieutenant-general? Wilt thou revoke thy trust? If thou dost, the offence were more grievous than the command which weds him to this damsel. That were not so readily forgiven. Trust me, he is one to resent a wrong done to his ambition, where he might submit to one inflicted on his heart."

"It may be so," was De Soto's answer to this suggestion, "yet I have resolved that he goes no longer as my lieutenant-general. I think of this office for another. It shall certainly be his no longer. He shall win his way to favor ere he gains it. What thinkest thou of Vasco Porcallo for this station?"

"Does he join the expedition?" inquired the other.

"Will such an appointment fail to persuade him to the enterprise? Such is the bait which I have passed before his eyes."

"His treasures are an object, surely!"

"He is brave also, and full of spirit."

"But he is old and capricious! a single skirmish with the red men will suffice for his ambition."

"Be it so; but he shall have made his investments! His castellanoes will have embarked in the expedition. These are not easily recalled. He may retire from toils which are too great for his years; but what shall restore him his gold when it shall have been expended in the enterprise?"

De Soto had made his calculations shrewdly. One of his vices—the greatest—was avarice. This impaired the dignity and virtue of his ambition. Don Balthazar was soon persuaded to see, in the argument of the adelantado, good reasons for confirming the office of lieutenant-general on the rich hidalgo, Vasco Porcallo de Figueroa, and for deposing from it the poor but gallant young cavalier who had so grievously offended. The subject, however, was soon dismissed, to give way to another of considerable interest to both the parties. But, for the discussion of this, we reserve ourselves for a fresh chapter, as it will need the presence of another of the persons of our drama.

CHAPTER II.

> "Go, Philostrate,
> Stir up the Athenian youth to merriments;
> Awake the pert and risible spirit of mirth;
> Turn melancholy forth to funeral;
> The pale companion is not for our pomp."—SHAKSPEARE.

"HAVE you sounded these Portuguese brothers, as I counselled you?" was the inquiry of De Soto.

The brow of Don Balthazar slightly darkened as he answered:

"It is not easy to sound them. They are suspicious and resentful. The jealousies of our people have made them so; and you have been able to offer them no position. I should have preferred, were this possible, that one of them should have this very office you propose to confer upon Vasco Porcallo."

"That is out of the question."

"I feel it; and yet, beyond the hope of profit, which is felt by the commonest arquebusier in the army, what is the motive for the enterprise on the part of these brothers? They are both young and noble—ambitious and full of valor. Their followers are few, it is true, but they will make good fight; and really, the abilities of the elder brother, Philip de Vasconselos, are probably of greater value than those of any of your cavaliers. The companion of De Vaça, he hath traversed all these wilds of Florida, and probably knoweth all the secrets of which De Vaça made such glorious boast and mystery. Besides, he speaks and understands the language of the natives; an advantage of which it is difficult to measure the importance. Of his valor and conduct we have sufficient testimony of our own eyes, even if the evidence of other witnesses were wanting; De Vaça himself spoke of him as one of the most prudent and valiant of his cavaliers."

"All this, I wot," answered the other impatiently, "but what of thy mission? what mean they by the reserve which seeks me not, and the change of mood which makes them declare themselves doubtful whether or not to proceed upon the enterprise?"

"They have spoken somewhat of the evident dislike and jealousies of certain of our knights, to say nothing of the rude disfavor of the common soldiers."

"This alone should show them how impossible it would be to give them command over our Spaniards. Are they not satisfied of this?"

"Yet doth it also afford sufficient reason why they should be unwilling to proceed in any enterprise with companions so unreasonable, for whom they will peril life and fortune, and from whom they can expect nothing in return."

"And thou hast gathered nothing further from thy inquiries into this matter? Hath nothing occurred to thy own thought and observation to add force to the difficulty which thou hast seen so clearly, and which thou hold'st so weighty? Bethink thee, Don Balthazar, hast thou not a niece, a damsel lovely as any that ever blossomed in bright Castile? These knights of Portugal have looked upon the maiden with eyes of love? Ha! Is't not so? Dost thou not see it?"

The brow of the person addressed again darkened as this suggestion met his ears. His lips might be seen more closely to contract together. He was about to speak when the rustling of silken garments at the entrance announced a new visitor; and the door opened, a moment after, for the admission of the lady of the adelantado. Both knights approached her as she appeared, with shows of the most profound deference.

"Am I permitted to attend these solemn councils?" was the inquiry of the noble lady as she passed into the apartment; her voice softly attuned to the playful question, and her lips parting with the sweetest smiles.

"To one who so admirably unites the wisdom of the one, with the virtues of the other sex—the strength and dignity of manhood with the grace and loveliness of woman—counsel her self must willingly incline her ear. We were foes to wisdom did we refuse to hearken to the words of her best favorite."

The stately compliment, so perfectly Spanish, was from the lips of Don Balthazar, upon whom the lady smiled most sweetly, not wholly insensible, it would seem, to the honeyed flattery.

"Now, verily," exclaimed De Soto, who beheld the expression in her face; "now, verily, hath this politician won thy whole heart by the silliest speech. He is like the cunning knave who possesseth counterfeit castellanoes, who, knowing their just worthlessness, yet circulates them for the value which they derive only from the ignorance of him who receives. He hath put his copper trinket upon thee, and will look for the golden one in return, even as we look to our Floridian savage for the precious metals, in exchange for others, which are as dear to his eyes, as despicable in ours. Is it not so, my lady? And yet, if thou art thus easily put upon, what shall be my security, leaving the government of Cuba in thy hands?"

"Oh! fear nothing, my lord; I shall ere long become schooled in all the subtleties of thy politicians, so that thy government shall have no wrong during thy absence. Be not deceived, my good lord, in the supposed estimate which our sex makes of the flatteries of thine. We receive the coin that thou offerest, not because we overvalue it or esteem it very highly, but simply as we know that it is quite too commonly the most precious which ye have to offer. Were sincerity one of the virtues of the man, we should perhaps never listen to his flatteries; but it were unreasonable to reject his false tokens, when we know that such constitute his whole treasure; and we receive the tribute of his lips only in the absence of all better securities lodged within his heart. It is something of an acknowledgment, in behalf of our authority, that he is solicitous to show the devotion which he has not always the nobleness to feel."

"Ha! Señor Balthazar, we gain nothing by this banter. Our lady knows that our gold is copper It is for such only that she takes it. Shrewdly spoken, by my faith; and yet it might be as shrewdly said, in reply, why receive the counterfeit at all, knowing so well its worthlessness, unless it were that the dependency of the one sex upon the other, rendered any gift of the man sufficiently precious, (though worthless in itself,) in the eyes of the woman."

"Now out upon thee for a heathen savage! Thou art not satisfied with shaming Don Balthazar with his tribute, but thou must shame me with the pleasure I feel in receiving it at his hands. I would thou wert fairly on thy march among the Floridian, that I might play the tyrant in thy government of Cuba, to the peril of thy insolent sex! But proceed to thy councils, if there be nothing unfit for the ears of the woman. I have need to sound the depths of all thy policy in other respects, since I am to play sovereign in thy place hereafter."

The noble lady, speaking playfully, had, in the meanwhile, with a grace peculiarly her own, sunk down upon the divan of orange, from which Don Balthazar had risen to receive her. Few persons, not actually born in the purple, were so well endowed to honor it, and to wield authority with sweetness. The daughter of Don Pedrarias Davila, a man distinguished, unhappily, quite as much by his cruel treatment of the famous Vasco Nunez de Balboa, the discoverer of the Pacific, as by his own deeds and successes, Isabella de Bobadilla, inherited the pride and dignity of her father's character, without those taints of vindictiveness and passion which had rendered him odious among his inferiors. She possessed that happy prudence which never forgets what is due to the humanities and the affections in the moment of power and good fortune. She was wiser than the greater number of her sex; calm in the hour of trial, full of provident forethought, with a mind quite equal to the government about to devolve upon her, and with a heart devoted to that lord who was about to leave her for a protracted season in a perilous progress, to which he was induced by the single persuasions of ambition. He had found her an admirable counsellor and ally, in making his preparations for the expedition; and, in penetrating his chamber of council without a summons, she was yet satisfied, from past experience, that her presence in such a place was never wholly unacceptable or unprofitable! When, therefore, she declared her pleasure to remain, unless the topics under discussion should prove ungracious in the hearing of her sex, the ready answer of her husband entreated her to do so, whilst assuring her against the exception which she expressed.

"Nay, Isabella," said he; "it particularly concerns thy sex, that of which we are to speak, and much of what has been spoken. Know then, in the first place, that thou art to prepare thy lovely handmaid, the damsel Leonora, for her nuptials with Nuno de Tobar."

"Thou hast then adjusted that matter?" said the lady, with a grave accent and demeanor.

"It is settled, and without anger or difficulty. It is for thee to decide upon the hour of the bridal. Let it be soon, for we must have dispatch, and advise with the damsel ere the day be sped. But there is yet another matter connected with thy sex which troubles me, and prevents my purpose. Their mischievous influence hath been at work upon my bravest cavaliers. Thou knowest these two young knights of Portugal. I need not tell thee of their worth, their valor, and the great importance to the expedition of the elder brother, Philip de Vasconselos, who hath already sped over all the territory of the Floridian, and is familiar with the heathen speech of its people. Now, it so happens that these two young gallants grow indifferent to the enterprise. They have held themselves somewhat aloof from me of late, and words have been heard to fall from their lips, which declare their doubts whether they will accompany the expedition, as was their purpose when they joined our armament at Seville."

"And canst thou not guess the reason for this change of purpose?" demanded the lady, with a smile.

"Ay, verily! Thy smile tells me that I am right in ascribing their fickleness of purpose to the persuasions and artifices of thy sex. Our grave Señor, Don Balthazar de Alvaro, will have it his only to the jealousies of our Spaniards, with whom these men of Portugal find but little favor. Something there may be in this, doubtless; but, I trow, it would never be sufficient to discourage such young gallants, known for their bravery, and ambitious of wealth and distinction, were it not for the charms of the Lady Olivia, his fair niece,——"

"It may be that thou art right in thy conjecture," said Don Balthazar, interrupting the speaker, his brow again darkening as if with displeasure; "but it will profit them little that they turn their eyes in the direction of my niece. Olivia de Alvaro is scarcely the proper game for either of these knights of Portugal."

"And wherefore, Señor?" was the quick inquiry of Doña Isabella. "These are brave and honorable gentlemen, both; of —as we know—a family as noble as any in Portugal. They have not wealth, it is true, but they have the qualities of strength, courage, and enterprise, which in these days of 'Golden Cathays,' everywhere achieve wealth, and make obscure names famous. I see not why you should so sternly resolve against the devotion which they seem disposed to offer to your niece."

Don Balthazar trod the floor in a stern silence, while the Adelantado took up the words,—

"Thou hast forgotten another matter, my lady, which seemeth to me of no small import in this case. If I mistake not greatly, the decision of the Lady Olivia herself will 'surely be more indulgent than that of her guardian, in relation to these young knights of Portugal."

"But I *am* her guardian, your excellency, and my niece is but a child.——"

"Seventeen is a goodly age for female judgment, Señor, in affairs of the affections," was the answer of the lady. "But thou surely wilt not oppose the authority of the guardian to the wishes of thy niece, when these fasten upon a person of whose worth and nobleness there can be no question."

"Ah! but I know not that," was the quick reply of Don Balthazar. "I see not—I believe not—that the affections of Olivia incline to either of these Portuguese adventurers."

"Deceive not thyself, Señor," said the Lady Isabella. "Men are seldom the best judges of such matters, especially where they are grave senators and busy politicians. You have quite too many concerns to demand your study—too many cares of business and fortune to suffer you to give much heed to the tendency of a young and feminine heart. I claim to understand it better, and I tell thee, Señor, that if ever woman loved cavalier, with all her soul, and with all her strength, then doth Olivia de Alvaro love this elder knight of Portugal, whom they call Philip de Vasconselos."

"I believe it not! You are deceived, Lady Isabella. I am sure that such is not the case. But if it were, I should be false to the duties I have undertaken to suffer her inclinations to have sway in this. This Philip de Vasconselos may have his virtues; yet what is he but a beggarly adventurer, who has squandered his birthright in wanderings where the better wisdom has always succeeded in acquiring it?"

"Not always, Señor, unless old proverbs fail us. The best wisdom is but too commonly the last to secure the smiles of Fortune. Have not your poets made her feminine, and with twofold sarcasm made her caprices to resemble ours? Say they not, that he is most apt to win her favor who less does for, and less deserves it; and shape they not their sarcasm in such wise as to salve the hurts of self-esteem, by recognizing the propriety of that favor which provides for him who would never be able, of his own wits, to provide for himself? You shall do no slander to this knight of Portugal, Philip de Vasconselos, who, verily, is a man of thought as well as of valor. I have enjoyed his wisdom with a rare delight, and if his valor keep any rate of pace with his judgment, he should be a famous leader in such adventure as that on which ye go. For the younger brother, I can scarcely speak so favorably. He seemeth at once less wise and more presuming. He speaks as one confident in himself, and I should deem him quite as rash and ill-advised as valiant;—nay more, he hath the manner of a man whom small griefs unreasonably inflame,—who is irritable of mood, suspicious of those about him, jealous of the good fame of his companions, and one of too little faith in others to be altogether worthy of faith himself. But it is not of him that we need to speak. He hath, I fancy, but little chance of success with our fair cousin, though it is evident he hath a passion for her quite as earnest as that of his elder brother."

"What sayest thou, Señor?" demanded De Soto, as his wife concluded.

"What should I say, your excellency," replied the latter, somewhat doggedly,—"save that my niece is in my keeping? She will not, I think, gainsay my judgment in this matter by opposing it with her own."

"Will she not?" demanded the lady, with a smile. "We shall see, Señor, who better understands the heart of woman. Bethink you, it is upon no ordinary matter that you ask her to forego her judgment. The fate of woman is in the resolve which she shall make for or against her heart. Her whole life is in the love which she feels; and this denied, or this possessed, determines her existence. She hath a rare instinct which teaches her all this. Submissive in all other respects, she here grows resolute and strong; and she whom you knew for many seasons the dove only, shall, when the heart demands such will and courage, assume the fierce courage of the falcon. Believe it or not, Olivia de Alvaro loves this knight of Portugal; and so loving, you shall not say nay to her desire, and find no resistance to your will."

"It may be," was the answer of the other, his brow still darkened, but a sinister smile at the same moment curling his lips, though scarce perceptible to those about him. That he was chafed beyond his wont, was still apparent.

"Verily, Señor Balthazar," said De Soto, "this thing hath angered you. You will do well to bear it calmly. Our lady is surely right. The heart of thy niece hath made its choice, as certainly as that Philip de Vasconselos hath resolved on his; and thou wilt be wise to put on a friendly countenance when they come to declare their desires. Thou wilt scarcely find a nobler cavalier in all Spain upon whom to bestow her fortune."

"And will you that I should encourage a passion which will tend to baffle thy own desires?" demanded Don Balthazar.

"How so,—what meanest thou?" was the inquiry of De Soto, who looked the alarm which he really felt.

"See'st thou not that the bridal of Philip de Vasconselos with Olivia de Alvaro is conclusive against his progress with the expedition? With her estates in Cuba to occupy his thoughts,—with her wealth in which to luxuriate,—wherefore should he incur the peril of the Floridian enterprise?"

"And wherefore should my lord himself incur such peril, Señor Balthazar?" was the quick and energetic reply of the lady. "Hath *he* not estates in Cuba, a government to demand his care, and wealth enough with which to procure all the luxuries of the island? Yet he will leave all these—he will leave *me*, but lately his newly-wedded bride—and one, I trow, not wholly without hold upon his heart—and go forth upon adventures of incomparable peril. But this belongs to the passion of a knightly ambition—a generous impatience of the dull paces of the common life;—an eager and noble appetite after conquest, and the glory which it brings! Of this same temper, seems to me the ambition of this knight of Portugal, who hath been regardless of wealth only as he hath been heedful of honor,—and whose pride it is rather to win a glorious name, than a golden habitation. Thou shalt not disparage this quest, Señor, since it is one which is ever precious in the sight of a generous knighthood."

"You speak it bravely, my lady; but shall not persuade me that this knight of Portugal would wed my niece only to depart from her. He shall need some time after the nuptials, ere his ambition shall assert itself. His love of distinction will doubtless bring him *after* the adelantado—but with slow footsteps, and when his lance shall be no longer needful to success."

"This is, indeed, a matter to be thought on, Don Balthazar," was the reply of De Soto, looking gravely, and evidently touched thrust it back a moment after, drew his cap above his eyes, and stretched himself along upon the sward, with his face downward. Here he lay in complete silence, and scarcely stirring, the full space of half an hour. Meanwhile, the day waned. The sun was at his setting, and the night birds began wheeling, with faint shrieks, about the place where he seemed to slumber. But slumber was not upon his eyelids, or in his thoughts. It was not his necessity just then. He rose, at length, with the deliberation of one who has recovered the full sway over all his moods, and, adjusting his garments, prepared to move towards his dwelling, which was still at some distance, and hidden wholly from his eyes by the sinuosity of the avenues, and the denseness of the thicket. But he paused more than once on his progress, and, more than once, did words of brief soliloquy break from his lips.

"At least, I must soon know all. There must be an explanation. I must fathom her secret. I must probe her heart to its core. If that be safe—if she be what she hath been sufficiently trained to be—what such training indeed should have made her,—" and a grim smile passed over his features as he spoke,—" then this Philip de Vasconselos can do no hurt. Let him live. He will scarcely linger here. But if there be sentiment in her bosom, newly born and from his agency, such as I would have trampled out, if need be, in blood and fire,—a sentiment hostile to my hold upon her—then must I strike,—strike fatally,—and crush the danger in its very bud. But, I must penetrate her secret. She hath grown subtle of late,—*that* is an evil sign. It is enough that she *hath* a secret, and from me. *That* alone is significant of danger! Doth her reserve signify distrust of me? Ha! what else? Do her tears manifest a feeling for another? Then is it a proof that she holds me in hate and loathing. I must search, fathom this mystery, and be as swift and stern as I am vigilant!"

This speech was not spoken all at once, but in snatches. during his walk, and each soliloquy compelling his momentary pause In this manner he went forward, his features and manner becom ing more and more composed as he approached the dwelling. At length the cottage and its gay verandahs opened before him. and he paused as he caught a glimpse of his niece, where she lay dreamily reclining, embowered in the grateful shades of the tall trees by which the dwelling was surrounded.

Olivia de Alvaro, as we now behold her, her form disposed at ease, stretched on ample cushions, in the airy recesses of the verandah, would seem, from the half-shut eye, and the almost motionless attitude in which she lay, to have been wrapt in the most grateful slumbers. She was evidently unconscious of the rays of the fast disappearing sunlight, which shot, faint and brokenly, through the intervening foliage. She was a pale, proud beauty, one whose high and aristocratic features seemed scarcely consistent with that despondency of mood and dependency of nature, which have been described as her present characteristics. Her features were not regular, but there was a strange harmony between them nevertheless; the lofty brow, corresponding well with the distinctly rounded chin,—the large and well-formed nose, and that 'drooping darkness of the Moorish eye,' which, as we know,—though it may slumber long in cloud and shadow,—is still capable of such sudden lightnings as consume at the single flash. We have already described her as very young—scarcely more than seventeen;—but this youthfulness was not marked by the usual frankness—the uncircumspect and exuberant flow, of that period. Her countenance was marked by an earnestness. an intensity of gaze and expression, which denoted a maturity of thought and feeling quite beyond her years. It is surprising how rapidly one lives, who has learned to feel, and been made to suffer. Yet what had been the sources of suffering in her? Rich, beautiful, well-beloved, what were the cares of Olivia de Alvaro, by which she had grown so singularly mature? This we must ascertain in future pages. Enough, if now we continue the description of her person.

She was tall, and of commanding figure and demeanor. Her features, significant of so much sweetness and beauty, were yet marked by a tremulous and timid sadness of gaze, which conveyed the impression of a sense of awe, compelling her fears, and depressing her elasticity. This expression, particularly at those moments when she seemed to become forgetful of every other presence, commended her to sympathy, rather than offended pride. There could be no jealousy of her superiority, in the evident feeling of apprehension which she displayed. A vague sense of danger seemed to accompany the consciousness of her charms; and the effect was rather to humble and subdue all the loftier indications that were yet inseparable from the graces of her manner, and the conscious nobility of blood and beauty.

To these she was by no means insensible. Her carriage was such as showed an habitual appreciation of all her possessions; yet so modified as to make nature more conspicuous than habit in her demeanor. The heart of a young damsel naturally, and very soon, becomes sensible of the beauties of her person. Her mirror, and the common language of society, read equally in speech and manner, soon teach her all the value of her charms. But a refined taste renders it impossible, if she really should be attractive, that she should escape this conviction. It is her merit when she does not presume upon her possessions, and is modestly content in their enjoyment. It is in due degree with the development of her intellect, and the experience of afflictions, that she schools her vanity. That Olivia de Alvaro had, in large measure, learned to tutor hers, might be gathered from many indications. That she was not insensible to her own charms, was equally evident from the exercises in which she employed them. Few damsels knew so well how to train the glance, to give variety and play to the expressive muscles, and the pleasing, persuasive action; to subdue to sweetness, and the most touching tenderness of tone, the murmurs of the obedient voice; to make the fingers speak, as with an endowment of their own, and to inform, with a nameless, but most winning flexibility, every movement of the well-regulated and exquisitely symmetrical figure. Half sitting, half reclining, in the western verandah of the dwelling, her eyes vaguely pursuing the soft and fluctuating play of the evening sunlight, that stele in golden droplets, as it were, through the slightly waving leaves of the anana and the orange, she yet appeared wholly regardless of the timid brightness that sprinkled, as with fairy eyes, the apartment all about her feet. She seemed to muse in far delicious fancies, that made her wholly unconscious of the actual world in which she lived. Her person, unrestrained by any human presence, had naturally subsided into an attitude equally graceful and voluptuous; and this was altogether the unstudied action of a grace, which, natural always, had yet always recognized in art only the appointed assistant, the tiring woman and handmaid, of the imperial nature. Her dark, glossy hair, hung upon her shoulders, from which it descended in waving but massive tresses. The art which had, without an effort, disposed their flowing and magnificent folds, had never been more successful in removing all proof of its own adorning fingers. Slightly stirred by the fitful zephyrs of an afternoon in May, that season which, in Cuba, recognizes the perfect presence of the full-bosomed summer, her ringlets played upon her neck like young birds, for the first time conscious of their wings, yet still fluttering, timidly and fondly, about the parent nest. And thus she reclined, clad in robes of white, slightly trimmed with blue and orange, seemingly unconscious of all things but those which were deeply hidden in her thoughts, at the moment when Don Balthazar drew nigh to the dwelling.

The shrubbery had enabled him to approach unseen, until within a few steps of the verandah. He could detect the familiar outline of her person through the leaves of a gorgeous orange, beneath which he stood silently beholding her. She dreamed not of his presence. His footstep had been carefully set down, as if not to disturb her; and thus unsuspected, he stood, for a few moments, watching her with a singular and intense interest. Even thus keen and concentrative the gaze which the fascinating serpent fastens upon the unconscious bird that flies or flutters in his sight. It was not malignity or hostility that was apparent in the expression of his eyes. Nay, to the casual spectator, there might have seemed fondness only, in the keen and earnest interest, which seemed to study her every feature, as if prompted by the most paternal affection. And yet there was a something bitter in the smile which occasionally played upon his lips; and the slight frown which darkened in his glance was significant of a disquiet or disappointment, the sources of which we may not yet comprehend. Suspicion, too, might be seen to lurk even beneath the smile of the observer, and his secret watch might have been dictated by a policy which was not above the indulgence of a baseness.

And yet his purpose did not seem to be espionage. A sudden and troublesome thought—perhaps a suddenly suggested curiosity—appeared to arrest his footsteps on his approach. Her appearance, her attitude, seemed to invite his study. It was to muse, to meditate, or, perhaps, to prepare his mind for some exigent duty, that he paused, without seeking to disturb the damsel in her vacant mood. She, too, had her causes for meditation; though one might readily ascribe the dreamy languor of her attitude to the bland and seductive influences of the climate. To the voluptuous idler, already familiar with that luxury of situation which suspends the thought, and strips the fancy of everything but wings, her appearance would seem natural enough, and her conjectured reveries would only be the most grateful, yet unimpressive in the world. It would be only to liken her bower to the wizard domain of that archimage who wove his perpetual snares in the Castle of Indolence, making all things dreamy and delusive in the half-shut eye. But the meditations of Olivia de Alvaro were of a sort, perhaps, even more deeply troublesome than those of her uncle. Big tears might be seen to gather in her eye—slowly, it is true, and few,—but they were such as we seldom look to see in the eyes of young and innocent loveliness. The great drops silently oozing from beneath their dark and drooping fringes, like some gradual stream gliding silently forth from the shade of overhanging alders, were not unseen by her uncle. His features became graver as he beheld them, and he looked aside—he looked down—as if anxious to shut them from his sight. He turned away hastily a moment after, and, with careful footstep, retreated silently from his place of watch. Teking a hasty turn through the deeper ranks of foliage, he again, after a little interval, was returning in the direction of the dwelling, when his ear was aroused by the sound of approaching voices. He promptly shrouded himself in a little copse of gren adilla. Here he could easily distinguish the persons of the visitors, himself unseen. In a few moments they had reached the spot where he stood concealed. They proved to be the young gallant, Nuno de Tobar, and his frail but beautiful betrothed, in whose behalf we have seen how greatly the anger of De Soto had been awakened. She was a pretty creature, light-hearted rather than wanton, whose happiness was now wholly complete, and whose faults were all about to be repaired. They walked unconsciously beside the stern Balthazar, and their prattle once more wrought his features into that sardonic expression so natural to a man who despises the simplicity of young affections. They were on a visit to the lovely Olivia, to whom, we may say in this place, the betrothal of the happy couple brought at once a pang and a pleasure. We must leave the explanation of this contradiction to other chapters.

It was with something of chagrin and disquiet that Don Balthazar discovered who were the approaching parties. He had almost spoken his annoyances aloud, as they passed onward to the cottage. His vexation was not long suppressed. As soon as they had passed into the verandah, he retired from his place of watch, to a spot of greater seclusion in the groves, and the passionate soliloquy to which he gave utterance afforded some slight clue to the nature of his secret meditations.

"Now," said he, flinging himself down upon the sward, a thick matting of grass, like that of the Bermuda, which completely protects the garments from the red stains of the earth. "Now will these fools, with happiness fancied in their grasp, possess her spirit with all the passions which they feel themselves. If her mind were yet free from any fancy in behalf of this knight of Portugal, they would do much towards its grafting. They will speak in raptures of hopes which they dream to be possessions, of realities which seldom live through a season, and of sentiments which few, however cheated at first, but live to curse and to despise in after times. This Nuno de Tobar is the sworn friend of Vasconselos. He will labor in his cause. He perhaps knows all his secrets. Perhaps he comes even now as an emissary. Demonios! But does it need this? Let me not deceive myself, though I would shut the truth from other eyes. Can I doubt that Olivia de Alvaro looks with favor on this knight? That she loves him—she, the —— but hush! The thing is by no means an absurdity. The insane passion does not stop to measure its own claims. The cloud that receives and swallows up the star, has no shame for such affrontery; and even guilt may worship with hope at the altars of the pure and beautiful. I cannot doubt that she loves him. Else why this change since he came upon the island? Why these tears—this despondency—this drooping fear,—this trembling and perpetual cloud and apprehension? She shrinks from other eyes—from mine. Her own are cast upon the earth, or closed from study. Could other eyes but read, like mine, she would have no secret to reveal! It is well that she dare not speak. The very passion that she feels for this stranger is my security. She must subdue these inclinations. She must stifle this working fancy which these meddling fools will blow into a flame. She *shall* stifle it! Fortunately, I am her *will*. I have ever led her as a child. She has known no impulses of her own, save those of infancy, until now; and she will scarcely now withstand that governing rule which hath hitherto swayed her as the breezes sway the leaf. I would, *now*, that this had not been the case. I have perilled upon a moment the security of a life; but regret is unavailing now. I must continue as I have begun. I must still assert the superior will of a master,—not simply to secure my slave, but to assure myself of safety. It will be easy, and why should I scruple to do it? Why this fear, this feebleness? I will overcome it as before! She shall bend, she shall bow, or break in the conflict! But there will be no conflict. She will offer no opposition—none that I cannot soon disarm. Had it been her fierce Biscayan mother, I should have no such victory. *She* would have defied me in her paroxysm, and in the very passion of her rage, she would have left no secret unrevealed, even though instant ruin followed on her speech. Fortunately, the child sucked nothing from the mother. She hath no such temper. She has the gentleness of poor Alphonso, all his meek submission, his dread of strife, his shrinking dislike of struggle and excitement. Had he not been so weak as to submit to *her* tyranny, he had never suffered wrong from me. Olivia hath his feebleness of will; but she hath warmer sensibilities. Still, they make nothing against my power,—I have schooled them to submission and self-denial. What if I have done her wrong—and she dreams not yet of its extent—yet, even if she knew all, no desperation of desire, or fear, could drive her to resistance. Here, I am secure! Unlike her fiery dam, she is too heedful of the world's voice to lift her own, where the very cry which would crush *my* fortunes, would leave hers wrecked on the same shoals. On this, I hold! Here, I am safe. I must still sway—still maintain the mastery—but I foresee the struggle. I see it in those tears, —in that deep despondency,—in the distaste which no longer suffers her eyes to meet the gaze of mine,—in the cold and chilling word which checks my speech,—and the reserve, almost like aversion, with which she encounters my approach. I must prepare for the struggle;—but shall we not escape it all if we once get these knights of Portugal embarked? But how, if they resolve to stay? That is a grief that must find its own remedies!"

We care not now to pursue our subtle politician in his walks or his soliloquies. Enough has been shown to develop the sort of temper with which he views the supposed conquests of his lovely niece, over the affections of two of the noblest adventurers in the train of De Soto. These had not been her only conquests. But none of her previous suitors had ever given her uncle any cause for apprehension. It has been shown that he is not simply averse to her marriage with either of the knights of Portugal, but is alike hostile to the claims of all. As the guardian of his niece, with small estates of his own, and ample possessions of hers, to manage, his disquiet on this subject may well be supposed to arise from motives of most singular selfishness or baseness. But Olivia herself, aware of his aversion to her marriage, has really no notion that avarice is the infirmity of her uncle. She knows but little of his individual resources, but much of himself. She has seen nothing in his expenditure, or conduct, which would make him appear in her eyes to be a mercenary. Her minority had been singularly managed, so as to keep her in a state of mental vassalage, quite uncommon on the island. She had been kept in almost complete seclusion until the appearance of De Soto and his lady, when it was impossible to withhold her from the court; her own wealth, her father's name, and the position of her uncle, equally requiring it. Up to this period she little dreamed of the treasures which the world had in its keeping. She little knew the value of her own. But in the course of a single night the germ of passion had blossomed, and Love rapidly maturing beneath its fervid warmth, had taught her a *grief* in teaching her a *faith.* Alas! she knew not till now how precious, how radiant white, must be the first offerings demanded for its shrine. Leaving the uncle to pursue his moody walk through the umbrageous grounds of his domain, let us return to the niece, and witness the reception of her guests.

CHAPTER IV.

> "But a month ago,
> I went from hence, and then 'twas fresh
> In murmur, (as you know what great ones do
> The less will prattle of) that he did seek
> The love of fair Olivia."—TWELFTH NIGHT.

THE pleasant laughter, and gay voices of Nuno de Tobar, and his betrothed, prepared Olivia de Alvaro for their approach. The trace of tears was quickly obliterated from her eyes, and she strove with smiles to welcome her visitors. Pride, as was alleged by her uncle, was one of the chief securities for her strength, no less than for his safety. She was one of those who love not that the world should behold or suspect their sorrows. But her pride was rather a habit than a passion. She had other and more fiery qualities in her nature, for which he failed to give her credit. He deceived himself when he thought he knew her thoroughly. Some of her characteristics were yet in abeyance, some moods and passions which are likely to confound and astonish him hereafter. But these in proper season. She, herself, is perhaps as little aware, as her uncle, of her natural endowments.

Olivia received her guests on the steps of her verandah. The cloud had disappeared from her face, the light had returned to her large and lustrous eyes, and with the sweetest voice in the world, she welcomed them to an abode which, to the casual visitor, would seem to be entirely secure from sorrow. The young creatures who now entered it, themselves newly made happy, were certainly not the persons to make any discovery of the latent troubles of its inmate; and assuming the happiness in other hearts, which they felt in their own, they poured out upon Olivia a torrent of congratulations, which it required considerable strength of endurance to withstand. She had heard of their betrothal, and of the forgiveness which De Soto had extended to the erring gallant. Society at that day in Cuba was not particularly jealous of propriety. That Leonora Bovadilla had sinned, found its sufficient excuse with knight and lady, in the simple fact that she loved; and it was only with that class of ancients, of her own sex, who had survived even the hope of a change from single to dependent blessedness—a number singularly few in every community—that censure claimed the privilege still to wag a slanderous tongue under the guise of a jealous virtue. Olivia de Alvaro had never been of the number to reproach the poor Leonora for her lapse, even when it was doubtful whether the sense of virtue, the sentiment of honor, or the feeling of love, in Nuno de Tobar, would prompt him to repair his wrong according to the worldly usage, by making her his wife. Having known her as a thoughtless child, without guile as without experience, a creature of extreme levity, but without any impulses to evil more than seemed naturally to belong to the mercurial temper, Olivia was not prepared to regard her as guilty, because she had been weak. She was indulgent in proportion as the world showed itself severe. She knew, according to a common history, that,

> "Every woe a tear may claim,
> Except an erring sister's shame,"

and rising above the prejudices of the world, as much through sympathy as generosity, she suffered her manner towards the frail offender to show none of those harsher aspects which forever insist upon its faults. On the contrary, a tender solicitude seemed desirous to soothe the humiliations of the sufferer, and make her forgetful of those public disgraces which she could not always hope to escape. Leonora felt all this, and repaid the kindness of Olivia by as much devotion as could distinguish a nature so thoughtless. The first visit which she made, after the reconciliation of her guardian with her lover, was that which we now witness. Of course, the peculiar case of the visitors was not one to be spoken of openly. The silent pressure of Leonora's hand by Olivia, the tender kiss which she impressed upon her cheeks, and the single tear which gathered in her eye, as she whispered a hurried word of congratulation, sufficiently assured the former of the continuance of that sympathy which had already afforded her so much solace. But she erred, perhaps, in ascribing the tear to the sympathies of friendship. Had she but beheld the big drops that fell from the same fruitful fountains, but a little while before, she might have suspected other and more selfish sources of sorrow in her friend.

Seated in the cool shadows of the verandah, the gay Leonora soon opened her stores of prattle. She had gathered all the rumors of the day, and she was impatient to unfold them.

"And O! dearest Olivia, have you heard of the tournament? The town is full of it. It is to be the greatest and the gayest of all the shows that we have had. They have begun the preparations already. Such a painting of shields and banners,—such a sharpening of swords and burnishing of lances,—such a prancing of steeds—it will be something to remember a thousand years to come! Nuno has been busy since noon making the arrangements. The adelantado cannot do without him. He will be busy for a week,—they will all be busy—your knight, as well as mine; for you know, Olivia, you have a knight."

The other shook her head very mournfully.

"Nay, never shake your head; you know it as well as I—two of them, indeed; and you might have a dozen, if you were not so proud"

"Me proud, Leonora!" reproachfully.

"No! no! I don't mean that! I *ought* to know, if any one, that you are any thing but proud. I should have said, so lofty—so superior——"

"Ah! you mock me, child."

"I am a child; but I don't mock you. It is so. I believe it all, and everybody else thinks so. I'm sure you'd have a thousand suitors, if they did not all feel that they are unworthy of your smiles."

The hand of Olivia was passed with a close pressure over her brows. Little did the thoughtless Leonora dream that the action was occasioned by a feeling of pain. She continued:

"But of the homage of the knights of Portugal, nobody has a question. It is in every one's mouth; everybody sees that both the brothers love you to distraction. The question with them all is, which of them you favor. Now, I am for Don Andres, the younger; but Nuno—"

Here she was interrupted by a look from her betrothed, for which Olivia was properly grateful. The subject seemed to annoy her.

"Hush, hush, dear Leonora!—Tell us of the tournament rather. This is not the season to talk of love, but of war. See how the adelantado treats the affections, when they come in conflict with his ambition. Who so lovely, so stately, s noble, so like a Queen, as the Lady Isabella?—yet will he leave her, a newly-wedded wife, to go on wild adventures against the Floridians. Fie upon such chivalry, such devotion, such love! What need hath he of further wars?—hath he not wealth enough from Peru?—hath he not grandeur enough as Governor of this goodly island, and reputed one of the noblest cavaliers of Spain? Methinks he wantonly flings from him a living and a glorious treasure, for a dream—for a shadow which will mock his hope, and defraud him of all his happiness."

Olivia had spoken rapidly, in order, possibly, to divert the interest of her companions to other subjects. In speaking, however, of the projected conquest of Florida, she yet trenched upon the province of Nuno de Tobar, and indirectly assailed his conduct also. He, too, like De Soto, had acquired the love of a young and beautiful woman; he had formed ties equally precious, which he was about to abandon at the calls of ambition; and though his state was neither secure, nor his possessions great like those of the latter, yet the imputation, in some degree, lay against him, of a like disregard to the claims of duty and domestic life. He answered Olivia after the usual manner of knight-errants.

"And how else, dear lady, can chivalry display itself, unless by deeds of arms and conquest? It is by these deeds and this conquest, that it brings home tribute to Beauty, and crowns love with its proper jewels. It is to make love secure in state and home, and refresh its bowers with lasting delight, that in encounters peril for a season, the laurels and rewards of which shall endure through future years. Love is not abandoned when the worshipper carries ever with him in his heart a passionate devotion, which makes him cry upon the beloved one's name in the storm of battle, and pray for her prayers in the tempests of the deep, which prompts him to build for her a temple in waste places, and to enwreathe chaplets of her favorite flowers in forests which she may never see. His devotion even warms with distance, and he remembers her beauties and her virtues the better when he no longer may enjoy them. If he goes forth, it is with the purpose that he may return full-handed with spoils, that he may lay at her feet in guerdon of his faith and homage."

"Ah! Senor, you phrase it well, and it is such fine eloquence that for a season reconciles the poor heart of woman to too many of the errantries of chivalry. For me, I confess, 'twould better please me should my knight leave to others the storm of battle and the peril of the seas. Let me have the devotions of his heart at the altars of home, rather than in the forests of the Floridian. Let me have the idol of my eyes always present to my sight. I should not need that he should wander away from my eyes to be able to recall his virtues and grow fond of his devotion."

"Oh! Fie, Olivia, dear,—you have no sort of idea of what belongs to true chivalry. Why, true chivalry lives on fighting and conquest, on long wanderings over sea and land, into places that were never heard of before, seeking all sorts of enemies to overthrow, and coming home with treasures of gold, great emeralds, such as they gather in Peru, and pearls,—pearls by the bushel. They gather them, Nuno tells me, by the basketful among the Floridians. Nay, you smile,—but the story comes from your knights of Portugal—Phillip, the elder, has been among the savages in that country."

"I have no knights, Leonora, and this reminds me that I have really no interest in this game of war that is called chivalry. Let those like it who may. Its splendid shows do not beguile or satisfy my imagination."

"Ah! but they will in the tournament, which is at hand. Don't tell me that you have no knight. I promise you, dear Olivia, that you will have knights enough to do battle for your smiles, and to wear your favors. These knights of Portugal will not be the only ones to break lances in your honor. But let them beware how they cross with my Nuno. If he does not unhorse every opponent, I will never, never, never love him any more. And that's a vow to the Blessed ——"

"Don't be rash, Leonora," interrupted Nuno, with a smile. "You may punish yourself by such a vow, much more than you could ever punish me!"

"Ha! How?"

He evaded the query, and went on.

"As for overthrowing these knights of Portugal, it is no easy matter. I should rather cross lances with any other foes! Philip de Vasconselos ——"

"How! Are you recreant? Will you allow these Portuguese to pluck the honors from Castile?"

"Nay, nay! not if I can help it. But I should prefer other hands than mine to make the attempt. The world has few lances which can safely cross that of Philip de Vasconselos, and mine, I fear, is not one of them; and I so love the man that I should find no satisfaction in depriving him of a single glory that he desires. But something, as you say, is due to the honor of Castile, and if Philip overthrows all other combatants, he must have a chance of including me among his captives."

The eyes of Olivia were cast upon the ground. But her ears drank in eagerly every syllable which had fallen from the generous lips of Nuno de Tobar. She did not speak when he had closed, nor for some time after, but remained apparently a silent listener to the gay and desultory prattle of Leonora, who, in the fulness of her heart, assured of her own happiness, and relieved of all doubts of the future, had given herself up to that fearless and roving method which but too commonly distinguished her mercurial temper. She was arrested when about to trench upon dangerous ground—when about to renew her *badinage* in regard to Olivia's feelings for the knights of Portugal,—by the appearance of one of them. Fortunately, his approach had been heard in season to prevent her speech.

The visitor was the younger of the two. Andres de Vasconselos had many of the qualities of his elder brother, Philip. Their persons were not unlike, their courage and the contour and expression of their faces. They had both served as well against the Moors of Spain as the red-men of the western continent. But Philip, the elder, enjoyed the high distinction of being usually understood when the family name was mentioned. He had done famous things under Almagro in Peru. He had once before traversed the neighboring continent of the Appalachian, at least as far as Cabeza de la Vaca had carried his explorations. He was wise, besides, prudent, circumspect and gentle, and these were virtues to which the younger brother, Andres, had but little claim. Of Philip we shall say more hereafter. Of Andres, the world spake with many qualifications. He was described as proud and passionate—quick of quarrel—arrogant in his assumptions, and of enormous self-conceit. We have already had it intimated that he, as well as his brother, was now in doubt whether to continue in a future progress with the expedition of De Soto. Yet they had both left Spain with this special object, coming over to the New World as a portion of the armament. Something of the reason for their change of purpose has already been suggested. They had, in fact, found but little encouragement from the adelantado,—less, perhaps, because of his inappreciation of their merits—for he thought of the brothers very highly—as in consequence of the bigotry and jealousy of the Spanish Chieftains—their clannish prejudices, and a somewhat painful sense of their inferiority, at least, to the elder of the knights of Portugal. The neglect of De Soto had followed, perhaps, inevitably on this feeling of his people. The brothers had been offered no distinctions in the army, and as their military passion became cooled, that of love made its appearance to assist in usurping the place of the former in their bosoms. Unhappily, their affections were fixed upon the same lady. The devotion of Andres de Vasconselos led him almost nightly to her dwelling. Philip was a frequent visitor; but he so chose his periods as seldom to cross his brother's progress. Andres little knew how much he owed to this forbearance. He was slow to perceive, what was seen by all the island, that, if the heart of Olivia de Alvaro inclined to either, he certainly was not the suitor whom she most preferred. His self-esteem was not willing to accept any such humiliating suggestion.

Olivia naturally received him with respect and kindness. She felt uneasy at his attentions, but she respected him because of her attachment to his brother. It was easy, with his temper, to mistake the sources of this kindness. But he was not suffered to presume upon it. A certain dignified but mild reserve, in the manners of the lady, served to check every feeling of overweening confidence, and to satisfy the bold gallant that the fortress must undergo a regular leaguer before the garrison would be persuaded to surrender. He endeavored accordingly to school his eager desires, with as much patience as he could command; and to lessen the duration of the siege, his attacks were rendered more and more frequent. It was seldom that a night was suffered to pass without finding him in her presence; and the gentleness of her reception, and the sweetness of her manners, seldom suffered him to leave her without giving his eager vanity sufficient assurance of favorable progress. She beheld this confidence with pain, and her reserves were increased accordingly;—but as these never put on harsh aspects, nothing was done to arrest the self-delusion of the lover.

A little awkwardness succeeded his first appearance within the circle. Nuno de Tobar was the friend of Philip de Vasconselos rather than his brother. He had never been altogether satisfied with the latter. He was aware of the attachment of both for his fair hostess—perhaps suspected the nature of her feelings for his friend—and knew, besides, that the younger brother had already begun to regard his senior with a feeling of rivalry Andres was naturally jealous of one whom he had reason to believe was in his brother's confidence; while Nuno de Tobar, though fond of Philip de Vasconselos, had anything but a friendly feeling for Andres. The imperious temper of the latter had, more than once, brought them to the verge of quarrel. Their interchange of civilities on the present occasion was cold and formal, and, though the fair hostess, seeing the feeling between them, made an amiable effort to interest the party, still the atmosphere for a while grew oppressive from mere stillness and formality. But the confidence of Andres de Vasconselos was of a sort not to permit this influence to prevail to his discomfiture; and a perseverance that suffered no discouragement from a freezing answer, was soon rewarded by a conversation, which, if not actually animated, was yet sufficiently so to keep the scene from becoming absolutely oppressive. By a strong effort of will, for which her previous exercise had not often prepared her, Olivia took a reasonable share in the dialogue, and Don Andres was encouraged to proceed as he found her interest somewhat rising in one of the subjects which was started. This was the affairs of the army and the expedition, and naturally enough of the tournament. The thoughtless speech of Leonora conducted her to an inquiry, the answer to which drew the eyes of Olivia directly upon the knight of Portugal.

"They say of thee and of thy brother, Don Andres, that ye are not minded to proceed on this expedition into the country of the Floridian?"

"Of what Philip de Vasconselos designs, fair lady, it would be presumption in me to conjecture. Of my own purpose I can say nothing, but that it is still subject to such moods as may prevail with me when the adelantado is about to depart."

"Well, for my part, I see not how such brave cavaliers, well renowned in sword, and battle-axe, and spear, can hold it doubtful what they shall do when the trumpet invites them to glorious enterprise; nor do I question that when the signal sounds, thou wilt be among the first to hear and answer. But, of a surety, thou wilt not be wanting to the tournament."

"And yet," answered the knight of Portugal, with a smile that might have been mistaken for a sneer, " were it not as great a rashness if I should venture in a passage at arms with such fortunate gallants as Don Nuno de Tobar, who wears the favors of one of the loveliest damsels of Cuba? It will need something more than skill and valor to render a poor knight of Portugal successful against the cavaliers of Castile, when they couch spear under the smiles of the most invincible beauty."

There was something equivocal in this remark that made Nuno de Tobar wince, but his betrothed did not perceive it. She went on, slily glancing, as she spoke, at the pale face of Olivia, which put on an increasing gravity as she listened.

"Yet seems it to me, Señor, that thou wilt scarcely lack in the auspices which befriend thy opponent. I doubt not but the smiles of Beauty will give thee sufficient encouragement. At least, it is scarcely fitting that a true knight should suffer from such want."

The eyes of Andres de Vasconselos followed those of Leonora, as she looked mischievously in the direction of her friend. The reference was quite unfortunate. There was no mistaking the resolute gravity which absolutely gloomed the features of Olivia. But her face was no longer pale. A warm flush rose upon her cheeks at the same moment, of the source of which Don Andres readily deceived himself. His vain and eager fancy easily construed this flush into a confession of weakness,—and a proud exulting glance, which he did not seek to restrain, betrayed to Olivia the delightful conviction which he felt. But her eyes made no answer to his own, and the flush passing immediately from her cheeks, was succeeded by an almost mortal paleness, which was by no means diminished while Andres continued to speak in answer to the grateful suggestions of Leonora. He had his reply, full of *empressement*, to the pleasing insinuation which she had conveyed, quite as much, perhaps, by the direction of her glance, as by the language which she had uttered. His reply, though the mere words might disclaim his sense of triumph, was yet distinguished by a manner which betrayed the most confident assurance.

"Alas! Lady Leonora, thou wouldst betray me to my ruin! Would I could rejoice in any such hope as that which thou encouragest. But how should it be for me, a poor knight of Portugal, by no means in favor with your proud nobles of Castile, to hope for better countenance from her proud and lovely daughters? Yet the bird will spread his wings for the mansions of the sun! The fond insect will dart, though it be to perish, into the blazing flame or pyre;—and I fear that, hopeless of the glory that I seek, and destined to equal peril in the pursuit, I too am ambitious of the prize that but mocks my best endeavor."

"Thou confessest then—thou lovest?" was the eager inquiry of the gay and thoughtless Leonora.

"Ah! wouldst thou possess thyself of my secret? That were only to make merry with my weakness. Surely, in the good fortune which has smiled upon thy heart, it were scarcely generous to find a pleasure to show to the world the disappointments which mock the desire now preying hopelessly, perchance, upon mine."

"Not hopelessly, not fruitlessly, Señor Andres! Verily, Señor, that is a speech more gallantly than truly spoken. I will not believe that thou thinkest so humbly of thy hopes, or of the noble qualities which thou bring'st into the field, as potent against the maidens as against the lances of Castile. As I know that our cavaliers esteem thee one of the best warriors in our array, so am I sure that our ladies look upon thee with a favor which does not misbeseem thy reputation as a knight."

The flattery was not lost upon the person addressed. He was in the mood to believe every syllable; and indeed, the thoughtless woman, rating the judgment of her friend by her own, was well prepared to believe that the preference of Olivia was bestowed rather upon the younger than the older brother. Don Andres was not unwilling to continue a conversation which seemed to bring him so much nigher to his object. He did not see the painful constraint which sat upon the features of Olivia.

"Ah!" was his reply. "But he who hath set his affection. upon the bird of paradise, can give but little heed to the plumage or the strains of inferior songsters."

His eyes again sought the pale countenance of the maiden whom he worshipped. Her glance was equally wandering and sad. Nuno de Tobar saw that she was troubled. He himself was dissatisfied with the thoughtless play of his betrothed. He felt its mischievous tendency, and his friendship for Philip de Vasconselos made him unwilling to behold a progress on the part of his brother which was adverse to his own. He interfered to effect a diversion of the topic, which the fanciful allusion of Don Andres now enabled him to do without an effort.

"Talking of birds and singing, dear Lady Olivia, reminds me that in the cares of the camp, and in my long term of disfavor, I have not enjoyed thy music for a weary season. I pray thee, favor us with some one of those many ditties which never come with due effect save from those who feel them. I would I could persuade thee to one of those antique ballads of El Cid; but I will not ask thee, remembering the flat denial which thou gavest, in my presence, to that fine courtier, De Sinolar, when he craved the ballad of Urraca, and the Moor who lost Valencia. Nathless, some other strain, I pray thee, if it be only to persuade Doña Leonora that Nuno de Tobar is not so entirely *her* slave that he dare not seek a favor at the hands of another beauty. I trust, Señor Andres, that thy ear, like mine, is accessible to all the charms of music."

"Verily, Señor," was the reply, "that depends entirely on the bird that sings. There are some whose plumage makes marvelously against their strains. That thou hast had the wit to entreat from the Lady Olivia that bounty which it has been my first thought to solicit, is a great vexation. But I must content myself now with repeating thy entreaty."

The cavaliers both looked pleadingly to Olivia as they spoke. But she needed no second soliciting. She was not one of those whose vanity requires persuasion, as well as audience; besides she was only too anxious to escape a further dialogue, which pained her something more than either of the parties present could imagine. She was not one of that common company who delight in the imputation, so grateful to the vulgar damsel, of conquests which they have made; and resented naturally, as offensive no less to decency than good taste, a reference of this nature in the presence of the very person who is suspected of feeling their authority. But there were deeper sensibilities besides these at work within her bosom, to prompt her to revolt at the conversation, and the diversion of Nuno de Tobar was eagerly seized upon as affording relief to troubled feelings. She had already taken the guitar ere Don Andres had finished speaking, and, after a few soft prelusive touches, with a voice that trembled with her emotions, though full of compass and power, she sang in the nappiest style of art, yet with the most easy execution, the following ballad, which seemed in some degree designed as a commentary upon the preceding conversation:

AMINA.

Now why does fair Amina,
   With gallant suitors near,
Still scornful hark the pleading
   That woos no other ear?

Great nobles seek her beauty,
   And knights for valor known,
And wealth displays its treasure,
   Yet still she keeps her own.

She answers sighs with silence,
   And heeds not, though she hears
The sorrows of the bosom,
   That worships her in tears.

A scornful song requites them,
   With answer such as shakes
The strong heart with its mockery—
   The feeble one it breaks!

THE SONG.

And thus, while all are watchful,
 Each eager in his quest,
She answers for the bosom
 In maiden freedom blest

" Ye call me now your mistress,
 Ye bow beneath my word ;
To change were sorry wisdom,
 The subject to the Lord.

" I know ye well, my masters,
 The gentlest of your kind,
To him who flies in freedom,
 The sternest where ye bind.

" 'Tis sweet to have your homage,
 'Tis sweet to hear you plead,
And know that for our beauty's prize
 Ye do each valiant deed.

" How well ye speed in tourney,
 How gallant grace the hall ;
How sweetly in the twilight groves
 Your pleading murmurs fall !

" Your eloquence how gracious,
 Your song forever sweet,
That lifts the heart on pinions
 As exquisite as fleet.

" Too precious to the maiden
 These treasures while they're true ;
And sad to think, if change in her,
 Should work a change in you.

" If 'tis to win our favor
 Your graceful arts are shown,—
If valor strikes thus nobly,
 That Beauty may be won—

" If 'tis for this the palace
 Your courtly graces sees,—
For this ye plead in twilight bower,
 With homage sure to please—

"How great the fear of Beauty,
  If, when ye gain the prize,
Ye deem no longer needful
  The grace that won her eyes.

"Ye sing but for your mistress—
  Ye sing not for your slave,—
And give no more, the object won,
  The worship that ye gave.

"I will not brook a peril,
  That sounds of joy the knell;
And will not yield my heart to love,
  Because I love so well."

The song was finished; and as the maiden laid the instrument aside, a storm of gentle reproaches fell upon her ear, as well from Nuno de Tobar as from the youthful knight of Portugal.

"Nay, nay!" exclaimed the fair Leonora de Bovadilla—"heed her not, heed her not! She thinks not as she sings. She has chosen this ballad in a perverse spirit, only to mock what I have been saying. She is sworn in her secret heart, well I know, against all such inhuman selfishness. Out upon your damsels like Amina! She was but a Moorish damsel, I trow, and her heart was given up to heathen divinities."

"And love himself is one of them," said De Tobar archly.

"Not *our* love, Don Nuno—not the love known to chivalry, and before whose altars the true knight first buckles on his spurs. He hath his birth in the gay regions of Provençe—a cavalier himself, belted and spurred, with the addition of a pair of wings. See you what John of Nostrodamus writes of him, and you will be satisfied that he is not of heathen origin—a pure Christain, a noble and a gentle—from whom comes the religion of the belted knight."

And the Portuguese chaunted the original description from the ballad of the Troubadour.

"Censure not the Moor," said Olivia to Leonora gently—"you know not that I somewhat share in the blood of that misguided people."

"But not of the infidel?" replied the other with a sort of holy horror, crossing herself devoutly as she spoke.

"No, surely, but of a family that haply beheld the blessed light of the Christian Church, and of their own free will sought baptism. But the ballad I have sung comes not from the Moor. It is pure Castilian. The damsel Amina was of the true faith."

"Ay, lady, but she sang not wisely, knowing the wants of our sex, and the better virtue in her own. Her ballad is in the perverse spirit of the Moor, who, with the true heaven in his eye, yet wilfully turned away his sight. In heart she was but a pagan. — It suits the creed of one who found in his slave the thing of his affections. Of such only is it permitted to think ill of knighthood, and to stifle all the free faith in the heart of woman. It suits for a reproach to a race of misbelievers, who, though they bore themselves manfully enough in battle, were yet little familiar with the laws of Christian chivalry. The true knight loves not less the treasure because it hath been won. If he keeps it no longer in his eye, it is because he hath conveyed it to his heart. If he boasts no longer of its beauty, it is because he fears to tempt the avarice of others to seek his treasure. If he sings no longer in her praise, it is because, when he hath wholly given himself up to her charms, as he doth by marriage, he hath said the most in her honor that could be spoken. Verily, I repeat, your Amina was but a wretched heathen in heart, cold and selfish, and her doctrine is only true of a people who believe with the infidel."

Such was the eloquent commentary of Don Andres, conveyed in a manner at once spirited and graceful.

"Thou hast made a right good and proper defence of thy sex and mine, Don Andres," exclaimed Leonora, "and I trow thou wilt never lack lady's favor to grace thy helmet in the fields of tourney. Thou wilt take thy part, I trust, in the tournament which the adelantado has appointed; thou and thy valiant brother, even if ye go not on the enterprise against the Floridian."

With the mention of his brother, the eyes of Don Andres were seen suddenly to sparkle with a keen and fiery expression. Nuno de Tobar, knowing the conscious rivalry that existed between the two, watched him with interest, but said nothing. But Don Andres was not so forbearing.

"Philip de Vasconselos must answer for himself," said he, somewhat equivocally—"we are both of us sufficiently old to adopt our resolutions without much consultation with one another."

With these words he passed quickly from the subject. The evening was not much longer protracted, and soon De Tobar and his betrothed took their departure, leaving the knight of Portugal behind them. They were not conscious, as they descended the verandah into the groves leading from the dwelling, of the movements of another who led the way through the shady thickets. This was no other than Philip de Vasconselos himself. Let us not imagine that he had been a listener. He had been making his way to the abode of Olivia, when arrested, almost on the threshold, by the voice of his brother. He was about to retire, as he had usually done under the same circumstances.

"Let him have all the chances," he murmured to himself, as he turned away. "He was the youngest born of our mother and had her fondest blessing. It were a grievous sorrow if he had not mine."

Just then the voice of Olivia in song, detained his departing footsteps. He leaned sadly against a tree while he listened to the satirical ballad with which the damsel had answered the solicitations of his brother. The sentiment of the ballad was no less ungracious in his ears than in those of Andres; and yet there was a secret feeling of satisfaction in the heart of Philip, that the ditty had been chosen in response to the prayer of a rival. He retired, with mingled feelings, from his place of watch, as the song ended, and strolled slowly through the alleys. In a little while he heard the footsteps and the voices of De Tobar and his companion, behind him, and perceived, with a pang, that his brother did not accompany them. His pace was hurriedly increased. He felt all the delicious opportunity which Andres enjoyed, and readily conjectured that it was with a special purpose that the latter remained after the departure of her other guests.

"Well!" he murmured to himself sadly, "be it so! If he

hath the word with which to win her, she is his! I will not envy my brother. I would I had the strength to pray that he might be successful. He hath wronged me—he will still wrong me— and I will submit. He shall find in me no willing rival, whether in love or war. Our mother gave him to my care. I will think of her love, though he may never do justice to mine."

The field was clear before Andres de Vasconselos. He was alone with the woman whom he loved. He was not the man to lose time, or dally long in a fruitless attendance at the shrine of his devotions without making his petition heard. He was one of those impetuous spirits whose fierce and eager will, in the assertion of its desires, is apt to blind to the prospect of defeat— to all prospect save that which is beheld through the medium of a passionate and almost frenzied hope. Scarcely had Nuno de Tobar and his betrothed disappeared, before he was at the feet of Olivia. But not for us to watch the progress of the brief but exciting scene which followed. Let it suffice that ere many minutes had elapsed, Andres de Vasconselos was also speeding away from the abode, darting headlong through the perfumed alleys which surrounded it, and hurrying almost madly in the direction of the neighboring hills.

With his disappearance, Don Balthazar de Alvaro once more emerged from the cover of the neighboring thicket. His espionage over his niece and her visitors seems to have been continued throughout the evening. He had been sufficiently near, in his place of concealment, to behold all that had taken place, and to hear every syllable that was spoken. An exulting expression was kindled in his face, and his satisfaction at the result was audibly expressed.

"So far it is well! He hath *his quietus*. I had expected this; but it is something to be sure. That danger is passed. There is yet another, and a greater! Were I as confident of the answer she would make to the prayer of Philip as of Andres—nay, were I *not so* confident—I should feel at rest. This accursed anxiety! It leaves me almost a coward. But I must arm myself for the worst, and against the final struggle. It will come, and I must be prepared. Olivia de Alvaro must wed with neither of these knights of Portugal. She must wed with none. The hour that finds her a bride, finds me ———. But it shall never come to this; we must baffle him, or he must perish. Both shall perish ere she wed this man!"

Did Olivia dream of the near neighborhood of her uncle all this while! Could she fancy what were his resolves and reflections, in respect to her future fate and fortunes! It might almost seem that she did from the pallid features of her face, the big tears swelling in her eyes, the drooping self-abandonment with which, as soon as Andres de Vasconselos had disappeared, she suffered herself to fall back upon the couch, her hands covering her face, and, as it were, seeking to stifle the deep moan of agony which perforce escaped from her lips. The sound reached Don Balthazar in his place of concealment. Slowly he receded from the spot and disappeared in the more distant shrubbery. He had not the heart to meet her at that moment.

CHAPTER V.

*"Uso a vedirmi
Tremar tu sei ; ma, più non tremo."*—ALFIERI.

It was past midnight when Andres de Vasconselos returned to the bohio or cottage, which was occupied by his brother and himself. His agitation was measurably subsided, but not his passions. The quiet was only upon the surface. A violent storm was still busy, raging in the depths of his spirit. His features were rigidly composed, but stern almost to ferocity, and his emotion was perhaps only concealed by the resolute compression of his lips. It seemed as if he did not dare to trust to them in speech. Though late, his brother had not yet retired for the night. Philip de Vasconselos was busily engaged writing at the table, the only one which the apartment contained. The light by which he wrote was peculiar enough, however common to the island. It consisted of a cluster of twelve or fifteen cocuyos,—that larger sort of phosphorescent insect. These were enclosed in a little wicker-work, or cage, made of the most delicate threads of gold-wire. They emitted a light, of a color brilliantly green, ample enough for all the purposes of the student. Philip looked up, at the entrance of his brother, and discovered, at a glance, that his emotions had been violently aroused and agitated. He welcomed him, however, with a gentle word and smile, the answer to which was at once brief and ungracious.

"Are you unwell, Andres?" was the inquiry, affectionately made; for the elder brother was touched, rather than vexed, by the repulsive accents of the other.

"And if I were, Philip de Vasconselos?" sternly and unsatisfactorily replied the younger.

"And if thou wert, Andres! This to me, thy brother?"

"Why not? Why should grief or suffering of mine concern thee? It is enough that thou hast neither."

"Nay, Andres, that I myself am free from cares and sorrows would be good reason only why I should seek to bring some remedy to thine. But there is yet another cause for my anxiety. The epistle, my brother, which is now growing beneath my hands especially reminds me of my duty to succor and to comfort thee. It is a letter to our mother, Andres; and I am even now about to speak of thy health and happiness."

"What warrant hast thou for assuming either? What knowest thou of my happiness or health?"

"Nay, Andres, that thou hast vigorous and youthful health, may not be denied. All who behold thee, speak loudly of thy full cheek, thy elastic form, and the brightness of thine eye; and these things speak for thy happiness also. It is vain to declare the presence of a grief which leaves the beauty and vigor of the form unwasted and untouched. Surely, my brother, thou art not unhappy?"

"Why troublest thou me with such questions, Philip? Write to our mother whatever it pleaseth thee to write. Say what thou wilt. It matters but little to me what thou sayest!"

"But it matters much to her, Andres," replied the other, somewhat reproachfully. "Besides, I dare not speak to our mother indifferently of him, her favorite son, whom she so commended especially to my affection as a younger brother."

"Philip de Vasconselos, both thou and our mother have erred greatly when ye claim to believe that I need guardianship. I tell thee, Señor, I am, like thyself, a man,—and fully capable of taking care of my own health and fortunes."

The reply to this rude speech was full of a sad solemnity.

"Something hath vexed thee, Andres, making thee unjust to thy brother and ungrateful to the tender fondness of thy mother for thy youth. Thou wilt find it less easy, when thou recoverest thy calm of temper, to forgive thyself than to procure her forgiveness or mine. I will finish my letter, making my own report of thy condition, which, until this hour, Andres, hath seemed to all the island, as to myself, such as it would be most grateful to any mother to behold or know."

"As thou wilt; and yet!—Look at me, Philip de Vasconselos! —look at me, ere thou writest down any delusive falsehood for my mother's eyes! Look I like one whom the Gods have marked for happiness?"

He approached the table as he spoke, and grasped, with some violence, the hand that held the pen. The eyes of the brothers encountered. Those of Andres were blood-shot, full of rage, and expressive of a fury that seemed about to break through all restraint. Philip rose, as he caught the fearful expression in the other's face. His own features were calm and firm, but filled with a tender concern and sympathy, such as spoke for the gentle and noble attachment with which the elder brother regarded the younger, and the favorite of their mother.

"Andres," he said, "I know not that I am wise, or like to be successful in asking thy confidence. Of late thou hast seemed to regard me rather as an enemy than a brother ——"

"Thou art! Thou art!" was the wild and reckless answer.

"Nay, I cannot answer thee, Andres, by any assurance in words. It becomes not me patiently to strive to disprove thy injustice. I look upon such speech as a sort of madness, on thy part, rather than a wrong done to me. Enough, that I tell thee I am here, ready, as thou hast always found me before, to serve thy cause, to help thy progress, to fight thy battles—if need be ——"

"I ask not thy help in battle, Philip de Vasconselos. I am equal to my own danger. But thou art willing to help my progress—to serve my cause?—How sayest?—Eh!"

"Yea! with all my strength, and all my heart!" was the eager reply.

"Hearken! wilt thou deign then to seek on my behalf, and to solicit from Don Balthazar de Alvaro, the hand of his niece in marriage? Wilt thou do this, Philip de Vasconselos?"

"Verily, of a truth will I do this, if the lady hath authorized
3*

thee so to solicit;" was the answer, in somewhat subdued accents.

"If the lady hath authorized thee to solicit!" was the mocking repetition of the infuriate young man: "Go to, Philip de Vasconselos, I well know that thou wouldst not, ay, thou couldst not, serve me in this. Would I need to solicit the favor of the uncle, were I sure of the favor of his niece?"

"Thou wouldst surely not seek the one, were the other denied thee?"

"Not through *thy* eloquence, surely, Señor Don Philip, lest thou shouldst haply forget thy client's claims in the prosecution of thy own."

"Andres, my brother," said the other calmly, but with a sterner show of expression than had before been apparent in his countenance,—"it will not be easy to make me angry with thee. It is in thy madness that thou dost me this gross injustice,—and I forgive it. But let us speak no more in regard to this matter. It needs not that I should tell thee what thou seemest already to understand, that my affections have been placed, as well as thine, upon the same lovely lady. I deny not this, though I have deemed it only proper that I should be silent on the subject, seeing thy secret in the same moment with mine own. It is surely our misfortune that we have so loved. But I resolved, from the moment when I discovered the bent of thy affections, that the field should be open to thee from any obstruction of mine. I stood not in thy way. I offered no rivalship to thee,—and, while thou hast nightly sought the dwelling of the Lady Olivia, it was enough for me to know that such was the course of thy footsteps, to turn mine in the opposite direction. This very night, when I learned that thou wast her guest, I left the garden of the lady——"

"Ha! thou wast there,—and thou hast heard?" was the interruption.

"I have heard nothing! When I found the verandah occupied by thyself and Nuno de Tobar, with his betrothed, I turned away in silence, seeking nothing farther. I left thee to thy own progress, with the resolution to give thee all the opportunity; and, if success were thine, to bury in silence, in the depths of mine own heart, the secret affection which has troubled it. Thy injustice hath not suffered this———"

A deep groan from the younger brother interrupted the speaker for a moment. The latter would have proceeded, but Andres broke in.

"Enough! Enough, my brother," he exclaimed with a returning sentiment of justice. "I am a madman and a fool. I have wronged thee! Pursue thy fortunes. It needs not any longer that thou shouldst yield thy hopes or purposes to mine. This night hath resolved me. It finds me denied, where I had hoped most strongly. It finds me destitute, where I had set all my fortunes on the venture. I dare not wish that thou shouldst be more fortunate. I am not generous enough for that. Yet I stand in thy path no longer. Within the hour I have made a new resolution; I will continue with Hernan de Soto. I will go with him into Florida. In Cuba I should find but wreck and sorrow only."

"Is it so, my brother!" said Philip sadly.

"Pity me not, if thou wouldst not madden me. Thou knowest my pride and temper. Beware, lest I forget what is due to thee —lest I forget thy justice, thy generosity, ever shown to me, even when my perversity was most. Enough, now that my mood inclines to thee, to do thee right, Philip; although I dread to think that I no longer love thee as I did. I see thee destined for success where I have failed—where I have been crushed and confounded with unexpected denial. I fear—I feel—that, but for thee, this had not been the case. Thou hast passed before me as thou hast ever done before. It matters nothing that thou shouldst tell me of thy forbearance. Thou hast given way to me—thou hast yielded me opportunity—and, in thy secret heart, perchance, it is like thou felt that thou couldst do so with safety. I know the strength of thy will and hope, Philip de Vasconselos, and fully believe that thou hast built thy expectations upon a confidence in thy superior fortune, which might boldly give every opportunity to mine———"

"Thou still wrong'st me, Andres!" mildly.

"Perhaps, perhaps!—do I not even wrong myself as well as thee? We will speak no more of this. Enough, that the field lies before thee—that I cross thy path no longer—that I go on the expedition with De Soto—and as, most likely, thou wilt be successful where I have failed, so thou wilt remain here, and we will cast our shadows no more upon each other. Write this to our mother, and say to her that my soul is now wholly yielded to the ambition of conquest. Tell her what thou wilt of those dreams of Dorado, which woo the adventurer to the wilds of the Appalachian."

"Brother ———"

"Think not that I would wrong thee, Philip. Is it not enough that even in my passion and my pang, I acknowledge thy forbearance? I blame thee not, even while I curse in bitterness thy always better fortune. It is thy fortune that prevents my love, and not thyself."

"But thou dost love me, Andres?"

"I know not that!—How should I love thee, when thou hast been the barrier to my love?—the only one passion on which all my affections have been set!"

"But I know not this, Andres; I have never spoken word of love or tenderness to the Lady Olivia."

"But thou wilt speak both; and she will hear thee, and respond to thee in accents like thine own. No more of this, lest I grow wild and foolish, and curse thee, Philip, for thy better fortune."

"Nay, thou shalt not, brother," and he threw his arms tenderly about the unreasonable youth, who submitted but only for a moment to the embrace; he shook himself free from it in the next instant. Philip's eyes followed him with a deep and melancholy interest, full of sorrow and affection, as he saw him preparing once more to leave the cabin.

"Whither go you, my brother, at this late hour?"

"Forth! Forth once more into the night!"

"Nay, Andres; were it not better thou shouldst seek sleep?"

"I cannot sleep! Thou knowest not what a stifling fullness harbors here—and here!" was the reply of Andres, smiting his head and bosom as he spoke. "I must hurry forth! I must have air and solitude!"

With these words he disappeared from the cabin. Philip de Vasconselos followed him to the door, and his eyes anxiously pursued the retreating form by the imperfect starlight, until it had wholly gone from sight. The elder brother then returned to the table, where, seating himself, he rested his cheek upon his palm, and sunk into a fit of melancholy, which was of mixed character, at once pleasing and painful. The perverse and willful pride of his brother, his suspicious and jealous temper, must necessarily have been productive of great grief to one by whom he was earnestly beloved; but it was in vain that Philip de Vasconselos tried to stifle the feeling of satisfaction which enlivened and pleasantly agitated his bosom, as he thought of the rejection by Olivia de Alvaro of his brother's suit. Love is certainly one of the most selfish and exacting of all the passions in the heart of youth; perhaps because it is the passion which most completely absorbs and swallows up the rest. Philip was really fond of Andres; fond of him by reason of natural sympathies, as a brother; fond of him by habit and association—fond of all that was manly in his character—proud of his spirit and youthful beauty—fond of him, on account of their mother, and particularly so, as, for so long a time, he had been the guardian of his youth and fortunes. But his heart reproached him for the still grateful feeling of satisfaction, which he vainly endeavored to subdue, and which continually reminded him that, in this quarter, there was no longer an obstacle to his own successes. It was to overcome this thought that he proceeded to resume the letter which he had been writing to his mother when Andres had first made his appearance. A few additional lines only were written, when he flung the reed from him and closed the portfolio. His nervous system was in too much agitation to suffer him to continue an employment which particularly demanded the utmost calm of the spirit. He went once more to the entrance of the cabin, and soliloquized, as if his brother were still in sight.

"Unhappy child of passion! forever erring and repenting—only to repeat thy error; what a destiny is thine! How shall I watch and save thee, when it is ever thus, that some cruel suspicion, the offspring of thy wild temper and fierce will, continually begets thy hostility against the hand that is outstretched in thy service! Thou wilt go with Hernan de Soto, and it may be that I shall not be with thee. Ha! Is this, then, a doubt? Is it so certain that mine shall be a better fortune with Olivia de Alvaro than was thine? She has refused thee,—thou, as brave, as noble, as comely as any of the gentlemen of Castile! Will she be more likely to hearken me? It is possible; and I have a hope, a hope in which I gladden—though I shame to own it,—based upon a brother's denial and defeat! Is there reason for this hope? Do I not delude myself—does not Nuno de Tobar, when he encourages my passion, does he not delude me also? The thought that I too shall be scorned, makes it easy to pardon the violent passions of my poor Andres. Well! We shall shortly see! Now that he no longer pursues the quest, it will be for me to know what is my fate. A few days, and it may be that I also go with thee, my brother, into the wild forests of the Apalachian. And yet, were there other fields of venture, Hernan de Soto should have no help of mine. He hath favored, rather than frowned upon, these jealousies of his Spanish followers. They hold me in their hate, if not their disesteem; and envy me the very skill and knowledge upon which they build somewhat for their hope of success. Let Olivia but smile upon *my* prayer, and I fling them off, with as little regard as I would fling off the most worthless thing, in my dislike or indifference!"

We need not follow Philip de Vasconselos in his soliloquy. Enough is given to show the temper of his mind and character. We will leave him to his slumbers, such as he may snatch, in the brief interval which now remains between the midnight and the dawn; while we retrace our footsteps once more to the **dwelling of Don Balthazar de Alvaro.**

It might have been an hour after we saw him retiring, silently, from his place of espionage among the groves which surrounded the verandah where his niece had received her guests, that we find him returning to the same spot. But it was no longer to find concealment and to play the spy that he now appeared. His step was set down firmly and fearlessly, and his lips parted with a pleasant catch of Castilian song, as he drew near the shrubbery. Don Balthazar was no mean musician. With no sensibilities such as are vulgarly assumed to be absolutely necessary to musical endowment, he was held to be something of a master, and could shape corresponding melodies to the most difficult ditties, with a readiness not unlike that of the Italian improvisatori. His song on the present occasion, which might have been a spontaneous utterance for aught we know, was sufficiently loud to be heard within the dwelling. But it did not reach the senses of Olivia, who lay stretched upon the divan, upon which we beheld her sink suddenly at the departure of Andres de Vasconselos, under the burden of a nameless sorrow, for which, with Beauty in her endowment, and Devotion at her feet, it would be very difficult to account. She beheld not the entrance of her uncle, and yet she slept not. Her eyes were open, but the glance was vacant; 'the sense was shut.' It was fixed within, upon the struggling passions of her own heart, and took no heed of external objects. Don Balthazar approached her—he stood before her—he spoke to her, yet she heard him not. He paused quietly, and surveyed her. Very peculiar was the character of that glance which he bestowed upon the lovely outline and perfect beauty of the features within his gaze. It might be pride and exultation, such as a father feels beholding the unsurpassable charms of a favorite daughter. But there was something still that was equivocal in the expression of his features. There was a mysterious significance in that look, at once of steady and circumspect watch, yet of eagerness and satisfaction, which baffled the curiosity that it continued to provoke. Some moments were consumed in this serpent-like gaze, and all the while she remained absolutely unconscious of his presence. She was only aroused from this unconsciousness as he sat himself quietly beside her, and folding his arms about her waist, lifted her with an air of great affection in his embrace. Then it was that she started, looked wildly about her for a moment, and then, distinguishing the intruder, fixed upon him a countenance expressive of any feeling but that of tenderness or regard. In an instant the full, quick, keen vitality, came like a flood of light into her great dark eyes; her lips quivered, and were suddenly closed fast, as if with sudden resolution. She started from the cushions, and shook herself free from his grasp, as if he had been a viper.

"You!" she exclaimed in a tone of suspicion and apprehension.

"Even so, Olivia. Who else? But what now? Why this passion? What has vexed you? What startles you?"

"How long have you been here?" she asked wildly.

"But this moment," he answered: "I thought you slept." She drew a deep sigh, as if suddenly relieved.

"It is late," she said; "I will retire."

"Late! what of that? Have you any cares for to-morrow? Sit, my beauty, and tell us who have been your guests—who hath been here? What are your tidings?"

"I have none," she answered coldly and timidly, still moving to retire.

"Now, saints and demons! what is in the child!" he exclaimed, as he endeavored once more to detain her in his grasp. She shrunk from him with a visible shudder. A heavy scowl passed over his forehead, and he spoke with closed teeth.

"What! still in thy Biscayan temper? Nay, nay, my precious one, thou shalt not leave me thus."

"Suffer me to go, uncle," she entreated, as he caught her hand.

"Why, so I will, when thou hast answered me what has put thee in this temper again? Methought, when I left thee last, that thou hadst been sobered—hadst grown wiser. What has wrought thee into this passion, at a moment when brave cavaliers grow humble in thy train? Or dost thou repent thee for having dismissed with denial this famous young gallant of Portugal?"

What a change in her aspect followed this speech from his lips! But a moment before she exhibited aversion, but it was coupled with timidity and a feeble, tearful apprehension. In a moment the timidity was gone—the tear—the apprehension. Her eyes flashed full with indignation as she replied:—

"What! thou hast again descended to the office of the spy? Thou hast once more placed thyself in secret watch upon my actions?"

"Not upon thy actions, child—not upon thee, but upon those who approach thee. I know thy danger from these gallants, and it is in degree as I fear them, my Olivia, that I keep watch over thee, as thy guardian—thy protector, child——"

He renewed the attempt to take her hand as he spoke.

"Touch me not," she cried. "Oh, wolf assigned to keep the lamb!"

"What wouldst thou have, child? It is surely needful that I hold ever present in mind the treasure that I am set to keep."

"Oh, fiend! and thou smil'st as thou speak'st thus dreadfully."

"Nay, nay, not a fiend, Olivia, only, I grant you, not exactly an angel. Believe me, I am not a whit worse than most other men."

"Thou slanderest thy race."

"No, truly, no. Most guardians, having such precious treasure in their keeping, would take care of it as I have done. Have I not kept thee well, my child—as tenderly, as closely? Shall others rob me of the treasure before mine own eyes? Ah, child! if I loved thee less, I had been spoiled of thee before. It is in my fondness, Olivia,——"

"Oh! cease to vex me with these cruel taunts! What gain is it to thee now, that thou shouldst add a sting to a sorrow? If to thee I owe the loss of hope, why jibe me ever with this loss? Why hold before mine eyes the terrible picture of the woe thou hast planted forever in my soul? Forbear thy mockeries. Suffer me to leave thee—suffer me to sleep—sleep—sleep! if this be possible to-night."

"Nay, I would not mock thee, Olivia. I but speak to thee the language of a sober truth. I do, indeed, love thee, my child—love thee as my own—would have thee ever as mine own, and thou mightst see in this fondness the secret of that distrust which dogs the heels of all others. Give not way to this blindness and madness, which can profit neither thee nor me, and see the love which I feel for thee, my child!"

"Peace! Peace! thou maddenest me when thou talkest to me of thy love!"

"A truce to thy passion, Olivia. Thou art not wise in its indulgence. It spoils thy beauty. It takes too much from thy charm of face, as it disturbs the peace of thy heart. Thus ruffled, thou remind'st me painfully of thy Biscayan mother, who was fiercer in her wrath than the hurricane of these tropic countries. She would suddenly grow convulsed like thyself, with a tempest that threatened everything with destruction; but she was not, as thou art, capable of soothing all down again to the most beautiful repose!"

"Her passion were much the most fitting to mate with thine! O! would that she were here! Mother! O! mother! Where art thou now? See'st thou thy child—into what hands—into what fate she has fallen—without hope—as one who drowns, with all the seas upon him, and no strength to struggle upward into life?"

She threw herself once more upon the cushions of the divan, her face downward. One single sob escaped her, but one, for at that moment the hand of Don Balthazar, in seeming tenderness, was placed upon her neck. His touch seemed to recall the more fiery feeling with which she had at first received him. She started up, and repulsed him with a spasmodic fierceness.

"Thy touch is like so much poison! Beware, lest I go mad! Thou wilt drive me too far, as if thou hadst not already driven me to perdition! Canst thou not pity—wilt thou not spare me? I have been weak—I know that I am weak still—but I feel that I have a strength in me that may become fearful for mischief, if not for good. Uncle, it were better, far better, ere you rouse that strength into exercise, that you should drive your dagger into both of our hearts."

The brow of Don Balthazar was contracted; but a determined effort dissipated the cloud. His *rôle* was that of conciliation. He was not unwilling to acknowledge and to respect that fearful strength which she asserted herself to possess, though latent. He felt that he had gone too far. He had given her no credit for that character of which she was now making a fearful exhibition. Nor, indeed, had he hitherto found any reason to suspect the presence of such fierce energies. She had hitherto borne herself so mildly, if not feebly, that he had come rather to slight, if not to despise, the weakness of a nature, which had been almost wholly controlled by his superior will. That he had been so successful hitherto, in this respect, was due to causes already glanced at—the seclusion of her mode of life, her extreme youth, and her imperfect education. The instincts of her heart, suddenly springing into birth, had opened to her eyes a new survey, and filled her soul with a consciousness not less overwhelming and oppressive than strange. He was beginning to discover the full extent of her developments, when it was perhaps too late. Regarding her as a child, a pliant creature in his hands, he had but too much given way to that satirical temper which marked his character. It was now his aim to soothe. He was not practised in this art, but he seriously addressed himself to the endeavor. "Truly, dear Olivia, thou art most perverse to-night. Is it at the moment when I am most grateful to thee, that thou wouldst repulse my acknowledgments? I do but seek to show how greatly I prize that dutiful affection which alone, I doubt not, has caused thee to dismiss this young and insolent knight of Portugal."

"Dutiful affection!" she exclaimed, interrupting him with a bitter look and accent, which effectually interpreted into scornful irony the two words which she had borrowed from his speech.

"And was it not this, Olivia?"

"Once for all, Señor, let this folly cease. There is no policy in this hypocrisy. Thou canst deceive me no longer. I have no need to deceive thee. We know each other. Thou knowest me—thou hast sounded the hollows of my heart, and the knowledge thou hast gained has been fatal to all my hopes. Thou knowest that I owe thee neither duty nor affection—that, if any thing, I owe thee hate only—an unforgiving hate that should dream of nothing but revenge. But I have no such dream. Give me but peace—such peace, at least, as may spring from thy forbearance, and if I meet thee with smiles no longer, I shall at least assail thee with no reproaches. I rejected the suit of Don Andres de Vasconselos simply because—— alas! why should I furnish thee with a reason for this rejection? Enough, that it was with no regard to thy interests, or thy desires, that I was moved to decline his prayer."

"And yet, that thou didst so, is a great gain to me, as well as to De Soto. Failing thee and thy *hacienda,* this knight will now be ready to seek for a slower fortune amongst the Apalachian of Florida. We had lost him but for this. He and his brother both—that more wily adventurer—had set earnest eyes upon thy possessions. I doubt not that they knew well the number of thy slaves and acres, and the exact annual product of thy lands."

"Oh! be silent, Señor—be silent, for very shame. It befits not thee, least of all, to impute such sordid passions to these noble gentlemen."

Even at this moment, when fully convinced of the necessity of conciliation, and really desirous not to offend, the habitual sneer of the uncle obtained the ascendency.

"And thou persuadest thyself—though I wonder not—that it is thy charms alone which have wrought upon the affections of these knights of Portugal."

The sarcasm smote sharply on the woman sensibilities of the damsel. She replied instantly:

"I think not of it! I would that I could think of neither them nor thee. Small pleasure, indeed, do I find in thinking of thee, and smaller the profit, in such condition as is mine, in giving thought to knight or noble, on whose scutcheon there rests no stain. Why wilt thou madden me with these things? If, for a moment, I have been weak and vain enough to think of any noble gentleman, Heaven knows how suddenly and soon my own heart has smitten me for the guilt and folly of such fancies. But if the deadlier tongue of Remorse were not speaking ever at my heart this language, there were rebuke sufficient in the consciousness that, whatever speech is addressed to my ear, must be heard also by thine;—that even did I presume to love, or to listen to the pleadings of a lover, the precious sweetness of such intercourse must be without secret or security. Thy watch is ever upon my footsteps, and thy miserable spies ——"

"Nay, but thou wrong'st me, child. I have set no eyes to watch thee but mine own, and mine watch thee only because thou art so precious in their sight."

She gave him but a single look, so cold—so freezingly sad, that he felt all its profound scorn and denial.

"Of a truth, Olivia, it is so. Hadst thou been my own child, I could not have loved thee better"

"Father! Mother! Hear him! Alas! wherefore *was I not* thine own! That might have secured me from this fate! And yet, I know not! I know not what thou holdest sacred! I know not what could have been safe in thy hands, from thy bad and brutal nature. Oh! Señor Balthazar—I will call thee no more mine uncle—when I look upon thee, as I do now, with eyes fairly opened upon thy cruelties and crime,—I feel a doubt, a dread, lest I be in the power of some fearful emissary of the enemy of souls, whose study is how to cut me off from repentance and salvation. Mother of God, be merciful! Jesu, descend to me and cover me with thy holy shelter. Oh! I feel that I shall madden, unless the white spirits whom I pray for shall come quickly to my aid!"

A passion of tears followed this wild apostrophe, and somewhat relieved the swollen heart and the overburdened brain. Don Balthazar felt that he must pause. He did not dare to address her in the moment of the paroxysm. He waited, watching her patiently, till her tears flowed freely, and then subduing himself to his policy—his bitter reckless mood to the necessity before him, and with which he felt that it would not do to trifle farther, —he carefully adapted his speech to the task of soothing. In some measure he succeeded. She grew calmer, and milder, and he now approached her where she sat upon the divan, and without interruption, save from her sobs occasionally, continued the glozing speech which was to quiet her anger. She answered him but seldom, and then capriciously—sometimes with tears only, and again with some burst of indignant speech, that drove him back to his first positions.

"Oh! why wilt thou, dearest Olivia, give way to these passionate phrensies? of what profit to conjure up such wild and gloomy reflections? They nothing help your situation or mine. They restore us nothing that is lost, but tend rather to embitter the only consolations that remain to us."

"What are they?" she asked fiercely.

"To economize the better feelings. To forgive where we can.—to spare when we can——"

"Ah! I owe thee much for thy forbearance."

"I feel that I deserve thy chiding; but, dearest child, I will do better. I will give thee no cause for anger henceforward. Only be merciful.—I owe thee much, Olivia,—much for the past.—That thou hast sent off this young gallant with denial, leaves me to-night with a light heart."

"And mine! mine is breaking!"—was the wild finish which her lips sobbed out at the conclusion of his sentence. The deep despairing agony of her manner admirably suited the language of her lips.

"Nay, nay, my child; not so! The world is but begun with thee. There is sunshine for thee, and flowers in abundance. Thou wilt forget——"

"Never! never! Oh! would it could break, break at once, that I may feel no more this terrible struggle—this pang that is worse than death! But its doom is not to break. There must be more agonies. I must undergo many deaths,—and that blight of all—that accursed bitter blight!"

The picture of her grief was beyond all practice. There could be no question of the terrible earnestness of her woe. With her face buried in the cushions of the divan, she lay silent or sobbing, without an effort to move, until he endeavored once more to raise her up. Again she betrayed that shuddering horror at his touch, which she had shown several times before; and, firmly repulsing him, she again abandoned herself to her afflictions. His soothing was in vain, or only offered new provocation to her sorrows.

"Olivia, dearest child, wherefore now this unwonted passion? What grief hast thou *now*, that thou hadst not yesterday, and the day before?———"

"Ay, Señor," she answered, with a fearful vehemence, "and last week, and months agone, even to that dark and damnable hour, when———"

And she closed the sentence abruptly, covering her face with her hands as she did so, as if to shut from sight some terrible presence.

"Olivia—dear child!"

"Child me not! I am not thy child. Thou hast known me as a child only to crush me as a woman. Away, I entreat thee—let me never see thee more. If thou wouldst not drive me into absolute phrensy, I implore thee to forbear—to depart forever. It is those days, those weeks, those months, when in my ignorance and weakness, I had not felt these agonies, as I feel them now, to which I owe them all! Blot these out, Señor, from my memory! make me forget them, I command thee, or take this dagger, and thrust it into this heart, which thou hast filled with death and misery. Do it, uncle—do it, if thou hast one spark of the man within thy bosom—if, indeed, thou hast one feeling of pity in thy soul for the poor orphan whose sire drew milk from the same bosom with thy own."

She clutched at the weapon in his girdle, and would have seized it, but that he grappled her by the wrist, and held her fast.

"Oh! thou *shouldst* do it—such a blow would never shame *thy* dagger. If thou wilt not, hence! Let me never see thee more. If thou canst not bring me the forgetfulness I implore, thou art my bane only, and canst bring no remedy. Thy words of soothing I despise. As I live, uncle, I loathe thy presence. Thy voice sounds hissingly in mine ears., like that of the serpent, who carries a deadly poison beneath his tongue."

The inspired priestess, drunk with the sacred fury, never looked so sublimely fearful. Her great flashing eyes, lighting up the paleness of her cheeks—her widely distended nostril, her lofty and erect figure, and the wild but beautiful action of her frame, actually seemed to confound and overwhelm her companion. He spoke—but how feeble now were his words of soothing—his entreaties—his arguments!

"Olivia! This is, indeed, wilful. Of what avail now all this horror, this professed loathing?"

"Professed! Oh! Man, man! Vain man! What seest thou in me at this moment, to make thee dream that I could say anything that I do not feel! But of what avail thou ask'st? Of what avail, indeed, except for curses—perhaps for death! But that the grief can bring no relief is sufficient cause for suffering. Could it avail—could anything avail—would I suffer thus? Would I seek no remedy? Would I not go through the furnace in its search, and gladly give up the life which is tutored to reconcile itself to all manner of sin and sorrow, as it is made to *see* that nothing can avail! Oh! Blessed Virgin, if my lips may now be permitted to name thy name, and to appeal to thee, what hast thou suffered me to see? In the brief space of a single week mine eyes have opened to the truth. I behold now what I neither saw nor dreamed before. Oh! Señor,—brother of my wretched father, what hast thou done! Thou hast slain the very hope—the life of hope and happiness of his only child, given to thee in blessings and in sacred trust, all of which thou hast trampled under foot in scorn."

"Not so, dearest Olivia. Thou seest this matter through a false medium. The evil is not of the magnitude which thou deem'st it. Who is there to betray our secret? Who is it that knows ——"

"Is it not enough that *I* know,—that *I* feel—that the dreadful consciousness is crushing me to the earth, making my soul a thing of constant fear, and apprehensions the most terrible?"

The wisdom of Don Balthazar was again at fault. He could not forbear a remark, which, however true in respect to the subject of her griefs, was yet very unseasonably referred to in the present condition of her feelings.

"Olivia, this dreadful consciousness of which thou speakest, never possessed thee until thine eyes beheld this Philip de Vasconselos. Beware—my child, lest ——"

The fearful spirit was roused again within her. She did not suffer him to finish.

"And I say to thee, Balthazar de Alvaro, unworthy and treacherous brother, base and cruel guardian—shameless and perjured man—do *thou* beware! If I am to be crushed and cursed by thee, I will not be reproached or threatened by thee! Thou sayest justly, indeed, that until I beheld this knight of Portugal, I did not well conceive the full extent of the wrong which thou hadst done me. That thy perfidy, thy stealth, thy cunning, thy pernicious malice and fatal power, which had wrought upon me in moments of oblivion, had done me the cruellest of evils, I well know! My tears, my reproaches have not been spared, as thou well knowest, from the beginning! But of the awful wrecks of which thou wert the sole cause, I had little knowledge. Mine eyes are opened, and, as thou sayest, with the moment of my knowledge of Philip de Vasconselos! Oh! make not my heart feeble by compelling my tongue to repeat that name. It was only when I knew *him* that I began darkly and hopelessly to know myself. I then, for the first time, heard the terrible voice speaking to my conscience as if from the depths of my own heart. It is in the birth of what had been my blessing and my joy, that I am made terribly sensible of what is now my privation and my curse! Enough! It is wonderful that I have speech for this! But thy wanton malice hath opened all the floods of my indignation. No more to-night! Let us separate—though I go not to sleep. *Sleep!* sleep! can I ever sleep again? Thou seest me changed; and such a change! I am no more a child,—blind, weak, submissive—overcome when my innocent sleep dreamed nothing of danger, and blasted by a guilt in which, Holy Mother, be my witness, I had no share! I am a woman now. I have risen to the highest intelligence of woman, only through despair. I now know thee for what thou truly art—base, brutal,—and oh! shame on thy pretence of manhood, with a corrupt selfishness that would keep me still a victim!"

"Olivia!"

"Follow me not—touch me not—look no more upon me—if thou art wise, and wouldst not see me a maniac beneath thine eyes, raving aloud to the abashed people of thy and my miserable secret."

Thus speaking, with arms extended as if for judgment, and eyes flashing almost supernatural fires, she waved him passionately aside, and defying the obstruction, which he was too much paralyzed to offer, darted headlong from the apartment

CHAPTER VI.

> "Now will these damned conspirators 'gainst Virtue
> Make such felonious traffic of her servants,
> As move the night to shudder ; cause her fair planets
> To blush with secret passion that they may not
> Come down with holy succor ! Oh ! that angels
> Might put on armor when they would, and strangle
> The enemy ere he strikes."—THE PARRICIDE.

She was gone from sight before he recovered himself. He stood abashed—stunned rather—pale and almost trembling, at the unexpected fury he had awakened. At length, but slowly, he began to recover himself; and his gathering thoughts betrayed themselves in broken soliloquy.

"This grows more serious. It must be looked to. It is a danger to be hushed by the shortest method, if it passes not off like all the rest. But I must prepare myself for the worst. She must not be suffered to destroy me, even if she resolves to destroy herself. I must cure these violences of passion—and I will."

His hand, perhaps unconsciously, griped the handle of his dagger. A moment after, he seized hurriedly the light, and left the room, pursuing, at first, the passage which Olivia had entered, as if about to proceed also in the direction of her chamber; but he paused almost as soon as he had entered it, wheeled about, passed once more into the apartment which he had left, and, opening a door in the opposite wall, entered another passage conducting to his own chamber. Here, setting the light down upon a table, he threw himself into a light chair of bamboo work, and with so little heed, and so heavily, that the slight wicker frame of the fabric creaked and threatened to sink beneath his weight.

"I was a fool," he said, soliloquizing moodily. "I was but a fool to confront her in her paroxysm. It is then that she hath as little measure in her anger as her fierce Biscayan mother. Yet how lately hath this sort of fury developed itself in her. How wonderfully to-night did she resemble her. There was the same dark, fiery eye, sending out sudden flashes; the same sudden swelling of the great vein across her forehead, till it seemed big to bursting; the same show of the teeth, gleaming white, close set, and gnashing at moments the thin lips that seemed to part and turn over, like those of a hungry tiger. What a resemblance! I never saw the like before. Yet, when I beheld the likeness, that I should have dealt in the old sarcasm; that I should not have forborne. I should have known enough of the mother, to have waited for the moment of her exhaustion. Who takes the fish will do wisely not to thwart him in the struggle. Why should he not struggle, since it avails nothing against his capture? He is so much the sooner in the toils. Let him beat the water while he lists, until it becomes easier to die than to strive. Such is the true art of dealing with women in their passion, especially when they carry tempers of such intensity. It is in her exhaustion only that she yields; and the exhaustion comes the sooner where the flurry is so extreme. With opposition, she finds new strength; but, taken in the lull, with fondness or persuasion, and she cannot help but yield!"

He paused, rested his elbow on the table, and supported his brow upon his hands for a while in silent meditation. A few moments only passed thus; his mood was too much excited for quiet. He started up from his seat, and again instantly resumed.

"Something has gone wrong," he muttered. "She hath discovered something of the secret. How much, it behooves that I should know. She knows the worst, that is certain; but can she have found out the agencies? I must summon Anita. That hag of hate hath not betrayed me, I know. She too much loves the evil to do aught which should prevent its exercise. She too much hated the mother to be merciful to the daughter. She hath too willingly served me in this matter to have repented of her share in the performance. But she may have kept her secret. loosely; she may have been watched; that Olivia has suspected her, I know; and, with suspicion once awakened, an intense spirit will be sleepless till it makes discovery. I must see and examine her."

He touched a tassel depending from the wainscot; then resumed his soliloquy, pursuing another train of thought.

"These accursed knights of Portugal! They vex me on every side. She hath dismissed one of them, but he is no less a trouble. Will he stay content with one rejection? These lovers,—deeply filled with the one image, and of rare arrogance,—are not easily satisfied with denial; but I will yet put my foot upon their necks; or, failing in this, I shall thrust my dagger to their hearts. Every man is haunted by some viper, or spider—venomous reptile, or spiteful insect. These are mine! Yet, but for this wonderful change in *her*, they should not give me cause of fear. But yesterday, so meek; and now, a tigress! Well, there is always, at the worst, *one* remedy, and *this* cannot fail me!"

Thus speaking, he drew forth his dagger from the sheath, and contemplated the weapon darkly as he spoke. There was that in his manner, and the cold intelligence in his eye, during this survey, which denoted the reckless hardihood of a nature, originally cold and selfish, and which had been thoroughly indurated by a long and terrible criminal experience. It is not for us to go back in his history, and recall the events of a life which have no absolute connection with the progress which is before us. Enough, that the past, once known, would leave us little doubt of the cool indifference with which the bold, bad man before us, would school himself to the execution of any crimes which it became his policy to contemplate. See him as he turns the dagger, and passes his finger over the rust-spots that darken its point, and dot the blade freely upward on both sides! A fierce smile,—a demoniac grin appears upon his face, as he makes the survey, and tells a sufficient story.

"Ay, it is there still!" he muttered—"precious proof of my revenge! Little did Nicolas de Vergaray fancy, when he triumphed over my heart, that I should so soon find the way to his! I would not cleanse the bright steel which his blood had tainted. I preferred that the stains should forever remind me of *my* triumph at the last;—ay, in the moment when he fondly fancied he had all to himself the happiness which he had despoiled me of! He, at least, enjoyed it only in his dreams!"

The door opened. The soliloquy was arrested. He restored the dagger to its sheath, and looked up at the intruder. This was an old woman of about sixty, a *mestizo*, a cross of the negro and the red-man. She combined, in very equal degree, the most conspicuous characteristics of the two. She had the high cheek bones, the thin lips, the full chin, the glossy dark flowing hair of the Indian, with the retreating forehead and flat nose of the black. Her eyes were of the sly, sharp, gipsy cast, the brows quite gray, and thus in singular contrast with her hair, which was quite as black as in the days of her childhood;—if, indeed, days of childhood had ever been known to her! She had not the appearance of one who had ever been a child. The wear and tear of vexing passions had scarred her face with every sign of premature old age. Her skin was a series of wrinkles, like the ripples of spent billows upon a gradually rising shore. Her teeth were gone, with the exception of a couple of very sharp snags, that stood out in front, between her thin lips, like those of a squirrel. She had no flesh upon her bones, and her clothes, thin and light, according with climate and season, hung upon her skeleton form as if from a peg upon the wall! A gauze handkerchief, wrapped imperfectly above her neck, suffered her skinny bosom to appear, but without increasing her attractions. Her figure, thus betraying the signs of age, was yet singularly erect. Her step was firm, though stealthy. You saw that she set her foot down firmly, though you did not hear it; and, though moving with caution, she was yet quick of movement. She did not wait for a summons, but advanced at once to her master, and stood up before him; her eyes lighting up beneath the gray brows, like lamps of naphtha in sepulchral caverns.

"Give me some wine, Anita," was his first salutation,

She brought it forth from a cupboard, and placed it before him; a flask encased in wicker-work of straw. The goblet was brought at the same moment. She said nothing.

"Get another goblet for yourself, Anita, and sit!"

She did as she was commanded, quietly, and without hesitation; as if to obey was a thing of course, and she had been accustomed to all manner of commands.

Don Balthazar filled his glass, and swallowed the contents at a single gulp. He filled it a second time, and seated it before him.

"Drink," said he, "Anita."

She did as she was bade, emptied the goblet as soon as filled, and her eyes glittered with a humid light, pale and intensely spiritual. After a pause, in which she seemed wholly to wait on his words, he spoke:

"Well, has she been troublesome?"

"No!" was the brief reply, in the short, shrill, yet soft manner of the red-man.

"It is strange! She has been showing me the image of her mother, as we both have seen it often, in other days; you, in particular, Anita!"

The eyes of the woman glared with an expression of hatred, which was absolutely fiendish.

"She shows the blood," he continued, "as I never saw it shown before! But how is it that she does not sleep? Has she ate—has she drank?"

"Yes; but not much! Very little! She suspects. She is uneasy. I see! She thinks something wrong."

This was spoken in a *patois* common to the persons of her class, but we do not choose to imitate her.

"Something more than *thinks*, I fancy! She *knows*. How has she discovered?"

"I don't know that she has discovered anything. She said to me once, about a week ago, that she wondered why she felt so drowsy every day."

"Ah!—and you?——"

"I wondered too! That was all!"

"There is something more. Are you sure, Anita, that she has not found *you* sleeping? Are you sure that you have not happened upon a flask of canary at the wrong moment?"

"No!"

"Well! I am sure that she has made some discovery! The question is what?—and how much? She knows the *worst*—that is certain."

The woman grinned.

"But does she know by what means we have worked? You say she eats and drinks little. Is this only the lack of appetite, or does she suspect her food?"

The woman avowed her ignorance.

"But she ate and drank yesterday?"

"Yes; but very little."

"Did she seem affected afterwards?"

"Very little! She was drowsy. She took her *siesta*; but when I came in to look at her, she rose up."

"Can she have become accustomed to it already? Does it cease to affect her? You must increase the dose, Anita."

"It may kill her!"

"Hardly! How much do you give her now?"

The woman took a small phial from her bosom and held it up to the light. It contained a slightly greenish liquor. She designated, with her finger upon the phial, the quantity given.

"That should be enough, certainly! But if she refuses the draught—rejects the food! That is the question. The next question is, whether she refuses from want of appetite, simply? You must change the food, Anita. Tempt her appetite. Get some new dishes, and forbear the drug, until her suspicions, if she have any, are quieted;—say, for the next three days Meanwhile, be vigilant, and see that you are not surprised. You note all who approach her?"

"All!"

"Now is the time for circumspection. She loves this knight of Portugal."

"She has just refused him."

"Yes; the younger brother. But the other——"

"*He* comes seldom."

"But is not the less powerful when he comes. They must be closely watched, when together. He must not be suffered to propose to her without interruption. If you find him, at any time, when I am absent, becoming too impressive, show yourself, and stop the progress. In that man I see my bane! She loves him. How has she concealed it from you?"

The woman answered by a vacant stare.

"Ah! I see! There are some things quite too subtle for you, Anita. But, let there be nothing which escapes your watch. If necessary, you must increase the potion."

"Unless you mean to kill her,—no! She now takes as much as can be safely given."

"Yes, if she takes it *all!* But, when she refuses to eat and drink, or does so sparingly, then more may be given. You must not forget what you owe her mother."

The eyes of the woman glared fearfully.

"You have not forgotten your own daughter?"

Anita seized the flask, unbidden, and again filled the glass before her, which she emptied at a draught.

"To-night, I have seen the mother in the daughter! She has all her passions, though as yet suppressed. She will give us trouble, unless we take heed to her. Our danger is in the passion which she feels for this Portuguese knight—the elder, I mean—not the younger. She cares nothing for him. If I can get them both away to Florida, or otherwise disposed of, all may go well; and she may subside into her old lethargy. Her passion for him has brought out all her other passions. They make her vigilant and thoughtful. They quicken her intelligence. She is not the same woman she was a month ago. She is no longer in my power, or in yours. If we heed not, she will escape us. She will marry this Portuguese. She will expose us!——"

The woman grinned with exultation.

"She dare not! To expose us is to tell——"

"Very true; but you remember that, when her Biscayan mother was aroused to passion, she had no prudence! She revealed every thing! It will be so with Olivia. I am sure of it, from what I have seen to-night. That is our danger. Let her, in this paroxysm, be assured that all her hopes of this Portuguese knight depend on escape from *us*, and she will rush into the market-place with all her secrets! She will destroy herself in the fury which would destroy us. And, Anita, if she can win belief, she will *not so surely* destroy herself. *We know* that she is guiltless, in her soul, of any crime;—we know that the whole wrong is ours!"

"Yes; but the shame?"

"Is something *in Spain;* not so much *here!* and pity and sympathy will lessen it anywhere! We must beware of any extremity. Now is the time for all your subtlety, if we would be safe. See to it; observe her closely; see that she and this knight of Portugal—the elder, mark you—from the younger, indeed, we have no cause of fear—do not meet, unless under *your* eye or mine; and that they do not come to any understanding. We must keep them from mutual confessions. They both love passionately; but better *for us* that they were both dead, than that either should speak of passion to each other's ears! Let her but hear and answer *him*, and she is happy, Anita—happy! think of that, Anita!—think of that! How will you relish to see the daughter of that mother happy in the arms of her lover, while you are led off to prison, knowing the fate of your *own* daughter—the debt of thirty years unpaid; while your son ——"

"Tell me of him! Have you heard?" was the eager inquiry of the woman, who, during the speech of the other—which was evidently designed to goad her passions into phrensy,—had risen from her seat, and moved hurriedly, with clasped hands, and in intense agitation, over the floor.

"Tell me of him! Of Mateo;—have you heard, my master?"

She approached him closely as she made the inquiry, and bent her face forward, almost touching his own. Her words, earnestly and impressively spoken, were yet in such subdued accents as barely to be audible to his ears.

"He is yet in the mountain fastnesses, and at the head of a formidable band. I have sent to him by a special messenger I have sent him money."

"Thanks, my master, thanks! But have you got his pardon from the adelantado?"

"Not yet! But if we can get these Portuguese knights fairly pledged for Florida, I shall succeed with Soto, or failing with him, shall do so with Doña Isabella when he is departed."

"You will not go with the expedition?"

"Until this night, I had resolved upon it. Now, my resolution is half taken the other way. There is too much to care for *here*. I must see to *her!*"

"Happy! She!" muttered the woman: "Ha! ha! As if I am living here for nothing. As if I had no memory to make bitter all my soul!"

"Drink, Anita."

The hag willingly obeyed. The instincts of black and red man, combined within her, made it easy to comply with such an order. When she had finished, her eyes glittering with a moist white light, her companion said—

"And now watch! She must eat and drink. If she will not eat as you provide, put things in her way to tempt her. Leave closets open to her search, only *prepare* what ye put there. Increase the dose."

"It will kill her, if she eats or drinks. But what then? Let her die!"

The light reddened fiercely in the vindictive woman's eye. Don Balthazar regarded her coldly and quietly for a moment, then, as if indifferently, remarked—

"No! not yet—not that! it might peril everything—it might subject us to suspicion——"

The woman approached him softly, and, with a significant lifting of the finger, said, whisperingly—

"No fear of that. I have a potion which shall so silently steal into the brain, that none shall suspect. It will leave no footprint, no finger-marks,—no blood, no blackness, no *sign* behind it, yet will it seize upon the life as surely and as suddenly, as if the dagger had been driven right into the close places of the heart. Say but the word——"

The dark-souled man shuddered, as he heard, and saw the fierce, eager, intense glare of the speaker's eyes. He said hurriedly—

"No! Anita! no! I will not that. I will that she should live—live—yes!—the time is not yet come!"

"It is as you say! Yet had I not forborne to give her this poison, but that thou hadst in thy power a more terrible death! I had rather thou shouldst slay her—thou, of her own blood:—and I saw thee do it."

"I slay her, Anita! Thou art mad! I tell thee, I would not touch her life, for the world, if——"

"Ay, if,—if she saves thee not the danger and the trouble. But it was the life of the heart and the hope, and the woman that I beheld thee bent to slay, and thy poison was so much more fatal than mine! Ha! ha! ha!"

"Oh! get thee hence, Anita! The wine begins to work in thee. But help thyself to another goblet, and to sleep now. Thy watch has been a weary one."

The woman yawned at the suggestion, filled the goblet, drank, and was about to retire without a word, when she seemed to recollect, and again spoke, as usual, in those low, subdued tones, which, when employed to utter passionate language, are so singularly impressive.

"Do not forget Mateo! let me see him once more—bring him to me—and I will drug for thee a thousand lives!"

Balthazar took her hand and wrung it warmly, nodded his head affirmatively, but said nothing. The woman went away, without obeisance or farther nod.

"Well, let the worst come!" muttered the Señor, after she had departed, "and Anita has her own remedies. If it cannot be otherwise, let her use the potion. She can burn afterwards to prove me guiltless. But the time is not yet—not yet. May it never be. I would escape that necessity, if I can!"

He seated himself, folded some strips of the fumous Cuban weed together, and lighted an extempore cigar, and still he soliloquized. Balthazar de Alvaro was a cold, unscrupulous villain; but though his thoughts ran upon crime, it would be an injustice to him now to suppose them dictated by hatred. It was not from any sentiment of hostility that he pursued his victim, as his language fully testified.

"It may kill her; true! What then? It will not hurt her; nay, it will help. It will save her. The quality of her offence is not such as will bring down punishment upon *her* head: and the wrong she suffers may well atone for that which she has done. If heaven be no fable, she is more worthy of its pity than its loathing; and if hell be not a dream of the priesthood, as I deem it, then my fate must assure her of a full revenge! Let these be her consolation. At all events, I must seek mine own safety. She must die, if needful to secure this! yet, we may escape this necessity. If we can chain her tongue, my fears perish; and if my fears perish, she may live. Time will show. I *must* have *time*. Let this old hag but prove faithful, and all may yet go well. These Portuguese knights disappear with the expedition. I must see to that. I must move Soto to show better favor to this Philip de Vasconselos than he hath yet done. He must encourage him; must give him some distinctions—some command—and win him from the paths of love, by opening better glimpses to those of ambition."

But we need not pursue the meditations of the subtle and bold criminal who sits and muses before us. They conduct us no farther in pursuit of the clues which are already in our grasp.

CHAPTER VII.

> Sir, in my heart there was a kind of fighting
> That would not let me sleep.... Rashly—
> And praised be rashness for it !—Let us know,
> Our indiscretion sometimes serves us well,
> When our deep plots do pall ; and that should teach us
> There's a divinity that shapes our ends,
> Rough hew them how we will."—HAMLET.

THE moment that Olivia reached her own chamber, she threw herself prostrate before a fine portrait of the Virgin that hung against the wall of the apartment. She uttered no prayer, no sob, no sound ; shed no tear ; gave no outward sign, beyond her prostration, of the object of her quest, or of the agony that preyed upon her ; asked not, in language, for the peace and security which she sought, but lay at length, her humility and grief apparent only in the one action, as if with the conviction that all her woes were known; her contrition ; the shame from which she suffered ; the faint hope which she dared not encourage ; the fond passion, which she felt to be pure as grateful, but which her conscience bade her not to entertain. She did not once look up to the benign and blessing features of that Mother of Love and Mercy, whose eyes, she yet felt, were looking sweetly and tenderly down, even into the secret recesses of her own full and bursting heart. And thus she lay, prone, motionless, as if her life and breathing had ceased in the utter prostration of her hope and person.

There is something very touching in the spectacle of a person totally ignorant of religion as a subject of thought and examination, who yet welcomes it as a faith; who believes with spontaneous consent ; who receives it as a mystery ; seeks not to analyze or solve it ; prefers it, indeed, *as* a mystery, and confides, without misgiving, to all its promises! Though wealthy, and of high birth and connections, Olivia de Alvaro was as little versed in the doctrines of the theologian, as the simplest peasant of the country. She knew not that there was anything needing to be understood. She simply felt. Her faith, as perhaps is the case always with the most pure of heart, was based wholly on the sympathies, and a natural sense of weakness. It was a thing of instinct, not of thought, and it reached her through a sensuous medium. Better, indeed, as it was so. Doubting her strength, her safety, and the good faith of those around her, she had no doubt as to whom only and certainly, she could turn for refuge. We may smile at her securities; we may hold her choice of the medium of communication with Deity, to be a mistaken one; but her confidence is unimpaired; and regarding the object sought only—peace of mind—reliance—confidence;—the end was quite to the full attained, in her case, as if the visible Saviour of mankind stood before her. Nor are we permitted to doubt that the benevolence of God accepts any medium of communication, with himself, which a pure faith, however mistaken, may honestly adopt. To suppose otherwise, would be to accuse his justice, making feebleness and ignorance objects of punishment, equally with offence and guilt.

Suddenly, while Olivia still lay in this position, the door of her chamber opened; and a person entered—a girl of sixteen or eighteen—a mulatto, who had been evidently just aroused from her slumbers. She came in yawning; her face vacant, her eyes still heavy with sleep. Her features were of a sort to show that sleep was not necessary to impair her intelligence. They were coarse and meaningless. She was one of those mulattoes, in whom the more sluggish characteristics of the negro race predominated over all others: and united, in singular degree, the qualities of cunning, with an excessive stolidity. Olivia rose at her approach, seated herself upon a little settle, and looked up into the face of the mulatto with eyes of inquiry, if not of hope. The suggestion occurred to her for a moment—"Can I possibly make use of this creature? Is she capable of the degree of faith and sympathy which I need in my present strait?" The inquiry was a natural one. Every young damsel inclines to put trust in her waiting maid, and in this relation Juana stood to her mistress. But the latter had too long had experience of the characteristics of the maid-servant. She was not ignorant of her cunning, but she had good reason to believe that this was all pledged to the service of her uncle, through the medium of the old hag Anita, who was the grandmother of the girl. As for her affections and sympathies, these Olivia had never yet been able to awaken. She had been indulgent and considerate; had bestowed her gifts freely, but beyond the single moment in which they were bestowed, she had no proof that the benefit was remembered with gratitude. The blank, indifferent, stolid features which she surveyed were full of discouragement, and after a brief examination of them, the unhappy damsel, with a sigh, averted her eyes, abandoned her purpose of solicitation—if she had entertained any—and submitted to be disrobed in profound silence. The girl was not disposed to break this silence. She performed her task drowsily. It was not a protracted one: and this done, she retired for the night, leaving her mistress alone, once more, to commune with her own sorrows.

"There is no hope!" she exclaimed, mournfully, sitting in her night dress where the maid had left her, her hands folded upon her lap, and her moist eyes looking vacantly up at the Virgin with an expression of the most woeful self-abandonment.

"Yet why should I hope! What is there to hope? What have I to live for? The light is gone, the love! I dare not love. It is criminal to love. It is now criminal to live! Yet, Mother of Mercy, I dare not think of death. I cannot die! I would not. Yet, it is not because I fear! Oh no! Yet, if it be not fear, can it be hope that makes me unwilling? Oh! weak and miserable sinner that I am, can I dream to unite the fate of any brave cavalier with mine? Shall I glide like a serpent into the bosom of so noble and gentle a knight as Philip de Vasconselos, and beguile him into love for so base a thing as I—I that live a lie to God and a loathing to myself! Shall I who know all that I am—and who hate my own knowledge—shall I delude such as he into a faith that I am worthy of his embrace and love? Alas! if love alone could make me worthy, then were it not unseemly that I should do so. Oh! I could requite his passion with a fervor and a truth that should leave him nothing to reproach, and nothing to regret! To grow to him—to cling to him forever—to pass into his very heart—to drink life and joy forever from his lips!—what a dream of happiness! Oh! why do I cherish this dream? Am I base enough to hope, or to toil for its fulfilment? Can I do so great a wrong to so noble a gentleman? Down, foolish thought! Be still! What is the wrong? Do I not love him? Will I not love him truly as never yet was knight beloved by woman? Knows he aught—will he ever know aught of what hath happ'd to me? will it lessen his trust or my fidelity? Who dare speak—who reveal the terrible secret?—not he—my uncle—my fate! my eternal enemy! whom——Mary, mother, take the wild thought from me!—whom I sometimes feel it in my heart to slay, even while he sleeps upon his couch under the noonday heavens!"

And, speaking thus passionately, she threw herself once more before the picture of the Virgin, whom she invoked, as with the hope, by prayer, to silence her tumultuous passions. But the refreshing mercies of prayer were not hers. Her soul was in too wild a conflict to be subdued to quiet, unless by a miracle of grace. There were other reasons for this conflict and this weakness. The unhappy girl was really feeble, and in want of sustenance. We have heard it intimated that she probably entertained suspicions with regard to the food proffered her. Such was the case. She now felt assured that her food was drugged; and she knew with what cruel object. She left much of it untasted, eating only in the necessity of life; and avoiding all those dishes with which she had reason to believe the lethargic potion to be mixed. Her caution and forbearance had not always availed for her safety; for so subtly was her food prepared by the dexterous agent employed in drugging it, that the drug had been introduced into fruits even, the integrity of which one would suppose could not be invaded unless by some external proofs being apparent. In this way only could she account for the dreamy and prostrating moods which she had occasionally felt during the day. Here, then, was a young woman, of high birth, proud connections, and ample fortune, an unsuspected prisoner in her own dwelling, denied, virtually, the necessary aliment of life. Truly the case was a pitiable one!—Olivia de Alvaro, sustained during all the scenes in which we have beheld her, chiefly by the intensity of her excitements, was now near to fainting from absolute want of food.

The cravings of nature were not to be withstood. She rose from her prostrate position; seizing her lamp, which she shaded carefully with a handkerchief on all sides but one, she cautiously opened the door of her chamber and entered upon the passage which, more or less directly, conducted to almost every apartment in the house. Adjoining her own was a small room, not much more than a closet, which had been assigned to the waiting maid Juana. Into this she looked boldly; intending, if the girl were yet awake, to speak to her of some object, any but that which she really had in view. But the girl, as she expected, from a previous knowledge of her habits, already slept profoundly. She closed the door cautiously behind her, and, with feet set down carefully, she stole along the passage leading to the opposite quarter of the house. The passage, at a certain point, divided, one arm conducting to the apartment of Don Balthazar, the other to guest-chambers; opposite to these was a saloon which was usually employed in the colder seasons of the year. The stairway, terminating the passage, led below to servants' apartments, kitchen, and store-rooms, and constituted, in particular, the province over which Anita presided. Hither were the footsteps of Olivia directed; but when she reached the place where the passage divided—her own lamp being shaded—she caught a glimpse of a light streaming from beneath the door of her uncle's cham from this quarter. Who could be the parties? Who but her cruel enemy, her uncle—the man who had abused his trust, and made the very ties of blood the means by which to violate them all,—who but he and the malignant creature whom she no less feared?—the unnatural cross of races, to neither of which had nature vouchsafed any of her most blessed and compensating qualities. And what should be the subject of their discussion?—Was she not their victim?—Were they not even then, as at all times, meditating how best to circumvent her innocence, and subdue her to the creature whom she could not think of but with horror and self-loathing? Perhaps she may hear what they meditate, may learn their secrets, and find a mean to escape their arts. Olivia did not suffer any doubts of propriety to prevent her from endeavoring to fathom their secrets. Her proceeding was fully justified by her situation. She set down her lamp at an angle of the passage, and covered it with the handkerchief; then stole forward to the door of the chamber which held the conspirators. Through a crevice—the joinery of that region, in that day, gave little heed to finish—she was enabled to see a part of the outline of her two enemies. They were both seated, and the wine-cup was before them. They were speaking earnestly, but in such subdued accents, that she strove vainly to gather more than a word at intervals. We have been more fortunate; and, except for her own sake, need not regret that she was disappointed. But she could see; and it so happened that it was even while she gazed, that Anita held up to Don Balthazar the little phial containing her drug, in order to indicate to him the dose which she usually bestowed upon her victim. Olivia beheld the phial and the action, and inferred the rest. Oh! how her eyes flashed and her soul flamed up as she beheld. Bitter was the feeling in her heart, which nearly drove the unuttered curse of her spirit out, aloud, through her closely compressed lips. But she grew firm, surveyed silently, and saw the phial restored to the bosom of the crone. After a while, as she found it impossible to hear what was spoken, her former resolve returned to her; and, though with some reluctance, she receded softly from the door, resumed her lamp, and proceeded by the little flight which conducted below, to the apartments in the rear, which were assigned especially to Anita. These were easily accessible; Anita never suspecting any visitor, and least of all the one in question, during her absence. Here, the poor girl, after curiously surveying the region into which she had not before often penetrated, began her search after food. She reasonably supposed that any provisions which she should find in these precincts would be found undrugged. There was a basket of cakes, such as had never been brought to her; of these she gathered a small number, taking care so to select them as not to disturb the general appearance of the pile. She found some "cold baked meats," also—some fragments of a bird-pie, and other matters of the same sort, such as had not been displayed among the cates usually provided for her. Anita, it was apparent, was by no means regardless of her own appetites. She had a taste for nice things, and, like most persons of inferior race, was in the possession of an enormous appetite. Olivia fed freely while storing her spoils away in a little basket which she had appropriated from a collection in the closet of the crone. With the basket in one hand and her little half-shaded lamp in the other, she prepared to effect her return to her own chamber; but hardly had she emerged from the old woman's apartments, when she heard the shuffling of feet upon the stair-flight, while a suppressed cough attested the approach of the very person upon whose domain she had been trespassing. Here was a dilemma. To say that she had any fears, in the event of discovey, would be absurd. The domain was hers. The food which she had seemed to pilfer was, in fact, the proceeds of her own estates. But the action would have betrayed her secret suspicions, which it was her policy for the present to conceal, and would only prompt her enemies to resort to new schemes which it might not be possible for her to detect and overthrow With the bitter feelings of her soul duly increased with the necessity which she now felt of concealment under these circumstances, Olivia silently receded along the path she had come. Still the shuffling of the old woman's feet was heard, the cough increased in frequency and force. There was but one course for the unhappy girl, and that was to hide herself in the very chamber of the enemy; if, indeed, this were possible. Fortunately, her strength rose with the emergency. Her mind became clearer under the pressure; indignant feelings gave her resolution, and she stepped back firmly to the *tabooed* region, as quickly as she might with safety, and there looked about her for a place of refuge.

She was not long in resolving upon a spot in which to shroud herself. The chamber was one of ample dimensions, and it had two spacious closets. But Olivia was prudently apprehensive that the old woman might look into these; she cast about for a place of better promise. Anita had the negro faculty of accumulation in high degree. To those who know anything of the habits of this race of people, it will readily be conjectured that a person in such a situation as that which she enjoyed, and of her age, had gathered about her an infinite treasure of the cast-off possessions of the whites. Her room was accordingly as well crowded with old clothes as the warehouse of a London clothesman. They hung about the walls; they lay upon the chairs; they were suspended upon lines crossing the room obliquely; and a huge wooden horse, occupying a large portion of one corner, was absolutely massed with them. Behind this convenient bulk Olivia succeeded in shrouding herself a few seconds before the light which the withered crone carried began to glimmer in the chamber. Here, scarce breathing, she crouched, with all the patience and resolution which she could command, awaiting the moment when the hag should sleep, in order to attempt her escape. The interval was sufficiently tedious, and trying to fear and patience. Anita had many things to do, and she brought with her the remnant of the flask of wine of which Don Balthazar and herself had been drinking. She had yet to try its quality when alone. She did so, and drank with a rare gusto. Then she munched of a biscuit, and then she adjusted her bed-clothes. Finally, she opened and looked into certain boxes, and carefully fastened them again, before she seated herself. In all these performances, the poor girl behind the clothes-horse was kept in continual apprehension. Several times the old hag approached the place of her concealment. Once she absolutely proceeded to take from it some of its articles of bed-furniture; to dispose of cloaks and shawls, and rearrange the disordered drapery. Olivia, all the while, cowering and crouching like a guilty person, dreading to be discovered and haled into the light. But she escaped; the crone receded to other parts of the room, having, it would seem, a variety of domestic cares, separate from those which concerned the young lady and the Don, her uncle. Meanwhile, the damsel watched all her proceedings with no small interest. With careful finger, she made for herself an aperture between the massed garments upon the horse, through which she could behold all that took place within the chamber. And it was with momently increasing interest that she saw what numerous cares occupied the soul of that old woman, momently hovering over the very verge of existence. How she had accumulated; with what method she examined and arranged; with what caution she put away; with what heed she counted and reviewed her treasures, as if she was required to provide for a thousand years. Olivia was confounded at the extent and sort of possessions which the aged crone could show; the constant spoliations of a long life. There were chests and boxes, all of which she opened and examined, lifting to the light, and surveying some of the contents, with the same gratification, no doubt, which she felt when she had first pilled them from the noble lord or lady whom she served, her master or their guests. Olivia beheld little trinkets there lifted up to sight, which she herself might claim. She recognized others, which had been the property of friends. These were all commonly associated with treasures of quite another character. Among the possessions of Anita there was quite an armory. There were hauberk, and helm, and lance-head, and dagger, and silver spur, and brass, and gorget, and coat-of-mail, and escanpil of cotton, and bright targe of polished steel. But we forbear the catalogue. Enough that this acquisitiveness of Anita had been for sixty years without restraint, exercised in a variety of situations, and of large opportunities, and that she had been as successful in concealing as she was avid in securing her spoil. Her treasures thus acquired, included fruits and spices, silks and satins, rare velvets, tiffany and lawn, jellies and syrops, tinct with rose and cinnamon, fresh from Samarcand and Ind. She had money, too, in considerable store, and into the slit of a box in one of her chests she dropped a newly-gotten castellano, probably the gift of Don Balthazar that very night.

Olivia now began to grow weary of her watch, which had yet proved so instructive. Her anxieties and apprehensions, as well as weariness, promised, however, soon to be relieved. The crone began to disrobe herself for the night. This performance, but for a single circumstance, would have been totally without interest to the spectator. But, one of the first necessities of Anita, after stripping off her outer garments, was to take from her bosom the little phial which Olivia had seen her exhibit to her uncle. This she placed upon the table, where it fastened the eye of the damsel, and held it with a singular fascination. In that phial lay her fate! *That* was the potent spell which had so chained her senses, until —— but the thought almost maddened her, and it was with difficulty that she restrained herself from rushing forth, and giving utterance to her wild passion in the wildest phrensies of speech and action. With a strenuous exertion of her will only, did she forbear; and, still keeping her eye upon the phial, she continued in her place of watch in quiet.

Meanwhile, Anita had assumed her night-dress. This done, she addressed herself to her prayers. She, too, could pray; but hers was not the prayer of agony, and a terrible strife. She simply obeyed a habit, which but too commonly deceives the miserable wretch into a false security. But her devotions seemed to her sufficiently satisfactory. They were coupled with a sort of penance, whether self-imposed or otherwise we need not inquire. Kneeling before a little image of the dying Christ, she entreated his mercy; then crawled on her hands and knees, without rising once, across the room to her couch, which stood opposite, and only raised herself that she might make her way into the bed.

No doubt her conscience was quite satisfied with the Deity which made her toils no weightier.

The soul of Olivia was in great agitation. Fettered in a constrained position, anxiously dreading and expecting discovery, excited by what she had seen, and moved by a purpose which she had not yet declared to herself, and which was still working in her thought, she was yet compelled to remain quiet until the old woman slept. Now, age does not sleep easily, or very soundly: and it was a long time still, before Olivia could be sure of the proof which taught her that Anita could no longer hear and see. At length, persuaded that she might venture out with safety, she did so. The light in the apartment guided her movements. She approached the bed, and surveyed the sleeper with curiosity. The withered features, though composed in the calm of sleep, still seemed to wear, in the eyes of the damsel, the expression of that malignant hatred with which she felt sure that Anita had always regarded her. She, herself, looked upon the sleeper with features of indignant loathing. She turned away quickly and proceeded to the table. The vague suggestion which had been working in her mind had grown into a resolution. She seized the phial, whose mysterious powers she believed herself to have felt, and without hesitation poured a portion of its contents into the wine-flask. There were still several draughts of the liquor in it; she knew the old woman's appetite for the juices of the grape, and pleased herself with the idea that she would drink, and sleep;—such a sleep as had been so often imposed upon her own senses, and to such cruel results. In that sleep of twenty-four hours—for such was the term which Olivia assigned to the action of the potion—she, herself, would enjoy a measure of liberty which had been long unknown. She would then explore the household, and provide herself—so moderate was her calculation—such a sufficient supply of proper food, from the stores of the housekeeper, as would keep her, for a while, at least, free from the necessity of partaking of her dosed dishes. Having executed her purpose, there was no longer a motive to remain, at the risk of detection, and seizing upon her basket and lamp, she disappeared in safety. The clasp of the door yielded, and was closed without noise; the passage proved free; the light nad disappeared from beneath the door of her uncle; and Olivia regained her chamber without embarrassment. Here she proceeded to satisfy her hunger, in some degree, upon the cates of which she possessed herself. For the remainder she sought a hiding-place, which she supposed to be unsuspected. These put away, the poor girl threw herself once more before tne image of the Virgin, in prayer. She could pray. She was conscious of suffering, but not of guilt; and, as she looked up, she fancied that the picture smiled upon her. Upon this smile she slept and dreamed pleasantly; and, in her dream, beheld the image of Philip de Vasconselos, occupying the place of the Virgin, and looking down upon her with even more loving sweetness.

5

CHAPTER VIII

"Oh, detu! Oh, sguardi! .. A gran pena repiglio
I sensi miei. Che mai diss 'egli? Avrebbe
Forse il mio amor?... Ma, no! Racchiuso stammi
Nel piu addentro del core."—ALFIERI.—FILIPPO.

Thus dreaming, the sleep of Olivia de Alvaro was fortunately a protracted one. Nature, thus, asserts for herself some happy hours, even in a life which is one of unfailing sorrows. She slept late. In the meantime, the girl Juana had been several times in her chamber. Her movements finally awakened the sleeper, who found that the day had considerably advanced. The morning repast was already awaiting her. She arose, and her toilet was assisted by the girl in waiting. This performed, Olivia dismissed her, preferring to take her breakfast alone. A portion of this she hurriedly put from sight, to be thrown away, or otherwise disposed of, at a fitting opportunity. Meanwhile, she pacified her appetite by a free use of the cates which she had appropriated from the stores of the old woman. A more buoyant feeling prevailed in her bosom, the natural effect of the temporary security which she felt. She had found a respite—had gained *time*—which, in the case of youth, is always felt to be a gain of importance. At all events, she was for so many hours safe, so she thought, from the dangers of that drugging influence which, for a long time, had been sapping her strength, and placing her completely at the mercy of those who had so terribly abused their advantages and power. Juana reappeared, removed the breakfast things, and proceeded to her household duties. Olivia, all this while, saw nothing of her uncle; and finally ascertained that he had left the dwelling at an early hour for the city. Her hope was, that, as was usually the case, she would see no more of him during the day. To be free from his presence was now always a source of relief to her. Whether she thought more favorably of the presence of another we may conjecture only; but we may mention that towards noon she proceeded to make her toilet anew, and seemingly with some regard to visitors. Her dress was carefully selected, and as carefully adjusted. She wore a rich necklace of pearls; and a bandeau of pearls encircled her forehead, twined tastefully in with the dark tresses of her glossy hair. She was, amidst all her grief, as the Greek poet describes Electra in her mourning, who clipt only the "extremity of her locks," "heedful of beauty, the same woman still!" Alas, Olivia de Alvaro was still a child only,—scarcely more than seventeen. Grief, and a terribly depressing sense of shame, had done much towards maturing her passions. But she had enjoyed too little communion with the world to have done much towards maturing her intellect. She felt shame and sorrow, but she felt love also; and girlhood was still strong within her; and hope was not wholly crushed within her heart. Yet, even while she habited her person as if with an eye to charm, she was troubled with misgivings such as, more than once, caused her to droop and sadden, and finally sink down upon her couch, and give way to a full flood of sorrows. What right had she to hope; what hope to be happy; how presume to dream of the precious affections of another, when these could be given with the presumption only that she was fully deserving of them all! The very truthfulness of her own passion prompted this just consideration of what was due to the affections of another. But youth and girlhood, and her own desires, finally triumphed. She rose amidst her tears. She completed her toilet. She arranged her tresses, and arrayed her jewels for conquest. Why should she not love, and loving, why not hope? Was not her love sufficiently warm,—her soul sufficiently devoted,—to render Philip de Vasconselos happy? She had, it is true, a secret, which it would be fatal to her hope were he to know; but how should he ever know?—And, "O! Blessed Virgin," she exclaimed, looking up at the benign mother, "am I to perish for the cruel deeds, the guilty passions of another!"

It was not difficult, though the subject of a long, secret struggle in her own soul, to reconcile herself to a conviction which promised her the happiness which she desired. Her passion proved too strong for her conscientiousness, and her reasons readily gave themselves, as they but too commonly do, to the requisitions of the former. Her philosophy is probably that of thousands in like situations. The fond heart of woman is too much dependent for its life on the affections, not to be easily persuaded by an argument which sustains the cause of the latter. The love which Olivia felt for Philip de Vasconselos was too precious to her soul to yield in such a struggle; and the result was, that she determined, though with shuddering and trembling, should he offer her his hand, to subdue her fears, her sense of justice, all scruples of whatever sort, and accept the blessing which her heart craved as its very breath of life. What could her uncle do? What could he dare? The word from his lips that would blast her, would seal his own ruin and disgrace forever! She would be true to Philip, as true as woman ever yet was to man;—he would protect her from all abuse and outrage—would rescue her from the hostile power from which she had most reason to fear both; and in the pure devotion of the future, might she not hope to repair the misfortunes of the past in which she could conscientiously affirm, that, however much she might have been the victim of the guilty, she had never been wittingly the participator in his crime?

Soothed, if not wholly satisfied, assured in some degree, by the solacing sort of argument through which her mind had past, Olivia proceeded to the latticed verandah, and from thence descended into the shrubbery. Ah! the innocent flower! ah! the unconscious bloom, and the unsuspected blossom! How they appealed to her! and whispered—such whispers as made her turn away from them with averted head, while upon her pale cheek there might have been seen a flush as deep and vivid as a warm sunset in a humid sky. She returned to the verandah, closing its lattices, letting down its curtains, and shutting out the sharper glances of the day. Then she threw herself upon the settee of wicker-work and cane, and covered her sad eyes with her hands in a sorrowful meditation. Leaving her thus abstracted for awhile, let us proceed to other parties.

That morning, Philip de Vasconselos had eaten his humble meal alone, and in silence. Andres was absent; whither he knew not, and the younger brother was of a temper, and just now in such a mood, that it was only a safe policy in the elder, not to seem too curious in any of his affairs. Philip, though naturally and humanely troubled about the fate of Andres, sympathizing with him very sincerely in his disappointments, was yet too *human* to be deeply grieved by the one misfortune —over all—which his brother felt, in the denial of his mistress. It would not, indeed, have been quite in nature, not to have felt his own hopes revive pleasurably at the knowledge. He was conscious of an exulting feeling in his bosom, accordingly; which, knowing its source, he labored, though unsuccessfully, to school and to rebuke. But this labor did not prevent him from making his toilet that morning with extreme care, and resolving to visit the fair Olivia. In this purpose he was seconded by the counsels of the gay gallant Nuno de Tobar, who suddenly broke in upon him, and finding him alone, gave free vent to his encouragements. Somehow, he too had heard of the defeat of Andres, and he urged it as one of the signs in favor of his friend. But Philip shook his head gravely. He valued the Lady Olivia too highly to fancy that she would be easy of attainment. His passion was too earnest, not to prompt him to a very severe questioning of his own merits, and to this effect was his reply to Tobar. But the latter loudly denounced his excessive modesty, and urged a thousand proofs, each conclusive to his own audacious spirit, for the encouragement of his friend. In the end, they proceeded together to the dwelling of the lady.

In the meanwhile, her uncle had suddenly made his appearance, bringing with him another visitor. This was a gaily dressed cavalier, sufficiently comely of person, and smooth of face, to be satisfied with himself; but who possessed few distinguishing traits by which to compel attention or respect. Still, if

Olivia was to wed with any body, this was the person whom her uncle was most pleased to tolerate. He may have had special reasons for this preference. Such, at least, was the belief of Olivia, to whom Don Balthazar had more than once spoken on the subject. He himself frequently afforded to the young gallant the means of being with his niece in private. Don Augustin de Sinolar was one of the passable gentlemen that go to make up what is called good society. He came of respectable family, enjoyed respectable possessions, obeyed the usual laws of fashion and never trespassed upon the proprieties of the circle. He was confident of speech, and was always in possession of the latest intelligence which could please the persons present by disparaging the absent. He was no less devotedly the lover of Olivia than were the brothers Vasconselos—that is, so far as concerned the externals of devotion. But the essentials of an earnest passion, of any sort, were not within the nature of De Sinolar. He was of marriageable years and person, and an establishment was necessary to his position, a wife was necessary to his establishment, and he required rank as a first condition in the damsel he should espouse. Other requisites were wholly subordinate. The ordinary secret of this ordinary gentleman, who, even in the workings of his passions, obeys rigidly a conventional arrangement, was that which made his policy; and to do the agreeable to his mistress, as a carpet knight, was the extent of his performance in the effort to secure favor. Had Olivia been of a like temper, De Sinolar would have proved a formidable rival to either of the Portuguese brothers. The small graces of society, the tea-table heroics, were in the possession of neither. Philip de Vasconselos was particularly deficient in such arts. He was of a grave, calm, reserved nature, too earnestly in love to meditate his conquests by any ordinary means. He could only show, as he did without his own consciousness, perhaps, how precious in his eyes was the object of his passion. The *woman of heart* soon distinguishes between two such suitors, and if she determines in favor of either, does not hesitate long in declaring for him whose earnestness is congenial with her own. It is the woman, whose character has been too feeble to withstand the coercive shaping of fashion merely, who is usually caught by him who is cool enough always to make himself agreeable simply as a companion.

The two friends found De Sinolar in possession of the ground, and eagerly displaying to the eyes of the languid Olivia a collection of silks and shawls, which he had purchased for the approaching tourney. The entrance of Don Philip and De Tobar afforded De Sinolar an opportunity of dilating to a larger audience upon the excellence of his tastes in the choice of silks and colors. De Tobar lent him a ready attention, the better to afford his friend the desired opportunities with Olivia. Her eye was cast down, but brightened, at his approach. He was not annoyed at the presence of the others, since it was not his purpose yet to approach the subject of his passion. The encouraging assurances of his friend had failed as yet to prompt him so soon to peril his hope upon the question. He seated himself near her, however, and spoke to her in those subdued tones which are so grateful to the ears of lovers; his deep, grave, almost sad glance, looking all the while, as it were, down into her heart. She caught a glimpse of this look, but suffered herself only a moment's gaze. That moment was enough to remind her of her dreams by night, when she had seen the same sweet, sad, soliciting glances gazing upon her from the place which was occupied by the picture of the Virgin. The approaching departure of the expedition for Florida became naturally the subject of conversation, and afforded a clue to De Sinolar, which prompted him to leave for awhile his satins.

"Ah! yes! we shall shortly hear of your departure, Señor," said he; "and yet, by the way, I know not if I rightly include you in the expedition. They say, Señor, that you have not yet declared whether you accompany Don Hernan or not; and some say, again, that you have half resolved *not* to go. Can it be so? Now one should think that there could be no doubt about your purpose. Else why should you come from Portugal, to the new Indies, if it were not to better fortune by conquest among the savages?"

"Unless," answered Tobar, with a laugh, "he might better fortune by a conquest among the saints;"—and he looked mischievously at Olivia as he spoke.

De Sinolar was for a moment at fault.

"Among the saints!—I don't see. Oh! yes! among the ladies! Saints and angels! yes! well, that were certainly less dangerous warfare, and one that I much prefer myself. If that is the game of Don Philip, he is wiser, I am free to confess, than most soldiers of my knowing. They have, methinks, precious small value of ladies' favors; and show but little wisdom accordingly. I beg you ten thousand pardons, Señor Don Philip, but I am bold to say I have regarded you as too much of the warrior to give heed to beauty—too fond of the tilt and spear, to hold in overmuch estimation the darts from lady's eyes, and the wounds they give;—wounds, I say it from my soul's experience, such as no army surgeon can be found to heal!"

Here he smote his bosom affectedly, and looked to Olivia; but her eyes were upon the floor. Even the sigh of the gallant, which followed his speech, was lost upon her heedless senses. They were all alive, however, the next moment, as the deep tones of Vasconselos answered De Sinolar.

"You do me wrong, Don Augustin, and you do the character of the noble warrior wrong, if you assume either me, or him, to be insensible to the charms of love, or the claims of beauty. Perhaps, it is the valiant man only, who is always prepared to sacrifice himself where he hates, who feels love to be a sufficient power to command self-sacrifice, if need be, also. But I trow there can be no occasion for me now to defend the tenderness and softness of the warrior's heart, which hath been sufficiently instanced in all stages of the world, and is a thing usually acknowledged among all classes of men. And for the soldier's regard for beauty, what need have we to look beyond a present instance? For what is this tournament provided, for which you are preparing those brilliant colors and silks, but that the valor of the soldier may make grateful appeal to the smiles of love and beauty?"

He paused. Olivia, looking down the while, said in low tones—

"But, Señor, you have not yet answered to the doubts of Don Augustin, touching your departure with the expedition."

"Ah! true," quoth De Sinolar—"They say that there are doubts, yet was it my thought that Don Hernan had shown you the better argument."

"They say rightly, Señorita," replied Vasconselos to Olivia, and scarcely noticing De Sinolar—"who say that I have yet determined nothing. I am truly but half resolved to depart, yet fully half inclined to remain. There be private reasons for this uncertainty. Whether Don Hernan will succeed in persuading me—and it is one of my doubts if he desires so to do—will greatly rest upon the force of other and opposite persuasions than those of war. Perhaps, it were only wise with me, to yield blindly to Don Hernan's arguments, and look nothing farther."

It was the tone with which this last sentence was spoken, and the look which accompanied, which held the meaning more significantly than the words themselves. The sweet, sad resignation in both went direct to the heart of Olivia. But she cast her eyes upon the floor and remained silent. But De Sinolar, who was conscious of nothing but the words spoken, and who was no adept in looking below the surface of any thing, proceeded in his usual manner.

"Well, Señor, it will be needful that you should decide shortly. In a few days we shall have the tournament, and in a few more, the caravels will be all ready to receive the armament. Then will you embark the horses and artillery. These the first. Then will the foot soldiers go on board, and at the last the knights and gentlemen. They are baking famous quantities of bread, even now, at Roja's, and la Granja's. The adelantado is eager to be at work among the heathen savages, stripping the gold from the altars and the treasure from the rich cities of the Apalachian. Ah! Lady Olivia, when these things are going on,

5*

we shall be as dull and quiet here as if we had never known either dance or music.

"These gay knights will all be on the path of conquest. Well For my part, I say let them conquer! I have no passion for conquest, and I have no faith in its fruits. I believe them to be all delusions. One man gets off with a sound head and a full pocket, but a hundred pays for him with deadly wounds, broken limbs, and beggary forever! If one could be sure that he should be the *one*, and not one of the hundred, why, it were pleasant to adventure; but where there's but one white bean to a score of black ones, I'm not the man to draw, if I can help it."

"But the fame, Señor—the glory?" said Olivia.

"Fame and glory! They will neither plaister my head, mend my limbs, nor find me in rations. My *repartimiento*, here, answers all my ambition. It lacks but a mistress to be all the empire I demand, and she, with the blessing of the Virgin, I hope some day to find willing to my hands."

And here he looked with a sudden tenderness towards Olivia.

"And have you never felt the eager desire for battle, Señor?" quoth Tobar:—"That joyous desire for the strife of swords and the crash of lances, which makes the head throb with delirium and the heart bound as if it had wings of its own, and was about to soar to heaven—that feeling which the adelantado hath happily described, from some old heathen Greek or Roman, as 'the rapture of the strife.'"

"No! indeed! no such raptures for me. Any other sort of rapture in preference! Let it be eating, or drinking, or dancing, or loving—I care not how vulgar or how simple—the bull-ring, the cock-pit—nay, the siesta,—any thing but the shouts and the struggle of combatants. The tournament is enough for me. I've tried that. I'll try it no more. When I want to break a lance, I have only to sally out into the mountains after some of my runaways. I use a blunt spear on such occasions. Then, I charge valiantly enough. Then, I overthrow and make captive. I don't kill unless I can't help myself; since it is more profitable and pleasant to beat my Indians than to bury them."

"Your humanity is commendable, Señor," was the somewhat cold response of Vasconselos, who, indeed, had scarcely heeded what the other had been saying; and now turned from him with a contempt which was sufficiently apparent. But the other was by no means discomfited by an expression which he clearly beheld. He replied very promptly and very indifferently, as if his social position—his wealth—put him quite beyond reproach.

"Ah! you scarcely mean that, I know, Señor Don Philip: but it matters nothing. I don't care who knows that I am resolved to live while I can, and risk no bones upon reputation. If heads are to be cloven, let them take the hardest: if brains are to be scattered, it needs only that you choose such as can waste little: if hard blows are to be struck, get those men only for the work who have been trained to the *boucan*. If you love fighting, Don Philip, it is well for you: not for me. I love it not. You have tried your hand at it, and it suits you. You have fought against the Moors. You have already had a taste of Floridian fighting, and I have seen you carry yourself, even sportively, against Bartolomeo de Gallegos, and Señor Nuno, here, and I am free to confess that you are the last person whom I should entreat to a supper of blades and lances. I am only at conflict with gentle woman," smiling sweetly on Olivia;—"and leave the pagan to such brave knights as yourself. By the way, Señor Don Philip, they tell me you served with Francis Pizarro in Peru! I had forgotten that."

"It mattered not," answered Vasconselos coldly.

"Now there is a man for you, that Francis Pizarro. He's the rough customer for a weak stomach. He's what I call a hero! Talk of Cortez, indeed! How should Hernan Cortez be a hero? I've seen him a hundred times when he was nothing but a farmer, and had a hacienda not half the value of my own. He was lucky, Señor—very lucky. I remember him well. I was but a boy when he worked his farm and drove his mule, like any other peasant,—though they make him now a born nobleman; and how could he have got these great honors, were it not for the blind fortune that puts one man on the horse while his betters hold the stirrups? No! no! If there be a truly great man of these days and countries, it is of a certainty the noble Marquis Pizarro."

Nuno de Tobar could scarcely restrain his angry impatience while the fopling continued to discourse thus freely of the great masters in the art of war, whom in that day it was the fashion to commend as above all Greek and Roman fame, and he sharply responded to the flippancies of De Sinolar in respect to Cortez. Vasconselos, on the contrary, gave him little heed, and seemed not to think it necessary to gainsay his opinions. He was content that he should "rabble on," as it afforded him an opportunity to murmur a quiet remark, in under tones, to his fair companion, whose responses, brief and timid, were always delivered in like subdued accents. It was only when his stock of small talk was entirely exhausted that Don Augustin was content to take his departure. This he did, when, at the close of a long rambling speech, he had emptied his budget of accumulations; what he said being only a repetition of what he had heard. He did not seem to apprehend any danger from leaving the field to his rival; persuading himself that Vasconselos, though good enough where lances were splintered, possessed too few resources of the courtier to make much progress where the game depended on the ease of the dialogue and the liveliness of the humor.

His departure was a relief to all the parties. Nuno de Tobar soon after rose, and upon some plea of flowers, passed from the apartment into the garden. The lovers were alone together. A wild thrill shot through the soul of Olivia at the consciousness. Her cheek flushed—her frame trembled with emotion. But she knew that she was watched—that the eyes of Don Balthazar were upon her from some quarter—that love had no security in that House of Fear. Vasconselos was free, of course, of all such apprehensions. He knew that Don Balthazar had entered the house with De Sinolar, but, as he had seen nothing of him after, he presumed that he had quitted it, or was elsewhere employed. He drew nigher to where she sate.

"The departure of this expedition, which threatens so much to lessen the pleasures of the ladies of Cuba, will give but little concern, I fancy, to you, Señorita."

"And wherefore not, Señor?"

"You take little delight, I fear, in such exercises as challenge the best regards of knighthood. I have seen you at very few of the gentle passages between the knights."

"True; but I am not insensible. I have heard full reports of their performances, and found delight in the accounts of such grace and valor, and courtesy and skill, as has been rarely seen."

"Yet would I have beheld you, Señorita, among the gay beauties of this island court, who have stimulated courtesy by their grace, and prompted achievement to great things by their approving smiles. I have looked for you, Señorita, very often, and,—may I say it,—have sometimes left the field, as, seeing you not, it has seemed to me to lack its best attraction."

"Ah! Señor, it is the wont of Cavaliers to use this sort of speech to foolish damsels. And why should you leave a field, where there have been so many beauties to cheer, and so many sweet voices to encourage?"

"Yet was there one, of all,—one only, lady, whom I most desired to behold."

"Ah! and why should the Señor Philip be insensible to the praises which have daily hailed his passages on every hand? Who has won the applauses and the prizes at the several tourneys? Whose lance hath been most honored in the conflict?—whose name been most sounded?—in whose fame have the multitude raised most frequently the shout of acclamation?"

"Alas! lady, all these tributes are of little value in the ears of Philip de Vasconselos, compared with the sweeter assurances that might fall from the lips of one, the loveliest virgin of all Cuba!"

The eyes of Vasconselos were fastened tenderly, as he spoke, upon those of Olivia. Hers sunk, bashfully, beneath his glance; and a warm red flush quickly overspread her cheeks. Her hand lay beside him upon the sofa, which she partly occupied. His fingers fell hesitatingly upon it; and it was not withdrawn. She was silent—the beatings of her heart were audible, and his bosom rose also and sunk, in impetuous responses, to the excited emotions which seemed to prevail in hers. He continued, more eagerly, and more tenderly.

"It may be that mine is the sin of presumption, lady; but of a truth it were a somewhat pardonable sin, since its hope is of favor at the shrine of as chaste and holy a passion——"

The hand was instantly withdrawn, and so hastily, as evidently to surprise the pleader. He looked inquiringly into her face, and, as he did so, her cheeks paled so suddenly, and to such an ashen white, that Vasconselos feared she was about to faint. But she recovered herself with great effort, yet not so completely as to prevent a sudden sobbing, like that of an infant in its sleep, from escaping into sound.

"You are ill, Señorita; or am I so unhappy as to have offended you?"

"You have not offended me, Señor Philip,—oh! no!" was the reply, tremulously and hastily spoken—"a momentary pain only."

He paused, waiting on her with a gentle and sweet solicitude that allowed no change in her face to escape his eyes. Hers sunk beneath his survey, and her cheeks were again suffused with blushes. This seemed a grateful omen to the knight of Portugal. He resumed his pleading—his hand again rested upon her own; and hers was unwithdrawn, in spite of the gentle pressure which detained it. She looked downwards as he pleaded.

"I trust, dear Señorita, I have not spoken too rashly. Better that I were dumb forever than now to offend. But, indeed, you must suffer me to speak. Indeed, you must hear me. Ah! if you but knew, Señorita, how pure is the tribute of affection which I now offer to your charms! Too well I know the chaste and holy homage which a virgin heart requires——"

The hand was suddenly withdrawn. An hysterical laugh escaped from the lips of the damsel, as she replied—

"Ah! Señor, you are all too serious. You sadden me much.

In faith, you do; and I must sing to you a merry song ere I grow gloomy as the night. You shall hear a cheerful ditty, such as will make you laugh, and make us forget—forget—be very forgetful."

She would have risen, and motioned to the guitar lying upon a table; but he held her firmly by the hand. He was bewildered by her conduct, but grew more and more firm as he contemplated her. He had seen too much of the world, and of human nature, not to perceive that there was some mystery in the proceeding. How else should he account for the feverish hurry of her manner, at such a moment, so utterly unlike her conduct, during all other periods?—how, for that sobbing sigh, that convulsive shudder, and those forced husky accents while delivering words ostensibly meant to be playful and sportive? Vasconselos was now not to be deceived. He saw that the gaiety was all assumed only;—yet wherefore? He was more ready to believe that there was agony, rather than merriment, in her spirit at that moment. Then why should she seek to sport with emotions, so sacred, in his bosom, when she had always before shown him a respect approaching to reverence? Vasconselos felt instinctively that the damsel sought under the guise of levity only to conceal the activity and presence of deep and painful emotions. He felt and saw all this; but it was not the moment, nor was his the mood, having advanced thus far, to be diverted from his object. He still kept his grasp upon her hand. He looked steadily into her eyes. They answered his gaze wildly. She trembled all over. He spoke.

"Olivia—lady—I cannot now be baffled—I must speak, and you must answer me. It is too great a matter, to me—too vital to my soul's life, to suffer me to be silent longer, or to leave you without having an answer. Yet you must not suspect me of unkindness. I see that you suffer. I am not deceived by this show of merriment. I feel that there is a secret sorrow which you vainly struggle to conceal——"

"No! no! no secret—I—O! Señor, release me—let me go!"

And she burst into a passion of tears, and buried her face in her hands upon the arm of the settee. Vasconselos bent over, clasped one of her hands in his own, and was about to pass his arm about her waist, when a sudden footstep was heard in the room. In the same moment Don Balthazar spoke,—but a single word,—but it sounded in the ears of Olivia like the voice of the Angel Monkir calling up the dead.

"Olivia!"

She started to her feet—looked wildly in the face of Vasconselos, who had withdrawn a pace, and was observing Don Balthazar—and then tottered towards her uncle. Philip darted forward to help her, when she recovered herself, bowed slightly to her lover, and followed her uncle from the room. Scarcely had she got into the passage when Don Balthazar said to her quickly—and she now observed that his face was very pale—

"When did you see Anita last?"

"Not since last night. Why?"

"She is dead!"

"Dead!"

"Ay, dead! of old age, I suppose. Died in a fit! But go to her. You will find her in her room. Meanwhile, I will excuse you to these gentlemen."

He disappeared. Olivia was frozen to the spot, and speechless. Her conscious soul was full of nameless terrors. She too readily divined the cause of the old woman's death, and though no purpose of crime was in her mind when she mixed with the contents of the wine-flask the potion from the phial, she shuddered with such a horror as might well become the guilt of the murderess. When Don Balthazar returned from speaking with Vasconselos and his friend, he found Olivia where he had left her, rather the statue of a frozen woman than a living, breathing sufferer. He was startled by her evident incapacity, and putting his arms about her, was about to convey her to her chamber; but the touch of his fingers recalled her energies. She revolted from the contact with as great a shuddering as she felt when first apprised of Anita's death.

"Touch me not!" she exclaimed solemnly—"I will go alone."

She did go, but not to the sight of the dead woman. She

felt that she could not endure that spectacle. She hurried to her own chamber, and when there, threw herself half fainting upon the couch. The new catastrophe, in which she had so much participated, added to the gloomy horrors which had already taken such full possession of her soul.

CHAPTER IX

" Mark me well :
I boldly tell thee that I bear a soul,
Prepared for either fortune. If thy hand
Be stronger, use thy power."   AGAMEMNON

Don Balthazar found no difficulty in sending off the two visitors. After the departure of Olivia, they had but little motive to remain. Her uncle was not much a favorite with them. He was known to be a hard and selfish man, who was believed, and rightly, to have no sympathies with either. Still, he was a man of the court, and could put on, when he pleased, the manners of a *preux chevalier*. He was now exceedingly courteous and conciliatory, and apologized warmly for the unavoidable withdrawal of his niece, and for those cares, of his own, which denied him the pleasure of giving them further entertainment. He told them, without scruple, the cause of the present confusion in his household; and made quite a pretty story of it.

"His venerable housekeeper, who had been almost a mother to Olivia, watching and tending her youth with more than parental solicitude, was suddenly found dead in her seat. Well that morning, to all appearance, at noon she had passed to judgment; and this without alarming the family. Olivia was, of course, terribly shocked by the event. She had retired inconsolable to her chamber. She was so tenderly attached to Anita, and Anita so tenderly attached to her! Her affection was very great,—great indeed;—so great, that he, Don Balthazar de Alvaro, was exceedingly anxious for her health;—and so forth." "And so good morning to you, Señores."

"An old hag!" exclaimed Nuno de Tobar to his companion as soon as they had got fairly beyond the premises,—"one of the ugliest and most fiendish-looking human vultures you ever beheld. As for her attachment to Olivia, or Olivia's to her, I don't believe a word of it. I never saw any proofs of it myself, and have heard many things which lead me to think there could be no attachment between them. In fact, Leonora tells me that Anita was no more than a spy upon the poor girl, whose steps were watched as carefully as if every bush concealed a lover, and behind every tree stood an armed man ready to snatch her up and make off with her. Be sure, Don Balthazar has no desire that she should pass from any keeping but his own. He enjoys too much good picking from the estates of Olivia to give her up without a struggle. There is a strange story about a silver mine which he has somehow wholly appropriated to himself; and by all accounts, he may well dread the day of reckoning with the man who shall become her husband. For this reason he keeps her immured as much as possible; and it is certain that no gentleman can obtain access to his dwelling without finding himself watched. You must continue, Philip, your visits when the uncle is known to be busy elsewhere. There is something gained, I am thinking, by the death of this old woman. It is a special providence in your behalf. See that you make use of it."

The calculations of Nuno de Tobar, in respect to the advantages gained in favor of the larger liberty of Olivia by the death of Anita, were somewhat those of Olivia herself; for, in spite of the shock which she had received by that event, and the natural horrors which were taught her by her own secret consciousness of the cause of it, she could not avoid reflecting upon the probable increase of her own securities in consequence. They were both deceived. That very night, the place of Anita was filled by another old woman, another creature of Don Balthazar, not so ugly, perhaps, or so old as her predecessor, but equally hard favored and unscrupulous. Sylvia was a mestizo also, brought from one of the haciendas of the estate, a few miles in the country. Olivia had seen and known her before. **The sight of this woman, in her new situation, left her little hope of profit** by the death of Anita. Sylvia was as subtle as the former, and no less the willing tool of her employer. She had all the fierce malignity of mood characteristic of the hybrid race to which she belonged,—a people usually of fierce passions, sudden impulses, capricious impulse, and tenacious of the sense of wrong and injury to the latest moment of existence. Don Balthazar knew his creatures well, and satisfied of this fact, Olivia, for the moment, resigned herself to despair again.

But she found an unexpected ally, where she least looked for one, in the person of the young serving girl, Juana. This girl was the grand-daughter of Anita. The event which put another in the place of her grandmother, had also its injurious consequences to herself. She naturally regarded herself as the heiress of her kinswoman; and knowing how large and various had been the accumulations of the latter, her expectations were correspondingly large. To her consternation, the successor to the place of Anita at once usurped possession of all her stores. Juana was driven out from the precincts altogether, and compelled to confine herself to the little chamber which she had long occupied, adjoining that of Olivia. Sylvia had assumed the entire control of the household, and her usurpations, in a few hours, were such as to satisfy Juana that her expectations from the savings of her grandmother were all cut off. She was held in no more favor than her mistress, and soon found herself under an authority which was disposed to submit to no questioning. Sylvia had her own children and grand-children to provide for. Juana was dreadfully indignant. She did not dare to approach Don Balthazar with her griefs; but she condescended to confide to Olivia. In her passion she revealed to her all the secrets of their mutual prison-house, all at least that she knew, and thus, in a measure, confirmed the unhappy girl in the conviction which she had already been compelled to feel, that she was the victim of a thousand cruel arts. Juana swore to have her revenges, and better to secure sympathy, she promised Olivia that she should have redress also. What were her plans of vengeance she did not declare; but when questioned in respect to her means and opportunities, contented herself with a knowing look, and a sagacious shaking of the head. She was naturally a stupid wench, but possessed that sort of animal cunning which is so frequently found in connection with a base and feeble intellect. For the present nothing could be extracted from her, and the business of the household went on without disorder, and with no apparent interruption. But, as we shall see in the sequel, Juana was busy after a fashion of her own.

But the day, thus distinguished by the startling events which we have recorded, was not at an end. Olivia sat alone in the verandah. The evening meal had been set before her by Juana, but had been carried out untasted. She had no appetite just then for mortal food. Her soul was still agitated to its depths, as the sea that heaves up tumultuously with all its waves, though the winds which have swept it with fearful strife, have wholly passed and gone. She lay reclined upon the settee of wickerwork where we beheld her during her morning interview with Vasconselos. There was no light in the apartment; none, in fact, was necessary, while the moon glinting through groves of orange and anana, sufficed for the desires of the sad and contemplative spirit. The gay gleams flitted over the floor of the verandah, and glided, stealthily and faintly, to the interior of the apartment, otherwise dimly shaded by the massive foliage which curtained the opening in front. Here, saddening under the sad sweetness of the scene, Olivia brooded,—absorbed in ruminating the events and the prospects of a life, which, at its very budding, seemed already shrouded with a blight. Her heart sunk within her as she thought; all was dark in the future; all gloomy, grievous, and reproachful in the past. At length she wept, and found a momentary relief in her tears. The big drops forced their way through her fingers,—tears of a bitterness which proved superior to all the sweets promised by an affection which was only too precious to her hopes.

"He loves me!" was her exclamation. "He loves me—he--the only man for whom this heart has ever felt a passion. I cannot mistake his silent admiration. I cannot doubt the broken meaning,—the imperfect sentiment—in these hesitating words, and oh! were it but that I could bear his glances with this dreadful and humiliating secret in my heart, how heavenly were such a love. But how to enjoy his affections, yet betray his confidence! How, unworthy as I am, to receive his embraces! —How place my head—how bury my face in the bosom whose faith I have deceived! Impossible! no, Philip de Vasconselos, —precious as I hold thee to my heart, I must deny myself even more than I deny thee. Thou wilt come, but it must be for denial only. I deny thee for thy better fortune. Thou wilt go hence; go upon the path of conquest; and ambition will rightly take the place of love! Though I die to own thee, yet I never will be thine."

She had spoken audibly this soliloquy. It made its way to other ears, though her own were scarcely conscious of its import. From the dense masses of shade at the foot of the verandah, came a voice in answer:

"A wise resolution, Olivia,—a very wise resolution! But one thou wilt hardly be prepared to keep. The morning sun will bring thee fresh hopes and fancies; the evening will bring thee thy lover with the moonlight; and thou wilt forget the vow as if it were written in water!"

At the first sound of the speaker's voice, Olivia half started from the settee on which she reclined. But, as she recognized the accents of Don Balthazar, she schooled her mood to indifference; drawing a long deep breath, and looking a mixed scorn and hatred, which, could her features have been seen at the moment, would have embodied a truthful portrait of those of Medea, about to take her flight for Athens, in her chariot dyed with the gore of her kindred. Intense and bitter was the momentary feeling of indignation which darkened her cheeks with red, only to subside, in the next instant, into a more than mortal paleness. The uncle advanced from the thicket and ascended to the verandah. He approached her, flung his cap upon a table, and seated himself at her side. She recoiled from him, retreating to the opposite end of the settee.

"So hostile still!" said he. "Well! It is perhaps reasonable enough, though it comports little with thy resolution. If thou wilt shake off the knights of Portugal, there is no need to send me with them. Nay, for the very reason that they depart, should I be suffered to remain. Let me say, Olivia, that I rejoice in thy resolution. It is wise—it is prudent. It would never do for thee to wed with Philip de Vasconselos"

"And wherefore not?"

"Ah! there are sufficient reasons."

"None which concern thee, at least. If I have so resolved, it is for a reason of mine own, the force of which it is little likely that thou shouldst feel."

"Be it so! It is enough that thou hast resolved. I care not to know the motive for a decision which is yet grateful to my mind. Thou hast resolved! and yet I somewhat wonder at thee Olivia."

"Thou know'st me not."

"Thou wilt scarce keep to thy resolution."

"Thou know'st me not."

"Ha! did I not see thee when he was urging thee, as still the passionate lover knows how to urge his suit? Did I not see thee tremble, even though thou recoiledst from his supplications? Did I not see the yielding weakness in thy lip and eye—hear it in the tremors of thy voice—know it in what I know of the passion for him which stirs in all thy soul? Thou wouldst have yielded, at one moment—nay, at another!—I am curious, Olivia. Wherefore, at certain moments, when his hand had taken thine into close keeping, and when thy whole heart was melting to his persuasive words—wherefore, then, didst thou break away, and speak of thy guitar, and of idle minstrelsy?"

"Said I not,—thou know'st me not?"

"But wherefore?"

"Thou didst not give heed to the words he uttered."

"Nay, but I did. They were words of passion and devotion, such as well befit such an occasion. They were well chosen words of love, I trow; and they were passing sweet, I am certain, in thy ears. Why just then didst thou recoil from him, even as from an adder thou hadst startled in thy path,—evade his supplications,—changing the course of his thought, and of thy own, and seeking to divert him from his purpose, only that he might hear how deftly thou couldst finger thy guitar?"

"And think'st thou I had such motive?"

"What else?"

"I tell thee again, thou know'st *me* not! Heard'st thou the words which he poured into mine ears?"

"What words? I noted that he was warming to thee with no doubtful purpose. Didst thou mistake him?"

"No! I knew—I *felt* his purpose; and had his words been otherwise chosen, I had probably been base enough to listen, and weak enough to yield! Ah! uncle! hadst thou not utterly hardened thy soul against all that is noble, the words which Don Philip employed had smitten upon thy senses equally with mine, and thou hadst felt a shudder and a cold shame pass over thee, such as made me, perforce, refuse to listen to the devotion of that love which I could not help but feel."

"What words are these? They spoke for his love only!"

"More! more! There were words in his speech which were as poisoned arrows to my heart."

"How! what?"

"For my—— but no! no! why should I repeat to thee? Thou wilt not feel as I do—thou canst not! Enough, that I strove to avoid the professions which I dared not trust myself to answer. I would have him abandon his purpose, and seek me no more. Let him find one who, though she may love him less profoundly, will be more deserving of his affections. It is because I so *much* love him, that I will deny his prayer. I dare not dishonor a heart which is so precious to my own."

The uncle rose from his seat, and stood intently gazing for a moment, in silence, upon the excited features of the damsel. She had exhibited to his mind a virtue beyond his understanding. He approached and laid his hand upon her shoulder. She recoiled from his touch.

"Verily, Olivia, thou art but a very simple child."

"Child! Oh! would to Heaven I were! but I am not. Thou hast forced upon me too dreary an experience of age—of *thy* age—to be a child—of *thy* sex, to be properly sensible of mine. Thou hast crushed me with a deadly weight of knowledge! Thy tutorship has taken from me all the sweet ignorance of childhood. Alas! I know too much for childhood as well as peace! neither shall I ever know again!"

"Thy fit is again coming on thee, Olivia!"

"Fit! I tell thee, Don Balthazar de Alvaro, that, though thou hast the power to destroy me, and every hope which is mine, I will not suffer thee to mock me with thy taunts! Fit! Verily, if it were foaming madness, it were in reason, in proper accordance with my wrongs and sorrows. Should I not be maddened! Should I not rave from the house-top of such wrongs as might move the heavens and the earth to shudder?"

"And wherefore rave? Thou seest how idle! I can well conceive how much thou feel'st the loss of such a knight as Philip de Vasconselos—for, of a truth, a more noble cavalier treads not the Isle of Cuba——"

"No more! no more!"

It seemed the humor of Don Balthazar to chafe the sore spot in her soul, and he continued:

"Well, what say'st thou to Augustin de Sinolar?"

"Why didst thou bring him hither to-day? He made suit to thee before. Said I not then, that I scorn this man De Sinolar?"

"So!—thou rejectest De Sinolar because thou scorn'st him, and Vasconselos because thou lovest him? This, my Olivia, is but child's play. Let me show thee thy folly. Thou hast a secret. It is my secret as well as thine, but I have every confidence that thou wilt keep it faithfully. Now, to have a secret, such as she never likes to reveal, is just the failing of every woman since the days of Eve. Just such a secret as thine, troubles every damsel fair as thou art!"

"Impossible!"

"True, my child! True! But should it make her miserable!

She has eaten certain fruits which are forbidden, but she has sense enough to wipe her mouth after eating, and who is the wiser? Now, this act of wiping the mouth is very simple. Shalt thou then deny thyself the privilege of eating again when it pleases thee? Shalt thou deny thyself, because of a past error—if it pleases thee so to call it—to partake of even more precious fruits, which thou dost really desire? Wherefore? What wisdom in it? No! no! I love thee, Olivia, and will teach thee better policy. I have resolved for thee, and if thou ever wed'st, thou shalt wed with De Sinolar."

"Name not that thing, De Sinolar, to me."

"True, he is a *thing*, that is certain;—and so far acceptable. I rather prefer him on that account."

"That thou may'st the better use him! For that thou may'st make a dog of him without endowing him with a dog's courage."

"Perhaps! perhaps!"

"But I shall never wed. So forbear this cruel talk, I pray thee."

"I cannot trust thy resolution, Olivia. I fear that when Philip de Vasconselos next approaches thee with the words of soliciting, thou wilt answer him with the words of consent."

"No! no! no!"

"Yet, verily, thou lovest that man!"

"I deny it not! It is my boast, when spoken to thy ears. It were my pride, were I other than I am, to make declaration of my love abroad to all mankind. I love him as man never was loved before; and it is, as I have said to thee already, it is even because I so much love, that I will not marry him. I will not do him such grievous wrong! Oh! uncle, thou hast destroyed my hope and happiness forever. Thou hast abused the trust of my dear father—thou the shepherd, that hast thyself been the wolf to destroy the lamb."

A paroxysm of tears followed this speech. The uncle smiled contemptuously. He knew that the more violent passion was usually weakened in the access of tears. She looked suddenly up and caught the expression; and a passionate pride rose up in her soul to her relief

"Thou mock'st, I see! Now, I say to thee, Don Balthazar de Alvaro! thou hadst better stay thy tortures. Thou know'st me not, or the fires which prey upon my soul like those of a volcano. Better thou shouldst, without weapon or preparation, arouse the she-wolf in the cavern with her young, than vex me farther with thy taunts. Beware! I have been weak, and thou hast taken me at 'vantage. But if I am weak, I am blind no longer; and if not strong to bear, I am, at least, tempered to resist and to resent. The very passions thou hast goaded into existence will be my avengers in the end. I counsel thee give heed to what I say. Beware! I am capable of things even more evil than thou think'st for, and there is a limit beyond which it were well for thee not to go. Once more I warn thee. I have had such bitter thoughts and feelings towards thee, that didst thou press me much further, I feel as if I could slay thee with a dagger, even as I would strike the serpent that crept to my bosom while I slept."

She had risen while she spoke, and stood before him, wild and passionate, with flashing dark eye, and white arm waving. He surveyed her with a stern and frowning brow, but somewhat coldly—his lips compressed, as if with a feeling of pride and power,—and his eye looking into hers with the bright fixedness which that of the serpent is said to show when fascinating the bird from the tree. There was a pause; the parties still regarding each other. She, standing, looking on him with a raised spirit, and wild, fiery glance; he, sitting, returning the gaze steadfastly— coolly if not calmly, and apparently reserving himself for the proper moment. At length, he spoke, very deliberately, as if measuring every syllable.

"I think I do know thee, Olivia de Alvaro, and something know of what thou art capable in thy passion. Have I not, of late, likened thee to thy Biscayan mother? and her I knew thoroughly. Let me convince thee that I do not estimate too humbly thy powers of evil. Sit down once more while I question thee."

There was something so calm and quiet in the authority of his voice and words, that, from habit merely, the damsel submitted and resumed her seat. Steadily looking into her face, he proceeded to speak again, as deliberately as before.

"Didst thou know, Olivia, that the poor old woman, Anita, was poisoned? She died from no old age, but from a deadly liquor which she was made to drink."

The listener grew white as death. Her knees shook beneath her. Her tongue was frozen.

"Ay, Olivia, some loving hand drenched her posset with a too bountiful allowance! Dost thou know this kerchief, Olivia?"

He showed it. It was her own. She was silent.

"This kerchief did I find where the person was concealed who drugged the old woman's draught."

He paused, as if awaiting the answer. But none was spoken.

"Thou hast nothing to say. Well! It is enough. Not to speak is sufficiently to answer at such a moment. But, let me say to thee farther, my child, it is known to me that thou thyself wast the last in the chamber of Anita last night! Shouldst thou think, now, that I am ignorant of what thou art capable? It was *thy* hand, Olivia de Alvaro, that drugged the old woman's draught with death."

"And if it were, Don Balthazar de Alvaro," exclaimed Olivia, rising, and resuming all her strength and courage, as she beheld the air and listened to the tone of superiority which he employed—"and if it were my hand, then were my hand rightly employed in punishing one who has been a murderess to me. And had my hand served thee with the same fatal drug, then were I also justified in the sight of man and heaven. Go to, Señor, thou shalt not alarm or confound me. I am prepared, when thou art so pleased, to listen to thee as thou reportest all thy story to the world. I fear thee not—I know not now that I fear anything in life. Thou hast brought me to this desperation. Yet know, that when I mixed the drug with the draught of Anita, I knew it not as a deadly poison. I knew it only, and believed it to be no more than a stupefying drug, such as wrap the senses in an unnatural and temporary slumber. As thou knowest so much, it is not unlikely that thou knowest, also, that I beheld thee and

Anita in secret conference in regard to my fate, on the night when that drug was mixed with her wine? I saw her, ay, and thee, as the fatal phial was held between ye to the light, and ye resolved together that my potion was to be increased. Was it unreasonable if I thought the goodly medicine which ye designed for me, in your charity, it was but fitting that ye also should partake? I wished to commend ye also to such blessed visions and dreams, as ye nightly and daily prepared for me. I would have ye too enjoy that insensible respose, which ye decreed between ye should lighten my cares, and keep me from the feeling of my cruel wrongs; and had it been possible, Don Balthazar, that I could have mingled the drug with thy own wine-cup, this hand should fearlessly have done it;—not, I affirm, as meaning that it should be fatal to thy life, but as forcing you to such trial of those sufferings of mine which have never yet compelled your pity and forbearance! Now, that you know of what I am capable, I again bid ye beware! You know the terms between us. I loathe you, and I fear you; yet so little do I fear the world of man, that, were it not for one who lives among ye, I should commission you freely to declare aloud all that you have made me and all that I am! Nay, the time may come, when, heedless of the shame which shall follow from this speech, I myself shall go out into the highways of the city, and speak aloud the truth myself!"

Don Balthazar was silenced. For the moment, he had no refuge. He rose and left the verandah, and passed into the groves around it; while Olivia, thoroughly exhausted, but no longer tremulous or fearful, rose with a firm frame and spirit, and moved quietly to her chamber.

CHAPTER X.

> "*Cymb*   The time is troublesome:
> We'll slip you for a season; but our jealousy
> Does yet depend."   SHAKSPEARE.

PHILIP DE VASCONSELOS did not, as was anticipated by Don Balthazar, and warmly counselled by Nuno de Tobar, return immediately to the attempt upon the affections of Olivia de Alvaro. It would have been quite enough to preclude his visit for that day and the next, at least, that there had been a death in the family; an event, however, to which his more reckless friend attached no sort of importance. But there was another reason for delay and hesitation: Philip had no such confidence in his own position, no such faith in his own powers, no such conviction of the favorable regards of the lady, as was asserted by Nuno. He was, on the contrary, troubled with many misgivings, which grew in difficulty the more he examined. The very fact that he really and earnestly loved, made him tremble at the thought of precipitating his fate; and the true lover is almost always prepared to think humbly of his own claims, in view of that supposed perfection which he recognizes in the lady of his love. Besides, with the natural delicacy of a proud and honorable mind, conscious of his own poverty, he felt the awkwardness of a suit to one who was in the possession of great riches. He felt how easy it was to suspect the motives of such a suitor, and dreaded lest such a suspicion should taint the mind of the lady herself. Not that he was disposed to forego his suit because of this, or any other consideration. On the contrary, he was resolved to bring it to the trial, and know the worst as soon as he could think it proper to do so. But all his conclusions counselled him to delay. Nor must we allow it to be supposed that he was without his encouragements.

He persuaded himself that there was much in what had taken place between himself and Olivia in that last interview, to show that she was very far from insensible to his pretensions. It is true that there were things in her carriage—some curious caprices of mood and manner, which he found it not easy altogether to comprehend. But there was still enough to please a lover; and to persuade one, even less bold and ardent than our hero, to continue a pursuit in which he had certainly suffered no repulse. She had evaded his application, but she had shown a peculiar sensibility at his approach. She had trifled somewhat when *he* was seriously earnest, but what was the meaning of her tremors when her fair white hand lingered within his grasp? and had she not encouraged his return?—and had she not declared an interest in his presence in Cuba, in language too impressive to be wholly without that desirable signification which the lover seeks? Vasconselos was very far from being discouraged—nay, without heeding the confident assurance of Nuno de Tobar, he felt a new hope springing within his bosom at every moment of increased reflection; and, ere the day was well over, he had resolved to bring his doubts to an issue, at least, before the departure of the expedition. It was his farther resolution, if successful in his suit, to abandon the adventure with De Soto. For that matter, he had partly determined thus, whatever might be the result of his courtship. This conclusion was reached that very night, and the next morning, when he was visited by Tobar, he unhesitatingly declared it, to the great consternation of that young gallant. The latter enabled him to do so, without effort, by rallying him on the score of his amour.

"Where were you last night, Philip? You promised to be with us, and broke faith. Truth to say, we had the merriest night of it in the tent of Juan de Anasco. Better flasks of Xeres were never opened to Don Ferdinand. All cried aloud against you, and cursed your drowsy courtship, which seems to be notorious throughout the Island. Now, my good fellow, if you must be in love, there is no good reason why you should be out of the world. Every body asks for you—they all look for you in vain. You are lost to all good fellowship."

"You are likely to lose me still more completely than you do now, Nuno. Some day you will fail to see me altogether. I mean, indeed, to separate myself wholly from such a band of vicious profligates, who have no faith in anything more lovely than a pearl oyster, and yield their hearts to nothing less persuasive than a gold mine. What should I do with such people;—I who still believe in love and beauty, and have a heart still open to the pleadings of a woman? That I do love is sufficient reason why I should leave such companions. From this day I am going to quit you all. I propose even to forego the expedition to Florida. It needs me not; and there are good reasons wherefore I should abandon it."

"Now the blessed saints forefend, that you should speak seriously this resolution, my friend. Why, Philip de Vasconselos, this is mere madness. What reasons can you have? That you love and would marry, and may marry Olivia de Alvaro, is not sufficient cause, I trow, since the one stands not in the way of the other, if there be any settled purpose in your mind to go."

"Aye, but there is none."

"How! I thought your going with the expedition was quite a settled matter. I know that the Adelantado counts confidently upon your going, and holds it of large importance to the interest of the expedition that you should go: for you are the only person of all the party who knows the tongue of the Floridian, and the passages to his country."

"I did, in some degree, prepare and consent to depart with the Adelantado, but if he counts upon my going and values my performance, he hath taken but a strange course for showing me the estimate he hath of my services."

"Truth, he hath neglected you somewhat."

"But this availeth little, and I have no regrets and no complaints. Let it suffice for you, Nuno, that, for the time, the passion for warlike adventure hath gone utterly out of my heart. I look with discomfort at all warlike panoply—I turn away from lance and sword with feeling of discomfort, and my shield glares at me with unpleasant brightness from the wall. Love hath subdued me to simpler and sweeter desires. I dream now of long floating hair and dewy eyes, and a sweet song and sweeter sigh in the shade of lemon groves in the star-light."

"Shame on thee, Vasconselos, that thou shouldst make such confession! I will report thee for a haggard through the army. I too have had my passions and my loves, as thou knowest, and I could, on occasion, play me a merry turn of sadness upon the guitar beneath my lady's lattice, even now; but that she should wean me from my love of shield and spear, were impossible! I must not believe thee."

"Thou shalt! thou wilt! I am the very thing that I tell thee, and care nothing for all the gold and treasure of the Floridian."

"It will greatly anger the adelantado when he hears of thy decision."

"Nay, I think he is somewhat prepared for it. He hath treated me with neglect from the beginning, in all substantial things, and he now shows me a cold courtesy, which argues hostility. This, of itself, were enough to move me to abandon his banner. But thou also knowest how much are we Portuguese the dislike of thy common soldiers. My brother, Andres, who leads a troop of our people, and a goodly one, hath a certain measure of independence. But I, who am only a single horse and lance, I have no power, and lacking power, have no security. I could only go as a simple volunteer, the aid to a superior who hath shown me aversion. Seest thou not how little motive is there left me for this adventure? Even the page who helped me buckle on my armor is withdrawn from me, since he waits also on my brother, and is his paid follower; and this reminds me, Nuno, that I am seeking to buy me a well-made blackamoor;— a boy who shall bring me water, unlace my helmet, and put on my spurs; a meek and docile urchin, who shall be quick as willing, and whom, by kindness, I can make faithful. Wilt thou make it known abroad that the Portuguese knight, Philip de Vasconseles, is willing to pay a goodly sum in Castellanos for this Moorish urchin?"

"It shall be done, Philip; but thou chafest me. I cannot lose thee from this expedition."

"It may be that the Lady Olivia will reject my hand. If it be so ——."

"Nay, I know her better. She will not reject thee. Leonora vows to me that her heart is full of thee only."

"Hath she said this to thy wife?"

"No! not in words; but she hath shown it in a thousand instances. My wife is a laugher, but she hath an eye. She sees, and I, too, see, Philip, and we have no doubts. It is your own modesty alone that seeks for them, and builds them up into a tower! I can tell you what the answer of the lady will be, and upon this you may count with certainty. But you will scarcely wed on the instant, even when she accepts thee. Some time will pass, and why not yield this to a campaign in Florida? How much better to bring home a dowry for your bride, in the pearl and gold of the Apalachian? Nay, hath she not a noble hacienda, one of the finest in all the island, at Matelos, which needs nothing but an adequate supply of slaves, to make it an empire? A single season in Apalachia will give thee any number."

"Nay, let her consent to my love, Nuno, and there shall be no delay. We shall instantly wed. I like not these long gaps between promise and performance. They make the heart sick and the soul weary. Unless there be good reason, there shall be no delay. She shall be mine as soon after she hath said the consenting word as the time will suffer for the coming of the priest and the preparation of the altar."

"And Don Balthazar! thinkest thou he is the person to suffer thee so easily to take possession? I look for trouble from that quarter."

"Trouble! I tell thee, Nuno, there is something in the aspect of that man which so offends my nature, that it will go hard with me if I do not take him by the beard on the first occasion. I have somehow, among men, an infallible instinct for knowing an enemy, even as most men have the instinct for knowing when there is venom in reptile and insect. My soul seems to lift my heel, as I behold him, with the feeling that I ought to crush."

"Yet beware! He is one who hath power and policy. He hath courage, too, and is known for a man of prowess in arms. You know that the adelantado hath made him Captain-General of the Fleet."

"Ha! then he departs with the expedition? I had thought this doubtful."

"The appointment hath secured him, and some thousands of Castellanos besides, drawn, I suspect, from the estates of the fair Olivia."

"Well, let him depart. It is even more important, if he goes, that I should remain. Let Olivia but yield me her favor, and I care not who departs. Nothing then should persuade me to this wild enterprise."

"Ah! Philip, thou didst not hold it so wild ere thou sawest the fair niece of Don Balthazar."

"I was but a wild person in that day myself."

"And why shouldst thou now deem it so wild an enterprise? Thou wert a companion with Cabeza de Vaça, and shared his spoils, and held with him the opinion that the mountains of Apalachia contained treasures of gold and silver even greater than those of Peru and Tenochtitlan."

"And think not otherwise now. But to me such treasures have grown valueless in comparison with others yet more precious. Thou shalt enjoy my share of them, Nuno. May they make thee rich and leave thee happy. But, for my happiness, I need not now to go on shipboard. I need not carry lance again among the savages. My ears shall not prick at the summons of the trumpet, and I shall soon learn to forget in the quiet shadows of my fig-tree, that I ever had communion with wild and profligate youth like thyself."

"Now am I half persuaded to implore the Saints that they move against thee, and forbid this damsel to give hearing to thy prayer. Thy passion for her bids fair to break the head from one of the best lances of Castile! What shall we do without thee in Florida—thou who know'st all about the country, and hast such sufficient knowledge of the infernal dialect of these savages of Apalachia? When this resolution of thine shall reach the ears of the Adelantado, he will surely madden. He will carry thee, perforce, Philip."

"Be thine the tongue, Nuno, to make him the report, that the first overflow of his anger will fall upon other heads than mine."

"Upon mine, thou meanest? Yet thou scarcely deservest this friendship from the comrade whom thou abandon'st at the entrance of the field! But thou wilt decide otherwise, I trust; and prove thyself true to thy vocation, if not to the sex. He who keeps faith with his comrade, need not concern himself in regard to pledges made to woman."

"Out upon thee for a heretic! But that I know thee to speak commonly a philosophy such as thou canst invent, and not such as thou believest, I should lift lance against thee, though I never strove in tilt or combat again! But get thee hence, and leave me to my meditations. Thou, meanwhile, may'st employ thyself, and amuse the island, by telling aloud this purpose of mine to abandon the expedition."

"But thou wilt take part in the tournament?"

"Ay, as a point of honor it is needful. We Portuguese have been too much held in disesteem by your proud Spaniards, and I am resolved to lower some of the haughty crests, which have abused the courtesy of knighthood. It will be, perchance, a solemn service, closing my career in chivalry. I will then dedicate my spear to the Gods of the Harvest—and set up an altar to peace, where hitherto I have bowed only to that of war!"

"*A Dios!*" exclaimed the young knight at parting. "I go sadly, Philip, to make evil report of thee to all good companions!"

"A Dios!" replied the Portuguese—"I wish thee no worse evil than that, in time, thou shalt come to be full believer in thy own report."

Nuno de Tobar needed no exhortations on the part of Philip

de Vasconselos, to spread abroad the news of his resolution to abandon the expedition. He was naturally given to talk freely all that he knew. But, in publishing the matter, he aimed really so to cause the expression of regret among the people, which he knew would be very general, as to move the Adelantado to review his conduct towards the Portuguese knights, and to repair the evils which had followed his neglect. It was the notion of Nuno, and it was probably not without justice, that a little more favor shown to these adventurers would have secured their attachments, and confirmed them in their desire for the adventure. It was not too late, he fancied, to win Philip back to the enterprise, and he resolved freely to declare himself, to this effect, to the ears of the Adelantado. The command of a score or two of lances, and an honorable appointment, would, he persuaded himself, so influence Philip de Vasconselos, that, even if he married Olivia, he would still accompany or follow the expedition. Was he not about to abandon his own wife, who was both young and beautiful; and did not the Adelantado himself do likewise, in respect to a woman no less beautiful than noble? He could see no reason why the Portuguese should exhibit a more feminine tenderness and affection than either.

In these views and this policy he seconded the desires and opinion of Don Balthazar de Alvaro. This person soon got tidings of the avowed determination of the knight of Portugal. Nuno de Tobar had given large currency to the report in a couple of hours; but Philip, who was not without his policy, and whose desire was to circulate his decision, set other agents to work in its dissemination. Scarcely had Nuno de Tobar disappeared when another visitor had sought his lodgings, and he was shortly succeeded by a third. To all of these our knight was equally communicative, and the news was soon dispersed, as upon the wings of the wind, all over the city. Don Balthazar was one of the first persons whom it reached.

"'Tis as I feared!" he muttered to himself. "This knight is hopeful of success. He is not willing to forego his chances. He grows confident: he will come again. He will propose. I cannot hide her from him. I cannot deny him entrance. I dare not hurry her off to the mountains. He must see her. Well! she has resolved, in her refinement of virtue, not to accept him—not to marry him or any other. She loves him too well, she says, to dishonor him. Very good! very satisfactory, could she keep her word—were she firm in her resolution. But, is it possible? Can I trust her? Is any woman to be trusted where her heart is full of the one object, where the passions are young and vigorous, and where the opportunities are free? She will tremble and hesitate, and be coy—recede, yet loiter,—listen, and finally, forgetting everything except the passion which she feels, she will fall into his arms, and he will drink the moist, warm consent from her burning lips. So it has been ever—so it will be ever—to the end of the history. I have studied the sex in vain if it be not so!—and how to prevent all this, for it must be prevented! The Adelantado must persuade this knight to continue with the expedition. He must win him. He hath the charm to do this, when he is persuaded to use it; and he must use it *now*. He must make him a captain of twenties—nay, hundreds—but he must bear him off; and meanwhile, it must be for me to encourage him with a promise of Olivia on his return from the expedition. To gain time is now the thing essential. The rest may be left to the thousand casualties of such an adventure as that on which we depart. But should these arts fail! should the persuasions of the Adelantado come too late—should the pride of this knight of Portugal reject our overtures with scorn, as perchance he may—should my promise of Olivia, on his return, not satisfy him—as, in faith, her encouragement hath been sufficient to make it unsatisfactory—what remains? Verily, but one remedy! We must try the sharp necessity of the dagger. There will be opportunities enough, I trow. It must either be my hand, or that of one whose soul and weapon I may buy against any bosom in Cuba!"

CHAPTER XI.

> "*Laf.* have then sinned against his experience, and transgressed against his valor, and my state that way is dangerous, since I cannot yet find it in my heart to repent Here he comes. I pray you make us friends. I will pursue the amity."
> ALL'S WELL THAT ENDS WELL.

We have heard the cold and cruel determination of Don Balthazar de Alvaro. We may be assured that it has not been spoken idly, or with a mere braggart spirit, and that his resolution and his will correspond too well, to make him pause, whenever it shall seem necessary to carry out his purposes in action. For the present, his conclusions led him at once to seek an interview with the adelantado. As he expected, he found De Soto already in possession of the rumor touching the withdrawal of Philip de Vasconselos from the expedition.

"Is this report true, Don Balthazar?" demanded the adelantado, who, proud as he was, and self-confident, could not help showing in his tone and manner that the affair seriously disquieted him.

"It is not improbable, your excellency: the report comes through several persons who have his ear. Nuno de Tobar himself assured me that his present mood inclined him to forego the expedition, but he thought that, with proper efforts made, Don Philip might be persuaded to review his decision."

"And am I to stoop to solicit this Portuguese knight to be my companion in my arms?" was the imperious demand of De Soto.

"Nay!" interposed, gently but earnestly, the more sedate spirit of his wife, the Lady Isabella—"nay, my Lord, this is an unreasonable spirit which possesses thee. Don Balthazar is surely too much thy friend to counsel thee to any dishonor, or descent from thy high dignity. He means not that thou shouldst sink the spirit of the noble and the knight, to conciliate an exacting spirit, or win the countenance of the unworthy. He but counsels, as I have striven to do, that in the case of these brave knights of Portugal, whom none hold to be less than honorable in very high degree, thou shouldst assume a different bearing from that which is but too common for our Spaniards to show to these gentlemen. Verily, I say myself, they have been quite too much slighted in this adventure, the more especially when we remember the claims of Don Philip, not merely as a brave warrior, and polished gentleman, but on account of the special qualities which he possesses from a former sojourn with the Floridian of Apalachia. And where is the shame and the discredit to thee of seeking and soliciting this noble and his brother? Dost thou not solicit many,—many who are far less worthy? What is all thy toil here, the parade which we daily make, the court which we hold, the feasts we give, the pageants and tourneys we exhibit, but the fruit of a solicitude which seeks men, and money and horses,—and all that is deemed needful to the success and glory of thy enterprise? Of a truth, my Lord, I see, as I have long seen, that there is no true wisdom in looking coldly on these brave spirits, who, I doubt not, will be most happy of thy favor, and most hearty in thy cause."

The Adelantado trode the floor with hasty strides while his wife was speaking. When she had done, he spoke.

"I see not what ye would have. I gave these knights all the countenance that was possible. They were entreated to our presence; they were dealt honorably with when they came. I could not strip command from other of my followers, born Castilians, who brought with them their own retainers. I could not for my own dignity, abridge my own command, that they should find the followers whom they did not bring. I dared not give them high places in the expedition, knowing well the jealousy of our people towards the foreigners. But, I trow, all this complaint of neglect had never been, Don Balthazar, had it not been for thy niece. It is the passion of this knight for the Lady Olivia, and, perchance, thy hostility to his object, which hath marred his purpose, and not any lack of my favor. He had gone, as so many do, as an individual adventurer, a single lance and sword, but for his passion for thy niece; and thou, I wot, hath put thy ban upon his affection."

"I have put no ban upon his affections, your excellency, nor upon hers. He is free to come and go, and he sees my niece when he will. I have not forbidden him; I do not purpose to forbid. If he seeks her in marriage, and she affects him, I withhold no consent."

"Thou hast changed in thy resolve since we last spoke of these parties!" said Donna Isabella.

"True, your Ladyship. I hearkened to your counsels, and resolved in compliance with them. But it is, perchance, for this very reason that he hath declined the expedition. Had I barred his passage to the Lady Olivia, he had been less hopeful. I am free to say that I believe she hath large power over him."

"And he over her," quoth the Lady Isabella, "or the woman's eyes have in this greatly mistaken the usual signs of the woman's heart."

"Well!" exclaimed Hernan de Soto, breaking in with impatience, "well, and what is to come of it? Will he sink into the drudge upon a vineyard? Will he become fruit-pruner on the hacienda of the Lady Olivia de Alvaro, and prepare his monthly accounts, as steward and agent, for the examination of the severe Señor Don Balthazar? Think'st thou to bring him to this? Can it be that one of the bravest and best lances in Portugal—ay, and Spain—will be content with this petty employ in life while great deeds are done in Florida—he who, but a month ago, had an ambition for conquest, and a passion for enterprise, equal to that of the most eager adventurer in Cuba? Then is knighthood greatly altered in spirit in the last *decade;* and one as he reads may well wonder if the deeds of Hernan de Cordova are not in faith a pure fable,—a silly invention of the poet. Go to, Don Balthazar, you shall not persuade me to this."

"I would persuade you to nothing, your excellency, which you deem hurtful to your honor or your interests, or which you find displeasing to your moods. You hear what is reported as coming from Don Philip himself. I believe the rumor, and think that he hath so expressed himself. It is for you to say whether the loss of this knight,—perchance his younger brother also,—be such loss as you can suffer without grievance."

"Of a truth, not! we want every man whom we can get, and every brave knight in especial,—particularly one who brings with him such manifold resources as Philip de Vasconselos."

"This being the case, your excellency, it may be well to ask in what way, without derogat' n from your high dignity, to persuade him to the adventure. I have shown you wherefore. I think he hath resolved to quit your banner;—the neglect of favor;—the jealousy of our Spaniards, and the passion which he hath for my niece."

"When thou sawest these things, and that the hope of thy niece was that which made him hostile to the expedition, why then didst thou give encouragement to this puling passion for the damsel?"

"Nay, my lord, thou art again unreasonable," interposed Donna Isabella. "If there be offence in that, the guilt of it lies at thy door and mine. Don Balthazar, as thou wilt recall, declared himself in opposition to the suit of the knight of Portugal, giving, as reason for it, the very peril which we now fear, that he would abandon the expedition if successful with the lady. Was it not so, Don Balthazar?"

Don Balthazar bowed assent, and then proceeded in reply to De Soto.

"I gave no encouragement, your excellency, to this passion. In truth, for many reasons I was greatly hostile to it. The calm, and, as seemed to me, as I trow it did to you, the insolent pride of this knight's bearing was rarely inconsistent with his poverty of position and resource, and I felt a pride of nation which revolted to think that the large possessions of my niece should fall into the clutch of a beggarly and grasping stranger. I had chosen another suitor for her—one Don Augustin de Sinolar, a worthy gentleman, and a handsome, whose estates lie adjoining those of my niece at the hacienda Matelos."

"And didst thou really seek to match thy niece with that thing of silk and straw, De Sinolar? Fie upon thee, Don Balthazar— fie upon thee, for designing a most unworthy sacrifice."

The face of Don Balthazar flushed to the temples, as he listened to the rebuke of the Lady Isabella, and felt the sharp indignant glance of her eye upon him. But he had his reply.

"He is rich, lady, and hath a good exterior. He hath the vanities of youth, perchance; I deny it not; but he hath few of the vices of youth. He hath meekness, and gentleness, and simplicity, and ——"

"Oh! hush thee, Don Balthazar; as if the qualities of a chicken or a hare were sufficient to satisfy the heart of a woman. Fie upon thee."

"Briefly," interposed De Soto, "she rejects your favorite De Sinolar, and must have your knight of Portugal."

"*My* choice was not hers, and, though the Lady Isabella rebukes me, I must say I am sorry for it. Olivia had been much happier, I trow, with De Sinolar, than she ever could hope to be with Philip de Vasconselos."

"And why not, I pray you?" again spoke the Lady Isabella. showing a feminine tenacity on a subject which so naturally interested the pride and temper of the sex.

"Nay, it does not matter to our present quest," said De Soto. 'The question is, does she resolve to wed the Portuguese?"

"She prefers him, beyond all question, but that she will wed with him is still—as who can answer for the caprices of the sex?"—and this was said with a sly glance at the Lady Isabella— "is still a very questionable matter."

"Nay. if she prefers him, and he seeks her, there is an end of the doubt. You do not bar the progress, and none denies. She will wed with him, I see, and he is lost to the expedition—a loss greater than fifty matchlocks!"

De Soto strode the apartment with a vexation which he did not labor to conceal. Now, that the loss of the knight seemed to be certain, he was at no pains to conceal his conviction of his value. The truth is that, as Don Balthazar had indicated already, the pride in the bearing of Don Philip de Vasconselos, and the stately reserve which he maintained to the Castilian leaders, De Soto among them, had touched the self-esteem of the latter. Yet this conduct of the Portuguese was not properly a cause of wonder or complaint, when it was remembered with what open jealousy he was regarded by the Spaniards. Don Balthazar watched his superior with keen eyes, but a calm, unspeaking countenance. After a brief pause, he spoke as follows:

"Nay, your Excellency, it does not seem so necessary that the Knight should be lost to the expedition, even should he wed with my niece. He may be persuaded to follow it after he hath wedded——"

"Better before!" said the Lady Isabella with a smile.

"Yes, I grant you, better before; and, whatever attempts we make upon him should be *seasonably* tried; but, failing to prevent his bridal—which, I repeat, is by no means an assured thing —then we may negotiate that he follow thee when the honey-moon is over. Thou wilt suffer one or more small caravels to remain from thy fleet, wherewith to bring stores after thee, and the sick soldiers, and in one of these he may easily depart with others. Thou wilt hardly feel his loss ere he is with thee. Thou wilt consume several weeks in thy progress along, and thy descent upon the coast—in the unloading of thy caravels, the landing of the horses, hogs and cattle, and in other needful preparations When thou art ready to penetrate the country of the Apalachian, he will, if we use the proper means of persuasion, be with thee in season."

"And these means of persuasion. Sant' Iago! Shall I go to this Knight of Portugal, and bend myself before him, and say, 'Sir Knight, wilt thou honor thy servant by taking thy part in this expedition?'"

"Nay, nay, my lord ——" began the lady, but the Adelantado waved his hand impatiently, looking to Balthazar. The latter did not delay his answer :—

"Will your Excellency leave this matter wholly to me? I will use what proper arguments I may. I will in no respect commit thy pride or honor. I will promise office, and the command of a troop, yet in no way conflict with thy engagements."

"How wilt thou do this?"

"Nay, will it not suffice that it shall be done?"

"In God's name, do it; I shall say no more. Thou wilt relieve me of an embarrassment; and if thou succeed'st with this churlish cavalier, will do help to the enterprise, as none better knows than thou! Away, Don Balthazar, and let the grass not grow beneath thy feet. To-morrow thou knowest the tournament begins, and there is much work for thee here as elsewhere. To thy papers, my secretary—my soul, rather!"

And with this superb compliment, the stately Don turned to his wife, and proceeded to dictate as she wrote. Don Balthazar, having *carte blanche*, made his bow and took his departure. He lost no time in visiting Philip de Vasconselos. The office was one which the uncle of Olivia would have cheerfully deputed to another; but this was impossible; and he proceeded accordingly to the work before him, with the promptitude of one to whom the duty is apparent. His hope lay in the temptation which he would hold forth to the ambition of the adventurer. Having himself little faith in the affections as sufficiently compensative to man, he persuaded himself that the aim of Philip de Vasconselos was the fortune of his ward. If he could hold forth a sufficient lure of the same character through another medium, he flattered himself that he should be successful. None doubted that Florida and the mountains of Apalachia concealed treasures in gold and silver, gems and precious stones, equal to any in the keeping of Peru. He knew that this faith was especially taught by the Portuguese who had been one of the explorers of that country with the Cavalier Cabeza de Vaça. All that seemed essential, therefore, to beguiling him to the enterprise, was to mollify his pride, and secure him the means of going thither in a style which should maintain his dignity and afford him an adequate command. For this money was necessary, and De Soto had none to spare. The resolution which Don Balthazar had formed, was to use the means afforded him by the large income from the estate of his niece, of which he had complete control. To employ the wealth of Olivia in ridding her of two dangerous lovers, seemed to him a perfectly legitimate measure; though, in respect to the propriety of the proceeding, he never allowed himself to doubt for a moment. Thus prepared with his general plan of action, he entered the humble dwelling of the Knight of Portugal.

Philip de Vasconselos beheld the approach of the unusual visitor without surprise. He had, in fact, anticipated the unwonted courtesy, and we may add, had partly designed it should be so, when he instructed his friends to declare aloud his determination. He knew quite as well as any other person, how necessary he was to the purposes of De Soto. The appearance of Don Balthazar seemed to assure him also of the conviction felt by the latter that his niece would favor the suit of the Portuguese. The instincts of Philip de Vasconselos on this subject had been strengthened by the positive reports of Nuno de Tobar. They were confirmed by the visit of the uncle. His hands were accordingly strengthened. He was prepared for the interview. Though yet a young man, hardly more than thirty, he had been a soldier; had travelled much; mingled much with men; endured those vicissitudes which strengthen patience, teach coolness, and give insight; and with a mind naturally acute, and a judgment well balanced and secure, he was more than a match for men of greater age and as much experience. He was a politician over whom the habitual cunning of Don Balthazar could obtain no advantage. It was a curious study to watch the interview between the parties—to behold the Castilian Don doubling like a fox through all the avenues of his art; to see him circling around his object, without approaching it; to note how warily he kept, in regard to his secret fears, while holding forth his most beguiling lures;—in particular to note how sweetly he could insinuate his flatteries of the man he hated in his soul, and had already resolved, simpler remedies having failed him, to treat with sharp medicine at the point of his dagger. He tried the pulse of Philip's vanity and ambition with most laborious art, and a skill of practice which had succeeded with ninety-nine in the hundred of the young men of the time. But he tried in vain.

Yet Philip de Vasconselos gave him no direct denial. The young man opposed art to art. He showed himself highly gratified with the praises of the other. He made no effort to disguise the ambition which he really felt, and suffered the old politician to believe that all his flatteries had made their way to his heart. He was never more frank and cordial in his life. He spoke to Don Balthazar as to the uncle of Olivia, and in the strain of one who regarded him as in no degree adverse to the free course of her affections. He did not say to him, "I love your niece,"—he did not even speak of her; yet he so shaped his speech, as to a confidential friend, and so governed tone and countenance equally as to indicate to the other the utter absence from his thoughts of any doubt that he, Don Balthazar, could be other than friendly to himself and objects. The confidence and ease with which he gave himself out—apparently—just forebore the look of self-complaisance, and expressed the sense and spirit of a man who felt that his chances with fortune were quite even, or at least looked so fair, as would render any reluctance to press them, a something too dastardly for the toleration of any brave man. In the end, all that Don Balthazar could obtain from the young knight was a promise to consider his proffers—to deliberate honestly upon them,—and resolve seasonably, giving his final answer before the departure of the fleet.

"Demonios!" muttered the Castilian to himself, when he had taken his departure: "This dog of a Moor thinks he already hath the rabbit in a sack. But he shall lose his own skin ere he hath. It is clear that he hopes for Olivia's consent. Now will it depend on her whether he tastes my dagger or not. If her virtue—Ha! ha! virtue!—if her virtue holds out to refusal of his hand, why let the dog drift where the seas may carry him! but if, as I fear, her passion for him proves too strong for her magnanimity, he must die! So be it! He shall never live to be her master--or mine!"

He returned with all diligence to the presence of the Adelantado, whom he found in the most joyous mood. The change of a couple of hours had effected wonders. When he left his presence De Soto was angry and sullen. Now his mirth was absolutely boisterous. In this merriment, though more temperately, Donna Isabella shared. Don Balthazar looked on with wonder, and several times vainly essayed to speak. He was always overborne by the laughter of his superior.

"Tell me nothing yet," cried De Soto, at an interval in his bursts of mirth,—"Nothing that shall qualify my pleasure. Ha! ha! ha! wait, good Don Balthazar, till I can recover breath, when you shall hear, and then, if it be not wholly against your principle, you shall laugh too."

"Ay, ay, your excellency, as Sancho counsels, 'Let not thy secret *rot* in thy keeping!'"

"Ere long it will be no secret. The story is too good to be kept from air. It must be sent abroad, and no doubt will gain addition as it goes. Thus, then, there were some *barques* that put into port, as thou knowest, from stress of weather yesterday. One of them had sprung aleak, and needed repair. On board of this vessel came Hernan Ponce, an old comrade of mine in Peru. We were dear friends in Peru, and we made a brotherhood between us, which is, as thou knowest, a copartnership for common interests and profits, to last through life. We were thus to share our gains and losses equally, our honors as our profits."

"Ah! and he now comes to claim of thee the half of thy state here, and thy command in the expedition?"

"Nothing half so good, Don Balthazar. He claims nothing at my hands, but his aim is to escape from claims of mine. Thou must know, then, that Hernan Ponce hath made great profits in Peru, and with immense wealth of gold and silver, jewels and precious stones, he hath embarked at Nombre de Dios for Spain.

It is greatly against his will that he hath put into Havana. So great was his fear of my demands that he made great offers to the Captain of the barque, Diego de Miruelos, who was an old fol lower of mine, if he would steer wide of Havana, though he should peril the ship's safety in doing so. But Diego, who has a keen scent for a rogue's secret, and who knew the danger of his vessel, was not to be overborne. So here he is; and yesterday he advised me, by secret message, of him he hath on board. Whereupon I sent a most courteous dispatch to Hernan Ponce, to compliment and congratulate him on his arrival, and to entreat him to come on shore, and in regard to our brotherhood, to share my dwelling, my command, and the honors and profits of my expedition."

"Ah! well—he hath complied?"

"No! no! There is something of the fox in Hernan Ponce, it appears, who showed himself a true comrade only when he was a poor adventurer. Now, that he hath grown rich, the na ture changes. He excused himself from coming ashore yesterday, pleading fatigue; but he is to visit me to-day. Meanwhile, Diego gave me to understand that Hernan held secret communication with the shore, and counselled me to set eyes abroad, such as might see clearly amid the darkness. Whereupon, I did so, until every inlet and landing-place was covered with my watchers. It was a wise precaution. Look at the fruits of it."

Drawing a curtain, De Soto showed to his guest a couple of goodly coffers, in which, the lids being removed, could be seen stores of gold, and pearls, and precious stones, heaped to fullness.

"These," continued De Soto, "were sent ashore last night, to be hidden somewhere. But, even as they were landed, my spies set upon the mariners, dispersed them, seized upon the treasure, and it is here. I learn from Diego that Hernan kept nothing on board but his coffers of silver. These, if pressed, he was to share with me in compliance with our articles o brotherhood. Have I not reason for merriment, think you? Ha. ha! ha! how will he stare when he beholds them!"

7

"Wilt thou show them?"

"Eh! why not? He shall see—the sordid runagate, that I know him! I will shame him with my discovery."

"Which is clearly forfeit."

"Nay, the dog.. I will not keep his treasure from him. I will spit upon it, and force his shame upon him."

"It is a gift of fortune. Thou wilt need it all, Don Hernan."

"Nay, teach not that," interposed Donna Isabella; "rather let it go, lest we be haunted by the prayers of hate and avarice. My lord will, I trust, need none of the treasure which is yielded grudgingly. I would not have his honor reproached by scandal."

"But it is his right, Señora."

"Yes! but one may well forego a right when there would be feeling of shame, and not pride, in its assertion. Better let my lord do as he nobly resolves,—spit upon the treasure, and so upon the baseness of the owner."

It was probably the advice of the lady that led De Soto to his determination. He was rather inclined to grasp at treasure from whatever source, and his reputation is not above the reproach of an unbecoming avarice. While they were yet speaking, the attendants announced the approach of Hernan Ponce, upon which Don Balthazar said,—

"My need requires me elsewhere. I will not stay to see thy treatment of this partner of thine, particularly, as it seems to me, thou dost unwisely in restoring him his treasure. Better wert thou to help thyself, and punish him thus. It were the most effectual manner for teaching him his baseness. He would then surely feel it. Such a wretch will go off exulting, even though thy spittle should somewhat stain his pearls."

"What of the knight of Portugal? Dost thou make any thing of him?"

"He speaks fairly, but does not yet decide. He will deliberate upon my counsel and proposals."

"Ah! he will deliberate. A curse upon the insolence of the

Moor—for all these Portuguese are of mixed blood, I think!—he will deliberate whether he will serve in ranks of honor—in the service of a Castilian knight. I would he knew nothing of the Apalachia, or that I had those about me who knew half so much, then should he never set foot in this enterprise, which is too great a glory for such as he.'

"Ah! my lord, thou dost this young knight a great wrong, I fear," said the lady.

"Break off," said Don Balthazar—"here comes your wealthy brother in arms and fortune. *A Dios*, your excellency. Señora, I kiss your hands."

"Let down the curtain upon the coffers," said De Soto hastily, as the footsteps sounded at the door without. In the next moment, the unhappy Hernan Ponce was ushered into the apartment. He had been apprised of the miscarriage of his treasure, he suspected into whose hands it had fallen—and, in his loss, he was taught to see his own baseness. His looks showed what he feared and felt. But in those of the Adelantado and his noble lady he saw nothing but cheering smiles, and a frank welcome. De Soto received him as an old friend, and betrayed no suspicion, and expressed no unkindness. He resolved to say nothing about the captured treasure until Ponce should speak. For a long time the latter forbore, talking about wholly indifferent subjects. But where the treasure is, there will the heart be also,—and out of the fullness of the heart will the mouth be forced to speak. The luckless adventurer, at length, delivered himself of his secret, and told the story of his misfortunes. The Adelantado had been waiting for this opportunity."

"What! Hernan Ponce, hadst thou then such a treasure as thou describest, and wouldst thou have hidden it from me? Was I not to share with thee in thy prosperity, even as I had shared with thee in thy adversity? Lo! now the difference between us. Behold these articles, properly devised, signed, and under seal, in which, as thou seest, all that I have expended in my present expedition, all the ships and munitions, the arms, the horses, the men and money; all the titles, commands, and privileges which I have obtained from the crown, I have set down and devised for our equal benefit, and made thy half secure to thee, according to the articles of fraternity and copartnership between us. Read the writings for thyself. See the names of the witnesses. Hast thou cause of complaint? Wilt thou say that I have not, in all things, fulfilled my part of the contract of brotherhood?"

Hernan Ponce read, and humbled himself. He admitted the justice with which De Soto had proceeded, and confessed that he had been unworthy of such a brother.

"It is not too late to atone, Hernan Ponce. The way is open to thee still. If thou art pleased to share the expedition with me, my titles and commands, my stores and possessions, I will yield thee such as thou may'st prefer. The one half of all shall be thine; the one half of the conquest and the treasures we may win."

The humiliation of Hernan Ponce increased, under the noble treatment of his old companion in arms, but he said mournfully—

"It is vain now, since, except the silver which is on board the vessel, I have no treasure of value left. It would be a shame and a wrong to accept the half of thine, when I held back thy proper share of what was mine."

"Nay, Hernan Ponce, it is not so evil with thee yet. Thy treasures hath fallen into friendly hands. Look, Señor, not a pearl is missing from thy coffers."

As he spoke, Donna Isabella raised the curtain, and the greedy miser gasped with joyous wonder, as he eagerly lifted the cover from the coffers, and saw that his gold and jewels remained untouched."

But this episode need not detain us longer. The history is briefly told by the chronicler. Hernan Ponce had no ambition for conquest. He was content with the treasures in possession. Now that his grasp was once more upon his coffers, he was for incurring no further risks. The Spanish equivalent for our English—"bird in the hand"—was tripping busily in his brain.

The honors proposed to him seemed to be rather too expensive. He had just left the land of savages and strife, and he had no reason to suppose that the Apalachians were like to prove more genial companions than those of Panama. He expressed himself very grateful to his brother in arms, the noble Adelantado, but really he could not think of depriving him of any share of his well-won honors—any of the results likely to accrue from his well-grounded hopes of conquest. For his own part, he needed change of air from the new world to the old. His health required it, and his treasures. He longed to air his pearls in the atmosphere of Seville; he thought his ingots would be improved by the coinage of his majesty. He was curious to look at the operations of the mint. And there were many other reasons equally strong and good. We do not mean to say that he urged all these aloud. They were the unspoken arguments of his secret soul. De Soto listened with contempt. Glad to get back his treasures, and perhaps feeling some compunctions of conscience, Hernan Ponce presented to the Lady Isabella ten thousand dollars in gold, which he entreated her graciously to accept. Had the story ceased here, we might have suffered Hernan Ponce to depart, with the reputation of being less base and unworthy than he originally appeared. But there is another scene in the drama which, though occurring afterwards, may very well be given in this place. His miser soul repented of this liberality, and waiting until De Soto had sailed for Florida, he brought suit to recover the ten thousand dollars from the Lady Isabella. But this brave woman, to whom he really owed the restoration of all his treasure, was not to be outwitted or alarmed. She replied quietly that there was a long account between her husband and the plaintiff, as might be seen in the articles of copartnership; that the latter owed De Soto more than fifty thousand ducats, being half of the outfit for the expedition; and concluded by demanding the arrest of the debtor, and his detention until the judgment should be given on the facts. Hernan Ponce got wind of this replication in due season, and without waiting the return of his ten thousand dollars, put out to sea, satisfied with his birds in hand, and leaving those in the bush to fly whither they thought proper. They had already taken wing with a hundred thousand more for the forests of the Apalachian. But we must not anticipate.

CHAPTER XII.

"Weep not at thine own words, tho' they must make
Me weep." SHELLEY.
"What cruel sufferings, more than she has known.
Canst thou inflict?" Ib.

THE household of Don Balthazar de Alvaro maintained its accustomed serenity to the world without. Its order had undergone no apparent disturbance since the death of old Anita, and Sylvia, her mestizo successor, seemed to fall as naturally into her habits, as if she had been trained directly under them. No doubt the stern discipline of her master had tutored her to implicit obedience, while his precaution had left nothing doubtful in the directions which he gave her for her government during his absence. But we may mention here, that the girl Juana, if not refractory, was inattentive, and the old hag who now superintended the household had occasion to notice her frequent and prolonged absences, for which the girl, on her return, was unwilling, or unable to account. Once or twice during the progress of the last twenty-four hours, had Sylvia felt it incumbent on her to administer an expressive cuff or two to the cheeks of the sullen servant, winding up these salutary admonitions with threats of more potent handling, and a final appeal to Don Balthazar. But blows and threats did not much mend the matter. They only increased the dogged obstinacy and sullenness of the girl; who, however, did not spare her young mistress the recital of her cruel wrongs. She concluded always, however, with a significant and monitory shaking of the head, winding up with the repeated assurance of redress, both for herself and mistress.

Olivia did not much heed these assurances, and listened, simply, in that mood of listlessness, which had followed her despairing determination not to wed with Philip de Vasconselos. She abandoned herself to this feeling, and its external exhibition **was** apathy. Still, she somewhat wondered that she did not see her lover—that he did not make his appearance, as her uncle feared, as her friend Leonora de Tobar had asserted he would appear, and as she felt it criminal to hope. A morning visit from Leonora, the thoughtless, the joyous, upon whom neither shame nor sorrow seemed to sit long, gave her all the little tattle of the town; and she ran on, with tongue at random, discoursing of a thousand matters in which Olivia took no interest. It was only when Philip de Vasconselos became the subject, that the visitor found an expression of eagerness and concern in the eyes of her suffering hostess.

"It is certain that he loves you to distraction, Olivia. Nuno says so, and he ought to know; and I suppose he could tell me a great many things to prove it; but he won't. He says Philip is his friend, and he can't betray his friend's secrets. As if a husband should have any secrets from his wife; and as if I couldn't keep a secret. Now you know, Olivia, nobody better keeps a secret than I. I never tell any thing—never! My mouth is sealed upon a secret, as solemnly and sacredly, Livy, as if it were a—a what?—why a kiss, to be sure. He might trust me, I'm sure, with every thing he knows—with every thing he's seen and done, and not a syllable should ever pass my lips. And yet, would you believe it, when I ask him about your Philip and his secrets, only to tell you every thing, why he tells me that Philip says he will tell me, and that I will tell you, and then every body will know every thing. The fact is, Livy, one thing is very certain to me, that if your Philip speaks in that way—though I don't believe a word of it—he's a very saucy person, and Nuno should not listen to him. But Nuno believes him the best fellow in the world, and says he loves him next to me. Not close, you know, but far off—that is, he has no friendship for any body betwixt him and me. Now I'll let you into a great secret that Nuno told me, and O! he was so positive that you shouldn't hear, of all the world, and I promised him not to tell you, Livy, but I didn't mean it, and I know better than all that;

for what is a friend meant for, if one is to tell them no secrets at all, and hear no secrets from them? Pretty friendship that, indeed! No! no! I know better, and I'll be faithful to you, Livy, and tell you every thing."

The necessity of stopping to take breath alone arrested the torrent. Meanwhile, Olivia had not the heart to reject the alleged secret. That which was stirring in her own bosom, and making her wretched, seemed to catch at every suggestion from without, as if it brought with it a hope; and, indeed, we are half inclined to think that very young girls, of the age of these two, have not often been persuaded to reject a revelation in which those great feminine interests, of love and marriage, are the understood elements. Olivia, however, sat incurious—seemingly so, at least —at all events, she was passive.

"Well! don't you ask what the secret is, Livy? you don't mean to pretend that you don't care; for, don't I know you're dying for this same Philip de Vasconselos, and that you think more of the plumes in his helmet than of the heads of all other men?"

Olivia shook her head.

"Oh! if you don't wish to know, Mary Mother, I don't wish to force it upon you. I can get any number of girls to listen to my secrets."

And she pouted and affected a moment's reserve. But she might as well have sought to stifle a volcano with a soup-plate, as to endeavor to keep down her tidings when they had once ascended to her tongue.

"Ah! I see you are sorry, now! Well, you shall hear it. You must know, then, that Philip has determined not to go with the Adelantado, and he told Nuno that it was because he loved you so much. And Nuno says it has caused a great hubbub, and the Adelantado is in quite a fix, and your uncle, the old Turk, has been sent to your Philip to persuade him; and Nuno thinks that Don Balthazar has made him a promise that if he goes with the expedition, and makes but one campaign, that he shall then have your hand. So that all is to end happily at last, Livy. My

7*

Nuno and your Philip will come home together, and when you are married, we'll buy a hacienda alongside of yours at Matelos, and we'll be as happy as birds of Paradise with our husbands. Isn't it nice, Livy, and won't we be so happy—so very, very happy?"

"Never! never!" exclaimed the poor girl solemnly, her head drooping upon her hands, through the fingers of which the big tears were seen to trickle.

"Oh! but we will, I tell you. None of your nevers for me. It must be so! Why, Livy, what do you cry for? Because you will have the very person that you love."

"No! no! I shall never marry, Leonora."

"Oh! I know better than that! Why, what in the world were you born for, Livy? What but to marry a noble gentleman, and—and—oh, you know what I mean; so don't look so like a simpleton."

"I have resolved not to marry, Leonora. I hope"—here her voice trembled—"I hope that Don Philip will never compel me to refuse his offer."

"Of course, he won't compel you to refuse. No, indeed; if I were he I'd rather compel you the other way, for say what you will, you love him, and you'll have him, if he ever asks you, and he loves you, and he will ask you; and I shall be at the wedding, and we will live alongside of each other, in our two heavenly haciendas at Matelos, and there shall be no more wars, and no more campaigns in Florida, and—and—"

There was another breathing spell necessary for farther progress. This found, the gay, thoughtless creature resumed.

"But I haven't told you half of my secrets. Nuno says that Philip and his brother Andres have quarrelled, and it is all on your account. He told Philip that you had refused him ——"

"He should not have done that."

"No! and by the way, Livy, that's what I have to quarrel with you about. You never told me, your own sister in love, a word about that business. Oh! you sly, selfish thing. To keep such a good secret to yourself, and never so much as give me a peep at it. I wouldn't have served you so."

"You would have told it to Don Nuno?"

"No, indeed! I can keep a secret as close, you know, as anybody. As for him, I never tell him anything. But, let me tell you about the quarrel. There were high words between them. Don Andres told Nuno himself. Philip never said a word;— and Don Andres went off from him and took away all the Portuguese soldiers, who were all followers of Don Andres. He has the money, you know, though he is the younger brother. Yet I doubt if he has any great deal of that! But Philip has still less, having spent all his patrimony in Florida before, when he went there with Cabeza de Vaça. Philip hasn't even a page to buckle on his armor, and he has given Nuno his money—all that he has, I suspect,—to buy him a negro boy to serve as a page to bring his horse and buckle on his armor. Think of that—a Moor to be the page of a noble knight. Oh! it is so pitiful! I am very, very sorry for poor Philip."

Olivia looked sorry too, but she never lifted her head and never spoke; a deep sigh forced its way from her bosom, and she thought—Oh! what dreadful thoughts were hers. How she would have rejoiced to take the poor knight to her bosom, and with her wealth to lift him into pride above the pity of the wretched multitude. Her thoughts took speech in tears; and every tear was wrung from a bleeding heart. Little did her thoughtless companion dream of the anguish which she caused by her wanton, though unmeaning babble. Unmeaning though it was from her lips, it was full of meaning in the soul of the hearer. It sunk deep, and settled firmly there, to be reproduced by a perpetual and unsleeping memory.

"But, dear me, Livy, how can you be so sad after all I have been telling you? Don't you see how every thing promises to come out well? Your uncle relents; Don Philip loves you; you love him; there will be nothing to prevent your marrying him now, and your happiness is sure. Do you weep for that? What a strange, foolish child, to weep because she is to be happy!"

"I shall never be happy, Leonora. I shall never marry Don Philip, or any man. I shall go to a convent."

"A convent! What! with your face and fortune? Now know you are crazy. But you don't mean what you say. Leave convents to the ugly and the poor, to those who have no hopes and no pleasures ——"

"I have no pleasures—no hopes!"

"And why not? It's because you won't have them, then. If I were you, I should have nothing else. I should live in hope all the day, and dream of pleasures all the night. The world should bring me nothing but love and sunshine, and every thought of my soul should be born in the odor of a thousand flowers. And why should your happiness not be like mine—you who have the means to make it so? Now don't think to cheat me with those vacant looks. This sadness is only a sort of cloud, behind which is the brightest moon of joy. The cloud will disappear with the first breeze, and the moon will shine out, bright and full of happiness. Wait a few days. To-morrow begins the sports and the tourneys. Oh! Livy, such great preparations as they have made. Nuno has had the arrangement of everything. He took me with him yesterday, to see the lists and barriers. They have raised them just without the city, in a natural amphitheatre among the hills. There is a great enclosure for the bull-fights. We are to have the most splendid bull-fights, as brave as any thing they have in Spain. They brought in a dozen great beasts yesterday from the mountains—the finest animals in the world; all as wild as tigers. Several famous matadors have come with them, and we are to have such sport. They have raised high scaffolds for the noble people and the ladies, and in the centre is one with a canopy for the Adelantado and the Lady Isabella, and their immediate friends; we are to sit with them, Livy, but on lower seats, and nearer to the lists, so that the gallant Cavaliers can draw nigh to us, after each passage of arms, and each select his Queen of Love and Beauty. Won't that be charming? Think of that, Livy. I'm sure I know who will be among the most gallant knights, and I'm sure I know who he'll choose as his Queen of Beauty. Ah! but, Livy, you mustn't put on that sad and solemn face! it will never do in such a scene as that!"

"I will not be there, Leonora."

"You can't help yourself. Your uncle will be compelled to bring you. I heard the Lady Isabella herself say to him that she will require you to be of her party, and he promised her that he would bring you. No! no! on such an occasion nobody will be allowed to stay away. In particular, what will be said if the greatest beauty and fortune in the Island were not to appear? Every body would say then, it was because Don Balthazar did not wish you to be seen—did not wish you to be loved—was not willing to give up the guardianship of your treasures. No! he cannot help but bring you. He knows what an outcry would follow your absence; and the blame would rest upon him. The Adelantado will see to that."

Olivia did not answer, but she felt the force of what her gay companion had spoken. She had already had it signified to her by her uncle, as a matter of course, that her presence had been required; and she felt, perhaps, that there was no mode of escape from the necessity. Possibly a lurking and natural curiosity might help to reconcile her to the duty. Nay, was it a natural reluctance, that which would forbear the sight of the noble performances of the man she loved? Let her resolve as she might, not to marry him, there was no need of a resolution to refuse to see him in a public spectacle where he was seen by thousands more. While they yet spoke of this matter, a servant appeared with a billet from Don Balthazar, and a case containing rich silks and ribbons. These amused the curious eyes of Leonora for half an hour. The note simply confirmed what had been said by the gay lady, touching the desires of Donna Isabella. In a short space after, a billet from that lady herself, conveying an expression of the same desire, was also brought her, accompanied by a brilliant necklace and cross, which she was entreated to accept, and wear at the tournament. Olivia received them, but without any show of interest. Not so Leonora, who gloated over them with a savage sort of admiration.

"You are the coldest creature in the world, Livy. Positively you have no heart. I could weep over such beautiful presents."

"And I too can better weep than rejoice over them, Leonora.'

"What can be the matter with the child? Livy, there is something wrong—it is unnatural that you should show such faces at such a time—you, so young, so beautiful, with such a fortune, and with such a lover—with every reason, too, for believing that nothing can now stand in the way of your loves. Livy, I do think that there is something wrong—something which I cannot guess."

For a moment the gay young woman forgot all her levity, and turning from the rich dresses and the jewels, fixed her eyes on the gloomy features of Olivia, with such intense and penetrating curiosity, that her cheeks flushed and her eyes fell; and she stammered rather than spoke—afraid of that suspicious gaze:—

"No! nothing; only I am sick—sick at heart, Leonora. I am very foolish and weak! Would to Heaven I were dead!"

"Shocking! was ever such a foolish child! But something is the matter, and it must be very serious to make you look and speak so;—and I must know it, Livy. As your friend, you must tell me all. You know how well I can keep a secret. Come, dear, tell me what it is that troubles you."

This recalled Olivia to herself. The very appeal to her experience in behalf of her friend's capacity to keep a secret, warned her of the danger threatening her. She did not philosophize except through her instincts; these sufficiently taught her that a secret, once supposed to exist, is already half discovered; and by a strong mental effort, she threw off her cloud for a space, and allowed herself to answer prattle with prattle. She diverted her friend's curiosity from herself to her garments, and in the examination of silks, ribbons and jewels, Leonora forgot that there were any other mysteries in the world. Thus the rest of the time was consumed while she remained.

When her gay visitor was gone, Olivia sank into a seeming stupor; yet her thought was busy all the while; the mournful, dreary, ghostly speculation, which aimed at nothing, settled upon nothing, hoped for nothing, and feared everything. The day passed thus. She was unconscious mostly when Juana made her appearance in the apartment, and only roused herself to reply to the salutations of Sylvia. Food was set before her, but she could not eat. Her appetite failed her wholly thus, for long periods, to be roused at periods into a sudden voracity. And she was alone—all alone. She felt her loneliness, with her other and severer griefs, and the image of Philip de Vasconselos only grew before her imagination to compel her tears. How tenderly did she think of him, yet how gloomily! He was at once her hope and her terror. She could have died for him with a bound and cry of joy; but she dared not resolve to live for him. On the edge of this *al Sirat* of hope and delight she loitered long, but the nobler sentiment rose superior to her love—nay, let us do her justice, rose out of her love, and had its birth only in her truth and fondness. The day passed and found her still resolute to deny him. "No!" was still the utterance of her heart and will—"No! I too much love him, and the nobleness which he loves, to dishonor him with hand of mine! Oh! uncle, to what misery hast thou doomed the orphan entrusted to thy keeping!"

While she broods, prostrate before the image of the Blessed Mother, scarce knowing where she lies—scarce praying as she purposes—her prayers, perhaps, more efficient from the very incapacity of her wandering mind, to fix, connect and breathe them, to the benign Being to whose maternal spirit she yet looks for saving,—let us turn to the movements of that cruel kinsman whom her condition loads with curses which her lips do not speak.

It was only after a long day of toil, public and private, that he returned to his habitation. He did not seek his niece, who had retired for the night. He proceeded at once to the apartment of Sylvia. The hag was prepared to meet him with complaints.

"You must send that idle wench, Juana, to the hacienda. She must be made to work the ground. She is of no service here. I can get nothing out of her. She is continually absent; when she returns, and I scold her, she is insolent. She is after mischief. These absences are for no good. You had best send her away, and get one more willing in her place."

At that moment Juana presented herself. Her first salutation was at the hands of Don Balthazar, in a blow from his double fist, which smote her to the earth. She rose with the blood spirting from her nostrils.

"Hence!" he exclaimed, with a voice of thunder and a brutal oath. "Hence! To-morrow you go to the country."

Juana disappeared—but not too far. She waited at the door and listened, her nose dropping blood all the while. She did not observe it. She scarcely felt the pain. The blood of the red man in her veins supplied her with one feeling only, and that was for the indignity. She listened. She reserved herself for her own time; but resolved that she would not go to the country. We shall see.

Meanwhile, a long conference followed between Don Balthazar and Sylvia, in regard to Olivia.

"She eats nothing that I provide her. I know not how she lives."

"She has supplied herself secretly from other sources. That girl——"

"Impossible! I have watched her. She has carried her nothing."

Juana, as she listened, reproached herself that such was the case. She had never thought of the wants of her young mistress. She now resolved to supply them from her own stores. She now became more resolved than ever to befriend the damsel, who suddenly rose before her eyes as an object of sympathizing interest. But she did not leave the door. She had still other things to hear.

"Here is more of the potion!" said Don Balthazar, giving the phial. "To-morrow I will see that she goes forth. In her absence search her apartments. If you find food, you know what to do with it."

This is all that need concern us of this conference. When Don Balthazar was about to leave the apartment, his eye caught sight of the blood upon the floor which had fallen from the nostrils of Juana.

"What is this?" he said, stooping.

"Ha! ha!" laughed the old woman as she looked down. "Her nose has caught it. Your hand is not a light one, Señor."

"She shall find it heavier yet. But are you sure?"

"Yes; see here—drop—drop—drop—even to the door."

The old woman pointed out the tracks; but on the outside they found it in a puddle.

"Ha!" exclaimed the Don, "the wench has loitered here. She has listened to all that has been said. But we must fix her for it. Mix the potion with her food, also. If she shares it with Olivia, well! our end is answered. That is the secret. Olivia has bribed her. She supplies her with food, so that the girl can well reject her own. Now we have her. But take all precautions; and when she goes forth to-morrow, search her chamber. Meanwhile, do you go to the room of Juana and see what she is about. Put on a gentle manner with her. Beguile her. Do not spare your reproaches of my violence. I will go to the chamber of Olivia, and see in like manner after her."

The old woman threw off her slippers and softly stole to the room of Juana. Don Balthazar waited awhile, and then followed slowly, on his way to the apartment of his niece, which was beyond it. When he drew nigh, he found Sylvia emerging from Juana's chamber.

"She is not there," said she in a whisper.

"Ha! she is then here!" He pointed to Olivia's door. "Go down and wait." He spoke in a whisper also. The old woman disappeared. Don Balthazar tried the door gently—it was locked within. He drew a steel probe from his pocket, stooped, and touched a secret spring in the panel. It silently unclosed; and crouching nearly to the floor, he succeeded, without noise, in entering the apartment. A dim light burned upon a table. The uncle looked up, and was confounded to see his niece seated, her eyes quietly beholding all his movements. Don Balthazar felt all the shame and meanness of his proceeding, in the unexpected discovery. Seared, reckless, indurated as he was, he could not suppress the sudden flush that overspread his cheeks, nor conceal the confusion which paralyzed his movement and for a moment arrested his speech. The face of Olivia declared her equal scorn and loathing. She never rose, but looking on him with pitiless composure, she exclaimed,—

"This, then, is the noble process for accomplishing my destruction!—worthy of a noble knight—thrice worthy a Castilian gentleman—and altogether becoming a guardian and a kinsman!"

The uncle rose, recovering himself, with the erect position.

"Thy destruction, girl! What dost thou mean? Dost thou think I come to murder thee?"

"And what else should I think, when thou comest in such fashion, at such an hour, and through an avenue which is secret to thyself? Why shouldst thou not murder me? and why, if such be not thy object, shouldst thou thus visit my place of sleeping? But thou well knowest I meant not that! Thou know'st that,—thanks to thy other means of destruction! I have now no fear of any hurt thou canst do to this poor life. Wert thou capable of a noble charity, I would entreat of thee to end it—to take thy dagger from thy girdle, and here, with no witness but the Holy Virgin, and that Heaven who will at last avenge my cause, strike me to the heart, and close the eyes which now see nothing but mine own shame."

"Olivia, thou art quite too passionate and wild!"

"Am I then, with the sight of thee, at this hour, knowing what thou art, knowing what terrible wrongs thou hast done to me, and seeing, for the first time, one of the secret modes by which thou hast destroyed the very life of my life,—my hope, my soul, forever!"

"Poh! Poh! How thou relatest these matters. I tell thee, were it not for thy own thoughts and fancies, thou hast suffered no wrong, no hurt,—nothing which should keep thee from being as gay as the gayest, and as happy as the best. Look at thy friend, Leonora de Tobar——"

"Speak to me nothing of her! Were it even as thou sayest, that my grief and shame are only in mine own thoughts and fancies, is it not the most terrible of wrongs that thou hast planted them there, so that their dreadful forms and images keep me from joy by day, and haunt my sleep by night with worse terrors than the grave! But, enough! Wilt thou not leave me to-night in peace—with such peace as thy crime may permit to a hopeless penitent?"

"Is no one with thee here? I look for the girl, Juana?"

"Did search of her bring thee hither? There is no one with us but the Virgin Mother, and the Saints who have pity on the orphan. Hence, and leave me."

"One thing more before I depart. The Lady Isabella has commissioned me to entreat thee to come to her to-morrow. She wants thy help and taste in certain draperies. I have promised that thou wilt attend her."

"And what if I say I will not? What am I, with the consciousness which I carry with me, that I should dare look in the face of such pure and noble person! But go—leave me. I will attend the Lady Isabella."

"'Tis well!—Thou hast not seen Juana? She hath not been with thee?"

"She is thy creature—one who hath helped for my destruction. What should I do with her? I loathe the sight of all who belong to thee!"

The Don, now thoroughly savage, replied—

"I go! But, mark me, girl, thou wilt one day so enrage me with thy insolence that I shall make thee tremble with such a terror as thou dost not dream of."

"Be it what thou wilt of violence, only let it not be shame and there shall be no tremors."

"We shall see! Open the door. I will leave thee."

"Depart as thou cam'st!" she replied, rising and taking the key from the lock, while for a moment the scorn upon her lips was lightened by a bitter smile. He looked furiously upon her, and made a step towards her, as if bent to wrest the key from her grasp; but a more cautious mood prevailed with him, and with anger that increased the awkwardness of his method of departure, full under her eyes the while, he scrambled through the panel, which instantly closed after him. Olivia hastily seized the light, and proceeded to examine it; but the secret spring was too well adjusted not to elude her search.

Full of anger, and with a fierce oath upon his lips, Don Balthazar rejoined the old woman, his creature and confederate, below.

"Well," said he, "hast thou found the wench, Juana?"

"She is gone. She is not within the house!"

"She shall taste the Calabózo to-morrow. See to what I have told thee when the Señorita goes forth, and make the search thorough. She hath concealments of which you know not. Do thy duty well, Sylvia, in this business, if thou wouldst be sure of my favor. In particular, do thou observe the outgoings of this wench, Juana. She hath questionless been bribed by her lady. See to her!"

Juana, meanwhile, was hidden in the groves with a companion. In the shadow of the great orange trees the features of neither were discernible; but he was a man, huge of size and bold of speech. He treated her as if she were a child; but tenderly, as if he were her father.

"Never you mind," said he, at parting with her; "the goods shall be had, and the blood shall be paid for! Only a little while. To keep from the meat awhile, is to strengthen the stomach. It is a strong man only who can wait. He drinks long who drinks slowly. Swallow thy tears, lest they blind thee. To-morrow is better for work than yesterday; and a good appetite better than a bad digestion. Take thy sleep now, my child, that thou may'st wake with both thine eyes open."

CHAPTER XIII.

"It is not safe
To tempt such spirits, and let them wear their swords."
BEAUMONT AND FLETCHER.

It is necessary that we should now take cognizance of other parties to this true history, whom we have suffered too long to remain in the back-ground. Our view is somewhat retrospective, the scene we are now about to depict having been sketched prior to the scenes which have occupied the two preceding chapters. Let us return to the well-known lodge of the young knights of Portugal, and see what are, if any, the changes which have occurred in the awkward relations which existed between them, the fruit of eager passions, and, unhappily, misplaced affections.

Several days have passed since the interview already described, in which they were the sole and angry actors. Though the scene on that occasion had terminated, if not amicably, at least quietly, yet Philip de Vasconselos, with great sorrow, perceived, on the return of his brother to the cabin which they occupied in common, that he had relapsed again into his condition of moodiness—a condition which did not always forbear rudeness. The elder brother, from long experience, well understood and dreaded the jealous, suspicious, and resentful spirit of the young man, which his impetuous passions were too often disposed to infuse with violence. He had striven, though without much good result, to soothe the evil spirit in the mood of Andres, and to mollify the disappointment which the latter still keenly felt in regard to his rejection by Olivia. It was under this desire that Philip had, in the meanwhile, forborne, however anxious, to visit the woman whom he loved quite as passionately, though with more generosity and prudence, than his brother. He made no allusions to her in his intercourse with Andres, and was studious so to select the subjects of his conversation, as by no possibility to prompt the mind of the youth to turn in the direction in which his heart had suffered hurt. But Andres exhibited no sense of this prudence and forbearance. He was one of those wilful and wrong-headed, but otherwise noble and generous spirits, who prefer, under disappointment, to suffer and complain; who, of themselves, irritate the sore places which they feel, and steadily tear away the plaster with which the physician would cure all their ailments. It was in despair of saying or doing anything which could be acceptable to his brother's mood, that Philip de Vasconselos finally forbore the effort. For the last two days, therefore, an ominous silence had prevailed in their cottage when they met. Nothing was spoken which either might well avoid; and Philip felt with sorrow, that the chasm between them was hourly growing greater in depth and width. But he felt with still greater sorrow that nothing could then be done to arrest its increase. It was to time only, that great corrector, that the matter could be left.

But time was not allowed them. The tournament approached, with all its excitements, appealing equally to their pride, their renown, and the somewhat peculiar position in which they stood in regard to the Castilian chivalry. Both of them, accordingly, might be seen, a few days before the event, busily engaged burnishing and preparing their armor. It had already been remarked, as discreditable to the Spanish knights, that their Portuguese auxiliaries were better armed, in a simpler and nobler style, and kept their mail and weapons under better polish than the former. De Soto himself had been compelled to refer to these knights in compliment on this account, and to urge their example, in order to prompt his Spanish cavaliers to get themselves serviceable armor, and to keep it in order. They were better pleased to show themselves in gewgaws and gilt than in the substantial coverings which were essential to warfare. One of the historians of this expedition thus contrasts the appearance of the knights of the two nations: " And he (the Adelantado) commanded a muster to be made, at the which the Portugales shewed themselves armed in verie bright armor, and the Castellans very gallant, with silke upon silke, with many pinkings and cuts. The Governour, because these braveries, in such an action, did not like nim, commanded that they should muster another day, and [that] every one should come forthe with his armor: at the which the Portugales came, as at the first, armed with very good armor, . . . The Castellans, for the most part, did weare very bad and rustic shirts of maile, and all of them head-pieces and steele caps, and verrie bad lances." The contrast mortified De Soto. In order to rebuke his Castilians into an emulation of the Portuguese, he distinguished the latter (perhaps unwisely) with unusual favors at the first, and appointed them places near his own person. This was the original source of that jealousy and hostility with which the Spaniards encountered the farther progress into favor of the Portuguese brothers. It showed itself so decidedly, and with marks of such serious discontent, that the Adelantado committed the further error of passing to the opposite extreme, and putting on such a cold aspect to our adventurers, as to forfeit in great degree their attachment to his cause and person, besides exposing them to the neglect and contempt of those who naturally take their cue from their superiors. We have not thought it necessary to detail any instances of the unfriendly or insolent treatment to which they were subject, but have satisfied ourselves with showing what has been the result of it upon their minds. Enough to mention that, in their own skill and spirit, their ability in the use of their weapon, and their promptness to resort to it, they found thus far a sufficient security against any outrageous contempts, while the friendship of a few of the Castilian knights, such as Nuno de Tobar, reconciled them in some degree to endure the slights and indifference of the rest. But the consequence of this false position in the Castilian army was to excite their national as well as individual pride; to make them resolve upon achievement; to keep their armor bright on all occasions; to be always ready for service with their weapons and to pluck the chaplet, on all occasions, from the helms of their boasting rivals. But their personal griefs were perhaps not necessary as incentives to performance, in the case of knights with whom chivalry still prevailed with all the force of a passion.

Our brothers pursued their task in silence. Occupying the same dwelling, and with but little space in their somewhat narrow limits for any performance unseen by either, this silence was an irksome one. The elder brother had made repeated efforts to break through the icy reserve which prevailed in the demeanor of the younger from that fatal night, the events of which have already been described. On that night, after their passionate interview, Andres de Vasconselos had returned from his lonely and gloomy wanderings, in no way improved for companionship. His affections were more stubbornly congealed than ever; his passions, if less explosive, not a whit more subdued or placable. A sullen rigidness was conspicuous in all his features; a gloomy inflexibility in his mood; a hostile reserve in his actions and deportment. This continued, increased hourly by the reports of the city, touching the supposed superior good fortune of his brother in respect to the affections of the lady of their mutual love. The kind words addressed to him by Philip were answered only in monosyllables, which were sometimes more than cold, and accompanied by looks which the truly warm feelings of the elder brother regarded as little less than savage. A becoming pity and sympathy, however, led him to be indulgent to a nature which, naturally passionate, was now suffering the stings of a peculiar provocation. Besides, was not Andres the last born, and the favorite, of a mother who was tenderly beloved by both? Philip did not forbear his efforts, because they were received with indifference. He felt that the moment was one which might form the turning point, the pivot, of a sad and serious future. The chasm left unclosed in season must only widen with time. The affections suffered to remain ruptured, or hurt, would only become callous from the lack of proper tendance, a gentle solicitude, a heedful care, the patient sweetness of a loving watch, which, never obtrusive, never suffered the proper moment of consolation to be lost. Such was the spirit with which Philip de Vasconselos regarded his wayward brother.

It was two days yet to the opening scenes of the tourney, the beginning of which we have already seen. The day was at its close; a day all flushed with beauty, and sweet with the warm breathings of the budding summer. The sun was at his setting His not ungrateful rays fell pleasantly gay upon the green slope which led to the slight *bohio*, or cottage, made of poles and reeds thatched with straw, which the brothers occupied. Soft flickering folds and remnants of purple, that seemed momently rolling themselves up, and disappearing with the breeze, only to re-appear and spread themselves out in increasing brightness, on higher slopes of hill, won, at the same moment, the silent fancies of the brothers. The hills were fringed with faint red tints that glorified them as with heavenly halos; the woods, flushed with the mingled drapery of spring and summer, lay gently waving in the breeze of evening, rocked in the arms of beauty, and canopied with the smiles of heaven. It was one of those delicious moments when the world without passes with all its sweetness into the heart, and takes the whole soul into its embrace of love. The brothers, as by a common instinct, threw aside their toils, and cast themselves down upon the hill-slope, their eyes ranging over the blessed prospect. Their shields, of bright blue steel, spotless, and shining like mirrors in the sun, reflected back the mellow softness of his beams. They hung upon the upright poles without the cottage, on each side of the entrance, to which they furnished a rich and befitting decoration. Their long lances, of well-sounded and seasoned ash, headed with broad shafts of bright steel, that shone like silver in the sun, were leaned against the wall of the dwelling, and also without the entrance. The page of Andres, a gay boy of fourteen, had just made his obeisance, and taken his departure, under instructions from his master; and for a moment, the two brothers, reposing from their toils of the day, seemed disposed to snatch a respite, in the sweet calm which had descended upon all nature in the grateful approach of evening. Andres lay at length beneath the slender shadows of a palm, which, at an earlier hour, could have yielded no shelter,—none was needed now. His eyes were shrouded by his arm, which was carelessly thrown across his brows. While in this attitude, Philip rose suddenly from where he lay, and moved by a brotherly impulse, approached him and threw himself quietly by his side.

"Andres, my brother," was the affectionate salutation of the elder, "it is naturally expected that we shall both do our devoir in the approaching tourney. It is due to our reputation, as good knights, and particularly to our position among these gentlemen of Castile, who would not be slow to remark upon any unwillingness which we might betray in entering the lists. They will do their best, and we must do ours. That we can maintain our own, and the honor of our country, in a passage-at-arms, whether with lance, sword, or battle-axe, with any of these cavaliers, I nothing question; though there be knights among them many who, like Nuno de Tobar, will honor, by their prowess, those who may strive against them. These will afford us sufficient exercise and honor. It needs not, my brother, that we should cross weapon with each other."

A grim smile passed over the features of Andres, as he withdrew his arm from above his eyes. The expression was an unpleasant one to Philip. A brief pause ensued. At length the younger replied:

"Verily, Philip de Vasconselos, it were not wise to suffer these knights of Castile to suppose thee unwilling to cross weapons with any warrior, even though he were of thy own blood and nation. Such reluctance, in the minds of persons sworn to cavil, might be construed into doubt of thy own capacity and prowess."

"I fear not, Andres," replied the other, calmly, "that any idle judgment of these or any cavaliers will do injustice to my reputation, since it will be easy, at any moment, particularly as I shall never be unwilling, to satisfy any doubting opponent, and to silence any unfriendly one. But no man will venture to think that any feeling but that of a natural attachment between kinsmen hath kept us from a trial of skill and prowess, which, though it be but the mimicry of strife, is yet too nearly like it, and is but too frequently apt to occasion the reality, not to plead against our indulgence, adversely, in the exercise. It is not, however, what the world without may think, my brother, but what we *feel* within, which should control our wishes in this matter. It is enough for me that, even in sport, I love not to confront with weapon the bosom of a brother who is so very dear to mine."

"Brother, mine, I do not quite understand these refinements. We have crossed weapons in the tourney a thousand times ere this, in our early exercises,—nay, in the very training which thou hast given me, and which, as a grateful pupil,"—this was spoken with a smile by no means pleasing in the eyes of Philip,—"I am only too glad to have received at thy hands. What is there now to make the difference?"

"Ask thy own heart, Andres," replied the other, sadly. "Art thou the same person that thou wast, when, without a care or thought but of the art which thou hadst in thy desire, thou took'st thy first lessons from my lance? Since that day thou hast mingled, for thyself, in the press of knights; thou hast shared the eager fury of the battle; thou hast won for thyself a name which thou must maintain, at all perils, to thyself and others. But thou hast other feelings, fears and hopes than those which possessed thee when a boy; thou hast grown a man of cares; and, I grieve to think it, my brother, thou no longer look'st upon me, thy Philip, as the loving friend from whom came thy first lessons in arts and arms. These make it prudent and proper that we should not strive against each other. The accidents of the tourney are, of themselves, sufficient to keep our arms asunder. Men have been slain, unwittingly by their rival knights, through false footing of their horse; through frailty and fault in arm; through haste; through indiscretion, and those nameless providences of the conflict, of which no man can well account, as no wisdom can foresee. But chiefly do I desire that we should not find our weapons crossed, inasmuch as I perceive in thee, my brother, a decline of that trust in me—that love, which, of old, made it pleasant to me to teach thy inexperience."

"I am no longer inexperienced, Philip de Vasconselos. I no longer need thy teaching, or that of any man! Thou talk'st of accidents from weakness, and defect of armor. Never better armor than mine, as thou knowest, came from the forge of the Milanese. It had its fashion from the same hands with thine, and is, I warrant me, as free from frailty. My lance is under thine eye. The sword which I carry has been a thousand times within thy grasp. Thou canst tell the weight of my battle-axe, and knowest the value of its tempered metal as certainly as thou dost thine own. What remains? Methinks, my brother, there is no such difference between the strength and size of my body and of thine. Take the muscle of this arm within thy grasp. Doth it show to thee a feebleness which should make it shrink from any struggle with any cavalier, even though he be of redoubtable prowess, like thyself? Thou speak'st of what is in my heart;—of a change in my feelings towards thee!—it may be there is such a change! Verily, I see nothing in my fortunes or in thine, Philip de Vasconselos, which should make me regard thee with feelings such as we bore to one another, when thou stood'st not in the way of my hopes, and hadst not yet shrouded my heart, in the overwhelming shadow of thy greater fame! I reproach thee not, that such has been thy fortune; but verily, it is no longer seasonable with thee, to discourse to me of the love of kinsmen; and I tell thee more, Philip de Vasconselos, thou hast but too much the habit of speaking to me as if I were still the boy, untaught, and only now receiving from thee, for the first time, his infant lessons in the use of blunt spear and shielded weapon."

"And is it thus, my brother?" was the mournful answer of Philip de Vasconselos.

"But I will not upbraid thee; and yet I will not forbear to entreat thee. The feeling which thou showest is most certainly enough to make me unwilling to encounter with thee in this tourney. Were it possible, without shame and discredit, to refuse to take lance in these gay passages, I should most surely withdraw myself from the field. But I am pledged to the encounter; with lance, sword, and battle-axe, three strokes of each; with Luis de Moscoso, with Balthazar de Gallegos, with Nuno de Tobar; and it may be with others, whom I now recall not."

"Thou canst not well escape thy devoir," said Andres, with a sneering smile.

"Nor, save on *thy* account," replied the other "would I desire to do so. But there is that within *my* bosom, Andres, whatever may inhabit in *thine*, which makes me shrink from the thought that we shall cross lances in the *melée*. I know not that thou designest such a conflict; but I know thy ambition—thy pride—and I fear that evil spirit which sometimes possesses thee, making thee blind to thy better feelings, and to the claims of those about thee, and which, I grieve to say it, has but too frequently shown itself in thy moods of late. Brother, hearken to me;—I pray thee let us not meet! Thou wilt find many noble knights to conquer, who will do thee honor. There will be no lack of the fit antagonist, even though Hernan de Soto himself shall take the field. Let us do nothing which may perchance lessen or change that love which our mother gave us, and which should be dear to us, because of her, as because of ourselves."

"It is on *my* account—for *me*—that thou wouldst avoid the encounter with me!" replied the younger brother. "Verily, Philip, thou hast betrayed thy modesty. Is it so sure that my lance must fail when it crosses thine?—is thy arm——"

"Nay, brother, why thus wilt thou mistake my purpose?—thus cruelly outrage my affections? I do not reproach thy prowess when I tell thee that it is on thy account, wholly, that I would avoid this encounter. I fear that thou wilt wrong thyself;—that thou wilt show a spirit in the field, which would not well become a brother;—that thy pride, wrought upon by sudden passions—by unjust suspicions—by unwise jealousies, will lead thee into deeds of unmeasured violence, such as——"

"Such as thou fearest, eh?" was the mocking interruption.

The other answered proudly—his tones growing instantly

calmer, and with a slower enunciation, while his eye flashed with a sudden fire, entirely different from its recent expression.

"I fear nothing, Andres de Vasconselos, as thou of all persons should by this time know;—nothing but shame, dishonor, and the reproach of knighthood;—nothing but a wrong done to our mother's fondness—and that wrong which thy evil mood seems resolute to do to our own. To escape this, I would have implored thee to forbearance; for I know thy temper in the conflict, and I somewhat dread my own! Unhappily, we share, in some degree, the passions of one another. Thus it is that we have both loved, where both may be luckless——"

"No! no!" exclaimed the other bitterly. Philip did not regard the interruption.

"With our mutual passions roused—our pride endangered in the field's regard, I dread the struggle that would follow: for, at such moments, Andres de Vasconselos, I cannot easily distinguish the kinsman from the foe! Love, pity, the ties of affection, and friendship, are all obscured in the wild passion when the blood rules triumphant in the brain, and I should bear thee down, my brother, as unsparingly as the least regarded among the ranks of all this Castilian chivalry."

"By the Blessed Virgin, thou speakest, Don Philip, as if I were already beneath thy spear——"

"Forgive me, brother, that I have done so! The Saints forefend that lance of mine should ever threaten thee in any conflict! I but——"

"And I tell thee, Don Philip, I no more reck of *thy* lance, than I do of that of the least famous of all these Castilian cavaliers! I know not of any prowess in thee that I have need to fear; and I promise thee, should it ever hap that our weapons be crossed, then look to do thy best, or I put thy boasted skill to shame."

"I boast no skill, brother!"

"Thou dost—thou art all a boast! What else is it when thou warn'st me that in the strife thou wilt be pitiless—that thou wilt suffer no thought of kindred to disarm thee? Is it not as much as if thy victory were already sure, and thou hadst me trampled under thy feet?"

"I have been in fault, brother; verily, I confess it. It is not for me to boast; and still less to seem to boast of advantage over thee. Believe me, I love thee too well to be pleased at any fortune which shall be, or seem, better than thine——"

The jealous spirit of the younger brother construed this sentence, which he interrupted, to refer to the disappointment of his suit with Olivia de Alvaro.

"Indeed, thou approv'st the truth of thy disclaimer by thy taunts. Have done, I pray thee, good Don Philip, and let the time bring its own brood; whether of hawks or sparrows, it matters not. I ask not of thy purpose, and feel myself scarcely free to tell thee of mine. I know not that I have any purposes. I know not that I shall oppose any lance in these passages. I but put myself in readiness, to obey my necessity—or my mood—whichever it may please thee best to believe. I only know, Philip de Vasconselos, that I am scorned and wretched, and thou triumphant, as well in the love of woman as in fame. Go to:—why wilt thou goad my sorrows, when such is thy own good fortune?"

"Andres, let not the sun set on this disagreement. I feel that thou dost me wrong, but I implore thee as if the wrong were mine."

Philip extended his hand affectionately to his brother, as he made this appeal. The other did not receive it; but, waving his own in the direction of the orb now rapidly disappearing behind the last distant billows of the sea, he said coldly—

"He sinks!" and, without another word, rose up and strode down the slopes which conducted to the city. The elder brother threw himself upon the earth, from whence, during the earnest portions of the dialogue, he had risen at the same moment with the other, and rested his aching forehead upon his hands.

"Verily!" he said to himself—"he is possessed of an evil demon! What is to be done? Will he put himself in harness against me? Can he purpose this? But no! no!—The evil mood will pass with the night. I will tent him no further with the matter."

That night beheld the two brothers, in the same apartment, praying ere they slept; yet they prayed not together, nor at the same moment. What was in their hearts while they appealed to heaven? Alas! it is our fear, that, while the lips moved in worship, the thought was foreign to the homage! Passion, rather than prayer, was in their mutual hearts;—the one dreaming, the while, of earthly loves and earthly distinctions;—the other, filled with a wild conflict, in which pride and vanity, confounded by defeat and humiliation, were busily brooding in worship at the shrine of a divinity which they did not yet presume to name.

The next day, without naming his purpose, Andres de Vasconselos withdrew from the place of lodging with his brother, and took up his abode with Antonio Segurado, one of his lieutenants.

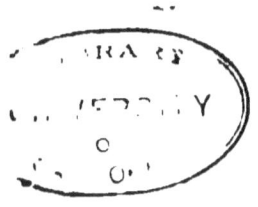

CHAPTER XIV.

"Now ringen trompes loud and clarioun
Ther is no more to say, but est and west,
In gon the speres sadly in the rest;
In goth the sharpe spore into the side:
Then see even who can juste, and who can ride."
THE KNIGHTES TALE.

HAVANA, at the period of the events which we record, was a growing hamlet of little more than a hundred dwellings. But a brief space before the arrival of Don Hernan de Soto in the island, there had been an invasion of the French, by whom the little city had been laid in ashes. It had been one of his duties, on his arrival, which had not been neglected in consequence of his preparations for Florida, to rebuild the town, which he had been doing with all his energy, and with a free exercise of his powers as Adelantado. To him the Habanese owe the erection of the first fort which the place ever possessed. It will be for the Cuban antiquarians of the present time to fix its location. As a matter of course, we are not to look to the works of De Soto, in rebuilding the city, for the evidences of his architectural tastes, or for any enduring proofs of the labor of his hands. The place then afforded but an imperfect idea of the noble and imposing city that we find it now. She then possessed none of those old gray towers and massive structures, which now assail the vision, and command the admiration of the spectator. Her heights and harbors were not then, as now, covered with the mighty and frowning fortresses that stretch themselves around her, with a hundred thousand guardian hands grasping bolts of iron terror for her protection. But, if less threatening and powerful, she was not less lovely and attractive. Her beautiful bay, then as now lacked but little of the helps of art to render it as wooing and persuasive as that famous one of the Italian ; and, in the luxuriance of her verdure, which covered, with a various and delicious beauty, all her heights; in the intense brilliancy and clearness of her moonlight, which seemed rather to hallow and to soften, than to impair the individuality and distinctness of objects, as beheld by day ; in the exquisite fragrance from her groves, and the soothing sweetness of the sea-breeze—which, in that tropical climate, one regards as the most blessed of all the angels who take part in the destinies of earth—playing like a thoughtless and innocent child among forests of vines and flowers—the fancy became sensible of a condition, in which life can offer nothing more grateful, or more fresh ; and, to be sure of which always, ambition might well be satisfied to lay aside his spear and shield forever. Her cottages, each as it were enshrined amidst an empire of fruits and fragrance, already wore that aspect which, in oriental regions, assures us of the *dolce far niente* in possession of their inmates, justifying vagabondage, and so irresistibly persuasive, that one who feels, ceases to wonder that a people, having such possessions, should be content to seek nothing farther—should demand nothing more from nature—should even, in process of time, become indifferent to the wants and appliances of art—should forget the civilization which they have won—shake off the convention which has fettered them, and lapse away into the stagnation, if not the savageism, of the aboriginals ; knowing life only in a delicious reverie, in which existence is an abstraction rather than a condition ; a dream, rather than a performance ; where living implies no anxiety, acquisition no toil, enjoyment no cessation ; in which nothing is apprehended so much as change, even though such change may bring with it the promise of a new pleasure. Such is the power of climate ; such the charm of that of Cuba ; but we must not be understood as assuming that such, at that period, was its effect upon the European inhabitants. The luxuries of society in that day had not so much accumulated, nor was the popular taste so much relaxed by the process of social refinement, as to enfeeble the energies and exertions of her people. They were still the hardy race which had been trained to endurance, strife, and all sorts of adventure, by the unceasing struggles of three hundred years. The benign climate had not yet done the work of emasculation—perhaps never would have done this work, if the surrounding savages had been left partially unconquered. Had the Spaniards with the profund policy which is said to have marked the history of Aztec supremacy, suffered rival and hostile races still to exist, upon whom periodically their young warriors could exercise their weapons, the vigorous energies of their people might have been trained to resist all the blandishments of climate. As yet, they remained unimpaired by its insidious sweetness. The savage still harbored in the mountains; the Caribbee still fed upon his captive along the margin of the gulf; the Apalachian, a fearless warrior, still roved unconquered in his mighty shades; and the Spaniard, still needy, with all his treasures, looked out, on every hand, for empires which he must yet possess. He was sensible of the delicious luxury of his Cuban climate, but did not yield to it his strength. That fierce, vigorous life which distinguished the Castilian character, at the period of the conquests of Spain in the new world,—to which was due such a wonderful constellation of great captains—Cortez, the Pizarros, Ojeda, Balboa, and a host besides — declared the energies of a people in their prime, with a startling mission of performance before them, demanding the equal exercise of the best genius and courage. The compound passion of avarice and ambition left them in no humor for repose. Without pause, yet not blindly, they pursued their mission; and the impatient and fevered restlessness which it demanded and excited, rendered them superior to every persuasion that threatened conflict with their strength. These could only prevail finally with the race which, with ample luxuries in possession, find no longer in their thirst the provocation to performance. For the present, no Spaniard can enjoy the sweets of Cuban airs with comparative safety. They have still a great work to do, are still goaded by fiery passions which will not suffer them to sleep, and they seize their luxuries with the mood of the hurrying traveler, in a strange land, who plucks the flower along the wayside as he passes, and hastens on his way. The **Spaniards** of that day gathered all their luxuries *en route*, and threw one acquisition away as soon as they made another. The fresh desires of achievements kept them from all loitering. Acknowledging the sweets and beauties of the scene, as proffered them by Nature—acknowledging with due appreciation the bounty in her gifts—they tasted only, and pressed forward. They were, then, far from yielding to that base faith (for humanity), which finds present possessions ample for their wants. It needed yet the riper experience of a hundred coming years, and enjoyments not yet within their grasp, to reconcile them to another moral—to the surrender of all such as might be rising to their hope! They are now driven by those fierce wants of Old Spain, such as naturally rage in a condition of society, which toilsome necessities still goad, and where the door to pride and power is open always to the staff of gold. Mere ease is not the object. This, in Cuba, is already in the possession of its people. They have only to live in the sunshine, and let themselves alone, and they live! But in the days of De Soto they did not hold such *life* to be *living*. They had then fiercer impulses to appease, and more exacting and earnest appetites to satisfy. They obeyed a destiny! They were still chiefly sensible of passions taught in the market-place; by the multitude; during the struggle; in which to hope is to contend;—strife, blood, conquest, glory and personal prominence, in all situations constituting the great argument to heart and mind. Hence the individuality of the Spaniard; his reference of all things to self; his swelling pride; his stern magnificence; his audacious courage; the unfailing hardihood of his adventure. How should a character such as this be sensible to the unobtrusive beauties of the natural world—to the insinuating sweetness of breeze and zephyr—to the charm of flower and landscape? How slow will he be to value that soft repose from all excitements, in which we are required to share, which belongs naturally to such a life as that of the Cuban, where the earth is always a bloom, where the air is always fragrance, where the skies give out forever an atmosphere of love! Flowers and fruits, the sweets of sky and air, and forests and oceans, all beau tiful in turn, all linked together by assimilative beauties, and all blessing, singly and together,—all nevertheless fail—perhaps, fortunately *then*,—to supersede, in the minds of our Spaniards, the habitual desires of their hearts. Still, the heroic pageant is in the ascendant; the human passion. The crowded spectacle, the strife of violent forces, the eager scene of human struggle and conquest, make them heedless of all that is simply sweet and lovely in their possession. Even women share the tastes with the passions of the sterner sex, and turn from their groves and gardens to the gory terrors of the bull-fight.

But why chide? These people are simply the pioneers for other races, who shall more securely enjoy what they neglect and despise. They work in obedience to laws of nature, which regard rather the uses of men than their pleasures. One race but paves the way for another. We blaze the pathways for future generations, happy if they should be the children of our loins, for whom we win empire and clear the way. The Spaniards of the time of De Soto, in consequence of a fatal defect in their morals, did not always conquer the inheritance for their *own* children. But of this they did not dream! How should they? Let *us* now return from our wanderings, and make generalization give place to detail.

Following out his plan, for increasing the enthusiasm at once of his own followers, and of the people at large of the island of Cuba, Hernan de Soto was now busied with his preparations for the public sports which he had appointed, and with which he was to delight the fancies of the Cubans. It was good policy that he should do these things; for it must be remembered that he was not merely Adelantado of Florida, and of its imaginary treasures and empires, but governor also of all Cuba; which beautiful and prolific island was to be left in charge of the Lady Isabella while he pursued his toils of conquests in the wild recesses of the Apalachian. He had designed his preparation on no ordinary scale of magnificence. Though reputed to be a close and avaricious general—proverbially so—he was yet fully aware that there are periods when it is necessary to be lavish and even profligate of expenditure. The objects which he now proposed to attain strongly urged and fully justified a large departure from his usual habits of economy. His wife, the noble Lady Isabella, was, however, in some degree the prompter of this liberality. She was no common woman, but one born with a princely eye to whatever is noble in the regards of man, whether in the externals or the substances of society and State. A generous impulse, at all times, made her anxious to satisfy the popular desires—that is, wherever their cravings led them to the appreciation of great deeds and graceful performance. Her knowledge of the present objects to be attained by her lord from the common sympathies, increased, in considerable degree, the naturally gracious and free affluence of her disposition. She bent her mind to the object, and consulted with all round her the various schemes by which to render the projected display one of a magnificence never before paralleled in Cuba; and though the Adelantado groaned in secret over the excess of expenditure which naturally followed from her plans, he was yet fully conscious of the good policy by which they were dictated; and his tastes readily acknowledged the beauty, skill and splendor which promised to be the results of her exertions.

The day was at hand, set aside for the commencement of the public sports, which had become official, and were to last three days. We are not to suppose that, because the higher forms of chivalry were dying out in Europe—because, in fact, the institution no longer cherished there any of the nobler objects of the order, and had sunk, from a social and political, into a mere military machine,—that its displays had become less ostentatious or less attractive when attempted. On the contrary, it is usually the case that, with the decay of an institution, its efforts at external splendor, are apt to be even greater than in the hour of its most unquestioned ascendency; even as the fashionable merchant is said to give his most magnificent parties when he has made all his preparations for a business failure! In the new world, in particular, where we might reasonably suppose that the imitations were necessarily rude and inferior, of all these pageants, which seem, over all, to require the highest finish in art and the utmost polish in society—which seem, in fact, to belong only to an *old* civilization, such as that of Christian Europe,—it was ordinarily found that the ambition for display was more than commonly ostentatious and expensive. Certain it is, that nothing of the sort in Spain, for a long time before, surpassed the promise, whether as regards the taste or the splendor, of the great preparations which had been made by De Soto for his three days of tourney and feats of arms, in the infant city of Havana. The lists, as our fair gossip, Donna Leonora de Tobar, has already told us, were erected in the beautiful amphitheatre just without the suburbs of the town. Here scaffoldings had been raised for the spectators, running half way round the barriers, inclosing a portion of the area. These were to be draped with showy stuffs. On some slight elevations, along the opposite space, a ruder sort of scaffoldings were reared for the common people. These, in those days, did not assume that what was given them in charity should be of a quality to compare with the best. There was yet a third distinction made in behalf of the persons in power, and their friends—the persons of noble birth and high position. Their place was something higher than the others, built of better materials, and in more careful manner. In the centre was a gorgeous canopy, which might have served for a prince of the blood. It covered a raised seat, richly cushioned. This was designed for the Adelantado and his noble lady. His immediate friends and chiefs, and the ladies of his court, were honored with private places on either hand. Before this seat were painted the arms of Spain, on a rich shield or escutcheon; its great golden towers, significant equally of its pride and strength, fronting the lists and the *oi polloi*, and forming a beautiful exhortation to the indulgence of the *amor patriæ*. Directly over the canopy, and streaming proudly from a staff that rose from behind it, flaunted, in mighty folds of silk heavily wrought with gold tissue, the armorial banner of Castile. A long series of escutcheons of a smaller size, but similar in shape to that in the centre, and not inferior in workmanship, formed a tier of very superb panels along the scaffoldings. These denoted the seats which were assigned to the noble families, whose arms they bore; each placed according to the rank of the owner, or the degree of power, or influence, which he possessed in the colony. Banners and bannerets, pennons and pennonceles, waved from spears whose broad and massive darts were fashioned sometimes of solid silver. The seats were cushioned with rich draperies; with shawls of brilliant colors, and cotton fabrics dyed in various unrivalled hues, such as the people of Peru and Mexico had learned to fashion in a style superior to anything beheld in Europe. Bright armor of various kinds, employed for ornament, glittered and gleamed at proper intervals, along the splendid scaffoldings; from which, at an early hour of the morning assigned for the sports, choice instruments poured forth peals of the most gay and inspiring music. The plan of the festivities required that the cool hours of the day only should be employed for the more active exercises of the combatants. The heat of the noonday sun, in that ardent clime, was, even at this early period of the year—the close of April—too intense to render agreeable any violent displays of agility, under heavy armor, for mere amusement. The first day was assigned to the young knights and squires, who were to run at the ring, joust with blunt spears, and smite the Turk's head—the English Quintain. There were to be sports also for the arquebusiers, and the crossbowmen,— the latter instrument of war not yet having been superseded by firearms. To these a certain time was to be allotted, and bull fights were to follow, and to close the day. The amusements of the evening, though all arranged, were yet of a private character, and did not fall within the plan of the Adelantado. They were also on a scale highly attractive and magnificent.

With the first glimpses of the dawn the spectators were to be seen assembling. The citizens were turning out in all direction. The people were crowding in from the country. The whole island sent a delegation of eyes to see, and hands to clap, and hearts to drink in and remember, long afterwards, the wondrous sights presented in that memorable spectacle—a spectacle which was to be not unworthy of the future conquests, in the country of the Apalachian. Very curious was the motley crowd that showed itself on all the streets and avenues leading to the great area of attraction. There were muleteers from the mountain; wandering tribes akin to the gipsies; retired soldiers; and half-savage groups, in which it was difficult to discern which race predominated most, the white man, the red man, or the negro. They constituted a curious amalgam; each exhibiting some trait or characteristic, picturesque, wild, individual, such as Murillo would delight to paint—such as would have risen into dignity under the brush of Rembrandt. Girls came bounding along with the castanets, by the side of mules on which sat tottering grandmothers; boys loitered with the crossbow, eager to pick up a *real* by shooting it down at twenty paces. Contrabandists showed open faces, as, on pack mules, they brought the *Aguardiente* for sale, in stone jugs, one on each side; its mouth opening from the bosom of a panier. The stately owner of a rich *hacienda*, where he marked his hundred calves each spring, rode on a brave barb by the side of his family, occupying a vehicle still in use, cumbrous but delightful of motion beyond all others, —the volanté. We must not stop to describe it. As at the present day in Old Spain, in the rural districts, nothing was more curious than the various costumes and characters exhibited by the appearance of the people from the country. Every department in the old country had its fitting representative, tenacious, in the new world, of all that distinguished his province in the old. The gay and vivacious Andalusian, ribanded at wrist and shoulder, breast and shoe;—the confident and swaggering Biscayan; the dull native of Valencia; the haughty Catalan;—you might mark them all at a glance. Groups wandered on together, the highways to the city being for hours never without its strollers. Old songs were to be heard, as they went, from natural musicians; sad touches, oddly mingled with lively *redondillas*, and sometimes, from some rude crowder, half soldier and half priest, or poet, you might hear extempore ballads devoted to the deeds of arms of Cortez and Pizarro. Mules in strings came down with fruit to the great market; lines of vehicles of all sorts, all adding to the clamor. Sometimes, but rarely, the beggar held out his cap for charity, and was laughed at as a cheat; for beggary in the new world must needs be so always. There was room and fruit for all. Sometimes the beggar, however, was a *manola* of the lowest class, who never asked for alms, but got her fee for the doleful ditties, which no one stopped to hear. There was better music forward; and the crowds hurried on their march. But, to enumerate is impossible. Fancy the most picturesque region of the world, filled with the most picturesque of all people, and the most contradictory; too proud for restraint, yet with a curious conventional arrangement, which, making every thing grave, admirably allowed of the mingling of the grand and the ridiculous;—all at once thrown into disorder, under conditions the most exciting;—all in highest state of emotion, yet all in the most amiable temper;—happy in the moment, and prepared to gather happiness from all possible sources.

Already, at early dawn, the trumpets began to pour forth their most lively *fanfares*. Already, a thousand cries of hope and expectation arose from the gathering and rapidly increasing groups. Some of the young champions were already on the ground, prepared for coursing, for shooting, for running with spears at the ring, and with swords upon the Quintain. Others were busy raising butts and preparing their shafts for the sports of archery. Some had chosen their rivals, in passages with blunt lance and muffled rapier. Jugglers and buffoons were on the ground—tumblers began their antics, and, ever and anon, a loud burst of clamor from the crowd announced some clever performance, or the appearance of some favorite champion. Murmurs, occasionally rising into shouts, declared the emotions which wrought restlessly in the bosoms of the multitude, like the billows of the troubled sea heaving up in the glorious sunshine. But we have to describe for the present, not anticipate.

The lists were made sufficiently ample for the conflict of horse as well as foot, and for the passages-at-arms of several as of single combatants. But these did not confine the various exercises of many who aimed at sports of their own, and who found favorite spots upon the sides of the surrounding hills. Rules had been published, prescribing the various forms of combat which were to be allowed within the lists, and the manner in which they were to be conducted. These were all to be pacific in character, however deadly might be the weapons which the parties thought proper to employ. In the hands of the good knight or squire, it was understood that the sharp spear, the sword, and the battle-axe, might be used with the noblest shows of skill and power, yet without hurt to life or limb. There were tilts appointed with the lance, and duels with the sword; contests of strength were to be tried with the mace and battle-axe, and of dexterity with the dagger and the knife. But, in each case, the contest was invariably to be decided, when one of the combatants should be put at such disadvantage as would place him at the mercy of his opponent, or render necessary for his relief a battle à *l'outrance*. To compel respect to this regulation was not always easy when the pride of the champion was mortified, and his passions roused; but De Soto had reserved to himself, as of right, to be the judge of the field, and his warder was Don Balthazar de Alvaro, a person no longer young, of grave aspect, of high authority, and quite learned, as well as experienced in the business of the tournament. It was reasonable to suppose, therefore, that a due regard to the regulations which had been published would be observed among the combatants. Of these hereafter; we must pause for the present.

CHAPTER XV.

> "Furious to the last,
> Full in the centre stands the bull at bay,
> 'Mid wounds, and clinging darts, and lances brast,
> And foes disabled in the brutal fray:
> And now the matadores round him play,
> Shake the red cloak and poise the ready brand:
> Once more, through all, he bursts his thundering way—
> Vain rage! the mantle quits the conynge hand,
> Wraps his fierce eye—'tis *past*—he sinks upon the sand!"—BYRON.

CHIVALRY is only another name for enthusiasm. The one never dies out in a community where the other may yet be found. Enthusiasm must exist where there is enterprise and courage; where there is zeal and sympathy; where the virtues essential for performance do not entirely stagnate. We do not make sufficient account of this great leavener of the passions and the virtues, which purifies the one and stimulates the other. When a people too greatly refines itself, it sneers at zeal and enthusiasm. *Empressement* is vulgar in the eyes of an aristocracy; and an aristocracy thus sinks into contempt! Whenever the tastes show themselves wanting in enthusiasm, they are about to destroy their possessors.

The Spaniards had not yet reached this condition in Cuba. Never were people more easily aroused, or more enthusiastic. To see them weep and smile, and shout and sing, without any moving cause, apparently, you would suppose them simply crazy; but their madness had its moving cause, however latent, arising from the active sympathy of the real life within their souls, and the grand and unmeasured passions which they daily exercised. Give me a people for performance, who have not yet learned to conceal their emotions.

Havana swarmed with life. At an early hour of the morning, as we have said—nay, long before the dawn—the hum and buzz of preparation were to be heard in every quarter. The country had poured itself into the city; the city had suddenly taken the voice and wing of liberty, such as the country usually enjoys. You might see, all night, the gleam upon the hill-sides of torches guiding the footsteps of long cavalcades over all the routes from the interior. Knights, nobles, artisans, peasants and mountaineers, arrieros and contrabandistas, banished rogues, outlaws, returning in disguise, and reckless of danger, in the passion which the tournament inspired; we have seen already how motley and various were the gróups. Crowds, from far and near, came on foot. A single mule sometimes contrived to bring a family; the cart, the sedan, the volante, were all in requisition; and very picturesque and beautiful was it to see the long trains, seeming, for all the world, one great continuous procession, winding along the circuitous paths; climbing suddenly to the hill-top, streaming through the plain, and vaguely reappearing—recognized by their torches only—in the deep dim avenues of the silent forest. After a group on foot, gay and rambling, would you see the stately and swelling hidalgo, on his great horse, showily caparisoned in gaudy and costly garments. Noble ladies in their carriages, of whatever sorts—sometimes in litters borne on the shoulders of the slender natives of the island—followed under the guidance of the Don. At a respectful distance in the rear, came groups of peasants, and there, heedless of all, rambled forward a savagely bearded mountaineer upon a donkey, whose horrid screams at intervals, causes the gorge of the knight to rise with the desire to punish the impertinence that dogs his heels so closely with such a beast. But even the Baron grows indulgent with the spirit of the scene, and the mountaineer rides nearer and nearer, without suffering from the wrath which, at another time, his approach would most certainly provoke.

But day opens the mighty pageant, and the sun hurries up with his purple banner, to be present at the scene. Fancy, now, the conflicting but mingling masses; the picturesque and oddly sorted costumes; the wild, but exhilarating mixture of voices, the hum, the stir, the billowy swaying to and fro, with roar and scream, and cry and hiss, and shout and laugh—that, however various, all fuse themselves together, as it were, into one universal voice of hope and enjoyment. The hills surrounding the amphitheatre are already covered with tents and booths of reed, thatched with straw; with vehicles of all sort; groups of mules and horses; stands for food, and fruit, and liquor; shows of mountebanks, and tables for the gamester. Gay steeds are fastened, and watched by liveried pages, under clumps of palms affording shelter. Gay banners stream from every tent or lodge, assigned to knights and men-at-arms. These, raised as if by magic, during the preceding night, occupied the more eligible vacant places contiguous. Each bears without the armorial insignia of the noble, whether he held due warranty from the legitimate herald, or owed his rank only to the persevering ambition of the *parvenu*, who seeks, under the shelter of a gray antiquity, to hide the short frock and coarse frame of the adventurer.

At intervals a sweet strain of music rises from a curtained verandah, and an occasional shrill blare of a sudden trumpet announces the setting up of some banneret, or the arrival upon the ground of the followers of some one of the many bold cavaliers who designed to take a part in the business of the tourney. Some of the pavilions of these knights are of silk, ornamented with figures of gold-thread and brocade; not less splendid to the eye are those of others, though made only of the cotton stuffs of the island, of Mexico and Peru; but these are all glowing with rich and living dyes of the new world, the art of preparing and using which was peculiar to the country. The pursuivants are busy, going forever to and fro, assigning places, according to degree and rank, for the pavilions of the several champions. Troops of cavalry flourished around, as a police, coercing order. Small detachments of infantry march to and fro, their matchlocks shining in the sun. The raised centre of the scaffolding around the amphitheatre, which is assigned to the Adelantado and his immediate circle, is already pavilioned with a gorgeous canopy

The banner of Castile and Leon is already rolling out, with its great, gorgeous and gold folds above it. Not so loftily raised, but yet so placed in the foreground as to attract all eyes, is the personal banner of De Soto: a sheet of azure, on which is painted a spirited picture of a cavalier, mounted on a fiery charger, both armed to the teeth, and about to leap a precipice. The picture illustrated one of the Adelantado's great feats in Peru. The motto is Italian, in gold letters—"*Fidati pur; che a trionfar ti guido.*" When De Soto was asked by Don Balthazar why he put so promising a motto in a foreign language, which was known to so few of his people, he answered—"That it may be more impressive!" The Adelentado was something of a philosopher. Hardly was the banner seen to wave than some one was ready to translate for the curious multitude the mysterious promise. When told that the gallant cavalier only swore in Italian that he would conduct them to conquest, there was not a syllable of the inscription that was not gotten instantly by heart, and that night it was sung as the burden of a refrain, by a native rhymester, who was content to encourage the enterprise upon which—he did not go himself!

Next to the pavilion of De Soto, on the right, was that of the Captain General, Don Porcallo de Figueroa, his banner shining above it, gleaming with a sun of gold. Don Balthazar de Alvaro had his place on the left of the Adelantado, whom he was to assist as warder or master of the tourney. We need not range the places of the rest, nor enumerate the good, the old, and the influential families, to whom conspicuous seats were assigned for the survey of the spectacle. Going without the barriers, we approach the tents or pavilions of the knights who were expected to engage in the several passages-at-arms. Here they were to dress and equip themselves; hither they were to retreat and rest when wearied, and take refreshment. Each was sacred to its owner, and great care was taken by the police of the field that they were never trespassed upon by the crowd. In the rear of each pavilion was a tent or shelter of more common material, where the horse or horses of the cavalier were kept and groomed.

Some of the knights, as the wealthy Señor Don Porcallo de Figueroa, for example, had a score of horses; but the greater number, like our poor knights of Portugal, had a single steed only. But he was generally a good one, of great strength and endurance, and admirably trained. We pass, in review, the several pavilions without the barriers, of the knights first mentioned: of Nuno de Tobar, of Balthazar de Gallegos, of Juan de Escalante, of Christopher de Spinola, and many others, each of which bears the especial shield and insignia of its proprietor. More simple than all the rest, made of crimson cotton, were the tents of the Portuguese brothers. It was remarked by curious observers, that these tents were no longer pitched side by side; they were now opposite each other, one on the right, the other on the left of the centre. The banner which floated above the pavilion of Philip, bore the image of a ruined castle, from which a falcon had spread its wings and was away. That of Andres exhibited a flight of meteors in a stormy sky. Both were significant. The shields of the several cavaliers hung each at the entrance of his tent, and in a situation favorable for that *atteint*, or stroke of the adversary's spear, blunt or sharp, which was the customary mode of conveying the challenge. At the opening of the passages, these were transferred to conspicuous places within the area. As yet none of the knights, challengers, or defenders, were to be seen by the multitude. Squires, leading horses, or pages loitering about the tents, alone were visible. It remains to mention only that the *torril*, or pen for the bulls, was constructed beneath the tiers of seats assigned to the common people. From this a closed passage, the door opening right upon the area, conducted directly to the ring. In the rear of the *torril*, pavilions were raised for the *toreadores*, *picadores*, *chulos* and *matadores*, each class separately; and these pavilions engaged no small degree of the curiosity of the people. From these parties they looked for their most grateful enjoyments. They knew the most famous *toreros* by name; Cuba could boast of *matadores* who were worthy to compare with any of Andalusia,—sons of her own mountains, who could administer the *coup de grace* to the bull, while in his maddening bounds, and never exhibit an emotion. But of these hereafter.

Drums roll, trumpets sound;—a wild burst of Saracenic music rises from the amphitheatre; and the crowds rush forward to seek their places. The Adelantado, at the head of a gorgeous cavalcade of knights, rides into the ring. Already have the noble ladies, with their several escorts, taken their seats upon the elevated gallery which has been assigned them. The people are fast filling up the humbler places around the barriers. De Soto, amidst fresh bursts of music, ascends to his chair of state. Don Balthazar seats himself below him. Both carry truncheons. The signals are given; the sports begin. A troop of young squires and pages are running at the ring. The old soldiers and experienced cavaliers look on with the natural interest of veterans; curious to see who are to be their successors in arms and distinction. The riding is very creditable; some instances particularly graceful and spirited; though one or two handsome youth are rolled over in the dust. The ring is borne off triumphantly several times; and this amusement ceases for a while. Then follows a less experienced class of youth, who ride at the Quintain. The Quintain is a lay figure, armed with a pole, which is freshly painted. The stroke, to be successful and safe, must be delivered fairly, in the centre of his shield or helmet. To miss these, or to touch them unfairly, is to receive a blow from the pole of the figure, who works upon a pivot, and is wheeled about by a moderate assault. The stroke of his pole leaves its mark behind it. It not unfrequently tumbles the assailant from his steed, and thus increases the merriment of the spectators. In England, the Quintain sometimes carried a bag of meal at the end of his pole, which, in a false *atteint*, covered his awkward opponent with flour. On the present occasion, the fresh black paint of his weapon is a more serious danger to the garments; and the Quintain left indelible proofs of his ability, and their own awkwardness, on the gaudy jackets of many of his inexperienced assailants. These exercises, which provoked a great deal of laughter, but did not much excite the spectators, were followed by a very pretty display of archery. In each of these performances there were, of course, champions to be distinguished; prizes were accordingly delivered, and the interest of the spectators was agreeably maintained to the close. But these were the mere preliminaries, the opening flourishes of the entertainment; pleasant enough while they lasted; but not provocative, nor calculated to appeal to those passions which lift a people to their feet, and force them to cry aloud their exultations, or their fears. The runners at the ring and Quintain, and the sports of the archers, were simply the prologues to the crowning entertainment of the day,—this was the Bull-Fight—the sport of sports to the Spaniard, one in which all classes delight,—which appeals equally to the sympathies and tastes of nobles and commons, of knights and ladies, and which, strange as it may appear to us, is said in no degree to impair the sweetness, the grace and gentleness of nature in the tender sex.

A few words on this subject. When we denounce the humanity of a people, who relish such an amusement, we commit the simple error of placing our tastes in judgment upon theirs. The truth is, that the question of humanity is really not involved at all in the subject, even by our own standards. Our *opinion* is simply superior to our *humanity;* and while society with us maintains an even course, we are thus critical in respect to its practices. Let events occur which disturb the habitual course of things, and our *opinion* gives way as readily to our passions as that of any people, and our moral sinks as low as our humanity. Men are very much the same, in all countries, as respects the appetites; and we have in our exercises, equivalent brutalities to those of any people in the world. A boxing match will appeal to the tastes of all of British blood as readily as bull-fight or knife match to those of the Spaniard; and a cock-fight, when announced, draws as large a crowd. We hunt the deer with a spirit quite as murderous as that which the Andalusian knows when he descends into the bull-ring with lance and rapier; and we course with our dogs after the fox nightly, with a pleasure that grows into a sort of madness, in proportion to the prolongation of the torturous sport. Opinion looks grave, and utters solemn humanities, when she reads of Gordon Cumming's horrible butcheries of the elephant, lion, gazelle, and giraffe—noble creatures all, harmless where they are found—but passions and appetites —our *human* nature, gloats over the murderous page; and we pass, with keen anxiety, in the footsteps of the *sportsman*, and hear with exultation the crack of his rifle, and rush in with wild eyes of pleasure, to behold his victim, ere his dying agonies are over. We take the fish by artful processes, so as to prolong his struggles, so that our delights shall be prolonged also; and we call the angler, " Gentle Master Izaak," while he details the several arts by which a worm may be made to wriggle, and a trout may be made to play, *in pain*. Our naturalists assert with wondrous **pains-taking,** their own *humanity*, while they transfix the living butterfly; and opinion, with us, sanctions with this definition, the indiscriminate slaughter of innocent song-bird, and beautiful fly, and wondrous insect, and curious reptile. Yet none of these sports, which include all the cruelties which belong to the Spanish bull-fight, involve the nobler conditions with which the man engages in the latter. In the bull fight he makes his manhood one of the conditions on which he wages the conflict. He perils life upon his sport. He does not claim the right to take and torture the life of the animal without giving the beast a chance in the conflict. The inhumanity in all these practices is pretty much the same; but much more may be said in favor of the bull-fight than of all the rest. The stakes of the opposing parties are equal in the game. Our opinion, in brief, is more humane than our humanity. The Englishman and the American, man or woman, who once witnesses a bull-fight, discovers that his tastes are superior in strength to his morals—that his virtues hold but little sway in the encounter with his blood—that his opinion is unsustained by his resolution—that his own habits are not a whit more heedful of the claims of the beast, than the Spaniard's. He hunts one class, and the Spaniard another; and whether he hunts more virtuously than the Spaniard, must be held very doubtful where he does not hunt half so bravely or at so much peril to himself.

Our purpose, however, in these remarks, is not to defend the bull-fight as a legitimate or proper amusement of men. We simply design to suggest to self-deception a little modesty, and to persuade cant to reconsider its pretensions. Humanity, nowhere, is equal to the encounter with temptation. Opinion, everywhere, is superior to humanity; and thus it is that the *morale* of a community will be superior to the sentiment in every individual composing the community. Our opinion excuses our brutalities, while it lays bare those of another nation. So long as this is the common practice of nations, so long shall we perpetuate both. Let us look to what is intrinsic, not what is specious, and we shall, perhaps, discover that in a comparison with our neighbor we have no great deal to boast—and something, possibly, to lose. But enough.

The bull-fight, as we have said, appeals equally to all conditions, and to both sexes, among the Spaniards. When the sports of the ring and the Quintain were over, and it was understood that those which properly belonged to the amphitheatre were to begin, there was a great increase among the audience. The groups, all of them, deserted the hills. Scarce a vacant seat was to be found in all the three high tiers of scaffolding which surrounded the barriers; and the spectacle became very brilliant, wild and picturesque, of that great and crowded circle. Beauty and knighthood were there in all their glory; while the multitude exhibited every variety of costume and character. The seats were so disposed that the entire person of the spectator in every quarter could be seen; each accordingly was clad in the richest dresses he could command. Banners and bannerets were waving; cavaliers wore their gaudiest colors; jewels flashed in such near connection with bright eyes that one could scarce distinguish between them; and ever and anon, long streaming flourishes of music, passionate phrensies of variously endowed instruments, .d soft, melancholy touches, at frequent pauses, from simpler pipes, conspired to raise the emotions, to excite the sensibilities, to lead the hearer and spectator out entirely from that common world which swallowed up his ordinary life in one dreary monotony.

"*Despejo!*" was the single word given out by Don Balthazar de Alvaro, as Corregidor, or master of ceremonies—equivalent to "clear the field"—"remove all obstructions from the amphitheatre."

There is sufficient reason for this order, which is always an ungracious one in the ears of "the fancy," "the swell mob," who have generally taken possession of the ring. They leave it with reluctance. But, at the order of the Corregidor, the splendid body of infantry which De Soto had been training for the Florida expedition, marched in, to the sound of martial music, and, with horizontal lances, swiftly swept the circle. Their movements were rapid; but the intruders retired slowly, simply clearing the barriers, around which they continued to cling, anxious to be nigh the scene; to see the minutest movements; and to take such part in the affair themselves as fortune would allow them;—their delight being found in beating the bull with their sticks, or thrusting at him with iron-pointed staves, from this safe entrenchment, whenever his course should bring him sufficiently nigh the barriers. This duty done, the infantry disappeared as rapidly as those whom they had driven out. But the ring was not left vacant, for a moment. Their places were soon occupied by the Toreadores, consisting of bands of *Picadores*, of *Chulos* or *Banderilleros*, and *Matadores*. These move in procession around the area, showing themselves to the spectators;—the *Picadores*, in the saddle, armed with lances. They wear short cloaks, the sleeves of which are partly laid open and left loose. Their small-clothes are of leather, the legs coated with a sort of greaves of plate iron;—shoes and stockings are concealed by white gaiters; and a flat, broad, round hat, well ribanded, completes their costume, which is quite fanciful and jockey-like. Not less so is that of men on foot, the *Chulos*, whose habits are more costly, if not more imposing. Their silk vests are trimmed with a profusion of ribands; brilliant scarfs fall over them; a silken net-work confines the hair, in place of which the fringes of the net stream down the shoulders. Their cloaks are, some of blue, and others of scarlet. In two parties they cross the arena, and make their obeisance to the Adelantado. They are in all—the footmen—about eighteen. This includes a couple of *matadores*, or killers. With these comes a *mediespada*, or half-swordsman, who is not often wanted. The *picadores*, or lancers, three in number, follow them on horseback, in the performance of the act of grace before the representative of the throne.

The *toreadores* take their stations, and declare themselves in readiness. First, you behold the *picadores*. These plant themselves on one side of the gate from whence the bull is to emerge, and at a distance of twenty-five or thirty paces. Those on foot, armed with their short javelins, called *banderillos*, meant to goad and torture the bull, and for their defence, their cloaks of blue and scarlet, take their places also, ready to assist the *picadores*, but along the barriers. A trumpet sounds; an Alguazil advances, and receives from Don Balthazar the key of the *torril*, or den of the bull. The Adelantado waves his gilded truncheon; Don Balthazar waves another; the bugles sound; wild shouts from the multitude declare the acme of expectation to be reached, the gate of the *torril* is thrown open, a rush is heard; and "*El Moro*"—"the Moor"—the great black bull of the Cuban mountains,—himself a mountainous mass of bone and muscle, darts headlong upon the scene, and hushes all to silence.

He stops suddenly; throwing up his head. He has passed from darkness into sudden light. The unwonted spectacle for a moment confounds him. He looks up; around; stares with dilating eye on all he sees; and then you may observe his tail rise, and wave, to and fro, the hairs starting up, like those upon his neck, and presenting a ridgy surface, a crested mane, showing his excitement, and gradually rising anger. As yet, he knows not where to look. On all sides, he sees so much! But, a tremendous shout from the multitude seems to decide him; and he answers it with a wild and sudden roar. Then, quick as a flash, he charges upon the nearest *picador*. His lance is ready to receive him. He is repulsed; he recoils. But not far; and with a fresh bound, he singles out his second enemy. He also meets him with a cool front, and a piercing weapon. A second time his neck is gored; but he darts upon the third *picador;* only to meet a fresh repulse! He has felt his enemy; and is either cowed or taught by his experience. Which? We shall see. He recoils from all, receding slowly: his eyes gleaming now with fire; his neck and shoulders streaming with blood; his head to the ground, as if with a heretofore-unknown feeling of humility. But do you think that he is humbled? No! He is only roused, —only contracting himself to spring; gathering his muscles into fold; gathering up his soul for newer effort, and growing momently more and more vicious and dangerous from his forbearance! Some of the spectators are deceived; as half the world is apt to judge and decide from first impressions, and because of their ignorance!

"A cow! a cow!" is the cry—"set the dogs upon him!" "*Ah! que! no vale ña!*" "The beast is worth nothing. He is a cow!"

"A cow, indeed!" cries the experienced mountaineer, who better knows the signs which the brute exhibits. "*Disparate!*—nonsense! Let me see the man who will milk that cow!"

He is right. "El Moro" is a hero, and has sense as well as strength. He has *felt* his enemy; he begins to know him. The *picadores* understand him better than the mob. They note his immense frame,—the great head,—the enormous breadth of neck,—the huge breast, like a rampart, which he spreads before them; the wonderful compactness of his whole figure. They see the lurking devil in his dilating eyes, looking up, though his horns seem directed only to the ground. They note other signs which escape the populace, and they prepare themselves, with all their address, for a second assault. Their horses, which have heard the roar of the bull, are trembling beneath them. They do not *see* the animal, as they have been blinded, the better to make them submit to the rein; but they *feel* their terrors the more. They are not the broken hackneys which are employed in the cities of modern Spain, not worth their forage;—but brave steeds, of fearless foresters, who have taken up the business of the *torero, con amore.* Sleek of skin, large of frame, slender of limb, with small heads, arching necks, bright, round, dilating eyes, clean fetlocks! You see that they come of Arabian stocks, and are not unworthy to carry fearless riders against the bull. They tremble, but they obey. The *picador,* meanwhile, carries his well-chosen lance beneath his right arm. He keeps a wary eye upon his enemy. He knows that he is to be expected;— that he *must* come;—that the struggle has not well begun, and that it will require his utmost skill to conquer—and escape! He does not mistake the ominous aspect in the sign of Taurus! He has not read the Zodiac of the ampitheatre in vain. These are all old stagers, these *picadores.* Each has a reputation to lose. They are known by name among the multitude, and these names have been cried aloud, already, by more than a hundred voices, in recognition and encouragement. "Bravo! Pepe!" "Bravo! little Juan!" "Bravo! Francisco Dias!" "Now shall we see which of you all will pluck *la devisa* from the neck of *El Moro.*" "*La devisa*" is a ribbon about the bull's neck, containing the name of his breeder.

"Which of you has a mistress with eyes worthy of a death? Bravo! good fellows! Let us see!"

The allusion, here, is to the practice of the *picador,* whose object it is to snatch away the ribbon as a trophy for his sweetheart. This is a great point gained; and a difficult one. The Bull, who is well aware of the honor of the thing, is, of course, always careful to resent, with particular malice, every such attempt upon the badge which proves his honorable breeding. It requires rare agility—which, in such a conflict, implies rare courage—to achieve the object.

But the crowd is clamorous. They are impatient at the delay of "El Moro." They regard him as too lymphatic. They shout to him their scorn, and some endeavor to assail him, from behind the barriers, with strokes of the *chivata,* or *porro,* sticks terminating in knobs, with which every rascal of the crowd goes properly armed to the circus. Their auxiliary assaults, in fact, are legitimated, and constitute a fair part of the exhibition. They contribute greatly to goad a timid animal to the necessary degree of desperation, work him up to madness; when, no longer dreading the prick of the lance, though it buries itself an inch deep in the flesh, he plunges headlong upon his enemies, not to be again baffled in the assault, not to be turned aside; and throwing all his brute force into one concentrated effort, puts the *picadores* to all their arts for safety.

"El Moro" is a bull of blood. He is a bull of discretion also. He has only paused to meditate in what manner to use his force against the skill of his enemies. He has concluded his plans; and, with a terrible snort, which ends in a roar, he rushes again upon the *picadores*. They meet him handsomely, their horses' heads a little turned on one side, their spears delivered dexterously, piercing the neck and shoulders of the beast. This is no pleasant sort of salutation. It is apt to turn off ten bulls in the dozen. They all remember, with keen sensibilities, the *garrocha*, or goad, by which the herdsmen have initiated them in the lessons of obedience. "El Moro" has not lost his sensibilities, or his memories; but "El Moro" has a prescience which tells him that he is doomed; and that to feel the pricks too keenly now, is only to prolong his tortures. He, accordingly, resolves to "come up to the scratch" valiantly. Skulking, he perceives, will avail him nothing. He must die, and he will not die feebly. The spear-point is in his neck deep, deep; and the blood spirts high, and crimsons his great swart breast and shoulders. But he resolves not to feel his hurts. He does not swerve: he plunges headlong forward; head downward; horns tossing and tail erect, and shaking to and fro like that of the lion in his bound, or the serpent in his coil.

"*Bravo toro! Bravo El Moro!*" is the delighted roar of the multitude, as they witness his spirit. The horsemen turn about like lightning; the first darts aside, with excellent skill, and sweeps out of the track.

"Bravo, Pepe!" cry the mob, as they witness this dexterity of the first of the *picadores;* but the bull sweeps on; he receives the spear-point of the second of his foes; but his own irresistible rush, his own headlong bulk, prevents his recoil now, even if his spirit quailed beneath the wound: but it does not. The *picador* tries to wheel and escape his assault, but too late:—the horns of "El Moro" are already buried in the flank of the steed; he rends his sides, snaps the defensive ribs like glass; steed and rider roll over upon the plain, the latter upon the off-side of the animal. The body of the horse constitutes his rampart for a moment. It is a fearful moment. Life and death hang on it. An awful hush envelops the amphitheatre; women shriek, men shout and swear; heads peer over each other; eyes are starting almost from their sockets; anxiety and appetite, fear and hope, horror and delight, are in wondrous strife in the multitudinous soul of the assembly. Every body looks to see the bull dash down upon the prostrate horse and rider. The latter lies close and quiet, expecting the assault: his hope of escape is in his insignificance. But "El Moro" is a bull of magnanimity—a heroic bull, worthy of the fierce and fearless race after whom they have named him. He disdains to touch the fallen victim. He spurns the sands anew; he dashes after the remaining *picadores,* who course round the amphitheatre, dexterously avoiding his charge, and seeking to double upon and wound him anew at every chance. Wonderful is the skill they exhibit, and great is the cheering which they receive. Both bull and *picador* receive it equally; nothing can be more fair than the applause; it is equally merited: and gratitude for the sport alone requires that merit should be equally acknowledged. "*Bravo toro!*" "*Bravo Picador!*" "*Bravo Little Juan!*" "*Bravo Moro!*" These and similar cries are heard from all quarters of the ring.

But "El Moro" is not content to share his fame with others, —he is greedy of glory. Another *picador* is overthrown; horse and man roll on the earth. Little Juan, who won the bravos lately, is scrambling over the barriers, partly assisted in the effort by the black brows of the bull himself—his horns just miss ing the haunches of the horseman, and grazing the barriers. It was a narrow escape. The horse of the *picador* flies wild, with his entrails hanging from a horrid wound in the belly. The bull pursues; at every bound he goads the blinded and terrified animal anew. Both are covered with blood. "*Mira!*" cries the "fancy"—the "swell mob" from the corridor,—"*Mira! que bel cuerpo de sangre!*" "See! see! what a beauteous body of blood!"

Thus goring as he goes, himself covered with gore, snorting with fury, his eyes like red fires, flashing in flight, his mouth full of foam and blood, his head tossing wildly, the blood and lather covering his whole body, the bull keeps on his way of terror, ripping and rending the wounded and agonized horse, until, with a terrific roar and effort, he fairly lifts the victim from the earth, dashes him down upon the sands, and strikes his hoofs on his neck, as he bounds over him in pursuit of the remaining *picador*.

There is no parleying with so headstrong a brute as that. There is no baffling him. He is not to be deluded of his proper prey. He is not the fool to put nose to the ground, as ordinary bulls do, wasting his fury upon the enemies he has already overthrown. The fallen horse or horseman attracts none of his attention. He sees and seeks him only who is on foot, in motion; and he gives the surviving *picador* no respite. Never was bull so determined, and so sensible. He is not merely a hero, he is a general; and the audience is duly sensible of his wonderful merits. They shout their *vivas* on every hand. "*Long live El Moro!*" he whom they have yet resolved shall die that very day. "Bravo toro! Bravo Moor!" They toss their hands aloft; they fling up their caps; *porros* and *chicatas* thunder their applauses against the barriers. "El Moro" seems aware of their applause, and resolute still better to deserve it. He gives the *picador* no moment of delay. He is upon him. The steed doubles with wondrous dexterity, and eludes the shock; and *he* now receives the *rivas*. But the bull is almost equally alert. His evolutions are as sudden as his rage is high. He wheels,— another bound, the lance of the *picador* but grazes him; the **horse darts away** but the bull is at his haunches, **and rends him**

—a terrible gash—in the rear. Bleeding and torn, the steed staggers forward, when a new thrust sends him over, and the rider flings himself off on the opposite side, to escape the inveterate assailant. It is a moment of extreme peril; every soul is hushed almost to stifling in the assembly; and now the *chulos* with their gaudy cloaks come fluttering upon the scene. They are to divert the bull from his victim. They glide between, almost like shapes of air. The red shawls flare before the eyes of El Moro. But El Moro is none of your common bulls. He is not to be persuaded that the shawl can work him injury. He has no vulgar bull-hostility to crimson. He darts at the *chulo*, and not his shawl. The *banderillo* flies—a little dart, ornamented with colored and gilded paper—and sticks into his neck. Another is planted directly opposite, buried deeply in the flesh. A third, a fourth, until the beast is fairly covered with these proofs of the dexterity of his new assailants, who trip along like dancing-masters about the scene; relying upon their wonderful agility to dart aside from his wild and passionate plunges. They scatter at his approach. He drives them to the barriers, over which the rescued *picador* has just clambered with a show of pain and labor, that proves he has not gone through the fray unscathed. There is a rent in his leathern breeches; there is an exceedingly sore place beneath it. But the *chulos* are dispersed,—El Moro remains the lord of the arena. He stamps as if for a new enemy; he roars as if in triumph! He darts, seeing no moving object, at those which lie still or writhing upon the plain. He tramples the gay mantles; he rends the prostrate and still struggling horse. He is impatient that they offer no resistance; for the goads still tear his neck and sides, and the wounds are a ceaseless torture. The amphitheatre rings with applauses of his prowess; but this subsides, and the appetite of the multitude craves a renewal of the excitement.

"*Caballos! Caballos al toro!*" is the cry. More horses are required for the bull. New champions appear upon the scene; and the battle is renewed. But we must not enter now upon details; "El Moro" maintains his reputation. Another horse is slain—another wounded—two riders are hurt with broken ribs, and the *chulos* again scatter themselves over the area for the rescue of the third. "El Moro" scatters them in turn: but he is exhausted by his victories. Covered with wounds, he staggers in the centre of the ring. His eye grows filmy, his head droops, his tail—but he is thus far the conqueror, and there is a moment of silent admiration in tribute to his prowess. But the signs show that he can make no more sport. He has done all that bull could do for the popular holiday; and nothing remains but to administer the *coup de grace*, and bring on his successors. The trumpet sounds. The *matador*—the killer—appears alone upon the scene. On his appearance, with lifted cap, he makes his obeisance to the Adelantado. In his right hand he holds a long toledo —a beautiful rapier, of the best temper—in his left hand he waves a little red flag, not much larger than a handkerchief, called the *muleta*. He receives the permission which he requires. "El Moro's" death-warrant is given out.

The matador exhibits the grace of a posture-master, with all the coolness of the executioner. He turns towards the victim, and advances slowly. He is pale; looks anxious; is evidently wary. Well he may be. Such an adversary, showing as much cunning as courage, is not often to be met. The *matador* stops, and with all the coolness of which he is capable, surveys the foe. He is a judge of character, and bulls have a character that requires to be studied. Antonio Pico also has a character at stake. He is greatly renowned among the Cubans. He has slain his hundreds, and he must show himself worthy of his renown. His movements were at once graceful and decided; and his thrusts were as swift as dexterous. He was the master of his art. But, sometimes, the master fails, and Pico was now evidently cautious. It is a duel which he is about to fight. The bull is still dangerous—his rage is still deadly. He has lost his energy, but not his malice. Pico has no shield, nothing but the *muleta*, and his beautiful rapier. His ball dress of silk, satin and ribbon, is at strange variance with the duty to be done; but that is one of the charming features of the performance. He commands himself;

restrains himself; a thousand eyes are upon him; he knows it, but he sees nothing but the eyes of the bull. Their tame, filmy expression does not deceive him. He fancies that "El Moro" understands the whole proceeding, what is to be done, and what is to be feared; and that he is preparing himself with more than bull subtlety, to make a fearful fight of it. It must be subtlety now, opposed to subtlety;—the wisdom of the man to the excited instincts of the beast. The expectation is, that the bull will run at the red flag; when the matador will receive him at the point of the weapon, which pierces him between the shoulder and the bone blade. If the bull has much spirit left, he will do this. The presumption is, if he will not, that he succumbs to his fate—that his energies are exhausted.

Pico waves his muleta in front of the animal. "El Moro" makes a single charge, but recoils—stops short, and stands with head down, as if in waiting. A shout of contempt, from the "fancy," assails him for this ignoble conduct. It encourages Pico. He advances, waves the flag anew; again the bull charges; the steel flashes, quick as lightning;—strikes;—strikes;—all see;—but it is an awkward stroke! Pico's nerves have been troubled. The steel strikes *the bone ;*—it flies from the hand of the matador; and, with a roar, the recovering bull is upon him, with a dreadful griding sweep. The brave fellow darts aside, but not unhurt. He staggers,—he makes for the barriers: the cunning "El Moro," with brightening eye, surges after him. The suspense is awful; the women scream; the men shout; the matador staggers forward to the barriers; falls, without catching them; and, but a moment remains for escape! a terrible anxiety prevails. In that moment, a gigantic form leaps over the barriers from the corridor. He is dark like the red man. He is of that race, mixed with the white and the negro,—a most unnatural and atrocious combination. But what he is, no one as yet can distinguish. They see nothing clearly. They only know that he stands between the fallen Pico and the charging El Moro. They see a common red kerchief waving in one hand. They see not the short, sharp knife in the other. They see, however, that he has succeeded in diverting the wrath of the bull, from the prostrate matador, to himself. A moment more, and the plunging animal stands where the stranger challenged. *He* has darted aside like an arrow, leaving his kerchief upon the horns of the bull, and waving before his eyes. The animal shakes his head, and thrusts it down. In that moment the stranger advances silently. A flash is seen; and the *machete* is fatally buried between the shoulders of El Moro. A hoarse sound issues from the nostrils of the mighty beast, and he sinks forward, the life gone forever, on the spot where he had stood terribly, but the instant before!

The crowd is relieved. They shout their gratification, and the "swell mob" without are particularly rejoiced with the exquisite feat of arms performed by one from among themselves. Scarcely was the deed done, however, when Don Balthazar de Alvaro, in a whisper to the sergeant of the guard, said,—

"Let that man who slew the bull be taken into custody. Let it be done secretly, so as not to cause confusion. Set a watch upon his footsteps, and when the crowd is dispersed, clap him up. He is a slave—an outlaw—the notorious outlaw, Mateo Morillo—slave of the estate of my niece. He has been in the mountains for two years. See that you secure him. There is a good reward to be got by his captivity!"

The sergeant promised obedience; but when he looked into the amphitheatre, the man, Mateo Morillo, had disappeared among the throng. He sought for him that day in vain.

Note.—For much of the detail in this chapter respecting the sports of the Spanish amphitheatre, I am indebted to the volumes of Roscoe, Ford, and the highly interesting and spirited sketches of Spain by our own countryman, Mr. S. T. Wallis, of Maryland.

CHAPTER XVI.

> The knight of the Redcrosse, when him he spide,
>   Spurring so hote with rage dispiteous,
> 'Gan fairely couch his speare, and towards ride:
>   Soone meete they both, both fell and furious,
> That, daunted with their forces hideous,
>   Their steeds doe stagger, and amazed stand;
> And eke themselves, too rudely rigorous,
>   Astonied with the stroke of their owne hand,
> Doe backe rebutte, and each to other yealdeth land."—SPENSER.

THE day's sports were by no means ended with the death of "El Moro." Other bulls were brought into the ring, and several fierce fights followed, marked by sundry vicissitudes and casualties. No less than six bulls perished before the day was over; and twice this number of horses were more or less seriously hurt. Three were killed outright. As many of the *toreadores* went off—were carried off, rather—with shattered ribs; so that, all things considered, the sports were highly satisfactory to the people. That night there was merry-making in all quarters of the city. The houses everywhere were thrown open for the reception of guests. The country cousins were made welcome. The voluptuous dances of the Spaniard succeeded to the feast, and were prolonged through the night. Wild and sentimental music burst from balcony and verandah, and the guitar tinkled sweetly in the groves of lime and orange. Olivia de Alvaro spent the night in the palace of the Adelantado, who entertained a large party. But Philip de Vasconselos, though invited, was not among the guests. Where is he? Why is he not present? These were the questions which Olivia unconsciously asked herself. Andres, his brother, was there; stern and gloomy; but he did not approach her. She danced and sang at the entreaty, or rather the command, of the Lady Isabella; but her heart was neither with the music nor the dance. She went through the performances mechanically, sick at soul, and longing to be away out of the painful glare of lights and company, and buried in the deep shadows of her domestic groves. We have no scene to exhibit, no picture to portray of the persons or events of this night. We hurry to the performances of the day following, which more immediately concern our progress.

The spectacle of the second day promised to exceed the first, in its splendor and state, if not in its attractions. It is doubtful, indeed, if any exhibition, short of battle itself, could, in that day, furnish attractions to the Spanish people to compare with those of the bull-fight. This was a strife of certain danger and frequent loss of life. There *must* be bloodshed; terrible wounds, great suffering, prolonged agonies, and momently increasing excitement. In proportion to the anxiety, the peril, the blood and agony, were the joys of the spectacle. But the tournament was only *a picture* of strife; *gentle* passages of arms and *joyous*, as the heralds described it; and, though full of noble displays, of grace, spirit, strength, skill and admirable horsemanship, it yet failed, usually, to provoke those intense anxieties which characterized the conflicts of the bull with the *toreadores*. But bulls are not to be slaughtered every day. The operation is an expensive one. The owners of fine horses do not very often wish to peril their ribs in the circus; and even the sorry hack has his value, to be considered after the first flush of excitement is over. The bull-fight, though the great passion of the Spaniards, is not, for these reasons, an affair of frequent occurrence. One day for this amusement was held quite sufficient for reasonable people and the "swell mob" were accordingly compelled to put up with the (to them) inferior spectacle of deeds of chivalry.

With the first flashings of the morning sunlight upon bright shield and glittering lance, a sweet, wild, prolonged and inspiriting burst of music issued from the amphitheatre, announcing the resumption of the sports. A thousand bosoms thrilled with delight, and a thousand voices hailed the signal with triumphant shouts. The sounds and clamors from the spacious area were echoed back from all the little hills around. They were all in motion at the music, and clapping their hands with joy. Soon, the fierce bray of the trumpet was heard mingling wildly with sweeter music. Anon came the roll of the drum; and steeds neighed, and squires shouted, and the mountain peasant began to sing, in his exulting unconsciousness, the rude ballads of his distant forests. There was shouting and clamor on every side; and the rushing of crowds, and the din of conflicting sounds, might have led the unadvised spectator to suppose that chaos had come again, so extreme was the confusion. But in all this confusion the truncheon of command prevailed. So well had everything been organized by Don Balthazar de Alvaro, and so native were such exercises to the multitude, that no conflict or disorder followed, where all things appeared to promise nothing less. The people knew their places; the officials their business. The heralds, and pursuivants, and alguazils were all in sufficient number and sufficiently active. But, where the popular consent is with the given purpose, it is surprising how multitudes work together to the common end. The officers skirted the barriers within as well as without, and kept them free from encroachment; and, gradually, the throngs, pressing forward like crowding billows of the sea, subsided calmly into their places along the galleries. The seats were filled as if by magic. The family groups, or special parties, each unobstructed in its wish to keep together, formed so many little domestic circles along the immensely crowded tiers; and the hum and buzz of conversation, free and unembarrassed as in private homes, went on. The merry laugh, and the smart jest, and the careless comment, were uttered aloud, as if none but friendly hearers were at hand to listen. It is a common error that the Spaniard is inflexible as well as proud. This is only true of a high state of convention in the old communities. In the new world, where all were adventurers, even nobility threw off some of its reserves, and accommodated itself to a more democratic condition of things;—

a result, indeed, inevitable from the necessities of the region. But to our progress.

Suddenly, the bands struck up the national air, and this was the signal for the approach and entrance of the Adelantado, the noble knights and ladies who immediately attended him and his lovely wife, and such favorites as were specially invited to the more elevated platform which was assigned to the representative of majesty. This platform, it may be well to state, though elevated above the lower ranges of the seats assigned to the multitude, was yet somewhat nearer to the circus. It was immediately above the corridor, which, in all other parts of the area, was uncovered. Indeed, it seemed to hang almost over the lists, and was not so high but that it might be easily touched by a lance in the hands of a knight on horseback. Along this platform, and in the foreground, on well and richly cushioned seats, the ladies were seated, occupying preferred places; the gallants in attendance taking position in the rear. In the centre of this former range, sate Don Balthazar de Alvaro, acting as warder; and immediately behind, but on a *dais* above him, occupying a richly garmented *fauteuil*, sate the Adelantado and his lady With the entrance of the two last, the *vivas* became wilder than the music, and De Soto bowed impressively and gracefully to the popular applause. His noble form and princely carriage, the splendor of his costume, and a proper regard to the immense amount of patronage which he had brought to the island, made him a wonderful favorite. Nor was his noble wife less so. She had virtues, indeed, superior to his, though of a less showy character; and her personal beauty, her noble carriage, the richness and exquisite taste of her dress, the equal grace and dignity of her bearing, served to make her an object of like and equal attraction with her lord. They took their seats, and the example was followed by those who accompanied them. When the places were all filled, the spectacle was one of wonderful brilliancy and beauty. The seats were so constructed as to show most of the persons of those who occupied the front, and these were all naturally solicitous to appear in their richest habits,

Olivia de Alvaro occupied one of these foremost seats, near her uncle, and a little below, but quite close to, the Lady Isabella. She too was splendidly habited; but she was perhaps the least conscious of the fact of all in that assembly. She had made her toilet with little heart for it, and little heed to appearances. Her thoughts were of the saddest; and her face now was pale as death. There was a brightness, however, in her eye, of singular wildness, and occasionally it flashed out with a vivid and peculiar intelligence. But she seldom trusted herself to gaze about the amphitheatre. She seemed to dread the encounter with other eyes. Beside her sate the frail, fair beauty, the wife of Nuno de Tobar, whose little tongue kept up a surprising discharge of small arms, without intermission. Her supply of missiles seemed inexhaustible, and as they were mostly addressed to the ears of Olivia, it is not a matter of wonder if she had nothing to say in return. The lack of opportunity, indeed, was rather grateful than otherwise. It saved her from all necessity of finding apologies for her taciturnity. Behind Olivia stood the provincial courtier, Don Augustin de Sinolar, redolent of perfume, and diffuse and gay in silks and glitter. There were other gallants in waiting: but we must not stop to enumerate. The anxiety of the multitude has brought them to that hush of expectation which, even more than military authority, is the best security for order. The Adelantado, like every good actor, well understood the impropriety of keeping the stage waiting. He rose gracefully and waved his truncheon. At the signal, a sudden blare from the trumpets, at the entrance, quickened the pulsation in every bosom. The blast was answered from a dozen quarters all around, the response from the tents of the challengers to the signal which required them to appear. But a few moments more elapsed when the trumpets within and without pealed in unison; a lively and prolonged strain of wild and cheerful music; and then was heard the heavy trampings of approaching horse.

"They come! They come!" was the involuntary cry from a thousand lately stifled voices. Then the heralds and pursuivants slowly cantered into the lists, skirting closely the barriers; and when expectation was at the highest, the challengers, six in number, made their appearance. And, truth to speak, they showed themselves right comely chevaliers to the eye, and seemed well able to carry themselves bravely and keep manfully the field. They were headed, as was fitting, by the Lieutenant General of the army, the stout and wealthy Hidalgo, Don Vasco Porcallos de Figueroa. This cavalier, whatever may have been his personal merits, was perhaps rather more indebted to his wealth, for the distinction he enjoyed, than to his genius as a soldier. We do not know that, up to this period, he had ever made any remarkable figure in arms. He certainly had, thus far, taken no such place in the popular imagination as was assigned to sundry of their famous men, who had proved even unfortunate—such as Alonzo de Ojeda, and many others. But wealth, with frequent *largesses*, a right generous spirit, and a gracious carriage, will work wonders towards achieving temporary distinction. The reader may not have forgotten the policy of the Adelantado, already indicated, by which he was moved to depose the amorous knight, Nuno de Tobar, from the office which he subsequently conferred on Vasco de Porcallos. We are not prepared to say that he rejoiced in the pretext which enabled him to do so. But, it was one certainly which he did not greatly regret. He was not displeased at having the means wherewith to buy the favors of the rich cavalier. And Vasco Porcallos did not defraud expectation. He did not withhold his treasures from the expedition to Florida. His *castellanos* were freely rendered to the wants of his superior, with whose ambitious views no man of the army seemed so deeply to sympathize. Vasco Porcallos was seized with a new-born desire for fame, without foregoing a jot of his old passion for acquisition. He was anxious to be known, hereafter, as one of the conquerors in Florida; and, at the same time, he made sundry shrewd calculations of the profit which would ensue from his landed estates in Cuba, by concentrating upon them the labor of the Apalachian savages whom he expected to make captive in his progress The two passions, glory and gain, strove equally together in his bosom; and, with such rare harmony, that neither could be said to be, at any time, in the ascendant. Vasco Porcallos was of a brave temper; and, though never distinguished in war, as a captain, had yet enjoyed considerable experience in the new world's conquests. Had he been a few years younger, he might still have hoped great things from his gallant spirit and generous ambition. But our cavalier was on the wrong side of fifty, and few soldiers have ever acquired reputation, or achieved successes in foreign invasion, after they have passed the meridian line of life. It may be reasonably doubted, if his prudence was at all conspicuous in his engaging in a long and hazardous expedition. That he would endure well enough the toils of a single campaign, was not questioned even among those who were jealous of his wealth and great appointments; and still less was it doubted that he would carry himself well in such passages of arms as it should fortune him to encounter. He was acknowledged to be a good lance and a proper horseman, and as now he appeared in the amphitheatre, portly of figure, tall, erect, covered with shining armor, riding a splendid bay, whose form and color were equally free of blemish—for the white spot, of crescent shape, conspicuous in the centre of the horse's forehead, was held to be a beauty and not a blemish—the loud shout of applause which welcomed him, seemed to give assurance of the popular confidence in his prowess. His steed was gayly caparisoned with his master's favorite colors, green and gold, and his own bearing seemed to exhibit a full consciousness of the distinction he enjoyed, in carrying so brave a rider. The portly knight bestrode him with an air and spirit worthy of so gallant an animal; and, as he pricked him forward with the formidable Spanish rowel and made him caracole to the balcony, where sate the Adelantado and his noble companions of the fair sex, the populace again shouted their unsuppressible admiration. Vasco Porcallos wore a brilliant armor, which betrayed never a stain of the soil. A rich surcoat of green silk (afterwards thrown off) hung somewhat loosely above his armor which was of polished steel, fretted in figures of gold and silver, vines and flowers appearing in the sort of jeweller's work which is known as variegated gold. His helmet was of like material and ornament, surmounted with a bunch of beautiful and costly plumes of the heron. The small shield which he carried lightly upon his left arm, was of steel also, inlaid with a circular bordering of gold, of vines and flowers, in the centre of which, splendidly illuminated, was the armorial ensign of the knight— a bright, keen eye, looking out from a sun of blazing gold. The arrogant motto spoke sufficiently for the insolent ambition of the cavalier. "*Es mio lo que veo!*"—("That is mine which I see!") But this confidence vexed no self-esteem in all the assembly. It was but the embodiment of the national conceit, and it was perhaps warranted by the fact. They *had* made their own all that they had seen. It was an encouragement to valor and enterprise, that the nation should thus believe, that there was nothing, in reserve, which its warriors could not, in like manner, make their own. The faith makes the victory. Vasco Porcallos, known by his *largesse* much more than by his valor, was readily assumed to possess a spirit and capacity worthy of his bounty; and his graceful obeisance before the *dais* upon which Hernan de Soto sate, was congratulated by the repeated *vivas* of the multitude, and acknowledged by the gracious smile and courtesy of the Adelantado. Backing his steed with an elegant and measured, yet free motion, Don Vasco gave way to his brother challengers to come forward.

He was followed by Balthazar de Gallegos, a stout and gallant adventurer; who, without being quite so matured by time as Vasco Porcallos, had, perhaps, seen quite as much service in Indian warfare. His carriage was good, and his skill and grace in managing his steed were quite equal to those of his predecessor; but there was a lamentable disparity in their equipments. The horse was a fine one, big-limbed, yet of lively motion; but his furniture was rusty; and the armor of the rider was distinguished equally by the antiquity of its appearance, and the numerous dints of battle which it showed. Even the slight decorations which Balthazar de Gallegos employed in honor of the occasion,—consisting of gaudy scarf and various colored shoulder knots and ribbons, served rather to expose than to relieve the defects and decayed places in his rusty harness. His shield was large and cumbrous, but carried lightly on his muscular arm. It was of a faded blue ground, on which was painted a volcanic mountain in eruption, the jets of fire ascending without falling— the motto indicative of a thoroughly Spanish ambition—"*Mas bien consumir que no exaltarme!*"—("Rather burn than not rise!") A few cheers followed the appearance of this cavalier; but they sounded very coldly and meanly, succeeding those which had honored the man of fortune; and after making his obeisance, Balthazar de Gallegos, drew his steed into the background, as if satisfied that his mountain would burn rather unprofitably at the present moment.

Very different was the welcome which hailed the appearance of the third challenger. This was our old acquaintance, the amorous young cavalier, Nuno de Tobar. Nuno was a favorite with all classes, poor and rich, men no less than women. His known grace and bravery,—his frank carriage, easy, accessible, playful manner,—the generosity of his heart,—the unaffected simplicity of his nature,—all combined to secure for him the most sweet voices of the multitude. These became clamorous as the spectators beheld the elegance and excellence with which he managed the iron-gray charger which he bestrode—the dexterity with which he led him, caracoling, almost waltzing, around the lists, to the foot of the gallery where the Adelantado presided. The steed himself was one to delight the eye of all who beheld him,— his symmetrical outline, his fiery grace, and the perfect obedience which he displayed, even when his spirit seemed eager to burst from the bondage of his own frame. The armor of Nuno de Tobar was bright and polished. He had taken some lessons on this subject from the Portuguese brothers, whom he aimed to rival. It was not rich, like that of Vasco de Porcallos, nor in such good taste. In truth, it must be admitted that the tastes of Nuno were inclined to be gaudy. The decorations of his armor, due probably as much to his gay young wife, as to his own tastes, were of a kind to suit the costume of a damsel rather than a cavalier. But liveliness and gallantry in youth will be permitted to excuse the offence of foppishness; and, where the tastes of a knight showed themselves doubtfully, a gentle judgment allowed his other personal qualities to repair the defect. The spectators beheld nothing but his graces, the known kindness of his heart, the strength of his arm, the spirit and the beauty of his horsemanship; and, while the men made the welkin ring with their clamor at his appearance, the damsels responded to their welcomes, by a pretty effort at clapping hands, and a swarming buzz of approving voices; for all which, our young knight exhibited a due measure of the most grateful smiles. His shield, we should mention, bore the representation of a ship drifting at sea, with the motto, "*El mar es mi puerto,*"—(The sea is my port,) conceived very much in the spirit of all the Spanish enterprise of that day. Having finished his obeisance, and made a laudable showing of his person and horsemanship, Nuno de Tobar reined his steed backwards, and took his position beside Balthazar de Gallegos; being the third of the knights on the list of challengers.

He was followed by three cavaliers of good repute: Christopher de Spinola, Gonzalo Sylvestre, (a youth not more than twenty-one, but of fine figure, excellent skill and great courage,) and Mateo de Aceytuno, a brave knight, who was also the largest in frame of all the cavaliers in the army. Whether on foot or mounted, his gigantic stature, like that of Saul, made it easy for him to tower above all his associates. His spirit and prowess were not unworthy of his size. Though somewhat slow of movement, apathetic, and not easily aroused, he yet never failed in any of the duties which were assigned him; and his behavior was such always as to secure for him the approbation of his superiors. He rode a famous steed, named Aceytuno, after himself, that had a reputation of its own. He was claimed to be of direct Barbary origin, and greatly valued by his owner, who, however, subsequently presented him to De Soto, in consequence of the frequent and warmly expressed admiration of the latter.

Accytuno was a brilliant animal; in color something between a sorrel and a bay, but of a blood so rich that it seemed rather to diffuse itself everywhere beneath the skin, through which it shone like a purple dye, than to pursue its bounded course through the ordinary channel of vein and artery.

Each of these knights had his motto and coat-of-arms. The shield of Christopher de Spinola carried a pair of huge wings, under which was written, "*A solus me sostingo,*" (Alone I sustain myself,) not a bad image for a modest bachelor, who had neither wife nor children, and was not required to feed the orphans of any of his neighbors. That of the gallant youth, Gonzalo Sylvestre, would be regarded in our day as something impious, even for a lover, who is supposed to be excusable, by reason of the amiable insanity under which he labors, for any infidelity except that to his mistress. His shield represented the face of a very beautiful woman, and the motto, "*Sin vos, y sin Dios y mi,*" (Without thee I am without God and without myself,) was considered by all the young damsels present as the most felicitous of all sweet sayings, to which, whatever might be the objections of the Deity himself, the Blessed Virgin ought by no manner of reason to object at all. The figure upon the shield of Don Mateo de Accytuno was confined to his profession of arms. A mailed hand grasps a lance; the device was, "*No hay otro vinculo que el nuestro,*" ("*There is no bond of union but ours,*"—or, as understood, if not expressed—" we part all bonds but our own.")

Mateo de Accytuno completed the number of the challengers. They now rode together around the lists, prepared to undertake all comers. The first passages were to be with the lance; to be followed by the battle-axe or sword, according to the pleasure of the contending parties; and the breaking of the lance, the blow fairly delivered without defence offered, of the battle-axe; or the sword wrested from the gripe of one or other of the combatants, in the struggle, was understood to be conclusive of the combat in each case, and sufficient for the victory.

By this time expectation was at the highest point of excitation in the assembly. The galleries were all filled with spectators;

the corridor girdled densely with the most reckless and eager; the superior seats shone, without vacancy, with beauty and splendor. Even along the surrounding hills, groups of the simple natives might be seen looking on and listening, though unable to catch more than a glimpse of events, and depending for their interest upon the expression of emotions among those who saw. Meanwhile, the eyes of the knights-challengers sought naturally the forms of the fair ladies in the galleries. Of these, indeed, the heralds kept them constantly reminded by their cries,—cries immemorially preserved by the heralds of chivalry—encouraging them to brave deeds for the reward of loving smiles.

"Bright eyes!" was the quaint form of the apostrophe;— "bright eyes for the blessing of brave lances! Brave lances for the honor of bright eyes! . Smile, fair ladies, that your noble lovers may take heart! Do brave deeds, noble lovers, that the ladies of your hearts may smile! a trumpet for brave lances!— and thrice a trumpet for the honor of bright eyes!"

Then blared the lively bugles in full blast together! Then burst in mighty gushes the full torrents of the wild barbaric music, which the Wisigoth had borrowed from the Moor, and the Spaniard from both—drums, and flutes, and cymbals:—while the excited pulses of the spectators were relieved by murmurs of delight; by sudden cries of exultation—by shouts of applause and encouragement.

The effect of all this was not less remarkable upon the knights-challengers than upon the crowd. The enthusiastic veteran, favorite of mammon, Don Vasco de Porcallos, could scarcely keep his seat, so eagerly did his ears drink in the stimulating sounds and murmurs, so fondly did his eyes traverse that fair assembly, to whose bright glances he was bade to look. Nor was the effect thus stimulating in his respect alone. Don Nuno de Tobar did not fail to note the perpetual waving towards him of the scarf of his newly-made and dutifully-loving wife; but it must be confessed that *his* eyes requited other spectators in that fairy circle, with quite as devout a regard as he paid to the beautiful, but frail, Leonora de Bobadilla. The young knights, Chris topher de Spinola and Gonzalo de Sylvestre, were not less heedful of charms to which they might more properly assert their claims; and, despite his rough exterior, Balthazar de Gallegos showed himself as eager of the notice of the ladies as any of the rest. Of whom, indeed, does not beauty, when it smiles, make the fool? The rough soldier, seasoned to ill usage and strife, callous to blows, and sworn to plunder, was quite as solicitous of the approval of bright eyes, as the young gallant just about to undertake his devoir to secure his spurs of knighthood.

But a rougher parley awaits all the parties. The Adelantado gives the signal for the assailants to appear. Don Balthazar de Alvaro waves his truncheon; the heralds shout, the trumpets sound, and the trampings of horse again are heard. Soon, the six assailing cavaliers begin to pass into the amphitheatre.

We shall be excused from such details, in respect to these, as we have given of the challengers, and for obvious reasons. They do not concern the actual business of this true chronicle, and enough has been shown to afford a general idea of the habits, manners, and characteristics of the times. We shall, accordingly, confine ourselves, hereafter, to such persons only as belong to our *dramatis personæ*.

Of the six assailants, then, we are required to report that Don Philip de Vasconselos ranked only as the fifth. His own modesty gave him this position. He might have led the party, had it pleased him to do so. But he preferred simply to take his place as one of several. His brother Andres was not of either party; but this, it must be remembered, did not affect his claims to take the field against all, or any, of those who might remain the conquerors.

Philip was mounted upon a coal-black steed of famous nurture; large of frame, strong of muscle, fleet of foot, hardy to endure, and of a beautiful symmetry. It was a pleasure to behold his form, simply as he stood, without motion, obedient to the rein. His eyes flashed fire as he darted into the ring, and heard the mingled cries and clamors from a hundred trumpets, and a thousand voices. Though docile as a lamb, his forefoot pawed the earth impatiently, as if emulous of the laurels also, and his breast heaved, like a rocking ship, that strains upon the cordage, as if anxious to break away upon the billows. But the firm hand of the rider was the anchor to his will. Very calmly did Philip de Vasconselos approach the *dais*, and make his obeisance with lifted lance, and graceful bend of his mailed stature, to the Adelantado. There was no curvetting, no aim to show either his riding or his bearing. De Soto received him with a graceful, but not a cordial salutation. The smile upon his lips was very faint and cold; very different, indeed, from that of the noble lady his wife, who curtsied frankly, and smiled cheeringly, while her eye declared her honest admiration of the character and bearing of the knight of Portugal. De Soto could not forgive the defection from his ranks of so experienced an adventurer; and though very impolitic to discriminate in the treatment of the knights, he was one of those men whose feelings but too frequently escape the fetters of their policy. With a further obeisance, Philip closed his visor, and rode back to his place in the lists—a place which brought him to confront the burly form of the gigantic Mateo de Aceytuno.

We must not forget to mention that his person was cased in a beautiful, but plain suit of chain armor, of the purest fashion. It was very brightly polished, and as free of spot or defect as of ornament. This suit he did not wear in Indian battle, but in place of it one of cotton, well wadded, which, strange to say, had been found better defence against the arrows of the red man, than the vaunted armor of the knights of Christendom. His helmet was surmounted by a single plume, long and waving, and black as the raven's. His shield was a series of circular steel plates, the centre of which revealed his crest and device,—the figure, a ruined tower, from which a falcon was about to fly, hovering above it,—the device, in Latin: "*Volucri non opus est nido*,"— (Having the wing, I no longer need the nest,)—a sufficient allusion to his homeless fortunes, and to the independent courage which enabled him to soar above them. He wore no lady's favor, no gaud, no ribbon; but with uniform costume, there was a sort of sombre nobleness in his aspect that compelled respectful attention. His known prowess, honored by those who were jealous of his nation, increased the admiration of those who surveyed his form and watched his movements. Of these he recked little, and perhaps saw nothing; but there were eyes in that great assembly whom it thrilled his bosom to feel were beholding him also. In the brief moment of communion with the gallery, where sate the grandees of the island and their families, his glance had encountered with that of Olivia de Alvaro. She had striven greatly to avoid the single look which she gave him, but a terrible fascination forced her eyes upon him. *His* grew brighter and prouder at the grateful encounter, and he did not perceive that hers sunk upon the instant of meeting, and that her cheek grew ashen pale. But her emotion did not escape the keen glances of her uncle; and a close observer might have noted the sudden contraction of his brows, which followed his discovery. Sitting where he did, just below the Adelantado, and immediately above the lists, he witnessed easily the sudden quickening of light in the eyes of the Portuguese cavalier, and the as sudden paling of the cheek of Olivia. But Philip and Olivia were, at that moment, wholly unconscious of the watch maintained upon them.

Here, let us pause and breathe. Our chapter is a long one, and having placed our champions in opposition, let us reserve the report of the joyous passage for another.

CHAPTER XVII.

'Son dunque," disse il Saracino, 'sono
Dunque in sì poco credito con voi,
Che mi stimate inutile, e non buono
Da potervi difender da costui?"—ARIOSTO

THE temptation to describe the scene that followed must be struggled with. It will not do for us to aim at successes, at this late day, in a field which has employed the genius of Tasso, of Ariosto, of Spenser, and Walter Scott, not to speak of hundreds more, whose practised pens have painted for us the full details of many a well-urged passages-of-arms between rival knights in the presence of nobility and beauty. The reader is already sufficiently imbued with such scenes to require no elaborate details; and we shall, accordingly, confine ourselves mostly to those portions of the tournament at Havana which concern immediately the persons of our own drama, making the general description as succinct as possible. With this caution to our audience, against unreasonable fears or improper expectations, we proceed to our task.

The champions, challengers, and defenders, being now confronted, and all prepared, the truncheon of De Soto was raised, giving the signal. The trumpets sounded the charge, and the opposing parties rushed to the encounter like so many vivid flashes from the cloud. The concussion threw up a sudden whirlwind of dust, while the solid earth shook beneath the thunder of their tread. At the very first encounter two of the assailing party and one of the challengers went down, and were dragged off the field by their squires. This result left Nuno de Tobar, whose opponent had been one of those overthrown, to turn his lance in whatsoever direction he thought proper; but, with the generosity of a noble nature, he preferred to keep himself in reserve for such other inequality in the struggle as might yield him an unembarrassed combatant wholly to himself. New lances having been supplied to those who had fractured them fairly in the passage and without disparagement to their arms, the signal was given for a fresh encounter; the vacancies, meanwhile, being supplied in the ranks of both parties. In this second passage, Don Vasco de Porcallos carried himself so handsomely against his opponent, who was a huge Fleming of nearly his own dimensions, that the latter was incontinently overthrown, and removed almost insensible from the field. A similar fortune, though not with such serious hurt, befell Christopher de Spinola, whose boast " *a solas me sostingo,*" was not justified by the result of the encounter. He was handsomely lifted out of his saddle by the lance of Diego Arias Tinoco, a brave captain, rough as a porcupine, who was honored as standard-bearer of the army. The latter, being now disengaged, was singled out by Nuno de Tobar, and his horse failing, and swerving in the shock, he was adjudged to have been worsted, and very reluctantly yielded for the moment to a conqueror.

The successes of Nuno were welcomed right royally by the cheers of the admiring spectators; whose comments, by the way, were administered unsparingly, whether for praise or blame, at every charge in the business of the field. Meanwhile, Philip de Vasconselos has borne himself in a second encounter with the gigantic Mateo de Aceytuno. In the first, a gentle and joyous passage, as the heralds styled it, the advantage was decreed to rest with neither. Their lances had been mutually well addressed, and had shivered at the same moment, both knights preserving their seats handsomely, though not, perhaps, with equal grace;—for Philip had few equals in mere carriage—and recovered their places in an instant; but proper judgments remarked, in the strong *patois* of the mountains, that the horse of Mateo had too little *bone* for his master's *beef*. In this, he certainly suffered some disadvantage. But the second conflict was decisive; and the knight of Aceytuno went down before his more adroit antagonist—his huge bulk thundering upon the earth like the concussion of some mighty tower. Something of this advantage was said to be due to a loosening of the girth, by which the saddle of the heavy knight was secured; but others more liberal, perhaps just, ascribed it to the better skill of Philip; at all events, the one opponent disappearing from the field, Philip de Vasconselos found himself in the presence of another, in the person of his friend, Nuno de Tobar.

Perhaps, the whole tournament exhibited no two warriors better matched in most respects. They were nearly of the same size and age; of strength apparently nearly equal, equally expert in the use of weapons, and equally accomplished in the management of the horse. These were the comparisons made by most persons; and as the two combatants, now almost alone engaged in the area, confronted each other with fresh lances, the people, and after them the heralds, sent up fresh cries of admiration and encouragement.

"Ho! brave cavaliers, for the honor of your ladies! Ho! bright lances, for the glory of the conquest!" And, sometimes, the cry, "Ho! Santiago, and the lance of Spain!" indicated the working of that feeling of nationality, which did not forget that the opponent of Nuno de Tobar was from another, and, at that time, a rival nation. The occasional murmurs, and snatches of dialogue among the crowds, declared this prejudice more strongly.

"I like not that these Portuguese should come hither to glean of our contests! Shall we find the countries and make the conquest of the natives, that these should gather the gold? Now, may the good lance of Nuno de Tobar send him from the saddle with such shock, as shall make him think no more of the pearls of Florida!"

Such was the sort of murmur occasionally spoken aloud.

"Out upon thee!" was the reply of some less selfish spirit. "There is room for all, and gold for all, and there needs all the brave men that we can muster for these wars with the Apalachian savages. They are no such feeble wretches as these of Cuba, or even of Peru, where Pizarro, I warrant you, and our Adelantado

10*

here, had work enough. They will make us glad of all the good lances that will crowd thither under our banner. The Portuguese is a good lance, and his brother, the younger, is a good lance; though where he hides himself at this time, and wherefore, I cannot guess. I had looked to see him here. Had he been opposed to our fat Vasco Porcallos, instead of that clumsy Fleming, I warrant you that he had made the other sweat! But, hark! they prepare! Go to it, good knights! Go to it with a stomach! Show that ye have fed on lances! That your daily meat hath been bolt and spear-head, and your drink hath been sword-blades, and Moorish scimitars! Ho! brave lances! Ho! brave steeds! To it! to it! brave lances, noble steeds!"

This was one of a hundred voices, eagerly urging the cavaliers to the conflict which was held so equal. Equal in many respects, there were yet some, in which the knight of Portugal, or as they called him, "the Knight of the Homeless Falcon,"—in allusion to his crest—had much the advantage. His steed had been better trained for such encounters; he himself had seen more various service; and he possessed a sedate and temperate coolness of mind, to which the somewhat mercurial nature of Nuno de Tobar could not lay claim. Above all, he knew just in what particulars he himself was strong and his opponent weak, and he prepared rather to exercise his patience and watchfulness, than his strength and skill. Nuno de Tobar, ambitious of excelling—fighting in the presence of the army, and of that beauty which was usually the source of his inspiration—resolved that Philip de Vasconselos should have need of both. Besides, he was to fight for the honor of Spanish lances. Though, personally, a devoted friend of his present opponent, he had heard the popular cries which insisted upon their *Castilian* representative, in opposition to the *foreign* knight; and he was determined that Spain's honor should suffer nothing at his hands.

But Philip de Vasconselos had also heard these cries. He had long since been bitterly made to feel the jealousy and prejudices which existed amongst the Castilians towards himself and his Portuguese associates, and the pride of self and nation, which rendered resolute his courage, was mingled with something of bitterness, which made him half forgetful that Nuno de Tobar was his friend. Thus it was that, as if in recognition of the peculiar wishes of the multitude, each knight was prepared to engage in the struggle with a sentiment approaching that of a *real* hostility. We have said nothing of the influence which the presence of Olivia de Alvaro had upon this feeling of Philip. It is enough to say that it did not, by any means, lessen his fixed resolution to employ all the prowess of which he was master in the approaching controversy.

The interval necessary in providing the champions with fresh lances, tightening the girths of their saddles, and otherwise making them ready for the combat, was consumed in much less time than we have taken in describing it. The knights were both in their places, and the trumpets sounded the charge. The passage was a very beautiful one, which greatly delighted the heralds. Both lances were shivered equally, the strokes being made at the same moment, and each delivering it fairly upon the shield of his enemy. Newly supplied with weapons, the encounter was renewed, and with the same results. By this time, however, Nuno de Tobar was growing impatient. He *felt*, rather than beheld, the *coolness* of his opponent; in which he knew lay the chief advantage of the latter; and with this feeling, it seemed quite in vain that he strove to preserve his own. Philip de Vasconselos discerned the restlessness of his adversary, in a little circumstance, which drew down upon the Spanish champion the thoughtless applauses of the multitude. In receiving a fresh lance from the herald, and while wheeling about to recover his position in the lists, De Tobar hurled the lance no less than three times into the air, catching it dexterously as it fell, and each time by the proper grasp. Such agility, which seemed conclusive to the crowd of equal confidence and skill, appeared in the eyes of Philip de Vasconselos a proof of a nervous excitation, rather than strength of will, or coolness; and he prepared himself, accordingly, to change somewhat his plan of combat. Hitherto, when his steed had rushed to the encounter, his lance, like that of De

Tobar, had been addressed to the *shield* of his opponent. This was the common mark in the tournament of that day; the want of exercise making the *atteint* more difficult when addressed to the gorget, or the helm; but the cavalier of Portugal had practised the one method as well as the other, and not designing a surprise upon his opponent, he shook out his lance, ere the trumpets sounded, and levelled it in the direction of De Tobar's *visor*. The hint seemed to be taken, for the lance of the latter was at once slightly elevated, receiving a new direction in his glance. Thus prepared, the signal was given, and they hurried to the shock. At the moment of crossing spears, his point still addressed to the *visor* of his opponent, Vasconselos threw suddenly the lower edge of his shield forwards, inclining it over his own head, and watching the object of his aim from beneath the very rim of the buckler. No time was left the other for providing against this peculiar interposition of the shield, which required him to have aimed so truly as to thrust his lance directly against the visor of his antagonist, the crest of which was totally covered, leaving the mark aimed at reduced to the smallest possible size. The skill of Tobar was not equal to such a manœuvre. The point of his lance accordingly struck the *edge* of the raised shield, and glanced upward, and onward, over the smooth surface, expending itself in air; while the point of Vasconselos, admirably delivered, was riveted in the bars of his antagonist's visor, so firmly, and so fairly, that there was no escape, no evasion of it possible; and the gallant Nuno was borne from his saddle, without seeming resistance. Indeed, the spear so fixed, the onward rush of both steeds gave it an impulse which no skill, no strength, at such a moment, could possibly withstand. It carried him headlong to the ground, and the steed went free from under him.

There was a cry, almost a howl, from the multitude, at the fall of their favorite, and the national champion.

"Demonios!" sang out the swell mob in the corridor, who flung up their arms with their voices, and swore, and tore their hair, with as much vivacity as could be shown by the most mercurial Frenchman. A few voices shouted their applause of the conqueror; not able to resist the emotion, more strong than nationality, in favor of a deed of manhood. But these soon died away; and then could be heard that angry sort of discussion, in all parts of the amphitheatre, in which, though all persons were agreed, there was yet no possibililty of settling upon the reason which should justify their anger, or soothe their disappointment. Meanwhile, Philip de Vasconselos had thrown himself out of the saddle, and was the first to hurry to assist and extricate his friend from helm and gorget, and raise him from the ground. The squires, however, were soon in attendance. The fall had been a really severe one, and the Spanish knight was somewhat stunned by it; but, otherwise, he was uninjured. But his head felt the soreness, not his heart. His gloved hand, as soon as he had sufficiently recovered to recognize his opponent, clutched that of Vasconselos, in token of that friendly sympathy between them, which such an event could never interrupt. He was assisted off from the field, and Philip now rode back to his place, prepared for the next encounter.

The caprices of the day had left him without other antagonist, of all the challengers, than the portly Hidalgo, Don Vasco Porcallos de Figueroa. In him, the Spanish multitude were disquieted to think, that they beheld the only obstacle, now, in the way of the knight of Portugal; who, if successful in *this* passage, would remain the master of the field. The vain and wealthy cavalier, thus distinguished by fate, as was Ulysses, to be "devoured the last" of his comrades, had hitherto maintained himself with equal spirit and success. He had been fortunate, perhaps, in not having been confronted with the most formidable of the knights by whom the challengers had been encountered. He was, perhaps, not wholly unconscious of this fact; and it was with some misgivings, accordingly,—which he shared equally with his Castilian friends,—that he prepared to contend, not so much for new conquests, as to maintain those which his lance had already achieved. He had seen enough of the prowess of the knight of the Falcon, by whom the favorite of the Spaniards had been so roughly handled, to entertain a reasonable apprehension of the consequences to himself; and, if the truth were known, he was in little humor for this last grand passage. Could he have retired from the contest without discredit, and without utter forfeiture of the honors he had already won, it is perhaps doing him no injustice to say that he would most certainly have declined it. He had not gone through his fatigues without suffering. His portly frame, for a long time unused to harness, was now shrinking beneath its incumbrance. He was reeking with perspiration, which a brimming goblet of cool wine of Xeres, which he had just swallowed, had not tended to diminish. But, with all his annoyances and doubts, he put on a good countenance, and, closing up his visor, prepared for the encounter, with his best hope and spirit.

"The fat knight adds but another to the trophies of our Portuguese cavalier. Philip de Vasconselos will remain master of the field; certainly, he hath most admirable skill of horse and weapon. He hath but a single joust before him, and then he may elect the Queen of Love and Beauty!"

This was said by Don Balthazar de Alvaro. It was addressed to the lady of the Adelantado. But it was meant for other ears. At a little distance, on the left of Hernan de Soto, stood Andres de Vasconselos. He had been a witness of all that had taken place; and had heard the significant words of Olivia's uncle. For a moment he gazed steadily upon the field; then, giving a single glance at Olivia, whose color had been greatly heightened by her emotions during the scene, he was about to leave the scaffolding, when the words of the Adelantado reached his ears, —not spoken aloud, but rather as if giving expression to a feeling which he could no longer suppress, and which was stronger than his policy:

"Now, would I give my best steed could Vasco Porcallos maintain himself to the overthrow of this Portuguese cavalier. It were shame to the lances of Spain should he bear away the palm; and I would gladly see that arrogance rebuked, which but too much distinguishes this stranger. Were it not for the position which I hold, I should myself take up lance, and mount steed in this combat!"

"To be thyself overcome," was the secret thought of Andres de Vasconselos, which he found it difficult to suppress. Hernan de Soto had not noticed the near neigborhood of the younger of the two Portuguese knights, as he made his indiscreet remark; but Balthazar de Alvaro was well aware of his presence. He saw, too, the meaning of that fierce glance which flashed from the eyes of Andres, when the speech of the Adelantado was made. It was his policy to divert the anger of Andres de Vasconselos from every but one object, and he quickly remarked, still seeming not to perceive the youth:

"It were no easy matter to wrest the victory from this knight of Portugal, at *this* moment. There are, if I mistake not, bright eyes in this assembly, the favoring smiles of which will arm him with invincible power. He who fights in the sight of beauty is always brave; but he who fights in the eyes of a beloved one, who, at the same time looks love in return, is unconquerable."

This was carelessly said, but the glance of the uncle led the eyes of Andres de Vasconselos to the spot where sate the niece. *She* saw nothing but the one presence in the field; and in her face, more than ever beautiful, glowed the fires of an affection which was not to be misunderstood. Her cheek was no longer sad and pale, as Andres had usually beheld it. It was now flashed with an emotion, betraying a joy and a triumph which was forgetful wholly of itself. Andres followed the direction of her eye, and he saw his brother, proud and eager, with visor uplifted, and gazing, with the most intent delight, upon the beautiful creature whom *he* had loved in vain. Bitter was the pang at his heart, and, with emotions of hate and envy, which could not be controlled, he dashed away from the stage, and disappeared among the pavilions in the rear. Balthazar de Alvaro beheld his departure, almost the only one of the assembly who did so, with a keen feeling of gratification.

"He **has** it!" muttered the wily politician to himself, as he once more addressed his attention to the business of the tourney:

"He has it—and the time is not distant, when he will make another feel the fury of that dark passion which is working in his heart."

Don Balthazar *judged* rightly of the feelings of Andres, when he allowed his own nature to provide the standards of judgment. Why had Andres gone to his pavilion? we shall see hereafter. Enough, that he summons his squire to his aid; that he cases himself in armor; that he bids them get ready his *destrier*, that he buckles sword to his side, and shakes aloft the heavy lance, and tries its burden with his hands. Let us leave him, and return to the amphitheatre.

CHAPTER XVIII.

> 'Clashing of swords. Brother opposed to brother!
> Here is no fencing at half-sword. Hold! hold!"
> BEAUMONT AND FLETCHER.

THIS episode, between parties not mingling with the action, offered no obstruction to the progress of the tourney. The preparations still went on for the passage-at-arms between our knight of the Falcon, and the redoubtable *millionaire*, Don Vasco de Porcallos. These were soon completed, and the knights took their places. "Laissez aller!" The signal being given, the two champions dashed forward to the encounter with a desperate speed that threatened to annihilate both combatants. There was no reluctance in the carriage and conduct of the rich cavalier, however great might have been his secret misgivings. While he, no doubt, questioned his own resources of skill and strength against an opponent who had always proved himself most formidable, yet the doubts of Don Vasco never once occasioned any *fears* in his bosom. He was brave enough when the trial was to be made. He was not destined to be successful, but he was spared some of the mortifications of defeat. A misfortune happened to him, while in mid career, which probably saved our corpulent cavalier from a much worse evil. His steed, which was as high-spirited as he was powerful, trod upon the barbed head of a broken lance which had been partly buried out of sight beneath the sands of the arena. The sharp point of the steel touched the *quick* of the animal's foot, and, with a snort of terror, he wheeled about at the very moment when the lances should have crossed. He became suddenly unmanageable. Quick as lightning, as he beheld the straits of his opponent, the knight of

Portugal elevated his own lance, and, having full control of his steed, drew him suddenly up, arresting him in his full speed so admirably, that he stood quivering upon the spot; the unexpended impulse which he had received now shaking him as with an ague. In another instant, Philip de Vasconselos was on his feet, and had grasped the bridle of the unmanageable steed of his rival, which, by this time, was in a state of fury, occasioned by the agony of his hurt, which threatened momently to unseat his rider. The timely service enabled Don Vasco to alight, and gratefully acknowledging the assistance rendered, he at the same time acknowledged himself vanquished. The courtesy of his opponent, indeed, had alone spared him this misfortune. Don Philip gracefully rejected this acknowledgment, and, ascribing the event solely to the sufferings of his rival's horse, proposed that Don Vasco should find another. But, by this time, the chivalrous feelings of the latter had somewhat subsided. He felt much less enthusiastic than before, and was rather pleased now at a means of evasion, which, while it lost him the final honor of the day, at least left him in possession of the credit which he had acquired in the previous passages. The knight of the Falcon remounted his own steed, and resumed his place within the lists. He stood alone, and in expectation. No champion stood before him, challenging the triumph which he had won,—the crowning triumph of the field. There was a sudden and deep silence throughout the assembly. The feeling was everywhere adverse to his claims and expectations; and it was with something of contempt, not unmixed with bitterness, that our knight of Portugal was reminded of the national prejudice, which felt reluctant to do justice to the achievements of the stranger. There was no other reason for the silence and forbearance of Don Hernan de Soto, who, in the case of a Castilian champion, or in that of one to whom he felt no personal prejudice, would, no doubt, have promptly risen in his place, and summoned the successful knight forward, to choose the Queen of Love and Beauty, and to receive the chaplet of honor at her hands. There was no reason why the award should not be promptly made. There was no challenge pending. No opponent had announced himself for the combat. All who had presented themselves had been disposed of. Yet the knight of the Falcon was allowed to stand in waiting, unemployed, alone, for a space of several minutes, not a word being spoken to him, and a dead silence hanging over the multitude, significantly declaring the general reluctance to make the necessary award. In the silence of the crowd, De Soto felt his justification. But the gallant Nuno de Tobar, who had, by this time, joined the ladies about the Adelantado, warmly interposed to demand that justice should be done to the conquering champion. It was with a cold severity of look that De Soto prepared to comply with a requisition which he could not longer escape with decency, when Don Balthazar de Alvaro interposed.

"But a moment more, your excellency."

"Wherefore?" demanded Tobar. "Will you keep the knight of Portugal in waiting all day, without a cause?"

"Let him wait!" said De Soto, sharply, though in subdued tones. "The warder hath a reason for it."

Don Balthazar whispered to Tobar:

"There *is* cause. The tourney is not yet ended. There is another challenger. He will soon appear."

"Ha! who?"

How did Don Balthazar know that there was another challenger? The simple Nuno de Tobar himself never dreamed of it; still less did he conjecture in what guise the new claimant for the laurels should appear. At that moment, silencing all further conversation and speculation, a sudden sharp flourish from a trumpet without awakened Philip de Vasconselos to the conviction that his crown was not secure. By this time, his feelings had become sufficiently embittered for genuine anger, and a real conflict. He turned his glance quickly, as he heard the tread of the approaching cavalier, and beheld emerging into the amphitheatre the form of Andres his brother. The spectacle was one of extreme sorrow and mortification to the elder brother. The moment he beheld him, Philip muttered to himself, closing his visor:

"Thou too, my brother! Thou hast then joined with mine enemies—ay, and *thy* enemies too—against me!"

The visor of Andres was already closed, and Philip could not behold his face; but he could readily conjecture the crimson flush which covered it,—the usual sign of his intemperate passion. He had been somewhat surprised, that Andres had taken *no* part in the tournament before; but the feeling was not one of regret, since, as we have seen, he had already entertained some misgivings that his brother might take the field against himself. We have not forgotten the fierce dialogue which had taken place between them on this subject. Of course, Philip de Vasconselos entertained no personal apprehensions from the encounter. His pride was in no way alarmed, lest he should meet with overthrow, in the passage-at-arms with his brother. Indeed, to speak plainly, Philip knew too well his own superiority of training, art, and muscle; though the vanity of Andres was such that he had persuaded himself to a very different estimate of their mutual powers. He was yet to be taught a better knowledge of their disparity. The reluctance of Philip to engage in such a contest, even though the tournament implied neither strife nor malice, was based upon his just knowledge of human nature; upon his thorough experience in respect to the mood and character of Andres—his passionate blood; his disappointments of heart; his jealousy of the superior influence and reputation of his brother. We can readily divine the several reasons which governed Philip in his anxiety to escape a conflict, in regard to which he yet entertained no fears. Now that they stood confronted, and the contest was inevitable, he endeavored to calm his own blood, and control his temper, somewhat excited by the circumstances which had marked his treatment by the Adelantado and the assembly. But this was not so difficult. The reception of Andres, by the audience, was of a sort to kindle in the elder brother a sentiment of passionate indignation, as it declared how grateful to the common feeling would be his overthrow. The multitude hailed the entry of the new champion with the wildest plaudits, not simply as he promised to prolong their sports, but as he afforded still another chance for the defeat of the person whose triumph had chafed the national pride. It was true that, even if Andres should succeed against Philip, the honor would be lost to Castile; but to this finality, their vision did not extend. All that they now required was the defeat of the one cavalier, to whom their own favorites had been compelled to succumb.

There was still another reason for the excitement of the multitude, on the unexpected appearance of Andres de Vasconselos. It is a curious fact, that the instincts of the vulgar rarely err in respect to the passions which goad and afflict the natures of distinguished men. The common people seem readily to conjecture in what points superiority is weak. They all knew, by sure instinct, that the brothers were rivals. They had seen and heard enough, touching their mutual attachment to the fair beauty, Olivia de Alvaro, to imagine that the approaching conflict was to be marked by other feelings than those of chivalrous ambition, and the pride that looks only to the momentary triumph. They guessed all the bitter vexation that stimulated the one champion, and they inferred like feelings in the bosom of the other. And the two were to fight in the presence of the woman whom they both loved. A thousand eyes turned involuntarily to where Olivia sate, pale and breathless with anxiety and apprehension. She, too, partook of the convictions of the multitude. They were brothers; they were rivals; and she had reason to fear that they were enemies. She had heard of the separation of their tents; and that there had already been sharp words between them. And now they stood, face to face, fronting each other with sharp weapons. What had she not to fear? The very manner in which Andres de Vasconselos appeared within the field; the moment chosen, when his elder brother was in full possession of the victory; when but a moment was needed to afford him the laurel crown for which he had striven! This was a circumstance full of significance. That Andres had not sought the conflict with other champions, or previously, at any period, was a sufficient proof that its *honors* were not the objects of his desire. Why should he take the field now, unless with the aim to pluck them from the brow of his brother? It was a bad passion—hate, revenge, anything but an honorable ambition —which prompted his appearance now, at the last moment.

Olivia thought all these things. Such were the thoughts of Philip also. But he strove to restrain and silence them; and, in the brief interval allowed him, his inward struggle was to subdue himself,—to keep his own bad passions in subjection, and to offer no such provocation to those of his brother, as would place him entirely beyond control of human reason. He resolved to be forbearing in all respects. But this did not imply that he would forego any of his resources of skill or strength in the conflict. He was not, by any means, to yield his claims to the honors of the field, in favor of *any* opponent. On this point he was resolute; and, thus resolved, it became him, if he would effect his triumph, and avoid giving unnecessary provocation, or inflicting mortification upon his brother, that he should maintain the coolest temper, and suffer nothing to disturb his passions. It required some effort to do this, for he had felt bitterly his isolation in the last few moments,—a feeling sadly increased, when, as he phrased it, his own brother had joined his enemies against him.

We must not allow it to be supposed that the Adelantado beheld the opening of the new issue between these parties, without being somewhat sensible to the strangeness of its aspects. His instincts, too, were at work; and remembering to have heard of the quarrel between the brothers, he began to think there was something unnatural in the approaching combat. His conscience reproached him for the ungenerous delay which had kept Philip de Vasconselos from the crown of victory, and afforded the opportunity for the event, of the results and character of which he had grown apprehensive; and he looked dubiously at the warder of the field, Don Balthazar de Alvaro, and for the first time felt suspicious of those motives, on his part, which had moved him to urge the delay in closing the lists. But there was now no moment for arrest and interposition, unless by the exercise of a seemingly arbitrary authority, which would show ungraciously in all eyes. Accordingly, the affair was suffered to go on. Both champions were already prepared for it.

Andres de Vasconselos, as we have already described him, was a handsome and vigorous youth, well made, of considerable muscle and agility, well skilled in arms, an admirable rider, and utterly fearless of soul. He was mounted on a fine blooded mare, of great hardihood and life. His armor, though sombre also, was more gay than that of his brother, and he wore a rich chain of gold, with a medallion pendant, around his gorget. A gay crimson scarf crossed his bosom, and contrasted effectively with his sable armor. His shield was very much like that of his brother; and crest and device equally declared that haughty ambition, which, in that day, marked pretty equally the Spanish and Portuguese adventurer. It bore for figure, a shower of meteors amidst cloud and storm, with the Latin words—"*Inter turbas illustris*"—"Glory amidst the storm." He was certainly the man to prefer always that his successes should be the fruits of the most unmeasured conflict. But we need linger no more in our preliminaries. The signal sounds; the truncheon of the warder is waved aloft; the trumpet sounds the charge; the heralds cry their encouragement.

"To it, gallant gentlemen! honor awaits brave deeds; your ladies look on you with smiles. Glory is for him that conquers, —'Glory amid the storm'— The falcon has her wings; why should he not soar to the heights of glory?"

These, and a hundred other cries, from the audience as well as the heralds, rang throughout the amphitheatre, as the brothers, parting from their places, rushed to the encounter with a shock that thundered along the earth. The lances were shivered famously; new ones were supplied in a moment; again, the wild rush was heard, rather than seen; and again came the fearful concussion. The lances were again shivered at the encounter, but it was observed that Andres de Vasconselos was nearly unseated in the shock. In truth, he had a narrow escape, and he felt it; and his anger was heightened, and, as he stood again confronting his opponent, a bitterer feeling of hostility than he had known before, worked within his bosom; and his teeth were gnashed together; and grasping the new spear with which he had been furnished, he muttered to himself, as he shook it aloft, —" If *thou* fail me, I will look to surer weapon."

The third passage was waited for with great impatience by the multitude. The previous combats seemed to have been mere child's play to these. Every one felt that the present passages were marked by passion much more serious than those of chivalric courtesy, even when stimulated by ambition, or urged by the desire of doing greatly in the eyes of love and beauty. The spectators were now hushed and breathless. The occasional cries of the heralds, repeating the old formulas of encouragement, seemed very unmeaning sounds in respect to such a conflict. They were felt almost as impertinences; and, indeed, by this time, the heralds themselves seemed to arrive at this opinion, for they suddenly became silent. All now was eager expectation. The signal followed, and the passage. There was the same fearful concussion, as before; the clouds of dust; the confusion. But the results were more decided, and the encounter was followed by a wild, sharp cry, full of rage and fury. Soon, Philip de Vasconselos emerged out of the dust-cloud, and coursed once round the ring; a moment after, Andres was beheld, on foot, with his battle-axe in his hand, and darting after his brother with the ferocity and speed of a tiger. The steed of the younger knight was down, rolling over in the sand; by what hurt or accident, no one could conjecture. He, himself, had all the action of a madman. His fine scarf was riven; his armor covered with dust, and his helmet thrown off. His hair, which was long, floated wildly; his face was crimson with passion, and his eyes glared with a fury which threatened to destroy everything in his path. He made headlong way towards Don Philip, who had now drawn up his steed, and stood quietly, if not calmly, awaiting him at the barriers, which was as far back as he could recede. Here he must stop and encounter what should happen, if he would not incur the disgrace of seeming to fly, which would have befallen him should he again put his horse in motion to escape from further assault. He had not long to wait. Blinded with rage and mortification, Andres soon made up to him, and at once sprang towards him, swinging the battle-axe above his head. Then it was that Philip exhibited, in highest degree, the wonderful spirit and activity which he possessed. In an instant he threw himself off from his steed, and, without weapon of any kind in his grasp, confronted his brother. The latter at first seemed not to perceive the unarmed condition of Don Philip, and all expected that he would strike, from the manner in which he shook his battle-axe and pushed forward. But, seeing ere he struck that his brother was unarmed, he cried out hoarsely—

"Get thee thy weapons!"

"Put down thine, Andres!" was the calm reply of Don Philip—"wherefore this madness?"

"Madness!" cried Don Andres; "if thou darest call me a madman, I will brain thee as thou stand'st! Get thy weapons, I tell thee; thy triumph is not complete. There must be other trials between us!"

"Go to, Andres: thou art foolish; thou art fevered! would'st thou strike at thy brother in anger?"

"I see no brother; I know no brother! I know thee as mine enemy only, and I will slay thee as a dog. Thou shalt have no triumph over *me!*"

With these passionate words, showing him entirely beyond control of reason, he at once strode forward, and struck, with deadly and determined aim and stroke, full at the crest of Don Philip! But the latter was prepared and watchful, though unarmed. He lightly stepped aside from the blow, which was such, that, if it had encountered his head, had certainly brought him down, powerful as he was. He stepped aside and escaped it; and, before the younger brother could recover his position, he grasped him by the arm; and with such a vigor as no one deemed him to possess, he wrested the axe from the grasp of the infuriate youth, with as little seeming effort as if the latter had been only a child in his hands. All this occupied far less time than we have employed in telling it; but the interval had been sufficient to have allowed the warder of the field to have thrown down his truncheon if he had pleased to do so, and for the heralds and guards to have interposed. Nuno de Tobar had entreated Don Balthazar to arrest the combat when it promised to be bloody, but he was unheeded.

"There is danger, I tell thee, Don Balthazar! Don Andres hath no control of himself in his passion, and see you not that the victory already rests with Don Philip?"

"Nay," said the other—"three strokes may be taken with the sword or battle-axe, according to the wishes of the combatants, after the passage with the lance."

"Only where the passage with the lance results in no advantage to either," was the reply of Tobar.

"Yet, I see not why they should be checked in a new passage, if the parties desire it."

"But Don Philip, you perceive, does *not* desire it."

"Then, by my troth, he loses some of his renown as a warrior. He should face his foe with any weapon."

Nuno de Tobar was furious at these words, and greatly apprehensive; and his passion might have exploded in a violent challenge of the justice and magnanimity of the Adelantado himself, to whom he now turned in impatient appeal, when he was arrested by the sudden termination of the combat, as we have described it. The next moment beheld Don Andres disarmed, and the battle-axe in the grasp of his brother. Then it was that Don Balthazar threw down his truncheon, and the trumpets sounded the retreat. But Don Andres heeded not these signals. He confronted Don Philip with a passion as reckless as before, but this time with the feelings of despair and shame, rather than of rage and hate.

"Slay me!" he cried, "strike, Philip de Vasconselos, as at thy enemy! Thou hast the weapon. Thou hast disgraced me eternally. Put a finish to thy work. Smite! my head is uncovered to thy blow!"

"Go to, Andres; this is folly; thou hast fever in thy veins, my brother. It is the madness of thy blood, not thy heart, that has wrought thee to this unhappy conduct. I cannot harm thee, Andres. I love thee, my brother, whatever thou may'st do, or feel, or say!"

With these words, Philip flung the battle-axe to a distance. Andres cast himself down, with his face upon the earth; but, as the heralds and squires came up, he rose again quietly, and suffered himself to be led out. He was borne away with a raging fever in his veins, and that night was in high delirium.

CHAPTER XIX.

"We charge these women leave the court,
Lest they should swoon."
MIDDLETON.—THE OLD LAW

THE effect of this scene was prodigious upon the whole assembly. Its events were just of that sort to fill the minds and excite the imaginations of such a swelling, earnest, grave yet passionate people as the Spaniards; and, for awhile, they were all hushed, as if overwhelmed with emotion, and still expecting other events of even greater excitement to follow. They were conquered by the Portuguese. The deportment of Philip de Vasconselos had been such as to impress every spectator with the full sense of his noble character and perfect heroism, and there were none now so bold as to challenge his triumph or his fame! Verily, he had gone through the most fearful of all trials for such a soul. He had survived them, though he suffered from them still. He had overcome those worst enemies, his own passions, which, wronged on every hand, and fiercely assailed by the one, above all others, who should have approached them with nothing but love and veneration, had been able to subdue themselves within just limits, and permitted him to rise equally above his enemies and his own rebellious blood! This was not lost upon the spectators. Their hush was only the prelude to their applause. Their instincts, kept in lively play all the while, and making them forgetful of all their former dislikes and jealousies, had brought their final judgments right. Their souls, as they beheld, became fully conscious of the rare beauty of his carriage and his performances throughout; and the gentle humanity, which, at the closing scene, had appeared so conspicuously in unison with the most determined courage and the coolest conduct. The wildest shouts testified their admiration, and declared the complete triumph of the hero of the day, not only over all opponents, but over their own stubborn and ungenerous prejudices. They did not see the bitter smile that mantled the face of Philip as he heard these uproars of admiration. He knew the value of popular applause, and quietly remounting his steed, he stood in silence waiting for the summons of the warder, to the foot of the *dais*, where the Adelantado was to place the crown upon the lance of the conqueror, who was required, in turn, to lay it at the foot of the lady whom he should designate as the Queen of Love and Beauty. It was her task to accept the tribute, and, lifting up the trophy so deposited, to place it on the head of her champion.

There was no reluctance, now, on the part of the Adelantado, to do justice to the knight of the Falcon. De Soto, it is true, had his prejudices as well as his people; and his pride had been somewhat stung by the reserve which had been exhibited towards him by Philip de Vasconselos; to say nothing of the offence which the latter had given, in announcing his doubts in respect to his farther connection with the expedition to Florida. But, though a proud and selfish person, De Soto was not a base one. He had his moments of prejudice and passion, but was by no means insensible to greatness of soul and heroic character, even in the instance of an enemy. He was thoroughly disarmed by the conduct of Philip; and some compunctious visitings of conscience now made him anxious to atone, as far as possible, by the most prompt acknowledgment, for his past coldness and neglect. He bade the warder do his duty, and, at a signal given, and amidst a passionate *fanfare* from the whole corps of trumpeters, the knight of the Falcon was led up to the foot of the *dais*. Here he dismounted, uncovered his head, ascended the rude steps, which had been hastily placed for the purpose, and presented his lance at the bidding of De Soto, who, in a warm and graceful speech, of a few sentences, placed upon it the trophy as signed to the conqueror. This was a beautiful coronet, or cap, of rich purple velvet, encircled with a chaplet of pearls, in the centre of which flamed a single but large diamond, surrounded by rubies and other precious stones. Don Philip received the prize with the most graceful obeisance, but in profound silence, then advancing to the foot of the seat occupied by Olivia de Alvaro, he knelt, and laid the coronet before her, dropping his lance at the same moment beside him. Again the trumpets sounded in a soft but capricious Saracenic strain, while the heralds cried aloud the name of the lady; and De Soto, rising, proclaimed her the Queen and Beauty of the tournament. We shall say nothing of the envy sparkling all the while in the eyes of the other fair dames in that fair assemblage; in the breast of each of whom, no doubt, there had lurked hopes more or less lively, during the progress of the day. However slight their hopes, when it was seen who was to be the successful champion, we can still easily understand how there should be many disappointments. Of course, there was much criticism, also, upon the choice of the knight of Portugal; and while most of them could admit cheerfully his superior claims as a warrior,—his skill, spirit, and address, in the tourney,—there were not a few to regret that so much heroism should be accompanied by so very bad a taste. But the multitude applauded the taste, no less than the valor and conduct of the knight.

It was now the task of Olivia de Alvaro to place the coronet on the brows of her champion. This was no easy task, however grateful. She had been an excited spectator of the scene; she had felt, with constant tremblings of heart and frame, all the vicissitudes of the conflict. These were rendered trebly acute in consequence of that secret history of grief of which we know something already; the action of which, on a system whose nerves were all disordered, was of a sort to enfeeble and excite at the same moment; so that but little strength was left her for the performance of her task at the closing scene of the day. But she arose, after a brief delay; the Knight of the Falcon still on his knees before her. There was a dead silence now in the assembly. All were curious to hear what she would say; for she was not simply to place the crown upon the head of the champion,—she was to accompany the act with words of acceptance of the honor conferred upon herself,—to bestow applause upon his performances, and to utter those exhortations to future deeds of chivalry and valor, which are supposed naturally to follow, where Beauty encourages, and Love is the gentle counsellor. She arose slowly, amid that general hush of expectation, which, by the way, increased her confusion; stooped to the crown which rested upon the footstool where Philip had laid it; lifted it, and advanced a step, in order to place it on his head. At this moment their eyes met; a sudden and ashen paleness overspread her cheeks; her heart, beating wildly but a moment before, seemed at once frozen within her; and she tottered, sunk forwards, and would have fallen to the floor, but that the swift arms of her lover caught and sustained her. She had fainted from the conflict of emotions which she could no longer sustain and live!

CHAPTER XX.

> "Invention is ashamed,
> Against the proclamation of thy passion,
> To say thou dost not . . . thy cheeks
> Confess one to the other."
>
> ALL'S WELL THAT ENDS WELL.

THEN it was, while all was commotion in the assembly, that the passionate love of Don Philip for the unconscious damsel in his arms, overcame and banished all the previous calm and steadfastness in his manner. He thought her dead. There was no color in her cheeks, no life in her eyes, no pulsation in her veins. He cried aloud for succor, while drawing her closely to his bosom, as if to warm her anew with his own tumultuous fires. Before any one could interpose, he had borne her back to the seat, supporting her with vigorous arm, and appealing to her consciousness by the most endearing efforts and expressions. He was at that moment freed from all the conventional restraints which had hitherto made his passion cautious, and taught concealment as the proper policy of love. He was now not unwilling that the world should hear what he had hitherto never declared to her, and with the sense of her danger and his loss, he became indifferent to the opinion of those around, a regard to which is so characteristic of the proud and sensitive nature. But he was not suffered long to indulge in a situation which he found so painfully sweet. He was brought to consciousness by the interposition of other persons. Don Balthazar de Alvaro was soon at his side, and, laying his hand with rather a rude grasp upon the shoulder of our knight, he bade him release the lady to those who could better effect her restoration, and who were the most proper persons to attempt it. Next came the wife of Tobar, followed by the lady of the Adelantado and others, to whom Philip was compelled to resign her. To these he yielded her, though with reluctance. He shook off the grasp of Don Balthazar, and answered his looks and words with an abruptness of manner, and a glance of fire, which declared the hostility and scorn which he truly felt, and in which the uncle was taught to read the language of defiance. Olivia was borne away by the female attendants. The Lady Isabella would have had her conveyed to her palace, but Don Balthazar, in a very resolute manner, resisted this arrangement, and she was conveyed at once to his own residence. The amusements of the day were over. The trumpets sounded the retreat; the audience slowly melted away; but long before the assembly was dispersed, Philip de Vasconselos had disappeared from the public sight.

He proceeded at once to the lodgings of his brother, but did not see him, as he feared that his presence would only increase the disorder of the latter. He ascertained, however, that his delirium and fever did not increase, and that he was well attended. The physician of De Soto himself had been sent him, and had administered some soothing drugs, after taking from him a goodly quantity of blood. He still remained with him, and would not suffer him to be disturbed. The attack had been severe as sudden, but it was not of prolonged duration; and judicious treatment, seconded by the youth and vigor of his constitution, enabled him, after a few days, to rise again to his feet. In a week he was able to resume his armor, and to exercise at the head of his little company. But he remained comparatively feeble for some time, and the mortification which he had suffered hung like a dark shadow upon his soul. He became habitually gloomy and morose; addressing himself wholly to military studies and exercises, and never suffering himself to be seen in society. Gradually he began to entertain more just and generous feelings towards his brother, though from this period there was no longer any cordiality between them. The events which were yet to occur served, in great degree, to disarm him of that jealous hostility to Philp which had been the sole cause of his recent madness. Philip, though solicitous of his health and safety, never obtruded himself upon him. He was content to leave to time the work of repair. But we must not anticipate.

The recovery of Olivia de Alvaro was much more rapid than that of her rejected lover. What remedies were employed in her case, were not suffered to be known; but the very next day found her able to sit up and converse. Leonora de Tobar sate some time with her. Donna Isabella was also pleased to visit her, and other ladies shared in their friendly attentions. But while recovering her consciousness, and in some degree her health, Olivia sank into a sort of sober melancholy, which no arts or attentions of her female companions could possibly reach. An exterior of the most stolid indifference encountered the friendly solicitude which sought to soothe and heal; and while her deportment was all gentleness and meekness, her heart was yet closed against all efforts to probe its secret, or ascertain its apprehensions or its wants. To Leonora de Tobar her case seemed a singularly mysterious one. She knew that she loved Philip de Vasconselos beyond all other men. She was now sure, as was all the world, that he loved her beyond all other women. What more? Why should either of them be unhappy? The whole affair was very incomprehensible to her, and afforded her a fruitful and constant subject for expostulation with the sufferer, and speculation with all other parties.

Don Balthazar was the only person who properly understood the whole difficulty. He had his fears of the case, as well as a full knowledge of its peculiarities. His hope of security, strange to say, was based upon what he knew to be the *virtues* of the damsel. He relied wholly upon her justice and magnanimity, to defeat the suit of the Knight of Portugal. But his fears were still active. He apprehended that the weakness of the woman would get the better part of her sense of justice. He knew the sensuous nature of the sex, and the paramount strength of their feelings. Could Olivia really be capable of rejecting the lover whom she preferred before all others, simply because of a cold sentiment of honor and propriety? Why should she not keep her secret, and thus secure her triumph? He still dreaded that she would resolve on this. He had too little nobleness himself to rely upon that of another; and the recent event lessened materially his confidence in the firmness of her virtue, which was at present all his security. Of course it is understood that he can never be reconciled to her union with Philip, or, indeed, with any man. We have but imperfectly unfolded our narrative thus far, if it be now necessary that we should endeavor to establish this fact. His selfishness, at once of avarice and passion, was a settled necessity, and utterly adverse to her finding happiness, according to the dictates of her affections.

But it was necessary to confirm her in her previously expressed and virtuous resolution of self-denial. He was required to strengthen her determination against the pleadings of her own heart, as well as of her lover, to lessen the strength of her feelings by stimulating her propriety, and to keep her virtuous magnanimity active, as a barrier against her passion. This he now perceived to be more powerful than he, or even she, had previously suspected. He had watched her through all the caprices of the tournament, and had seen the warmth and violence of her feelings, written in her face and action amidst all the changes of the struggle. "She is not to be trusted to her own sentiments," was his reflection. "She may resolve as she pleases, in her quiet moments of thought; but let Philip de Vasconselos kneel imploring at her feet, and she will probably forget all her honorable resolves. She will yield to his entreaties, before she is conscious of the extremity of her admissions. I must provide against this." Let us see what are his processes for effecting his objects.

Olivia was reclining upon a couch in the apartment opening upon the verandah. There Don Balthazar suddenly presented himself. She looked up at his appearance, with eyes full of so sad a reproach, that, had he been capable of a generous impression, would have made him instantly contrite. But he was not capable of the nobleness of self-reproach. A more cold, selfish, heartless nature, never dwelt in the breast of man. He took his seat beside her, and assumed his most conciliating manner.

"Well, my child, you are better, and I am glad to see it; but you have quite too many chattering visitors. They will only weary and distress you. The tongue of that silly wife of Tobar is enough to madden any invalid, and there are others of like sort, who do not so much desire to soothe or amuse, as to exercise their tongues and curiosity. What you want is peace and quiet."

"Peace and quiet! where am I to find them?"

"Why not? There is no reason why you should not find both, if you are only moderate in your expectations. It is the unreasonable and extravagant hopes of youth alone that keep peace and quiet from any bosom."

"Hopes! Do you really suppose that I entertain any hopes?"

"Indeed! Do you not? and why, if you entertain no hopes, do you encourage these painful and oppressive sensibilities, that keep you only in a continual agony?"

"It is for this very reason, that I can entertain no hopes, that these agonizing sensibilities are mine. But I surely need not say this to you"

"My dear child, do not deceive yourself. You do entertain hopes and expectations, and it is these that keep alive and active these moods and sensibilities. I know you better than you do yourself. You may deceive yourself, in moments of solitude, with the idea that you have nothing to live for. But events will be apt to put all these notions out of your head. You are now so much better that you will soon have other visitors."

"Who! what mean you?"

"Your Portuguese cavalier will soon be here, no doubt, and on his knees before you. It is inevitable, after what has taken place, that he will come, and must. He has fairly committed himself in the eyes of the world; he will soon find it necessary to complete his progress by a formal offer of his hand."

"And you think I will accept him?"

"Well; there is some danger of it. The truth is, my dear child, you are not the mistress of your own affections. He has too much enslaved your imagination to suffer you to escape him. You love him quite too intensely to reject his prayer."

"Alas! It is because I so much love him that I will reject him

I may be degraded, uncle—I am—and you well know why I am, and who has degraded me;—but I am not base! I will not sink lower in my own esteem, in doing such a terrible wrong to a nature so noble as that of the knight of Portugal, by uniting his honor with my shame!"

"Who knows that there is any shame?"

"God!"

"Ah! perhaps! But you have no apprehension that he will be at any pains to make it known?"

"I know not that. Guilt is ever in danger of exposure. Shame is like the cloud, that, whether the star will or will not, rises at any hour, with the winds, to blot its beautiful surface. But whether the world knows or not—whether God permits the truth to be revealed or not—alters not the case to me. It is enough that *I* know the terrible shame that hangs upon my soul like night. Enough, that I too much love Don Philip de Vasconselos to bestow my consciousness of ignominy upon him."

"This is all mere sentiment, my child."

"Sentiment! But you speak as if you really desired that I should wed with the knight of Portugal?"

"No! By Satan, no! I hate, I loathe the man, and I love you, my child. Never, with my consent, shall you take him to your arms."

"Why, then, leave it to doubt? Why impose upon me the task which you yet think me too weak to execute? Forbid him the house—forbid him the quest—and put an end to all your apprehensions."

"Would that process be effectual? No, no! my child, that will never answer. Our customs here, in Cuba, would not suffer it. What would everybody say of me? It would wrap me in a thousand strifes and embarrassments. Besides, Don Philip de Vasconselos would not suffer any such evasion; and the Adelantado would sustain him in the assertion of the right to see you. No! no! he must not be denied every opportunity, and the whole matter must be left to your own decision."

"That is already made! I can never be the wife of Don

Philip. Were I other than the thing I am, I should know no greater happiness. As I am, it is impossible that I should think of happiness, or should so wrong him in my desire for it, as to unite my grief and shame to his honor and his fortunes."

"And I repeat, you know not yourself. You have not the strength for this. You mean as you say, no doubt, now that you are comparatively calm, and when he is not present; but when he appears, and you see him before you—at your feet,—where will be your fine resolutions? You will yield. You will consent,—you will forget all your nice sentiments, and keep your secret, and be happy!"

"Leave me," she said calmly. "You do not know me. Still less do you know how you annoy and humble me. Enough for *you* that you are secure in *your* wishes, whatever may be mine. I cannot marry Don Philip; I *will* not; though I tell you frankly, that I should know no greater secret of happiness than this, were this possible. You have doomed me to loss of all! Leave me now."

"But you must take your medicine, Olivia."

"I will take nothing at your hands."

"Why not?"

"You have drugged me enough. I fear to drink—to eat—almost to breathe—knowing upon what poisons you have fed me."

"This is foolish. On my honor, you have nothing to fear now."

"Oh! if you asseverate so solemnly, I am sure there is danger! Take it away! I will not drink, though I perish."

"Obstinate! I tell you, this is the potion provided by the physician."

"It has passed through your hands."

"Am I poison?"

"Ay, death! worse than death! shame, horror, hell! Do not vex me;—leave me! I will trust you in nothing, I tell you! Is it not enough that you have destroyed every hope; would you torture me without a purpose?"

"You are mad! Is it torture that I should give you the very medicine which has been prescribed for you?"

"I am not sure that it is the same! You have the art to alter the nature of all things that approach me. You change the helpful to the hurtful—the good to the bad. By the Holy Virgin, uncle, were it not for the wrong that I should do to another, I should wed with the knight of Portugal, if only to find an avenger—to be sure of one to whom I might say—Slay me this monster, who has destroyed me, soul and body!"

Don Balthazar hurled the cup of physic to the floor, and with a look of the fiercest anger, and a half-muttered curse, he strode hastily out of the apartment.

"Thank God!" said the poor girl as he disappeared, "I breathe more freely!"

And she sunk into a long, sad revery; and the thought of Don Philip came to her, and brought with it fancies of the most bright and cheering felicity. She fancied him at her feet; she thought of herself in his arms. The world shut out, in the lone security of their mountain hacienda, she said to herself—"Surely this is happiness,—this is security and peace! And why," she asked of herself, "should I not enjoy this peace, this security, this happiness? What have I done that I should deny myself to live? Am I guilty of this crime—this shame? Is it mine? Am I not a wretched victim only of the toils, and the arts, and the superior powers of another? Have I, in my own soul, consented to this surrender of my innocence to the spoiler? Wherefore should I suffer more? Have I not suffered enough? Why should I not be happy with him I love, true to him ever, and never willingly false to Heaven or myself? It is a secret from all but one, this shame that is my sorrow; and that one, for his own sake, dare not whisper it to the bird that flies! Alas! alas! my heart, whither would you carry me? Would you have me abuse his noble trust for your pleasure? Oh! be still, lest in my weakness I commit a wrong as great as that which I have suffered!"

Such, in brief, were the prolonged meditations of the unhappy woman throughout the melancholy hours of her solitude. Her passion for Philip de Vasconselos was now perpetually suggesting to her mind fresh arguments against the virtuous resolution which, in cooler moments, had been the conclusion of her thought. She felt that her resolution was growing momently more and more weak; but still she combated herself; argued with her own thought, strove nobly against her heart, and all its really innocent desires, and bewildered finally, and exhausted, she surrendered herself at last to the dreamiest revery, such as naturally occurs to the sensuous nature, in the delicious climate in which she dwelt. In this revery, in which every breath was soft, every glance fair and wooing, every influence possessing the magic of a spell upon the affections, she found temporary refuge, against that severer virtue which counselled nothing less than self-denial and sacrifice! Ah! who is strong for such a sacrifice when every passion of the dependent and loving nature wars against it! Will Olivia de Alvaro be able to keep her vow, when Philip de Vasconselos bows before her? She trembles as she thinks of it; but still—she thinks of it! Her thought evermore recurs, after long wandering, to his expected coming! *Will* he come? will he *not?* Can he otherwise? And, should he come,—and when he comes,—then—shall she find the strength to say to him "depart!"—And should he linger—should he deny to go—should he ask "wherefore?"—what answer shall she make? Can she say, I have no love to give in return, when she really has nothing in her heart but love for him? And if she cannot, in truth, and from her heart say this, what plea shall justify her denial of his prayer? It is thus that she begins to conjure up, for her own conscience, the difficulties which stand in the way of her own self-sacrifice. It is thus that the ingenious passions argue the case with the honest thought. Which shall triumph in the end? Olivia de Alvaro is a most weak, most loving woman—she is passionate, too, with all the intense fires of the south. She means nobly, her thought is rightly advised; and she would act according to the dictates of a justly governed conscience; but, when the passions strive, what mind is strong against them?—

when the heart loves, with entire devotion, where are the thoughts which shall extinguish its glowing fires? As well say to the rising floods of ocean—"Sink back, with all your billows, and rest calmly in the bosom of your floods." The struggle between soul and heart, in the case of Olivia de Alvaro, is but begun. How will it end? Verily, there is very good reason why Don Balthazar should be apprehensive. Truly, he knows, better than his niece, how great is her weakness! But he will not leave her wholly alone, to fight the battle with her passions. He will frequently come mockingly to her succor, and, by torturing her pride into passion, will seek to subdue the force of other passions. He has all the subtlety of the serpent: will he use it successfully? It is very certain that he will spare no arts to defeat the hopes of the two young hearts, who, but for his evil working, had long since been rendered happy.

CHAPTER XXI.

"Hold thee: there's my purse. I give thee not this to suggest thee from thy master thou talkest of: serve him still."

ALL'S WELL THAT ENDS WELL.

THE public sports which the Adelantado had provided for the gratification of the people of Cuba were all finally ended. We have not thought proper to describe the amusements which followed on the third day, however interesting to the spectators; for the simple reason that they do not immediately affect the condition of our *dramatis personæ*. They still demanded the personal attendance of Don Balthazar de Alvaro, however, as warder of the field; and this gave a little respite to the suffering Olivia in her solitude. We have already noted an interview between the niece and her uncle, after the third day of the tournament; but there was one event, occurring at the close of that day, which it becomes us not to suffer to pass unnoticed. After the passages-at-arms, of all sorts, were fairly over, and the trumpets had merrily sounded the signals for the dispersion of the assembly—while the crowd, moving to and fro in all directions, resembled the shifting scenes of a panorama—Don Balthazar called to him an officer, and, speaking aside, said:

"Has the slave, Mateo, been taken—the mestizo, the matador, whose capture I confided to thy hands?"

"He has not Señor. He has eluded all our efforts."

"Thou hast suffered these sports to keep thee from thy duty; else, how should he escape thy search?"

"No, Señor——"

"It must be so, I tell thee; for the fellow is not likely to leave Havana so long as these amusements last; and there should be no places of hiding in the city which should be beyond the reach of a good officer! See to it! This night is all that is left thee to effect his capture. Half of these people will be off to the country by the dawn; he, probably, among them. Seek him at the tents and tables where they game. All of his class have a terrible passion for cards and dice. At the cockpits he may be found. He hath possibly brought with him some favorite birds from the country. He drinks, too, with a rare passion, which will no doubt carry him to the shops where the *aguardiente* is to be had. Get thee a dozen of thy fellows, well counselled, who know the man, and set them on the quest for him in all these places. If you take him, you shall all be well rewarded. If not, I shall endeavor to find officers who need no exhortation to their duty. There is no reason why he should not be found. He showed himself quite freely and fearlessly at the bull-fight, relying, I suppose, on certain changes of dress and costume. He is hardly in hiding any where, and, while in Havana, will no doubt be found at one or other of the places I have mentioned. Stint not your efforts, nor the numbers of your men, nor the needful money; and, if you take him, bring him to me at "the Grove;" at midnight, even; so that ye delay not after you have taken him. Enough! see to it, Diego, as you would be sure of my favors!"

"Señor, I will not sleep in this search."

"Good! to it at once, for he will doubtless soon leave Havana for the mountains."

The Hidalgo separated from the Alguazil, and both disappeared from sight. Within the same hour Don Balthazar might be seen riding, on a famous black charger, towards the retreat, without the city, where the Señorita, his niece, maintained her solitude. It was but a little before this, that the very outlaw, the mestizo slave, Mateo, might have been seen, on foot, pursuing the same route. The latter had fairly entered the woods, when he heard the sound of horse's feet behind him. He immediately sheltered himself from sight in a dense thicket of bamboo, and, from his place of retreat, beheld the knight ride slowly by. The outlaw grinned savagely as he perceived his old master, whom he remembered by numerous cruelties, such as, in that day, but too much distinguished the fierce warriors of Spain when dealing with their Indian and negro slaves. We have already mentioned that Mateo was a fugitive; having fled, not simply from the cruelty of his master, but from the consequences of his own crimes. He had murdered, in a sudden broil, one of the officers of the estate of the Señorita Olivia, to which, indeed, he belonged: the control of Don Balthazar over him resulting only from his being the guardian of his niece. From that moment, Mateo disappeared, having sought shelter in the contiguous mountains, which were, at that early period, entirely unexplored. He had been subsequently heard of, on several occasions, but only in the character of a robber. A price had been set upon his head, but he had always contrived to elude the pursuit of justice. His mother, the old woman Anita, in the employ of Don Balthazar, as we have seen, and the willing creature of his infamous arts and practices, had not forborne to plead the cause of her son; and she probably would have succeeded, long before her death, in procuring his pardon, could she have been successful in persuading Mateo to take the essential initiative in such a matter, by surrendering himself to the estate. But Mateo was not ready to incur such a peril, and distrusted all the assurances of the Don, whom he too well knew readily to confide in. Besides, the violent and brutal character of his passions kept him continually working against his own pardon, by the commission of new crimes and misdemeanors. Like all of his race, he was too fond of the pleasures of the crowd, and such as were promised by the exhibitions of the bull-ring and the tournament, to forego the temptation, at whatever hazard, of being a witness of the grand spectacles offered to the public by the magnificence of Don Hernan de Soto. But Mateo relied upon his disguises; upon the shaggy hair, the wild beard, and the strange costume which he wore; and upon the fact of a three years' absence from all the eyes that knew him. He felt himself sufficiently estranged from all eyes, and did not doubt that even his mother would fail to recognize her son. But he did too little justice to the keen sight and tenacious memory of Don Balthazar. Of the death of the old woman, Mateo had learned nothing until he reached Havana, a few days before. But, in that time, he had seen his sister, the sullen girl, Juana, on several secret occasions had heard all her tidings; had listened to all her complaints, and had decided upon the course to be pursued for attaining all necessary remedies for his own and her alleged wrongs. Of these remedies we shall learn hereafter. We need not say, perhaps, that he laughed at all the labors of his mother, in striving to procure his forgiveness, as a fugitive slave. He was one of those reckless persons, too savage for subjection, too indolent for toil, who prefer to appropriate the labors of others to the exercise of any of his own; and, by the strong hand, or sleight of hand, contrived to extract a very comfortable living out of a world which he thought good for nothing else. Now that he was in Havana, he was resolved to bring about the settlement of all his affairs in that city; and his own and sister's accounts promised to employ him actively for a time. His old master was his chief debtor; and, that he did not emerge from his bamboo shelter, and insist upon immediate payment, while the knight was passing, was simply because he thought it very possible that Don Balthazar did not carry a sufficient amount in funds about with him, to enable him to make satisfactory settlement. It would have been, otherwise, quite as easy to spring out from his hiding-place upon the Don, as, from the corridor into the bull-ring, giving the *coup de grace* to *El Moro!* The knight was suffered to proceed in safety to his house, whither Mateo followed more slowly, and not until the darkness had fairly covered the hacienda.

We shall suffer several hours to elapse without reporting their events; but we must suppose that they have not been suffered to pass unemployed either by the Hidalgo or the outlaw. Nay, we beg to state that both parties have been busy, though we do not just now care to go into a narrative of their several doings. Enough, that towards midnight Don Balthazar ceased from his labors for the night; and in his chamber, with his dressing-gown about him, and his limbs released in some degree from the gar ments worn throughout the day, he rests at length upon a wicker settee of bamboo, and meditates through the graceful clouds of aromatic smoke that ascend volume after volume from his much beloved cigar. Don Balthazar, though somewhat *blazé*, is yet not wholly insensible to the *good things* of this life, speaking only of the physical enjoyments. Indeed, it is to the *blazé* chiefly that the "creature comforts" rise into paramount value and estimation. It is when the purer tastes and the proper desires of the mind have been perverted, or abused, or lost, that one seeks recompense by appeals to appetites which, until then, are kept in honest subjection. Don Balthazar did not rely on his cigar wholly for his happiness; a flask of generous wine rested on a table beside him, from which, ever and anon, he replenished his goblet. He emptied it, perhaps, much more freely than he was aware. The troubles of his mind made him somewhat unconscious of the frequency of his potations, and their effects working favorably upon his mood, seemed to justify the appetite in still further seeking succor from this source. Don Balthazar had survived all the proper tastes. His appetites were wholly artificial. His tastes had become prurient; his passions had been succeeded by mere desires depending upon his diseased fancies. These, as chronic, always exert a tyrannous power over their possessor, and compel him to pursuits and objects which, in calm moments, seem wholly undeserving of any effort. A thousand times did the mere reason and common sense of the knight counsel him to throw off habits and desires which were equally evil and profitless; but in vain. A single moment of dreaming revery brought back the tyrannous fancies in all their power. The cigar, the wine,—these were potent influences, though unsuspected, in behalf of his evil moods; and his will no longer seconded the suggestion of his better moments. It would be doing him great injustice to say that he did not repeatedly deplore the weaknesses of his nature, and the crime and the cruelty of which it was the source. But his strength was not a strength in behalf of virtue. It was the strength of evil passions only—of passions arriving at sole power by reason of their un scrupulous exercise, and in their dying embers exerting a new and more evil sort of influence in consequence of their very decay and feebleness. He knew, and felt, and reproached himself at moments for his terrible abuse of authority and advantage in the case of his unhappy niece. He was sometimes made conscious of the awful spectre of his deceased brother, looking down upon him with loathing and anger, and the saddest reproach in his face; sometimes he fancied his voice in his ears, and at other times he beheld suddenly, as it were, a glimpse of the fierce visage of "the Biscayan mother" of Olivia, flaming with indignation, before his eyes. His conscience thus, at times, came to the assistance of his better reason, and filled him with virtuous resolution. But it is not easy for one accustomed for thirty years to give the full reins to his moods and passions, to re-conquer them and recover the ascendency of thought and will over habit. Habit is the most unbending of all mortal tyrannies, and the better genius of Don Balthazar struggled vainly against the appetites which he had so constantly fed in its despite. And now, when some better feelings were endeavoring to assert themselves in his bosom—when a lingering feeling of commiseration for the poor child whom he had so cruelly abused had prompted him to reflections upon his own selfishness, which, seeking a momentary and even mocking gratification, was destroying the very life of hope in the bosom of the girl—destroying her peace for ever, and all the gladdening impulses which make youth happy—he hardened himself against the kindlier impression by a recourse to some of those hard philosophies, which, in his case, had already overthrown all the authority as well of humanity as religion.

"What matters it," said he to himself, filling his goblet with a fresh supply from the wine-flask,—"what matters it in the end? These passions of love are in fact nothing but the caprices of fancy; a brief space will reconcile her to the loss of this knight of Portugal, whose youth, grace, and noble bearing are the only attractions; when he has fairly embarked for Florida she will forget him, and she will then remember me with as much tenderness as any other lover. She will feel that, though I have wronged her, it was because of my passion that I did so; and my love will justify in her mind the exercise of the power which I had upon her. If not, what is she but a woman, created for the pleasure and the delight of man; and why should she not minister to my delight as well as to another? Women, if well treated, kindly, and without neglect, readily reconcile themselves to the condition from which they cannot escape. She will hereafter consent willingly to that which she has vainly thought to oppose; and in the necessity of her case will become aware of what is grateful in it. Already, I think, she begins to improve. She grows milder every day. For a week she has exhibited none of those fitful bursts of passion which she inherited from that tigress mother; and her eyes, though they still look sadly and reproachfully, show no longer that fierce hate and loathing which distinguished them before. She grows pliant—she is yielding. Let me but baffle this knight of Portugal, and I have her wholly in my power. He must depart. She must reject his petition; and if not, then I must find a way to silence him forever."

Don Balthazar deceived himself in one thing. The mildness of Olivia's present aspect was scarcely in proof that she was now more reconciled to his power than before. We may say, in this place, that she was schooling herself to a more cunning policy—that she was opposing art to art, and was never more resolved, against her uncle, than at the moment when she appeared most resigned to her fate. Her game was to lull to sleep his vigilance by appearing more submissive. She was resolved to escape from his tyranny as soon as she might hope to do so with safety. As yet, however, she had formed no deliberate plan for doing so. She had vague projects and purposes in her mind, ill-defined and aimless at present; but, in any scheme, to quiet his suspicions and disarm his vigilance, were the first objects, necessary to the success of any other. These, in the end, might ripen into something definite and clear, and in the meantime, her policy was single, and thus far evidently successful. Don Balthazar was fatigued with a struggle which brought only fear and exhaustion even with its successes; and was quite willing to believe in the shows of resignation, on the part of his victim, by which he hoped to enjoy more easy triumphs.

As thus he lay, weaving conjectures, and hopes and doubts, in the most intricate meshes for his own fancy, he was surprised by a sudden and most unexpected visitor. But it becomes us to speak of the proceedings of this visitor, before we formally introduce him to our Hidalgo. We have seen that the fugitive, Mateo, was on his way, pursuing a like route with Don Balthazar, when the appearance of the latter drove the outlaw into shelter. He saw his ancient master speed forward, and followed him at his leisure. A little after nightfall, stationed in a lemon thicket near the dwelling, Mateo gave a signal whistle, and in a few minutes after, was joined by the servant girl, Juana. She was his sister; and, rude and sullen in her intercourse with all other persons, on him she bestowed nothing but tenderness and affection. Her whole deportment and character seemed to change on their meeting. She clung fondly to his neck; kissed him repeatedly; called him her dear brother, and would have continued her transports, had he not, with a sort of good-natured violence, shaken her off.

"That will do, that will do, Juana. There's no time now for kissing and foolishness. I have come for work. What can be done? Is there a good chance? Is there anybody in the house, any man body I mean, besides Don Balthazar?"

'No! nobody! There's my young lady, and the old hound, Sylvia; and there's the cook and Pedro; but she's in the kitchen, and Pedro is gone off somewhere. There's nothing to prevent, now."

"Well, you must show me a way to get in, and come suddenly upon the old woman. The master's in his room, eh?"

"Yes, he's planning some more wickedness, all to himself. Even if Sylvia was to cry out, he could hardly hear where he is; and you need'n't go near him at all."

"Ay, ay; but I *must* go near him. I've got some accounts to settle with him, now I'm here."

"Don't trust yourself with him, dear Mateo. He's got arms

in his room; matchlocks and guns, and sharp, bright swords He's never unprepared for mischief; and if he sets eyes on you, he'll shoot you."

"If I don't shoot him : but that's a game that two can play at just as well as one; and I hope to take him by surprise. I must try to do so. Don't you fear. I have arms too, just as well as he, and I know just as well how to use them; and I'm not afraid of his wickedness. I've got some of my own."

"And you will get all the things of poor mammy?"

"Won't leave a hair for the old hag that robbed you. You shall have everything. I'll have them carried off and hid away for you, where you can get them when you want them."

"But you will carry them with you to the mountains, Mateo."

"And how will you get the use of them there?"

"Why, ain't I to go along with you, brother?"

"You go along with me? to the mountains? Why what would you do there, poor child?"

"Why, live with you, and take care of your home for you.'

"Home!" with a fierce chuckle. "I have no home. I am never a week in one place together. I pass from mountain to mountain; and hide in one cave after another; and go in all sorts of weather; and sleep twenty nights under the open sky, where I sleep once in a human cabin. The outlaw has no home, no place where he can sleep in safety; except where the wild beast keeps watch for him along the mountain-top, and frightens off the pursuer."

"I don't care, Mateo! I am not afraid! I want to go with you wherever you go, and I'll live with you, and work for you, and *fight* for you, too; just as if I were a man and not a woman."

"Well, I suppose you *can* fight; you've got the strength for it, and I reckon you're not afraid; but——"

"And I may go with you?" eagerly.

"No, Juana, child. Not just yet. I'll come for you, whenever I'm ready for you, and can fix you in some certain place."

"Oh! but I do so want to get away from *this* place. You don't know what I suffer. It's only a week ago that my Lord beat me with his whip over my face and shoulders."

"Pooh! Pooh! what of that! Do you suppose if you were with me, I shouldn't beat you too when you deserved it?"

"But I didn't deserve it, Mateo."

"Oh! that's all nonsense. Women always deserve a whipping, and should get it once or twice a week to keep 'em sensible and proper. You don't know when you're well off. With me, you'd want bread often enough; and there would be no safety. You'd have to start out of your bed at midnight, to fly, when you hear the bloodhounds barking up the hills. It's sometimes monstrous hard for me to get off. How would it be with you? You'd be caught by the dogs. You'd be torn to pieces; or I'd have to risk my own life to save you. Then, if you fell into the hands of the hunters, you'd be a thousand times worse off than ever. They'd send you to the Calabooza, and sell you to a hard master, who'd put you into the fields, and whip the blood out of your body, and the very heart out of your bosom. You'r well off as you are. You've got a good mistress, and a comfortable place, and plenty to eat and drink. But the master beats you, you say. Well, once in a way, perhaps he does; but that does you no harm. I'd have to beat you ten times as much, Juana, if you were with me. 'Twould be for your good, I'd do it. I'd know you wanted it; I know you of old. You'd be the last person in the world to try and quit this place, if it hadn't spoiled you. You've been treated too well here; that's the whole of it. You're best off where you are; I know all about it. I'd have been better off at the hacienda from which I ran away, but that I was a bad fellow, who couldn't be satisfied anywhere, and would rather steal than work. It's easier to me, and I feel better after it. But I know it's not the best thing for me; and I know it would be the very worst thing for you. It's because I love you as my sister, Juana, that I'd rather you'd stay with the Señorita, and be honest and quiet. *She's* good to you, *I know*. No! No! you cannot go with me. Just now, you'd only be in my way, and in the way of danger and all sorts of trouble. But I hope soon to get a safe hiding-place, and then, if you'r ready and willing, I'll take you off. For the present you must keep where you are."

It was in this way that the outlaw answered the entreaties of his sister. He, no doubt, came to a right conclusion on the subject. But she was not satisfied, and submitted sullenly to the authority with which she had never been accustomed to contend.

"But," she added, as a last argument,—"it's not the Señorita only; she's to be married, they say, and there's to be a new master."

"Well: he won't eat you! There can't be any worse than Don Balthazar; and no master in the world will hurt the slave that serves him faithfully. He'd be a fool to do it."

"But I don't like a new master; and I don't like to be under a master that's a Portuguese."

"Ho! it's one of the Portuguese that she is to marry! Well, if it's the one that tumbled the handsome cavalier, Nuno de Tobar, she'd be well officered. He's a noble soldier, I warrant—rides a horse, and handles a lance, as if he was made for nothing else. If I were sure that Don Balthazar would not go to the country of the Apalachians, I'd volunteer to go in this same knight's company. But if he went, he'd be sure to find me out in time. I could serve such a man as the Portuguese, and cheerfully acknowledge him my master. Every man, I think, is born to have a master, and is never quite happy till he finds the right one. I like this knight of Portugal. I don't see what you've got to be afraid of if he marries your lady."

"Ah!" said the girl stealthily,—"he'd never marry *her*, if he only knew what I know."

"What do you know?—But if it's any harm of *her*, Juana, don't say it, for your life. The Señorita, you say, has always been good to you. Don't you turn upon her like a snake. Hush up, and keep her secrets, as if they were your own."

"Well, it ain't so much her secret as my Lord's! Oh! Mateo, if you knew what a born devil he is, and how he's killing the poor young lady—murdering her very soul and body!"

"Ha!" exclaimed the outlaw, musingly—"Ha!" A new

ight seemed to dawn upon him; and he paused, and laid his hand upon Juana's shoulder. "I see! Don't you say a word more! Don Balthazar—but no matter. Show me now how to muzzle this old hag, Sylvia."

In a few moments, the two had disappeared within the dwelling.

CHAPTER XXII.

'Here be rare plottings. There's more mischief in that one head, and that oily tongue than in all the country."

THE PARSON.

SYLVIA, that arch beldame, as Juana esteemed her, in the sovereignty of her domain, below stairs, was, at this moment, in the enjoyment of her highest felicity. She had a good supper before her; her toils of the day were ended, and she was congratulating herself upon the ease and security with which she could command all the comforts which were necessary to the creature. Supper over, she would sleep, and the dreams that would follow might reasonably be expected to be all very pleasant ones. But Fortune plays fine tricks with human securities, and the Fates are always busy to thwart pleasant anticipations; making no sort of difference between those of the nobleman and those of the drudge. Humble as was Sylvia's secret of happiness, it was destined to disappointment; and care nestled in the cup, the grateful beverage of which she was about to carry to her lips. In this very moment, the cruel and capricious fortune, in the aspect of the mestizo, Mateo, stood quietly behind the old woman, prepared to cast the sack over her head. Suddenly she felt a rude gripe of huge, strange fingers about her throat, utterly denying her the privilege to scream ;—almost to breathe! Hardly had she been thus surprised, when a shawl was passed about her jaws, effectually shutting out the supper, and just as effectually shutting in all sound. She strove desperately to shriek, but the voice died away in a hoarse but faint gurgling in her throat. She was in the hands of an adroit enemy. Mateo was dexterous in his vocation. He had enjoyed some practice in his outlawed life. The eyes of the old woman were soon enveloped in another bandage, and as completely denied to see, as her mouth to speak or swallow. A stout cord was then passed about her arms, and thus rendered *hors du combat*, she might be trusted safely. Every obstacle was thus removed from the way of the conspirators, and Mateo now gave the signal for the appearance of Juana, who, till this moment, had kept in the background. She was not long in showing herself. Mateo, in the meanwhile, coolly took his place at the table which bore the supper of Sylvia, and his appetite being invigorated, we may suppose, by long abstinence and previous toils, he proceeded to its demolition in a manner which would have shocked the true proprietor, could she have seen. She suspected no doubt what was in progress, but there was no remedy. She had to submit with as much resignation as she could command.

Meanwhile, Juana was otherwise busied in making inquest into the secrets of the prison-house. Mateo soon joined her, and the leading purpose of the conspirators was soon made apparent. There were closets thrown wide, and boxes torn open. All the goods and chattels, the accumulations of old Anita, to which Sylvia had so quietly succeeded, were brought out from their hiding-places. One may conjecture the variety of treasures which had been accumulated by both these ancient beldames, in the course of half a century of peculation. But the details must be left to conjecture. Our purpose is not a catalogue. Mateo and Juana were equally busy. The latter knew where to look, and the former how to secure. His *machete* did good service in forcing open boxes; and every sack which could be found, was appropriated to the compact accumulation of the scattered treasures. Slung upon the broad, strong shoulders of the outlaw, they disappeared one by one; transferred, in brief space, from the house to the adjoining woods, where, it seems, the mestizo had seasonably provided a sort of cart for their better conveyance to other hiding-places. The work was done by a practiced hand, and very effectually.

Sylvia could readily conjecture what was going on, but she was only able to groan and grieve internally. She did not remain passive, however, and rose up, blinded and muzzled, and corded as she was, with more than one effort to interfere. It was only by one or two emphatic exhortations from the heavy fists of the outlaw, that she was persuaded of the better policy of submitting, without farther struggles, to her fate.

Supposing this work to be fairly over, and Mateo in full possession of all his mother's chattels; perhaps of others also, to which that amiable woman could never assert any claim, the outlaw found it becoming to transfer his attentions to another of the household. His next work was with the master.

We have seen that Don Balthazar de Alvaro was disposed to indulge in a somewhat meditative mood; one, however, in which conscience was allowed to play only a subordinate part to philosophy. The pleasant fumes of the cigar, the grateful potency of the wine-flask, the genial sweetness of the climate, had together, as we have seen, induced finally a very grateful condition of revery, in which the thoughts of the mind accommodated themselves, with a rare condescension, to the humors of the body. The result was a condition of complacent happiness, which was stripped of all apprehensions. There were no clouds in his sky, that he could perceive; and for the troubles of his hearth, it was surprising how slight they seemed, and how soon they were dispersed, as he meditated his good fortune, his own resources, and brought the energies of his will to bear upon the future. It was only to get Philip de Vasconselos out of his path;—and for this object he had several schemes, even if the love-sick damsel should fail to assert her virtuous resolution to reject him;—to get Olivia out to her plantation, and under proper surveillance there; and then for the gold regions of the Apalachian, and one or two campaigns. His ambition was not asleep during all these speculations. His appetites demanded free floods of gold; he required captive red men for slaves; he had fancies of royal favor, and did not see why he, too, should not become the Adelantado of newly-discovered and treasure-yielding provinces. It is rarely that ambition is satisfied with a single field of conquest. It throws out its antennæ in all directions; it grasps wide, right and left, and baits for all the fish in the sea; is as eager after power as money;

after slaves as conquest; after love, or lust, as in the soul-starving search after gold. Don Balthazar, reclined on his cane sofa, head thrown back, cigar in mouth, and wine-flask at his elbow, was in the enjoyment of a great variety of very grateful anticipations. How the coldest and sternest of men may become dreamers, it is scarcely necessary to insist, with the experienced reader.

It was the very moment when his dreaming mood was most active, and most serenely secure in the possession of the most teeming fancies, that Mateo, the outlaw, chose for appearing in the presence of the knight. Now, we must do the mestizo the justice to say that it was no part of his design to disperse the pleasant fancies of the Don, or to overthrow the castles of delight and strength which his imagination was erecting. To Mateo it would be of no sort of moment, how wildly, or how pleasantly, the knight might dream. He might smile contemptuously upon such employments, but that he should deliberately set himself in hostility to the worker for their overthrow, is really not to be thought of. Bad fellow as he undoubtedly was, Mateo was not so malicious. He had very different, and more solid purposes. If, in his prosecution of these, the dreams of Don Balthazar happened to be dispersed, the evil was unintended; and, we have no doubt, if properly apprised of what he had unwittingly done, he would have expressed his devout contrition. Certainly he little conjectured of what a golden domain he dispossessed his ancient master in the course of a very little space of time.

Mateo entered the apartment of the Hidalgo without disturbing his revery. He did not enter, after the fashion of ordinary visitors, through the door. Mateo was no ordinary outlaw. Not that he preferred the more laborious process of ascending a column of the verandah and climbing in through the window. But simply because the door was bolted on the inside. Don Balthazar was a man of precautions—a politician who knew that reveries were not properly to be enjoyed, unless with all reasonable securities first taken. That he left his window unfastened, which opened upon the verandah, was simply to admit the breeze, and he never once fancied that his reveries could render him oblivious to the approach of any less light-footed visitor. He was mistaken. Mateo made his way in, without disturbing his sense of security. Not that he was not heard. Don Balthazar was sensible to the rustling of the orange-tree beside the verandah; he heard the branches scrape rather roughly upon the column. But that might be occasioned by the puff of wind that smote just then gratefully over his brow and bosom; and so believing, his eyes were shut, and the thick volume of smoke went up from his cigar, increasing in mass as the exciting vision of future lordships in Florida rose before his imagination.

On a sudden he was awakened to full consciousness. His atmosphere grew heavier. It seemed as if his fancies found some obstruction, and could no longer spread their wings as freely as before. He felt as if there were some antagonist influence in his sky, which had suddenly darkened all his bright stars. And this consciousness certainly preceded the opening of his eyes. He had not yet opened them, when his ears were saluted with the tones of a strange speaker, and in language well calculated to startle and drive him from his world of visions.

"Well, I must say, your Excellency, that you are very comfortable here."

We have preferred putting the *patois* of our mestizo into tolerably correct language, taking for granted that the reader will readily suppose that there were certain differences between the speech of the outlaw and his superior. This will suffice for explanation. We have no taste for that sort of literature which makes the vulgar speak viciously, when what they have to say can as well be said in tolerable phrase and grammar.

Don Balthazar forgot to smoke. The cigar dropped from his opening lips. His eyes unclosed. His head was partly raised. Never did visage more express confounding wonderment. There, quietly seated on the settee directly opposite, was the outlaw, whom he had given it in charge to his alguazils to arrest. How came he there? Was he not in bonds? Were the alguazils in waiting? They had probably taken the fugitive, and were at hand. All these conjectures, and many others, passed through the brain of the Hidalgo in a single moment of time. But they were dismissed as rapidly as conceived. The outlaw had no appearance of constraint. He looked rather like a conqueror than a captive. There were no chains about his body or his wrist. Never sat mortal so perfectly at his ease, his great bulk covering half of the slight cane settee of which he had taken possession. There was a good-natured mockery, too, in his face, that betrayed no sense of inconvenience. It was evident, at a second glance, that he was not only no prisoner, but not aware, himself, of any risk of becoming one. There was a great knife in his belt, conspicuous, which the eyes of Don Balthazar fastened upon. It was the very weapon with which the matador had slain the bull. The Don began to feel uneasy.

"Who is that?" he inquired; though he need not have done so; for he knew the intruder the instant he set eyes upon him.

"Don't your Excellency know?"

"No!—who?"

"Your Excellency has a bad memory for old acquaintance. Don't you remember Mateo, that once belonged to the estate of Don Felix?"

"You?"

"Yes, Señor, the same! I was a bad fellow, you know, and wouldn't work. Work don't suit me. If it hadn't been for that, I'd have kept on the estate forever, for I rather liked the place, and the living was very good. But it's too hard to have to work for the bread one eats, and I always preferred to take it where I could get it without work. I don't object to other people doing all the work they can. It's necessary, perhaps;—some must do it, indeed, where all must feed; but I am for leaving it to those that like it. I don't like it, and as long as I can get my bread without digging for it, I'll do so."

"You killed Pedro Gutierrez?"

"Exactly: because he would make me work! It was all his fault. I warned him that I wouldn't work; that it didn't agree with me; that I didn't like it. He tried to force me, and blows followed; and he got the worst of them. If he was killed, he brought it on his own head."

"You are a murderer, and an outlaw."

"Good words, your Excellency,—good words! What's the use of fouling your Excellency's mouth with bad ones? I don't care much about words at any time; but sometimes they make me angry. I don't want to be angry now, as I'm in a special good humor, and there's no need to quarrel with old acquaintance. I have not seen you so long that it does me real good to look upon you. Your Excellency don't seem to be much changed. There's a little more of the salt in your hair, your Excellency, and it shows a little in your beard, now that you let it grow so long. You should use some of our black root die, which will make the hair as young as when you were only twenty!"

The blood of the knight was boiling in his veins. But he tried to be cool, and with great apparent calmness, said—

"Do you know, Mateo, that if you are once taken you will be garoted without trial?"

"One must take the tiger, your Excellency, before you can draw his teeth."

"But they will take you! You cannot resist a dozen men—a troop—an army. Now, I happen to know that you have been heard of in Havana, and that the alguazils are in search of you."

"Ah! well! They will hardly look for me here, your Excellency, and I shall not be here very long. I shall soon be off for the mountains. Meanwhile, I must take my choice. Alguazils are very fine trencher men, but scarcely of much account where the only feed is steel and bullet. I shall probably escape from these of Havana."

"But what brings you here now?"

"Well, you're something concerned in the affair, though perhaps you don't know it. I heard of the death of my poor mother, Anita ——"

"Ah! yes; true, she was your mother."

"I rather think your Excellency ought to know, since you've been promising the old woman to get me pardoned for a long time past. I suppose you had good reasons for not keeping your promise."

"Yes; your mother knew. I told her that no pardon was possible until you should come in."

"Very clear, your Excellency; and now that I've come in, you tell me that the alguazils are already looking after me, and that I shall be garoted if caught. How do the two stories tally, your Excellency?"

"To come in and surrender, is quite a different thing from coming in as you do now."

"Perhaps so; but it don't matter much any way. As for my surrender, your Excellency, before I have the pardon under the seal of the king's governor, it's not to be talked of, it's so foolish."

"Then what brings you now?"

"Ah! I was telling you. My mother died, your Excellency very suddenly, nobody knows how. I hear that she was poisoned, Señor."

"From whom do you hear this?"

"That's not necessary to be said. She was poisoned, and have to find out the poisoner and settle with him "—here he handled his *machete*. "It's his blood or mine, your Excellency."

This was said with significant emphasis, and such a look as showed the Don that he himself was the object of suspicion.

"But suppose she was poisoned by a woman?"

"Then it's only a little harder upon my conscience, and I must use a smaller knife than this. But what woman, your Excellency?"

"Nay, I do not *know* by whom the deed was done. I have a suspicion only."

"Your Excellency's suspicions are like to be as good as another man's evidence. Was it the woman Sylvia?"

"No, I think not; and as I suspect only, I cannot say."

"The thing *must* be found out, your Excellency. I am not the man to let my mother be baited, like a dog we hate, with poisoned beef. Your Excellency will find it necessary to give me help in this discovery. You have not done right by me. You let this woman Sylvia take possession of all my mother's property."

"Property! Why, what property had your mother? She was a slave!"

"Yes, by the laws, I know; but your Excellency knows I don't mind laws, and have my own. Now, I have already taken possession of all my mother's property."

"The devil you have!"

"Exactly; I took possession just an hour ago. I tied up the old hag below——"

"You have not murdered the woman?"

"No! . Only tied her up, hand and tongue. You will find her after I am gone rather stiff in her limbs, and feeling the want of her supper, which I have eaten. The goods I have carried off already, and the plunder, were worth having, I assure you. There will be fine sights of treasure in the mountains when I get back.'

The knight grew more and more uneasy. The cool insolence of the outlaw was almost intolerable. He looked about him with impatience, and his eyes turned involuntarily to the wall upon which he had hung his sword and dagger. To his surprise they were gone. How had they been taken away? It was evident that Mateo had been in the chamber already that night, or some emissary; and he found himself completely in the power of the ruffian. Don Balthazar did not lack for courage; but the gigantic frame of his companion discouraged at a glance the momentary impulse which he felt suddenly to spring upon and grapple with him; and he now gazed upon the person whom he feared with an eye of vacancy. Mateo seemed to read his thoughts. He had followed his glance to where the weapons had been wont to hang, and divined his feelings. The outlaw laughed securely, with a bold, honest chuckle of security and triumph.

"'Twont do, your Excellency; the game's in my hand. I could strangle you in a moment, and slit your pipe before you could make any music out of it. But that's not what I want to do. I'll not be hard upon you; that is, if it is not by you that the old woman was poisoned. I don't say 'twas you, but I have my thoughts. I know you deal in poisons sometimes, and I've got a trail to some of your secrets. What do you think now of the Señorita, the Lady Olivia? She's a beauty, I know; —but what do you think?"

The knight winced.

"I certainly think with you. She is a beauty."

"Ah! Don Balthazar, what a pity it is that you are her uncle, and that your hair is so salty!"

"Hark ye, Mateo!" said the Hidalgo, suddenly rising to his feet.

"Sit down," cried the outlaw imperatively, and putting his hand to his knife. "You can talk, and I can hear just as well when both of us sit."

"Do you think I mean to harm you?"

"Oh! no! that you can't. I could settle your accounts in a moment; but don't want the trouble of it. I want you to get my pardon, I tell you, for I want to be free to come and go where I please. I am sometimes cut off from a good bull-fight and a *festa*, because of the trouble with the alguazils."

"You want a pardon, do you?"

"Exactly; and something more, your Excellency. I said that I liked the sort of living at the old estate, and I should like it still if I had no work to do. Now, what I want of you is not only to get me a pardon, but to make me overseer for tl estate of the Señorita."

"Demonios! What more does your modesty require?"

"Very little after that."

"Put the wolf to take care of the sheep, eh?"

"Not quite so bad as that, your Excellency. The fact is, you can't do a better thing for the interests of the estate. It's a good rule to set a thief to catch a thief; and the man that won't work is either too lazy or too knowing. Now, your Excellency, it's not because I'm lazy that I won't work. It's because I'm too proud; and I'm too proud because I'm too knowing. I can make others work, and I know as well as any man how the work ought to be done. Try me, and you shall see. If you had tried me before instead of putting a blind bull over me, you'd have done better, and Pedro Gutierrez would never have had his skull opened suddenly, to his great disgrace showing that he had no brains in the shell. Many a man don't do, and won't do, because the right work is not given him, and the right confidence. Now, do you try me, and you'll see what I can do. Make me your overseer, get my pardon made out with the royal seal, and give my sister to live with me, and you will find Mateo as faithful as a dog. Refuse me, and you keep me the tiger and the outlaw that you have made me."

Rapid were the thoughts which coursed through the knight's brain. The philosophy of the outlaw began to strike him favorably. He reflected—"This fellow can be bought. He will do any service in return for these things. He will strike my foe, as coolly as butcher smites ox; he will obey my finger without questioning. I leave for Florida. Olivia retires to the hacienda. There, he is supreme in my absence. Ah! well! I see!"

Then aloud:

"'Pon my soul, Mateo, you are moderate in your wishes. But suppose I comply with them?"

"It will be wise!"

"Perhaps so! But are you prepared to show your devotion to him who will do for you all this?"

"Am I prepared to make a profitable bargain?"

"Suppose there be a hateful serpent in my path?"

"I will put my heel upon his head!"

"Suppose there be a wolf in my close?"

"I will put my knife across his throat!"

"A mad bull, fierce as El Moro, and as strong?"

"Here is the very machete that slew El Moro!"

"It shall be done! Fill yourself a cup of wine, and we will speak farther of this matter. We understand each other. It is a bargain between us!"

CHAPTER XXIII.

*"This day is ominous,
Therefore, come back."*

TROILUS AND CRESSIDA.

It will not be difficult to conjecture what were the terms which Don Balthazar was prepared to make with the outlaw, or the character of the services which the latter was to render, by which to secure the pardon which he desired and the office which he claimed The knight saw, in the appearance of Mateo, the means by which to relieve himself from all danger at the hands of Philip de Vasconselos. He was one of those persons who readily adapt the tool to their uses which offers itself most readily to their hands; and saw, at a glance, in what way the outlaw could promote his purposes. We are not now to be told that he was a man of few scruples when he was eager for his objects; his fears and virtues equally failing to suggest considerations of doubt to a very ductile conscience. Strange to say, the conditions which he demanded of the outlaw, were not so readily accepted by this person. Mateo was not without his own rude virtues. He had been impressed with the knightly graces and valor of Vasconselos—had seen with delight his wonderful skill in the tournament, and had hailed his successes as if he shared in them. Besides, he was aware of the isolation of the Portuguese cavalier, and well knew the reluctance with which the Spaniards had acknowledged his superiority. Mateo had too little of the Spanish blood in him to feel with them, and adversely to one whose isolation so much reminded him of his own; and he gave him his sympathies on this account, as well as because of his valiant bearing. But he was a person in a situation which did not suffer him to withstand the tempter; and, though slowly and reluctantly, he, at length, yield ed to the temptation. He was bought by the promise of pardon, and the hope of reward; and consented to become the assassin of the knight of Portugal. That night he confided the whole secret to his sister, Juana, expecting her to be gratified with an arrangement which promised him security and trust, and freedom to herself. But he was confounded to find that she saw the affair in a very different aspect.

"Don't you believe Don Balthazar, my brother!" said the girl. "He has some snare for your feet. It was because you had him in your power that he made this bargain with you. He keeps terms with no one; and I am only afraid that he throws dust in your eyes, while he puts the alguazils upon your footsteps! Besides, you don't know what a noble gentleman this knight of Portugal is."

"Don't I, then! Haven't I seen him with lance and sword; on horse and foot; and don't I know how these Spaniards hate and fear him? Jesu! It did my heart good to see how he carried himself;—how he managed the horse and lance, and made the sword fly, here and there, at every point in the heavens, wherever the enemy attacked. Oh! but I *do* know him, and I was very loth to promise to lift knife against his breast!"

"And why did you do it?"

"*Demonios!* What was I to do? Here was my own pardon offered me, your freedom, and the whole charge of the hacienda."

"You will get none of these! Don Balthazar means only to betray thee. He wishes, no doubt, to get this knight of Portugal out of his way; for there are precious reasons, my brother, why he should fear the presence of the Portuguese. Ah! if thou knew'st! But when thou hast done the service, then will he be the first to denounce thee. He is a bitter traitor. His whole life is a treachery. His heart is full of serpents. He has lied to thee with sweetness, and thou hast tasted of the sweetness till thou dost not feel the poison! He is a poisoner! Ah! if thou knew'st! Know I not that he keeps many poisons in his closet? Did I not tell thee that our mother died by poison? Whence did it come?"

"He says a woman poisoned her."

"A woman! He might just as well have said that I did it, or the Lady Olivia. There was none other to do it; for Sylvia came hither only after our mother was dead. No! no! Mateo, *he* was the poisoner, be sure; and thou hast sold thyself to do this bad man's bad work, making the good man thy victim, only to feed on his poison thyself, when thou little dream'st of such danger!"

"Hush up, child! He dare not deceive me! Let him try it! Let me but find him at his treachery, and I will slit his throat with a whistle."

"Ah! if he be not too quick for thee. I nothing doubt that he will have the alguazils upon thy steps before another day is over."

"I shall keep mine eyes about me, girl; and, hark thee, I shall hide here in these thickets, and thou shalt feed me from the house. They will never dream of looking for me here. I know the hours when to steal forth, but hither will I come to sleep. Dost thou hear?"

"Yes! It is best, perhaps. The plan is a good one. But thou wilt not kill this knight of Portugal to pleasure this bad man?"

"It must be done! I will do as I have said; and if Don Balthazar, then, does not as he hath sworn to me, I will cut out his lying tongue, and he shall see me eat it ere he dies!"

We need not farther pursue the conference, which ended in an arrangement by which the outlaw, unknown to any but Juana, was to find his nightly refuge, in the groves and harboring places belonging to the grounds of the knight's own dwelling, and be supplied with food at her hands. He was also to time carefully his moments of sallying forth; and it was deemed only a proper precaution that Don Balthazar was not to know where he harbored, or be permitted any knowledge of his movements; at all events, until it was certain that Juana's suspicions were groundless.

This conference took place outside of the house, and among

the thick groves by which it was environed. While it was in progress, Don Balthazar contrived to find his way into the domain of Sylvia, and free her from her unpleasant bandagings. He affected great surprise at her condition, and gave her no clues to the secret of it. Nor, while he was present, did she conjecture who was the bold ruffian by whom she had been plundered. But scarcely had the knight retired, when she received a gleam of intelligence from a simple discovery enough. The bandage about her eyes was a scarf which she had often seen in the possession of Juana—that, or one very much like it. Now, where one is disposed to dislike, or suspect, the proofs rapidly accumulate. This discovery, though by no means conclusive—since the ruffian might very well have caught up, and made use of, the scarf of the innocent serving-maid—yet set the memories and wits of old Sylvia busy. She saw the mystery at a glance. Was not Mateo the brother of Juana;—was not Mateo an outlaw;—and had she not heard that Mateo had been seen in the bull-fight, and that her excellent master—ever to be honored—had actually set certain alguazils upon his footsteps? Nay, did not Don Balthazar, only two nights before, give her warning to keep a close eye upon Juana, for that the outlaw, her brother, was at hand? And, O, shame to her prudence, had she not been too careless of this counsel; and was it not for this very incautiousness that she had fallen a victim to the robber! Now it was that she remembered the frequent stealthy absences of the girl at night—her window open—her chamber empty—and a hundred other matters; which, in her present keen suspicions, were proofs like holy writ—confirmations strong—not to be gainsayed in any court of justice.

Sylvia was resolved in her suspicions. They were clear enough as proofs. "And now," mused the sagacious old woman, "how to recover my property—how to enjoy my revenges! I see through the whole affair. Juana harbors her brother *here!* Truly, a most excellent notion, that of making the house of the most noble knight, Don Balthazar, the place of refuge for the very outlaw whom he has sent the alguazils to find! But I will be too much for them both—they shall see! they shall see!"

Her plans were soon devised, and the very next morning, bright and early, she sallied forth on some professedly innocent pretences. We need not follow her footsteps, but content ourselves with reporting, in brief, the object of her expedition. It was to seek out the alguazils—the chief of them, rather—and bestow upon him the benefit of her discovery. She made an effort to see Don Balthazar, and to enlighten him on the subject; but, to her surprise, he seemed to have left the hacienda after relieving her of her bonds. He did not again, that night, occupy his own chamber; possibly, because of its assumed insecurity; and during the day following, he did not re-appear. He was busy in the city.

Meanwhile, what of Olivia—the poor victim, torn by love on the one hand, by a bitter consciousness of wrong and shame on the other; by passions which she could not control, by fears which she dared not name; by vague, vain hopes, which fluctuated in a sort of shadowy existence in her soul, keeping her restless, dreaming of possibilities, and the most mocking fancies, which left her, half the time, in the greatest uncertainty of reason! Her health seemed to improve, however, and, though pale and sad as ever, there were symptoms of better spirits and a greater cheerfulness. Love itself was her only stimulant, while it was also one of her most disturbing griefs. The image of Philip de Vasconselos was ever present to her imagination, coming always clothed with promise. The more she reflected upon the probability of his addressing her, the more she began to doubt of her own strength to say him nay. But, even then, her conscience smote her with the criminality of consent; and she would thus sink back into hopelessness and sorrow. But why was it that he came not? To this inquiry, which again suggested a painful doubt of her conquest—painful still, though she had resolved to reject his suit—her lively friend, Leonora de Tobar, brought a sufficiently explanatory answer. He was close in attendance upon, and anxious for the safety of, his sick brother. Now, how ever, that Andres was out of danger, Olivia might look to see him soon. She spent that morning with the unhappy damsel, and her lively prattle alternately cheered and depressed her. When she was gone, Olivia made her toilet with more than usual care. Why? The words of Leonora assured her that she might surely look for Don Philip's coming soon—that very day perhaps; and it was with an interest which the poor girl dared not acknowledge to herself, that she arrayed her charms to the best possible advantage; and gazed with a sorrowful sort of satisfaction into the mirror which reflected them to her eyes. Then she sighed, with the sudden rush of her fancies from the seat of conscience, rebuked by the stern judgment of that sacred monitor.

"Wherefore," she murmured to herself; "wherefore this beauty—this solicitude to appear beautiful in his eyes? Alas! my soul, I cannot do him this great dishonor. I can never doom his noble heart to such infamy as embrace of me will bring!"

She sank away from the mirror—she threw herself upon her couch, and buried her face within her hands. The next moment the girl, Juana, was gazing upon her with a look of sympathizing interest, which touched her soul. The girl looked into the chamber only to disappear.

"*Madre de Dios!*" Olivia murmured to herself: "Can it be that she knows—that she suspects?"

And with the doubt, the apprehension grew to terror.

"I am at the mercy, O! Heavens, of the meanest slave!"

The fear was followed by an agonizing burst of grief! The day was one of perpetual doubts and apprehensions. But it passed away without events. Vasconselos did *not* appear, as Leonora had conjectured, and as Olivia had hoped—and feared! Her doubts and fears grew strengthened. If her secret was in the possession of the slave, Juana, it was a secret no longer! That it should have reached the ears of Philip, was her new terror! It prostrated her for awhile! Half the night was passed in tears and terrors, which were so many agonies. She could bear his loss—she could be content to give him up forever—but that he should *know* her shame; that his noble soul should become conscious of the deadly stain upon hers—*that* she could never bear, and live! She prayed for death. In her secret thought arose a vague feeling, which brought, and commended to her, the fatal poison, with which, unwittingly, her hand had bestowed death upon Anita. Were there not other drops of silence, and sleep, and safety in that fatal phial? Where was it? She would look for it! She would find it, and at the worst, she would *sleep;* and all these terrible agonies of thought would have an end! In the deep stillness of the midnight hour, the unhappy damsel resolved on suicide. But there were other drops of bitterness in her cup of misery, which she was yet to drink to the dregs. Let us not anticipate, but follow the fortunes of other persons of our drama.

Sylvia had made her way to the alguazils, and had put them in possession of all the clues which she had procured, leading to the pathways and hiding-places of the outlaw, Mateo. Once roused to suspicion, she had found numerous reasons for confirming her in her conjectures. She noted all the outgoings of Juana. She watched her with secrecy, and comparative success; and though she did not see Mateo, she yet arrived at a very shrewd notion of the thickets in which he might be found. The hacienda which Don Balthazar and his niece occupied, though smaller than the estate which he cultivated for her, was yet one of considerable range in grove and forest. It had numerous dim avenues of shade and silence. There were solitary walks which no one frequented. There were hollows among the wooded hills which might have harbored a hermit. It seems that Mateo knew the place. He possessed himself of its various haunts; and, but for the too eager desire of Juana to seek him out, and be with him when there was no necessity for it, the old woman would probably never have guessed his propinquity. Had the girl been content to seek him only at night, and to carry him food but once in the twenty-four hours, and then under cover of the darkness, he had been safe. But the girl loved her brother.

and was very proud of his prowess. Besides, after the death of Anita, she needed the solace of association with the only kinsman left her. She gratified this desire, and sought to gratify him, twenty times a day, perhaps; stealing forth with fruits and delicacies, with nice morsels from the kitchen, and with an occasional wine-flask, or the remains of one, whenever she could appropriate it with impunity. But the eye of Sylvia was upon her; and she noted the direction taken by the footsteps of the girl. It was surprising with what correctness she conjectured the harboring places of the fugitive, from these observations, and her own knowledge of the grounds. She put all her clues into the keeping of the alguazils. The result was, that before sunset, some half dozen of them were quietly skirting the hacienda, divided into two parties, and gradually contracting their circuits about the suspected place of refuge.

Mateo, meanwhile, never dreamed of danger from this source. It is true that Juana had her doubts of the good faith of Don Balthazar, and labored to inspire him with similar doubts. In some degree she succeeded, so as in fact to make him circumspect as possible. But the great gain of security, of freedom, and high trust, which the Hidalgo had promised, were considerations quite too grateful and tempting not to prevail in the argument addressed to the confidence of the outlaw; who, besides, seemed to understand very well why the uncle of Olivia should desire to get Don Philip de Vasconselos removed from the path. It was not with any satisfaction that Mateo contemplated the duty assigned him. He would rather have killed any two other men in Havana than this one Portuguese. But, as he said, "What am I to do? I can't be a fugitive always, flying for safety; and to be my own master is a great deal to one who don't like to work; and to get into a snug office, where I can compel others to do the thing which I don't like to do myself, is certainly very pleasant! Besides, if I don't take the Portuguese in hand, Don Balthazar will only employ somebody else—some bungler, who will not do it half so well; who will botch the business; who will give the good knight unnecessary pain, and perhaps keep him lingering. Now *I* will dispatch him at a blow. It is but a stroke over the shoulders, and he is caught up by the angels; for he is a good young man, and in a very proper state to die! It must be done—and shall be! But let Don Balthazar beware how he plays me false. If I have one death for Don Philip, whom I rather love, I have a dozen deaths for him whom I hate; and he shall taste them all if he tries to make a fool of me!"

In this state of mind was he musing, while the alguazils were skirting his hiding-place; which happened, at this moment, to be on the verge of the hacienda, the point nearest the city. Here the thicket was most dense; without pathways or avenues, except such as nature had left in a very tangled piece of forest, portions of which were clothed in a mass of brush and vine almost too closely for the progress of a wild-cat or fox, but through which Mateo fancied he could burrow with tolerable ease, assisted by a few strokes of his *machete*. The common pathway from the city to the hacienda ran along the margin of this thicket, and was skirted by some very lofty trees.

It happened that Philip de Vasconselos had taken this very evening to visit the damsel whom his admiring fancies had chosen as the Queen of the tournament. The duty would have been done before, but for her indisposition, the reports of which, abroad, had been very contradictory. Philip, though anxious, and now hopeful, was too generous, whatever his anxiety, to appear before her while she suffered. He had learned that day, however, from Nuno de Tobar, that she was at length well enough to receive visitors; and he had chosen the most delicious of the hours of the day, in that clime and season, to approach her with his congratulations, his thanks, and possibly with the assurances of a sympathy, far beyond any thing implied by these, in his love and admiration! The purpose, not wholly decided on—for the truly chivalrous are always timid in an affair of the affections—of offering her his hand, and imploring hers, yet fluctuated as a restless impulse in his bosom. It would be idle to say that he did not hope, and hope strongly, for success. Even

13

the modesty of his character could not be deceived on a subject on which the common voice of society allowed no doubts, and he was resolved to bring his own doubts, if any, to a close, as soon as possible, and terminate a condition of suspense which had many vexations. But, whether he should address Olivia that evening or not, was to depend upon his reception, her health, and other circumstances which need not be mentioned. Enough, that he is at last on his way to her hacienda.

He had just entered upon the estate, and, with slow step, and musing spirit, was penetrating the avenue of great trees which led to the dwelling, when he was startled from a pleasant revery. by a sudden outcry from the depths of the thicket on his right. There were clamors, as of threatened violence; the shouts of man to man; a rushing and crackling among the shrubs and branches of the wood, followed by a fierce, wild, savage oath or two, which came very distinctly to his ears, and which declared for angry passions ready to do mischief. The sun had set. The interval of twilight is brief in that region. A sudden glory suffuses the sky, as the great eye of day is about to close; the glory disappears, a faint misty light lingers in the sky, which gradually deepens into dusk. Such was the hour. The dusk was nearly darkness in the wood; and, for a moment, Don Philip could see nothing, though he impulsively took a few steps into the thicket in order to trace the secret of the outcry. He was not left long in doubt. Suddenly, a gigantic figure, that seemed to rise from the earth where he had fallen, bounded close beside him. He was followed by three others, who now rushed out of the wood and made after the fugitive, armed with swords and knives. They were close upon his heels, and he turned about to confront them. Three upon one! The struggle was too unequal. The chivalry of Don Philip was aroused as he beheld. With the natural impulse of a brave man, sympathizing with the weak, he drew his sword, and threw himself in the way of the pursuers; the outlaw, for it was he, being some twenty steps in advance.

"Stand aside!" cried one of the alguazils, who seemed to be the leader:—"we are officers of justice."

"I know not that!" was the answer. "Where is your warrant? Let me see your authority."

"No time for that now! We are under the authority of Don Balthazar de Alvaro, and these are his grounds. We are to arrest yonder outlaw."

"Ha! Ha! Ha!" was the fierce chuckle of the outlaw, who, taking advantage of the diversion in his favor, had sheltered himself among the trees, but who did not seem disposed to fly much farther. He had obtained a momentary respite, which, probably, was all that was now necessary to his safety.

"Ha! Ha! Ha! Send Don Balthazar himself to me, and we shall see who is the outlaw!"

Don Philip heard the words distinctly.

"Who is the man?" he asked.

"Mateo, the outlaw, the fugitive, the murderer. Beware, Señor, how you arrest the officers of justice, and help the escape of the criminal! I know you, Don Philip de Vasconselos; you will have to answer for it if you delay us."

"If you know me, you know than I cannot stand by and see three men opposed to one. Show me your authority for taking this man, before you pass me. The penalty be upon my head!"

It is probable that the alguazils would have attempted to beat the knight out of their path, but knighthood had its *prestige*, and they well remembered the potent weapon of the Portuguese. The officer remonstrated.

"You cannot read the paper," he said, "by this light. But it is here. Let us pass, or there will be trouble."

"Let them pass, Señor," cried the fugitive. "They will have fleeter legs than Spanish Alguazils usually carry, if they hope to overtake Mateo; and better skill and courage than usual, if they conquer when they overtake! Come on, rascals, that I may carry you with me to the devil."

The confidence with which the outlaw spoke determined Philip to oppose the officers no farther. He probably saw that it would be prudent only to forbear a quarrel with the public authorities knowing, as he did, how doubtful were his own relations with the Adelantado, and how small his popularity with the Spaniards at large.

"You are right," said he to the officers; "I have nothing to do with this business!" and he turned aside, and put up his weapon. The alguazils started again in pursuit. A shrill whistle sounded from the opposite quarter. It was the signal of the other party in search of the fugitive. The outlaw was between two squads of enemies, and he bounded away to the covert, both parties after him. For several minutes, Don Philip listened to their outcries, as they severally crashed their way into the thickets. He half regretted that he had not still farther delayed the chase after the bold outlaw. In a little while the sounds ceased. The alguazils were at fault, bewildered in the wood; and the fugitive laughed at them securely in its deep recesses. But, of this escape, Philip knew not at the moment. He resumed his progress towards the dwelling, his mood having become somewhat sterner by the momentary excitement. Hardly had he advanced a dozen steps, however, when he encountered the girl, Juana, wringing her hands, and showing many signs of terror.

"Who is this?"

"Oh! Señor Don Philip, how I thank you! You have saved my poor brother. They will give him to the *garote vil*, if they take him; and it is I who have betrayed him."

"You! Are you not the girl, Juana, belonging to Don Balthazar de Alvaro?"

"Oh! not to *him*, but to the poor young lady, the Señorita Olivia?"

"And he is your brother? And why do they pursue him? What has he done?"

"Oh! nothing in the world, Señor; nothing in the world; only he is too good to do work at the hacienda. They charge him with murder and other things. But it is not true. He is the best person in the world, Señor, and the best brother, and he killed the great bull, El Moro; and would be as good a Christian as Father Paul himself, if they'd only let him have his own way."

The knight smiled at the moderate conditions which were required for Mateo's Christianity.

"Certainly, Juana, they are very unreasonable with your brother."

"Oh! I knew you'd think so, Señor. He is only too good for the like of them. He is the best brother in all Cuba."

"Well, you are a good girl for believing thus of your brother.— But how is your lady—how is the Señorita de Alvaro? I was just going to visit her."

"Ah!" said the girl quickly—"But you can't see her this evening. She is not well, and she bade me leave her, and that's the reason that you see me here. I stole off, as the Señorita retired —only to see and talk with Mateo, and the alguazils—may the Devils burn them in pitch and sulphur!—they followed after me and I led them to the very place where he was sleeping. Oh! they had so nearly caught him; and if they had, and they had put him to the *garote vil*, I would have drowned myself in the sea, forever and forever!"

The visit of Philip de Vasconselos was arrested by the intelligence which Juana gave him of her lady; but the girl deceived him. Olivia had not retired; and we may add that she really expected the cavalier. She had been taught to look for him by the garrulous assurances of Leonora de Tobar, who had gathered from her husband's report that Don Philip would surely come that night. And, but for this interruption, how might the events of this truthful history have been altered!—whether for good or evil we do not pretend to say. But altered they must have been. Don Philip might have made the visit in vain; he might have been denied; probably would have been; though it is difficult to say. The task of denial would have been a hard one to the poor damsel, loving him as she did; and reluctant as she was to say him nay—to say nay to the pleadings of her own passion, no less than his. She had dressed herself for Philip—she had been solicitous of charms which, perhaps, needed little help from art or ornament for conquest. Yet she had adorned herself richly with her jewels! Would she have had the firmness—the virtue

—to refuse the prayer of one whom she was yet so anxious to please? It is probable that Don Balthazar knew her weaknesses better than she did herself. At all events, the lie of the girl, Juana, told with no malignant purpose, but simply to prevent the discovery of her unlicensed absence by her mistress, changed, very completely, the whole current of our history—changed the fortunes of Don Philip, no less than those of the lady of his love. Not that he did not again seek her—but this must be a matter for future revelation. Philip de Vasconselos turned away from Juana, and from the hacienda, and with a parting word of kindness to the girl, slowly took his route back to his lonely lodgings.

"Praise the Holy Virgin that he is gone! and the Saints be all praised because he came. If he had not come between these cursed alguazils, they would have been, all of them, upon poor Mateo. They can hardly take him now, it is so dark, and he knows the thickets so well. He will escape. He is safe. I don't hear them now. Oh! I am so glad that the good knight of Portugal came! And Mateo wanted to kill him, and all to please that great cayman, my master. But he shan't touch him now. If he's to kill anybody, I know who it shall be. It shan't be the good Don Philip, I know. He is a good knight. I love him. And my lady loves him too, better than all things in this world. But if he knew! If he only knew what I know! But he shall never know for me! And if he marries her I shall be so glad."

CHAPTER XXIV.

> "Now help ye charming spells and periapts,
> And ye choice spirits that admonish me,
> And give me signs of future accidents."
>
> SHAKSPEARE.

DAY passed, night came and went, with all her train of thoughtful stars, and the hours grew more and more sad to Olivia de Alvaro, in the solitude of her chamber. The sense of pain and apprehension increased to absolute terror, as it became certain that she was not to see Don Philip that night. She sate beside the verandah below stairs till a very late hour; and O! the hopelessness and woe of that sick suffering soul, left to its own miserable musings, and struggling against its own terrible consciousness. Youth has wonderful resources against every evil but the sense of shame. Beauty maintains a glorious elasticity in its own ecstasies of hope, provided you do not crush it with a doubt of its own purity. But if this doubt be present, it hangs above the heart with all the threatening terrors of the thunder-cloud. You dare not trust the sunshine. You cannot confide to the breeze. The whispers of the grove seem to repeat the secret of your fears. The stars seem mournful witnesses against you, and you dread lest the fierce glances of the noonday sun will suddenly penetrate your prison-house, and lay bare to the world its dreadful mysteries. Shame is a haunting spectre that will down at no man's bidding. It is thus terrible to man; but to woman, young, beautiful, pure in spirit, and hopeful still, in the possession of generous passions and loving sympathies, it is the demon that implies all horrors, past and future; that mars all felicity with a voice of doom, and threatens every breath of hope and feeling with the tortures of eternal sorrow. The soul thus haunted cannot well be said to live. It enjoys nothing. It distrusts all pleas friendships, loves, associations. The eyes that look upon them spies, the voices that address it seem accusers. The very passions and sympathies, thus overshadowed, grow to scorpions, that fasten upon the being in whose heart they harbor. To describe the sorrows of such a being, in detail, would be impossible. This would be to analyze every emotion, thought, fancy; and to discern the self-suggested doubt and apprehension which the mind continually conjures up for its own agony. If, from such a knowledge of her situation as we have been enabled to give, the reader cannot conceive of the miserable melancholy of Olivia's mood, nothing now may be said more fully to enlighten him. There are some agencies which are indescribable; beyond which we may not go—beyond which we may not see—over which the curtain drops of itself, and which we thence only venture to contemplate through means of conjectures, which still, for the sake of humanity, imply uncertainty. We give to the sufferer the benefit of the doubt, and in some degree feel a relief from having done so. It is a relief not to believe too much. We prefer to suppose that the victim has some alternative by which to escape from a situation the agonies of which are too exquisite for endurance.

How, in what gloomy wakefulness, and torturing thought, Olivia passed the night, we shall not pretend to describe. Nature at last, in her utter exhaustion, compelled thought to silence. She slept, but not till a very late hour. It was midnight when Don Balthazar reached home. She heard him enter the house, and immediately proceeded to assure herself that her door was fastened. The secret door leading to her chamber, of which she only recently had knowledge, she also contrived to provide against by a heavy piece of furniture, which promised to render it unavailable to the intruder. This done, the eyes of the damsel grew weary, and after a sobbing prayer, she soon sank to slumber. She slept late the next day, and was awakened by Juana tapping at the entrance. Don Balthazar had already departed for the city, and Olivia felt relieved at the intelligence. She took a light breakfast but was oppressed by heaviness after it. Her eyes drooped, and her spirits. She looked about her, made efforts to shake off the feeling, which she ascribed to her previous wakefulness, and bustled accordingly about her chamber. But the feeling increased. She remarked with surprise that the beaufet, in which she kept certain little delicacies, sweetmeats, cocoa, bon-bons, and other trifles of like sort, was unfastened She had secured it, as she believed, the night before, and as she had always been particularly careful to do so, she was annoyed by the circumstance. It flashed across her mind that some one must have visited her chamber while she slept. But it was evident that the secret door could not be penetrated from without, fastened as it was by a massive piece of furniture, and the ordinary entrance had not been disturbed. She was compelled to dismiss the suspicion, which, could she have entertained, might have led her to another mode of accounting for her drowsiness. This increased as the day proceeded. She was, however, somewhat kept alive by the unwonted freedom of Juana's communications. Hitherto she had kept the girl at a distance; holding her to be an object of as much suspicion as her mother, Anita. But of late, and since the advent of the hateful Sylvia, Juana had been more devoted to her young mistress, more solicitous to serve her, and had shown her sympathy on several occasions, when sympathy from the humblest source must necessarily be grateful to the torn and suffering heart of the unhappy damsel. Juana's own heart was too full now, any longer to keep the secret of her brother. She told the whole story of his presence in Havana, his discovery, the pursuit of him, urged by the beagles of the law, at the instance of Don Balthazar, and his lucky escape. But she said not a syllable of the interposition of Don Philip de Vasconselos. Her communications did not rest here. She told most of the particulars of the midnight conference between Don Balthazar and the outlaw, the lures held out to the latter, the promises made of freedom for himself and her, and the future management of the estate,—not forgetting the criminal condition by which the outlaw was to secure these benefits. Once opened, the stream of revelation was unbroken until the whole fountain was emptied. But there was another reservation which the girl made. She did **not** say *who* was the victim whom the hate of Don Balthazar required the outlaw to assassinate. In reply to the eager and apprehensive inquiry of Olivia, she professed not to know. But Olivia knew. Her instincts readily divined the secret, as she, better than any body else, knew well what were her uncle's necessities and danger, and how naturally he regarded Philip de Vasconselos as his worst enemy.

"Holy Maria!" murmured the poor girl to herself: "Will he murder him because he hath destroyed his hope as well as mine! Oh! surely, I must do something here!"

Then aloud, to Juana, she said—

"But your brother will never do this horrid deed, Juana?"

"No! no! Señorita; not *now*, I'm thinking. He might have done it yesterday, perhaps; but now, when he finds that Don Balthazar keeps no faith with him, and puts the alguazils at his back, just as he has made a solemn bargain with him before the angels,—Mateo will never trust him, or work for him in any way."

"Hear me, Juana! I will give Mateo and yourself freedom. It is to me you belong——"

"Yes, Señorita, to be sure; but you are not of age yet, you know, and your uncle is your guardian till then; and he——"

"I know all that, Juana; but do you and your brother serve *me* faithfully—do all that I shall require in the meantime, and I will provide that you shall both have your freedom as soon as I am of legal age. Meanwhile, I will see the Lady Isabella, who is very kind to me, and through her I will get Mateo's pardon for the crimes of which he has been guilty."

"Oh! will you, dear Señorita, my most dear Señorita? But what do you want us to do?"

"I will tell you hereafter. At present I hardly know myself. I must think. I see that there is something to be done, but now, I scarcely know what. My head feels very confused, and I am so drowsy. I slept but little last night. I shall think of everything during the day. Meanwhile, do you contrive to see your brother, and tell him what I have said. Tell him, above all things, not to lift hand or weapon against Don Philip——"

"But I didn't say 'twas Don Philip, Señorita."

"No matter! I know! It can be no other. If he hurts one hair of Don Philip's head, I will have him hunted up in the mountains by all the troops of the Adelantado, and I will never sleep till they bring him to the *garote vil*. Now, warn him. Let him be faithful to me, and I will make you both free. See him soon. Go now. Hasten! Find him. Do not rest till you tell him all. But whisper not a word of this to any other living soul."

Juana did not need a second command to depart in search of her brother. Her absence was noted by Sylvia, who was furious at the escape of Mateo from the alguazils. She was soon upon the track of the serving-girl, whose superior agility, however, enabled her finally to elude the pursuit of the old woman. Meanwhile, Olivia had a visitor in the gay young wife of Nuno de Tobar, who found her sinking back into that state of languor and apathy from which the communication of Juana had momentarily aroused her. Her energies had risen, with the temporary excitement, to subside as suddenly; and the lively prattle of Leonora seemed to be wasted entirely upon the ears to which it was addressed. The gay young woman came in with a bound, full of anticipations in respect to her young hostess."

"Well, my child," said she, "it is all settled, I suppose?"

"What is settled, Leonora?"

"Why, that you are to be the bride of Don Philip."

"No! It is settled only that I am *not* to be the bride of Don Philip!" was the sad reply.

"What! Olivia, you have not been so foolish as to refuse him? You who really love him so!"

"He has not given me the opportunity, Leonora."

"How! But he has been here?"

"No!"

"Is it possible! Well, that is very strange! I got from Nuno that he was *surely* to come to see you yesterday."

"He did *not* come!" was the answer, in sad tones.

"That is certainly very curious. He told Nuno that he would visit you in the evening. That was yesterday morning. Nuno spent the morning with him, and said he was in the greatest spirits; that he did nothing but talk of you, and of your beauty and sweetness, and grace and innocence!"

"Ah!" exclaimed Olivia, with a sudden flushing of the cheek, while she pressed her hand upon her side as if in pain.

"What is the matter? Are you sick?"

"A sudden pain!"

"You have these sudden pains too frequently. You keep too much at home. Home always fills me with pains. It don't agree with the health of any young woman not to go frequently abroad, where she can see and be seen. That's what I tell Nuno when he wants to quarrel with me for going out so much. Though, in truth, I do not go out so very often. I visit nobody but you, and the Lady Isabella, and Donna Vicente de Ladrone, and the Señoritas Guzman, and dear little Maria de Levoine, and Theresa Moreno, and a few others. But I tell Nuno that it is not for the love of it that I visit; it is only for my health. I should have just those sort of pains that trouble you, if I did not show myself everywhere every day; and I tell Nuno I am not going to make myself sick by minding what he says. Oh! he's like all other men, and would be nothing less than a tyrant if I'd let him. And do you be warned in time. When you marry Don Philip take your position firmly at the outset; and seize the first opportunity of putting your foot down *so*—and saying, 'Twont do, Don Philip! You are quite mistaken in your woman. I am my own mistress, Don Philip, and if you were a wise gentleman, and a gallant, I should be yours also!' That's what you must say and do, Olivia, if you'd be a free woman and a ruling, happy wife. It's the only way!"

And she stamped very prettily, with a properly graceful emphasis, with her pretty little left foot, and tossed her tresses with the air of a sultana. But Olivia only smiled sadly in reply, and shook her head.

"Oh! don't shake your head so pathetically. You are troubled with the blues only, and will recover as soon as Don Philip comes singing—'Will you, will you—won't you, Olivia?' And he will come, I assure you. I only wonder, after what he said yesterday, that he was not here last evening. He will be sure to come this, so take care and see to your toilet. Put on your best smiles, and be sure to wear your pearls, they are so becoming to you. Oh! when he goes to Florida he will send you bushels of them. Nuno promises me any quantity; and what do you think, Olive? he tells me that, in that country, the Apalatchies raise them from the seed. Think of that. I can hardly believe him. Only think of planting your garden with seed-pearl, and raising them in any quantity and size. He says that they can be grown larger than the largest fowl-egg, only by manuring them with star-dust. But what is star-dust? He wouldn't tell me that. Only said there was a plenty of it to be had in every country, and more in Cuba than any other."

To all this Olivia had to smile only, but in such a sort did she smile, that even the lively visitor was somewhat chilled by it."

"Oh do!" said she, "Olivia, shake off these gloomy fits. I tell you he *will* come, and will be at your feet within twenty-four hours; and you will pout, and hesitate, and tremble and say nothing. Then he will take your hand and he will carry it to his lips, and you will tremble more than ever; but you will never think to draw your hand away, which is a thing so easily done that it does not seem worth while to do it; and then he will rise and seat himself beside you on the settee, and with one hand holding yours he will put the other about your waist, and suddenly he will mistake your mouth for the hand he has been kissing, and he will kiss that; and after he has gone so far, you will see that there is no sense in refusing him the use of the things that he knows so well what to do with."

"Never, Leonora. Do not speak of it. I do not think that Don Philip cares for me, and I assure you we shall never be married."

"Oh I know better! You mustn't refuse Don Philip on

any account. He will take you out of the custody of your uncle, who is only a sort of great Moorish bull, such as fought the other day in the ring; and a monstrous pretty fight he made, indeed! If I could see Don Balthazar fighting in the same manner, till he was killed, and dead outright, and lying sprawling in red blood, and with his neck and shoulder stuck full of *banderillas*, I think I should like him a great deal better. But now I don't like him at all. Here he keeps you no better than a prisoner. In fact, Olivia, I half suspect he likes you better, as a woman, than as a niece, and would rather not see you married to anybody."

Olivia started at this random shaft; rose from the settee; and with staring eye and flushed cheek, gazed her answer; vague, wild, utterly unmeaning, as it seemed, to the remark of Leonora.

"What! dear child, another of those cruel pains? I must send you some famous drops I have. Sit down again! Lie down, Olive, dear. I can speak to you just as well when you lie as when you sit. There, rest yourself for awhile. Poor, dear creature, how your cheek pales and flushes, in an instant, and what an odd look you have in your eyes! You must take some of my drops, and take more exercise, and take advice, Olive, and what's more and better, take Don Philip. Oh! he will cure you of all these infirmities. That's the good of a husband! Now don't be looking so woeful and low-spirited. Positively, there are big tears in your eyes! What have I been saying to make you so sad? I'm sure I meant to be very lively and very goodnatured, and to tell you only such things as would please you. By the way, something odd of your Don Philip. You must know that he has the most eccentric tastes in the world. What do you think? He gave Nuno a commission to buy him a negro boy, a sort of lacquey, fifteen or sixteen—a lad to go on messages, and polish his armor, and help lace him in it, and perhaps dress his hair—who knows what sort of duties the page of a young gallant has to perform? Well, Nuno, who knows every body, busies himself to procure this lad for him, and sends him half a hundred, more or less, of the best black boys, for such a purpose, in all Havana. And none pleases our excellent Don Philip. He has a taste, would you believe it, even in the choice of a negro. He requires the boy to be graceful and good-looking, as if such a thing was to be found! He must needs have a negro handsome! Was ever such an absurdity! Such a whim! So ridiculous! To one, he objects because he is bowlegged; to another, because he squints; to a third, because his forehead is back of his ears; to a fourth, because his mouth is like a cavern, as huge as that of Covandonga, and forever open. He says that sleeping some night in Florida, a cayman will go down his throat, and he shall lose his negro and his money. And thus, positively, he has refused every negro that has been brought him. What's to be done with such a man? But I tell Nuno, these are only his humors, because he's unsettled. He's not thinking of the negro at all; only of you, Olivia—only of you! Now, for my part, as I told Nuno, I don't wish a good-looking negro about *me*. The idea of a handsome negro is unreasonable and unnatural. The uglier the better. Beauty and good looks would be entirely out of place in such an animal."

We despair fully of success, in the endeavor to keep pace, as a reporter, with the tongue of the lively Leonora. Enough that, after a certain period, its exertions were relaxed. Even she herself tired finally of the fruitless effort to provoke interest or curiosity in what she said, in a mind so utterly absorbed, a spirit so utterly subdued and sad, as that of Olivia. The latter drooped, and became more and more apathetic in proportion to the efforts of Leonora to arouse her; and, giving up the task, in no satisfied humor, she at length took her departure, with a promise to return as soon as she could hear that Don Philip had made his visit.

Olivia yielded to her apathy as soon as her companion had gone. It grew to absolute drowsiness, in spite of sundry efforts which she made to arouse herself; which she did the rather to shake off a feeling which oppressed her, than with any necessity for doing the several things about the house which she undertook. But, as the hour for the *siesta* drew nigh, she yielded to the subtle influence which possessed her, and which she persuaded herself was due to the heat of the day, and the absence of the freshening breezes of the sea. She had disposed herself on the settee as for sleep, when Juana reappeared, much flurried and exhausted. She had failed to find her brother, after a long and very fatiguing search in all the well-known places. It was probable, so Juana thought, that the late pursuit of the alguazils had driven Mateo from the estate. We, however, knew better. He had simply found it necessary to shift his quarters, and to exercise a little more caution. He may have temporarily left the grounds, but he did not abandon them. In truth, to state a fact which poor Juana did not conjecture, he found it necessary for his own safety to elude *her* search. She it was, who, with a foolish fondness, had brought old Sylvia and the alguazils upon his track. He kept from her sight, and changed his ground at her approach. The girl was very much troubled by the failure of her search. Olivia might have felt and shown quite as much concern on hearing her report, but for the torpor that had now seized upon her faculties. She repeated her commands to Juana to find her brother, and arrest his knife, in so many murmurs.

"It is very warm and oppressive, Juana. We shall have a thunder-storm. I am very drowsy."

Juana shook her head. She ascribed her mistress's drowsiness to a very different cause. She had enjoyed some of the experience of old Anita, and she muttered to herself—"She has had the spice!" Aloud, she said,—

"It is warm, Señorita, and close, but I don't think there will be any thunder-storm. In a little while the sea-breeze will wake up, and you will feel better, perhaps."

"I will go to the summer-house, Juana, and take my *siesta*, if you think there will be no thunder-storm. Carry my dress for the evening over there, and my jewel-case. I will make my toilet there. We need apprehend no visitors now until evening, I think, and you need not disturb me until the proper time to dress."

She gave other directions—had some oranges, now in their prime, carried to the summer-house, and with languid limbs went thither, after awhile, herself; her whole appearance being that of one not only indifferent, but insensible to external things.

The summer-house was a retreat happily conceived for a climate like that of Cuba. It held a neatly furnished, airy apartment, surrounded by a colonnade which effectually excluded the sunlight from its floors. It was surrounded by ample thickets, which added to the shade, and seemed to give security. It was a sweet solitude, the chosen retreat of contemplation. Here silence had full empire. A happy succession of small courts and avenues through the thickets, opening in all directions, gave free admission to the breeze. These avenues ran through long tracts of the palm, the orange, the grenadilla, and the anana. Their several fruits, more or less ripe, hung lusciously in sight, in close proximity, and drooping to the hand. On each side, the passages were cut through seeming walls of thicket, affording arched walks of the most noble natural Gothic. These all conducted to the one centre, in the light and airy octagon cot to which Olivia had retired. This fabric was very slight, a mere framework of wood; the columns around it being more solid than the structure; and at a glance seemed to be constructed literally of palm, bamboos, and other flexible and tenacious shrub trees, peculiar to that region; which, lopt from their roots, will sometimes bud and blossom, like the miraculous rod of the prophet. The bamboos were artfully interwoven, and roofed with the thick leaves of palm, and plantain, and fig. These were all so many plates and shields, green, broad and with glossy velvet coating that might effectually baffle the fierce glances of the sun, even if there were no loftier shadows from great trees, that stretched their broad and massive boughs between. Art had done its best, within the cottage, to emulate the handiwork of nature without. There was no lack of the necessary supply of curtains and cushions. The former drooped in green or blue before the several openings of the cottage, which was, in fact, only a group of verandahs, placed in parallelism, shutting out the light, but readily yielding to the pressure of the breeze. Upon one of the piles of cushions Olivia sunk down, taking naturally an attitude of grace, and exhibiting an outline exquisitely rounded, such as frequently distinguishes the figure of the woman trained in a life of luxurious ease, and in that delicious climate. She seems, at once, to sleep. Her eyes close. Her sense is steeped in oblivion. She dreams, yet she does not sleep. She feels, but she is not conscious. Her blood stagnates in her veins; yet it works potently in her brain. She is in a morbid and unnatural condition. She is under the influence of "periapts"—spells, which steep the sense in oblivion—in unconsciousness of evil,—making the victim deaf to the very thunders that roll above his head, and blind to the forms of terror, or of danger, that flit before his eye. She has partaken of "the insane root that takes the reason prisoner." The potent medicine which now seals up her consciousness was one of the secrets of her fearful uncle. She has suspected him;—she has,—as we have already seen, endeavored to evade his arts; but they have been too much for her. She little dreams that he possesses avenues to all her hiding-places, keys of power to persuade to yielding, every lock and bolt which she deems secure. At the very moment when she fancied herself most safe, and was beginning to exult in the conviction that she could baffle and defy his arts, her strength failed her—her powers all frozen by his terrible spells. Late that day he reached home and asked for Olivia. He was told by Juana that she was in the summer-house—that she slept. A knowing smile slightly curled his lip. Dinner was served him in his chamber. The wine of Xeres sparkled before him. He drank with the manner of one who enjoys a temporary respite from all the cares of life. He finished the goblet; refilled it; finally emptied the flask, and threw himself into his hammock, with a cigar. He smoked for a while, then rose, drew forth another flask of wine, broached it and drank freely; finished his cigar in his hammock, and after a little while, restlessly worked himself out of it. His eye was humid, his cheeks flushed, his steps uncertain. He looked about him with an air of hesitation, then repeated his draught from the flask, and, with a sudden impulse, hurried out into the verandah, and down the steps into the garden. The keen eyes of Juana followed him from below.

She saw that he made his way towards the summer-house, while he fancied himself unseen.

"Oh!" she muttered *sotto voce*, as she watched, "Oh! if the *garote vil* only had its teeth in the neck of the right one, I know who would never drink two whole wine-flasks at a sitting, and then!— —" The sentence was left unfinished, unless the final ejaculation, after some pause, may be considered a proper part of it :—"Oh! the poor Señorita!"

Juana was not much given to pity. It was nate to the uncle, rather than sympathy for the niece, that caused her ejaculations!

CHAPTER XXV.

> "Approach the chamber, and destroy your sight
> With a new Gorgon."
> — MACBETH.

THE day had been one of considerable bustle in Havana, and Don Balthazar had been very busy all the morning. Juan de Anasco, the contador, a brave, choleric little fellow, who united all the qualities of the soldier, with the experience of the sailor, had been a second time dispatched to coast the shores of Florida, in order to find a proper harbor to which the expedition might sail direct. He arrived the previous night, after a protracted voyage of three months, during which great fears were entertained that he had been lost at sea. His escape had been a narrow one, and it will illustrate the superstitions of his time and people, to show how he returned thanks to Heaven for his restoration and safety. In fulfillment of a vow, made at a moment of extreme peril, he and all his crew, the moment they reached the shores of Havana, threw themselves upon their knees, and in this manner crawled to church to hear mass. Then he made his report of disasters and discoveries, and described a secure harbor which he had found in Florida. The armament of De Soto had been nearly ready for several days before. It needed now but little further preparation, and waited, in fact, but a favorable wind. The report of Anasco stimulated the industry of all parties. De Soto was impatient to depart, and his desires were so many keen spurs in the sides of the lieutenants, keeping them incessantly employed. Don Balthazar, as we have mentioned, had been very busy all the morning, and hence, perhaps, his rather free indulgence in the pleasures of the wine-cup after the toils of the day were over.

That night there was a great feast to be given by the Adelantado, to the cavaliers and chiefs of his army, and the principal persons of Havana. It was the policy of De Soto to keep up the enthusiasm of his people in regard to the expedition, and to conciliate the affections of those whom he was to leave behind him under the government of his wife. To this feast, as a matter of course, the two Portuguese brothers were invited, and Andres, the younger, though just recovered from his illness, had resolved to attend. Not so, Philip. He had fully resolved *not* to accompany the expedition;—we have seen with what reason. He enjoyed no command, and felt that he had not made himself friends among the Spaniards, and that he could never become the favorite of the Adelantado. But his chief reason, perhaps, lay in the growth of his hopes of favor in the eyes of Olivia de Alvaro. If she approved and consented to his prayer, the conquest of Florida would possess no attractions in his eyes. His ambition had grown moderate, as his love increased in fervor. His passion for adventure had suddenly become subdued in the birth and growth of a more powerful passion. If Olivia smiled, what was Florida to him? He cared nothing for its golden treasures. The pearls which it seemed to proffer were worthless, in comparison with those of love. And he was hopeful. That Olivia loved him he could scarcely doubt. Her eyes had shown it—her emotions—the public voice seemed to proclaim it; and Nuno de Tobar, who brought him the favorable reports of his gay young wife held it to be beyond all question, and solemnly assured him to this effect. But Nuno was not prepared to countenance the lover in his refusal to take part in the expedition. He himself was about to leave the young and beautiful creature whom he had just wedded; why should Philip de Vasconselos be more anxious than himself? Why should so brave a cavalier refuse all opportunities of glory and conquest, and great treasure, and power, simply because he was a lover? The notion seemed to him perfectly ridiculous, and he greatly resented the absence from the feast upon which Philip had resolved.

"It will never do, Philip," said he.

"But it must do, Nuno," answered the other gayly. "What should I do at this supper? I shall not be a favorite, if present. I shall win none of De Soto's smiles, and, in truth, I care not to win them;—and I shall not be missed if absent. There will be enough to shout their hopes and desires, and to respond, with sweet echoes, to the fine promises of De Soto. There will be enough for the wine, at all events, and I should be only out of place in a scene for which my temper does not fit me. Besides, my presence will only have the effect of persuading the Adelantado that I will yet accompany the exposition."

"And you must, Philip; we cannot well do without you."

"I have not been treated, Nuno, as if such were the common opinion."

"But it is, no matter how they have treated you; such is their conviction, no less than mine!"

"Then are they the most ungrateful rascals in the world, and the greater fools, too," replied Philip. "But not to vex you, Nuno (and for your sake I should really wish to go, were it proper that I should, under the present circumstances), I am grown too tender-hearted for war! Its image now offends me. I see nothing persuasive in the aspect of glory; there is nothing sweet in the music of a trumpet charge, though it leads to victory. My dream now is of repose, of a sweet solitude in the shade, with a pair of loving eyes looking ever into mine, and the voice of a true heart breathing ever in my ear the music of a passion which asks first for peace—peace—peace! This dream haunts me ever. It takes from me the passion as the pride of arms. It compensates for all I lose. With Olivia in the country, I shall be too happy to repine at any of your conquests."

"Now do I almost wish that she may refuse thee."

"No, thou dost not."

"Thou deservest it!"

"What, for being truer and more devoted to love than to ambition?"

"No, but for thy desertion of thy comrades."

"Comrades! Oh! good friend and brother of mine, as I will call thee, for thou hast been true to me, and full of brotherly loving since I have known thee—dost thou not smile within thyself at thy own folly, when thou speakest of *my comrades* among the cavaliers of De Soto?"

"Am I not thy comrade, and wilt thou suffer me to go alone on this expedition of peril?"

"Thou goest with *thy* comrades, Nuno, but not with *mine*. Thou art a favorite, where they look upon me with ill favor. They will serve thee with loyalty, and support thee; and follow thy lance to battle with a joy; and exult in thy victories. But on mine they look only with evil eyes. Follow thy bent, Nuno, and cherish thy passion for conquest; and none will more truly rejoice in thy successes and good fortune than the poor knight of Portugal. But thou obey'st a passion which I do not feel, and thou hast encouragements in which I do not share. Art thou not unreasonable, *mi amigo*, in thy demand that I shall partake of the peril of an expedition which promises neither pride, nor reward, nor favor of any sort?"

Nuno de Tobar was silenced. His friend had spoken but the truth. He changed the subject.

"So, none of the Ethiops that I send thee will answer? Verily, Philip, for a wise man thou hast strange notions of thine own! Of what matter to thee that a negro slave should be handsome?"

"Not handsome, but well-looking. Now, all those that were offered me were among the ugliest and most ill-looking knaves in the world—models of deformity and ugliness. I confess such as these offend my sight."

"It is the common aspect of the race."

"Ay, but there are degrees, in which these aspects do not offend."

"It will be long ere thou art suited. But the silly knight, De Sinolar, hath promised to send me some passable urchins for inspection; but he will require a great price for his wares, particularly when he knows they are for thee. He regards thee as a dangerous rival."

"What! aspires he to Olivia?"

"Yes, indeed; and with the approbation, it is thought, of her uncle. De Sinólar was greatly annoyed at thy success in the tourney, and would have taken lance himself—he avowed—to encounter thee; but that he had no horse to be relied on, and lances, he thought, were things quite too frail for a man to peril his honor upon. He hath every confidence in his own skill, strength and courage, but doubts if the wit of man hath yet conceived any adequate weapons upon which these may securely rest themselves in the tournament. He holds himself in reserve, however, when the becoming implements of battle shall be made."

"There is wit in the knight's philosophy. Think you it came from himself?"

"Verily, I do not. He reads much in Amadis and other adventures of chivalry, and the excuse hath an antique fashion. And thou didst not see the Lady Olivia yesterday?"

Philip told of the encounter with the outlaw and the alguazils, and added,—

"But, with the blessing of the Virgin, I will seek her to-day. While you are preparing for your feast I shall speed to her dwelling, resolved to put to hazard all my hopes."

"She loves thee, Philip! I know it, if I know anything of the heart of woman. She will accept thee, my friend, and thou wilt be happy! But should she refuse thee?"

"Then, perchance, thou wilt find me beside thee when thou liftest lance against the Apalachian."

"I could almost pray, Philip, that she should send thee from her with the blessing of Abaddon, which is said to be very much like a curse!"

And he grasped vigorously the hand of his friend. They separated after some further conversation, and Philip retired to the recesses of his humble lodging.

The day passed slowly to our knight of Portugal. He had

appointed to himself the afternoon for his purposed visit to Olivia. He was impatient for its approach. His soul was teeming with delicious fancies. Truly, as he had said to Nuno de Tobar, he was delivered up to softer influences than those of war. The sweet and balmy atmosphere he breathed, grateful though enervating, contributed to the gentle reveries of the lover! The hour chosen for his visit to the beloved one was especially appropriate to such an object. Nobody who has not felt, can possibly conceive of the balm and beauty-breathing sweetness, in such a climate, of the hour which just precedes the sunset; when his rays, bright without heat, stream with soft beauty through the green forests, and wrap them in a halo, that makes them as gloriously sweet as golden. There is a delicious mystery to the soul that delights in gentle reveries in the shadows at this hour—in the smiling glances of the sun, when he suffuses all the horizon with the warmest flushes of orange, green, and purple. In a region where the excessive heat and glare of his light at noon are ungrateful to the eye and oppressive to the frame, the day necessarily offends, even at early morning; and the soul necessarily sympathizes with its several agents, even as one spares his slave or servant the task which exposes him to pestilence or storm. Thus the spirits sink as the form suffers. The sunset hour in the same region redeems the day. It *is* the day—the all of day that the eye requires. It is by a natural instinct that, in this region, he who seeks for love chooses this hour, or the night which is lighted by a moon, for his purpose. These naturally suggest themselves in all climates as the periods when the heart may go forth in quest of its kindred. But here, these are the *only* periods. Nobody could find eloquence for love-making in Cuba during the noonday. No damsel would believe the loyalty of the heart that so lacks discretion as to prefer its suit at such a time. The day is obtrusive, and love demands secresy It is a thing of tremors and timidities. It haunts the shade. It has a consciousness of something in its quest which it holds quite too sacred for exposure, or the risk of exposure; and as it only *whispers* when indifference would *speak*, so it *shrinks* and *hides* when audacity and pride *go forth.*

The delicious softness of the hour sunk deeply into his soul, as Philip de Vasconselos passed into the shady and silent defiles leading through the thick woods which girdled the hacienda of the lady of his love. The sweet light from the slant beams of the declining sun flitted from tree to tree before him, like the butterfly wings of a truant fancy. The bright droplets fell, here and there, through the groves, lying about like eyes of fairies, peering through the thick grasses along the slopes. Philip's heart was fairly open to fairy eyes. His soul warmed and was thawed beneath the spells of that winged and fanciful sunlight. He had thrown aside all the restraints which held him in check, through policy when amid the crowd. Here was solitude, and silence, and the shade;—and the pathway led to love; and the smiles of heaven were upon his progress! His step was free as air; his soul buoyant with hope! He would soon feast his eyes upon those precious features of the beloved one, which seemed to them to make a heaven of the place where they inhabited! And the great shadows gathered behind him as he went; and the trees grew motionless; and the woods ceased to breathe and murmur; and the silence deepened; and the pathways darkened; and all was harmony and security! These transitions increased the sweetness of the scene, and as the glances of the sunlight grew less frequent, they seemed brighter, and softer, and more tender and touching in the eyes of the lover. Philip went forward, meeting with no interruption. He passed from pathway to pathway along a route well known. The avenues widened: he was approaching the dwelling. In a few moments he would be in the sight, would be at the feet of her, upon whose word hung all his world of hope and fear. Well might he tremble with the increase of his emotions. What heart is wholly brave at such a moment? and who does not feel, with great misgiving, that, where the anticipation is so pregnant with delicious life, its denial and defeat must bring a pang far greater than that of **death?**

It was in the midst of his wildest anticipations and most trembling hopes, that Philip was suddenly aroused to more common associations, by the appearance of a man suddenly springing out of the lemon thicket beside him. He drew back, and laid hand upon his sword. But the voice of the stranger reassured him. It was that of the outlaw Mateo, who was almost breathless, evidently greatly excited, his eyes dilated, and his tones trembling with emotion.

"Don't be alarmed, Señor. I am not your enemy! I am your friend! You have done me service, and helped me to escape from my enemies. I would not *now* harm a hair of your head. I would serve you—ay, do you good service—would save you from a great evil."

"What evil?"

"Come with me!" and he laid his hand respectfully upon the knight's arm, as if to conduct him forward.

"It is thither I am going," said Philip, "but I must go *alone*, my good fellow."

"Yes, you must go alone! I know *that*. But you were going to the *house*. *She* is not there. She is at the bower in the woods. It is there you must seek her. You were going—pardon me, Señor, —to declare your love for the Señorita."

"How, sirrah!".

"Pardon me, Señor, I say again;—but I know it;—everybody in Havana expects it. I mean not to offend. I tell you I want to *serve* you. I love you and honor you, and owe you gratitude. It is this that makes me say what I do,—and lead you this way. You must *not* make love to the Señorita. She is not for you, Señor,— she is not worthy of you!"

"How, fellow! Do not provoke me to anger!"

"Forgive me, Señor; but give me time, and give yourself time. Just come with me now;" and he almost dragged him forward. "There,—into that avenue—follow it—it will lead you to the summer-house. Go forward—go *alone*—go quickly— but go *softly—softly*—say nothing, but *look;*—see! Then, if you will,—tell the Señorita that you love her—that you come to make her your wife!"

There was something in all this proceeding which was so earnest and so startling, that, though it offended the proud knight because of the freedom of the outlaw's manner, he did not feel like showing anger. Indeed, he was too much startled, too sensibly impressed with a nameless terror, to be altogether conscious of the extent of the liberty which Mateo had taken. He fancied that Olivia was in danger, and vague notions of serpents and tigers rose before his imagination. Intuitively, he obeyed his tutor, and darted into the alley.

"Softly, softly!" cried the outlaw, following close behind. In a few moments he reached the summer-house.

"Go up the steps—*in*—the Señorita is *there*. Go—look—see, but softly, very softly, and do not speak!"

Philip obeyed, and ascended the steps of the verandah; the curtains were lifted; he disappeared among the columns, and Mateo waited without, among the groves. He had not long to wait. Scarcely had Philip disappeared from his sight, when his form was again seen, emerging from among the columns. A single hollow groan escaped him. Mateo darted forward to meet him, and the knight staggered down the steps, almost falling into his arms. The outlaw hurried him into the thicket.

"Quickly, quickly!" said he.—"He will have heard that groan."

Philip staggered away, without offering opposition. His head swam; his knees tottered beneath him.

"I am very faint!" said he.

"Rest here," answered the outlaw, conducting him to a wooden seat enveloped in shrubbery, and almost forcing him down upon it, while he plucked an orange from the shrub-tree above him, and in a second laid its rich juices open with a knife.

"No!" exclaimed Philip, after a pause, rejecting the orange, and staggering up from the seat—"I cannot rest here, nor anywhere! Let us away! away from this place!"

"You have seen?"

"No more! Do not ask me;" and the knight of Portugal covered his eyes with his hands.

"Stay for a moment!" said the outlaw—"while I go back, and give him this!" and he lifted his huge *machete* as he spoke, and looked the matador about to strike.

"No!" hastily answered the knight,—laying his hand upon the arm of the outlaw. "It must not be! Put up your knife. What is it to us? what is it to us? Let us go hence!"

And he started forward, blindly, and once more in the direction of the summer-house.

"That is not the way! That leads you back——"

With a shudder, Philip wheeled about, and hurried off in the opposite direction; the outlaw following him respectfully, and in silence. In the same silence they wound their way through the thickets of lemon and orange. When they approached the verge of the estate, Mateo stopped suddenly:—

"I must go no further. Here I must leave you, Señor. I must not risk exposure."

Philip grasped his hand.

"Thanks, my good fellow, thanks! I have nothing more to give. You have done me good service; but at what expense—what suffering!"

"Could it be otherwise, Senor?"

"No! I thank you. It is well! you have saved me from a great misery, by giving me a great hurt. I would I had the means to reward you. But I thank you! I thank you!" and he groaned heavily.

"I ask no reward, Señor. I am only too happy to serve you. I wish I could serve you forever. I feel that I could work for *you*, and for any true man like you! But I can't work for a bad one, and a beast! I would be happy to go with you to Florida. But there, Don Balthazar would know me through any disguises. And yet, I might get over that. Let me go now, Señor."

And a new impulse seemed to seize upon the outlaw, the ex

pression in his face declaring, as fully as words, the renewed purpose in his mind.

"No! not till you promise me you will do nothing in this matter. I see what you mean. But, if you slay *him*, you expose *her!* Let him live. You cannot go with me to Florida. I know not that I shall go myself. Stay where you are. Get back to your mountains. But, as you live, and as you love me, breathe not a syllable of this! Farewell!"

With these words, and having received the outlaw's promise, Philip de Vasconselos turned away.

"It is gone!" he murmured to himself as he went. "It is gone, the hope, the brightness, and the joy! all gone! Oh! Jesu! what a ruin!" and he again covered his face with his hands, as if to shut out a spectacle of horror. "Oh! would that I had the monster in a fair field, with only sword and dagger!"

Thus exclaiming, he disappeared from sight. Mateo sank back into covert, and soon he heard the voice of Juana in the thicket. He suffered her to approach him. She had followed the steps of her brother and the knight. She had seen them as they left the summer-house, upon which it would seem that she, also, had been keeping watch.

"What have you seen, Juana?" demanded the outlaw sternly.

"All!"

"Ah! all! You do not mean that——"

"Yes! I saw when you and Don Philip went towards the summer-house. I was in the thicket. When the knight of Portugal came down the steps and groaned so loud, it roused Don Balthazar. He came out soon after you, and looked about him, and I lay close. But, seeing nothing, he went back again."

"Well! what's done can't be undone; but look you, Juana, if you whisper a word of this to anybody, I'll slit your tongue. Do you hear now? Well! remember; I am just the man to do what I promise, though you are my own sister."

CHAPTER XXVI.

> "I've done my journey *here*; my day is out,
> All that the world has else, is foolery,
> Labor and loss of time. What should I live for?"
> BEAUMONT AND FLETCHER.

"WHAT remains, but that I should seek Florida—seek the wilderness—the solitude—the strife!—forget—forget! Oh! Lethe, would thou wert not a fable!"

Such were the muttered exclamations of Philip de Vasconselos, as he went, almost blindly forward, on his way to his lowly abode.

"It is all over! all blasted! The dream—the too precious dream! Jesu! that it should end thus! How should it be so! How should she—so fair, so gentle, so seeming pure and angelic!—Ha! Ha! Ha! It is not wonderful! It is a truth—an experience old as the hills! When came the tempter ever save in garments of an angel of light! It is the one power which he possesses, over all others, of seeming, to mortal eyes, the thing he is most unlike! And how nearly had I fallen into the snare! How blind, neither to see nor to suspect! But for this outlaw—this slave—I had been a lost man—sold to a delusion—expending my soul upon a phantom—laying my best affections in tribute upon an altar which devotes them all to shame! Yet, I cannot thank him! He hath, at a word, in a moment, by a spell, robbed me of the one glad, joyous vision of my life! I had but one hope, and he hath destroyed it! I knew but one desire, and he hath made it death! What now should I live for? Of what avail that I am young, and fearless, and skilled in arms, and all noble exercises? The motive for performance is gone, and the life goes with it. All is a blank before me; all cheerless, all bitterness; a long waste of darkness and denial!"

And he threw himself down hopelessly by the way-side. Darkness had settled down; but the stars were coming out, silently and palely, looking like the spectres of past pleasures. The distant lights of the city were present to his eyes also. There were torches flaming upon the farthest hills, and pyres were burning before booths and camps, from which rose faintly, at intervals, the sounds of merriment. Gay laughter and shouts, he heard, or fancied, rising from rustic groups engaged in the fandango; and anon, but more faintly, he caught the tinkle of a guitar rising from some bohio or cottage, in the contiguous hollow of the hills.

"They laugh! they shout! they sing; as if there were not a shadow upon the earth—as if guilt and shame had not fouled the fairest aspect under heaven! Jesu, to be so beautiful and sweet to the eye—to acquire such power, through sunniest charms, over the soul, and yet to fail in the one great virtue which alone makes all dear things precious to the heart! But, is it so? Is it true? Have I not been deceived? Am I not betrayed by treachery and cunning? May it not all be a delusion of the senses? Is it sure that it was she? Did not mine eyes deceive me; and, while there is a doubt, shall I give faith to an assurance so terrible—so revolting—so fatal to the loveliest work of heaven! It was dusk—the woods were thick—the sunbeams did not pierce them—the curtains hung around, darkening the chamber!—there was a woman, but is it certain that she was Olivia—my Olivia! the pure, the proud, the beautiful? Was I not too ready to believe the accursed suggestion of the outlaw; was there no contrivance for my ruin—for *her* ruin? What if I return and see; and, if it be true, what should keep me from slaying him, at least, and looking her to stone with eyes of scornfulness and hate!"

But he did not rise. He could not doubt. He could not delude himself into the thought that what he had seen was a mere delusion of the senses. It was too true—too real—and the more he strove to dispel the conviction, the more it grew to strength, and took possession of his soul; filling it with a nameless and indescribable horror. For an hour he lay thus upon the earth, delivered to despair. There was no refuge for hope in thought, and he lay brooding, with an aimless mind, and an agonized spirit. At last, he rose. The strong man rarely sinks below a certain point. He may be overwhelmed, like the weakest, by a shock, at once terrible, revolting, and unexpected: but the heart gathers its forces after a season, and nature compels the proper efforts for her own recovery and repose. The grief may remain, but it does not overcome. It may prove a lasting blight to the hope, the fancy, the affections; but there is a calm resolution which enables the sufferer to live and to perform; for performance is, beyond all other things, the natural law, and the necessity of the true man; and even the sorrow, which wounds and blights the heart, serves to strengthen the noble courage and the indomitable will. Philip de Vasconselos rose from the earth at last. He had become somewhat more composed. His will and character were beginning to assert themselves. He was still the master of *himself!* He rose and went forward, sadly, slowly, but resolutely; endeavoring, with all the calm he could command, to shape the course for his progress in the future. This was soon decided in his mind.

The lights of the city grew before his eyes. The torches and camp-fires, along the hills that skirted the city, became more glaring, and cast their great red shadows upon his path. The voices of merriment, the songs, the shouts, the joyous cries and laughter, with the tinkle of pleasant instruments, became louder and more frequent on his ear. Suddenly, his eye caught a glimpse of the long, temporary structure, of poles, covered with palm branches, and the broad leaves of other trees, in which the knights were revelling at the last festivities of the Adelantado.

"What remains," murmured Philip, "but that I go with this expedition? What matters it to me, now that I am no favorite? I ask no favors. There are blows and danger to be encountered among the Apalachian, and he who is armed as I am now, against all terrors, can make himself a favorite, by making himself fearful. What better region in which to bury my sorrows, and hide my anguish from vulgar eyes? Where can I more surely escape from this agony of thought? In the fierce strife, there will be forgetfulness; and forgetfulness will be the most precious of hopes, even though it comes only through the embrace with death. I will go with Nuno!"

Under this new impulse, he hurried forward rapidly towards the scene of festivity, as if fearing to trust himself to think further upon the subject of his progress. It was not long before he reached the place; the shouts from within, the music, assailing his ears with a sense of pain, without, however, impairing his resolution to join the revellers,—to engage in their expedition.

The structure in which the Adelantado and his Floridian chivalry held their feast was, as we have said, a rude, simple fabric, designed only for the temporary purpose. It consisted of slender shafts, green trees freshly cut, and thatched with bamboo and fresh bushes. It was fantastically adorned in a style which the climate and productions of the country naturally suggested to the eye of taste. The flag of Spain, the banners of De Soto, and of the several captains, were disposed happily around the apartment. Green leaves and gorgeous flowers were wreathed about the columns, declaring visibly the wealth of the delicious region of which they were the natural tribute. Fruits in gay festoons hung down within reach from the rafters: the luscious pine, the mellow banana, the juicy and fragrant orange. Of the provision for the feast, it will be much easier for the reader to imagine than for us to describe. Enough that the Adelantado and the knights of the expedition had done their best to requite the hospitalities of the Islanders in a fashion worthy of their own. They had expended no small part of the treasures remaining from their outfit, in doing the honors gallantly and with becoming ostentation. They not only provided, as it was the custom of the gentry of the city and country to provide, but they studiously procured dishes such as they had merely heard described, and fancied others, the better to outdo description—" Exhausted *cates*, and their imagined new." The turtle, fresh from the sea, furnished the only soup,—a first course, which was served up in the uncouth monster's own shell; game and domestic poultry, including doves from the côte; young peacocks, their plumage artfully disposed about the birds after they were made ready by the cook for the table, so as almost to represent the living creature his gay streamers of green, and purple, and gold, looking as bright and fairy-like as when he unfolds them to sight, strutting and spreading himself abroad from court and verandah. Some dishes were prepared formed wholly of the tongues of singing birds; and we may add, were eaten with an appetite such as might be assumed to originate only with a hope to win the musical powers of the member thus hushed forever. The unripened plantain was sliced and browned in sugar by the fire; or, roasted, was macerated with the inspissated juices of the cane. This course, by the way, was preceded by one consisting wholly of sea and shell-fish, and was succeeded by fruits of more than twenty kinds, all natives of the island. Fresh guayavas, fragrant ananas, bananas and sapadillos, yielded themselves to delighted palates in delicious sympathy with wines of Xeres, which had already began to circulate with potency before Philip de Vasconselos entered the assembly.

He entered at a moment when De Soto was addressing his audience. The Spanish language is one of equal grandeur and beauty; the Spanish character is necessarily one of ambition and hyperbole. The language of a people usually declares for its character in its best days. We know from other histories how a language may exhibit more vitality than a people; how gloriously it survives them. A language, known through its literature, is perhaps the only durable monument of a people. De Soto, as is well known, was an accomplished cavalier, greatly distinguished at a period when Spain could claim a host of heroes. It is not so well known that he was an accomplished speaker, thoroughly master of the arts of language, versed in its delicacies, and practised in all its graces. His audience listened to him with ecstasy, and rounded his sentences with their *vivas* and *bravas*. He dwelt upon that superiority of character which exulted in adventure. The art of war, he contended, and its prosecution in new lands, was, perhaps, the very noblest and most god-like of all human arts. He spoke of the greatness of his nation, as particularly renowned for the use of this art, in its most inspiring exercises. He painted fame and glory, brightly and purely, and grandly, as they appear always to youth and enterprise, and dwelt upon the progresses of Cortez and Pizarro in Mexico and Peru—subjects, in hearing the report of which, the Castilian ear could never tire. By a natural transition he came to speak of their present adventure in the wilds of Florida. He did not disparage the valor of the red men of Apalachia, nor seek to lessen the picture of danger which he drew as a necessary consequence of the enterprise; but he insisted upon the utter impossibility of any valor of the red-men as able to stand for a moment before such warriors as he led to the encounter. He particularly dwelt upon the great treasures of the country, its glorious cities hidden in the bosom of mighty mountains; its treasures of gold and silver; its pearls to be gathered in heaps along its shores; arguments which, he well knew, were beyond all others, in persuading young ambition and greedy avarice to his banners. At the close, seeing Philip de Vasconselos enter, he took the opportunity of throwing out a few bitter sarcasms upon the timid, the laggard, the weak, the souls deficient in true courage and noble enterprise, who hung back when an occasion so glorious was offered to their eyes.

The glances of the assembly followed those of the Adelantado, and rested upon the flushed countenance of Philip. He saw the direction given to the words of De Soto, and felt the purpose of the latter to inflict a sting upon his pride and heart. He rose proudly when the Adelantado had finished, and looked sternly around the assembly. It was surprising how composed he was. He appeared fully to have recovered himself, and though very grave, as the occasion seemed to require, he was quite as firm and calm as if he labored under no other provocation than that which he had just received. Never was individual less daunted by the circumstances in which he stood. He saw that there was dissatisfaction —certainly constraint—in the faces of nearly all around him; reflecting that in the countenance of the Adelantado, who scarcely acknowledged, with a stately bend of the head, the measured but courteous approach of our hero, and the deepening shadows upon whose brow argued no friendly welcome for what he might say. But Philip was little moved by these unfriendly auspices. He respected De Soto as a brave and noble cavalier, distinguished equally by talents and graces, and high in favor of his sovereign; but his respect and admiration were not so profound as to cause him to suffer any mortification from the loss of his favoring countenance. He advanced towards the *dais* which had been assigned to the Adelantado, raising him a little above the rest of the assembly,—passing through the crowd with exceedingly deliberate pace, until he stood but a few paces from the person he addressed.

"Your Excellency," said he, "has been pleased to indulge in certain remarks of censure upon that unambitious, unperforming and timid class, who, bred to arms, are yet reluctant to engage in the honorable adventure to which you invite them. I cannot deceive myself as to the fact, that certain in this assembly are disposed to make these remarks applicable to the person who now addresses you. I trust it is not necessary to say here that for any one who would impute to me the want of courage, I have but a single answer, and that lies at the point of my weapon; be it lance, or sword, battle-axe, or dagger. I am ready to encounter any questioner. That I have been slow in resolving to accompany this expedition, has been no fault of mine. I came hither from my own land for this very purpose; and until I reached Havana, I knew no disposition to change my determination. It will be admitted, I think, that the encouragements offered to me for this adventure, however, have been very few; and, perhaps, were I to say the truth, I should describe the course taken with me as designed specially to rebuke the presumption which had prompted me to seek a place under the banner of Castile."

"Not so, Señor, not so, by God!" exclaimed De Soto, interrupting him energetically.

"Be this as it may, your Excellency, it is one of those things upon which I do not dwell; for, to me, war and adventure carry their own encouragements; and it is found, always in the time of danger, that no one's sword is amiss that does good service on our side. I have no fear that in the day of trial, I shall fail to prove my right to be present where blows are given and received. Encouragement I need not,—discouragement will never chill my enterprise or lessen my strength. That I hesitated to engage under your banner when I came here was due to other influences, which ——"

De Soto smiled grimly. Philip saw the smile, and his face was suddenly flushed with crimson.

"But it matters not," he proceeded, "to say wherefore I hesitated to declare my purpose. It will suffice, your Excellency, to say that I am now prepared, if permitted, to accompany your expedition to the country of the Apalachian—a country which I somewhat know already—a people with whom I have already had fierce as well as amicable intercourse,—and among whom, it may be found, that my presence shall work for good to your Excellency's enterprise."

This said, Philip de Vasconselos bowed courteously, and calmly wheeling about, made his way back to the place where he had entered the apartment. The Adelantado—the audience—was taken completely by surprise. Nothing could have been more unexpected to all ears. De Soto spoke in reply approvingly, and with warm compliment. Other voices followed with the same burden. But Philip neither heard nor listened. He was making his way out, when his hand was suddenly seized by that of his brother Andres.

"Brother!" was all that the latter said.

"Andres, my brother!" exclaimed Philip, throwing his arm around the neck of the youth, while a sudden gush of tears from overfull fountains blinded his eyes. No more was said between them. Such was their reconciliation. The speech of Philip had taught Andres—strangely enough—that the passion of his brother for Olivia de Alvaro had proved as fruitless as his own. Why? This was the mystery which none could solve. Philip tore himself away from the brief embrace, and was hurrying out, when Nuno de Tobar rushed up, and, warmed with wine, caught him exultingly in his arms.

"But how is all this, Philip?"

At that moment Don Balthazar de Alvaro suddenly entered, and was passing very near them. Instinctively, Philip grasped the handle of his sword, and his eyes were fastened upon the uncle of Olivia, with such an expression as made the latter start, as at the approach of a famished tiger. Philip recovered himself in a moment, turned away from the face of him whom he longed to destroy, and was followed out by Nuno into the open air.

"Tell me," said the latter, "how comes this change?"

"Do not ask me, Nuno; enough that I go with you."

"Holy Mother, but your looks, Philip ——"

"Heed them not—heed me not—let me leave you, Nuno, I am not fit for this assembly."

"But you have been to see Olivia—you have seen her?"

"I *have* seen her!"

"And she refused you?"

"No!—I have not spoken with her."

"Seen her—but not spoken!—What! Your courage failed you at the last moment—you had not the heart?"

"I had *not* the heart!"

"Jesu! man! What weakness is this?"

"No weakness! No more, Nuno. There is that which puts an eternal barrier between Olivia de Alvaro and myself—a barrier deep as the grave, impassable as hell. I can tell you nothing. You but distress me when you ask—ask nothing. From this moment name her not to me, Nuno, unless you would make me your foe for ever!"

CHAPTER XXX.

Cenci. Speak, pale slave! what said she?
Andrea. My Lord, 'twas what she look'd. She said;
      Go, tell my father that I see the gulf
      Of Hell between us two, which *he* may pass;
      I will not,"
                          SHELLEY.—*The Cenci.*

DON BALTHAZAR was greatly surprised by what he heard in the assembly, of the declared purpose of Philip de Vasconselos to accompany the expedition. It was a surprise to everybody—how much more to him! Such unexpected good fortune was hardly to be hoped for. The danger, now, of a suitor to his niece, so likely to be successful, no longer threatened him. At the first moment when he learned the fact, he felt an exhilarating sense of triumph. But soon he asked himself, how was so sudden a change wrought in the purposes and feelings of the knight of Portugal? But a day before he was known to be eager and determined in his purpose to address Olivia. His hope of success was good, and every voice encouraged the prosecution of his suit. Why the change in his purpose? That Philip had *not* addressed his niece, Don Balthazar was quite certain. That they had no interview, he was assured. That she had received no written communication he was equally confident. It was clear that Philip, without testing his hopes at all, had suddenly abandoned them. Wherefore? The question began to stagger the inquirer. Guilt is always a thing of terror, and the discovery of such guilt as that of Don Balthazar, was doubly terrible to the conscious fears within his bosom. He now saw the significance of that look which Philip had cast upon him as he came into the assembly, and readily divined the mystery which puzzled all other persons.

"He has discovered all!" was his secret thought. "Yet how?" Here was the farther difficulty. "What was the discovery which Philip had made?" "To what degree was he committed by it?" His anxieties increased with his unuttered inquiries, addressed to himself. But Don Balthazar had a rare faculty of self-concealment. His secretiveness was a large development in his moral organization. He could smile, and look calmly about him, and engage in the frivolous conversation of society,—in all the business of the crowd—seemingly unmoved,—while the vultures of doubt, and dread, and conscience, were all at work tearing at his vitals. He joined in the talk going on in the assembly. In this way he might obtain some clues to the secret of Philip. But he learned nothing satisfactory. One fact, however, he gathered from all that was said, which seemed to weigh upon his thoughts; and that only related to the sudden appearance of the knight of Portugal, at a late hour, in fact not many minutes before himself. "Where had he been till that hour?" While asking himself this question, Nuno de Tobar reappeared within the circle. "I will sound *him!*" was the unexpressed resolution of the Don, as he sauntered around, gradually winding his way towards the place where Nuno had taken his seat. The countenance of the latter was troubled. His mind was in some confusion, as well from the wine he had taken, as from the conference with Philip. But the approach of Don Balthazar served, in some degree, to steady his intellect, and make him cautious. He knew that Olivia's uncle had been hostile to his friend. It had not escaped the notice of Nuno, that the glance with which Philip had met Don Balthazar, but a few moments before, was that of a determined, if not a savage hatred. Sympathizing earnestly with his friend, Nuno shared, in some degree, his hostile sentiments. He had himself never been the friend of Don Balthazar, and was now more than ever disposed to regard him as an enemy. In some way, he felt assured that the present sufferings of Vasconselos, and his abandonment of Olivia, were due to the evil influence of her uncle.

Thus feeling, he was sobered by the approach of the Don;

made reserved and cautious; as the good soldier is apt to feel when in an enemy's country, and marching through a region proper for snares and ambuscades. Besides, by prudent management, might he not find out something in respect to this mystery? Don Balthazar probably knew the cause of Philip's conduct. There might have been an open rupture between them:—Don Balthazar, like Philip, had been absent from the festivities until a late hour. They had reached the assembly at nearly the same time. Might not their mutual absence, and arrival, have been due to a common cause? Nuno determined to search this matter. He would probe the inquirer. His mind co-operating with his feelings and his instincts, became cool, searching and vigilant, and Don Balthazar extracted nothing from him. That he was as little successful in penetrating the bosom of the Don—habitually cool and circumspect—was, perhaps, to be expected. They separated after a profitless and brief conference, which satisfied neither.

But if Don Balthazar extracted nothing from Nuno, the young wife of the latter was something more successful. From her he had few concealments. Scarcely had he reached home that night, warmed with the festivities in which he had shared so freely, and excited by the nature of the mystery which oppressed him, when he began his revelations.

"Would you believe it, Leonora, it is all over with Philip and Olivia? There is a breach between them, which Philip says is impassable! He has joined the expedition. What has caused it, he does not say; but he tells me that there is an end of the matter; that she is nothing to him now."

"Blessed Maria! what does it mean? Has she refused him? Foolish, foolish creature! But she always said that she would."

"But she has not! He has not asked her! He told me so in so many words."

"And I don't believe a word of it! You men are so proud and vain that you never like to confess to a rejection. It's the way with all of you. Be assured that Philip has been refused. She said she would refuse him, but I did not believe her. I know she loves him. But she is so strange. It does appear to me, sometimes, as if she were not in her right mind. And to refuse so nice a cavalier! I wonder where she expects to find another like him. But it's not her doing, I'm sure, not her own heart! It's that cross-grained uncle that she has. He has done it all. I wonder what is the secret of his power over her. I'm sure she hates him. But he rules her in spite of it; and he has compelled her to refuse him."

"I don't believe it, child; for I believe Philip, and he positively assured me that he had not asked her. He's not the man to lie, or to be ashamed of rejection. He has no such weakness. He was very earnest about it—very miserable,—and entreated me never again to speak to him on the subject."

"Then I'm sure she has refused him. Did he say he had not seen her?"

"No! I knew that he went to the hacienda late in the afternoon, and he admits that he saw her, but did not speak to her."

"Now, as if that were reasonable, Nuno."

"It is certainly very strange. I can't see into it."

"But I do; and the whole mystery lies in the one fact that he has simply been rejected, and his pride will not confess it. He has been mortified by refusal, when he counted confidently on success. And I confess, I counted on it too; for though Olivia always said that she would refuse him, yet I know that she loves him desperately, and as she will have no other man. But it is all the doing of Don Balthazar. He hates Don Philip—he hates both the brothers—I have seen *that* a thousand times. But what are his hates to her, and how has he succeeded in making her sacrifice her love to them? What is the secret of his power to control her against her own happiness and will? That is the secret which I should like to find out!"

"You are right, I suspect, in ascribing it all to her uncle. Philip is not the man to be rejected by any woman in a hurry, and I am convinced, like yourself, that Olivia really loves him as she will be likely to love no other person. But there is some mystery in the whole affair. The poor girl is very unhappy. That I have long seen, and Don Balthazar is at the bottom of all her troubles. He manages her property, and has, I suspect, but little of his own. He will be very unwilling to resign the power which this gives him into the hands of any other person. The only wonder is that she does not see this, and assert her independence. She has sense enough to understand her rights; but she is so weak,—so timid——"

"You mistake her there! Olivia is a woman of very strong passions, and can be very firm and obstinate upon occasion. What surprises me is, that she does not assert her will, and show the strength of her passion, in an affair which so deeply concerns her own happiness, and where her heart is evidently so much interested. This is the difficulty. I do not wonder that Don Balthazar should oppose and deny, but that she should submit; and the question is, how does he obtain this power, by which to rule her as he pleases, against her own affections, when he himself is possessed of none of them."

"Yet, it is his influence certainly, that has somehow brought the affair to this unfortunate conclusion, and Philip feels this. Had you but seen the look which he gave Don Balthazar when they met to-night. His fingers clutched the handle of his sword convulsively, and the gleam of hatred in his eyes was mixed up with such an expression of horror and disgust, as I never saw in mortal eye before. I shall never forget it."

"Still, I think that they will come together yet. She loves him, I tell you, beyond all other persons. She will never suffer herself to be deprived of him, if she can help it; and I don't think she could survive it. I tell you, Nuno, she idolizes Don Philip, and she will marry him yet, in spite of Don Balthazar."

"Yes, perhaps;—and yet, from what Philip said to-night, it will hardly depend upon her. He used the strongest language—"

"Oh! a fig for the strong language of a lover. I know what it means always! He will forget his resolution as soon as he lays his eyes upon her, and looks into her pale sweet face, and hears the soft silvery voice that answers to his own. He is now only under the first feeling of vexation and anger. He talks as if he would tear her to pieces, no doubt; but let him sleep upon it, and he will rise in the morning to renew his worship."

"Philip de Vasconselos is like no other man, I know."

"Ah! you are mistaken. In some things all men are pretty much alike; and in an affair of love—where there is real love—your strong cavalier and stately Don are just as feeble as the man of silk and velvet. You are all pretty much alike—all easily overthrown—where women are concerned."

"It is a very strange affair throughout."

"I'll find it out to-morrow, if I live. I'll see Olivia in the morning, and she must have sharper wits, and greater strength, than I believe, if she can hide the secret much longer from my eyes. You will admit that if Philip has seen her, then the probability is that she has refused him."

"He himself admits that he has seen her—seen her this very day, but denies that he has spoken with her. *There* is the difficulty—*that* is the surprising fact."

"Seen her, but not spoken with her! You say he went to see her, and *did* see her, but said nothing?"

"Yes; that is precisely what he asserts."

"Oh! he means no more than this—that he did not propose."

"It may be—yet he spoke very precisely and positively."

"Well, Olivia will be able to answer that. She will, at all events, confess that there was an interview; though she may tell me nothing of what passed between them. If she says so much as that, you will readily suppose that Don Philip has simply kept back something which his pride will not suffer him to confess."

"Yes;—though how to believe it of Philip—how to suppose him so weak, or to think that he should keep back the truth from *me*—that is what troubles me."

"Well, leave it till the morrow!" said the wife.

With the morrow, eager to penetrate the mystery, Leonora de Tobar prepared, at an early hour, to visit her friend. She found, unexpectedly, the uncle and niece together. Olivia was looking paler than usual, and wore an exhausted and suffering appearance. Her eyes were dull, heavy, unobservant and expressionless. Her whole mental nature seemed stagnant; she moved like an automaton; welcomed her guest as one in a dream; and sunk back upon the settee, after the exertion, like one worn out with long watching. Leonora was quite as flippant as ever, and for a while talked about a hundred nonsensical matters quite foreign to the one which filled her thoughts. She longed and waited anxiously for the moment when the withdrawal of Don Balthazar would afford her the opportunity which she desired for broaching the one subject for which alone she came. But, as if he divined her object, he seemed no ways disposed to take his departure. He bore patiently the torrent of small talk, which, with the hope of driving him away, she poured out from a most inexhaustible fountain. But in vain. He fortified himself with a pile of papers, which he displayed upon the parlor table soon after her arrival. Busying himself in army and navy estimates,—for Don Balthazar filled several different departments in the bureau of the Adelantado—he strove to busy himself in the midst of details; and, though the incessant buzzing in his ears must certainly have defeated every attempt at thought or investigation, he persevered in the appearance of both, with unwearied industry. The patience of Leonora was not of a sort to contend with that of the veteran, resolved upon an object. She gave way at last, but by no means with the intention to beat a retreat. She only prepared to change her operations, and, failing at blockade and starvation, she determined boldly to effect her purpose by assault. Olivia, all this while, seemed quite unconscious of—certainly indifferent to,—all that was going on. She neither looked up nor listened, nor had a word to say. Never was there a more perfect exhibition of apathy, or we might say despair. What to her was all this childish prattle, of her child friend? What cared she for that small personal talk which made the burden of all her conversations? She had neither mood, nor heart, nor head, nor memory, nor sense, for all that was saying or had been said. She was, in truth, laboring under a sort of aberration of mind, the result of drugs and evil practice, of the whole extent of which, though, in her sane moments, she had suspicions, she had really no conscious knowledge except by her prolonged sufferings day by day. But, very soon, the conversation aroused her. The daring Leonora, according to her new plan of operation, now addressed herself to the uncle. Turning to him very abruptly, and when he was least prepared for the assault, she said—

"So, Don Balthazar, we are to lose Don Philip de Vasconselos after all. The report is, that he joined the expedition last night, after a very eloquent speech. But you must have heard it all, and can tell us much better than anybody else."

Olivia looked up with a wild and vacant stare, but the sense seemed to be slowly kindling in her eyes. With a frown, Don Balthazar replied:

"I do not see what there is to tell. No more, it appears, than you know already. Your husband was present. He, perhaps, remembers the speech, since he regards the knight of Portugal as something of an orator. Let him report it."

"Well, I suppose, after this, the fact may be held undeniable; and now the wonder is why he should have left his purpose doubtful so long. Why, but a week ago, it was in everybody's mouth that he was not to go at all—that he had abandoned the expedition altogether."

"Well, you admire him the more, I suppose, because of his feminine caprices," was the surly answer.

"No, indeed, though I don't see anything amiss in caprices now and then. They are rather agreeable, to my notion. But, in his case, people found good reasons for his refusal to go; better, indeed, than I can find for his present change of mind."

"Ah! well! good reasons?"

"To be sure! Very excellent reasons, Señor; they gave him credit for discovering more precious treasures in Havana than he was like to find in Florida, and at less peril of life and comfort; and these were surely good reasons for staying."

"Humph!" quoth the Don, looking askance at Olivia, in

whose eyes the returning light of thought was momently growing more intelligent.

"The truth is," continued Leonora, "nobody could question the admiration of Don Philip for our dear Olivia here. Everybody saw it; it was in everybody's mouth; and to confess my conviction, I was very sure that Olivia had just as much regard for Don Philip as he felt for her."

Olivia sighed involuntarily. The knight looked very savage, and turned over his papers diligently. After a pause, he said,—

"I know no law which forbids fools to talk about their neighbors. I suppose it is hardly punishable, since such people are not to be held strictly to account for what they say; but I trust my niece has given no sufficient reason for the assumption, on the part of any body, that she had given away her affections gratuitously to any man—to one, indeed, who had never sought them."

"Well, Señor, that is well said by a guardian; but hearts are not always regulated by the strict letter of domestic law. They are like birds, which will break out of cage if you leave the door open. Affections are strangely wilful things, Señor, and very apt to fly in the face of authority."

"*You* have good reason for saying so, Señora!" was the scornful sneer of the Don in return, emphasising with a pause the pronoun, and thus making an allusion sufficiently obvious to her amour (which the church had not sanctioned) with Nuno de Tobar. But she received it with a cool indifference that silenced all further attacks of the same sort.

"Oh! if you allude to me, I confess that I have been wilful enough and sinful enough, and that my affections very readily ran away with my prudence; and but that Nuno was a blessed good boy, and loved me for my heart, and not for my wisdom, I should have been a sad piece of scandal for all Cuba. I was born a woman, Señor, and I believe I will always be one, let me live never so long. Now, a woman has a natural faith in man, as her born guardian, and protector, and lover, and friend; and if he wrongs her faith, he discredits himself, not her. That's my notion in such cases. Don't suppose that you make me feel at all uncomfortable by your hints; for I am willing to admit, to all Cuba, that I was very weak, and very loving—too loving to believe evil of the man I fancied! So now, Don Balthazar, if it pleases you to talk of *my* affairs, I can't prevent you. It's the fool's privilege, as you have just said, against which there is no law, to say what one pleases of his friends; and you have certainly the same rights as other people; but, in truth, if you will suffer me, I will speak rather of Olivia and Don Philip, as being just now much better subjects, and about which I feel much more concerned."

The little woman's good nature actually endowed her with wit and wisdom. Don Balthazar was quite astounded by her audacity. She was invulnerable to his shafts. He looked up, and glared upon her more savagely than ever, but remained silent; and in a moment after, seemed more than ever busy with his documents. But Leonora went on, and somehow, his instincts prompted him to listen. She might have heard from her husband what the latter had withheld from him; and his doubts had been by no means quieted by the reflections of the past night. Leonora now especially addressed herself to Olivia.

"I confess, dear Olivia, that I am surprised and disappointed. I feel vexed at this strange determination of Don Philip, knowing that he loves you, and believing that you love him, that he should resolve to go without addressing you. But perhaps he *has* done so, and you have been so foolish as to refuse him! Ah, my child, can it be possible?"

The sad eyes of Olivia, now full of expression, anticipated the reply of her lips.

"He has *not* addressed me, Leonora; he has not even been here. I have not seen him since the moment when I was taken sick at the tournament."

"Is it possible?"

"True!" said Olivia, very mournfully. "True!"

"Nay," continued Leonora, after a thoughtful pause—"nay, there must be some mistake in this. You certainly *have* seen him within the last two days, though he may not have proposed to you."

"No! I have not."

"That is strange!"

"Why strange?"

"He has certainly seen *you* since the tournament."

"Why do you think so?"

"He told Nuno that he had! Told him so only last night."

Don Balthazar could not keep his eyes upon the papers. He looked up inquiringly to Leonora. She noted the curious expression in his eyes, and was determined to withhold nothing which should either obtain for herself the secret which she desired, or should goad the haughty Don with revelations which she somehow fancied would annoy him. When, therefore, Olivia anxiously besought her, as to the alleged visit of Philip, she prepared to tell all that she knew.

"Well, I know that he has been to see you twice in the last two days. He came day before yesterday, and was a party to an encounter which took place in your grounds here between a troop of alguazils and a certain outlaw."

"A slave—a mestizo?" involuntarily asked the Don.

"Even so: one Mateo! Philip told Nuno all about it. He interposed, finding half a score of persons upon one; until the officers told him how the matter stood, and then he suffered them to proceed. The outlaw made his escape, however; and Don Philip then proceeded to visit you, when your girl, Juana, met him, and told him that you were sick and had retired for the night."

"When was this?" demanded Olivia, with strange calmness.

"Two days ago only."

Olivia rose and called Juana. The girl was close at hand—had been listening, in fact, at the door. She made her appearance, and on being asked, confirmed the story.

"Why did you speak a falsehood, Juana?"

The girl hung her head and made no answer. Olivia turned to Leonora.

"You say that Don Philip came here again, Leonora? Was here yesterday?"

"Yes—so he assured Nuno last night."

"When? at what hour?"

"Last evening—about dusk."

"And saw *me?*"

"So he said; but, strangely enough, he mentioned that though he saw you, he did not speak to you. Yet he came to speak. He came to offer you his hand."

Olivia pressed her hands upon her heart, with a look of indescribable suffering. Don Balthazar arose, somewhat agitated, and approached Leonora.

"You say, Señora, that Don Philip was here last evening? Last evening!"

"Yes."

"And at dusk?"

"About that time. He came hither about sunset. Nuno saw him when he left his lodgings to make the visit, and he told him all about it."

"And he saw *me?*" said Olivia. "Where was I?"

"In the summer-house, Señorita!" was the voluntary reply of Juana, who had been eagerly waiting to speak.

"It is a mistake!" said Don Balthazar—"He was not here. I tell you, Señorita, it is altogether a mistake."

This was said with a vehemence meant to cover an agitation which the knight could not otherwise subdue. Olivia beheld this agitation through the effort to conceal it. His asseveration went for nothing, particularly as Leonora insisted that Don Philip had declared the fact to her husband, only last night, and after the former had made his speech.

"It is impossible!" said Don Balthazar, in a manner meant to silence all further discussion; but the malignant element in the bosom of the slave, Juana, was not prepared to suffer him to escape thus easily. She could not suppress the grin of malice from her features, as she hastily replied :—

"Oh! yes, Señor; Don Philip was certainly here; and was at the summer-house. I saw him when he was leaving it. It was there he must have seen the Señorita. You came out of the summer-house just after Don Philip had gone."

"I!" exclaimed the Don with troubled aspect—"I!"

"You, Señor!" cried Olivia, rising and striding across the interval that separated her from her uncle—while her eyes, dilating beyond their orbs, were fixed upon him with an expression of mixed agony and horror.

"You!—you!—were you in the summer-house last evening—you,—when I was there!"

He was silent . . . . Juana supplied the answer.

"Yes, my lady—the Señor went to the summer-house after he had dined. But it was dusk before I saw Don Philip. I did not see Don Philip when he came, but only when he was coming down the steps of the summer-house, and was going away; and I was quite frightened to see his face. He looked like a man that was going crazy; and O! how he did groan! I heard him! I was quite afraid to go near him."

"What did he here at that hour!" cried Don Balthazar, furiously—"How dare he intrude upon my privacy!—— How dared you ——"

He was arrested in his speech by the action of Olivia, who suddenly pressed closer to him, so as almost to touch him, her hands clasped together, and with such a look—so like madness, in her face—that, involuntarily, the uncle recoiled from her, and the words died away upon his lips.

"Oh! you have done your worst now!" she exclaimed. "I see it all! I know it all! Fiend and monster as you are,—you feel it, too, do you not! You see it! You will burn for this! Your rages shall be endless! There shall be no drop of water for your tongue! There *must* be a hell, if it be for your use only! There must be devils, if it be only for your torture!

Oh! do not start, and recoil! I will not harm you! Daggers would be no punishment for such crimes as yours. Hell! hell only! Hell! hell! hell!"

She clasped her head with both her hands, and reeled about dizzily. Leonora caught her in her arms in time to save her from falling upon the floor. She was in a swoon! It came seasonably to save her from madness. We close the scene. Let us suppose that Leonora clung lovingly, and nursed heedfully her suffering friend; and that Don Balthazar fled from the presence which, with all his brutal heartlessness of character, he dared

CHAPTER XXVIII.

"I swear
To dedicate my cunning and my strength,
My silence, and whatever else is mine,
To thy commands."   SHELLEY.

Don Balthazar fled into the recesses of the thicket, and buried himself amid dark and savage thoughts.

"He knows all, indeed!" he exclaimed, when he felt himself alone. "Where was that scoundrel, Mateo, that he did not slay him before this! But for those bungling alguazils! they have marred his purpose. I forgot to warn them, and hence all the mischief. But, if it were necessary that I should have him put out of the way *before*, it is trebly necessary now! He knows too much! He could blast me, at any moment, by his speech! He must die! *She* must die! It is now the only means of safety! Oh! would it had been done the very hour that I resolved upon it! I should have done it with my own hand, if I had only dreamed of this danger. I was mad, blind, oblivious,—a very dolt,—not to see that his existence was perilous to my safety!—Hers too! But I must be heedful in this matter. It will not do *here*. It will not do till I am gone. Then, I shall contrive it. I will send her off to the country. She shall depart as soon as she is fit to travel. Sylvia shall see to the rest. It shall be done. For him! ah! how shall I manage that? Shall it be *here?* Shall it be in Florida? Here, best, if Mateo can contrive it; but in Florida it will be quite as easy. He has no followers;—few friends! If he is found, with a knife in his bosom, it is by the hand of the red man that he dies! Who will doubt? None! and he *must* die! That is settled. It is *his* life or mine! Would I could see that scoundrel Mateo!"

The devil is said to answer promptly whenever he is called. The person invoked stood the next moment before the Don.

"Ha! Ha! You want Mateo, do you?—the scoundrel Mateo!—well, you see him, I hope. He is here, and not so much a scoundrel as some that wear much better reputation."

The reckless outlaw laughed irreverently at his own sarcasm. He felt his securities. Perhaps, he would have even relished a hand-to-hand struggle with the knight; but he seemed to entertain no hostile purpose, and stood quietly confronting him, looking good-humored enough, considering the genuine feelings of hatred which he felt for his superior. Don Balthazar was not a timid man,—was not easily startled by any event or presence,—and certainly had no fears of any individual foe; but the appearance of the outlaw, so apropos to his summons, brought up to his mind a vague image of the satanic presence, which, in fact, was the true meaning of his requisition. It is the hellish agent which we summon always when we design a hellish deed. Don Balthazar, however, welcomed the fugitive after his own fashion, with the air of a master who knew his rights, and had reason to complain.

"You are here at last! But you have done nothing. You promised finely! Where are your performances? Had you done according to your pledges, I had been saved from a very unpleasant affair!"

"Had I done!—and who is to blame, I beg to know, that I have not done? You make a bargain with me, and when I set about to do my work, I find your alguazils upon my heels. *Your* alguazils, bearing *your* orders to seize and bind me, and have me properly dressed for the honors of the *garote vil!* Ah! indeed! The *garote vil* for your own ally—the man who is to risk his life doing your business! What do you say to that?"

"What do I say! Why, that the thing was wholly a mistake. The rascals did not understand me."

"A mistake! Oh, it would have been precious consolation to me, with my neck fitted with an iron cravat, to hear that it was done wholly by mistake! I had as lief die by the law, as by mistake, any day!"

"I tell you that the alguazils were ordered after you, *before* I had spoken with you; I only forgot to see and speak to them, and they continued the search in consequence. But I will put a stop to their pursuit."

"Oh! you *forgot* only! But that was strange on your part. You're too much a man of business to forget such things in common. But you'll remember *now*, you say; and I'm to be pursued no more?"

"Yes: I shall see to it this very day; but you are to do the business you undertook?"

"Ah! that business!"

"Yes; you will dispose of this knight of Portugal, *shortly*, as you do your prayers;—send him to God by a quick conveyance? You are not afraid? You will not shrink from your engagements?"

"Afraid! O, no! I'm not afraid of *your* alguazils! As for keeping *my* engagements, that will depend upon the way you keep yours. I don't see that, so far, you've been very keen to remember them."

"You make too much of this forgetfulness of mine."

"Oh! you may forget again! I never trust a bad memory; not even my own. See this handkerchief; there are three knots in it. Every one marks a life. This is one I put in it when I engaged with you to send Don Philip by a short cut to paradise. You must knot your handkerchief too, before I take this knot out of mine."

Don Balthazar received the suggestion rather literally. He coolly took out his handkerchief, and proceeded to knot it; but the outlaw laughed.

"Look you, Don Balthazar, the man who can't *write*, makes his knot in the handkerchief; but that's not the rule for you. You must make your knot on paper, with pen and ink; and there must be a great seal to it. Get me the pardon, under the hands of the Adelantado, for all *past* offences; that's one *knot* you're to make. Prepare me the paper that proves mine and Juana's freedom, and when you give me these, I shall take out my knot here, and Don Philip will fly off to join the angels in paradise; *that* will save you from finding him in your way hereafter."

And the fellow chuckled greatly at his own wit. Don Balthazar was not so well pleased at these requisitions.

"But, when I have got you these papers, what security have I that you will do what you promise for me?"

"Security! Well, it seems to me that your security will be quite as good as mine. What security do you give *me*, when I have slain Don Philip, that you will do for me what you have promised?"

"Slave! Do you count the word of a nobleman, and a soldier, as of no more value than that of a mestizo and an outlaw?"

"Pooh, pooh, Señor; that sort of talk won't do between *us!* It's you that are the outlaw, not me! I am to kill Don Philip on *your* account, not on mine; because *you* hate him, and not from any hate that I bear the Portuguese. Were I to kill him on *my own* account, *I* should be outlawed: killing him *for you*, it's *your* act, not mine, and *you're* the outlaw! Don't speak to me as if there was any difference between us. There's none, I tell you, but what's in my favor! I think myself a much better man than you any way. I don't get other people to fight my battles, or avenge my wrongs—there's where I'm the better man: and as for strength and skill with the weapon, why, I could slit your throat in the twinkling of an eye, and before you could mutter an *ave.*"

Thus saying, he flourished his naked *machete* in fearful proximity to the knight's face. The cheeks of the Don flushed crimson, and he hastily drew his sword half-way from the sheath.

"Oh! put up," said the outlaw; "it's no use—and besides, it's not necessary. I'm not going to kill you; and if I were, you could do nothing to help yourself. I wouldn't give you the smallest chance. I'd be into you, and through you, before you could get your toledo out of the scabbard. I'm none of your fine knights of Castile and Portugal, to let you put yourself just in your own attitude to fight; all *that* seems to me only foolishness. Here's my enemy, and I'm to kill him. If I don't kill him, he kills me. Now, I don't want to be killed, just yet; and I rather he should die than me! What then? Will I give him a chance? Not a bit of it! I'll slit his throat without saying, 'By your leave, señor.' And if it was my profit to slit yours, I'd have done it without all this palaver. Don't be afraid. We're on terms. I've a contract with you; and I'm willing to work for you, on conditions. But you must get down from the great horse when you speak to me. I can't bear to be ridden over by any Don that ever came from Spain! and I won't! There now; you know me. Is it a thing clear between us? Will you get me the pardon, the free papers, with the big seal? *Shall* I kill the knight of Portugal for you?"

"You're a bold fellow, Mateo;—it's a bargain!"

"Very good. When shall I have the papers? I must have them, to see, and to show; for I can't read, señor, and must get some one to read them for me, to see that all's right, before I do my share in the business."

"You are hard in your conditions, Mateo; but you shall have your own way. Meet me here, at this hour, two days hence, and you shall have the pardon and the papers!"

"Good, señor; I'll be punctual to the sun."

When the two separated, the knight proceeded, almost immediately, to take horse, and ride into the city; the outlaw disappeared within the thickets. Don Balthazar did not return to the hacienda that night. In his place, Olivia had another visitor. While Sylvia slept, Juana conducted her brother to the chamber of her mistress. The latter appeared to expect him; she was certainly not unprepared for his coming.

It was surprising to behold her countenance, as the bold outlaw entered the chamber. Where had she acquired that wonderful composure—that strength of calm—so suddenly?—after

the overthrow of her hope and pride, so terrible and so recent?
—after that wild compulsion which seemed to have racked
equally the body and the soul, how had she so soon and
thoroughly recovered? In the utter wreck of her pride, her
sensibilities seemed suddenly to have become blunted. She
had the look of one who felt nothing. There was not in her
countenance the slightest show of suffering. Her eyes were
strong in their glare,—not sad. The muscles of her mouth
betrayed not the slightest emotion. She looked like one of
those wretched persons whom we sometimes encounter in society,
who grow prematurely wise—who never know youth or childhood—who spring, at a single bound, into manhood, and the full
possession of their minds; and who do so, in almost all cases,
at the expense of their hearts—nay, to the utter death and burial
of their hearts! Such premature development always makes
monsters. The look of Olivia was that of one whose heart was
utterly dead within her, and who has survived and forgotten—if,
indeed, she ever knew—its loss. It was—to sum up in a word
already used—all stony! The calm was that of death—the
composure, that of insensibility—not apathy! Yet there was
life in her. There was a new-born energy working within
her soul. That had survived the heart—had acquired its
strength—only in the utter annihilation of the hope, if not the
affections. These still lived, however;—but in what manner?
We shall, perhaps, see as we advance; but they were not now to
declare themselves in the ordinary way, as is the case with those
who do not live to denial—who still indulge, if not in hope, in
dreams—in delirium! Olivia had her purposes still; and, through
these, her lingering and blighted affections were still destined to
exist, and work;—but she had no more feminine emotions. The
blissful though deceiving reveries of her woman heart were all
at an end! There were now no delicious fancies, tripping, like
nimble servitors, in obedience to thought or will; bringing gay
colors, and creatures of the element, to beguile her saddened
moods. Fancy had been stripped of all its wings—ruthlessly
stripped—and life now crept on like the worm deposited beneath
the precious flowers, to which it can no longer fly. But the
worm still had life; and a will, which continued to incline in the
direction of its former fancies. Olivia de Alvaro, we repeat,
has still a purpose,—whether of hate or love we have yet to
learn! Enough, that it is the purpose of a broken heart,—well
knowing how complete has been its ruin,—how utterly hopeless
is its condition—how dread its humiliation,—how unrelieved
by solace, whether of mind, or heart, or soul. She is without

aspirations; yet she has a purpose! And *that* purpose? We shall see as we proceed.

Whatever it is, she pursued it with such energies as she has never before displayed in the prosecution of any object. They are such as might become the strongest-willed person of the other sex. She bends her whole soul upon the task. She excludes all fears, all doubts, from consideration—everything which may impair her efforts. Perhaps, we should rather say that, feeling as she does, her soul is no longer accessible to fears. She has endured the last sorrow, and the worst; and death has no terrors, in a season, when life is not only without hope, but without inspiration of any kind. She wrought, nevertheless, as one dedicated to duty; as one, too, to whom the strength came, physical and spiritual, only with the duty! An hour had made her a new person; and, with the due consciousness of a fresh impulse, she has no time for sorrows. Sorrows! How should tears, or wailings even, or prolonged watching, give testimony to such a woe as hers! To have been capable of either would have implied very inferior sensibilities, or a smaller degree of heart and suffering!

A night of stunning and strange sensations, that seemed rather to afflict the body than the mind, and she stood up, a new being! With the dawn she found herself employed,—active, watchful, vigilant,—speaking few words, but firmly,—allowing no questions,—willing, and causing to be done, according to her will! Juana, now honestly prepared to serve, was put in requisition, and kept busy. At night she was required, as we see, to bring her brother, the outlaw, to the chamber of her mistress. When there, the latter had few words, but they exhibited her in a wholly new attitude, to both brother and sister. Juana she dismissed to another chamber. From Mateo, now alone with her, she demanded an account of his interview with Don Balthazar. He revealed its purport—all! Olivia listened without seeming emotion. When he was done, she said.

"I have presumed on your fidelity, Mateo. You dare not lie to me! You will not! I am willing to believe you. You are too much of a man to deceive me."

"By the Blessed Virgin!"—he began.

"It does not need, Mateo, that you swear. I *will* believe you. You shall work for me, and shed no blood! There is your pardon, which I have procured for you through the Lady Isabella, and there is the paper, which makes you and Juana free people— no longer slaves of mine. Take them, and then listen to what I would have you do."

The outlaw fell at her feet,—seized her hand, and covered it with kisses. She withdrew it, indifferently, without emotion.

"Enough," she said: "Enough! How long, Mateo, will it take you to procure me a supply of the roots for making the tawny brown dye of the mountains?"

"I can get you any quantity, Señora, in a short twelve hours."

"Be it so. You must set out for it as soon as I dismiss you."

Juana here peered within the chamber, but the lady motioned her away, and then, in a whisper, gave Mateo some other instructions. Her manner was calm, resolute, emotionless wholly; her words clear, though whispered; her purpose made fully evident to his understanding, though at present it is withheld from ours. He argued with her purpose, but in vain. He finally submitted;—Juana was called in, and her brother hurriedly disappeared. He returned by noon of the next day, and brought her the roots of a native dye, such as she required. He had other trusts to execute, which kept him actively employed. Meanwhile, Juana kept diligent watch. The espionage of Sylvia was baffled; and, more than once during the day and night, Mateo penetrated the dwelling in safety,—sometimes with a package beneath his arm; sometimes with only certain tidings on his lips. He wrought submissively, beneath a will which it was neither his policy nor his desire to disobey. Meanwhile, his eyes filled, rough and savage as he was, as he gazed upon Olivia, and remembered that it was by his agency that her pride had received its fatal blow—to say nothing of her hope—in the terrible moment when Philip de Vasconselos had entered the summer-house. But he dared not make this confession.

"Yet, how could I help it?" quoth the outlaw, to himself, by way of apology. "He had saved me, had served me, and was a noble gentleman. Then, I knew her only as the kin of that scoundrel, Don Balthazar! Yet, I wish it had not been so!"

The regret was unavailing, but it strengthened the desire in the heart of the outlaw to serve her faithfully in all things; and it softened him to survey her, so wholly changed,—a woman no longer,—stern, inaccessible, hopeless,—having but one idea; and that—he shrugged his shoulders as he thought of it. But he was forbid to argue it again.

"I have heard of such things before; but, after all, it's only a sort of madness! She will break down in it, or break out,—and that's pretty much the same thing,—and then it's all over with her! Oh! it is so pitiful! and she so young, so beautiful, and of such a great family! *Demonios!* How I should like to cure all the trouble, if it could be done, by making three cuts with my machete on the black heart of that monster, Don Balthazar!

I would make a cross for him should cross him out forever! Well, let her break down, and I shall do it yet! *He* can't buy me now, at any price. But I shall sell him at just what price I please! Who'll buy on these terms? Who? Why the devil, to be sure! Who else?"

CHAPTER XXIX.

> Soffri, che poco
> Ti rimane a soffrir. Non ti spaventi
> L'aspetto della pena: il mal peggiore
> E de' mali il timor."
>
>   ARTASERSE.

It required, in fact, no effort on the part of Don Balthazar to procure the pardon of Mateo, the outlaw, from the hands of the Adelantado. He had only to place the paper before him, with a crowd of other papers, for signature, and the sign-manual was set down without scruple or examination. This was the usual process. It was thus that, at the entreaty of Olivia, the Lady Isabella had already procured the pardon of the mestizo; and thus it was that the affair had escaped the knowledge of the knight. In neither instance had De Soto been made aware of what he had done, and Don Balthazar was thus naturally kept ignorant of the peculiar interest which his niece had manifested in the outlaw, and of her intimacy with him. He was utterly without suspicion in this quarter; the consequence of his impression of her ignorance of affairs, and of her utter indifference and apathy upon most subjects. The pardon procured, the Don prepared the legal discharge of Mateo, and his sister, from the service of his ward. He signed the latter papers as her guardian, and, as usual, without consulting her. The deed of emancipation which she had prepared was, in fact, void, in consequence of her minority; and this was quite as well known to Mateo as to herself. But it was understood between them that he was to keep aloof until she should reach maturity, when he could boldly defy the uncle. The parties did not deceive themselves, or one another; and though the discharge of Olivia was, for the present, of less value than that of Don Balthazar, still Mateo much preferred to receive the boon at her hands, though of questionable validity, than to incur any obligation at the hands of a person whom he meditated to murder at the first decent opportunity. Armed with the desired papers, Mateo did not think proper to keep his engagement with the Don. He was to have met him in the thicket, where we have already beheld their interview, but the knight waited for him in vain; and, after lingering for an hour, becoming impatient, he took his way towards the summer-house, and thence proceeded to the dwelling. He little dreamed that the person he hoped to see was closely following and observing all his movements. So was Juana. Mateo had counselled the latter carefully on certain points, and the watch maintained by one or the other of them left no single proceeding of Don Balthazar, when at home, unnoticed! While at the summer-house, the Don had divested himself of the papers with which he had proposed to meet the outlaw. As it was in this neighborhood that he still calculated to encounter him, he thought to have them always ready by leaving them there. He fastened them up securely in a huge chest which he kept in a closet. But Mateo, who watched all his steps, soon wormed his way into the closet and the chest. He was armed with a bit of iron wire, his *machete*, and a small drill and mallet; and it was surprising with what rapidity he persuaded locks to give up their secrets. Such is the advantage of being in high practice, wherever the arts are concerned. The worthy outlaw, however, did not immediately possess himself of the documents of the Don. For the present, he was content to know where they were hidden. He preferred that their loss should not be discovered until the last moment, when the Don should be ready for departure to Florida, and he to his native mountains. He had much yet to do in Havana, and did not care to be disturbed again by the alguazils, while pursuing his pleasant occupations. He continued in the employment of Olivia; and her present purposes, steadily pursued, with a mind now profoundly concentrated on the one object, found him enough to do. But there was a slight interruption to their intercourse. In carrying out his purposes, Don Balthazar, as we have seen, had resolved to send his niece to the plantation,—the hacienda, or country-seat of his ward at Matelos,—where her large estates chiefly lay. This was in order to his own security. Here, he might best practise against her peace—perhaps her life. Here, she would be removed from frequent association with the Lady Isabella, who had taken a greater interest in her happiness than Don Balthazar cared to see, or to encourage. She was to proceed thither under the conduct of De Sinolar, whose hacienda was contiguous, and whom Don Balthazar was not unwilling that Olivia should marry. De Sinolar was his creature,—silly creature, as we have seen,—vain and weak,—who feared the Don, and whom the latter regarded as a useful mask to shelter his own proceedings. If she would wed with De Sinolar, she might live; and the latter was to be allowed every opportunity of winning his way to her favor. Don Balthazar, however, had now but little hope of this, unless through her utter despair of the knight of Portugal, and the desperation of soul which his own cruel conduct had occasioned. The expedition once departed, carrying with it Don Philip, and the uncle was satisfied to trust somewhat to time. Time might effect his object, and if not—the dagger! This latter remedy was to be entrusted to Mateo; unless, indeed, Sylvia should prove herself as expert with the bowl as her predecessor, Anita, had been.

According to these plans, Olivia was suddenly apprised that she was to travel that very day under the escort of De Sinolar. She was silently submissive. She was not allowed words of parting with her friends, the Lady Isabella, or the fair, frail wife of Nuno de Tobar. To this also she was reconciled. She had no desire to see either. She had survived friendship. Mere society had no attractions for her, and nothing compensative. She lived but for a single purpose, and this was of a nature to be rather helped than defeated by her removal from the city;—that is to say, by her seeming or temporary removal. She was prepared to go,—but her secret resolution was taken to return; and that, too, before the sailing of the expedition. We shall see, hereafter, in what manner. Don Balthazar was rather surprised at her submission. He had expected a struggle. But she heard his requisition with a cold indifference, and answered it with a single word of resignation.

"I am ready now!"

He was surprised, and said something about her friends.

"Would you not desire to see and part with the Lady Isabella,—with Leonora de Tobar?"

"No! What are friends and friendship to me?"

"It might be done in an hour. It were proper, perhaps."

"I do not care to see them."

"Well, as you please! You can see them as frequently as you think proper after I am gone. Indeed, as Leonora will remain in Cuba, you might have her as your guest."

Olivia was silent. The uncle proceeded:

"De Sinolar has gallantly undertaken to be your escort, and you can command his services during my absence, in any matter in which you may need assistance. He has kindly volunteered his good offices. I have given him instruction."

"When does the expedition sail?" she coldly inquired.

"Within two days. We are all ready, and the wind promises to be fair."

She asked no more.

"When we separate, Olivia, it may be forever! I go upon an expedition of great peril. I may never return. Do you forgive me, child?"

A terrible scorn rose into her stony gaze.

"Forgive!" she exclaimed—"Forgive!—ask it of the ghost of my murdered happiness;—at the grave of my wronged innocence; of the hope which you have banished from my heart forever; of all that I was, and might have been, and am not! Ask it not of me, as I am, Don Balthazar, lest I curse you with a doom!"

"We are now to part! Perhaps never again to meet. My life is henceforth to be one of constant peril. You may hear of me as a victim to the darts and fiery tortures of the Apalachian! Will you not forgive me, Olivia?"

"Play the hypocrite with me no longer. Do I not know that, in your soul, you scorn the very prayer for forgiveness which your false lips utter? Hence! Better that we, should both forget! So long as I can remember, it is not possible to forgive!"

And little more was spoken between them, ere they separated. De Sinolar soon made his appearance. The vehicle was packed, and stood in readiness at the door. Don Balthazar conferred privately with De Sinolar.

"You will have her pretty much under your own eye at the hacienda. You will have her to yourself. Play the *bold* lover, if you would succeed with such a woman. Make her your own at every hazard. These Knights of Portugal once gone, she will show herself less coy."

De Sinolar curled his moustache, and grinned gratefully

"I flatter myself, señor——"

"Pooh, pooh! Don't flatter *yourself*, man! Flatter *her!* The man who perpetually flatters himself offends everybody. This is your fault. It is in the way of your own successes."

The carpet knight was a little discomfited by this abrupt speech, but he contrived to conclude his sentence, and succeeded in saying that he flattered himself he should finally succeed in flattering her; and so they parted. It was but half a day's journey to the hacienda. We find nothing to interest us along the route, since the wit and humor of De Sinolar are of a sort which is too ethereal to keep, or too heavy to be borne, and Olivia could only listen, and did not reply to his gallantries. But we must not forget that Juana accompanied her mistress, and that Mateo, on a fine horse, hovered along the track, keeping the party in sight, but being himself unseen. It was some consolation to Olivia, that Sylvia was no longer her guardian. The poor girl never dreamed that she was destined to follow her; having been kept back only to receive the final instructions of her master in respect to his victim.

The hacienda of Matelos was reached in safety about dusk. Olivia, pleading fatigue, dismissed Don Augustin to his own abode, which lay contiguous, on an adjoining plantation. She retired to her chamber for awhile, but it was not long before Mateo made his appearance. Certain signals, previously agreed upon, announced his arrival to Juana, and he was stealthily conducted by that damsel to the chamber of her mistress. Olivia was sitting with hands clasped, and eyes fixed upon a picture of the Virgin which hung upon the wall opposite, when the outlaw entered the room. She at once rose.

"You are true, Mateo, and I thank you. You must now get the horses ready."

"Ah! my lady," said the outlaw, "I have been thinking you can never stand this trial. It is a hard life you propose to undertake. You will never have the strength for it. You do not know the toil, the danger. You will surely sink under it; you will perish, and there will be no one to help you."

"I shall need no help, Mateo; and if I perish, it is only an end of a long and terrible struggle."

"But why engage in this struggle, Señorita? Of what avail?"

"The easiest form of death is in the struggle, Mateo. Do not argue with me now; I am resolved."

"But, I must argue, dearest mistress—I, who know what are the toils of such a life, day by day, on the back of a horse."

"You forget, Mateo, that my father taught me how to ride; that I have been a horse-rider from my childhood, over the ruggedest mountain passes. I fear no steed that was ever bridled. My poor father, you remember him, Mateo?"

"Ah! my lady, do I not? Had he lived, I should never have been a bad fellow; never been an outlaw,—never shed human blood."

"Well, as he had no son, he made a boy of me, and taught me the exercises of boyhood. He showed me the uses of the matchlock and the cross-bow, until I ceased to fear the shock and the report of fire-arms, and could bring down the mountain eagle with my arrows. I have grown into the woman, but I have never lost the spirit, nor the practice, which he taught me. Toil, trial, danger, have no fears for me. I am bolder and braver now than ever Do you have no apprehensions, my good Mateo; for there is that in my soul now which makes me laugh at danger."

The outlaw continued to expostulate, when she abruptly and sternly silenced him.

"Have you not sworn to serve me, Mateo, without questioning?" she demanded, with an air of calm authority.

"And have I not done so, dearest lady? I will still do as you require, if you command me; but I would entreat you—would show you what it is that you propose to encounter and to undertake."

"No more! You mean well; but you know not. You speak in vain. I am resolved! My life is on it, Mateo! I live now for the one object only, and this executed, I shall gladly lay down my life. But while I do live, I must thus work, thus toil, thus peril life, and know life only in this peril. If there be storm and strife, and battle—ay, blood—it is even so much the better. I can now better endure the tempest than the calm. It is in this calm, that I can encounter a thousand terrors worse than any which the storm may bring."

He would have still entreated, but she spoke decidedly.

"No more! I tell you, I am resolute as death. Do as I command you, or tell me that you will do nothing. I will then seek some servant who thinks himself less wise, and proves more faithful."

"Ah! be not angry with me, dear Señorita. I am not wise, and I am faithful. None can be more so. It is because of my love for you——"

"Enough, Mateo; I do not doubt your fidelity; and to any other woman,—to a woman in any less wretched case than mine, your counsel would be sensible and proper. But—you know, perhaps, Mateo—but mine is not the common fate of woman! If you knew my misfortune, you must know that I am doomed to a ceaseless agony while I live; and that toil, and physical pain, and death itself, have no tortures such as I must inevitably endure in life! I have resolved! Let me hear if I may hope for further help from you?"

The big tear gathered in the eye of the *Mestizo*, as he looked into her sad, wan face. She was tearless; and the intense spiritual gleam from her eyes almost filled him with terror. How should such a glare,—such an expression—gleam forth from such beautiful, such childlike eyes! How should such a resolution inform so delicate a creature!

"I'd sooner fight for you, a thousand times," he exclaimed "but I'm ready to do what you ask, and what I promised."

"Do it, then! We have little time to lose. Leave me, and procure the horses."

He obeyed sadly, and in silence. The horses were soon ready, and she was apprised of it. She did not delay. One moment in silent prayer she sank down before the image of the Madonna, then rose with a step of firmness and walked forth into the grove where the saddled steed was in waiting. It was an hour short of midnight. The stars were few in heaven. The gusts swept, with a sad soughing, through the woods, and seemed filled with mournful and warning voices. The ear of the outlaw was sensible to the sounds, and his more superstitious nature held them to be ominous. But Olivia seemed not to hear or heed them. She wrung the hand of Juana in silence, leapt into the saddle, and, followed by Mateo on horseback also, she turned once more in the direction of Havana. Juana remained behind to plead the indisposition of her mistress, and baffle, for awhile, the curiosity of De Sinolar.

The wayfarers rode hard and fast. In a low and seemingly unoccupied hovel in the suburbs of the city, we find Olivia safely housed before daylight. The place had been selected and procured for her by Mateo, agreeably to previous instructions. There was a rude couch, upon which she rested for awhile. But not long. She was soon up and busy. Mateo was summoned, and was promptly in attendance.

"Are all the things here, Mateo?"

"You will find them in that box, my lady."

"Have you prepared——"

"Every thing, Señorita. I have done all; I am ready for all things: but O! my lady, it is not yet too late."

"What do you fear, Mateo?"

"Every thing for you, Señorita—nothing for myself. Nay, if you will believe me, I would sooner cut for you the throats of a dozen such villains as Don Balthazar, than see you go on this fearful business."

"Nay, Mateo, I wish no throats cut for me! Still less that of——"

"Oh! if you would only listen to me, Señorita."

She answered with a strange smile, and so calmly, that he was disturbed by the very repose of her voice and manner, as it argued a resolution so utterly immovable.

"Well,—what would you say, Mateo?"

The poor fellow could only repeat what he had so idly urged already.

"Say, my lady, say?—Why, I would say that you know not what it is you are about to undertake and undergo! That you are not fit—not strong enough!——"

"Is it fatigue, pain, peril, loss of life, the agony of wounds? I am prepared for all these! Must I repeat to you that I should gladly welcome either, or all, of these, if I could lose those horrors which oppress me now! Horrors! but if you know not——"

"But if you are discovered?"

"Ah! that is the terror! that!"—after a pause: "But I must brave it! I tell you, Mateo, I cannot remain here! I cannot survive thus! I must extort from new griefs, troubles, privations and dangers, such excitement as shall obliterate the past! I know not what you know, of my cause of agony; but I suspect, Mateo, that you know enough to understand that I can fly to nothing worse, in the shape of woe, than I have already had to meet! If you *know* this, be silent! If you are prepared to serve me faithfully, be submissive! Let me have no further entreaty."

"The Virgin be with you, my dear lady, and bring you help and succor! I go to do all as you have commanded."

With these words he left her. She closed and fastened the door behind him; and, for a while, stood where she had been speaking; wholly absorbed in thought; looking like a statue rather than a breathing woman! Then she spoke, half in prayer, half in soliloquy:

"Ay! the Blessed Virgin! Succor! Succor! I surely need her help! Would she have come sooner! Oh! how wild the pathway seems before me! What clouds, how torn! How flitting with the wind: and what a crowd of changing and frightful aspects! They drift along, with the force of the tempest, which they vainly offer to resist! Now, they cry to one another for help and succor! But they disappear, even as they cry, swallowed up in the fearful void, and making way for other forms and aspects! There is no sun, no moon, no stars; but there is a light as from the eyes of death; sepulchral, and filled with myriads of floating spectres! What can it mean! Where am I! What do I see? Ah! these are Hernan de Soto, and his troops and followers! That is Nuno de Tobar: yonder rides—Oh! how my heart loathes him as he rides!—and, yonder is—Oh! Blessed Virgin, it is myself I see! But the spectre lives and moves,—and *serves!* It is Don Philip that charges away in front—away! away! and—see, how the boy follows him! Ah!...."

The highly wrought and febrile condition of Olivia's brain, must account for her apparent vision, in which she sees the known and the conjectured; in which she mingles a past knowledge with her own future purposes. The madness lasted but for a brief space! She seemed suddenly to recover, and sank upon her knees before the image of the Virgin. She now prayed inaudibly; then rose, calm,—rigid rather in every muscle, and then proceeded to unfold the contents of trunks and chests, as if with the view of making her toilet. Let us leave her to this performance

CHAPTER XXX.

"I have surely seen him :
His favor is familiar to me.
Boy, thou hast looked thyself into my grace,
And art mine own."
                                   CYMBELINE.

The eighteenth day of May, in the year of grace, one thousand, five hundred and thirty-nine—more than three hundred years ago!—was marked with a white stone in the calendar of Don Hernan de Soto; for, on that day, his squadron, eight large vessels (small-sized schooners of our days), a caravel (a sloop) and two brigantines—things with scarce a deck at all—sailed from the noble harbor of Havana, with their prows turned east in the direction of the opposite coast of Florida. But it was rather late in the day before they took their departure; and though the armament had been supposed in readiness several days before, yet, when the time came, there were many things that required to be hurried. Of these, the Adelantado had his share: and Don Balthazar more than his share; all needing to be attended to, and sped. But, of the cares of these great personages, we will say nothing in this place. They scarcely affect our narrative. We shall confine ourselves to those of Don Philip de Vasconselos, chiefly; and relate how he was provided with a Moorish page, almost at the last moment, and on the most liberal terms.

The sun was just warming the tops of the Cuban mountains, when the good knight was summoned to the entrance of his lodgings, to hearken to an unexpected visitor. This was no other than our old acquaintance, Mateo, the outlaw. Don Philip was on the alert, and was not found napping even at that early hour. He was busy brushing up his armor; condensing his wardrobe into the smallest possible compass; preparing his steed and furniture; for transfer to one of the caravels where a place had been appointed him; and adjusting his affairs, in general, for that removal which had now become inevitable.

Don Philip met the outlaw with a grave, but gentle welcome; spoke, and looked him kindly; and asked what he could do for him. The sight of the features of the Portuguese knight, seemed to occasion some difficulty in the speech of the outlaw. The sadness, approaching confirmed melancholy, which his face wore, and when the tones of his voice so well expressed, reminded Mateo of many matters, and in particular, of one very terrible scene, in which he had beheld the brave cavalier wounded to the very soul; crushed, as it were, into the earth, and partly by his proceedings. The whole scene came back to both parties as they met; and, as the gloom darkened on the visage of Don Philip, the mind of Mateo became agitated and confused, in a way wholly unwonted with the rough, wild, half-savage character of the *Mestizo*. But he plucked up resolution to reply, and in tones as simple and unconstrained as possible.

"Well, Señor, it's not so much what you can do for me, as what I can do for you!—You've been wanting a page or squire, Señor," said the outlaw, "and you haven't got one yet?"

"It is true, Mateo. I did not like the looks of any that were brought me. Can you help me to one? Do you know?———"

"I *can* provide you with a Page, Señor; not a servant; a young lad, a kinsman, a nephew of my own; brown like myself, but the child of a free woman of the mountains; who has heard of you, and would like to see a little of the world, and of armies, under such a brave leader; but he can't be bought. He's the son of a free woman, Señor, as I tell you, and will serve you for love, not for money; and will bring his own horse, and provide his own means; and will only expect to be treated kindly, and to be taught the art of war; and———"

"Will he submit—will he obey me?"

"Certainly, as a page, Señor: and will be happy to do so. I can answer for all that, Señor. He will do for you, I am sure, as no bondman would ever do—will be faithful always—and be very glad when you employ him, for he is pleased with you, Señor,—he has seen you often, and admires you very much! He longs to go with you, and hasn't let me rest, for the last week, for urging me to come to you and make the offer. He don't want pay—he has means of his own, as I told you: his mother, a free woman of the mountains, Señor, has property; cattle and horses; and though the boy is quite young, and slightly built, yet he has health and strength, and can stand a good deal of trouble and fatigue; all he wants is to be with you;—that is, to see war under your lead;—and as he's the son of a free woman, Señor, I thought it right, perhaps, that he should have such desires, and should learn from the best teacher."

"Bring him to me, Mateo."

"He is here at hand—I could not well keep him away, Señ. He is *so* anxious!"

Here the outlaw turned away for a moment from the lodge of

the knight, and, stepping down to the highway, he gave a slight halloo. In sight, stood a boy holding a stout and spirited steed. He approached at the signal, leading the horse. When he drew nigh, the knight, who had retired into the lodge for a moment, reappeared, and gazed steadily upon the new-comer.

"Let the boy fasten the horse to yon sapling, Mateo, and draw nigh, that I may have some talk with him. He has a fine horse, Mateo."

"Yes, Señor, I raised him myself. He walks like the wind, and will go like an eagle to the charge. Suppose you step out, and look at him closely, Señor. You must love a fine animal, Señor, and this is one for a brave man to love, without feeling ashamed of his choice."

How the heart, already vitally sore, applies the most remote allusion to the cause of its secret suffering! This casual remark of Mateo, smote on the sensibilities of Philip de Vasconselos, like a sneer. But the face of Mateo was innocent of any occult meaning; and Philip showed that he felt, simply by an increased solemnity of voice and visage. He followed the outlaw out to where the horse stood, still held by the boy in waiting. The first regards of the knight were given entirely to the steed.

"He is certainly a very fine animal, Mateo. You do not praise him more than he deserves."

"See what a chest he carries, Señor, broad like a castle. See what legs, so clean, so wiry. There's not an ounce of fat to spare from those quarters. There's not a long hair that you'd like to pull out from those fetlocks. And, look at his eye! It's like that of a great captain! Cortez, I warrant, does not open a finer when he looks down from the towers of the Mexican. See what a mane of silk! It is like the hair of a Princess. And he's young, but a quarter over four, Señor; and he comes of a breed that lasts till forty."

"Unless no shaft from an Apalachian savage cuts him short;" was the remark of Vasconselos, sadly made, as he turned to bestow a look upon the boy.

There seemed to be a new interest springing into the eyes of Philip as he gazed. The boy was of fine, dark bronze complexion, looking more like the native race of Indians, than the *Mestizo cross*, from which he was said to have sprung: he was well made, and symmetrical; with good limbs and much grace of outline. But Vasconselos dwelt not so much upon the form, as the face, of the youth. This seemed to rivet his attention for a while. And the effect of his gaze was to disquiet the boy himself, and Mateo, his uncle. The former closed his eyes, involuntarily, under the steadfast glance of the knight; and the outlaw hurriedly said:

"The boy is bashful, Señor: he has never before stood in the presence of a great captain, or a knight, or even a fine gentleman. He is from the mountains, as I said, and don't know about the fine behavior of a young man of the city, who is always expected to look up, you know, as if he was born to say to the sun—'stop a little—I must talk with you.' Now, Juan——"

"Juan?—Is that his name?"

"Yes, Juan, Señor; his mother's name is Juana, a free woman of the mountains, Señor——"

"His face reminds me very much of one that I have seen somewhere. I have certainly seen him before, Mateo."

"Never him, Señor,—never!" replied the other sturdily. "Juan has never been to the city before last week; and you, I know, have never been into the mountains, Señor. He is a mountain boy, your Excellency,—son of a free woman of the mountains. He has seen *you*, but you could not have seen *him* before. But what's in a likeness, Señor? You will see them every day, every where. I have seen thousands of likenesses, in my time, for which there was not the slightest bit of reason. Now, Juan looks like several people I know, and you may have seen *them*. He looks very like Antonio Morelos, a creole of Havana, here. You must have seen *him*. Then, he looks monstrous like his mother, and she has been a thousand times to the city. Oh! likenesses are nothing now, we see so many. You never could have seen our Juan's face before, Señor."

Mateo talked rapidly, rather than earnestly, as if against time and the wind. Vasconselos did not seem to hear half what he was saying. He still kept an earnest eye upon the boy, as if deeply interested; evidently communing with every feature of his face—as far, that is to say, as he was allowed to see them. But the boy's eyes were cast down. *He* saw nothing; yet felt, evidently, that the keen eyes of the knight were upon him.

"The boy is young, very young, Mateo, and I very much fear will hardly be able to stand the fatigues of such a campaign as that we shall have to endure in Florida."

"Oh! he is strong, Señor. His looks are deceptive. **He** comes of a hardy race. He can stand fire and water."

"But he seems unusually timid. Art thou sure that he has courage? Will he look danger in the eye?"

The boy seemed disposed to answer for himself. He looked up—he looked Don Philip in the eye, and without blenching

16

Nay, there was so much of a settled calm—an unflinching resolution in his sudden glance, that the knight was struck with it.

"Certainly," quoth he, "that was something like a lightening up of the spirit. He is capable of flashes, Mateo."

"Ay, and of fire and flame too, Señor! Faggots! Give him time, your Excellency, and you will see the blaze. But he's naturally bashful when you're looking on him. It's not a bad sign in a boy, Señor."

"No, truly! But I like his looks, Mateo. There is something in those features that please me much. Were I sure of the strength and courage of the boy,—his capacity to endure,—I should not hesitate: I should feel sure of his fidelity."

"Oh! that I can promise, Señor. He's as faithful to the man he loves as if he were a woman."

"Pity but he were more so!" responded the knight quickly. The outlaw felt that he had blundered, and he promptly strove to recover his false step.

"As a woman is expected to be, your Excellency; that's what I mean! I can answer for Juan; for his courage, his hardihood, not less than his honesty, Señor. He's a boy of good principles."

"Let him answer for himself! Somehow, Mateo, I am a little doubtful of your answers. You are too quick to be quite sure of what you say! Hark ye, Juan, are you sure you desire to go with me, to Florida?"

The boy evidently trembled: but promptly enough, in a rather hoarse voice, answered—

"Yes, Señor! I wish to go with you."

The voice was a strange one, yet, its tones seemed to interest the knight, as if there was something familiar in them also.

"He has a very peculiar voice, Mateo."

"Yes, Señor, strange enough to those who heard him only a year ago. Now, his voice is getting the cross 'twixt man and boy. It's rather more a squeak than a song, your Excellency. But I reckon, Señor, we all underwent some such change about the same time in our lives."

Don Philip. But, my good boy, you don't know the toil and trouble; the daily marching in that country; where there are no roads; only rank forests, great swamps, wild beasts, deadly reptiles; where, half the time, you may be without food; and perhaps, quite as frequently without water.

Juan. Yes, Señor, but if one would be a soldier, it's a part of his education to taste these things. I am to be a soldier, you know

Philip. True; but you begin early! There is a certain hardening necessary before one can be a soldier

Juan. This campaign will give it me, Señor.

Mateo. You see, your Excellency, his heart is set on being a soldier.

"True; but one does not begin training for it, in the midst of a campaign," quoth Philip, not heeding the outlaw.

Juan. You forget, Señor, that I was bred among the mountains.

Philip. If you had been bred upon the plains, my boy, it might be more in your favor, going to Florida. But you forget the danger.

Juan. It is that of war, Señor, and I am not afraid to die.

Philip. So young, and not afraid to die? but you speak what you cannot know! Bethink you of the terrors of the strife; the savage arrows,—his cannibal sacrifices,—his bloody rages,—the scalping knife,—the fiery torture!

Juan. Yet *you* are to encounter them, Señor.

Philip. I am a *man*, boy, accustomed to the encounter; and life is to me of little worth. I have survived its hopes.

Juan. And I have none, Señor.

Philip. Thou no hopes, at a season when the heart is all hope, or should be?

Mateo. Ah! you don't know Juan, Señor. He was always a saddish sort of boy; loving the glooms; the dark woods; the lonely rocks! He never played like other boys! He was never *like* other boys.

Philip. But he will outgrow this sadness, Mateo. He will grow to hopes. It would be cruel to peril one so young, so tender yet, in such a warfare as that with the Floridian savage!

Juan. You allow nothing for the *will*, Señor,—the heart—nothing——

Philip. Every thing, boy! will and heart are the great essentials of all achievement. Can it be that thou art already ambitious?

Mateo. That he is, your Excellency. It's his great folly, Señor; I've told him so a thousand times. For what can his ambition do, *for him*, a *mestizo?* Let him be as brave as Francis Pizarro, and as wise as Hernan Cortez, who'll give *him* command of armies, and authority in counsel? Here am I now, as brave, *I* think, as any man that ever stepped in leather; yet what am I but an outlaw! I don't think I'm wanting in a sort of sense either, yet who listens to me?

Philip. The boy talks sensibly, Mateo, yet he is very young

Mateo. If he lives much longer, Señor, he'll grow much older. And if he don't live long, he'll only be more sure of being young all the days of his life.

Philip. Logical enough, Mateo; yet I have no wish to shorten his days.

"Try me, Señor," murmured the boy, in very low but earnest tones, not daring to look up. There was a pleasant change in the voice, which seemed to interest the hearer. He put his hand on the head of the boy, who started from under the touch, and visibly trembled. But Philip was not permitted to see his face.

"Do you not overrate both your courage and your strength, my boy? You start and tremble at my touch."

"'Tis not with *fear*, Señor!" was the subdued reply, still in the same low, sweet accents.

"No! For why should you fear *me*, child? But you seem naturally timid—nervous, I should say;—and such wars as that we go upon, require hardihood above all other things. There must be no agitation when the trumpet rings the alarm. There must be no faltering when we are bade to charge. The page of the knight will be expected to do good service, and to follow close after his master, even if he does not emulate him. Canst thou carry a lance, Juan?"

"I am provided with a cross-bow, Señor, and can shoot. The lance will come——"

"Thou art so eager for it, Juan——"

"Oh! take me with you, Señor!"

"I like thee, boy. Thou hast something about thee which appeals strangely to my imagination."

And the good knight sighed deeply. His instincts, rather than his memory, perhaps, guided his asseverations. The boy hung his head also. He dared not, at that moment, look up in the face of Don Philip.

"I will take thee with me, boy, and fight thy battles, if need be; will keep thee as much from harm as possible, and share with thee my spoils——"

"I ask nothing, Señor!" said the boy hastily.

"Oh! no, Señor!" quoth Mateo. "My sister is a free woman of the mountains. Her son is able to pay his own way. He wishes to go to see service and learn a profession, and will share no one's spoil. He hopes to make his own. Besides, my sister is resolute that her son shall take no pay for his services. Remember that, Señor. She has provided him, as you see, with a good horse. She has given him a well-filled pouch besides! she has made all provisions for his support and equipment; and I am commissioned to get even the needful weapons and armor. So you see, Señor, he is to go with you for *love*, not for money."

"For love!" murmured the boy.

"Be it so, Juan," said the knight, taking his hand. "Be it as thou wilt. Thou shalt go with me, boy. Thou shalt be my companion, rather than my page. But thou wilt find me a sad companion, Juan—a melancholy master. I tremble for thee, besides, when I behold thy slight frame, thy timidity, thy tenderness and youth. We must be true to each other, Juan; for we go with those who are true only to themselves. We must love each other, Juan; for in all that assembled host, there will be few worthy of any pure heart's love. Wilt thou love me, boy, spite of my gloomy visage, and melancholy moods?"

"I will love thee, Señor—I *do* love thee!" was the murmured reply, and this time the boy looked up. The glances of the two met. Then it was that the knight saw how large and expressive were the eyes of the boy, and what a soft and dewy brightness shone through the dilating orbs. But they sunk in a moment beneath the searching gaze of the knight. They sunk, and the boy again trembled.

"Truth, Mateo, he *is* bashful! But a campaign soon cures that infirmity. Well, Juan, you are mine now."

And he gave the boy his hand, who kissed it passionately, murmuring—

"Thine! Thine!"

The knight turned away to the tent with Mateo, the boy leading his horse and following. Before the close of the day, knight and page were upon the waters of the gulf, rolling forward in a good vessel towards the gloomy shores of the Apalachian.

CHAPTER XXXI.

> "*Æsop.* What do we act to-day?
> *Latinus.* Agavi's phrensy,
> With Pentheus' bloody end."
> MASSINGER. *The Roman Actor.*

BUT we are not yet permitted to depart, and must follow, for a brief space, the fortunes of some other of our *dramatis personæ*. The novelist cannot do always, as he would, with his own creations. He cannot linger always with those whom he prefers. We must suffer the Fates to exercise their controlling agencies just as certainly as they do in real life, and among the living people whom we know. He may create, but he cannot control. It is upon this very condition that he is permitted to create. The Being, once filled with the breath of life, and having made his appearance upon the stage of human action, must thenceforward conform to necessities over which the author exercises no authority. These will have their origin in the character, the actions, and the impulses, of his persons; in the events which flow from their performances; in their conflicts with rival actors on the scene; in their strength or imbecility; with some allowance made for the operation of external causes, which, we are told, will always, more or less, affect the destinies equally of mice and men! Let us leave Philip de Vasconselos, and the dusky page, Juan, to their progress over the blue waters of the gulf, while we follow the steps of Mateo, the outlaw.

As soon as the Mestizo had closed the arrangement, by which his "nephew, the son of a free woman of the mountains," had been secured a place in the service of the knight of Portugal, he disappeared from the vicinity of the Spanish encampment. He had, we may mention, used some precautions when "about town," by which he had kept his person from all unnecessary exposure. He had still some decent regard for the existence of a class of persons, the Alguazils, with whom he entertained few special sympathies; and, in leaving the lodgings of Vasconselos, he had stolen away into covert, by the most secluded passages. A single moment, in private, and under the cover of a clump of trees, densely packed with shrubbery, had sufficed for his parting with Juan. There he might be seen wholly to change the manner of speech and address which he had employed, with regard to the boy, when the knight, his master, was a looker-on. He seized his hand and kissed it repeatedly, and there was a reverence in the expression of his face, and in the words of his mouth, which denoted the existence of relations, between the parties, very different from those which he has been pleased to assert in the conference which has been reported. On leaving the boy, he concluded with a promise to see him, and the good knight of Portugal, at the shore, in the moment of his embarkation.

"It may be," he said, "that I shall follow you—nay, go with you, to the country of the Apalachian; for I long to see great things; and be where the good knights rush to the meeting of the spears! It may be! We shall see!"

When they had separated, and while Mateo pursued his way through the woods, alone, his lips opened in frequent soliloquy.

"Yes!" quoth he, "were it not for that devil of all the devils, Don Balthazar de Alvaro, I should follow the expedition. I would take lance under this good knight. I would fight like the best among them. He hath no followers; but, with me, he should have at least five. I am as good as any five of these men with the cross-bow. And would I not have a good horse of my own? worthy to be straddled by any cavalier in Don Hernan's army? Ah! it would be glorious! How I should smite! Verily, I have a strength in my arm, and a skill with horse and weapon, that would show where blows are thickest. I could clear the track with a sweep! And I am a young man, and in my best strength. It is hard that I should have nothing great to do! Very hard!"

And his speed was accelerated; and his arm could be seen waving, as if he were about to make a mighty swoop with the broadsword.

"But I dare not go, while that black wolf is with the army! He hath an eye to see through me. He hath already known me in a disguise which had baffled the eyes of my own sister; and, failing to do for him this murder of the good knight, he would have me *garotted* without a scruple! Would his throat were cut! I have half a mind to slip off with the rest, and put my knife into him, the first dark night he walks alone. Were I now to meet him, I would slay him!"

And he felt in his girdle for his *machete*, and looked up, and around him, with glaring eye, and distended nostril, as if already snuffing the atmosphere breathed by an enemy. But all was still and quiet where he walked, among the thick groves, inclining to the hills, and now beyond the city suburbs. It was still the cool of early morning, and the whole realm of nature around him seemed to murmur of repose. The inanimate life of the forest declared no unrest—no unruly passions,—no wretched discontent. The sky was now beautifully clear, and if a voice was heard besides his own, it was that only of some very tiny bird, such as harbors only in the stunted shrubbery, where a single leaf will afford instant and close shelter for its form. But the very repose spoke to the violent passions of the outlaw, with a stimulating accent.

"Ah!" said he, "if I only had him here!" and he clenched his fist savagely.

"But I must get those papers! He will be in the camp *soon* to-day. He will be among the last to sail. In an hour, he will have left the hacienda. But may he not return to it, in the hope to see me, and to learn that I have done his work? Perhaps; but hardly! He will scarce have time! Humph! Done *his* work! I must do my own! Verily, if I meet him *there*, I will do it thoroughly! Shall I cut throats except to my own liking? By the Blessed Devils, no! I will cut *his* throat if I can! And if I do, what is to keep me from the expedition? I am a man for the wars. I will see how the lances cross with the shock of thunder. But I must get me those papers. He little dreams that I know their hiding-place. When he goes to the city this morning, it will be to make ready. He will hardly return to the hacienda. Then will I take possession. Juana knows what to do. When the ships have all gone, she goes off to the mountains. She will be doubly safe with the papers of the Señorita, and of that Uncle-devil. She *shall* be safe! Then, if I should find him *there*, and feel my way into his ribs, we are all safe! Oh! If I should only find him there! If he goes on this expedition, will my poor lady be safe a moment? No! No! There's no blinding his snake-eyes! He will see, and I know there will be trouble—and more than trouble;—there will be a great danger always in the path of the good knight Oh! it must be that I shall split his black heart with my knife, and let out all its poison with its blood! It must be, when there's so much good to come of it—when there's no safety for anybody while he lives! I owe him a stroke of my *machete!* And if the Blessed Devils give me half a chance, I will pay him with a vengeance!"

We have here the passions of the outlaw's soul, and the plans of his mind, fairly mingled up together, in that sort of web of thought, which is the usual mental process in the sensuous nature. Don Balthazar, at this moment little dreamed of the danger which threatened him. While Mateo, making his way to the hacienda of the knight, was thus soliloquizing, the haughty Don was savagely meditating, in his turn, upon some of the disappointments which he had experienced. That the Portuguese knight still lived, was a present annoyance, and a vital danger. He now knew himself to be at the mercy of this cavalier, so far as his moral position was concerned. The revelation of his secret, he well knew, would be fatal to his reputation in Cuba, and the army;—so long as the government of both was administered by persons so severely virtuous as he believed Don Hernan de Soto and his noble wife to be. True, he had a certain security for his secret, in the very regard which Philip de Vasconselos evidently entertained for Olivia. So long as she lived, Philip would probably be silent, in respect to that which would hurt her reputation. But who was to secure the unfaithful guardian against the speech of Olivia herself? Her passionate blood had evidently escaped wholly from the control of her tyrant. He had made her desperate, in making her desolate; and he felt that, in death alone, could his safety be made certain. He knew the nature of passionate women too well; and now perceived that Olivia, in this respect, too much resembled her Biscayan mother, of whom his experience was sufficiently vivid, and who, he well knew, in the madness of her awakened passions, had neither fear nor prudence, nor scruple of any sort. He trembled, accordingly; proud, fearless and powerful as he was; lest the reckless, or the thoughtless word of either the knight of Portugal or Olivia de Alvaro, should, at any moment, hurl him headlong from position, making him odious to all, and subjecting him to legal, as well as social, persecution. Why had not the outlaw, Mateo, done his work upon the knight? There were surely opportunities enough; and Mateo was too well known, as a desperado, to suppose that he had either moral scruples, or personal fears! The question troubled the Don, since, from his own conjectures, he vainly sought an answer.

While he meditated these doubts, an *aide* of the Adelantado arrived, and brought him despatches from Don Hernan, which required his early presence in the city. He dismissed the messenger with a reply which promised that he would soon be there, and was now simply making his final preparations for joining the expedition, and superintending the work of embarkation. The officer disappeared, riding fast, and was seen at a distance, as he left the hacienda, by the approaching outlaw.

"Demonios!" muttered Mateo, between his closed teeth, "there goes my last chance! Had I come an hour sooner!"

He had mistaken the rider for Don Balthazar. He now more

leisurely continued his progress, and at length found himself amidst the silent groves surrounding the summer-house of the knight,—that lovely and secluded lodge which had been so fruitful in events affecting the destinies of some of the persons of our drama. It was fated to furnish yet another scene of deep interest to the parties.

Don Balthazar, burning or preserving papers, arranging arms, and armor, was busy and thoughtful in his chamber, when the old hag, Sylvia, suddenly burst into the apartment. He looked up at the intrusion, with a haughty frown; but she was not appalled by it. She was wild with excitement; and her sinister and withered features were now absolutely fiendish in the expression of rage which they exhibited. She could scarcely speak, so agitating were her emotions. When she did succeed in giving utterance to the cause of her excitement, she was surprised to find that her master did not partake of her wrath, and seemed lightly to listen to her communications.

"He is here, Señor;" she exclaimed,—"the villain, Mateo; the outlaw; the murderer; the robber of the old woman! He is here, Señor, in the groves; he is even now gone to the garden house!"

Mateo had evidently neglected his usual precautions. Satisfied that the horseman whom he had seen pushing for the city, at full speed, was Don Balthazar himself, he had been at no pains to make his movements secret.

"Ah! he is here, then,—Mateo?" and the knight smiled with a grim complaisance, and muttered, *sotto voce*—"He has done it, then, perhaps, and comes for his reward! Good! He knows his time, and has, no doubt, done it efficiently! Well! I must see him."

He at once rose, and, with his sword only at his side, moved quickly from the chamber. Sylvia was quite confounded; and followed, muttering her surprise as she went. Don Balthazar never once looked behind, and did not see her; or he would have dismissed her with severity. And then!—But we must not anticipate!

He hurried on; and so rapid were his movements, that the stiffened limbs of the old woman utterly failed to enable her to keep any sort of pace with the progress which he made. He was soon in the groves; had soon overpassed the space; and, walking in the buckskin shoes, the use of which the Spaniards had borrowed from the red men,—wearing them commonly when in their peaceful avocations,—he entered the garden house unheard.

He was confounded at what he beheld. The outlaw had coolly

taken possession of the premises. He was on his knees, in the recess where stood the army chest in which Don Balthazar had stored the papers which the outlaw sought; his head was fairly buried in the chest, and he was busily engaged evidently in the examination of all its contents. The surprise was complete. For a moment, the knight stood motionless, watching the cool intruder! He saw the secret of the proceeding at a glance.

"The scoundrel," said he to himself, "has seen me put away the papers in the chest, and he now comes to steal them, without having done the service!" Then, aloud, advancing as he spoke, and laying his hand upon the outlaw's shoulder, he said—

"How now, rascal, what are you doing here?"

The cool, hardy, daring character of Mateo, was such as to render surprises less dangerous to him, and less difficult of evasion, than would be the case with most people. At the sound of the knight's voice, he immediately conceived the predicament in which he stood. But, that Don Balthazar *spoke*, and only laid his hand on his shoulder, when he might have run him through the body, as a first salutation, was an absolute surrender of all the advantages of the surprise; and afforded to the bold ruffian the chance of operating a surprise in turn. Certainly, most persons, taken thus at advantage, would have lost something of their moral resources in consequence of their position. But Mateo was not an ordinary ruffian. The forbearance of the knight showed the outlaw that the former would not be likely, under the circumstances, to anticipate resistance, still less assault, from the person he appeared to think so completely in his power;—and the exercise of his thought, to this effect, at such a moment, exhibited Mateo in possession of a more deeply searching mind than his superior. In the twinkling of an eye, with a rare agility, which, in the outlaw, was a possession fully equal to his wonderful strength, he suddenly slipped from under the grasp of the Don, and, before the latter dreamed of his danger, had changed positions with him; had thrown himself upon him, and forced him down upon the chest, with his head buried among its recesses. To do this was the work of an instant only. Fortunately for the knight, the assailant had not a single weapon in his grasp. He had been using his *machete*, in prying open the cover of the chest, and had thrown it down upon the floor a few feet distant. But his fingers seemed to be made of steel, and these grappled the throat of Don Balthazar, with a gripe so close and fierce, that in a single moment of time, the latter had grown purple in the face, while his eyes dilated wildly in their sockets.

"Villain, would you murder me?" gasped the cavalier, vainly struggling to rise, and making efforts as desperate as unavailing.

"You have come for it! I thought you safe, and I cursed the Blessed Devils, that helped you off. But I did 'em wrong! They have delivered you into my hands! You thought to buy me, did you, to kill the good knight of Portugal? I'll kill *you* for him! I'll kill you for the poor young lady, my mistress! Oh! didn't I see, with my own eyes, just as Don Philip saw? You ought to die a hundred deaths! But, as it's only once for you as for other men, the sooner you taste it, the sooner you get your wages. You shan't have time to say a prayer; not one: for you shan't have any mercy from God any more than from me! Die! I say; die! Die! Die!"

The knight succumbed; he had neither room nor strength for struggle. Hands and head buried in the chest, and face downwards, he was helpless! The hoarse gurgle of his breath in the throat was already painful to the ear, and the writhings of his form were those of a man vainly struggling with the last potent enemy; when, suddenly, a sound was heard by the writhing and almost suffocated man,—a sound,—a stroke!—another, and another!—and the gripe of his enemy relaxed; and there was a wild yell above him;—but one!—and Don Balthazar felt relieved. He began once more to breathe. He felt no longer the incumbent weight of the gigantic ruffian upon his back! Gradually, he recovered consciousness. He heard a voice calling him by name. He felt hands officiously helping him to rise; he felt a cool but grateful shock of water. His eyes opened to the day once more. He looked about him: slowly, but fully, at length, his glance took in the objects around him. He found himself seated beside the chest, from which he had been rolled out rather than lifted; and, before him, stiff in death, lay the corse of the outlaw, who, but a little before, had been so completely in his power! The old hag, Sylvia, stood at hand to help her master, and soon explained the agency by which his life had been saved. She had followed him to the summer-house, curious to see and hear, and anxious for the recovery of her goods, of which Mateo had deprived her. She had come not a moment too soon! Seeing the knight's danger, she had caught up the hatchet which was employed for trimming the trees and shrubbery of the grove, and which lay in the verandah of the summer-house, convenient, with saw and other implements; and, without a word,—governed by instincts which always prompt to decisive action where the mind has few thoughts to trouble it,—had stolen behind the outlaw. **He, bent** only on strangling his enemy,—with passions **which** deadened the sense,—heard nothing of her approach! A stunning blow from the hatchet made him conscious of his danger, while almost taking all consciousness away! He was not allowed a moment. Stroke after stroke followed, with the hammer, as with the edge of the hatchet; delivered without regard to the appropriate use of the weapon, but delivered with such a will as made every stroke tell fatally; until the head was cleft wide; the skull beaten in;—and the strong, fierce, wild, savage man rolled upon the floor;—a ghastly spectacle of death; wallowing in blood; —in a moment, torn from life; in the moment of his greatest strength of arm and passion; and, by the withered arm of a despised old woman! The outlaw knew not by whose arm, or by what weapon he perished. He saw not his assailant. He was not allowed to turn and face his danger: the reiterated blows fell crushingly and fast, and he sunk under them, a helpless mass, in less time than we have employed in describing the event.

CHAPTER XXXII.

"*Master, go on, and I will follow thee,
To the last gasp, with truth and loyalty.*'

As You Like It.

It was a goodly hour after the event, before Don Balthazar had sufficiently recovered from his sufferings to resume his activity, or comply with the summons of the Adelantado, to return to the city. When able to rise and look about him, he gave his orders with customary *sang froid*, for the removal and disposition of the dead body of the outlaw, which was publicly exposed during the day, and finally hung in chains by the public executioner. But this exhibition did not take place till after the departure of the expedition; and the good Knight of Portugal, and his page Juan, were somewhat surprised at not exchanging farewells with the bold outlaw, as he had promised them should be the case. They little anticipated for him, such a short and hurried transition, from the extreme health, hope and vigor of impetuous and eager manhood, to the stagnating and corrupting embrace of death; and did not learn, until they had arrived in Florida, the history of the bloody and fatal conflict which we have narrated. It was with a feeling of disappointment, that they turned their eyes upon the wide waste of waters before their prows, from the crowds upon the shore, gradually melting into masses, and to be individualized no longer. As the night came on, Philip de Vasconselos threw himself upon the deck of the caravel, musing sadly upon the stars as they silently stole out to sight, and hardly knew that the boy Juan crouched as silently behind him. There was scarcely a word spoken between them that night, yet, somehow, this silent attendance, and simple devotion of the page, strengthened, at each moment, the feeling of sympathy, with which the knight, from the very first, regarded him.

"The boy hath a heart," quoth Philip to himself;—"he can feel. He hath not yet survived his tenderness. But it will not be for long. The world rarely leaves us long in possession of such a treasure. Were he wise, now, the sooner he flings it from him, or puts it to silence, the more sure were he to escape its sorrows. What profits it to us that we have the wealth that keeps us wakeful; when sleep,—sleep,—is the best blessing that we need, and ought to pray for? Oh! that I might shut out thought when I shut mine eyes; or hush the heart into silence that only wounds me with its cries!"

Thus, the knight. The boy, no doubt, had his musings also. They both slept upon the deck, nightly, in close neighborhood, throughout the voyage. Neither spoke much; but they grew silently together. If Don Philip showed himself wakeful and restless, and strode the deck at times throughout the night, the boy watched him the while, and sometimes followed his footsteps; though always at a distance. Gradually, this distance lessened between them. The page followed close his master. Voyagers in a frail barque, upon the lonely wastes of ocean, rarely observe the restraining barriers which keep the souls of men apart on shore; and the devotion of the boy, his silent watchfulness, his unobtrusive attention, at length, won the knight's regard; and he called him to his side in frequent remark; and he bade him observe the stars; and he called them by their several names; and taught him their uses to the mariner; and he discoursed of the winds; of their mysterious birth and origin: how some of them were gracious, always, in regard to the seaman; how others brought poison to the atmosphere. Then he spoke of the new wild world of the Apalachian to which they were approaching, and of which Vasconselos taught the page many strange things; all of which he had learned from his own experience, in the famous adventure which he had pursued along with Cabeza de Vaca on his famous expedition;—thus teaching his young companion various matters of which one so young and untutored could not be expected to know. And the boy reverently listened, and loved to listen, though in sooth, he knew much more of these things than the good knight supposed, and had enjoyed much better sources of knowledge than might beseem his present position. Of this Philip de Vasconselos had no conjecture, though he could see that the page was by no means an ordinary boy; was quick to conceive, and to apprehend; and when he replied, did so shrewishly, and with an intelligence and thought as much beyond his apparent age, as beyond his situation and race. But, it was in the delicate sensibilities of Juan, that the knight took most interest. Now, these sensibilities of youth do not declare themselves usually in words, or in ordinary fashion. Where the heart feels quickly, and the emotions wait ever in readiness for the summons, words are not always present to serve the wants or wishes of the superior endowment. This must show itself to the eye and mind of him who would understand and love it; and it requires, accordingly, mind and eye, capable of reading a very subtle, profound and mysterious language. Now the secret of this capacity is to be found only in very active susceptibilities, on the part of him who reads. His open sensibilities must be keen and watchful; he must possess a gentle spirit at the core: he must have loved and suffered; must still love and suffer; must be full of pity and sorrow, though he speaks little and doth not complain; and there must be a rare delicacy of sentiment in his soul, so that there shall be no change in the aspect of the other whom he seeks or esteems, however slight, that he shall not see, and comprehend at a single glance. Nor wants he to see, except to be solicitous; nor comprehend that he may slight. It is enough, here to say, that these conditions, by which kindred spirits seek, meet, and link themselves with one another, were all found in the respect of Don Philip and the boy Juan; so that a look, a tone, a gesture, of one or the other, did not fail to make itself fully understood by both, and to command at the same time the most genial sympathy. And it shall be no long time, after such is found to be the case between two such parties, when it will be impossible to maintain cold barriers of society, keeping them separate; when the two hearts shall so yearn for the close communion, that the mind shall forget all the distinctions of men on land, and there shall be a gentle law controlling both, which shall do away utterly with all common usages of constraint, substituting others of a finer fabric, more subtle, apparent, and not less strong; which shall grow out of veneration and sympathy. Thus it was that Philip de Vasconselos soon learned—even in that short voyage—to love the boy, Juan, as a boy of truly loyal and devout soul; as of tender and sweet sympathies; and of tastes so delicate, as equally to confound the knight at their possession by one of his sex and race. The boy, on the other hand, might be supposed to love the knight because of his justice, his noble purpose and princely thoughts; his great courage and skill in arms; his graceful carriage; and for all that was manly and great in his character. It might be that, had Philip been of the other sex, these traits would have proved less imposing in the estimation of the page! But it matters little as to what were the causes, respectively working, by which the two gradually grew to be so well attached to each other. Enough, that such is the fact, and that they held frequent communion. With whom else should Philip commune? Never was noble knight more desolate of soul, and lone of place, than he. Often did the eyes of Philip rest searchingly upon the bronze features of the boy, with a curious and tender interest. It seemed to him that the features which he perused, were such as had been known to him before; that they were, in some sort, precious to his memory, as they were grateful to his sight. At such moments, the eyes of the page would be cast down, and the knight fancied that there was an expression of emotion, in his countenance, amounting to compassion, when he was conscious of this silent study. But Philip spoke nothing of the thoughts which this conduct occasioned : yet he did not the less continue to examine the features of the youth ; and he found a strange secret pleasure in this study. Nor did he, because of the study, continue the less to teach, and to commune with the young mind which he was pleased to instruct. And thus it happened that the two scarcely sought, or found, much communion with any others of the ship. The boy knew none, of all in the army, but Philip, and he, with few friends in the expedition, had, as it happened, none of them in the same vessel with himself. Nuno de Tobar, his only close associate in Cuba, and his own brother Andres, had both been taken on board the same barque which bore the Adelantado and Don Balthazar de Alvaro.

The expedition, according to one of the accounts, had set sail from Havana on the 12th of May, 1539 ; other authorities say the 18th of the same month. In all probability the latter was the true date. The fleet, in safety, reached the coast of Florida on the 25th, being seven days at sea. But whether it sailed on the 12th or 18th, in either case, the voyage had not been a long one, for that period, in those capricious seas,—and in that season of the year. The fleet entered the Bay of Tampa, to which De Soto gave the name of Espiritu Santo. The soul of the Adelantado was greatly lifted at the success of the voyage,— all his ships arriving in good order, and at the same time ;—and at the noble display of his armament on the shores of the Apalachian. Never before had so splendid an army been sent from the old world to the new. It consisted of no less than a thousand men, of whom three hundred and fifty were cavaliers on horseback. These were, many of them, of the noblest families of Castile. The knights were provided with helmets, and cuirasses, and shields, and steel armor ; armed with swords of the best temper, and with well-tried lances of Biscay ; a complete and admirable equipment. The great body of the troops wore coats of *escaupil*, a sort of thick buff coats, wadded with cotton, the better to resist the fearful arrows of the red men. They were armed with arquebus or crossbow, and carried with them a single piece of artillery. Fleet greyhounds were provided to run down the fugitives, and well-trained bloodhounds were held in leash, to do good duty in the thickest of the fight,—to rend or devour the naked savages, upon whom they had been taught to feed. The chivalry of that day found nothing inhuman in the use of such an agency in war. But, as mere conquest were nothing without taking heed to its acquisitions, workmen, and the necessary apparatus, were carried, for the purpose of smelting and refining the precious metals which they confidently expected to find. Nor were the chains, handcuffs, and collars of iron, forgotten, by which their captives were to be secured, in order to be shipped safely to the plantations of the Cuban. Droves of cattle, mules, and hogs, constituted a more benevolent provision, made for the wants of the expedition, when it should reach the country, where the hogs and cattle were to be let go free.

Accustomed to the easy conquest of such feeble tribes as the Peruvian, De Soto felt that such an armament, so far surpassing those of Cortez and Pizarro, was quite equal to the conquest over the whole country of the Apalachian. Never a doubt of this result crossed the mind of the haughty Adelantado, and he made instant preparations for throwing a body of troops on shore, and taking possession of the territory in the name of his monarch, the Emperor, Charles the Fifth. The wealthy knight, Vasco Porcallos, claimed the high honor of leading this party, and performing this act of sovereignty; and the privilege was conceded him. He was to have the command of a force of three thousand men, being, in fact, all those who could be prepared for disembarkation during that day. The shipping, meanwhile, were gradually warping in shore, a performance not so easy on account of the rapid shoaling of the water, and for which they had to depend upon the tides. Meanwhile, more for the purposes of solemnity and state, than because he felt the need to be taught anything, the Adelantado called a council of his chief officers. Philip de Vasconselos was invited to this conference. He, by the way, had been one of those designated to land with Vasco Porcallos, the better that he might act as interpreter, should there be any meeting with the red men. With regard to this sort of service, De Soto now more than ever felt the importance of having one with him who not only had some knowledge of the country, but who could thus become a medium of communication with its people. Though still a little too lofty and reserved towards our knight of Portugal, he yet descended somewhat from his pride of place in order to solicit him. He had already distinguished him by the request, that he would serve about his person as one of his Lieutenants,— a request which the other had no motive to refuse; and he cheerfully consented to disembark among the first with Vasco Por callos. His first counsel to the Adelantado, and the other chiefs, was that every step should be taken with great circumspection; that there should be horse patrols on every side; that the most unrelaxing watchfulness should be required of every sentinel; that the troops should sleep in their armor, and have their weapons constantly at hand.

"These Apalachians, Señores," said he, "are a fierce and fearless race; they are no such feeble and timid people, as those of Cuba and Peru. They love the fight with a passion which prefers it as their best delight. They ask no mercy, and they accord none. It will need all our valor and prudence, and we shall triumph rather less through our valor, than our modes of delivering battle,—the peculiarity of our weapons,—the terrors inspired by our arquebuses,—which shall seem to the savages no less than thunder and swords of the subtle lightning; and the awe with which they shall behold our horses; to them so many unknown and devouring monsters; which they shall endeavor to escape in vain, and whose speed shall mock their own fleetness of foot; which, compared with that of other men, is truly marvellous!"

The Adelantado smiled rather contemptuously at this counsel, having, as he thought, sufficient experience himself, in warfare with the red men, to know what precautions to take, and how to manage the encounter with the enemy.

"Truly, we are thankful for your zeal and wisdom, Don Philip, though with some experience of our own, in the warfare with the heathen, and some small reputation gained in other wars, it might be held reasonable to suppose that I should omit none of the precautions which are needful to the safety of my followers when embarking on the shores of the Floridian."

There was no pique in the tone or manner of our knight of Portugal, as he replied calmly:

"Your Excellency says rightly, and I were greatly deserving of rebuke, had I designed to cast a doubt upon your perfect sufficiency for the toils of war in any land: but I meant nothing more than a general warning that the circumspection which would suffice against an ordinary race, will hardly be adequate for security against this of the Apalachian, whose subtleties far exceed those of all other races of red men, and who are as valiant in perilling their persons as they are ingenious in their warlike devices."

With this apologetic speech, he paused, seeing that he spoke to an unwilling auditory. The Adelantado addressed his council without giving the slightest heed to what had been urged by the knight of Portugal; and the latter, shrugging his shoulders, consoled himself with the reflection, that the lesson which he strove in vain to enforce, would probably be taught, though at a greater cost to his hearers, by the Apalachian himself.

"The experience which tutors pride to a just humility," he mused within himself, "is perhaps, the best sort of lessoning; and he who would succeed, when the warfare is somewhat with his own vanity, cannot be saved from the punishment which follows close upon its indulgence. It is well, perhaps, that he will not hear, since it is only right that he should be made to feel; and our safety and success, perhaps, must equally depend upon our being made to feel, at the *beginning* of the adventure, rather than at a later time, when we are too deeply engaged in it. But, so sure as there are Fates, Hernando de Soto will be certain to receive his lesson before he hath gone very deeply into his books."

The conference,—such as it was—where there could be no dissent and no deliberation,—was soon at an end. De Soto simply detailed his plans at length, and gave his order for the disembarkation, the conduct of which was entrusted to the wealthy Don Vasco Porcallos; and never was ambitious mortal more eager than he to set forth on his adventures. His appetites for gold and captives had been growing with every league of progress which he had made on the watery waste, and still less than the Adelantado was he prepared to apprehend the possibility of failure or reverse of any sort in his present frame of mind. He dreamed only of riding down myriads of naked and panic-stricken savages, selecting the most vigorous captives and spearing the rest. But Vasconselos better knew the danger, and hence the duty. He knew they were not to triumph without hard fighting, great firmness, and constant caution.

Scarcely had the vessels appeared in sight of the coasts, than the balefires smoked on all the heights and tumuli that lined the shore, attesting the watch and vigilance of the Floridians. These were signals of danger, and announced to the warriors in the interior to gather from all quarters. Philip pointed out these signals to the page. "See you, Juan," said he,—"already the red men have taken alarm. Those smokes that rise every where in sight, will kindle other smokes, which shall give warning to all the separate tribes. They will fire piles throughout the mighty forests, until the answering smokes shall ascend from the great mountains of the Apalachian. Where a people are thus vigilant to note and prepare for the first dangers of invasion, they are warlike; they will fight famously; they will give us work to do, and task equally our skill and valor. So, be you watchful always, my boy, that you be not at any time surprised. In a country of deep forests, and great swarded meadows, such as we shall here encounter, filled with races of fearless hunters, there is no moment secure from danger; there is scarcely a position safe against surprise. One lies down never at night, without the apprehension that he shall suddenly be summoned by the deathly whoops of the savage, to face the danger in the dark. It needs to sleep always, lance or sword in hand, and with one eye and one ear ever open to sights and sounds of most terrible import. Be watchful, as you shall behold me ever; and be sure that you cling closely to my footsteps, when the work of death begins."

Could the good knight, at this moment, have felt the quick, deep beatings of the boy's heart; could he have seen the tremulous quiver of his lips; could he have conjectured what emotions, strange and oppressive, all crowded for utterance in that young bosom;—all, however, kept down by a will that was perfectly wonderful, in so young a frame! But the eyes of Philip were scarcely set upon the boy as he addressed him. He spoke while they were both busy, preparing their equipments, and getting in readiness to obey the command to disembark. It was with prodigious effort that the boy controlled his emotions sufficiently to speak.

"And are we, even now, to land upon the shores of the Apalachian, Señor?"

"Within the hour, Juan, a party of three hundred men, commanded by Don Vasco Porcallos, will take possession of the country in the name of the Emperor, and I am to accompany him, as interpreter of the speech of the red man, should we happen to meet with any of his race. But he will be more apt to speak through his darts and arrows, than with civil tongue; and now I think of it, Juan, it is perhaps needless that you should go with me on shore, until the whole command shall disembark. You are yet quite young, and had better gather glimpses of the strife from a distance at first, than be a sharer in one of which thou hast no experience. Keep thine ears open, and after midnight thou shalt hear the hellish clamors of the savage as they howl and rage around our camp. I shall not need thee in this adventure, for which thou art yet scarcely well fitted."

The boy's lip quivered, but his words were firmly delivered.

"Señor, when shall I be fitted, if I never begin? Some time I must begin, and the longer the day is put off, the slower will be my teaching. I do not fear. I shall be with you, Señor; if you please, I will go on shore with you to-night."

"In God's name, boy, have your wish. You say rightly. There must be a time, when this lesson must be taught, and learned, and the sooner, as you say, the better. Get on your escaupil, and see that your weapons are such as will serve to risk a life upon. Bring them hither, that I may see."

We must not linger on these details. Suffice it that all parties were soon prepared for the landing. It was on the last day of the month of May, soft, serene and sweet, that the gallant Hidalgo, Don Vasco Porcallos, led the way for his detachment of three hundred, and took final possession of the soil of the Floridians in the name of Spain. The solemnity was a very stately one, but needs not that we describe it. The banner of Castile was unrolled and elevated in the free air of the Apalachians, and was planted upon one of the elevations nearest to the shore. The region was thickly wooded, the forests were all clad in the freshest verdure of the opening summer; the breeze was charged with odors from worlds of flowers, the choicest natives of the country; and a natural delight filled every bosom, and exhilarated the spirits of the soldiery with an enthusiasm that seemed already in possession of the fullest successes. In pitching their camp, Philip de Vasconselos again ventured to give such hints to Don Vasco, as became his experience and caution. But the latter was even more sanguine than De Soto, and less heedful; and the manner in which he received these counsels of the knight of Portugal, seemed to have been borrowed from that of the Adelantado on the occasion already shown. He was civilly scornful, and Vasconselos saw, with chagrin and apprehension, that the ground chosen for the night was such as would rather invite and facilitate than discourage from attack. But he could do no more. He had only to submit, and hope against his fears, and provide as well as he might, against the emergency that he anticipated. But lacking all command, with but the single follower, he a child, inexperienced and evidently tired, what could be done?

"Come," said he cheerfully to Juan, "come, my boy, and let us seek out our quarters. We are limited to a certain precinct, but this affords choice of sleeping-place, and upon this choice may rest chance of safety."

The boy followed in silence. The knight rambled over the ground assigned for the encampment, and chose a little clump of wood, which afforded sufficient cover for a small group, yet stood apart, as it were, from the rest of the forest: affording an interval, over which the eye could range with tolerable freedom for some space, and thus note any hostile approaches. To find this par ticular spot, Vasconselos made his way to the very verge of the encampment, but not much farther from the shore than any of the rest of the detachment. Here he hung his buckler upon a bough, while, in the rear of the thicket, he secured his steed. He was one of the few, but seven in number, who had succeeded in bringing their horses ashore that evening. "The good knight must love his good steed, and care for him, Juan, as he values his own life. Help me now to rub him down. Bring me some of those dried grasses, my boy. His legs are stiffened by his narrow lodgings, and ship-board, and lack of exercise. The rope? Hast thou brought it?"

"It is here, Señor."

"Ah! now this will give him range to feed, yet keep him fast; but an armful of these young reeds, with their fresh leaves upon them, will help his appetite. Let us cut them, boy."

The grass was quickly cut with their *muchetes*, with one of which each was properly provided, and the soft green cane-tops were spread before the haltered animal, who fed with eagerness.

"It rejoices the knight's heart to see his charger feed with appetite. The grateful beast knows what we do for him. He will be content through the night. Thine own shall be brought ashore to-morrow, and then, if thou hast never practised these little toils, thou shalt learn from me. But evermore be careful of thy steed. In a strange wild country like this, of the Apalachian, if he fail thee, thou art lost. Never feel thyself at ease until thou seest him eat and drink with a will; and it were well always to give him chance to wallow in the sands. A little toil, nightly taken, ere thou sleep'st thyself, and thy steed sleeps well also; and thy own conscience is at peace in thy bosom, and thy safety is so far secure. But remember thy beast, always, if thou wouldst sleep with a good conscience."

And thus, as they cared for the wants and comforts of the gallant destrier, did Vasconselos speak to his page; and the latter occasionally murmured a sentence in reply or inquiry; but it was a delightful thing to see how, first, they cared for the animal, before seeing how they themselves had wants. Juan found a strange satisfaction, thus employed, the more perhaps, because he toiled for such a master; and as he passed the rough, dry grasses of the forest over the animal's sides and thighs, his arms sometimes crossing with those of the good knight, and their eyes meeting, and the gentle words of the latter melting into his ears, the heart of the boy beat with emotions of a singular pleasure, such as he had seldom felt before. The horse stripped and chafed, and his furniture hidden away in the thicket at hand, but always con venient, they selected their own place of repose. The dried leaves of the forest furnished a sufficient couch; the forest pines and other trees yielded a goodly shelter. The evening was calm and grateful. The warm serenity of the season required no closer lodgings. The most perfect repose prevailed throughout the forest, and save the clamor made by the troops, not a sound was to be heard, whether on land or sea. The soldiers dispersed themselves about the woods, chose their places of repose as Vasconselos had done, but without any regard to his precautions. They saw no danger, and apprehended none, as they beheld no foe, and all was confidence, and all was excitement.

"Surely, Señor," said Juan, "these quiet woods harbor no enemies."

"It is in the quiet seas, Juan, that the shark prevails. In the tempest he retires to his ocean caverns. The wolf prowls in the stillness of the night. The adder is a great traveller in the dark hours. It is because these forests are so quiet now, that I feel there are enemies at hand. But let us sup ere we speak of them, lest we forfeit something of appetite. Where is thy wallet?"

It was produced. The page displayed its contents, and stood in waiting.

"Sit, boy, and eat with me. Thou art my companion, child, not slave. Sit!"

With a strange tremor in his limbs, and vacant look which did not escape the eye of Philip, the boy took his seat before him, but scarcely nigh. This emotion the knight ascribed to the humility of the page. He strove to soothe this by condescension, by the utmost gentleness of manner and fondness of discourse; but the effect was not such as he expected—not just then, at least.

"Time will wear off these fears," said the knight to himself, as he broke the bread and passed it to the boy.

"Eat, Juan! Thou wilt need to learn how to eat and sleep at all seasons; if thou wouldst become a soldier. We shall have to wake and fight, when it shall not please us, the summons; and shall *not* be summoned to our food always, or our sleep, when most the appetite shall call for both."

When they had supped, Philip said—

"Now, Juan, thou wilt watch while I sleep. I will take advantage of the early hours of the night, when the red man seldom prowls or strikes, and in the middle of it, I will wake, or thou shalt waken me, that I may take thy place as watcher for the rest of the night. See, from this place, where we both lie concealed, you are enabled to note all that happens around you for some distance You will observe who approaches; note all things that seem unwonted; and arouse me instantly. Do not trust to your own courage, or weapon, wholly, if it need that any thing be done! See, on every side but one, lies the encampment. On the left, the interval is open which separates us from the denser forest. From that quarter the danger may arise. Watch *that* well! Behind us, at a little distance, is the sea; in which, with a few fleet bounds, we may bury our forms from an enemy, and be within speech and succor from the ships. Thou canst watch for three goodly hours, without feeling the heavy weight of sleep upon thee. That time over, I shall surely rise to relieve thee, and should I not, do thou then awaken me."

Without further speech, Philip de Vasconselos, in his armor, as he stood, threw himself at length at the foot of the great tree. His hand grasped his sword, which he had unstrapped from his shoulders. It was not long before he slept; for he was one of those to whom the experience of such a life had taught the wisdom of securing and encouraging the blessings of sleep whenever he could, knowing, as he had said to Juan, that the summons to arouse for battle might come at any moment in a savage country, and might not always please the sleeper; and he possessed the faculty of commanding sleep at almost any moment.

He slept; and gradually the boy drew nearer, crawling softly, to the head of the knight, whose face was turned upon the side opposite. But with this scarcely audible movement, Philip showed himself restless. The boy receded, and gathering up his cross-bow, raised it to the level of the eye, and ranged it from side to side, upon the open spaces between the trees in front. The stars shone very brightly, and in that region served to reveal objects of small size at considerable distance. Juan meditated within himself very seriously the question:

"What if some red warrior should suddenly appear?"

His heart beat with quickened pulses, as he asked the question.

"Should I have the strength, the courage, the confidence to shoot?—But he bade me not! I was to awaken him. I was to watch only, and report the danger."

He laid the bow aside, and once more crept closely to the sleeping cavalier. The face of Philip was still averted. But the boy did not seem anxious to gaze upon it. His object appeared to be attained when he was beside him. There he sate, quietly, his eyes looking out with sufficient watchfulness, intent enough, but with a sense wandering in quite other fields of survey. With hands clasped upon his lap, he yielded himself up to fancies, dreaming and delicious, yet so touched with a peculiar sadness, that the bitter predominated over the sweet, and the big tears might be seen, moulding themselves into melancholy jewels in the starlight, rounding themselves gradually upon his cheek, and dropping one by one, as they grew to brilliants. The hours swam along with the stars, and the stars waned in their silent progress for the blessing of other eyes, and the eyes of Juan drooped at last with the heaviness upon them. He strove to shake off the drowsiness which he felt; but there was something in that foreign atmosphere which could not be withstood, and while he strove to range along the barrel of the cross-bow, (which he had taken up with some vague notion that it would keep him wakeful,) over the intervals which spread between him and the gloomy shadows of the wood which he had been especially enjoined to watch;—it seemed to him as if the wood itself were swimming, like waves of the sea, and as if the stars descended to the plain, only to ascend once more; to and fro; upward and downward and onward, till all things appeared to mix and mingle in his sight. Then suddenly, he started, with a strange confusion, as he fancied he heard the voice of Don Philip. This, for a moment, aroused him; but looking down, he saw Don Philip still sleeping; and, satisfied to see thus, he was conscious of little more after this for some time, though he might have been just as watchful as before. But very soon after this, Don Philip really awakened. He found the boy fast asleep, with his arm thrown over his neck. He gently unloosed it, and rose.

"Poor boy!" said the knight—"Thou hast taken on thee a perilous labor, which thy slight figure will scarce endure. But sleep, and I will watch thee. I could wish thee stronger, for my sake, no less than thine; for verily, of all this host, I have now none but thee!" After a pause—"And there is that about the child which binds me to him; which makes me love him almost Wherefore? It is because I am alone! It is because the nature of the strong man requires a charge, a trust, a burden, so that his strength shall be healthfully at exercise; so that his muscles shall not shrink, lacking due employment! Well! I will protect and help him so long as I can help any thing, and in.—but why look into the vast vacancy of that dark realm of the future, in which no flower shall ever grow for me?"

He rose suddenly, as if startled; seized his sword, buckled it to his side, and caught up the cross-bow of the page. He stole forward a few paces, and seemed to listen; then returned to his place, and laid the bow again by the side of the sleeping Juan. His next attentions were bestowed upon his steed The beast had eaten plentifully, and now slept; but raised his head, and seemed to recognize his master as he drew nigh. Philip patted his neck affectionately, then bade him rise, and proceeded with the utmost care and silence to put on his war harness, his saddle and bridle, and have him in readiness for instant use. But he did not loose the animal; simply shortened his halter that he might not again lie down. Meanwhile, every thing was still as death in the encampment. Philip saw no sentinels; heard no guards relieved; knew nothing of the cautionary steps which Don Vasco Porcallos might be supposed to have taken. The night was lapsing towards the dawn. This he felt in the coolness of the atmosphere. He stole cautiously out to the edge of the wood in his quarter of the camp, and looked to the black range of the forest beyond. Nothing was stirring, not a leaf seemed to be disturbed, in the cold thin air of the morning.

"Well," said he, as he returned to where he left the boy sleeping, "it may be that we shall escape to-night. The savages, perhaps, have not yet had time for a gathering of their warriors. They would otherwise have never suffered the night to pass, without giving us a taste of battle. I know them of old; fierce, restless, impatient, fearless: cunning as valiant; and never relenting in their purposes. We shall see enough of them yet, though we escape them now."

He returned to his late resting-place. Juan was still bound fast in the embrace of sleep. He threw himself beside the boy, and in the imperfect light of the stars, which looked down through the openings of the trees, he steadily perused his features. In this examination the interest of the knight appeared to be very great, and the study seemed to sadden him. But the bronze features, in the imperfect starlight, revealed nothing. The face was sweet and girlish, and the face, if fair, might be counted beautiful. So the musing knight thought, during the long watch of hours which he maintained beside the unconscious boy. But he was not suffered to continue the unembarrassed study, until the better light of the morning should enable him to peruse the intelligible features. He fancied that he heard unwonted sounds; a stick was broken in the woods. His steed whinnied. There was an interruption of the silence which he could not define, and seizing his sword, he rose to his feet, and quietly stole away to where his steed was fastened.

Meanwhile, Juan slept on, never once conjecturing aught of the sad and silent watch which the good knight had kept above him. But he was awakened rudely from his dream. At that moment, Vasconselos heard a cry, that sounded in his ears like the voice of a woman. It appeared also to proceed from the spot where Juan had been left sleeping. He, by this time, had ventured out again to the edge of the wood, and was looking over the intervening space towards the dark forests lying beyond. The cry alarmed him; though it bore no resemblance to the usual whoop of Indian battle. It might be that some wild beast had found his way to where the boy slept—the panther's cry is like that of a child or girl,—and, with excited pulses, and the blood rapidly coursing through his veins, Philip darted back to the place where the boy was left. He reached the spot just in time to discover two dark forms,—clearly men,—who were drawing Juan away to the thickets. He readily divined the purpose in the action. Again a shriek: and this time he knew it for the boy's; but so full of a feminine terror, that his heart sickened as he thought of the strange simplicity and ignorance which had prompted one so feeble to venture upon an enterprise so perilous. He thought and felt thus, even in that moment of alarm. He saw that the boy struggled, and he further saw that the dusky forms, by whom he had been seized, were brandishing, each, a heavy mace above his head. There was no time for further thought, or for hesitation. To dart forward, and with a single stroke of his keen sword, to smite down one of the assailants; to grasp the other by the throat and tear him from the boy, then, as he staggered back, to run him through the body, —was the work of a few moments. The two savages lay at his feet in the agonies of death. The boy staggered, gasping, towards him, an hysterical sob only breaking from his lips. With a stern voice, the knight said:—

"Seize thy cross-bow, Juan, and collect thyself. This is no time for fears. The Apalachian is on us."

To confirm his words, at that very instant, the wild yells of the savages rose up in all quarters of the encampment. The Spaniards struggled out of sleep only to encounter their enemies. The sentinels had slept. Few were awake. The surprise was complete.

"Follow me," cried Philip to the boy, and his stern accents, by enforcing obedience, in some degree disarmed Juan of his terrors; at all events, he obeyed. He followed by instinct, cross-bow in hand, and was at the side of the knight as the latter leaped upon his steed.

"Up with thee, behind me, boy—we have not a moment."

And the light form, assisted by the powerful arm of Philip, sprang at once upon the steed. The spur was instantly driven into the beast's sides, and he was made to go! The wild rush, the monstrous form, the gigantic bulk, of the animal, made its impression. A hundred naked savages darted out of the wood through which he went, and fled before his path. The knight shouted aloud, in the language of Castile; then blew a wild flourish upon his bugle, and joyed to hear the answers of the Spaniards from sundry quarters. Vasco Porcallos was soon on horseback, for though vain as a peacock, and pursy as an alderman, he had the blood and energy of a true cavalier. The other five troopers were soon in saddle, and, charging among the red men, now yelling and darting amidst the forests, in the doubtful light of morning, they soon changed the character of the event. But, until this demonstration of the knights on horseback, the affair was seriously against the whites. The Spaniards had been not only surprised, but fairly routed. Started out of their profoundest sleep, they had made but little opposition to the savages. They fled in tumultuous confusion to the sea-side, clamoring for succor to the ships. Many of these were wounded; all would have perished, but for the spirited charge of the knights on horseback, and the strange terrors occasioned by the horses, animals whom the red men had never seen before. The savages disappeared in the forests, as soon as they found themselves seriously resisted, almost as swiftly and suddenly as they had appeared. Vasco Porcallos was greatly delighted with this, his first essay in arms against the Floridian. But, even while he boasted of his prowess, his noble steed fell suddenly dead beneath him, slain by an arrow which had buried itself out of sight in his body. When they reached the shore, the red men all dispersed, and the troops issuing in boats with drum and trumpet from the shipping, Juan slipped, from behind Philip de Vasconselos, upon the ground.

"Art thou hurt, boy?" demanded the knight.

"No, Señor, thanks to your care, I have no hurt."

"But thou tremblest still, Juan."

"Yes, Señor, but it is not now with fear. I think I shall never be afraid again."

"Ay, boy, thou hast tasted of the strife. Many a warrior who grew famous afterwards, has felt the terrors of thy heart, Juan. But I had never forgiven myself hadst thou been slain. I but left thee for a moment, and thou seest how these cunning savages came upon thee. I had watched thee for two goodly hours as thou slept'st, and fancied we should hear nothing of them."

"Alas! Señor, thou left'st me to watch, and I slept. I knew

not that I slept. I knew not when mine eyes closed, and I knew not of thy awakening."

"I had too much tasked thee, Juan," answered the knight gently. "Thou slept'st ere I awakened. It was thy arm falling over my neck that awakened me."

"My arm over thy neck, Señor! Oh! what have I done?" and the boy hung his head.

"Foolish boy, and where is thy offence in this?"

But the boy turned away without speaking, and little did Philip fancy how wildly the tides were rising and falling in his bosom.

CHAPTER XXXIII.

> "Methinks amongst yon train,
> And habited like them, I well could pass,
> And no one mark me."
> VAN ARTEVELDE.

It does not lie within the plan of this legend to follow in detail all the progresses of De Soto in his weary marches, his long wanderings and fierce battles with the Floridian and other Indian races of our country. These details must be sought in other histories, and are available in many, to the reader. We shall only notice the general route pursued by the expedition, through what regions, and dwell upon those events only, which concern the persons of the drama, with whom we have already travelled through so many pages.

The encounter with the red men of Apalachia, which, as we have seen, took place almost on the very moment of De Soto's landing in the country, was only the beginning of a long history of conflicts. From tribe to tribe, from village to village, he pressed onward, only to encounter the fiercest foes, or the most treacherous friends. But, at the very outset of his career, he recovered a Spaniard, one Juan Ortiz, who had been a follower of Pamphilo de Narvaez, and had become a captive to the Apalachians. In a captivity of several years, he had acquired the language of many of the tribes, and almost lost his own. This acquisition rendered De Soto somewhat independent of the services of Philip de Vasconselos. The latter was soon made aware of this consciousness of independence, on the part of the Adelantado.

Eager for the attainment of the great objects of the expedition, the famous cities, and the golden treasure, which were believed to be locked up in the Apalachian mountains, Soto lost no time in unnecessary delays. Dispatching his largest vessels to Havana, with the view to cutting off all thought on the part of his followers, of returning home—in this policy, emulating Cortez, and other great leaders,—Soto retained but a single caravel, and two brigantines, to keep possession of the sea-coast and the bay where he had cast anchor. To this charge, he appointed Pedro Calderon, an old soldier. He next proceeded to send forth various small expeditions into the country, seeking gold and information. None of the parties thus sent forth failed to experience curious and exciting adventures; but they do not affect our legend. We must not forget, however, that, from this moment, we lose our famous millionaire, Don Vasco Porcallos, whom an adventure in a swamp, in which he narrowly escaped suffocation, cured effectually of all his warlike ambition, and who returned with the fleet to Cuba.

Soto set forth himself, after no great delay, for the interior. His splendid cavalry were free for use, by the employment of hordes of captive Indians who carried the heavy luggage of the expedition. His foot marched at an easy rate, the cavalry procuring supplies, and clearing the forests as they went. In this way, the army marched from Tampa to Anaica, near the modern Tallahassee. The brigantines, meanwhile, coasting the shore, discovered the harbor of Ochoa, now Pensacola. Moving from Anaica, Soto marched east, and successively crossed the rivers Ockmulge, Oconee and Ogechee. He finally reached the Savannah. These marches were not made in peace. War and terror hung upon the footsteps of the Spaniards. Every where they met with foes;—not such foes as the feeble Cuban or Peruvian—but fierce, stern, strong, implacable enemies,—accustomed to hard blows, and to a life of incessant warfare. The advantages lay with the Spaniards, but only as a consequence of their superior civilization. They owed their victories to their cavalry and firearms, rather than their valor. In this quality, the Apalachians were equal to any people that ever lived. The Spaniards proved merciless conquerors. They mutilated where they did not destroy, or desire to make captive. They had brought with them handcuffs of iron, for securing their prisoners, and thus ironed, the miserable wretches bore the baggage of their captors through the wilderness. Their conquest was not easily made. Thousands of the red men perished in the conflict, and the Spaniards did not always escape. It was not easy to ride down these fierce savages. Many of the whites perished. De Soto, himself, had several narrow escapes in close personal conflict, in which, but for his companions in arms, he must have been slain. We need not say that, on all these occasions, Philip de Vasconselos maintained himself according to his reputation. He suffered no disaster. His page was equally fortunate. The latter had risen in his master's esteem, as he had subsequently shown more courage than had been promised by his first encounter, at the landing of the troops. From that moment, he exhibited no signs of fear. He was ever near the good knight, and proved always ready with the cross-bow. Of what effect were the arrows he discharged, we have no means of knowing. Enough that he contrived to satisfy the spectators—if any may be thought to have been spectators at such a time, and in such fields—of his stoutness of heart and readiness of aim. Philip de Vasconselos himself was satisfied, and felt more at ease in respect to the boy's safety, than he had been at the first opening of the campaign.

He was more than satisfied in other respects. The boy proved an intelligent companion. In his society the knight found solace, and often did he feel surprise, at the equal taste and intellect, so different from his race, which, as they grew more and more intimate, the boy betrayed. Of course, Philip had not forgotten what Mateo had told him, that Juan, the son of a free woman of the mountains, had been carefully nurtured, and had not been wanting in such education as could be procured by money, in such a region, during that early period. But the intellect of the boy declared for gifts, quite as much as acquisition—such gifts as were not often found in any other than the white race. But, though such exhibitions surprised Philip, quite as much as they delighted him, yet his moods and present employments were not of a sort to suffer him much speculation upon them. He was, after a while, quite content to enjoy their benefits, in the solace which they brought, without questioning their source; and he needed all this solace. He was still alone, and still, in spite of his services and valor, quite as much as before an object of jealousy among the Spaniards. Nuno de Tobar, indeed, was still his friend, and he knew others in the army, who were kindlily inclined; but it was not often that the parties saw each other. They were in different commands, and frequently detached on expeditions, aside from the main route. There had been no absolute reconciliation between the Portuguese brothers; and Andres still kept aloof; though we may state that his bitterness of mood had been modified. But they rarely met. Philip was a frequent volunteer when perilous or adventurous service was required. It was in this way, mostly, that he exercised his skill in arms, save when summoned to the special assistance of the Adelantado, to whom he was nominally an *aide ;* but this rarely happened except when captives or embassies were to be examined, and interpretations made from their language. This requisition, too, had been of unfrequent occurrence since Juan Ortiz had been recovered. He, however, sometimes failed to understand the tongues of foreign tribes, and thus it was that Philip was needed. But for this, his uses in the army, according to the estimates seemingly put upon them by his superior, were of little moment.

Philip felt this treatment, and his boy showed that he felt it

17*

also. The two lived to themselves apart. They lay beneath the same trees at night: they harnessed their horses in the same glade. They sat together at the same repast; Juan retired behind his lord, and speaking with him thus, except when, at times, as finally was frequently the case, Philip bade him to sit beside him, or before him—a proceeding which the knight adopted, the better to encourage the boy, and to overcome his excessive shyness. And he gradually succeeded. The boy, who shrank from all other associations, gradually grew to him, as the vine grows to the mighty tree. Soon he came to speak freely even of his own secret fancies and emotions, and it really pleased the knight to hearken the language, still timidly spoken, of a young confiding heart, possessed of the deepest and tenderest feelings, which the isolation in which he lived, and the wild seclusion of that realm of shade and forest, seemed rather to expand and develop, than subdue and overcome. The deep solitude which received them as they went, seemed to open the warmer fountains of their human nature, as society rarely opens them. Thrown together incessantly—forced to communion by the repulsive treatment of the rest—sleeping near each other by night, encountering the same toils and dangers by day,—breaking the same loaf when they ate, and naturally inclined to each other by kindred sensibilities,—it was soon evident to each that the charm of their lives lay chiefly in the regards of one another. There was a sad simplicity in both their natures,—a grave tenderness of soul, which still further helped to cement their intimacy; and it was soon felt—by Philip, at least,—that, in this new and seemingly incongruous relationship, the peculiar pangs and disappointments which he had experienced in Cuba, were fast losing the sharpness and severity of their sting. He sometimes wondered at himself that he so much craved the companionship of the boy; but he was too much pleased with the enjoyment of it to question its sources. When they were apart he mused upon his fondness with curiosity. Why should he, a knight of Portugal, feel such sympathy for this Moorish urchin? It was in vain that he recalled the boy's devotion to himself,—his goodness of heart, his gentleness of mood, the quickness of his mind, the delicacy of his fancy, and his general intelligence. These did not suffice to account for the hold upon his affections which the boy had taken. In all his meditations when left to himself, he found no solution of his problem. When the boy was at hand, and they spoke together, there was no problem. It seemed to him quite natural, at such moments, all the affection that he felt,—all the sympathy that warmed him to the dusky page.

To all others, Juan was a stone,—insensible, unattractive—a sullen, reserved and silent boy,—submissive, but retiring; humble, but not soliciting; one of whom nobody entertained thought or question; of whom the common speech in camp was, that this page was just suited to the haughty and sullen master. There was an exception perhaps to this general judgment. Don Balthazar de Alvaro was observed to note the boy with a persevering eye. Juan was the first to be aware of this. It did not finally escape the notice of Philip; but it did not occasion his surprise or curiosity. In the case of Juan, however, it was something of an annoyance. Had he been watched, it would have been seen that he sought to avoid the eyes of Don Balthazar—that he was somewhat agitated when they met suddenly—that he spoke with a slight tremor of voice in the hearing of the Don, and especially when, as was sometimes the case, he was required to answer his demands. It sometimes happened that Don Balthazar sought Vasconselos at his post, or where he had cast himself down for the night. On such occasions—as he considered the ostensible subject upon which the former came,—he could not forbear musing upon its inadequacy as a plea for coming. The parties did not love each other. Their instincts were hostile. There could not be any cordiality between them; and, such being the case, why Don Balthazar should seek him, unless with reasons of necessity, was a frequent subject of Philip's surprise. At such times, he always drew an unfavorable augury from his coming.

"He means mischief," said he aloud, one evening, after the departure of Don Balthazar from the place where he had laid himself down to rest. "Why should he come to me, and on such pretext? What is it to me whither we move to-morrow, or what new dreams fill the brain of the Adelantado? Let him march, east or west, along the plains, or among the mountains, I care nothing! and, sure, he knows it. He knows, too, that I love not his serpent nature, and his subtle and treacherous eye. He knows, too, that I am not to be deceived in him! Besides, what can he seek of me? I am poor and powerless. He can win nothing from my weakness. If he comes, he can only come in hate! Yet what have I to fear? Him I fear not, and he knows it too. Verily I believe, that did he not fear me, he would have sought to slay me ere this,—nevertheless—I feel it—by sure instinct. I feel it—this man means mischief."

"He is a villain!" was the bitter speech of Juan from behind the tree, where he had crept quietly.

"Ha! Juan, are you there, boy? But what do you know about Don Balthazar? Ah! Juan, if you knew what I know of that man—had you but seen what mine eyes have looked on——"

"Seen, Senor?——" was the faltered inquiry.

"Aye, boy, seen! But it is not for you to hear—not for mortal to hear. Yet, were it not for another—his victim—one dear to me once as my own eyes,—but for her,—I had long since taken the monster by the throat, and declared his crime aloud, while I strangled him in deadly punishment! You say right, Juan; though you know nothing. Don Balthazar de Alvaro is one of the blackest of all the black villains that poison and deface the blessed things of earth. He hath been my fate—that man!"

The boy sobbed, "And mine!" but the words did not reach the ears of Philip, and when he looked round, and called again to the page, he was nowhere to be seen. Ere he returned that night, Vasconselos was asleep. The boy had eaten no supper. He crept close by his sleeping master, and watched over him for weary hours, with big tears gathering fast in his eyes the while. When, at the dawn, the knight awakened, he saw Juan sleeping, with his head sunk against his own shoulder, and the stain of tears was still upon his cheek.

CHAPTER XXXIV.

> 'Hell put it in
> The enemy's mind to be desperate.'
>
> MASSINGER.

WE can only give glimpses of a progress, every form of which was distinguished by its own interest and capricious varieties. We have shown, thus far, the relationships of our parties; and how they grew, and what were their developments. Each day gradually contributed to unfold the increasing dependence of Don Philip and his page upon one another; and both were watched, though neither perhaps saw to what extent, by the serpent eyes of Don Balthazar de Alvaro. Meanwhile, Philip de Vasconselos seemed to grow less and less in favor with the Adelantado, who now rarely summoned him to his service; and, except when they met, seemed to have forgotten his existence. On such occasions there was an evident distance of manner in the bearing of De Soto, amounting almost to repugnance, which increased the regrets of Philip that he had ever joined the expedition. His mortification at having done so, would have been unendurable, but for a certain indifference of mood, which rendered him reckless what became of him,—reckless of all things, indeed; and made him just as well satisfied to rove without a purpose, and fight without a cause, as to sleep beneath his tree, when the day had closed in exhaustion. Latterly, his feeling grew less indifferent. He seemed to be slowly acquiring a new interest in life. He was conscious of more impulse, of aim, and objects, vague, indeed, enough, and which he did not seek to pursue, but which served to show that life for him still had its resources, even its attractions, and was not wholly denied an object. But if the question as to that object was asked of Don Philip, he would have been without an answer. Enough that under existing circumstances, he could find his associations still endurable;—without an object in life, he could yet find life not wholly a burden and a curse!

The brooding mind was not suffered much opportunity for exercise, in the progress pursued by De Soto. That ambitious chieftain, in his appetite for conquest and power, kept his followers sleepless. We may now, with tolerable certainty, follow the route of the Spaniards upon the map, and trace their course from the Bay of Tampa, into and through Georgia, even to South Carolina. Their progress was erratic. They were easily tempted aside by lures of gold, in this or that quarter; and the imperfectly understood reports of this or that Indian guide, frequently misled them from the direct course, to wild adventures, and strange episodes, which diverted them from the true discovery. In all their progresses danger hung upon them in the rear, and disappointment stood in waiting for their approach. One or two adventures briefly narrated, will serve to illustrate their daily history; and we linger over a single instance, which enabled Vasconselos to recover a portion of De Soto's favor.

There was a Floridian Chieftain, or King, named Vitachuco, who had stubbornly resisted all the approaches of Soto. The latter, by treachery, contrived to secure the person of this Chieftain. His next object was to win his favor—a measure conceived to be by no means difficult, inasmuch as the Adelantedo, in making captive the Chief, had slaughtered near a thousand of his warriors, who had sought to rescue his person. Vitachuco, though kept as a prisoner, and watched, was still allowed certain privileges. He ate at the table of Soto. He was still able to commune with his subjects, hundreds of whom were employed about the Spaniards, as slaves and drudges. To these Vitachuco communicated his secret thoughts and purposes. He was not a willing captive. But he was politic. He met subtlety with subtlety. He suppressed his indignation,—appeared not to see the restraint put upon his footsteps, and so behaved, as entirely to disarm the suspicions of his captors. But the fiery indignation was working in his soul, and he only wanted the proper moment and opportunity, in which to break his bonds, and avenge himself upon his captors. This design was reserved for a day of feasting, when Soto entertained his captive along with other nobles and princes of the Apalachians, held in similar bonds with their superior, or of other tribes whom he desired to conciliate. Vitachuco was too impatient of his injuries to think wisely, or to resolve with prudence. He did not heed the fact that himself and followers were unarmed, and were to grapple, if grapple they did, with foes who never laid aside their weapons or their mail. The fearless savage resolved to try the struggle at all odds, unprepared as he was, at the approaching repast; of which he had due intimations. The four pages, or servants, that waited upon him, were all boys, but he entrusted them with his secret. They communicated with such warriors as he himself could not see; and the plan was rapidly matured for execution the very next day, being the day assigned for the feasting.

According to their plan, Vitachuco was to spring upon the Adelantado, and kill him if he could, while they were at dinner; his followers doing the same good service for all the Spaniards present—and, without, for all others upon whom they could lay hands. The village of Vitachuco was to be the scene of action.

It happened, the evening before the event, that Juan, the page of Vasconselos, remarked the activity of Vitachuco's pages, and that they held frequent communications with their people. Crowds of the red men were seen coming to the encampment, or crowding stealthily about it. The place where Vasconselos found shelter, usually, on the verge of the encampment, was favorable to observation; and the constant coming and departure of the Floridians, compelled the boy's observation, and prompted him to communicate with the knight, his master. They both watched, and discovered enough, at all events, to render them suspicious. They redoubled their vigilance, and found that some provisions, rather novel for a feast, had been made by the savages. They found hidden in the contiguous woods, large bundles of darts, barbed with flints, that were ready for use; and scores of huge macanas or war maces, edged with flint also, a single blow from which, in a moderately strong hand, would cleave the skull of any Spaniard, though covered with helm of steel.

To effect these discoveries, and to guard in some degree against the designs of the savages, by putting the army on the *qui vive*, was a work of time, and the Adelantado was already at dinner with his treacherous guests, ere Philip de Vasconselos was prepared to unfold his discoveries. Now,—speaking of things without regard to persons—the Spaniards were quite as treacherous as the Floridians; and it was with a bitter smile and sneer that Philip, commenting upon the small claims of the former upon his fidelity, said to Juan:—

"It is liar against liar, serpent against serpent!—what have we to do with it, boy? It were just as well that we should see them strive together, and clap hands equally to behold the good stroke delivered by Floridian or Spaniard!"

But the sympathies of race and education prevailed, and the white chieftain, with a feeling of unutterable scorn, which he concealed under the most courtly demeanor, suddenly appeared at the place of feasting,—to which he had not been invited,—when all was most hilarious, and the Adelantado as little dreaming of the *dessert* which the Floridian had provided, as of any other good blessing, with which he might profitably dispense. Vasconselos, as we say, suddenly appeared within the circle, and for a moment, quietly surveyed it without speaking.

Whether it was that the scorn which he felt, somewhat showed itself in his features, or that the Adelantado was in no mood to behold *him* with toleration, whom he had not received to favor, is not easy to be said. It is certain, however, that Soto somewhat forgot his courtesy in the reception which he gave the knight of Portugal. With a stern look and chilling accents, he cried out, as he beheld him:—

"How now, Sir Knight of Portugal, what is it brings you to this presence at this unseemly moment? We had not anticipated the honor of your attendance."

The brow of the knight of Portugal grew black as he replied:

"Señor Don Hernan de Soto, Philip de Vasconselos asks no favor or courtesy from any man alive! He comes not now as a courtier, or as a guest, but as a soldier, who shrinks from no duty even when it needs that he should appear where he is never welcome! What I have to say, by way of apology for my presence now, is soon spoken. Ask of the savages whom you feast, why our camp is girdled by a thousand red warriors, why the pages of their prince have been in such frequent communion with them, and why, all on a sudden, such provision as this is made, at convenient places, in all the neighboring woods?"

Saying these words, he took from an attendant, and threw down upon the board, and amidst the guests, bundles of darts, wrapt in skins of the rattle-snake, and a score of the heavy macanas, such as we have described already. At the sight of these objects, and before the Adelantado could reply to what he conceived the insolent speech of Vasconselos—insolent in sense as in tone—the war-whoop rang wildly through the hall; a terrible yell that shook the hearts of the assembly, as with a sudden voice of doom. Vitachuco, from whom the signal came, started to his feet at the same moment, and, in the twinkling of an eye, he sprang, like a tiger, full upon Soto. With one hand he seized him by the collar, while, with the other, he dealt him such a blow between the eyes, as made the blood fly, and prostrated the Adelantado to the floor, as heavily as falls the ox beneath the stroke of the butcher!

All was confusion in that moment. Terribly did this war-whoop of the savages ring throughout the hall;—and without— through all the avenues of the village, where the followers of Vitachuco were collecting at the signal, as had been agreed on among them. The Spaniards, never dreaming of attack from unarmed savages, were taken completely by surprise. The Adelantado lay stunned and senseless beneath the grasp of Vitachuco, and all was confusion, and uncertainty, within and with out. The Indians, everywhere, seized whatever implements they could lay hands upon for weapons. Some grasped the pikes and swords of the Spaniards; others snatched the pots from the fire, and emptied the contents over their foes, while beating them about the head with the vessels. Plates, pitchers, jars, the pestles from the mortars wherein they pounded maize; stools, benches, tables, billets of wood; in the hands of the fierce Floridians became instruments of war and vengeance! Never had such a fight been seen; so promiscuous; urged with such novel weapons; and so full of terror and confusion. The terror and danger of the scene were duly increased by others yet, who, plucking the flaming brands of *lightwood* from the fire, darted into the thickest of the fray, shouting like furies, and looking more like demons from the infernal regions than mere mortal combatants!

Such was the scene and the character of the struggle throughout the village. The Spaniards recovered themselves promptly and fought desperately, and conquered finally; but they suffered severely. Besides those who perished, many were terribly bruised, scalded, burnt, and maimed. Arms were broken, teeth knocked out, faces scarred for ever; the very handcuffs on the wrists of many of the savages, becoming fearful means of injury and assault in the promiscuous and close struggle, hand to hand.

In the hall of the great house of the village where the Adelantado had feasted the Cassique, the conflict, though involving smaller numbers, was no less fearful and savage in its character. But for the presence of Philip de Vasconselos, and his active energies and vigilance, Soto, and all the party, must have perished. The Adelantado, as we have seen, was stunned by the first desperate assault of the Indian Chief. The latter clung to his victim, and would very soon have finished his work, but for the quick movement of Philip, who darted to the rescue, and passed his sword through the body of the savage, while, tiger-like, he was tearing the neck of the Adelantado. The Spanish knights, at this sight, recovered from their consternation, and a dozen swords were crossed in an instant in the body of Vitachuco. The furious savage died without a groan, glaring, with fellest rage, upon his enemies, in the very moment when his last breath was passing. The Indians who remained in the hall were dispatched in like manner, but not before they had inflicted hurts upon the Spaniards which left their ghastly marks through life. The end was massacre. Discipline prevailed over rude and ferocious valor. The people of Vitachuco, thirteen hundred warriors, the

flower of his nation, perished in the affair, or were butchered
after it. Such is a sample of the fierce character of the red men
of Florida, their desperate valor, and the sleepless passion for
freedom, which they indulged at every peril. The character remains unchanged to this day. The people of Vitachuco occupied
the same region which the Seminoles maintained, with such surprising skill and courage, for five years, against the army of the
United States, in recent times.

CHAPTER XXXV.

> PAUL.—"Did you note
> The majesty she appears in.
> CLEON.—Yes, my good Lord;
> I was ravished with it."
>
> MASSINGER.

This event had a considerable effect in restoring Vasconselos to the favor of De Soto. The Adelantado could not ungraciously forbear to acknowledge a service to which he owed his own life and probably the safety of his army. He, accordingly, thanked Philip in stately language, hidalgo-fashion, in the presence of all his troops. But his pride kept him still in memory of that haughty reserve of the Portuguese cavalier, which had so offended his *amour propre* at first; and as Philip, while as courteously receiving the compliment of the Adelantado, in a style not dissimilar from that in which it was couched, abated nothing of his own dignity, it followed, that the debt which De Soto felt, of gratitude, was rather irksome and burdensome, than grateful to that haughty cavalier. He had, besides, ever at hand, whispering insidious suggestions in his ear, the wily Don Balthazar de Alvaro. This knight did not suffer the natural feelings of De Soto to have full play at any time, in his relations to the Portuguese. But for *his* constant labors, it might have been that what was naturally noble in the bosom of the Adelantado, would have asserted itself to the extent of doing full justice to the merits of Philip; and giving full exercise to his own proper courtesy and honor. As it was, the intercourse between the knight of Portugal and the Spanish Chief, though more courteous and gracious than before, was scarcely more cordial; and Philip remained, as before, companioned only by the page Juan, who clung to him more closely than ever, and grew daily more and more necessary to his affections.

We pass now over a considerable tract of time, of which we shall make no record, but which, though full of toils and strifes, trials and vicissitudes, found our *dramatis personæ* unchanged in their several relations. The army, meanwhile, had marched from Florida into Georgia, had crossed that State, and at length approached the waters of the Savannah. In the province of Cofa, however, De Soto experienced an embarrassment in his progress, which rendered it necessary that Philip de Vasconselos should be again conciliated. The dialect of the red men changed, and the nterpreter, Juan Ortiz, was no longer competent to act in this capacity. Philip had traversed this very region. He took the place of Ortiz; negotiated with the Cassique of Cofa; and once more had the satisfaction, if any it were, of seeing the eyes of the Adelantado turned upon him with favor. But the Portuguese knight regarded these kindly demonstrations with indifference. He had survived all care, in respect to the carriage of the Castilian Captain, and his followers; and simply contented himself with the performance of his duty, as it rose, without giving any heed to the profit or the loss which might follow upon his toils. With the Cassique of Cofa, he concluded an amicable treaty, which secured the support and friendship of a very potent savage. From him, however, it was learned that there were more powerful potentates, yet beyond them, to the east, whom it was even more necessary to conciliate. Much was said of a Princess, or Queen of Cofachiqui,—a province just beyond; the population of which was very numerous, and the territory very fertile. It was reported to be very rich, also, in gold, pearls, and other precious treasures. The young Princess who ruled the country had lately come to her throne. She was pronounced to be beautiful beyond description, and the imagination of the Adelantado was greatly inflamed by what he heard, of the surpassing beauty of the maiden, her vast empire, her great treasures, and the wealth and power of her connections. Her blood mingled with that of the great Chieftains and Princes who ruled along the waters of Chatahoochie, Alabama, and Mississippi. The Cassique of Cofa, very powerful as he himself claimed to be, yet acknowledged his inferiority to this Princess; his incapacity to encounter her troops in war, and the fear which he felt of provoking her hostility. Patofa, the chief in question, hated as he feared; and we may add that, with savage cunning and ferocity, he continued, under the sheltering wing of the Spaniards, to execute no little mischief upon the people and country of the power which he loathed and dreaded; butchering without remorse, and plundering, whenever he had the opportunity of doing so in secret. For these reasons, De Soto was compelled, however reluctantly, to dismiss the savage chieftain to his own country, with all his followers. His policy was conciliation; particularly in the case of a Princess so beautiful, so well connected, so wealthy and powerful, as her of Cofachiqui, whose territories he had already penetrated, and whose chief settlements, on the banks of the Savannah, he was now approaching with all possible expedition.

It was at a spot on the west side of the Savannah, just where **the river sweeps** boldly beneath the shining walls of Silver Bluff, that the Adelantado, with a select detachment of a hundred cavalry, and as many infantry, emerged from the great forests, with the view to the passage of the stream. The noble river lay broad before him in the cloudless light of a noon-day sun On the depressed position which he occupied, an esplanade of swamp, liable to occasional overflow of the freshets from the rapid rising of the waters, he looked up to the high banks on the opposite shore —now of Carolina—and surveyed a prospect before him with unqualified admiration. The mighty forest ranges had been scarcely broken in any quarter; and the gigantic oak, the hickory, the mulberry, and black walnut, stood up, and spread away in mighty ranks, solemnizing the scene as far as the eye could reach. Terminating long vistas, rose the rustic cots and cabins of the people of Cofachiqui, stretching in a half circle, which followed the course of the stream, and sufficiently nigh to enable the inhabitants to take their fish from its waters, without inconvenience, to their homes. Conical mounts, and terraces, artificial areas, consecrated to religious rites, or public sports and gatherings, relieved, with the villages, the monotony of the unbroken forest. Upon a bold promontory to the right, surrounded by trees of the greatest age, and most remarkable aspect, rose up the temple of the tribe: a rude but picturesque edifice of logs, encircled with pillars, around which the wild vine had been trained to run. So that the whole fabric, relieved of all rudeness to the eye, seemed to be the handiwork of the endowing Spring herself; a green and purple trophy, vines, flowers and fruit, worthy to be the scene of innocent rites, and the religion of a pure and simple-hearted people. It was surrounded by tumuli—by the graves of ages, overgrown in like manner with shrubs and vines. In the recesses of the temple, were other treasures of nature and trophies of art. There, subsequently, the Adelantado gathered heaps of pearl—bushels of treasure to the Spaniards;—and there also were found some melancholy memorials of their own and other European people. Shields, and helmets, and daggers, and spear-heads, cast away by the followers of Cabeza de Vaca, or more probably by those of the cruel and luckless Vasquez de Ayllen, at the mouth of the Combahee, which, according to Indian computation, was but two days' journey from Silver Bluff. But we must not anticipate.

When the brilliant cavalcade of the Spanish Chieftain arrived at the west bank of the Savannah, he found the opposite shore covered with groups of the red men, looking out and watching his approach. The signs of vigilance and confident strength were everywhere present to his eyes. The boats were numerous

along the banks, but they were all on the eastern side of the river.
Bands of warriors might be seen hastily arraying themselves in
their rude armor, and hurrying,—each as he made himself ready
—with javelin, and spear, and bow, to join the crowds that gathered by the river. Conspicuous among those upon the banks,
were to be noticed a group of six persons, of very noble appearance, all of whom had passed the middle period of life. To
these, great deference was shown, and soon a great canoe, pro-
pelled by several strong rowers, approached the spot where they
stood. They entered the canoe in silence, and, a moment after,
it shot across the stream to the spot where De Soto had arrived,
at the head of his array. The fearless chieftains of the forest
approached him with a calm dignity, and a noble grace, which
struck the Adelantado with surprise, and compelled his respect.
He soon perceived that he stood in the presence of a people, very
far superior to those whom he had hitherto encountered in the
forests of the Floridian—superior in grace and art, if not in valor.
De Soto hastily seated himself in a chair of state, which he carried
with him for occasions like the present. The deputation of Chiefs
made three reverences as they drew nigh,—one to the east, a
second to the west, and a third to the Spanish Chieftain. Then,
they spoke through one of their party, a lofty and venerable man,
whose brow and bearing declared for habitual authority, and the
consciousness of power. He demanded briefly—

"Wherefore do you come, stranger? Is it for peace or war?"

Philip de Vasconselos interpreted, and reported the answer for
the Adelantado in the language of Cofachiqui.

"For Peace! we are friends. We ask only for a free passage
through the lands of your people, and their help, with raft and
canoe, in crossing your big rivers. We will pay for these helps
in goods of our country."

A long and pacific conference followed. The red men were too
well assured of their own power to dread the small array of
strangers before them. They knew not of the fearful weapons
which they bore, and the powerful arts which they possessed.
At the close of the conference, the Chief of the deputation, repeating his friendly assurances, said that he must receive the
commands of Coçalla, the young Queen, his mistress. She was
young—had but lately assumed dominion over them, and they
were required to consult deliberately before they perilled her
authority, or the peace of the country, by any action of their
own. But he did not doubt, that, from the generous nature of
this princess, she would do all in her power to promote the ob
jects of the strangers.

They did not err in this conjecture. Perhaps, their own report prompted her compliance, or, at all events, provoked her curiosity. It was not long after their return to the settlements, when the attention of the Spaniards was drawn to shows of great bustle and preparation along the opposite shore. The crowd continued to gather. There were sounds of conchs, and the occasional clamor of rattle and drum, regularly timed, and significant of a gathering and a march. While the Spaniards gazed, curious and anxious, a procession was beheld emerging from the woods, in the midst of which, seated upon a sort of palanquin, and borne upon the shoulders of six able men, was the form of a young maiden, who was readily conceived to be the Princess of the country. The palanquin was wreathed with vines and flowers, and gay streamers of stained cotton floated above it on every side. The cushions upon which the damsel half reclined, rather than sat, were spread with robes of the same richly dyed material. She was clad in similar stuffs, but of finer quality, and rich fringe depended from her skirts and shoulders. Her hair, black as ebony, and glossily bright, floated free, but was woven thick with ropes of pearl; frequent strands of pearl encircled her neck, falling free upon her bosom. Her sandals were also sown with pearl, and she wore anklets of the same precious decorations. Numerous young girls, bearing baskets of flowers, and habited like herself, followed in her train; and she was attended by goodly bands of spearmen and archers, all richly and picturesquely habited, and equally prepared for action and display. Before her, went several musicians, who blew the conch, shook the rattle, beat the drum, and played upon a rude sort of syrinx made of reeds, which gave forth a long succession of sweet but melancholy sounds. Others kept pace close beside the litter, whose office it was to wave before her huge fans of particolored feathers, the plumage of the wild birds of the Floridian, gathered from all quarters, and wrought with an art which leaves the modern fan of Europe but little of superiority to boast.

In this state, the Spaniards were allowed to behold her progress through the forests for awhile, when she suddenly disappeared in its deeper recesses with all her train. But her disappearance was for a brief space only. Very soon a great canoe, of the largest size and most magnificently decorated, with cushions, and canopies, and broad fringes and streamers of richly and variously stained cotton, was seen to emerge from the mouth of a creek that ran close beside the promontory on which stood the sylvan temple of Cofachiqui. In this canoe, under the canopy, reclined the princess in the stern, upon a pile of cushions. She was attended by eight beautiful girls, only less richly habited than herself. Her barge was accompanied, or rather led, by another of like dimensions, in which sat the six chieftains who had constituted the deputation. A cloud of canoes, of all sizes, filled with warriors, followed after and closed the procession, which now, under the impelling strokes of hardy rowers, soon made its way to the opposite shore. When arrived, the young princess, unassisted, but followed by all her train, stept fearlessly to the land, and the Spaniards were greatly struck by the elegant grace of her movements, the admirable symmetry of her form, the beauty and innocence, as well as intelligence of her face, and the picturesque appropriateness of her costume. De Soto made the most imposing preparations to give her corresponding welcome. Her obeisance to the Adelantado was full of grace and dignity; and this made, she seated herself on a sort of stool, which her attendant had brought with her for the purpose, though De Soto motioned her to the chair of state from which he himself had arisen.

A long and interesting conference ensued between the parties, carried on through Philip de Vasconselos, on whom, it was observed by more than one, that the fair princess bestowed the most encouraging smiles, speaking with as much sweetness, as ease and dignity. But the sad face of Philip never once changed through the whole conference. He was gentle and respectful, but calm, subdued, and too melancholy to note how flattering to himself were the looks of the beautiful Cassique. But Juan, the page, noted it as well as others; and he turned away from the sight as if disquieted, and retired into the rear, seating himself gloomily, beneath the old trees of the forest. Juan Ortiz, the former interpreter, too, was among the persons who thought the princess was quite too gracious in her bearing to a poor knight of Portugal, when an Adelantado of the Castilian was present; and De Soto himself more than once looked on with cloudy visage, as he beheld the smiles given to Philip, which he thought were properly due only to himself. The conference was long, but satisfactory in high degree to the Spaniards. At the close, and when the princess was about to depart, she rose, and unwinding the strings of pearl from about her neck, would have thrown them over that of the interpreter, but he recoiled from the dangerous honor, and motioned to De Soto. But the princess hesitated.

"Will not the warrior who speaks of strange things in the ear of Coçalla, the Queen, wear the pearls which have been about her neck?"

"Such gifts, beautiful Coçalla, are only for a great chief to wear. In the noble person who sits in the chair of state, you behold the great chief of our people. He will be proud to wear the pearls of the Queen of Cofachiqui."

She looked reproachfully at the knight of Portugal, and still hesitated, the pearls hanging from her hands. De Soto had observed her movements keenly. He suspected the truth.

"What says she, Don Philip?" was his stern and sudden question to the knight.

It was with a blush that Philip felt the necessity of evading, or suppressing, the truth.

"The princess would bestow upon the Adelantado the pearls which she carries in her hands, but fears to violate decorum. She would have *me* bestow them; but I have counselled her that the honor will be more graciously felt, if she will make the gift with her own hands."

"Thou art right," was the reply of the Adelantado, and he approached more closely and bowed his head. Slowly and reluctantly still, but obeying the sign made by Don Philip, the princess cast the heavy strands over the shoulders of the Adelantado, who, seizing her hand as she did so, passed a rich gold ring, with a ruby, over one of her fingers.

With this ceremonial, the conference ended. The princess had complied with the desires of the Spaniards. Her boats conveyed them across the river; her people brought them provisions; she received them in her village with favor; and, for a season, there was nothing but mutual pleasure and gratification among the parties. The Spaniards were delighted with the grace and beauty of the queen, at which they greatly wondered; and she, as well as her people, was equally charmed with the curious strangers who brought with them so many strange and charming objects. In particular, she thought long, and dwelt much, to her attendants, upon the handsome warrior, whose voice was so sweet within her ears. She likened his speech to that of the 'trick tongue' (the mock-bird), when it is the season for him to seek out a mate, and win his favorite by the pleasings of his song.

But Philip retired to sad, rather than sweet thoughts and fancies. That night, as he sat at his evening meal beneath a tree, with Juan in attendance, he was unusually sad and spiritless. Juan was very gloomy, too, but made an effort to revive the spirits of his master. He was curious, too, and he chose for his subject the beautiful queen, who was the topic of universal eulogium among the Spaniards.

"Think you, my Lord, that this woman is so very beautiful?" asked the boy.

"Woman? Forget you, sirrah, that you are speaking of a great Princess among her people!" was the sharp reply.

"Pardon me, Señor, but I meant not to offend;" answered the page with becoming humility—"but—does my Lord think her so very beautiful?" he persisted.

"She is very beautiful, Juan."

"That is to say, for a savage Indian?"

"She is one of God's creatures, Juan, and there is no race without its beauties."

"But these beauties do not suit the better tastes of a refined people, Señor. They are too rude; and besides, these beauties are of the form only; they lack the correspondences of education and learning, and the charm of accomplishments, such as are needful to satisfy the desires of a Christian people."

"Aye, boy; but if the tastes lack, the virtues are not wanting. There is heart, at least, in the savage rudeness, though it may lack the artful accomplishments of the refined European. There is no treachery here—no false faith—no base, degrading passions, nursed, though they are felt to be vicious, and practised by those who boast of their higher virtues and their purer tastes. Better far that there be no accomplishments, such as thou pratest of, if they are to be allied with foul lusts, practised in secret, to the grievous peril of the soul, and in despite of that very education of the mind, which teaches the sin, and the shame, and the horror of such practice. Better far, the embrace with the rude and simple woman of the Apalachian, than the whited sepulchres of Christendom, where all is smooth and shining without, and all loathsomeness and corruption within. I would rather lay my head upon the bosom of the simple savage, who is innocent as she knows nothing, than upon hers, who sins with all her knowledge, and is treacherous to the very faith which she professes and believes. Ah! boy—speak to me no more. Thou little knowest into what a gaping wound thou hast thrust thy torturing fingers."

The page said no more that night. He stole away to the solitude of another thicket, and bitterly did he weep the night away, with his face buried in the long grasses of the plain.

CHAPTER XXXVI.

" Deh ! non tradir' mi, amico."
                                ARTAXERXE.

At first, nothing could exceed the mutual satisfaction of the red men and the Spaniards in their commerce and communion. The latter delighted their simple hosts with gifts of curiosity and use, which were at once new to them and serviceable. The Indians, on the other hand, stript their houses and persons, and even their graves, of the pearls which they possessed in great quantities, to glut the desires of the strangers. To these gifts were added others which still further aroused the cupidity of our adventurers. Bits of gold and silver were mingled with their spoils, prompting a thousand curious inquiries as to the region whence they came. When told of the provinces of Xualla and Chalaque, where the gold grew, De Soto resolved upon the exploration of these regions also. But he proposed awhile to remain where he was; satisfied that he was even now in a world of great mineral treasures. The very appearance of the bluffs of Cofachiqui, shining with isinglass and mica, led to dreams of silver ore, which, a few bits found along the shore, seemed greatly to encourage; and while he remained in this neighborhood, he actually undertook the prodigious toil of cutting off an elbow of the river, and turning its water for several miles, in order to lay bare the bed of the stream for the possession of the precious treasures which were supposed to pave it. The proofs of this great labor, pursued with stern industry and a large body of workmen, for awhile, are still to be found in the canal, shown to this day in these precincts, and which still goes by the name of the Spanish Cut. But the Adelantado was compelled, though reluctant, to dismiss this pleasant fancy, and abandon the painful labors to which it led. His silver proved to be even less valuable than lead. It crumbled away at his touch. Better accounts reached him from the interior; accounts which we now know to have been strictly true.

Meanwhile, the pleasant relations between the red men and the white underwent a change. The Spaniards soon began to show the simple natives the sterner aspects of their character. Their eager, grasping, despotic temper, began to manifest itself, as they grew more confident in their position, and more familiar with the people. Violence took the place of kindness. In wanton mood, in mere levity, the intruders usurped the possessions of the savages, defiled their women, and brutally assailed their persons as their pride. Strife followed, and frequent struggle. The granaries of the red men lessened under the wasteful demands of their visitors, and the beautiful Princess herself, who had been at first so much charmed by the pale warriors,—and who still craved to be permitted to love and honor—her feelings, perhaps, being much more interested than her judgment—even she found how difficult it was to keep on terms with a people, so avaricious, so tyrannical, and selfish. She looked sternly upon the Spaniards in general, she looked coldly upon the Adelantado, whom an equal inflexibility of will and appetite made hard-favored and perpetually exacting. It was upon the noble interpreter, only, that she cast always sweet and loving glances. To him she spoke freely of the respects in which the Spaniards vexed and troubled her.

"They rob and wrong my people; they destroy their fields; beat them when they complain, and murder them when they resist. It is no longer easy to procure the provisions which shall feed so many mouths. My people grow very impatient. My chiefs counsel me to expel the intruders; my warriors would take up arms against them. It remains only that I give the signal, and the shout of war would rise above the forests, and the shaft of death would fly from every thicket. But, I am silent, noble Philip, as they call thee;—silent! I feel for my people, and I chafe at the insolences of thine. Why am I silent? It is because I would not harm thee: because I would not see thee depart, Philip."

Philip beheld her with a sad and drooping eye. What a history of grief and hopelessness did her tender words and looks recall!

"I am but a leaf in the wind, noble Coçalla; a bubble upon the stream; a spent arrow, whose course through the air is lost as soon as made. Think not of me. Persuade thy warriors to forbearance. The Adelantado will, I think, depart soon from thy provinces. Better not provoke his anger. He hath a power of which thy people know nothing: to which they must succumb in strife, or perish. He hath but little reason to remain here much longer, and will most likely depart ere the coming moon! Till then be patient—keep thy people in patience, and let them bring in good supplies of provisions, that we may the sooner leave thee."

"But *thou* need'st not leave Cofachiqui, Phil'p. Thou wilt stay here, and dwell in the village of Coçalla. It is a Queen among her people who implores thee to stay."

Before Philip could reply, his page Juan, with aspect gloomy and anxious, suddenly entered the apartment, and after a hurried obeisance, said—

"Señor, your presence is needed without. There is trouble. The Indians are arming and surrounding some of our people. There have been blows already between them, and there is danger of insurrection."

"I must see to this!" said Vasconselos. In a few words he conveyed to the Princess what he had heard from Juan, and hurriedly took his departure. Juan was about to follow, when the Princess beckoned him, and throwing a rich robe of furs upon his shoulders, motioned him to accept it, in a sweet and gracious manner. But the boy shook the garment from his shoulders, and with a single glance, of a strange and almost savage sternness, at the noble giver, wheeled about and hastily followed his lord.

The Princess was confounded at this treatment. She had bestowed the gift upon the boy as she had beheld his devotion to his master. It was a tribute prompted entirely by her regard for the latter. She could not conjecture the meaning of the boy, or the dark and savage look which he gave her; and the rejection of her gift, apart from the manner in which the thing was done, was itself an insult. She expressed her wonder, in her own language, and hastily summoned her attendants. These had hardly made their appearance, when one of her grave and venerable forest councillors entered also. His brow was full of trouble. He hurriedly confirmed the report which she had just heard from Vasconselos, of the difficulty between her people and the Spaniards, and, anxious about the result, she hurried forth also with the aged chief, in the hope, by her presence, to quiet the aroused passions of her subjects.

When Philip de Vasconselos appeared upon the scene of commotion, the conflict seemed inevitable. The red men were arming every where, and gathering to the conflict. They had been goaded beyond their endurance, by the brutalities of some of the Spanish rabble, had resented with blows an unprovoked injury; and, unwillingly restrained so long, by the authority of their queen, it was now apparent that the outbreak would be proportionately extreme, from the enforced authority which had hitherto kept in subjection their usually untameable passions. The warriors had submitted to the presence and the aggressions of the Spaniards, against their habitual practice, and against their nature. Fierce, proud, always prepared for, and fond of, war,— the conquerors of all the surrounding tribes,—how should they submit to the insolence of his handful of strangers, whom it seemed so easy to destroy? The moment had arrived, at last, for the assertion of their strength and independence!

The moment was inauspicious for De Soto. One half of his forces had been despatched in different bodies, and directions, in the exploration of the country. Nuno de Tobar was probably fifty miles off, with a select body of forty horses, on the route to Achalaque. Juan de Anasco, with a similar force, was away on another route. So was Gonzalo Sylvestre; so was Andres de Vasconselos, with his Portuguese, and other knights. The remains of the army, with De Soto, at the moment of commotion, were scattered along the river banks, or in the forests, fishing or fowling. Unless he could quell the commotion without the extreme of struggle, without absolute violence, he was in danger of being utterly destroyed. The princess of Cofachiqui could bring several thousand warriors into the field. It was under these circumstances that the Adelantado hurried forth, as Philip de Vasconselos had done, in order to interpose his person and authority for the prevention of the strife. It was here that he showed the resources of a good head and a long experience. To the surprise equally of his own soldiers and the red men, he seized a cudgel and began to belabor the Spaniards, seconded in the operation most heartily by Philip, who had reached the scene in season for this proper, if not pleasant exercise. The princess appeared at this juncture, and clapped her hands with a sort of girlish delight, which contributed to the success of De Soto's policy. The chiefs and sages went amongst their warriors with words of counsel; and the outbreak was quelled almost as soon as it had taken place. The red men retired to their woods, hardly satisfied, but subdued, they knew not well in what manner. The Adelantado escorted the princess to her dwelling, and partook of a feast which she had prepared. For the moment harmony seemed restored. But it was a hollow amnesty. There were wounds that rankled on both sides, and refused to be healed. Pride was at work equally in the hearts of the Spaniards and red men, and passions, of even a worse order, which the artifices of both only labored to conceal—not overcome.

That night, the Adelantado called a council of his chief officers at his quarters. Philip de Vasconselos was present with the rest.

"I have summoned you, Señores," said De Soto, "that we may confer together as to the policy before us. You have seen to-day what is the temper of these savages. For some days past we have witnessed a rising spirit of insolence among them. They bring in their maize and beans very reluctantly. With all our exertions, we scarcely get an adequate supply, and the return of the several parties, we have sent out, will find too many mouths for our granaries. The princess, herself, no longer looks on us with friendly eyes. She treats us coldly; she denies herself, sometimes, when I seek to see her; and there can be no question that she looks upon our continued presence with dislike. Speak forth, Señores; declare your opinions freely, and say what is left to us in this condition of our affairs."

There were many speakers, to all of whom the remarks of the Adelantado furnished the key-note. All were agreed that the queen and her subjects were changed in temper towards them; that it was evident they were regarded no longer as grateful guests, but as burdensome and offensive intruders. But no one suggested the course of action. They all well knew that, while De Soto listened patiently to all, he followed no counsel but his own, or that to which he fully inclined himself. Vasconselos alone was silent.

"We would hear from Don Philip," said De Soto, with a smile which had in it something of a sneer. Philip quietly and promptly answered.

"There is no question but it is true that these people are tired of us. We have worn out their patience. We have consumed their provisions, occupied their houses, controlled and commanded their labor, enjoyed their hospitality to the full extent of their resources; and in return, have beaten and despoiled their men and women, and shown ourselves very ungrateful for all that they have done with us. For my part, I only wonder that they have tolerated us so long. The admirable drubbing which your Excellency administered this day to some of the runagates who have turned the hearts of this simple people against us, was quite as much due to justice as to good policy. It might have been well to have administered a little more of it, and to a score or two of other offenders."

"Well, but admitting the truth of all this, Señor Don Philip," responded De Soto, rather impatiently,—"the question is, what are we to do,—how repair the evil—how put ourselves in security against such mischance as had so nearly befallen us to-day?"

"The question is an embarrassing one, your Excellency, and, perhaps, were better addressed to some of your older and closer councillors. The solution of it will depend upon your objects. Why should we linger here? The silver which we hoped to gather from these banks of earth turns out a delusion. The gold, as we learn on every hand, is to be found many leagues above, and in the region of mighty mountains. You have abandoned the idea of changing the bed of the stream, since there is no probability that it will afford a treasure which the banks on its sides do not possess. Wherefore, then, remain in a region which promises nothing, and where we have evidently exhausted the hospitality, with the provisions of its people? Our delay can give us neither food, nor profit, nor security."

"True again, but still not satisfactory. There is a subject besides which we need to consider. If we depart from these people thus, and while they keep their present mood, we lose credit among them. They will feel that they have had a sort of triumph. It will make them insolent. Their runners will precede us where we go; they will disparage our arms and valor; they will lose us that authority which makes our progress go without question; and we shall have to fight every step of our way."

"We have had to do this already in most cases. In the country of the savage this can scarce be otherwise. We can look only to our arms and courage to carry us through. But where this needs not—where we are received in kindness—it is scarcely wise to force hatred upon the people that welcome us at first with love. This is what we have been doing. We have manacled, maimed, and even burned these people, for small offences, which, in their ignorance, they have committed. Yet they have borne with all, through the kindness of their Queen. They cannot endure starvation. We have brought them to this. Let us leave them in season, before we have made them desperate; and carry their friendly wishes with us, if we can carry nothing better. They have yielded to us all their treasures of gold and pearls."

"Ay, but their favor is already lost. They will send us forward with no good wishes. They will rather send before us tidings of evil which shall prejudice our progress wherever we appear. The Princess Coçalla has grown haughty and indifferent, Señor Don Philip, to all among us, but yourself."

Philip regarded the savage smile upon the countenance of the Adelantado, with a quiet, cold, immovable look. He did not attempt to answer. Don Balthazar de Alvaro now took up the parole.

"I suspect that few will doubt the necessity of our leaving this place, your Excellency; and just as few will be prepared to deny the danger of which your Excellency speaks, from the malicious and unfriendly reports of these people. We have had sufficient proofs of their growing hostility. The mother of this Princess keeps aloof from us, and has eluded pursuit and search.

The young Indian Chief whom we sent to her with a message, slew himself rather than approach her after he had been forbidden; and I am sure that we should have lost the favor of the Princess here, but for the special regard which possesses her soul, in behalf of one of us. How long this will secure us is a problem which we shall soon be able to solve, if it be true that the natives are out of provisions. Now, we are all agreed to depart from a region in which we shall find famine only instead of gold; and we are agreed also, that we may have to fight our way at every step, and get our provisions only at the end of our weapon. Well, with your Excellency's leave, we are in precisely the same strait with those great men, Hernan Cortez and Francis Pizarro, and I see not that we can do better than adopt their policy."

"What policy?" quoth the Adelantado.

"That of seizing upon the sovereign of the country, and making her a hostage for the good behavior of her people. This Princess of Cofachiqui is in your power. Her people hold her in an esteem little short of reverence. Seize her, keep her in close custody, under watchful guardianship, and you secure the good conduct of her people. You are required now to traverse hundreds of miles over which she possesses acknowledged sway: as you pass west, if you need to do so, you are told that she is closely allied to the great powers of the Apalachian, the Alabamous, the Mechachebe! What follows? The people, in all these places, obey her decrees, bring provisions, bear burdens, submit without blows. The policy of Cortez and Pizarro must be that of Hernan de Soto, if he hopes for like success with these heathen savages. It is the only policy for safety."

"And I deem it a base and horrid policy, Señor!" cried Vasconselos, rising, and speaking with all the warmth of a noble and ingenuous soul, shocked at the cold cruelty and baseness of the counsel given. "O! Don Hernan de Soto, beware how you stain an honorable fame, by the adoption of a policy so shameful, so shocking, so dreadfully ungrateful. This young Princess has received you with highest honors, has treated you with unvarying kindness, has yielded from her stores all that she possesses. As a Christian gentleman, and loyal cavalier, you cannot follow counsels which shall violate every trusted virtue, every security of feeling and of honor."

The brow of De Soto darkened terribly.

"You employ strong language, Don Philip de Vasconselos; but you may have special reasons for doing so. *You*, at least, would seem to owe special favors to this dusky Princess."

The pale cheeks of Philip reddened, but he was silent. The Adelantado proceeded:

"But our obligations are general only, and shared with all the chiefs of my army. You hear how they express themselves, and what they counsel. In great necessities, nice scruples are vicious impediments, and we may not apply to great embarrassments, the principles we submit to when the currents of life flow smoothly on as we would have them, under ordinary laws. I hold the counsel of Don Balthazar to be the only means of escape and progress in this our emergency. It is our necessity, which we cannot escape."

"O! say not so, your Excellency——" began Philip de Vasconselos, but the truncheon of the Adelantado came down heavily upon the table,—and he thundered out—

"We have decided, gentlemen—we are resolved—the council is dissolved. We shall see to these things with early morning. Be you each prepared, in armor, to second all my orders."

The council dispersed, each to his own quarters, all leaving the Adelantado, except Don Balthazar, who had other matters to insinuate when he did not counsel. Philip de Vasconselos, grieved to the heart, retired to his lowly lodgings, where he sat down to his silent supper, of which he scarcely ate, attended by Juan in silence.

"O! boy, boy!" he exclaimed, suddenly—"thou little knowest, boy," he proceeded—"but if the heart of woman be incurably false, that of man is terribly base! If her heart be weak as water, his is more hard and unfeeling than the pitiless rock. am sick, Juan, very sick of all things that live!"

And the supper was pushed away; and the knight threw himself on his couch of reeds and brush, under the roof of his simple Indian lodge which had given him shelter, and he felt to what a base use his ruler had put all the benefits of the simple and confiding red men, and their sweet and lovely sovereign. And Juan lay between two rustic pillars, in the shade, half watching the words of his master all the while. And he drowsed while watching: but Philip slept not. He could not sleep because of too much thought, and long after midnight he arose, and he muttered to himself—

"It shall not be! I will prevent this dreadful treachery!"

And he stole forth even as he spoke, carrying his sword beneath his arm, and he made his way, amidst the dim woods, guided only by the starlight, and certain scattered fires of the village, until he was lost in the thickets that lay between the

Spanish encampment and the grounds which environed the abode of thé Princess. He knew not that the only half-sleeping Juan, aroused by his exclamation, had started to his feet, and caught up a weapon also, and was following stealthily upon his footsteps.

CHAPTER XXXVII.

> "E chi poteva,
> Mio ben, senza vedir-ti
> La patria abbandonnar?"
> ARTASERSE

MEANWHILE, the Adelantado and his prime minister, Don Balthazar de Alvaro, sate late at their private councils, after the rest of the noble Knights and Captains had retired. They had much to discuss and determine which was not proper to be submitted to the common ear. But a portion only of this conference properly concerns our drama. It was at the close of their discourse that De Soto gave it in charge to Don Balthazar, to arrest the Princess and put her under safeguard.

"There need be no violence, Señor Balthazar, if your proceedings are prompt and secret. All outward forms of respect must be maintained. We must only see that she does not escape. See to it by sunrise."

"Better an hour or two before," was the answer of the Don. "The Indians may be put on the alert by sunrise."

"What! you do not suspect Don Philip?"

"He is a favorite with the Princess."

"But I should think her no great favorite with him. He seems to treat her with great reserve, if not coldness."

"Reserve is apt to be only a prudent masking of the passions."

"But would he dare to play us false!"

"Ah! this would scarcely be considered a treachery; or only such as were becoming in a good knight. We can, at all events, better guard against than punish such a treachery."

"Ay, by the holy cross, but I should punish such a treachery, were the offender the best knight in Christendom."

"Verily, and I should hark on, and say well done, your Excellency; but still I repeat, better in this case prevent, than have to punish such treachery. In brief, the Princess must not be allowed to escape. Were she to do so, we should fare badly in our future progress through her dominions. With your Excellency's leave, I will make the arrest before the dawn of another day."

"It is as you please. You are no doubt right in the precau

tion; though, let me find this Knight of Portugal playing me false, and ——."

The threat was unspoken, or was sufficiently expressed in the angry gesture, and the heavy stroke with which, with clenched fist, he smote the rude table at which the parties were seated. In a little while after this, Don Balthazar took his leave.

He proceeded almost instantly to collect a select body of his followers, all armed, for the capture of the Princess Cocalla. This labor occupied some time. He had to move with all precautions, rout up soldiers who were sleeping, and hunt up others who were scattered; and this brought him to a tolerably late hour in the night. By that time Philip de Vasconselos had already proceeded on his generous mission, of arousing the Princess to the necessity of flight, and ere Don Balthazar had set his little squad in motion: but the latter was not delayed much longer. Still, the Portuguese Knight is in season for his object, if there should occur no embarrassments.

It was no small one, however, that of finding access to the Princess. She occupied a centre mansion, rude enough for royalty, so far as we refer to the agencies of art, but a most royal abode if we look only to the natural accessories. That great home of forest oaks, and hickories, and walnuts, towering masses of wood and shrubbery—a mighty colonnade of gigantic forms, conducting through numerous airy avenues to the lowly mansion of logs, surrounded by a shady roof of thatched poles,—an ample verandah of green, surrounding the habitation, which nestled in the great shelter of the ancient forest—was an abode for an Emperor. In this verandah slept a score or more of warriors always ready, armed with feathered shaft, and flint-headed spear, and obsidian bludgeon, stone tomahawk and knife of flint. No Emperor ever possessed subjects more faithful and devoted. The space of forest surrounding the abode of the Princess was filled up with scattered parties of other warriors, who slept beneath the trees when the weather was fair, and who kept watch from hidden huts, when the storm descended. They were as vigilant as faithful.

Hardly had Philip de Vasconselos entered the tabooed precincts, when a dozen spears were at his breast.

"Lead me to your queen," he said in calm, but commanding accents—" she is in danger. I must see her."

A brief and rapid consultation ensued among the forest watchers. The result was favorable to the wishes of the knight, simply as all knew him to be the favorite of Cocalla. He was scarcely a less favorite among her people. He was conducted silently through the green glades, and amidst the dark avenues of thicket; the boy Juan stealthily and closely following, unnoticed by Philip, and permitted by the red men, as a matter of course, as he was the attendant of the master. When they reached the lodge, a conch, which hung from one of the pillars of the verandah, was sounded by one of the watchers at the porch. A door opened, and a whispered conversation ensued between the guard and some one within. A brief space, and Philip was admitted to an antechamber, a great hall, indeed, at one side of which stood a maiden with a blazing torch. Juan remained in waiting without the verandah, anxious to press forward, and trembling with anxiety, yet dreading what he should behold. But, for awhile, his courage failed him, leaving his anxiety unrepressed.

But a few moments had elapsed, after Philip's entrance into the hall, when the princess made her appearance. She was clad in simple white cotton garments, hastily caught up. It needed but little time or effort to adjust the costume of the native princess. She was followed by a group of damsels, and one or two matrons. In a few moments after, several old men made their appearance from contiguous dormitories.

There was a joyous eagerness in the face of the bright-eyed Coçalla, as she looked upon the knight.

"Philip!" She had learned to call his name very prettily— "Philip!" and the rest she spoke in her own language, taking his hand frankly as she spoke.

"What would the voice of the Spaniard with Coçalla? It is not the hour of council. The bird that sings by day, sleeps in the darkness. The warrior sleeps, with the spear beneath his arm. Why comes Philip to me now? Would he make his home with the red warriors of the forest? Philip shall be a chief for Cozalla."

"It is not for that I come, noble Coçalla. But there is danger for the princess. My people have said Coçalla must be ours! She must march with our army to the great mountains. She must be the hostage for her people. She must follow the path as we mark it out for her footsteps. Let Coçalla fly to the great thickets and escape from captivity."

"Does the Spanish chief say this of the Queen of Cofachiqui?" was the indignant answer.

"The Spanish chiefs have so spoken!"

"What! They see not my warriors? They know not their valor, their skill, their numbers, and the fatal weapons which they carry."

"Neither numbers nor weapons will avail against the arms of the Spaniards."

"Ha! say'st thou! Thou shalt see." And she whispered to her attendants, one of whom disappeared.

"The princess must fly to the deep forests," continued Vasconselos. "There alone can she be safe from our people."

"Fly! and from my home,—while my warriors are around me? Never! never!—And yet—" speaking quickly—"Will Philip go with me to my lodge in the great forests? Will he become a warrior of Cofachiqui? Say, Philip,—wilt thou go with me, and find a lodge among my people—and become a chief—*the* great chief—the '*well*-beloved of Cofachiqui?' And she caught his hand eagerly.

"Alas!" he said, "I cannot, beautiful Coçalla—my lot is cast among the Spaniards."

"Then will I meet them here. I will gather my warriors. They shall fight these Spaniards—they shall fall upon them, and slay them all—all but thee, Philip. Thou shalt be a great chief of Cofachiqui."

A group of old men entered at this moment, and were apprised of what Vasconselos had reported. They received the information gravely. They heard their princess as she inveighed loudly against the insolent purpose of the Spaniards. She bade them gather the warriors together, and meet their enemy. She was resolved not to fly, unless——and she turned again to the knight—

"Will not Philip go with Coçalla to the great forests of her people, and be a chief of Cofachiqui?"

He shook his head mournfully. The old chiefs interfered. Philip understood all that they spoke, though in low tones, to their queen. They, too, exhorted her to take the counsel of Vasconselos, and seek safety in flight. At the moment, they were unprepared for conflict. Their warriors about the village were few in number, hardly more than necessary for a body-guard of honor for their sovereign. It required time to call in the warriors, and to prepare for such enemies as those with whom they had to deal, and the terrible resources of which were already, in part, known to the chiefs. But the princess grew unreasonable; still recurring, at the close of her speech, to the one burden, in the appeal to Philip—" to find a lodge among, and be a chief over her people—*the* chief!" The old warriors looked grave. They renewed their counsels and expostulations. They were seconded by the earnest entreaties of Vasconselos. She said to him reproachfully—

"Does Philip bid me go from him where I can see him no

more? Does Philip say to Coçalla—let the forests grow between us, so that our eyes shall never meet again? Ah! Philip!" and she laid her hand, as if with pain, upon her heart. The knight felt very wretched at the wretchedness he was compelled to inflict, and a vague but beguiling thought passed through his fancy for an instant, with the rapidity of an arrow of light.

"And why should I not depart with this true-hearted and innocent princess?—She is young and beautiful, and powerful, and more than all, pure of thought and feeling. Why should I follow in the steps of those who hate, when I am persuaded by those who love?"

But he dismissed the seductive argument with the resolute exertion of his will. The very thought of love, and of another woman, while his heart was still so sore with the most humiliating experience of the sex, was a revolting thought. He hastily expelled it from his mind.

"Heed not me," he said, "noble Princess:—I am but an insect in thy path. I am nothing."

"Thou art every thing, Philip, to Coçalla. My people will honor thee for my sake, and thou shalt be a chief among them. And thou shalt dwell in a lodge with Coçalla, and there shall be no Spaniards in the great forests where we go. Thou shalt be a chief of my people, Philip,—thou shalt be the only chief for Coçalla."

And with these words, in the eager impulse of a passion which was no less pure than warm,—the passion of a nature wholly unsophisticated, no longer able to restrain her feelings, she threw her arms around the neck of Vasconselos, and laid her head upon his breast. Her long, dark tresses fell like a shower of starry night over his shoulders.

At that moment, and before the knight could recover himself, he felt his arm plucked from behind, and the voice of Juan sounded huskily in his ears.

"See you not, Señor, that unless you tear yourself away from her, she will not depart? She will be captured, unless you leave her at once! Already Don Balthazar is gathering his troop to surround the village of the princess. Fly from her in season, or she is surely taken. These moments are fatally lost."

Vasconselos heard, and tenderly but firmly he unwound the arms of the princess from about his neck. At this act, silently performed, she turned, with a sudden revulsion of feeling, and threw herself on the bosom of one of the matrons, while her sobs sounded distinctly through the apartment.

"Now—now!" cried Juan, in quick, eager accents, as Philip lingered—"Now is the moment, Señor. She will fly when you are gone from sight."

"You are right, boy, right!" answered the knight. The hand of Juan eagerly grasped that of his superior, and led him away from the apartment and into the woods, without a moment's delay. They were within a few paces of the lodging of Vasconselos, when they heard a slight blast of a trumpet in the thicket between them and the abode of the Princess.

"It is the signal of Don Balthazar," said Juan hurriedly. "We are safe;" and he drew the knight into the lodge.

"But Coçalla?" said Philip.

"She has had time enough for escape if she willed it; but methinks she would rather be a captive were Don Philip the jailer, than be the free Princess of all these forests."

There was something of bitterness in the accents of the boy. Philip noted it, but his mind was too full of anxiety, in respect to the escape of Coçalla, to dwell upon minor matters.

"Now may the Saints forbid!" he ejaculated.

"This princess seems very precious to the Señor!" quoth Juan, moodily.

"As nobility, and generosity of soul, and true virtue in a woman, should ever be to every noble knight!" responded Philip, somewhat sternly; and Juan shrunk away, as if an arrow had pierced him suddenly in the breast; and Vasconselos heard no more words from him that night. The boy had gone aside to bury his face in the leaves of his couch, and to weep in secret, as was his nightly custom and necessity.

CHAPTER XXXVIII

"*Val se hai cara la vita.*"
ALFIERI.

THE effort of Don Philip had been made in vain. The Princess Coçalla gave herself up to a passion of grief, that resisted argument and entreaty. She became fully conscious of her danger (of which even the assurance of Vasconselos had failed to possess her mind)—of the danger which awaited her, only when it was too late. It was only when the shrill blast of the Spanish trumpet, speaking in signal to the co-operating squad, and the crash of conflicting weapons, had struck upon her senses, that she consented to make the attempt to escape. But, by this time, the building was entirely surrounded, and she was seized by a group of common soldiers, as she strove to steal away from the rear during the struggle between her warriors and the assailants. Her people fought desperately, even the old chiefs and counsellors, but only to be butchered. The dawn saw her village smoking with blood, and herself a captive.

The Princess was from this moment kept under close restraint, well watched and guarded, but treated with forbearance, if not with kindness. She was allowed a litter to be borne upon the shoulders of her own people, when she was indisposed to walk. The Adelantado, for awhile, paid her a morning visit, as Cortez had done to Montezuma, in which he maintained all the most deferential externals. She did not reproach, nor entreat; but from the moment when she became a captive, she habited herself in the stern reserve of character so peculiar to the red men of America, and haughtily refused communion with her treacherous and ungrateful guest. But her captivity disarmed her people. They dared not rebel against the authority whose simple decree might destroy the head of the nation. They submitted every where—submitted as *Tamenes*, or porters, to bear the luggage of the army, and brought in provisions throughout the country, wherever the Spaniards came or sent.

The army was set in motion soon after the arrest of the Princess, and the young and noble Coçalla was borne along with it, unresisting, as recklessly as the tides of ocean bear away upon their discordant billows, the beautiful and innocent flower which the tem pest has flung upon them from the shores. In this manner was she conducted up the Savannah to its sources, passing into that region of glorious scenery which we now find in the county of Habersham, in Georgia. Pursuing a direct western course across the northern parts of that State, the expedition reached the head waters of the Coosa. From town to town—still submitted to wherever it came—the Spanish army proceeded to the Conasauga, the Oostanaula, and other streams. They explored the country as they went, lodged in the villages, and secured the submission of the chiefs; some of whom they also kept in captivity, the better to secure the obedience of their people. Occasionally, De Soto sent out detachments, right and left, in quest of gold and silver.

It was while two of these detachments, under the knights, Villabos and Silvera, had gone forth to explore the mountains of Chisca, that the Spanish army rested for a space of more than thirty days, at a populous Indian town, called Chiaha, the chief of which was a cousin of our Princess of Cofachiqui. This chief, influenced by the situation of his kinswoman, had received the Spaniards with a seeming good-will, which left them wholly without cause of complaint. But, with the rest from their fatigue, the passions of the invaders passed beyond all ordinary limits, and they made a formal demand upon the Cassique for a certain number of the young women of the nation. Hitherto, the men had not been denied to serve the Spaniards, in the capacity of Tamenes. The demand for women, implied a reckless disregard to all the sensibilities of the people; and, in a single night, the Cassique of Chiaha, who was also held somewhat in the position of a captive, found himself abandoned by all his followers. Wild was the rage of the Spaniards at the flight of their destined victims, and vain were all the efforts of the Cassique to propitiate their anger. They ravaged his country, with fire and sword, slaughtering and burning without mercy.

It was at this moment, and while the invaders were showing themselves most licentious and reckless, that the Princess Cocalla, still a captive, and still watched, though more carelessly than usual, attempted to make her escape. She had been confided to the guardianship of two soldiers, Pedro Martin, and Gil Torres. Her followers had laid down her litter, and she had descended to drink at a spring by the wayside. The two soldiers, meanwhile, had taken advantage of the pause to produce their dice, and were busily engaged in perilling some of their pearls and other acquisitions, as was the universal practice, upon the hazards of the game. Suddenly, they missed the Princess and her followers.

They instantly sought, by a vigorous search in the neighboring woods, to repair the consequences of their fault. Unfortunately, they had missed the captive too soon after her flight, to enable her to escape very far. She was found; her followers gallantly threw themselves in the path of the pursuers, and armed only with sticks or billets, hastily snatched up in the forest, endeavored to defend their mistress. But they were immediately butchered. Coçalla, who had continued her flight, was soon overtaken, and violently seized by Pedro Martin. The bold ruffian, goaded by licentious passions, dragged her into the covert, while Gil Torres stood by, as if keeping sentry. Her cries rang through the woods, and not in vain. They called up a champion in the perilous moment.

Don Philip de Vasconselos had not lost sight of the beautiful Princess who had so fearlessly shown him how precious he was in her eyes. But he forbore to trespass upon the indulgence which she had shown him, and, with a rare modesty and forbearance, a delicacy of consideration, which had few parallels in that day amongst these wild adventurers, he steadily rejected the temptations which were held out to him by the warmth of her affection and the confiding innocence of her nature. He studiously forbore her presence, except when specially required to communicate with her by De Soto himself. In fact, there was a policy, as well as propriety, in this forbearance. Vasconselos had discovered *that he was watched.* Juan, his page, had made some discoveries to this effect, and had made them known immediately to the knight. He was watched by the creatures of Don Balthazar. This was the amount of the discovery: and there were suspicious circumstances, coupled with the conduct of Juan Ortiz, the interpreter, whose jealousy had been kindled, at the expense of Vasconselos, in consequence of the better knowledge of the Indian tongues which the latter possessed. He had lost some of his authority with the Spaniards during the period when the Portuguese knight served wholly as the medium of communication between the red men and the white. Ortiz possessed, however, a rare natural capacity for the acquisition of language, and, with a strong motive to goad his industry, in his pride, his mortification, and his love of ease—for, when not interpreting, he was required to serve in the ranks as a common soldier—he addressed himself to the task of picking up the dialect of the people of the new regions into which he passed. He had become to a certain extent successful, so that he was now able to understand and conjecture the purport of the various conversations between the Princess and the knight, whenever they took place in public. On all these occasions, Coçalla freely gave vent to her affections, and spoke with Vasconselos as frankly in respect to her love, as if no other ear but his own could comprehend the purport of her speech. All this matter was reported to Don Balthazar, who, by the way, had been repulsed by the Princess in every approach which he had made to familiarity with her. How Juan, the Moorish page, had ascertained these facts, may not now be said, but he had learned enough to set his master on his guard against the subtle Ortiz and other spies employed by his enemy.

But though cautious, and avoiding as much as possible all intercourse with the Princess, Vasconselos watched over her safety as tenderly as if he returned her affection. He had seen the growing indifference of De Soto to the claims and character of the Princess, and he strove, whenever he could do so without provoking suspicion, to lighten her bonds and soften her mortifications. The boy, Juan, was sometimes sent with tributes to Coçalla, with delicacies which she might not else procure; and we may add that, though he obeyed the knight, he yet did so with some reluctance. More than once he expostulated with Philip upon the risk which he incurred, by his attentions, and strove to alarm his fears; but he soon found that such suggestions only inspired the knight with audacity. He then ventured to change his mode of attack, and would speak, with a sneer, about the incapacity of the red woman to appreciate either the delicacy of his gifts or his attentions. But to this suggestion, also, the reply of the knight was apt to silence, for awhile, the presumption of the page.

"Cease," one day he said to Juan—"cease, boy, to prate of what thou knowest not. I tell thee that this heathen princess is a more beautiful soul in my sight, than any that I know of paler blood. And why shouldst thou, a blackamoor, presume to sneer at the complexion which is more akin to that of the Christian than thine own? Go to, for a foolish boy, and say nothing more in this wise; for verily, sometimes, when thou speakest thus, I am almost tempted to hold thee an enemy to this most gracious yet luckless princess; whom I hold in such esteem, boy, and regard, that if I had yet a heart to give, or a faith to yield, to woman, I should prefer to trust in her, than to any living beauty in all Spain or Portugal."

Such speeches were always apt to humble and to silence the page for a season. The knight no ways withheld his kindnesses and protection from the princess, because of the counsels of the boy. Yet he suffered her not to see that he watched over her and now, when the passions of the rude and licentious ruffian Pedro Martin had dragged her into the deep thickets, and she shrieked aloud in her last and worst terrors for a champion to save her, she had little reason to think that the chief whom she loved before all, would suddenly appear to her rescue.

Philip de Vasconselos was fortunately at hand. He heard the cries of the captive princess. He recognized the voice. He knew the present licentious moods of the Spaniards. He had denounced, as a terrible crime, that requisition upon the Cassique of Chiaha, which had outraged his people, and driven them away to the shelter of the woods. His instinct instantly conceived the danger of the princess; the neglect and disregard of De Soto tending to encourage the audacity of those who were appointed to watch over her. He called to Juan, and hurried with sword drawn into the thickets. He was suddenly confronted by Gil Torres.

"It is nothing, Señor Don Philip, but the cries of the heathen woman, the Princess of Cofachiqui, who has been seeking to make escape from us, and whom my comrade, Pedro, has just secured."

"Stand aside, fellow—I must see this comrade of thine."

Martin raised his lance, and caught the knight by the wrist to detain him. With one blow of his gauntletted fist, Vasconselos smote him to the earth, where he lay senseless. Philip hurried into the thicket, where Coçalla still struggled with all her might against the brutal assailant. But she was almost exhausted. She could no longer shriek. She could only oppose. Her long black hair, which swept the ground, was floating dishevelled, her garments were torn, her hands were bloody. At this perilous moment she saw the approach of the knight of Portugal. She knew him at a glance. She could only murmur, "Philip," and her strength failed her. She sank down senseless. At the sight of Vasconselos, the ruffian fled.

The knight raised the princess from the ground.

"Bring water, Juan."

The boy obeyed, bringing the water in the knight's helmet, which he threw to him for the purpose. He dashed the face of the princess with the cooling sprinkle. He poured the grateful draught into her lips. She opened her eyes. They lightened with joy. She threw her arms round his neck, and cried—

"Philip! O Philip!"

"You must fly," he said—"fly, Coçalla. Do not waste the precious moments now. It is your only chance. Use it. I will keep off these villains."

He shook himself free from her, and darted away. She stood mournfully looking at him for a while, then waved her hand to him, and cried—

"Philip! Philip!"

He disappeared in the opposite woods; and she turned away, with clasped hands, and moving with slow footsteps, bending form, and a very mournful aspect, murmuring as she went, the one word "Philip." She too was soon buried, out of sight, in the sheltering bosom of the mighty forest.

CHAPTER XXXIX.

> "There is my pledge! I'll prove it on thy heart,
> Ere I taste bread, thou art in nothing, less
> Than I have here proclaimed thee."
>
> KING LEAR.

WHILE these events were in progress, in and about the precincts of the Indian town of Chiaha, Hernando de Soto was absent from the place. He had led a portion of his forces in pursuit of the fugitive red men, who had left their village in consequence of the brutal requisition to render up their women; and a report of the gathering of a large body of the savages, in a hostile attitude, not far off, had aroused all the eager fury of the Spanish governor, to pursue and punish them. He had pursued with his usual energy, but without encountering the subtle enemy, who, when they pleased, could readily cover themselves, in such perfect concealment in the deeper forests, that the whole army of the Adelantado could never ferret them out, or bring them to battle. De Soto rested his troops, after the fruitless pursuit, in a beautiful wood, about half a day's journey from the town of Chiaha. Here he waited the return of certain of his officers, whom he had sent on exploring journeys higher up the country. Nuno de Tobar was thus absent with twenty lances: Andres de Vasconselos had been sent forward with his Portuguese, to feel his way along the banks of the Coosaw, and to prepare for the coming of the army. There were a few other leaders of the Spanish host, who, like these, might have had sympathies with Philip de Vasconselos, who were also most inopportunely absent. There was probably some design and management in an arrangement, which, at this juncture, removed from the neighborhood the few persons who might have resisted the perpetration of a cruel wrong, and brought back the moods of De Soto to such a condition, as would, at least, have tempered the severities which he might else suppose were required by justice.

The star of Don Balthazar de Alvaro was, at this moment, completely in the ascendant. He had been left in charge of the village of Chiaha, when De Soto undertook the pursuit of the fugitive Indians. It was his task to assign the guards to the Princess of Cofachiqui; to regulate and control, in fact, all the operations within his command, according to his own discretion

It was not the purpose of De Soto to return to the village, but to proceed onward, following the footsteps of the pioneer force of Andres de Vasconselos to the country of the Alabamas.

With this large discretion in his hands, Don Balthazar was not the person to forego the gratification of any of his passions. The persons whom he had appointed to take charge of the princess Coçalla, were his own creatures, the most despicable of the common soldiers of his division. Don Balthazar had been scorned by the princess. He knew the wild licentiousness which at this time possessed the army. He knew the character of those to whose tender mercies he entrusted her. He might have predicted the event, if he did not,—perhaps he anticipated it; perhaps he anticipated other fruits from the epidemic of license which prevailed among the soldiers. It is not improbable that when he was found by the ruffian, Pedro, who fled from the rapier of Don Philip, conveniently in waiting in a lonely lodge on the edge of the forest, that he himself had prompted his myrmidons to their brutality, and that he had other passions to gratify, not less wild and intense than that of revenge.

Great was the wrath of Don Balthazar when Pedro Martin made his report. Gil Torres, with a bloody sconce, made his appearance soon after, which confirmed it. The report was such that, by their own showing, no good Christians could have been more innocent of evil, or virtuously set upon doing good. The subordinates saved their superior from much of the necessity of invention; and where they failed as artists, he supplied the defects in their case. They were prepared to affirm it with due solemnities; and, thus armed, Don Balthazar smote one hand with the other, and exclaimed exultingly,—

"Now, Señor Don Philip, I have thee at extremity. Thou canst not escape me now."

He dismissed the two soldiers. He called up Juan Ortiz, the interpreter, to a private conference. He had secured the agency of this simple fellow, who was naturally hostile to the Potuguese knight, as the latter had so often superseded him in that employment, from which he derived so much of his importance with the army. Don Balthazar had tutored Ortiz already to his purposes, while persuading the interpreter that they were entirely his own. He, too, had certain evidence to give in respect to the treason of Don Philip—for this was the serious charge which Don Balthazar was preparing to bring against our knight of Portugal. For some time he had been concocting his schemes in secret. Like some great spider, lurking unseen in obscure corner, he had spread forth his numerous, silent, unsuspected snares, like fine threads,

19

to be wrought by patient malice into meshes, so strong as to bind utterly the unwary victim. His meshes were now complete. The victim was in the toils, and he had now only to proceed to destroy him at his leisure.

Furious that the Princess Coçalla should escape, he was yet delighted that the event afforded him evidence so conclusive against Vasconselos. He prepared his despatches with all care to De Soto. He set forth the facts in the case, and *his* inferences He suggested the course of procedure. He knew but too well in what way to act upon the enormous self-esteem of the Adelantado, already sufficiently provoked with Don Philip, and by what subtle artifices of suggestion to open to his eyes the most vast and various suspicions of the guilt of the man he sought to destroy. Yet all this, though done boldly, was done adroitly, so that De Soto never fancied himself taught or counselled; and, acting promptly, on the very suggestions given by Don Balthazar, he yet fancied, all the while, that he was the master of his own purposes.

He sent back instant despatches in reply to those which he received. It followed that, at midnight, Philip de Vasconselos was summoned, in most respectful terms, to the quarters of Don Balthazar.

He prepared at once to obey. Juan, the page, would have followed him; but the summons of the Don had entreated him to a secret conference, and Philip gave the boy in charge of his lodge, and commanded him to remain where he was, awaiting his return. The quarters of Don Balthazar might have been half a mile from those of Philip; but the latter took horse to compass the interval. He went in armor also. Such was the practice; and, in seasons of excitement, and with doubtful friends around them, such was the proper policy. But Philip was not at his ease. His instincts taught him to dread treachery. He knew Don Balthazar too well to put faith in his smooth accents. He knew that the latter must hate, and would strive to destroy him. Juan, the page, had like instincts, and an even better knowledge of the man than had his master. He plucked the knight by his sleeve, and whispered—

"Beware, Señor:—this summons—this man——"

Philip laid his hand gently on the boy's mouth, and said, also in a whisper—

"The good knight must be bold, Juan, and being so, must always beware that he is not *too* bold. But to caution him at one hour of a danger which he must confront, by force of duty, at all hours, is surely an idle lesson. Hear me, boy:—do thou beware that thou neglectest not the duty which I now assign thee.

I have, for a long while, meditated to give thee a solemn charge, in anticipation of this danger of death which walks ever, side by side, with the soldier. There are three letters, sealed with my signet, and folded in silk, which you will find in the little leathern case with which I travel. When I have left thee to-night, detach them from this case, and take them into thy own keeping. They are addressed, one of them, to my mother, in Portugal:—another to my brother Andres; and a third to a lady of the island of Cuba,—whose name—but thou wilt read it on the missive. These thou shalt, if thou survivest me, in good faith deliver. All other papers in the case shalt thou this very night destroy, as soon as I have left thee, and thou find'st thyself alone. Swear to me, boy, on the Holy Cross, that thou wilt do these things which I have bidden!"

The knight held up the cross hilted sword as he spoke, and the boy, with a convulsive emotion, seized and kissed it. Then, with a sob, he cried—

"Oh! Señor Don Philip, suffer that I follow thee now—that I go with thee to this meeting with thy enemy."

"Not so: but I will send thee word how and when to follow, should I not return before noon to-morrow. For this night, boy, farewell!"

And he laid his hand gently on Juan's shoulder, and turned off a moment after. But the boy caught the hand quickly in his grasp, pressed it fervently in both of his own, then released it, and turned away. The knight looked at the Moor with almost loving eyes.

"Verily," he murmured to himself—"verily, this boy hath a noble heart and soul, and he is very loving; and with such a depth of feeling as is seldom witnessed at his years. Where the heart groweth so fast, and drinks in so much, it is rarely destined for long life. Life lingers only with the hard, and the cold, and those who are economical with the affections. The cold toad, it is said, remaineth—it cannot be said that he liveth—for a full thousand years, locked up in stone."

Thus musing, the knight left the lodge, and joined the young Lieutenant who brought the message from Don Balthazar, and who awaited him at the entrance. They mounted horse instantly, and went towards the village; but scarcely had they entered the narrow streets, when Vasconselos found himself surrounded by a score or two of horse, from the centre of whom advanced a Captain, who said, in stern accents—

"Señor Don Philip de Vasconselos, some time of Elvas in Portugal, and now in the service of His Most Catholic Majesty, the King of Spain, &c., I arrest thee, by orders of his Excellency, Don Hernando de Soto, Governor of Cuba, and Adelantado of Florida, under a charge of High Treason. Yield thy sword!"

"Treason!" exclaimed Don Philip indignantly. "Treason! Where is my accuser?"

"Thou shalt see and hear all in due season! At present, I am commanded to bring thee, without speech with any one, to the presence of the Adelantado."

Resistance,—even if Don Philip had been disposed to offer any—would have been perfectly idle. He submitted with quiet dignity.

"Be it so!" he answered, quietly yielding his sword—"conduct me to the Adelantado."

The party set off that very instant. The knight of Portugal did not once see Don Balthazar until they met in the presence of De Soto. The wily spider had only waited to see Vasconselos fairly in the clutches of the party placed in waiting for his arrest, when he set off, with another party of horse, bringing up the rear, and watchful that the captive should find no means of escape.

It was nearly noon of the next day when they reached the army. It was encamped on a pleasant plain, overshadowed every where with great trees of the forest. De Soto, with pride and passion equally roused, was impatiently waiting for the arrival of the offender. No delay was allowed him; and the preparation for his trial had been made before he came. A rude scaffolding, upon which the chair of state had been placed in readiness, had been raised for the Adelantado. His chief knights were grouped immediately around him. The troops, horse and foot, including the parties just arrived,—all under arms,—were dispersed so as to form a half-circle about the *dais*, in which every thing could be heard and seen by the meanest soldier. There they stood, in grim array, with burnished weapons, in mail and escaupil, banner and banneret flying, and the gorgeous flag of Spain floating in the midst. De Soto was not the person to omit any of the blazonry and pageantry, the state and ceremonial, which belonged to his authority. Seated in his chair of state, surrounded by his knights, he ordered that the prisoner should be brought before him.

Philip de Vasconselos, conducted by his guards into the circle, abated nothing of his dignity or noble firmness, as he stood before the presence in which he could see none but enemies. He looked around for the few persons whose sympathies and sup port be might have hoped for, had they been at hand. Where was Nuno de Tobar at that moment? Where was his brother, Andres? In their absence, he readily divined that no precautions had been omitted by his enemies, for effecting their object. He saw that his doom was written.

This conviction, which threw him so completely upon God and his own soul, raised him, with a strength of will and character, to face the event, whatever it might be.

"I am here, under bonds, as a criminal, Don Hernan de Soto," spoke Philip, in clear, manly tones, his eye fixed brightly the while upon the face of the Adelantado:—"I demand to know of what I am accused, and that my accuser shall be set before me!"

"Thou shalt have thy wish, Philip de Vasconselos. The charge against thee is that of high treason to His Catholic Majesty, with whom thou hast taken service."

"I brand the charge with falsehood. I am no traitor."

"That shall we see. Thou shalt behold and see thy accusers, and the witnesses shall be brought before thee, who shall prove thy offence."

Vasconselos folded his arms patiently, and looked coldly around the assembly, while Hernan de Soto, who did not think amiss of his own eloquence, descanted in a sort of general speech upon the affairs and necessities of the army; the duties of a good knight, and faithful subject; the high trusts and confidence which had been given to the knight of Portugal, and the imperative necessity for condign punishment, wherever trusts had been forfeited, and the trusted person had shown himself unfaithful. Philip smiled scornfully, in a bitter mood, as he listened to certain portions of the speech; and the cheeks of De Soto reddened as he noticed the expression. His conscience smote him, though not sufficiently, when he reflected upon the notorious slight to which the knight of Portugal had been subjected from the beginning, and how small had been the trust and favor shown him.

His speech over, he proceeded to his specifications under it.

"Thou art charged, Philip de Vasconselos, by the noble Señor, Don Balthazar de Alvaro, with having betrayed to the Princess of Cofachiqui the secret councils of the conference, when thou wast present as a member, and when it was resolved that the safety of the army required that we should take that person into close custody. It is alleged that thou didst betray that conference to the Princess, in order to persuade her to escape from our hands."

"It is true, that I did so endeavor to persuade the Princess Coçalla to escape, and in this was I faithful to my oath of chivalry. I were no true knight to have kept silence, when so gross a wrong was meditated against that gentle and lovely young Princess. But the council knew my sentiments in reference to that measure. I did not conceal what I thought, that it was a baseness which would forever dishonor the Spanish name."

"That gave thee no right to betray the councils to which thou wert admitted on the implied condition of thy secrecy. Thy faith was pledged to us; and the crime, if crime there were, fell upon our heads, not thine. Thou hast admitted the charge, which we should else establish against thee by no less than three reputable witnesses."

"It is admitted," said the knight.

"It is next charged that thou didst recently set upon the two soldiers appointed for the safe keeping of the princess, didst assault them with naked weapons, didst wound one of them, and put in mortal fear the other, and didst succeed in wresting this princess from their keeping, so that she has made full escape from our care and custody, thus depriving this army of all the benefits which grew naturally out of our charge of her person."

"I found the two ruffianly soldiers to whom the princess had been confided, setting upon her with brutal violence and foul purpose, and as true knight and gentleman, I did so rescue her from their keeping. I had no purpose in this, but the safety and innocence of the noble woman."

The two soldiers were brought forward, and loudly protested their innocence, making affirmation on the Holy Evangel.

"Thou hear'st?" said De Soto.

"I hear, Señor. Is it to be allowed to these wretches, thus charged with a heinous crime, to acquit themselves by their own asseverations?"

"It is thy offence, Señor, and not theirs, which is now before this tribunal." Such was the interposition of Don Balthazar.

"And it is in answer to the charge against me, that I do accuse these ruffians and acquit myself."

"Were such privilege awarded to the criminal, there would be no witness to be found innocent," replied De Soto. "Thou dost not deny the rescue of the princess from her keepers?"

"I glory in the act too greatly to deny it," was the answer. "I am proud of the noble service."

"Ha! We shall see how far thy exultation in the deed will suffice to acquit thee of its penalties! Hear further:

"It is charged that thou hast been a wooer to this princess for her love; that the tie of marriage exists between thee, according to the fashion among the heathen Apalachians, and in despite of all Christian rites; and that she hath pledged to thee, and thou hast accepted the gift, of the whole empire of the Apalachian, which thou mean'st to hold adversely to the crown of Spain, to which thy sworn faith is strictly held."

"The charge is no less false than foolish!"

"There shall be proof to confound thee! There are yet other charges. It is alleged—and this shall be proved by Juan Ortiz,—that on a certain occasion, when at Cofachiqui, thou wast called upon as an Interpreter to demand of the princess that her people be required to bring in supplies of maize and beans; that thou didst counsel her *not* to comply with our demands; and didst tell her that, by this means, she could starve us out of the country, or so enfeeble us that the very children of the Apalachian should then be the masters over us in fight."

"The charge is wholly false! By whom could such charge be made, seeing that no one of the army but myself understood the language of the people? Who, then, could say what words were spoken between the princess and myself?"

"That will not avail thee! Our interpreter, Juan Ortiz, hath a keen ear and quick comprehension; and so far hath he learned of this language, that he hath been enabled to follow thee, and scan thy proceedings, and detect thy treacheries. He asserts boldly that such was thy speech to the princess."

"He hath misunderstood me," replied the knight of Portugal, "from a too imperfect knowledge of what he heard. What, in truth, was spoken, was to the effect that the Spaniards were *not* a people to be starved out, because of the refusal of the red men to bring in their supplies—for such had been the nature of the princess's own speech—and that they would seize them where found, and, would never suffer themselves to starve, even though they fed upon the children of the tribe. I was only too faithful to the Spaniards when I spoke to the princess."

"Ha! in painting them as heathen cannibals?"

"It was but a threat, your Excellency."

"A threat! But wherefore, when this princess spoke in threats to thee, didst thou not repeat her language to us?"

"Of what need! the provisions were brought."

"But we should have been allowed to judge of the propriety of thy arguments, Señor. It were a matter to be weighed solemnly, whether we should suffer thee to depict, even to the Heathen, the Christian warriors of Castile, as so many cannibals, eager to feed on human flesh."

"If your Excellency is pleased to speak of this bold threat with so much solemnity, I can make no answer to thee."

"Ay, thou need'st not! Thou hast made answer sufficient for thy ruin. Thou hast thyself admitted the charges which would condemn thee; and if thou did it not, here are the witnesses who should prove thy treachery. Hast thou any who can say aught in thy defence?"

"None, Señor; since I see that the few gentlemen who have best knowledge of my nature and performances, are not in this assembly; it will be for those to answer to their consciences, by whom they have been sent away at this juncture."

"Does the Knight of Portugal impute to me a wrong?—for it was I by whom they were sent away, and by the Holy Cross, I swear that when they were thus sent away, I had no thought that thou, or any other, should be arraigned for trial, on these, or any other charges."

"Your Excellency is, no doubt, free of offence in this matter, but there is one person, at least, for whom truth could never say so much, and who hath wrought this scheme for my ruin. There is one proof that I might offer—one witness—" and he paused. De Soto quickly said—

"Speak, Señor, and he shall be brought. I will gladly accord them all chance of speech and hearing."

"Nay, Señor, I know not that it will need or avail. It was of my page, the boy Juan, that I had thought. He knows best of my acts and motives. Besides, he hath gathered even more of this language of the Apalachian, than this man, Ortiz, could possibly have done."

"The boy is a slave, your Excellency—a wretched Moor," interposed Don Balthazar; "he can give no evidence in a case affecting both Christian knights and Castilian gentlemen."

"But I would, nevertheless, have had him here, Señor Don Balthazar," answered De Soto, with some asperity in his accents. "Why was he not brought?"

"It was not known, your Excellency, that his presence would be required as a witness, or for any other purpose. The Señor Don Philip did not signify any wish upon the subject."

"And how should I have done so, your Excellency," answered Philip, with a scornful look at Don Balthazar, though addressing De Soto, "when I was not suffered to suspect the strait in which I stood—when I was beguiled from my lodgings, upon false pretences of kindness and counsel, and seized without warning or summons, by a troop of cavalry at midnight? I saw not the boy after my arrest, and until the moment when I met with him here, Don Balthazar de Alvaro did not permit that I should see him."

"I trust, Señor," said De Soto to Don Balthazar, "that thou hast not proceeded in any way in this matter unbecoming a true knight."

"It were sorry policy, your Excellency," was the cool reply, "to give warning to the traitor of your purpose to tie his hands till the cord is ready."

"Surely there is no hardship in such proceeding. The suspected person is not to be suffered chances of escape; but when the knight of Portugal was in thy hands, thou shouldst have seen that he lacked no proper agency in making his defence. Not that this Moorish boy could serve thee, Señor, for his evidence could not make weight against the better testimony of Christian witnesses."

"And I know not that he could say any thing, your Excellency, in my behalf. He could only asseverate his own ignorance of all treachery on the part of Philip de Vasconselos, such as would discredit knight or gentleman. I have no witnesses but God and the blessed Saviour. To them I make appeal against my enemy. But I claim the privilege of combat, your Excellency, with my accuser, my guilt or my innocence to rest on the issue of the combat. I throw down my gauntlet in mortal defiance, and challenge to the field of battle, his body against mine, with lance or sword, and battle-axe and dagger, or with any other weapon that he pleases, the foul, base, dishonest, and perjured knight, Don Balthazar de Alvaro, as one who has done me cruel wrong, and has sought, by false slanders, suborned witnesses, to do me to death, and to stain with shame a scutcheon that has always hitherto been pure and without dishonor. There is my glove! Your Excellency will not deny me to assert my truth according to the laws of arms. I claim the wager of battle!"

He advanced calmly and firmly as he spoke, and throwing down his glove at the feet of Don Balthazar, exclaimed, *sotto voce*, but still loud enough to be heard by others than the person addressed—

"Lift it, Señor, if thou wouldst not be known for the **dastard**, as I know thee for the villain and the knave!"

CHAPTER XL.

"Take this life,
And cancel these cold bonds.'

CYMBELINE.

There was a marked and lively sensation throughout the assembly. The savage and mercenary soldiers of that day were not wholly insensible to the courage of a truly noble soul, and, little loving, as they were, of the foreigners who had mortified their pride, on such frequent occasions, the Castilians were compelled to acknowledge how admirable, calm, fearless and chivalrous was the whole bearing of Philip de Vasconselos.

But Don Balthazar did not lift the glove. There might have been seen a red suffusion coloring suddenly his swarthy cheeks as he heard the epithets applied by the knight of Portugal; but, otherwise, he was apparently unmoved. He answered with a cool and quiet indifference, which betrayed the long and hard training of his political life.

"Nay, Señor, thy glove is no longer such as an honorable knight and gentleman may lift without stain upon his fingers. Thou hast not the right to claim the ordeal of battle. This would be thy right were I the accuser, and the only witness against thee! Then mightst thou claim to put thy body as thy word against mine, and cry upon God to defend the right! But such is not now the case. Thy crimes, partially confessed by thyself, are also proven by sundry Christian witnesses, sworn on Holy Evangel. I claim the judgment, your Excellency,"—turning to De Soto,—" upon the arch traitor, Philip de Vasconselos, who hath betrayed the counsels and the trusts of His Most Catholic Majesty, given him in keeping, and hath meditated and devised still further treasons, as hath been shown by sworn witnesses. I claim the judgment upon the said traitor, and that he be done to death without delay!"

There was a momentary start,—a slight recoil on the part of Vasconselos, as he heard the words. It is barely possible that he had not apprehended that the malice of his enemies would attain to this extremity; but, if his emotion expressed surprise, it was without fear. He looked on and listened, without other show of emotion.

"What hast thou to say, Philip de Vasconselos, against this plea for judgment?" demanded the Adelantado.

"What should I say, Señor?—what *could* I say, that would avail for my safety? To endeavor to speak at all—to seem to hope, indeed, any thing from my speech, or any speech, in this juncture of affairs,—would only show me as ignorant of the malice of the base, as they are of the virtues which are always hateful in their sight! I would not seem weak and foolish even in the eyes that hold, or pretend to hold me, dishonored! I have no more to say. I am in the power of mine enemies. I shall only speak to God!"

"You are in *my* power, Philip de Vasconselos."

"And you, Señor," replied the other boldly, "assured as you deem yourself of the powers which control your will and passions, are yet serving the passions of others—passions which make thee as fearfully mine enemy, as if thy deliberate will and thy own bitter prejudices and dislike had made thee so. The power that is passionate and proud, and the pride that is prejudiced are thus ever the instruments of injustice, and the blind creatures of the cooler and subtler criminal. The cunning arts which, taking advantage of thy passionate moods, have made thee to look coldly and even harshly upon me from the beginning, have not been unseen by me, though unsuspected by thee. They have triumphed, in this present consummation over my life and honor, as they have triumphed over thy magnanimity and prudence. I can in no way oppose them. No words of mine can now enlighten thee. Thou must work thy will, according to thy sense of what is justice. I yield to the fate to which I can oppose neither argument nor valor. But, if I perish by thy doom, and by the arts of that foul and subtle knave and slanderer, who has woven around me these snares and meshes, I perish without shame or dishonor. Nor do I perish without redress. Here, now, in the last words which I address to thy ears, Hernan de Soto, I cite thee for judgment with myself before the Sovereign of Judges, whom no arts can mislead, whom no pride, or passion, or prejudice can turn from paths of justice! Thou shalt meet me before God's tribunal! There shalt thou behold that traitor confounded eternally, who now sits, smooth and smiling, cold and cunning, exulting in the base consciousness of a triumph over one who knows his baseness, and who could, this day, as he well knows, speak of him such things as should make the foulest heart in this assembly turn from him with horrid shudder, and a hideous loathing. I shall say no more. Do with me as thou wilt."

The patient submission which resigns itself calmly to in

evitable fate, always wears an aspect of great nobleness. When Philip de Vasconselos was led from the presence of the assembly, he was followed, on all sides, by glances of silent admiration and a compelled respect. He was withdrawn, by the guards, while the Adelantado and his council sate in private judgment on his fate. Long was the conference that followed. Don Balthazar strenuously urged the doom of death. But De Soto, filled with chivalrous notions, was not prepared to yield to the malignant suggestion. It is possible that he somewhat suspected that there was some truth in the charge of malignity and slander which Philip had brought against Don Balthazar. He had long been aware of the dislike which they mutually felt for each other. He said to the latter—

"Verily, Don Balthazar, this knight of Portugal hath bitter thoughts of thee."

"When had the criminal other thoughts of him who declares his crime?"

"But I somewhat fear that thou hast pushed this matter to the uttermost."

"Grant it be so, Señor;—there is enough, besides, in the confession which he made to suffice for his conviction."

"True! True! He hath confessed to the betrayal of our purpose to the princess, and to the charge of assault upon our officers, and her rescue."

"These are crimes worthy of death! This is treason! What had Cortez or Pizarro done to the knight, or knights, who had rescued Montezuma and the Inca from their guards, and set them free to work the ruin of the army and the enterprise?"

"They had been made to taste of the sharp edge of the axe! —But I will *not* slay this knight of Portugal! He hath done us good service, and there is some rebuke of conscience that I feel, for his too much neglect, and for the cold aspect which I have shown him. Besides, I owe him a life. But for his succor I had probably perished under the savage assault of the fierce Floridian, Vitachuco. I cannot forget these things. I will *not* take the life of this man!"

"What! Wilt thou forgive such treachery? Wilt thou suffer this traitor still to harbor with thee and devise new treasons?"

"No! the army shall be purged of him! nor shall he escape without due punishment. He is proud! He is a belted knight, and hath won his spurs in Christendom! I will degrade him, according to the proper laws of chivalry, which he holds in such veneration! His shield shall be reversed; his scutcheon shall be defaced; his armor shall be taken from his breast, and shall be battered into shapelessness; his sword shall be broken before his eyes; his helmet shall be fouled in the morass; and, with rope about his neck, his spurs shall be hewn from his heels, by the axe of the common executioner! Then shall he be driven with blow and buffet from the army, and, tied to a tree of the forest, he shall be left to the mercies of these red savages of Apalachia, to whom he hath shown such favor. Doubtless, they will remember the service, and take him into some sheltering wigwam!"

De Soto having declared his purpose, there was no further argument. Don Balthazar, however, though confounded for a moment at the novel terrors of the proposed punishment, would yet have greatly preferred the sharp and summary judgment of the axe. 'Dead men tell no tales'—and so long as Philip de Vasconselos had the power to speak, so long did he feel for the safety of his terrible secret. He did not appreciate the hurts of honor so highly as De Soto.

The knight of Portugal was once more brought before the Adelantado. From the lips of his haughty judge he heard the doom pronounced, even as we have already heard it. Then did the cheeks of the brave cavalier grow pale; then did his lips quiver; —then was his soul thrown back upon itself, without being able to find support! Hoarsely, with a cry almost, as he heard the judgment, he implored for a change of doom!

"Death! Death, rather than such doom as this!"—was the passionate entreaty.

And shuddering, he knelt—the proud man knelt—humbling himself before man—before the man who had already wronged him,—who wronged him still;—but in whose power he stood, and who, alone, in that world of wilderness, possessed the power to save him! In our day, we should fail justly to appreciate the terrible character of the doom pronounced by De Soto upon the knight of Portugal. The fantastic chivalry was still a religion with its sworn followers. Such degradation as was decreed by the Adelantado, was the obliteration of the whole previous life! It inured to the future. It tainted the name of fame forever! It was the reproach of all former deeds of valor! It was the death of the soul, and of all the hope, and pride, and glory, which the spirit of chivalry held most precious in esteem! Philip de Vasconselos succumbed beneath it! He sank upon his knees—he humbled himself as we have seen,—he prayed for the axe—for death,—for any doom but this!

He was denied—denied with words and looks of scorn! Then he rose, stern, silent, **resolved**—and strong to endure, be cause of that denial, and those words and looks of scorn! He arose, erect, and looked coldly on his judges. But there was a terrible glare from his eyes, which made all other eyes look aside! His lips were now compressed, but big drops of blood could be seen slowly to ooze from between them, and to form themselves in beads upon his beard. He stood, and for a few moments there was a deep pause in the assembly. Then, at a signal from De Soto, the executioner came forward with his assistants. They passed a halter about his neck. He offered no resistance. He did not even turn his glances upon them, when they laid hands upon his shoulder. But as they led him out, he looked steadily at De Soto, and said solemnly:

"A Dios!"

The words were not spoken by way of farewell. They were in the nature of a citation; and so De Soto understood them; and a sudden paleness, the shadow of a presentiment, overspread his face. But the emotion passed from his soul. The drums and trumpets sounded. The assembly was broken up, and the army, forming a grand procession, was marched at once to the place of execution.

And there, the central object of that great array, stern, lofty, helpless, but resigned, stood the noble victim—resolute to submit, but not wholly able to conceal the terrible emotions which racked his soul! There, bound by the degrading halter to the tree, by the hands of the common executioner, he was subjected to all the details of the cruel and malignant judgment, as we have reported them. His sword was broken, his shield reversed, its blazonry obliterated, before his eyes! The armor was torn from his person, and battered with blows of a club; his helmet was hurled into a neighboring morass. And he saw and was silent,—looking the while steadily upon the Adelantado with eyes of a deep mysterious solemnity, that spoke for dread and terrible thoughts, as well as sufferings!

But when the executioner approached with his axe—when the prisoner was made to lift his feet and place them upon the block, and when, one by one, the golden spurs of knighthood were hewn from his heels by repeated blows, then broke the groan of agony from his overcharged bosom, and he threw out his powerful arms and grasped the stalwart executioner, even as he had been an infant in his grasp, and hurled him away, staggering, while a howl, rather than a cry, following the groan, seemed sent up to heaven —by way of reproach, for that it looked on, and beheld this terrible injustice, while the great eye of the sun peered down from the noon-day skies, as bright and serene as if all below was becoming in heaven's eye as it was beautiful to that of man! Vasconselos hurled away the executioner, but not before his task was done! The spurs had been smitten off, clean at the heel, and the work of degradation was complete. His violence was the sudden impulse of an accumulated despair, which was no longer suppressible.

A moment after this one demonstration of agony and violence, and the knight of Portugal remained passive. Still fettered by the cord of the hangman, and, by the neck, to a sapling of the forest, he looked on the rest of the proceedings with a strange, but not unnatural calm.

Then De Soto made a speech to his army, the substance of which we may conjecture. The bugles sounded; the cavalry wheeled into compact squadrons, the infantry shouldered arms, and, to the sound of triumphant music, the whole army marched from the ground. Fettered to the tree, with only a sufficient length of rope to enable him to sink down at its foot, Philip de Vasconselos was left alone, in the centre of that now dreary forest.

The army was under marching orders. Preparations for the renewal of its progress had been made before the trial, and that act consummated, the legions of De Soto departed the spot to see it no more! Philip was left to his fate—the fangs of the wolf, the scalping-knife of the savage, or the crueller death, by remorseless hunger! He could hear the distant music, gradually growing fainter: finally, the faint bugle-note advised him of the movement of the rear-guard; and soon, this too melted away in the great world of space, and he remained with silence, in the depths of the Apalachian solitudes!

CHAPTER XLI.

<blockquote style="text-align:center">
"Had they known,
A woman's hand secured that deed her own.
The worst of crimes had left her woman still."
CORSAIR.
</blockquote>

The army of the Adelantado proceeded on its march along the waters of the Coosaw, but Don Balthazar de Alvaro returned, with his detachment of cavalry, to the village of Chiaha. To him was allotted the duty of bringing up the rear-guard, with the heavy baggage; and he was required to remain in Chiaha until the smaller bodies which had been sent forth on exploring expeditions, under Nuno de Tobar, Andres de Vasconselos and others, should return. Chiaha was the appointed place of their rendezvous.

There was an exulting spirit in the bosom of Don Balthazar, as he led his troopers away from the field where he had witnessed the degradation of Philip de Vasconselos. He had triumphed over his enemy; and there was now no danger that the knight of Portugal would ever cross his path in the progress of the expedition. The penalty of his return was death. Don Balthazar would have preferred that this punishment should have been the one inflicted. He did not, himself, attach much importance to what he thought the fantastic notions of honor and shame, which were taught by the laws of chivalry; and, were it not that the punishment of Don Philip implied his utter banishment from the army, and his almost certain death, in the condition in which he had been left, from the fierce fangs of the wild beast, or the reckless arrows of the savage, he might have been still ill at ease in respect to some of his securities. In truth, he still had some lurking apprehensions that Philip de Vasconselos was yet, in some way, his evil genius; destined yet to re-appear, and confront him with that danger which had so long haunted his imagination! With this fear, it occurred to him, more than once, to send back one of his troopers to dispatch secretly the degraded knight; but this was placing himself too completely in the power of his creature; and he well knew that such a fact, revealed to De Soto and the army, would be necessarily his own ruin; would confirm, to the Adelantado, the accusations made by Vasconselos, and would arm the few friends of the latter—few, but brave and powerful—with perpetual hostility and vengeance! He was content to leave the doomed noble to his fate, as it had been pronounced by De Soto, and executed before his eyes.

Persuading himself that his death was inevitable, or, at all events, that the danger from that one source had been driven wholly from his own path, he went on his way to Chiaha with rejoicing and exulting spirit. He reached the village late in the night. There was still an eager mood hurrying him to other performances; and when he had dismissed his troops to their several stations, received the report of the officer left in command, and refreshed himself with a bottle of canary, he threw himself once more into the saddle. The soldier on duty before his quarters, asked, "Shall I mount and follow you, Señor?"

"No! Keep your post. I want nobody."

The expedition which now prompted the nocturnal movements of Don Balthazar, was of a sort to require no witnesses. The arch-fiend, now working, more than ever powerful within his soul, and stimulating a crowd of passions into eager exercise, was all-sufficient for his companionship. Don Balthazar galloped off, in the direction of the cabin which had been occupied by Philip de Vasconselos!

The page, Juan, did not sleep. He had fully executed the trusts given him in charge by his master; had possessed himself of the three papers, and destroyed the rest. This employment, and the contemplation of the several addresses of the latter, had filled the boy with the most melancholy mood. One of the letters he did little but contemplate. With perpetual tears in his eyes, he did nothing but read over the superscription. The day was passed in sorrows and vague apprehensions. Vasconselos did not return by noon. The boy inquired for him in vain, and could only learn that he had ridden out with the detachment of horse upon a secret expedition. But why had he not been permitted to accompany this expedition? The privilege had never before been denied him. There was a mystery in the affair which troubled him, and he neither ate during the day, nor sought for sleep during the night. He was sleepless from intense nervous excitement, and sate, or walked, as the night advanced, in the loneliness of that rude chamber of the red man, which was dimly lighted by the brands of pine which blazed flickeringly upon the hearth. While thus moodily employed, he heard the gallop of a horse approaching. He trembled, and clasped his hands; then felt that all the letters were safe within his bosom, and experienced a strange and sudden dread lest the knight should resume the charge of them. There was one letter which he would not willingly give up,—the contents of which he dreaded, yet desired to peruse.

"It is he—it is Philip!" murmured the boy, recovering, and relieved of the apprehensions which had troubled him for the safety of the knight. "It is Philip!" and he hastily undid the fastenings of the entrance. The horseman threw himself off the saddle at this moment, and hastily pushed his way into the cottage.

"Señor!" said the page, somewhat taken by surprise at the manner and hurried movement of the knight, so unlike that of Vasconselos. "Señor Philip!" he said, timidly and inquiringly.

"Not he, my good lad, but one quite as good, I fancy!" answered the stranger, grasping the boy's wrist and dragging him towards the light. In the next moment, Juan identified the person of the intruder. To recoil was an involuntary act, as he exclaimed—

"Don Balthazar!"

"Ay, methinks, my good boy, I should be as well known to thee by this time as the cavalier whom thou servest. But why dost thou recoil? Dost thou fear me?"

"No, Señor, but——"

It was with very great effort that the boy was enabled to say these latter words, which he did with husky and tremulous accents, the sounds dying away in his throat.

"Ay, but thou dost. Yet thou shouldst not. Henceforth, thou shalt look upon me as thy best friend and protector, since thy late master can take care of thee no longer."

"My late master! the Señor Philip—Don Philip de Vasconselos! Speak, Señor, tell me what hath happened to my master? Where is he? Hath he been wounded—is he——"

"Oh! thou hast got thy voice of a sudden. But I am too slow of speech to answer thy rapid inquiries. No more of thy late master, boy! Thou art henceforth to be *my* page. I shall give thee lodgings as near my own as thou hast had to those of Don Philip. Thou shalt be a sharer of my chamber, boy, as thou hast been of his! Ay, and I will caress thee and care for thee quite as tenderly. I know thy great merits as a page, and I see thy virtues beneath the unnatural black coating which wrap them up from all other eyes. His eyes never looked on thee more tenderly than mine shall look, boy; and thou shalt lose nothing of pleasure and indulgence by the exchange of one master for another. What say'st thou? Is the thing pleasing in thy sight?"

"I know not what thou meanest; I do not understand thee! Only tell me, Señor, where is Señor Philip—Don Philip——"

"Señor Philip—Don Philip! nay, why not say to me, as thou hast doubtless said a thousand times to him—Philip—Philip—my Philip—dear, dear Philip! Is it so, my very perfect blackamoor? Was it not thus that the dulcet accents ran, in every possible variety of sweet and pleasant change? And by what sweet name did our Philip requite thee, my gentle Moor?"

The boy was bewildered. It did not lessen his disquiet and bewilderment, that the wine was evidently doing warm work with the brain of the questioner: but Juan had acquired a strength and confidence in army life, and in the daily communion with Vasconselos, which now rendered him comparatively cool in moments of difficulty, and under embarrassing relations. He strove successfully to combat his nervous tremors and apprehensions, and to answer calmly.

"The Señor Balthazar speaks very strange things to me, which I do not understand!"

"Ay, but I will not leave thee in such blessed ignorance, my good boy. Know then that thy old master is disposed of."

"Slain! slain! Thou dost not tell me, Señor, that my master——"

"No! no! not exactly quiet yet, unless, indeed, the red men have been about him with their stone hatchets and macanas,—or unless some stray wolf, or pard, hath followed a keen scent to where he lies on the field where the Adelantado hath but lately camped."

"Señor, for the love of the Holy Virgin, tell me truly of my Lord!" And there was no restraint, now—no measure, in the wild, earnest pleadings of that passionate voice. "Tell me what hath happed—how he hath been circumvented—if still he lives!"

"Ha! ha! Thou canst speak out now, in thy natural voice of love and passion. Thou forget'st the blackamoor policy! Well! Thou art in growing condition to hear the truth. Thou shalt hear. Thy lord, thy master, thy Portuguese Don, hath paid the penalty of his crimes—he hath been disgraced from knighthood, stript of sword and armor, his spurs hewn from his heels, his neck haltered to a tree, and beaten with blows of the executioner, he is left to the storms of heaven and the hatchet of the Apalachian!"

"Jesu! have mercy! And thou hast done this thing?"

"Nay, but a little towards it. I but sped the progress and nodded to the judgment, and smiled on the execution. I put the arrow on the string and found the mark. 'Twas De Soto that sped it from the bow!"

The boy clasped his hands wildly together. The knight began to sing a vulgar ballad then current in the army. There was something very fearful in the strong glance which the page set upon the face of the singer, whose every look and tone betrayed the full consciousness of his triumph. He stooped, while singing, and threw fresh brands upon the fire. Juan suddenly darted away as if to pass him; but the knight was not unobservant, caught him by the arm, as he went forward, and whirled him back to the corner of the chamber beyond him.

"No! no! thou dost not cease to be page, boy, in the loss of one master! One but makes way for another; and I am instead of thy Philip; with all his rights and privileges, my sweet Moor. But thou shalt lose none of thine in becoming page to me. Oh! no! thou shalt share my lodge, my couch, an thou wilt, for my taste revolts not at thy dusky visage, when the features are so fine, and the good faith of the owner so perfect. Thou art mine, now, my boy!"

"Señor! I must go and seek Don Philip!" was the calmly expressed resolution of the boy.

"Thou wouldst go in vain. Thou wouldst find his bones only. He hath given rare picking to the panther."

"Señor, I must go!"

"Stay where thou art!"

"If thou hast compassion in thy soul——"

"Pshaw! I know not such folly."

"As a knight, thou know'st it is my duty to seek my lord."

"Not when he is dishonored, boy! Henceforth, I am thy knight, I tell thee! Thy master—in whose hands thy life lies, even as an egg, which I can crush to atoms with a will! What! thou pretendest that thou know'st me not! Thou wouldst not admit to thyself that I know thee! Does thy imposture tickle thee so much, that thou art resolute not to see and believe?"

The page, indeed, had seen but too well! Yet he was resolute, as Don Balthazar had said, *not* to see! It was still possible—so he persuaded himself—that his persecutor spoke from his drunkenness, rather than his knowledge;—and that his secret,—for he had one—was still unsuspected, or, at least, unknown. He answered accordingly, with as much calmness of temper as he could command.

"Señor, I know not what thou mean'st or intend'st; but thou

surely canst not design to keep me from the good knight, who hath been my kind friend and benefactor,—my preserver frequently,—in this weary march through the country of the Apalachian? You tell me that he is gone from me and lost to me—you tell me that he hath undergone a cruel judgment, for, I know not what offence;—but you tell me that he still lives! Let me, as in duty bound, go to the service of the good knight, Don Philip, and succor him, if I may, and wait on him as I should! I entreat this of thy nobleness and mercy, as a knight thyself, who well knowest what the dutiful page oweth to the cavalier he serves!"

The eyes of Don Balthazar answered the speaker with a wicked leer.

"This passeth belief!" he exclaimed. "Well, it is a sort of virtue to hold out denial to the last; though, when the mask is torn from the face, it is but a stupid sort of virtue to do so! And thou, too, who knowest *me* so well,—thou, Olivia de Alvaro—to dream that I should not know *thee* through any disguise! What a foolish child thou hast been, and art! But I knew thee from the first day that we landed! I watched thee and thy paramour in all thy progress! Thou hast slept with him beneath the same tree; in the same shady thicket; under the same tent; in the same hovel of the red man; and the same considerate handmaiden, the night, hath drawn the curtains gently, to conceal the loving embraces of the gallant Don and his Moorish page!"

"Foul-mouthed, as false! It is untrue! We have slept together in a thousand places, and the good knight hath watched and sheltered me as a noble gentleman, but he hath never done me wrong. Even now he knows me—wherever he be, and whatever be his fate,—only as the boy that I appear to other eyes! But I hope not to teach the truth of this to a soul so incapable of virtue as is thine! It is enough that it is known to me, and to the blessed angels, who have watched us from above!"

Don Balthazar passed to the door, and finally fastened it within. He approached the damsel.

"It matters little, Olivia, whether he knew thee as boy or woman. He will know thee no more. Thou art henceforth mine. Thou shalt appear in the army as my page; and,—child,—thou shalt sleep in my tent, and under the tree with me; and the night shall yield us the same friendly veil which she granted to thee and thy cavalier. It was no fault of the handmaid, I warrant, if the knight made no discovery of thy secret! But I am wiser than he; and my knowledge shall the better profit us both. Nor need thou put on the airs of thy Biscayan mother with me *now!* We have no such restraints here, as restrained our raptures and made us fearful in Havana. Here, there is something more than freedom! Thou know'st the license of the army. Thou hast seen that it could not save a princess of the people. Suppose it said to the soldiers, This blackamoor page is the girl whom Philip de Vasconselos entertained *par amour*—and what will follow? I tell thee, girl, in very love of thee, they will tear one another to pieces, and tear thy delicate limbs to pieces also! Art thou wise to see this, and to understand how much better it will be, still to keep thy secret, and to serve me as a page, even as thou hast served this knight of Portugal?"

For a time, a strong despair sate in the eyes of Olivia. But she gathered strength and comparative composure, while he was speaking, and when he was done, she said with closed lips and teeth,—

"I will perish first!"

"Nay, nay, thou shalt not perish! I have done too much to secure thee in my keeping to lose thee now; when I have at last securely won thee. I have pursued this knight of Portugal, until I destroyed him, because he knew the secret of thy shame and my dishonor! He is no longer a danger to either of us.—And thou art won! We are here, alone—in the deep midnight,— with no eye to see, no hand to rescue thee from my grasp,—and, with the treasure thus won,—and the precious beauty thus in my embrace,—shall I now recoil from my possessions?—shall I withdraw my claim, and abandon the very bliss for which I have toiled in such secret ways, and perilled so many open dangers? No, my Olivia, thou art now mine, more certainly than ever. It needs now no subtle opiate to subdue thy senses. It needs now no future watchful anxiety, to watch the paths, and dread ever more the danger and detection! Here, we have perfect freedom. Life means privilege, to take and keep! We have no laws but such as justify the passions; and just now, the passions are the only laws that require to be obeyed. Thou art mine, girl,— mine, Olivia,—and I seize thee with a rapture, which, sweet as thy embrace hath been of yore, promises now a blessing as far beyond the past, as the joys of heaven are claimed to be beyond those of earth! Wilt thou be mine, and submit to be my willing page, as thou hast been, *par amour*, the page of Vasconselos?"

"Touch me not, Señor!"—she said as he approached her. "Touch me not!"

"Ay, but I will touch thee, and take thee, and wind thee in my embrace, I tell thee!——"

"Touch me not!" as he continued to approach.

"Thou art mine, I tell thee!" and he laid one hand upon her shoulder, and tore wide the fastenings of the jacket of escaupil, or cotton armor, which she wore, until the white bosom escaped from its bonds, and grew revealed to the eyes of the satyr! At the same moment, the three letters of Vasconselos escaped also, and fell upon the ground.

"Ha!" said he, stooping to lift them, while he still kept one hand upon her shoulder——"Ha! What love chronicles have we here?"

He was about to gather them up, when, with broken accents, she cried—

"It must be so! It hath been decreed! It is a command! It is from God-himself! I must do it! There is no escape! I knew it would come to this at last. I felt sure that I should have to do it!"

And while speaking thus, as if to herself, she drew the dagger of the page, and smote the knight upon the neck, even as he stood stooping. Had she been taught by anatomical science where best to plant the blow for immediate death, her hand could not have been more effectually guided than by its sudden instinct. She smote but once, and while a husky and gurgling sound issued, with a volume of blood, from the throat of the victim, he fell forward upon the earth, and lay motionless at her feet! She hastily gathered up the letters which his hands had only touched—they were already spotted with his blood,—thrust them once more into her bosom, opened the door, and darted from the cabin! In a few moments more, she was mounted upon her own steed and flying—flying far and fast, into the cover of the forests! and ever as she rode, she murmured to herself, gasping and breathing heavily—"I knew it must be so!—I felt that it had to be done! It had to be done! It had to be done! Holy Virgin! It had to be done, and by my hands!"

CHAPTER XLII.

*"Now shall we pluck him from his wretched plight,
And make misfortune favor."*   OLD PLAY

THE army of De Soto marched down the west side of the Coosa, and were soon buried deeply in the virgin wildernesses of Alabama. They gave but few thoughts to the noble victim whom they had dishonored and left to perish in the ravening solitudes of the forest. To him, the short remnant of the day passed in such a dreariness as may better be imagined than described. Fettered rigidly to the tree, at the foot of which he was barely suffered to repose in a half-crouching position, Vasconselos was scarcely conscious of the hours as they glided from daylight into darkness. A savage gloom covered up his soul, and shut out the ordinary transitions and aspects of external life from his vision. In the case of one so noble of soul, so proud of spirit, so sensitive to shame and honor, we may fancy how terribly intense were the horrors of such a doom as that which he had been made to endure. We may equally understand how regardless he had become in respect to the future, from his endurance of the past. The day passed blankly, before his eyes; the stars came out, looking down upon him with sad aspects through the overhanging boughs of the forest trees, with like blankness of expression. He heeded not, he did not behold the tender brightness in their looks. He lay crouching, a grim savage, denied the only prayer which his soul could possibly put up in that dreary trial, that of a manly death, through a fierce and terrible struggle with his enemies.

And so, hour after hour, in a hopeless craving for freedom of limb, and the exercise of a mighty muscle in the deadly strife! and the hopeless craving became at length debility. Mental and physical exhaustion began to supervene. He became conscious of aspects and influences which taught to his waning faculties the fear of approaching madness. He was conscious of an incertitude of thought and sense, which was the most oppressive of all the painful feelings which he now endured. He felt that his senses were escaping him, or becoming so diseasedly acute as to confound his judgment. He felt that he could no longer bring to bear upon his faculties the exercise of a controlling will and a sober mind. Strange hues and colors, and gleams, were flashing before his eyes; strange sounds, and murmurs, and voices, were mingling in his ears; and he could feel, as it were, the touches of tongues of flame that were put out to meet the ends of his fingers, thrilling them with curiously painful sensations of cold and heat alternately. It was not the stars that he saw, but great eyes that swept down to him from above, wheeling about him in mazy dances, and pausing in troops to look down into his own. In the midst of these aspects, which were those of the mind rather than the eye, his physical senses were made conscious of the flight of some great bird whose wings he heard, as they wheeled about him in slow gyrations, gradually ceasing, as the heavy frame settled down upon the bough of the tree just over him, whence he heard the great wings flapping, the sound soon followed by a piercing scream, which seemed the utterance of a savage voice of exultation—that of the vulture already in possession of his prey. And with a natural instinct, the knight threw up his arms, and waved his hand feebly aloft, as if to scare away the obscene and voracious cormorant. There was a momentary creeping of his flesh in horror, as he reflected upon the hour—not long to be delayed—when the winged savage would fasten upon his heart, and when he should not possess the power to struggle against his blood-seeking beak. But the lingering thought still strove to reconcile him to a probability, however terrible, which yet promised him release from the mortifying consciousness of the moral doom which his life had received—the shame, dishonor, and humiliation of his present situation.

The strife of thought and consciousness, though but for a single moment, in such a condition as that in which he lay, was itself a long eternity of torture. It was not to be endured for a longer period with mortal consciousness; and insensibility soon came to the relief of a misery which human strength found it impossible to sustain. Thought left him, and murmuring insane things, Philip de Vasconselos sunk at length prostrate, and in utter senselessness, at the foot of the tree.

And the great bird dropped heavily beside him from the bough, and walked about him, and stood with gradually shutting and unclosing wings above his head, as if fanning him into deeper slumbers. But suddenly he strode away, and lifted himself lightly again into the tree, as he heard a child-like cry in the thicket. A moment after, a stealthy cat-like tread was to be heard upon the leaves; and soon a long gaunt form, beautifully spotted, stole forth, and approached the unconscious cavalier.

And the wild savage of the woods,—the most savage, perhaps, in all the forests of America, the panther, encircled the sleeping man; and he stooped his nose to the unconscious ears; and there was a faint murmur of speech from the lips of the knight; and once more the panther retired into his thicket, and the great vulture again dropped from the tree-top to the ground. And he, too, encircled the sleeper. And once more he spread his great wings above his head, and he fanned slowly the drowsy air about him: then he sounded a fierce wild note—a great shriek through the forest—and the sleeper stirred slightly with a lifted arm; and the vulture resumed the fanning with his wings. But soon another shriek from the depths of the night was heard in answer to the signal of the watchful bird; and another followed after it. And ere many moments there was a family group of the ravenous birds about their victim, and each spread forth his wings, beating slowly the drowsy atmosphere, and drawing nigher momently until they stood about the head and breast of the unconscious knight, like so many hooded priests about the corse of a brother. And still it seemed as if the knight were not unconscious, though unable. A murmur broke from his lips, and ever and anon his arm was thrown up spasmodically, but only to fall supine upon the earth beside him.

Again was the child-like cry heard in the forest, and the savage panther once more issued from its depths, stealthily as the cat, passing along timorously beside the edge of the wood, and pursuing a circling course towards his victim; and this time he came not alone. He was accompanied by his more savage mate, followed by her cubs, and they drew near, whining as they did so, like kittens that are beckoned to their food. The obscene birds angrily flapped their wings and shrieked at their approach; but still retreated, and once more lifted themselves upon slow pinions to the trees above, where they looked down, watching the common prey, and waiting for their moment with impatience.

Now, could we see clearly the condition of the exhausted cavalier, we should behold him covered with a cold and clammy sweat, the proof that there was still a lurking consciousness, a faculty of life, which, though lacking every essential capacity for struggle and defence, was yet not wanting in the acutest sensibilities of horror. Again was there a feeble murmur of speech from his pallid lips, and again were his nerveless arms stirred, but this time unlifted, as if striving to defy or to drive away the assailant.

He was not thus to be expelled. Heedless of the murmur,

needless of the moving arms, the savage dam, crying to her cubs, planted her stealthy foot firmly upon the bosom of the victim. The male panther, meanwhile, stood above his head, watchful of every movement, and ready to rend with fierce teeth and talons, at the first shows of life or struggle. And the cold sweat breaks in great drops from brow and bosom of the knight, and his eyes open, and he shouts,—or strives to shout, but how feebly!—and his arm strikes out wildly, but with the most child-like feebleness; and on the instant the grim savage who stands above his head, leaps terribly upon his breast. And the eyes of the knight are now widely open, and he sees and feels, but he has no strength, no hope! He murmurs a prayer to Heaven, and his eyes close upon the rest! He resigns himself to the fate which he can no longer oppose, and from which he sees no means of escape. Not that he desires escape from death. It is the animal instinct only that would struggle now, and for this the animal is incapable. It is the manner of the death only from which the mind revolts, and the mind rapidly lapses into trance. In his latest consciousness he hears the sharp, shrill cry of the gigantic and savage beast upon his breast.

He little dreams that the cry is one of annoyance and fear, and not of triumph. Suddenly the vultures scream from the tree, and the beasts cry angrily beneath it. They are startled from their prey. The woods gleam with sudden lights, that flash offensively in the eyes of the midnight prowlers of the jungle. The great natural alleys of the forests echo with cheerful voices. The lights dart from side to side; they are torches borne by troops of the red men that gather at the summons of a group that now approach, armed with flaming brands also, towards the spot where the Portuguese cavalier lies at length unconscious. The beasts growl and whine, fiercely glaring upon the backward path, as they retire from before the gleaming torches. Blazing brands are flung at them by the red men, to hurry them in flight, and they slink away from the victim whom they were just about to rend. The vultures in turn lift their vans and sail off to higher trees of the forest. There they sit, brooding sullenly on what they see. So the panthers, with their savage young, disappointed of their feast, lurk angrily upon the edge of the dark jungle in which they make their abode. They still lurk, watchful, hopeful of their victim; and woe to the Indian, particularly if a woman, should he or she wander too nigh the spot where he crouches, and neglects to wave before the path the brand of fire which offends his eyes!

In place of obscene bird and savage beast, groups of the red men surround the prostrate knight. In the midst, bent over him with solicitous care and passionate affection, kneels a young and beautiful woman of the dusky race. Her cares revive him. He opens his eyes to see, by the light of the blazing torches, the fond and sweet features of Coçalla, the Princess of Cafachiqui.

"He lives! His eyes open to Coçalla! Oh! Philip, thou shalt be mine now, and forever, and a great chief among my people!"

He swoons again, but he is in fond and faithful keeping.

CHAPTER XLIII.

"Faithful, she flies, in search of him she loves,
But droops at last! Ah! hapless, that the soul
Finds no sufficient succor from the frame.
T' achieve the wondrous virtue that it wills!"
OLD PLAY.

OLIVIA DE ALVARO—or, as we shall continue to describe her in her assumed character and sex—Juan, the Page of Vasconselos the deed done which avenged the wrongs of herself and lover upon one, at least, and the worst of their enemies; fled upon her fiery steed, with blood more fiery and wild, bounding madly in her own bosom. She drove the rowel into the eager *destrier*, unwitting what she did or where she flew. For a time, her progress was the work of madness. Certainly, she gave herself no single moment of thought. She obeyed an impulse—an instinct. She made no moment's pause, she asked herself no single question. It mattered not to her, in that fearful hour, with her hands dyed deeply in kindred blood, and thick billows of the same red sea, seeming to flow in upon her throbbing brain, in what direction she flew, or what fate awaited her. There was a power, seemingly beyond, if not foreign to her own, which drove her forward recklessly. The passions held the reins. She followed as they bade. The horse flew beneath her, yet it seemed as if she would have flown beyond him. His speed was nothing to the wild and headlong flight of her moods. She was scarcely conscious of his movements. On, on—no matter whither—she goads him terribly forward—and he snorts as he bounds away, and the thick flakes of foam gather about his mouth, and the white streaks rise upon his flanks, and yet the rowel rakes and tears his reddening sides.

But the instincts of horse and rider are equally true. Juan knew the general routes of the army. In forest countries, the military traces are few and soon defined. The tread of a corps of horse or foot through the woods soon makes itself perceptible. The horse readily detects the beaten pathways of his fellows. Our page, besides, had been previously advised of the route of De Soto. He knew from the taunts of Don Balthazar, that Vasconselos had been summoned to camp,—that it was there he had been dishonored—and left;—and beyond this he desired no more knowledge to give him a general notion of the route he should pursue. He had become skilled, from the sinuous progress which he had made with the army. He had gradually—perhaps without his own consciousness—acquired all those general laws of travel which the wayfarer in the great forests can hardly forbear to learn. But to these he made no reference in the present progress. His lessons came to him through his impulses. They served him as instincts. In the ordinary processes of thought and induction, he certainly did not once indulge during the long, wild, but well-directed flight, in which we are to trace his course.

He dashed headlong through the village of Chiaha, where the command of Don Balthazar was still quartered. Little did his cavaliers dream of the bloody fate of their superior. The fugitive was challenged by the sentry as he entered one of the sylvan avenues, and again challenged as he hurried through the opposite end into the wilderness again. He heard not the demand—he made no answer to the summons, and the matchlock was emptied at him as he flew, and he knew not that he had escaped any danger. The great thickets once more receive him with such shelter as they afford. The dim lights of heaven suffice for the steed, but he sees nothing, nor is he conscious of any lack of light. If he does not reason, he is yet not unenlightened by aspects that sufficiently fill his mind. Even as he speeds, he sees, still receding as he approaches, yet still conspicuously distinct before his eyes, the great encampment of De Soto—the amphitheatre of trees and tents, and grouped soldiers surrounding and grim warriors presiding in judgment, and a cruel executioner with bloody axe prominent over all, and in the midst a noble form, about to sink!—and he cries hoarsely as he spurs the steed—hoarsely and feebly,—his voice subsiding to a whisper—

"But one moment, Philip—but one moment—and I am with thee. With thee, Philip! with thee! To die with thee, Philip—to die *for* thee! One moment, Philip—one moment—one!—"

And at each period of pause,—when the steed stopped to pant,—or, with nose to the ground, to scent, or to feel, his way—such would be the apostrophe. Then the dark or bloody aspects would seem to rise more conspicuously and urgently before the gaze of the fugitive—the arrested motion of the steed making him feel that the delay was dangerous—that the event was in progress which he alone could arrest—that not a moment was to be lost! and this was all his thought! Then it was that the lingering beast would be made anew to feel the severe inflictions of the rowel,—and, snorting with terror to plunge forward with his bur den—fortunately a light one—resuming a flight which, for five hours, had known no cessation.' In this flight the rider had no terrors—no consciousness of any danger. The beast had many. Sometimes he shyed from the track, while every limb shook with emotion. His keen scent had caught the wind borne to him from the lairs of the wolf and panther. They, too, might have been upon his track; doubtless were,—but that his flight had been so fast and far, and that he seemed to their eyes to carry on his back a wild terror, with eyes of madness, much more fearful than their own. Of such as these the fugitive never thought. But, when the steed swerved aside, he irked him with spur or dagger,—indignant—crying out in shrillest tones—"Beast! we have not a moment to lose. See you not they hasten!—ah! Philip, but a moment more! But a moment!"

And with every word there was rowel stroke, or dagger thrust, till the flanks and neck of the steed were clammy with the red blood oozing forth.

And while the eyes of the rider stared out, dilating, wild and red, into the infinite space and vacancy—filled only with confused and dreadful aspects to his gaze—the day suddenly opened the great portals of the world, and the steed went forward with more confidence; but Juan saw not a whit more than had been quite as apparent to him all the night. Nay, he saw less, for night and darkness, and the solitude, had been favorable to the creation of such illusions as had occupied his mind, and the glare of day, and the sounds and sights of waking and creeping things, did somewhat conflict with the mental power to create and make its own individual impressions.

It was a dreadful ride, like that of Leonora and the Fiend Lover, in the weird and fantastic legend of Bürger. And, if the dead lover accompanied not our fugitive, there were yet terrible aspects that rode beside, and fearful cries followed on the wind, while ever and anon the voice of Don Balthazar thrilled in the ears of the page, crying, "Back, you are mine! You are too late!"

Then would the fugitive set his teeth closely together, and clutch his dagger with determined gripe, and hiss through his shut lips—"What! you have not had enough? You would taste again, would you!"

And so muttering, he would behold the amphitheatre once more, wherein De Soto's knights and soldiers environed the noble victim; and so seeing, the boy would set on, with driving spur anew, repeating his hoarse whisper in his throat the while—"But a moment, Philip—but a moment! and I will be with thee and die with thee!"

The day dawned, and the horse sped over a beaten track. He was in the very route pursued the day before, when Don Balthazar returned triumphant after the degradation of his enemy—returned, as he fancied, to delights, and the safe renewal of criminal but intoxicating pleasures, never once dreaming that Fate stood with open arms welcoming him to the bloodiest embrace.

The steed of our page felt himself sure at every step. The track was readily apparent. He went forward more confidently and more cheerfully, but with less rapidity, for now it was that the rider began to feel the gradual exhaustion of that strength which had been too severely taxed by such a progress. The page was no longer conscious of the diminished speed of the animal. His own growing feebleness reconciled him to the more sluggish pace of the beast. But ever and anon he would start out of his stupor with a sort of cry, and using the rowel, would expostulate—"Would you stop now, beast, when we are nigh the spot? What, do you not hear him call to me? You know his voice. Hear! He says—ah! what does he say! But I know, I know. Wait but a moment, Señor,—but a moment—but a moment!"

And the bridle grasp would relax,—and the form would seem to turn in the saddle,—while the eyes would close for a while, to open anew, only at the sudden short stopping of the horse, to graze along the wayside. Then would the rider show a moment's anger, and send him forward anew with prick of dagger, and mutter as before—the poor beast submitting, with the wonted docility of the well-trained war-horse, pursuing meekly the beaten track until he stood—coming to a full halt—on the very ground where De Soto's encampment had been made.

Then the page opened his eyes, and was about to smite the beast and goad him forward—when the rude scaffolding which the Adelantado had made his dais—on which had stood his Chair of State, and where he had delivered judgment—became suddenly apparent to his glance. With a sudden shriek as he beheld, the boy stretched out his hands and plunged forward, falling heavily upon the ground, with a sad murmur—

"It is too late! too late!"

He swooned away; while the horse, stepping carefully backward, wandered off in search of water. And, for an hour, the beast wandered thus from side to side. He found streams in which he slaked his thirst. He found tender grasses in the shady woods, which he cropped at leisure. And the day thus wore on. The animal now began to be a little restive, and he whinnied for companionship, looking round, from side to side, for some one to approach, and strip off his furniture, and show that solicitude for him to which he had been accustomed, and which the beast craves no less than his master.

His whinny made its way to other ears than those of his late rider. The page still lay insensible, in the shadow of a great tree; nature thus seeking relief from the sufferings which it had undergone, and obtaining respite from the fiery stress of thought upon the brain. Soon, a figure emerged from the thicket, stealthily approaching the spot where the horse had again begun to feed. The stranger was one of the red men, a subject of the Cassique of Chiaha. He was followed by two others, one of whom was a woman. The leader of the party made his way towards the steed, observing the while the greatest precaution. To the red men the horse was still an object of terror. He had been wont, at first, to confound him with his rider. He had thus perfectly conceived the idea of the ancients of the East, to whom we owe the classical monster, the Centaur. Disabused by experience of this error, he did not yet divest the horse of all those powers which really belonged to his rider. He fancied still that fire issued from his nostrils. He did not doubt that his teeth were quite as fearful as those of the tiger or the wolf. It required, accordingly, no small degree of courage to approach the monster of which so little was known, and of whose powers so much was erroneously thought. But one red man did approach; the horse seeming so innocent—so gentle and subdued—so quietly grazing, and altogether inviting approach by the general docility of his air and behaviour. The grasp of the forest hunter was at length fairly laid upon the bridle of the steed, and he was a captive.

The red man laughed out with delight. He called his comrades to him, and they approached with trembling. He grew bolder as he beheld their fears. He encouraged them. He stroked the neck and mane of the beast, who seemed grateful and submissive, and they all laughed. And they chattered among themselves like parrots; until made bolder as he became familiar, and as the animal continued to crop the grass, showing himself quite passive, the captor leapt upon his back, and crept forward to the saddle, and wreathed his hand in the mane, having abandoned his grasp of the bridle, of the use of which he had no notion. Pleased with his elevation, the savage persuaded his comrades to follow him, and his brother warrior leapt up, then the squaw followed, and as the horse moved slowly from side to side, cropping the grass, and seemingly heedless of his burden, but still walking, the simple savages clapped their hands and yelled with delight.

But that yell awakened the destrier to new sensations. The beast knew that he was in the power of his enemies. His character changed on the instant. His moods, his passions, were all stirred with excitement. He threw head and tail aloft. He shook out his mane; the blood of the war-horse was aroused as with the shrill summons of the clarion, and he dashed away at headlong speed, to seek the spot where he had left his master. At the first bound he shook himself free of the squaw, who rolled away over his haunches, suffering no hurt but a prodigious fright, as she settled down in a heap upon the earth, hardly knowing whether she was dead or alive. The Indians yelled again with sudden terror; and the shrill cry increased the speed of the animal. Away he dashed with the headlong rapidity of a charge. The foremost of the savages clung to his back like a cat, while he wound his hands more firmly within the animal's mane. The other clung to the body of his comrade. Then the animal threw his head down, and both of them went over his neck. They rolled away, on opposite sides, quite unhurt, but horribly alarmed. The steed flew, as he felt relieved of his burden, and he was quickly out of sight.

The two savages lay for several minutes upon the earth, not daring to look up or speak. But as the sounds of the horse's feet grew more distant, one of them rose to a sitting posture. He called to the other in under tones. It required some thought and examination to be assured of the fact that both of them still lived, and that no bones were broken. One of them went back for the squaw. She, too, was unhurt. They were soon brought together, and a rapid consultation determined them to pursue the monster who had treated them with so much indignity. Bows were bent, arrows got in readiness, the stone hatchet was seized in sinewy grasp, and the two warriors went forward—the woman following at a little distance, and trembling for the event.

It was a matter of course that the red men should fasten instantly upon the fresh track of the horse, and follow it with unerring certainty. The beast, meanwhile, had made his way back to where the page had fallen, and when the pursuers drew nigh they found him smelling at the hands of his late rider and pushing them with his nose. The boy was stirring slightly. Suddenly, the horse receded. He had winded the red men. He dashed backward, and as he did so, seizing their moment, they both darted upon the half-awaking Juan, and had seized him by the arms before he had become fully conscious. The rude assault brought him back to consciousness. He strove to shake off his captors, but his struggles were feeble; his arms fell uselessly, unperformingly, beside him; and he showed his submission by signs. Why should he struggle against fate? What had he to live for? Why should he dread the death which he now fancied to be certain?

The red men possessed themselves of the page's dagger, the only weapon which he carried. With their stone hatchets waving in his sight, they motioned him to rise. By signs they bade him recover the horse, which he did without effort, but they were sufficiently wary not to suffer him to mount. The beast was led accordingly, and the boy proceeded with his captors all on foot; the squaw having joined them in compliance with their repeated halloos.

The destrier was now docile enough, following his master. The page feebly led him on. But he soon sank down by the way. One of the red men would have brained him with his hatchet; but the other, who was the older, and the woman, interposed. The latter soon perceived the boy's exhaustion, and while one of the men went off in search of a spring or rivulet, the squaw darted into the woods, bringing back with her, after a little while, some leaves, and a small round acid fruit. The latter she squeezed into the page's mouth. The leaves she pressed upon his forehead. Water was brought in a leaf shaped like a slipper, of which he drank freely. In a little while he was revived. When he recovered sufficiently, he motioned them by signs to let him ride, one of them taking the bridle within his hands. The proposition was a startling one, and led to a long discussion among the captors, which was finally settled by the eldest of the party, who seized the bridle with the most heroic air of self-sacrifice, in one hand, while with the other, waving his stone hatchet, he threatened the head of the horse with sudden stroke, at the first suspicious symptom. Juan mounted with feeble heart and limbs, indifferently, and only resigned to the wishes of his captors.

And thus the four travelled for six or eight weary hours. Noon came and went. The sun at length was faintly smiling farewell over the forest, at the closing of his pilgrimage, when the party came in sight of the beautiful river, the Coosa, at the spot where it first acquires an individual existence, from the junction of the Etowah and the Oostanaula.

Here was an encampment of the red men. They could be seen in crowds along the banks of the river. But the eyes of Juan were fastened upon a group that was gathered beneath a sort of canopy upon the hillside. They slowly approached this station. The page's eyes brightened as he drew nigh. Surely, it is Don Philip that he sees, seated upon the ground in front of the canopy, while the red men wander about in the background. But the page doubts. Can it be that the savage-looking man whom he sees,—woe-stricken, with matted and dishevelled hair and beard,—is his noble master—the accomplished knight of Portugal—the man of grace, and stature, and beauty; of ease and sweetness, and clear bright eye, and generous aspect? Can he have so altered in so short a space? Juan could scarcely believe. But he had no conception of the change which he had himself undergone. With a cry he threw himself from the steed at the feet of the cavalier—

"Oh! Señor! Oh! Don Philip——"

The knight looked up for the first time as he heard the cry.

"My poor boy, my poor Juan, is it thou, indeed!"

And he took the boy suddenly to his embrace. He shrunk from the grasp: he trembled like a leaf; tottered, and would have fallen but that the knight held him up.

"God be praised, Juan, that thou art again with me! I had feared that I should lose thee forever, my poor boy; and surely, Juan, if there be any that I can now love, it is thyself."

He again grasped the page and drew him to his embrace. The head of the boy sank upon his shoulder. His eye was bright with tears. The head was relieved. The heart enjoyed a strange and sudden sensation of happiness. At that moment his ear caught the sound of a well-known voice.

"Philip!" said, in the tenderest tones, the beautiful Coçalla, the Princess of Cofachiqui; and she laid her hand affectionately upon the shoulders of the knight.

"Philip!"

The word went like a dagger to the heart of the page. The tenderness of tone in which it was spoken filled her soul with bitterness. There was an agony in her bosom, as sudden and extreme as the rapture which had filled it but a moment before, and, with the seeming recovery of all her strength and senses, she withdrew herself from the embrace of Vasconselos, who gently released her.

"Go within, Juan," said the knight, pointing him to the rude tent of bushes before which stood the canopy of stained cotton;

" go within, boy, and await me, for I have much to hear from thee."

With the big tears gathering in his eyes like great pearls of the ocean, the page did as he was commanded, having, ere he went, beheld Coçalla take her place by the side of the knight, while one of her hands rested proudly on his shoulder, and her large brown eyes seemed to drink in rapture while gazing deeply into his.

CHAPTER XLIV

> "*Auf.* Say, what's thy name?
> Thou hast a grim appearance, and thy face
> Bears a command in 't; though thy tackle's torn
> Thou show'st a noble vessel. What's thy name?"
> *Coriolanus.*

MEANWHILE, the Spanish army pursued its progress into the rich, wild provinces of the Alabamous. They were now approaching the territories of the great Indian Cassique, called Tuscaluza, or the Black Warrior,—a ruler at once remarkable for the extent of his sway, his haughty valor, and his gigantic stature. He had heard of the approaching Spaniards, of their power, their wonderful arms and armor, their strange appearance, and the mystery which seemed to envelop their origin. He was naturally curious to see the strangers, and was too great a potentate himself, and too valiant a chief to entertain any apprehension of their power. Of their treatment of his kinswoman, Coçalla, he had up to this period heard nothing, and his invitation, accordingly, through his inferior cassiques, was cordially extended to the Spanish commander to visit him in the recesses of his wild domain. His chief settlements were along the banks of the river which still bears his name—his territories stretched away indefinitely, even beyond the waters of the Mississippi. As the strangers drew nigh to his royal precincts, he despatched his son to give them special welcome—a youth of eighteen, but tall like himself, his stature far overtopping that of the tallest soldiers in the Spanish army. His bold and noble carriage contributed, with his stature, to compel the respect and admiration of the Adelantado and his cavaliers.

But ere the arrival of this youth, as an ambassador, there was some stir in the Spanish camp, in consequence of the treatment which Philip de Vasconselos had received. The return of Nuno de Tobar, and Andres de Vasconselos, led to warm words, angry passion, and finally to a re-examination of the affair. If Andres felt coldly towards his brother—and no doubt his conscience had long since rebuked him severely for his conduct, for which his boyish pride would suffer him to make no atonement—his feelings of kindred were by no means subdued. Now that his brother was dishonored, and had probably perished in consequence of the exile and exposure which followed his sentence, the better nature of the young man obtained the ascendant, and he felt his error to its full extent, and bitterly lamented the little sympathy which he had shown to a brother to whom he was indebted for the best training and affection of his early years. Nor was Nuno de Tobar less eagerly aroused than Andres to the necessity of vindicating the fame of Philip, and, if possible, of recovering and restoring him to the army. To this end their earnest efforts were directed. The woods were scoured where the victim had been left to perish, but in vain. He was already in the close keeping of the Princess of Copachiqui—not so far, indeed, from the camp of the Spaniards—not so much beyond their reach—but that, had he himself been willing, he might have been found. But in what way could it be conveyed to him that he was not pursued with malice, and that justice should be done to his worth at last? He might well question the motives for the search on the part of those from whom he had never yet experienced sympathy or confidence.

Coçalla and her followers were all well aware of the neighborhood of the Spanish parties sent out in search of Philip—nay, he himself was not ignorant, and he might possibly have suspected their better motives, knowing as he did that his brother and Nuno de Tobar were at the head of these detachments; but he now no longer cared to resume a connection with the associates who had abandoned him, and with an expedition whose daily progresses revolted all his human and chivalrous sentiments. Besides, he had been inexpiably disgraced according to all the laws of chivalry, and there was no adequate power to do him justice, and to restore his honors. A savage scorn of all social relations took the place in his bosom of the gentler sympathies he had once so loved to cherish. A fierce mood preyed like a vulture upon his thoughts, and he brooded only upon revenge. This was now the atoning, the compensative sentiment which he encouraged, and his thought was wholly addressed to the modes by which he should wreak the full measure of his vengeance upon the two whom he regarded as the principals in his great disgrace, and the bitter defeat of all his hopes and honor. His thought by day, his dream by night, found him ever engaged in the hot struggle of the gladiator with Don Balthazar de Alvaro and the haughty Adelantado; and he sat or wandered with his savage associates, grim and silent, following the progress of the Spaniards with eye and mind; a Fate, himself, threatening but too truly the melancholy doom which attended upon their footsteps.

It was with a gloomy feeling of bitterness and self reproach that

Andres de Vasconselos and Nuno de Tobar gave up the search after the fugitive. They naturally concluded that he had perished—the victim of the red men. But they addressed themselves to the business of the inquiry touching the charges brought against him, and, in particular, as concerned the agency of Don Balthazar in the affair. In respect to this person, Nuno de Tobar could give considerable evidence. The conviction that Don Balthazar had been the vindictive pursuer of his brother to destruction, prompted Andres de Vasconselos to hurry to the village of Chiaha, where the former had been left in command, resolved to disgrace him by blows, and force him to single combat. He was met on his arrival by the intelligence, already known to us, of the murder of the knight, and of the flight of the page Juan—the latter being supposed by some the assassin; by others, the red men were credited with the achievment, the boy being thought their captive.

Andres de Vasconselos was disarmed by this intelligence, which had the further effect of relieving Hernan de Soto of much of the responsibilities of his situation. Though bold and haughty enough, it was yet quite too important to the safety, not less than the success, of the Adelantado, to venture to defy the complaints and indignation of some of his bravest knights. He now began to feel that he should need the very meanest of his force to carry through the objects of his expedition, and in propitiating the captains who had interested themselves in the case of Philip, the death of Don Balthazar afforded a ready agency. He was, in fact, the chief criminal, and De Soto was really but his creature. Facts were exposed by Tobar, showing the bitter malice of Don Balthazar; and the very creatures whom he had suborned against the knight of Portugal, were now not unwilling to expose the influences which were brought to bear for his destruction. De Soto, after the farce of a solemn reconsideration of the case, was brought to revoke his judgment; but it was too late! Philip de Vasconselos had undergone a fearful change of character. He was now the vulture of revenge, hovering in the rear of the devoted cavalcade, waiting his moment when to swoop down in blood upon the quarry.

Close and ominous watch, indeed, did he keep upon the movements of the Spaniards through the agency of the red men of Cofachiqui. They were gathering daily in numbers, well armed, and eager for revenge. They were joined by the warriors of Chiaha, and tacitly, as it seemed, did they refer the whole conduct of their people to the direction of Philip de Vasconselos. In this they naturally obeyed the wishes of the Princess; but this influence might not have sufficed to confer upon him this authority, were it not that they were instinctively impressed by himself, by the great injuries which had made him the incarnation of that wild revenge which the red men so much love and honor, and by his unquestionable ability as a commander. He, himself, seemed to take their lead as a matter of course. He neither asked them nor himself in respect to the matter. He willed, and they submitted. He pointed with his finger hither or thither, and they sped. They saw his purpose in his look. They took their directions from his eye and hand; and there was that of the terribly savage in his fearful glance, and so much of the sublimely fearful in the embodied woe which seemed to speak in every silent look and gesture, that to submit and obey was the voluntary impulse of all who looked upon the noble outlaw.

The one purpose which occupied his mind, sufficed to concentrate all his faculties. The Spaniards now began daily to experience the influence of a will and a power which threatened them with the greatest dangers, the more formidable, as it was still impossible to conjecture what shape the danger was to take, or when and where the blow was to fall. An ominous gloom seemed to hang upon their hearts. Superstitious apprehensions haunted their souls—a cloud seemed to hang upon their pathway, in no degree relieved by the courteous invitations of the great cassique, Tuscaluza. Weariness, exhaustion, daily toil and march, and continued disappointments, no doubt combined to render them especially sensible to such fears and doubts. But there were external evidences daily offered them which had their effect, also, in compelling and arousing their superstitious fears. The red men seemed to have altered their whole policy. They hovered about the advancing army, but without coming to blows. They no longer rushed out boldly from beneath the forest trees, in groups, or single men, challenging the invader to the crossing of the spears. But if they did not fight, they did not fly. There, in front, and flank, and rear, they might be seen to hover like so many threatening clouds, retiring into safety when approached,—not to be overtaken,—but still giving proofs that they were unrelaxing in that haunting watch and pursuit which they had begun from the moment when Vasconselos took command. It may be that De Soto and others suspected his presence and authority among the red men, and that a gloomy prescience, and vague terrors, were the result of this suspicion. To these feelings, each day added large increase. The Spaniards now longed for the strife; they felt how much easier and more grateful it would be to bring this annoyance to prompt and desperate issue, which vexed their pride and perpetually troubled their securities. But they strove for this in vain. Many were the efforts which they made to beguile the savages to battle,—to ensnare them in ambush,— to run them down with their mounted men; but the vigilant generalship of the Portuguese cavalier held them in close hands, and they hung about the wearied Spaniards like clouds of voracious birds, sufficiently nigh to seize their prey when occasion offered, but at a safe distance from any danger. Daily they succeeded in picking up some victim from the ranks of the invader. Not a loiterer escaped the bow-shaft or the macana. The straggler invariably perished—pierced with sharp arrows, or brained with the heavy hatchet of stone. It was death to turn aside into the covert; it was fatal to charge beyond the ranks which offered immediate support. One newly adopted policy of the red men seemed particularly ominous to the Spaniards. They now addressed their shafts to the breasts of the horses, rather than the cavaliers, and every now and then some fine steed fell a victim under the unexpected arrow, despatched from unsuspected coverts where the assailants found impenetrable shelter.

Thus haunted, thus troubled with evil omens, the Spanish army made its way into the thickly settled countries of the Alabamous. This people, under the sway of Tuscaluza, were probably composed of the Choctaws, Chickasaws, and the remnants of other tribes. They were numerous, in comparison with the other nations of the red men, and were as fearless and practised in warfare as they were numerous. De Soto, in entering their great towns and villages, did so with unusual precaution. His mind was impressed evidently with a far greater sense of the responsibilities and difficulties of his situation than had ever been the case before. His apprehensions and disquiet were greatly increased at this period by a new evil; an epidemic appeared among his troops, which was fatal to many. They were seized with a low fever, which seemed to prostrate them instantly. At the end of a very few days they perished; the skin, even before death, becoming of a discolored and greenish hue, and their bodies emitting a fetid odor. A terrible fear possessed the army, that they were poisoned—that the subtle savages had mixed their maize, or the waters of the streams, with some vegetable poison of great potency. We may imagine the terror that seized upon all hearts from a conjecture so full of horror. Some of their Tamenes, however, suggested a native remedy for the disease, which was probably due rather to exhaustion and unsatisfactory food. A ley, made from the ashes of a certain herb, and mingled with their food instead of salt—of which they had none—was found to afford security against attack. But many of them perished of the disorder before the remedy was made known.

Tuscaluza met De Soto at one of his villages, at some distance from his capital city. He probably did not design that the Spaniards should penetrate to that place. But he did not know the character of the invaders. The haughty chieftain welcomed the Adelantado in a truly royal manner, with great show of forest state, and a dignity which might have furnished a model to the noblest sovereign of Christendom. His immense stature, erect carriage, haughty demeanor, perfect composure, insensibility to surprise of any kind, had the effect of awing the Spaniards into something like reverence, for a season. The Adelantado presented him with a dress of scarlet, and with a flowing mantle of the same material. These he wore with a natural grace which showed him superior to the efforts of the artist. With his own towering plumes, he became the crowning and central figure, of right, amid the grand assemblage of native chieftains and steel-clad warriors by whom he was surrounded. The Adelantado added to his gifts that of a horse also; though it was with great difficulty that a beast was found sufficiently powerful to endure the weight of so colossal a warrior.

The courtesy of De Soto, his gifts and attentions were not unpleasing to the haughty Cassique, and he cheerfully accompanied them in a march of three days, to one of his first-class villages, called after himself, Tuscaluza. This village stood upon a peninsula of the Alabama River. The river was crossed without difficulty, and the army encamped for the night in a beautiful valley, about a league beyond the place of passage. There was feasting and great state for some hours in the Spanish camp, and Tuscaluza was a guest at supper with the Adelantado. But when he retired, it was without the precincts of the camp, and Spaniards, though on the watch to discover his place of resort for the night, failed to trace his progress through the wild forests through which, with his attendants, he made his easy way. But there were other watchers more successful, and when Tuscaluza entered his sylvan lodge, but two miles from the Spanish camp, he found the beautiful Princess Coçalla, his own niece, awaiting him in the lodge; and seated upon a pile of bear-skins, a stern, silent, savage-looking man, one of the pale-faced warriors, in whose grim aspect we recognize the once gentle, graceful, and courtly knight of Portugal.

Coçalla threw herself upon the neck of Tuscaluza, and was

welcomed with such a degree of fondness as was consistent with
the pride and power of so haughty a monarch. He received her
with tenderness even, and she wept sweet tears upon the breast
of him who had been the well-beloved brother of her mother.
What fool was it who first taught that the red men lacked the
sensibilities of humanity?

But we must defer our further report to another chapter.

CHAPTER XLV.

"Up, sword, and know thou a more horrid hent."
Hamlet.

The gigantic and haughty sovereign of the Alabamous was sensibly awed by the stern aspect which encountered him, when he turned from the beautiful Coçalla to welcome to his abode the outlawed knight of Portugal. Stern self-possession, calm inflexible endurance—as significant of the big heart and the unyielding courage—are among the master virtues of the red men. In brief words, Coçalla had conveyed to her uncle the simple outline of the fortunes of Vasconselos, as well as her own, since she had first come to a knowledge of the Spaniards. Tuscaluza had heard enough to compel his respect for the knight, and to secure his gratitude and confidence in consideration of what he had done for the Princess. But when he looked on Philip, he saw before him no ordinary warrior. He felt himself in the presence of a Fate—of a terror and a power, the resources and purpose of which he could instantly conjecture from the mixed aspect of concentrated woe and vengeance which confronted him. He welcomed the knight, but the latter had no answer; and the savage prince, who seemed at once to comprehend the nature and the necessity of the cavalier, sate quietly beside him upon the bear skins, and yielded himself composedly, while Coçalla proceeded to unfold the details of that long history which she had hitherto rendered him in the briefest possible manner.

To one who should regard only the outer aspects of the red man, the features of Tuscaluza betrayed not the slightest secret of the impression which this narrative made upon his soul. But the pride, anger, fierce hatred, and eager impulse to war, were not the less active in his bosom, because there were no external signs of their presence. At the close of the story, he simply rose and threw off the scarlet robes with which De Soto had decorated his person, cast them contemptuously upon the earthen floor of his cabin, and, as he paced the apartment to and fro, he walked over the rich silks unheedingly. Then, after a brief interval, he stretched his hand out to Vasconselos. The latter took it without a word and rose. He laid his own hand upon his breast, and said, in the Choctaw dialect:—

"Philip is a warrior. He will fight the battles of the great

Tuscaluza. Will the Cassique say to his warriors—Go! follow Philip, that we may drive the Spaniards to their homes beyond the sea?"

"That we may drive them into the sea!" was the fierce response, as the savage monarch again eagerly grasped the hand of the knight. He added—"Philip shall be a great chief of the Alabamous. He shall have many warriors to go with him to battle. He shall show to the Black warrior of the Alabamous how we may best feed on these Spaniards, and capture the mighty beasts upon which they ride."

"It shall be done. Let Philip be clad in the war-paint of the Alabamous, and bring him garments for a chief of the red men."

When Philip had spoken these words, Coçalla threw her arms about his neck. He did not return her caresses, but he looked into her face with a tender sadness, which for a moment smoothed the terrible expression from his visage. At this moment the page Juan entered the apartment. Coçalla caught his glance, and instantly withdrew her arms from the neck of Vasconselos. How subtle are the feminine instincts. The forest Princess seemed to know that Juan looked not favorably upon the passion which she felt for Philip. The page, meanwhile, recoiled from the glance of Tuscaluza, who, as he regarded the intruder, stopped in his walk, exclaiming—"Hah!"

Coçalla calmly bade the page enter, and explained his relation with Vasconselos.

"It is good," replied the Cassique, resuming his walk. "It is good; but let him go, till one shall come to him and say, 'thy master hath use for thee,' and his finger conveyed the same directions to the page himself. With a sad, longing look towards Philip—who did not seem to heed him, or, indeed, to heed anything—Juan turned away, and left the hovel.

It was then that Tuscaluza brought forth sundry rich garments of native furs and cotton, the latter stained brightly with yellow, the color of the nation, and crossed with bars of blue. The banner of Tuscaluza was thus designed, the bars of blue being three in number. These were presented to Philip, who received them as a matter of course, with something of indifference in his manner, while he stooped carefully and picked up the scarlet robes upon which Tuscaluza had so scornfully trampled. These he restored to the Cassique.

"Why should the great warrior show to the Spaniards that he is angry, and cast his gifts upon the ground? Let the robe disguise the wrath. Let the great warrior rather persuade the

Spaniards that he is a friend; nor tell him when he means to strike."

The suggestion corresponded happily with the genius of savage warfare.

"Good!" said the chief, resuming and shaking the robes, but without freeing them from the stains which they had already taken from the earth. When the next day, these stains were visible to the eyes of the Spaniards, the cavaliers enjoyed a pleasant laugh at the expense of the grim warrior.

"He drank quite too much of the Canaries last night, your Excellency," said Nuno de Tobar. "He hath been rolling down hill, and methinks hath had a taste of the river, which doubtless failed to relish after the wine."

"Nay, Señor Nuno," was the reply, "he walked away with all the erectness which he showed at the beginning."

"Yes; but did you not see that he never trusted himself to the back of his horse. It was led off by one of his followers, and he strode away on foot."

"Yes; and had thine eyes but followed him as he sped, then wouldst thou have seen that his movement was solid and square, like a tower. He went not to the right nor to the left, till the great forests received him."

"Then hath he had a brew of his own ere he slept, for verily those stains of the scarlet are those of a man who hath wallowed upon the bosom of his mother, without knowing well what arms have embraced him. All these savages possess the art of making strong drink."

"And upon that thou found'st thy argument for its necessity and justification. Go to, Señor Nuno, and let not this heathen Prince suspect that you laugh at his weakness—if such it be—for verily he is as proud and jealous of his state as ever was Lucifer, when he had sway among the stars. Away to thy post, and see that thy detachment be in marching order! Remember, he is not to suspect that there are guards upon his person."

Such was the policy of the Spaniards. That of Tuscaluza tutored as he was by Vasconselos, was a few shades more profound. All that night these two chiefs communed together in the hovel; Coçalla, after a while, having retired. Juan was kept in waiting, but in an adjacent cabin.

We design that the strategies of the red men shall gradually unfold themselves. It is enough to mention here that Philip conveyed to the Black Warrior a full idea of the importance to the Spaniards of their horses, and the necessity of capturing them, **or slaying** them. He counselled the latter course as by far the best, but urged, in the meanwhile, that, in the event of a conflict, the scene of action should always be so chosen as to deprive the cavalry of all share in the battle. It was this counsel that finally determined Tuscaluza to conduct the enemy to one of his largest towns, named Mauvila. This was a walled town, and is supposed to have stood upon the northern bank of the Alabama, at a place now called Choctaw Point. The town of Mauvila occupied a noble plain. The walls were rude, being high embankments of earth and wood, filled in between great forest trees; the wood being fastened in piles with vines and reeds, and the face of the wall being plastered with a thick coating of native clay or earth, which hardened into smooth consistency in the sun and air. The defences were slight, of course—such as strong arms and good axes could hew down in short time, and through which the small falconets of that day could have easily blown a capacious opening. But the Spaniards were without artillery of any kind. Still, they had adequate implements for breaking their way, if time were allowed them. The wall was pierced with loop-holes for arrows, and at certain moderate distances it was surmounted by numerous towers, each capable of holding a score of fighting men. There were but two gates, one on the east, the other on the west side. In the centre of the village was a great square, or parade-ground, around which the buildings were erected. These did not exceed a hundred in number, but they were mostly vast fortresses, capable of containing entire tribes, from five hundred to fifteen hundred persons in each—great halls only, without rooms; the red men lodging together as in caravanserais.

To this place, thus constructed, the Black Warrior conducted his destined victims. He was accompanied by few personal attendants, and no warriors. To this he had been counselled by Vasconselos. But he had made preparations elsewhere for the part which his followers had to play, and the consciousness that he was held a close prisoner by the very courteous knight who attended him, did not lessen his purpose of giving the Spaniards such sauce to their supper as would effectually spoil their appetites. When the vanguard of De Soto's army appeared before the town, the Adelanta lo leading and accompanied by Tuscaluza, a splendid array of the native warriors, flaunting in feathers, in robes of fur and cotton, of various and brilliant colors, came forth to meet them. To these succeeded long lines of beautiful damsels—and they were beautiful though dusky—"dark but comely" as was the maid who was sung by the erring muse of Solomon the Wise.—These came forth with songs and dances,— rude pipes of reed, the simple flutes of the region—cymbals and drums, made of the gourd, covered with skins tightly drawn, and long clarions, hollowed out of the soft woods common to the swamps.

So far, all seemed to go as merrily as marriage bells, and De Soto had no cause for apprehension; but he had some occasions for doubt, when, on entering the town, he found that, while he, himself, his officers and immediate attendants, were assigned a couple of the best houses of the place, his troops were to be lodged in cabins *without* the walls. The great body of the army had not yet arrived, but followed on, somewhat too tardily, under the charge of Luis de Moscoso.

Hanging closely, but unseen, upon the steps of Moscoso—like a gathering thunder cloud that marshals its mighty legions on the very verge of the horizon—Philip de Vasconselos followed with a force of some three thousand warriors. A dozen times was he tempted by the heedless manner of Moscoso's march to dart upon him with his cloud of savages, and destroy him, if possible, before he could unite with De Soto; and long afterwards did he reproach himself with not having done so. Could he have seen the banneret of Don Balthazar de Alvaro flaunting amidst the gay array, he could scarcely have foreborne the effort. It was against Don Balthazar first, and De Soto next, that his concentrated vengeance was directed. Neither of these were present to stimulate his rage. Besides, he might mar the plot concluded upon with the Black Warrior, by anticipating the designated moment, and some fugitives might escape on horseback, and convey to the very victims whom he sought, the intelligence which should enable them to guard effectually against the attack. Hungering, therefore, for the action, he was compelled to control himself and his red followers—no easy task—and which he, perhaps, never could have done but that he was supported by the presence and authority of Coçalla, the Princess. She kept close beside him as he went, the two followed by Juan, with wild emotions of a passionate love and anger mixed. The wretched boy! He, too, had his temptations, and more than once he found himself meditating to lift his lance, and strike it into the back of the beautiful Princess, though with the certainty of immediate death himself, that he might end his pangs of jealousy forever. Verily, they were great, and the tender devotion of the Princess to Philip, never suffered them to sleep for a single moment. It was still a feminine consideration that restrained him. How should his dying eyes meet the anger in those of Philip, were he thus to strike?

Tuscaluza had a considerable body of warriors with him at

Mauvila—possibly three or four thousand. There were still other bodies collecting. The always extravagant statements of the Spanish and Portuguese authorities, by which they have sought to exaggerate the importance of the event, and to lessen the seeming losses of the Spaniards in the struggle, are to be received with many grains of allowance. Let it suffice that the Black Warrior was embodying, and had embodied, a considerable number of warriors, quite enough to have devoured his enemies—using his own language—had there been any equality in their defences and armor. But the Spaniards were clad in mail, covering the most vulnerable parts; their faces only partially exposed, their thighs and legs. The darts and arrows had but small marks. The savages, on the other hand, might as well have been naked. Their furs, bear skins, and even shields of hide, afforded no sort of protection from the bullet of the fusileer, or even the sword-cuts, the lance-thrusts, and arrows of the horsemen and archers. Philip de Vasconselos knew too well the greatness of this inequality between the combatants. and felt that the very numbers of the savages, within a certain range, were rather hurtful than helpful in the action. The very valor of the red men was a danger, since they had not yet learned to appreciate their foes. He strove, in every possible way, and by every argument, to teach this to the Black Warrior, and his favorite captain, without offending their self-esteem. Unfortunately for them he succeeded but imperfectly. The pride and passions of Tuscaluza both operated fatally to precipitate events and make him forgetful of all the counsels of the Portuguese knight.

It was early in the morning of the 18th of October that De Soto, with the Black Warrrior, and the vanguard of the Spanish army, entered the village of Mauvila. The town, as we have seen, was strongly fortified, impregnable, indeed, to such assaults as were common to the experience of the red men. The arrangements of Tuscaluza for the disposition of his troops were such as to offend the military caution of the Adelantado. He was advised, too, of other suspicious circumstances in the conduct of the red chief—of the gradual accumulation of large bodies of troops—of the collection of vast piles of weapons of war, shafts and macanas—and of several missing soldiers—stragglers who had probably been massacred. De Soto was aroused and anxious, but felt that it was necessary to temporize until the coming of Moscoso with the main body of the army. He affected to be satisfied, and felt that he was safe so long as he had Tuscaluza in his custody. But the haughty spirit of the

Sovereign precipitated the issue. They had scarcely entered the town when he signified to De Soto the abode which had been assigned him, while he indicated his own purpose to occupy another. But the Adelantado replied, cavalierly perhaps—that he did not approve of the arrangement.

"The Black Warrior will remain with me."

The haughty soul of Tuscaluza then blazed out—

"The Black Warrior is the king in all these countries. It is for him to command. It is for all others to obey. The Spanish chief is at liberty to depart, but he must not pretend to say to Tuscaluza, here shalt thou remain, or thither shalt thou go. Does the Spaniard hear? Such is the speech of the Black Warrior."

The moment was not auspicious for a decisive reply to this speech, such as, under other circumstances, De Soto would have given. Tuscaluza waited for no answer to his words. He entered the dwelling which he had indicated as his own abode, leaving the Spanish chief to find his way to the other. That in which he took shelter contained a thousand warriors. De Soto quietly proceeded to the dwelling appointed for his use, and instantly sent out his officers to go secretly among his troopers, and command them to hold themselves in readiness for action. Meanwhile, he resolved still to keep up the appearance of friendship and cordiality. Breakfast being prepared, he sent Juan Ortiz, the interpreter, to invite the Black Warrior to his table. He was refused admittance, but his message was delivered, and the reply was civil—"The Black Warrior will come."

But the Black Warrior did not come. Some time elapsed, and Juan Ortiz was sent with a second message, receiving the same answer as before. The same result followed. There was a long delay; and again Juan Ortiz was despatched with a third message. Now, whether it was that the interpreter, vexed at his repeated miscarriages, became insolent in his tone and language, or whether the red men now found themselves ready for a change in theirs, must be a subject of conjecture; but, when Juan Ortiz, standing at the door of the Sovereign, cried aloud to his subjects—"Tell Tuscaluza, that the food grows cold upon the table; that the Adelantado awaits him, and sends to him to come forth at once,"—then the long suppressed storm broke out in fury. A red warrior sallied forth to the entrance, crying aloud, while his eyes flashed fire, and all his face was inflamed with anger—

"Vagabond and robber, begone! Is it such as thou that darest clamor aloud at the doors of a great chief, crying, come forth, come forth! Away to thy robber master, and say to him, that when Tuscaluza comes forth it is to destroy him. Hence, vagabond!" And as Juan Ortiz, half frightened out of his senses, sped away, he could hear the grim savage exclaim proudly—

"By the sun and moon! This is no longer to be borne. To your weapons, warriors of Mauvila, and let us put an end to the insolence of these wandering wretches!"

The speaker was the great leader of the Mauvilians—their general—in their own phrase, the Big Warrior. He had led them in a hundred conflicts. He had won fame and glory from them all. His triumphs were about to end with his conflicts. Having spoken, he beheld a group of Spaniards in the great square, closely huddled together. There were other Spaniards near at hand, but passing singly. He did not notice these, but making a signal to one of his followers, a bow and arrows were handed him. He seized the bow, threw back from his shoulders the flowing mantle of skins which he wore, and was about fixing the arrow to the string, when his purpose was arrested and his movements anticipated by the action of one of those cool, always ready and prompt warriors, to whom constant strife has served to impart resolve and instantaneous action—one Balthazar de Gallegos. The sword from this warrior, already bared in his grasp, flashed in air the moment, when the Big Warrior grasped the bow, and before the arrow could leave the string, the sharp blade was ranging through the vitals of the red man, who fell dead upon the spot. And thus commenced a conflict of a character the most terrible and bloody, destined to paralyze the fortunes of Hernan de Soto. The fate which had been hovering like a storm-cloud above his head, was swooping down at last upon his victim.

CHAPTER XLVI.

"Ha! what shout is this?" *Coriolanus.*

THE soup of the Adelantado that day was cooled uneaten. Scarcely had Juan Ortiz entered the dwelling which his master occupied, and declared his tidings, when the war-whoop rang throughout the village, echoed by five thousand vigorous voices. The warriors poured forth from a thousand unsuspected vomitories. They slaughtered the scattered Spaniards, as, heedless of their leader's order, they lounged about street and square. The latter fought, but vainly. They were driven from the town; numbers of the cavaliers saw their horses slain, shot down before their eyes; a loss which they held to be even more serious than of the soldiery. To slay the horses was especially the labor of one large portion of the savages. To this had they been counselled by their chiefs, under instructions of Vasconselos. Unluckily for themselves, this was almost the only part of his instructions which they seem to have remembered. But, for a time, their successes were too flattering to suffer them to pause. The vanguard of the Spaniards expelled from their walls, several slain, many more wounded, more than thirty horses killed outright, or maimed forever, and the whole of the baggage of the invading army, with the single exception of one knight's effects; these were successes calculated to turn the heads of any savage people, ignorant of their enemy, and incapable of any true estimate of the means by which they had won success.

And such had been the advantages gained by the red men in their first demonstration against the Spaniard, at Mauvila. They had lost their general, the fierce brave who had so summarily dismissed Juan Ortiz with defiance to his master, and who had perished under the sudden sword-thrust of Balthazar de Gallegos. His son, a noble young warrior, had perished also, in the effort to avenge his death, but not before he had pummelled Gallegos about the head and ears with his bow, until the Spaniard was blinded with his blood, and stunned, almost to perishing, beneath his blows. The gallant savage had in vain sent his arrows at the mailed bosom of the Castilian knight. In slaying half a score of Spaniards the red men had lost hundreds; but there was no lack of numbers to take their places, and they scarcely felt their losses. It was not so with the white warriors, who were too few, not to feel severely the loss of such a large proportion of their whole disposable force. The result, whatever the inequality of loss, was a temporary triumph with the Mauvilians. They had beaten the invader from their fastnesses, and they were in possession of all the spoils of the field. They had also released the captive Tamenes from the chains of their masters, had put weapons into their hands, and thus more than made up for the number which had been lost by the battle to their ranks. Exulting in the successes which they had won, the red men closed their gates, displayed their *spolia opima* from the walls, and running to and fro along the parapets, brandished their arms with exultation, while the welkin rang with their wild shouts of triumph and defiance.

Goaded with fury by what they saw, the Spanish chivalry without the walls, organizing themselves, rapidly dashed forward to the gates with the view of assailing them, or, at least, for the purpose of covering the foot soldiers, who advanced with their axes for this purpose. But the brave Mauvilians—too valiant, eager and exulting to observe a becoming prudence—never suffered them to approach the gates, but leaping the walls in hundreds, resolutely took the field, exposing their naked bosoms fearlessly to the superior weapons of the Castilians. A desperate conflict ensued: the numbers and reckless valor of the red men proving quite a match for the superior civilization of their foes, while the struggle was confined to those who fought entirely on foot. Fierce, indeed, was the affray. Mercy was neither asked nor expected. The shafts of the savages answered to the lances of the Spaniards; the stone battle-axe and thundering macana did not recoil from the sharp collision with the polished blade of the Toledan. It was only when the cavaliers of Spain dashed in to the support of their comrades that the Mauvilians gave ground, and retreated to the cover of their fortress. Thither the mounted men pursued them, but were driven back by showers of stones and arrows from the walls and loop-holes of the town. As they wavered and recoiled, the Mauvilians again sallied forth, closing with the cavaliers, seizing on their very bridles, grasping their lances, tearing them from their hands, and clinging to the retiring horses until dragged away hundreds of paces from the walls. Such a conflict, valor so inflexible, afforded but small encouragement to the hopes of the invader, and De Soto groaned over the tardy progress of Moscoso, and the absence of more than half his little army.

In this manner had they fought, without decisive results—unless in favor of the Mauvilians—for three mortal hours, when Luis de

Moscoso made his appearance with the main body of the Spanish forces, and at once engaged in the *melée*. But with his appearance in the field, that of Philip de Vasconselos took place also.

For a moment let us pause in this place, to say that none of the relations of this great event, as given by the Spanish and Portuguese narrators, are to be entirely relied on. The history which the lion might give of his achievements has yet to be written. The accounts of the white men are grievously confused and contradictory, for the simple reason that they labored to obscure, to modify, and even to pervert the details whose results were so disastrous to their progress, and, as they fancied, in their national pride and vanity, so discreditable to their arms. Now, the reader will please to understand that our version of the story is drawn chiefly from the narratives of the Mauvilians themselves, as contained in the celebrated MSS. of the Great Iawa, or High Priest of Chickasah, Oolena Ithiopoholla, who wore the sacred symbols, somewhere about the year 1619, only about 70 years after this event. The narrative is written on the bark of trees, in the Choctaw character, and, bating some few injuries from exposure and time (which do not affect it in the portions relating to the battle of Mauvila), may still be read in the keeping of my excellent red friend Mico Tuskina Ithiopolla, a lineal descendant of the venerable Iawa, by whose hands it was written. Our account of the affair, which we modestly venture to assert is the only one deserving of perfect confidence, is drawn almost entirely from this ancient and veracious chronicle.

To resume from its pages :

" Now had the battle lasted three mortal hours, when another and a larger army of the Spaniards, under one of their great generals, by name Luis de Moscoso, made his appearance in the field. He had been closely watched and followed during the march from Tuscaloosa by the white chief, to whom had been given the name of Istalana, and of whose cruel treatment by the Spaniards, and happy escape, by the help of the great Princess Coçalla, of Cofachiqui, we have already related the account. Istalana (or 'the chief that broods') led a force of three thousand brave warriors of Tuscaloosa and Cofachiqui, full command over whom had been given him by the Great King. Now, so soon as Istalana beheld the warriors of Moscoso preparing to join with the troops under Soto, the Castilian, and to advance against the walls of Mauvila he set upon him suddenly, with a terrible assault from behind. Moscoso was greatly astonied at this assault, for he knew not that he was so closely watched and followed. But he turned upon Istalana and his men and made good fight for the victory; and he was joined by the men upon the horses of Soto, the Castilian, and great were the deeds of arms that followed, and many were the blows given and received, and glorious was the slaughter. The earth and sun drank great streams of blood that day; and, for that the warriors of Mauvila were too brave to need coverings for their breasts against the darts of their enemies, the slaughter fell most heavily upon them; while the Spaniards, being covered with scales of hard metal, or wrapped in many folds of a thick garment, which shook off the shafts of the Mauvila warriors when delivered from a distance, they suffered less grievously, and many were but hurt and wounded, when, but for reason of their armor of metal, they would have died outright. But the Mauvilians hurt and smote them sorely, and bruised them with many blows, so that none of them utterly escaped, while many were slain with shafts rightly delivered between the eyes, and, when they chanced to turn their backs, with arrows that drove through the body beneath the shoulders and rested against the metallic plates in front. Hundreds carried with them grievous wounds in the legs and thighs, which were less sheltered by armor; and wherever the warriors of Castile and Mauvila strove together hand to hand, the one with bright sword shining in the sun, the other with the heavy macana, or the thundering stone hatchet, then did the armor prove no help, but rather a hurt to the white warriors, and they fell crushed beneath the blows of Mauvila, and they fled before the might of her warriors. And great was the destruction of the strange beast which they call the horse, of whom the Spaniards took great account, and, for which reason, the warriors of Mauvila smote and slew them without sparing. Verily, they slew more than seventy of these giant beasts in the course of the day's fighting, sending the arrows right through their huge bodies, so that the feathers only lay hidden in the bowels of the beast.

"And when the warriors within the walls of Mauvila, who were commanded by the great king himself, beheld how that the Spaniards were set upon by the troops of Istalana from behind, then did he rise and cry aloud:

"'Now is the time for ye to go forth, ye warriors of Mauvila, and all the followers of the great king! Now send ye up the great shout of war which leads to victory, and get ye out from the fortress to the fight, while your women, and the young daughters of Mauvila gather upon the walls and cry to ye with words of love and welcome, and sing the while sweet songs of victory and vengeance! Now to your arms! and go forth and fight against the Spaniards from the walls, while Istalana, the white warrior, who is our general, deals death upon them from behind!'

"'And they went forth, even as he commanded, with a mighty whoop of victory, which shook the earth and struck terror to the hearts of the pale faces. And the Spaniards, who rode the mighty horses, rushed together, like a great hurricane, between the warriors of Mauvila, who came forth from the fortress, and the footsoldiers of the chief Moscoso. And they rushed over many of our people, and they trampled them under the iron hoofs of the mighty beasts; but the rest parted each way from before them, then closed behind them as they sped, delivering swift arrows that pierced the beasts to the bowels, and pierced the riders to the brain, so that they rolled together in sore agony, and with grevious cries upon the stricken earth. And even as the warriors of Mauvila sank down beneath their beasts, other braves darted hotly forth to take their places, and it gladdened the big heart of the great king that day, to behold with what a joy his braves died for his honor, and to save his country from the Spaniards. Verily, it is too much to tell; for they alone who saw could truly report what glorious deaths were that day given and received, and how the blood gushed from the big heart, and the brains of brave warriors were beaten out, and how the bowels of the mighty beasts fell down at the sharp passage of the lance and knife; for the cunning warriors of Mauvila, while they lay wounded beneath the horses, smote them suddenly under their great bellies. And then the beasts grew maddened, and they fled swiftly as the arrow flies, with a horrid scream, and grievous groans, the bowels trailing as they sped, until they could fly no more, and rolled over their riders, the chiefs in armor, whom they crushed beneath their own weight. And at every horse thus slain the women and the maidens upon the walls of Mauvila made a new song of rejoicing. And they sang—

"'Great is the Brave of the Mauvilian who hath slain the mighty beast of the pale faces.

"'He shall be named the Slayer of the Beast forever, and there shall be a totem for his bosom, with the picture of the beast.

"'And his name shall be sung forever by the maidens of Mauvila; and the warriors shall go ever into battle with a cry upon his name.

"'Verily, he shall pass the blue mountains upon the spirit of the beast that he hath slain. He shall hunt in the Happy Vallies on the body of the beast; and when he enters the lodge of the Great Master of Souls, then shall a voice welcome him with a cry, saying, make way there—give place all of ye, for hither comes the warrior that hath slain the Great Beast of the Pale Faces.'

"'Verily, as the Mauvilian hearkened to this song, great was the desire of many to become the slayer of the beasts which the Spanish warriors rode. Yet there were some who sought rather to take them captive; for wherefore should the warriors of Mauvila not bestride them, even as the Castilians? But the greater number preferred to slay them, for they knew not by what words to make the beasts know their masters, and they feared the danger from their heels, and they wist not how to guide them in their flight. So they slew them, whenever they could, save in few cases, when, as was the counsel of the chief Istalana, they caught them by their bridles after they had slain their riders, and led them off into the thickets.

"Now, Istalana, the white warrior, himself had one of these beasts, upon which he made to ride a strange boy who followed him in silence—a creature black as the great bear of Nolichucky. But, when the battle drew nigh, and when he was about to set upon the troops of Moscoso, he bade this black boy take shelter with the Princess Coçalla in the thicket, which was at hand, and where many harbored close unseen. And Istalana raised himself with a single bound upon the back of this beast; and he had strong thongs of bear skin with which to guide him; and a great chair of bear skin, with horns, but without feet, was beneath him, and upon the back of the beast. And Istalana armed himself with a long lance which he had made, thrice as great and heavy as that borne by our people. And he carried besides a great battle axe of metal which had been taken from the Spaniards. And, thus armed and mounted, he prepared to ride into the battle even as the Spaniards rode. But first, he put large bodies of our warriors in ambush, close in the woods, but beside the field of battle; and he bade them not show themselves until he gave them command to do so. And he led but one third of the Mauvilians into battle against Moscoso, being but a thousand men. And to these he gave command that they should greatly scatter themselves; that they should shelter themselves beneath the trees, wherever these stood, and thus escape the wrath of the mighty beasts, whom they were to transfix with their arrows. And he taught them truly, moreover, to aim their darts only at the faces and the thighs of the Spaniards, for 'Verily,' said he, 'What matters if you slay them not outright. Wound them only, so that they shall become disabled, and how easy then to run in and brain them with the hatchet of stone.' And, of a truth, had they followed this counsel of Istalana, then had not so many great warriors of Mauvila fallen on that day. But it was in the wildness of their valor, which suffered them to fear no danger, that so many of them yielded their naked life to the death shaft of the Spaniard.

"Now, it was even in the moment when the Spanish warriors who rode were trampling down the braves of Mauvila, striving to keep them back from the conflict which had begun between the troops of Istalana and Moscoso, that the chief Istalana appeared in front, mounted on one of the great beasts of the Spaniards. Verily, the beast was of a beautiful strength and majesty, and he had a name with his master, and he was called Bajardo. And when the Spaniards beheld the beast—though they knew nothing of the great chief Istalana, (for he was no longer of the pale sickly color of the white men, but had been made comely by the war paint of the Mauvilians, and he wore feathers of the birds of Mauvila and Apalachia, and a robe of saffron-cotton of our people, and upon his shoulders a rich robe of fur which the Great King had given him when he made him a chief,)—when, I say, the Spaniards beheld the beast, they said one to another, 'Is not that Bajardo, the horse which was ridden of old by the Blackamoor Juan, the Page of the knight of Portugal?' And they answered, 'Verily, it doth seem so. Yet hath he long been missing.'

"But they saw nothing of the Blackamoor, and they knew not the knight of Portugal, in the costume and the war paint of the Mauvilian. And the knight of Portugal, now the chief Istalana, rode forth towards the warriors of Spain, even to where was seen, making great show above the rest, the chief, Soto, of Castile, their general and great warrior. And Soto and his warriors marvelled much when they saw a red warrior of Mauvila so gallantly riding towards them; and they wondered more when they saw him shake out his lance in defiance, waving it towards Soto himself, and, in the manner of the pale warriors, thus seeming to bid him come to the conflict. And the captains and chiefs around Soto were angry, and they said, 'Let us go and punish this insolent savage;' but Soto said—

"'Nay! It is for me to punish his insolence!' And he rode forth alone, a little ahead of the rest; and, seeing this, Istalana said to the Mauvilians—

"'Get ye back all, and leave Soto, of Castile, to me. Only see that others come not between us. If I slay him, or ye see me overthrown, then fall fiercely upon the chiefs that follow him; and heed ever the things that I have told ye.'

"And the warriors of Mauvila fell back. And Istalana pre

pared himself for Soto, though he carried no weapon but the heavy lance, and the great axe of metal, such as the Spaniards bore. And he had no armor upon his limbs, and he wore no buckler upon his arm. And he went unafraid to the encounter with Soto, of Castile. And Soto came on briskly, with his lance couched for the encounter, and he little wist of the enemy who stood before him; and knew not but that it was a brave native warrior of Mauvila; for he saw that they were a people the most daring of all the world, who were willing to fight with any foe, and with any weapons, or according to any fashion. And knowing this, Soto said within himself—

"'Now, verily, these warriors of Mauvila have a world of impudence. Here is a savage that hath gotten him a beast which he knows not how to manage, yet would he undertake the warfare with me after my own fashion. Yet, in sooth, he keeps his seat with a tolerable grace and steadiness, and with proper teaching might be rendered a right comely and formidable cavalier. Yet shall I have to punish him with a death thrust, that I may rebuke the overweening presumption of his people.'

"And so thinking and speaking to himself, Soto, the Castilian, spurred his beast forward to the meeting with Istalana, who, nothing loth, or slow, made his beast go to meet him, with a great rushing. And the two leveled their long lances, and there was a great cloud that wrapt them; and lo, when the cloud lifted, there could be seen Soto, the cavalier, falling upon the ground, and Istalana wheeling his great beast backward, and making towards Soto, with his lance ready to do him to death with a thrust."

CHAPTER XLVII.

"Turn thou the mouth of thy artillery
Against these saucy walls."   KING JOHN.

WE have given a sufficient specimen of our Choctaw chronicler for a while. Relying on his authority as heretofore, we shall yet forego the stately simplicity, and the quaint solemnity of his style, as far as possible in the future, and trust to that which is more natural to ourselves and readers. We need repeat, after this sample of our authority, that his account is the most trustworthy of all the parties; and our materials will show that he supplies a thousand deficiencies, in the details, which the vexed vanity of the Spanish invaders would never allow them to put on record. We proceed now to our history.

The fall of De Soto occasioned naturally a tremendous sensation. The wild exultation of the red men rang throughout the field as for a victory already gained, and a most unexpected triumph rendered certain. The Adelantado of the Spaniards was considered by the simple natives in the light somewhat of a god man—a demi-god, who was in some degree invincible, or like Achilles, only vulnerable in some small region not easily reached by dart or tomahawk. They were now disabused of this superstition, and their spirits rose in consequence to the highest pitch of hope and enthusiasm. They knew not but that he was already slain; at least, he was in the power of their champion; that seemed certain, and a single stroke of the terrible lance which Vasconselos carried was alone needed for the *coup de grace*. Istalana, now doubly glorious, and a favorite in their eyes, seemed prepared to satisfy their expectations. Wheeling about to return to the charge, his lance was couched, and the vulture, commissioned by the fates for his destruction, already threatened De Soto with the consummation of his doom.

But the Spanish chivalry were not prepared to suffer the conqueror to complete his work of vengeance. They had seen the fall of their governor; and, with a mixed howl and shout, the gallant cavaliers who had attended him, and who had only remained a short distance from the scene of the passage between himself and Istalana, now dashed forward to his rescue. They were just in season. Our Portuguese Mauvilian was already upon his enemy. De Soto who had succeeded in recovering his feet, had drawn his sword, and was ready to defend himself.

"Hernan de Soto," cried Vasconselos, to the complete astonishment of his opponent, "thy hour is come! The doom for thee is written! Thou shalt die beneath the hand and curse of the man thou hast basely dishonored!"

He knew the voice. He could no longer doubt the person.

"Philip de Vasconselos!"

"Ay! and thy fate! Prepare thee!"

"I fear thee not, renegade and traitor!"

"Ha! thou shalt feel me!"

And the lance was couched at his breast. De Soto raised his sword in defence. Philip would have sprung from his steed and encountered him on more equal footing with the battle-axe, but just then the rush behind him required him to guard himself. The Spanish knights were upon him. There were Nuno de Tobar, and Balthazar de Gallegos, and many others. Philip gave the rowels to Bajardo. He dashed through the thick array. Gonzalo de Sylvestre was rolled over upon the earth; Alonzo de Piños was reached by the lance which failed to slay him, but knocked out several of his front teeth, and greatly disfiguring his mouth, spoiled the prettiest face in the army. Others were handled only less roughly, and thundering through them as the great buffalo thunders through a forest of prairie dogs, the wonderful cavalier of the red men broke away from the network of foes which for a moment seemed to threaten him with captivity or death. His forest followers were not idle. The warriors of Mauvila launched themselves, with desperate valor, into the thickest of the wild array, and the battle, with all its terrors, was resumed on every side.

It raged with no abatement for more than an hour, and with no seeming change of fortune. Many of the Spaniards perished; many of their horses. Hardly one escaped without wounds; but the naked red men suffered death, and not wounds, with every hurt. More than a thousand had perished in the strife, when Istalana, whose plans had been wholly baffled by the impatient pride and haughty valor of Tuscaluza and his general, succeeded in drawing off a portion of his forces to the shelter of the forest, into recesses where the horses could not pursue, and whence the arrow could be shot with unerring and unexpected aim. The red men disappeared almost in the twinkling of eye, leaving the field strewn with their bodies.

Coçalla was the first to receive Vasconselos. But where was Juan? Philip looked about him with inquiry. The page was behind him carrying bow and arrows, and was covered with the dust and blood of the field.

"Ah! boy; and I bade thee not?" said Vasconselos reproachfully.

"I saw them as they surrounded thee, Señor, and I could no longer remain away."

Philip smiled sadly on the Moor. But when he looked a second time on Coçalla, he beheld that she too had had shared the dangers of the fray. She had been more fortunate than Juan, and had been wounded in the arm. Oh! what were the pangs of that young attendant when he beheld Vasconselos take the beautiful arm of Coçalla into his hands and carefully help to bind up the still bleeding limb. The hurt was fortunately slight. But it was a wound received in his defence; and, more fortunate still, it was an arrow from her bow that stuck in the thigh of De Soto himself, giving a painful wound, which would have driven from the field that day any cavalier of merely ordinary courage. Vasconselos had seen, before the action was over, that De Soto was hurt. He saw it by his riding, though he knew not the nature of the wound. Little did he dream what hand had sent the shaft. When he did know, when he conceived fully that page and princess had both gone forth to his rescue the moment that they beheld his peril, the heart of the melancholy knight was very full. No tears gathered in his eyes. He had forgotten how to weep; but never did eyes declare such tender emotions; and he looked from Juan to Coçalla, and he took the hand of the princess and kissed it, while he drew the trembling Moor to his bosom, and said to him fondly—

"Boy, thou shalt evermore be brother to me. I have no other brother now but thee."

Andres de Vasconselos had been one of the cavaliers whose ranks that day he had so fiercely broken through. But he had raised no lance against that young kinsman's bosom.

Juan trembled with terrible emotions as, for the first time, he was strained so warmly to the breast of his lord. He felt that the heart within him was like a molten sea—all fire, all tears, scalding and streaming, but ready all the while to break through all barriers and be poured out like water on the sands. But the tenderness was for a moment only, and even while the knight strained the Moorish page to his bosom, the Princess Coçalla interposed, and laid her hand first, and then her head upon his shoulder, and said in the most melting manner—

"Ah! Philip! Ah! brave Philip."

But, just then, Juan cried out with a change of feeling :—

"Oh! Señor, thou art wounded."

The red stain was apparent through the white cotton of his vest. The garments were sticking to the wound upon his bosom.

"Let it remain," said Philip, as page and princess, now both excited with fear, proposed to attend the hurt.

"Let it remain. It is nothing, and now bleeds no longer."

It was but a flesh-wound made by the partly spent shaft from a cross-bow. He had pulled out the arrow during the fight, and, pressing the garments upon the wound, had succeeded in stopping the flow of blood. There was no time now for surgery. The Spaniards had renewed the action, and Istalana was required to go forth again.

Furious with the sanguinary courage of the Mauvilians, conscious of the peril which awaited his own and the fortunes of his army, and mortified deeply with the disgrace of his overthrow in the sight of foes and followers, Hernan de Soto only delayed the action long enough to enable his followers to recover from exhaustion. It was necessary to obtain possession of the town. There his people would find shelter and provisions, both of which they began to need. There had the red men stored their supplies for the winter. Several of the houses were great granaries of maize, beans, and potatoes. There, too, were their great armories—arrows, arrow-bolts, and macanas, darts, and stone hatchets. To possess himself of these, was to supply his own soldiers, and greatly to impoverish and enfeeble the red men. There, too, exulting in his savage pride and power, was the hateful and insolent Tuscaluza, the only cassique among the native princes who had ever shown himself really formidable to the Spaniards in Apalachia, up to the present moment. All his passions and all his reflections conspired to goad him to the most desperate efforts to make his way into the fortress of Mauvila. To remain without, exposed to the perpetual assaults of thousands of enemies, springing up in the twinkling of an eye, and melting away as suddenly into their great forest shelters, was a prospect that threatened nothing short of ruin.

But it was necessary to plan the attack upon the fortress with a due regard to the thousands who guarded it, and of the other thousands who swarmed throughout the forests in his rear. The latter, too, were led by one who knew equally well what was proper to the warfare of the red men and the Spaniards. Bitter and savage were the moods which possessed De Soto as he thought of Philip de Vasconselos.

"And I have fallen beneath his lance this day; and, but for my followers, I had been slain by the very man whom I had doomed to dishonor and left to death!"

His gloomy musings were interrupted by the entrance of several of his cavaliers, Nuno de Tobar and Andres de Vasconselos among them. He was about to declare the secret which he alone possessed, that of the identity of the red warrior Istalana with the outlawed knight of Portugal. But the sight of Andres, and the recollections of the old affectionate intimacy between Tobar and Philip, led him to a prudent secrecy.

"No!" said he to himself. "Not yet! Let them once know that Philip lives, and that this is he—remembering too that he hath been wrongly doomed—and will they strive so bravely against him? will they not, rather this brother of his, strive in his behalf? May he not go over to him? May he not carry others? In the moment of disaster, who clings to an old leader? What numbers will gladly seize the moment to pass into the embraces of the successful party? And know we not that many have sought occasion to drop away upon the march, and wiving with these savage women to grow to power among the tribes? No! no! I must hush and hide this damnable discovery close in the heart, where it only works to torture."

Such were the brief, hurried, and natural, but unspoken thoughts which occurred to the Adelantado, when he beheld his knights enter to receive their orders. De Soto could not throw off the savage gloom that possessed his soul and filled his countenance, but he gave it an expression of swift ferocity.

"Well, señors, you are ready. It is time. Let us now to work, with all our soul and strength, to scourge these savages to the uttermost. Before the sun shall set this day, we must be in in possession of yonder fortress. If we fail, our day has ended! Do you heed me, all? While this sun lasts we must conquer yon town, and hold it in possession. Yonder forests,"—and he shuddered as he pointed to them—"harbor ten thousand enemies, hateful and hating us, without pity or affection; with numbers destined to hourly increase, pouring in ever as the vultures throng about the carcass. Let us go forth."

They were soon in full array, and in the field. De Soto had already matured his plans. He had detailed the greater and better portion of his cavaliers for the defence of his rear, while a chosen body assailed the fortress. The horsemen were particularly reserved, the better to avoid the shafts shot securely from the walls. They were appointed to that better service upon the plain in which the steed can exercise the chief faculty, that of fleetness, which confers upon him his peculiar uses in war.

The battle was resumed. Tuscaluza and his warriors prepared for the Spaniards along the walls. Istalana led forth his troops from the forest, and against their rear. He was encountered by the picked chivalry of De Soto which, in separate bodies of ten men each, occupied the plain in their front, and, cased in armor—all the vital parts protected except the eyes—offered but small marks for the archery of the red men, while in their successive charges they swept down hundreds. The horse was more vulnerable, however, though some pains had been taken to protect him in the more exposed and sensitive regions of his body. Istalana, or, as we shall henceforth prefer to call him, Vasconselos, aimed at two objects—to bring his troops, only as archers, into full play, and at the same time to cover them as much as possible with the trees of the forest from the sweeping charges of the horsemen. But, if he kept the cover of the forest wholly, he failed to reach the cavalry with his arrows, the plain being of such extent; and not to drive them from it, was to leave the garrison without succor, or diversion, to endure the whole weight of De Soto's assault. He accordingly prepared to throw a body of five hundred active warriors, good with spear and battle axe, between the detachment of cavalry in front of him and the forces with which De Soto assailed the walls, while the rest of his troops, covered as much as possible by the forest, kept the horse in full employment with their arrows. He, himself, on foot, prepared to lead his spear-men into the thickest of the fight, and between the two divisions of the Spanish army.

"And now," saith our old Choctaw chronicler, "the glorious fight began once more, with a shock as of many thunderbolts. And Soto, of Castile, led his great men close up against the walls of Mauvila; and the great king confronted him there with a terrible flight of arrows; and with heavy stones he drove him back from the fortress. And when Soto, of Castile, was thus driven back, he fell upon the warriors of the great chief Istalana, and very terrible was the battle that ensued between these mighty men of war. But, though many of the Spaniards were slain and more hurt, yet, by reason of the armor of tough metal which they wore, many escaped, who else had been done to death, by the valiant strokes of Istalana and his spearmen. These, on the other hand, being all men of naked valor, were sore stricken by the Spanish bolts and darts; and the wise chieftain, **Istalana**, when that he beheld how the battle went against his people, he drew them cunningly away from between the ranks of the Spaniards, and gave them shelter for a season among the great trees of the forest. And De Soto, of Castile, again strove with the great king against the walls of Mauvila, and his axe-men toiled to cut though the walls, and to beat down the gates of the fortress; and a second time were they driven back, sorely smitten, because of the heavy stones delivered from the fortress. And again did the brave Istalana give battle to the retreating Spaniards, and to those who fought from the backs of the mighty beasts. And the battle went now one way, and now the other, and, for a season, neither party prevailed in the conflict. But great was the loss, and grievous the blows of blood which were delivered on both sides among the champions. And, among the people of Mauvila, there was great slaughter. Many cassiques of fame perished in valiant agonies, crying to the gods to open the blue mansions in the happy valley, and to send for them the bright maidens, each bearing a cheering bowl to quench the thirst of the wearied spirit. The mighty Oolenoe Ifisto was the first to fall, having slain many foes. Then Chinabee Himantla gave up the ghost, wearing more than thirty scalp locks upon arm and thigh; and there were many more, brave like these, who sang that day the song of the last fight. And many other great chiefs were stricken and hurt in the fighting of this day. Istalana, the great chief himself, was stricken twice, but he said nothing of his hurts, while he gave death to other men to drink, sorely against the will of him who hath no thirst.

"But it was not only to the chiefs of Mauvila that the hurts and the death were given. The Great Chief of the Spaniards, Soto of Castile, felt the sharp arrows in his thigh and side; but he was not slain. The lying prophet of the pale faces was scored with a flying shaft, like a coward, in the back. But he lived, that men might say, this is the mark of one who fled. And there was a goodly youth, a kinsman of Soto, of Castile, one whom they call Carlos, whose throat the arrow filled, so that he never called for drink again. And many were the warriors and chiefs besides, for whom they made bitter moaning that night in the camp of the Spaniards.

"But the truth demands that I declare, that, on the third assault upon the walls of Mauvila, the warriors of Soto, of Castile, prevailed. And they prevailed by reason of the fact, that the Great King was hurt with a lance that entered his bosom even where he strove with a great warrior at the gate of the fortress. And when the warriors of Mauvila beheld the Great King fall, they sent up a mighty cry. And the women, with foolish tongues spread it along the walls and through the town, that the **Great King** was slain, even Tuscaluza; but, of a truth, it was not so. Grievous was his hurt, and glorious, since it was made upon his open breast, in full front, and even in the moment when, with his mighty stone-hatchet, he clove the brain of a great warrior of the Spaniards. But, nevertheless, men thought him slain; and when his people bore him away from the gate to a place of safety without the walls, and into the forests on the other side—as was counselled by the prophet—then the women lamented, and the foolish warriors broke their weapons and fled from the walls which they were bade to defend, and went hither and thither, not knowing what to do; and, by reason of this folly, the followers of Soto, of Castile, broke their way through the walls, and beat down the gates, and their great captains, on their mighty beasts, rode headlong through the streets of Mauvila, smiting as they went. Then was it too late, when our warriors hastily caught up their arms, and renewed the fight.

"And the women of Mauvila strove, too, in the ranks of battle, and very great and glorious was the slaughter. But the Spaniards prevailed in battle against our people, and when this was beheld by the brave women of Mauvila, they seized bright torches of the living flame. And they gave it wings; and they sent it from housetop to housetop; and they hid it away in the hearts of the houses. And where they had their husbands slain, they flung themselves into the burning houses, and they welcomed the coming of the Spaniards with arms of flame, waving them on, as they passed over the walls and through the gates with songs of triumph and defiance. It was a day of rich blood. And the people of Mauvila left for the Spaniards only a feast of famine, and music of agony and groans, with a raging fire to quench the thirst which they knew, from eating at such a banquet. The brave Tuscaluza, the son of the Great King, was slain; but the Great King himself was made safe in the big forests lying toward Chickasah. Thither came also the mighty chief Istalana, who had grevious hurts upon his breast, upon his face, upon his arms and side. Sorely was he stricken; and they brought him upon the shoulders of the Tamenes toward Chickasah, and the princess Coçalla, of Cofachiqui, tended him, while he lay hurt, and the strange black page, Juan, watched beside him nightly when he slept."

CHAPTER XLVIII.

*"He bears
A tempest which his mortal vessel tears."*

PERICLES.

SUCH was the terrible battle of Mauvila. The Spaniards had obtained the victory. They had won the chief fortified city of the Mauvilians. They had expelled the inhabitants or destroyed them. Thousands of the redmen had perished—not so many, by thousands, as the conquerors claim to have destroyed, but still the havoc had been terrible, and the victims were five times as numerous as the whole army of De Soto. The rash valor of the Mauvilians, their naked bosoms, the superiority of the Spanish arms and armor, had naturally rendered the defeat a massacre!

But the triumph of the invaders was dashed by their own terrible losses, and De Soto lamented his victory in the language of Pyrrhus. Nay, it did not require such another victory to leave the Castilian conqueror undone. He was already undone, and he felt it. The gloom of despair was on his soul. His face wore a perpetual scowl. His language was harsh to all when he spoke. He was no longer the confident, frank, impulsive cavalier, who could sweetly smile upon his friends, and who bore in his bosom an exulting hope and consciousness of desert, which filled all who beheld with unvarying auguries of success. He was now stern, savage, suspicious; distrustful of friends and fortune; with the mortifying conviction that he had not only failed, in the great hopes which had inspired his enterprise, but doomed to other failures, involving fame as well as fortune; perilous to life as to success. He thought of the noble woman, his wife, left behind him in the Government of Cuba, and bitterly remembered that between her and himself rolled the great sea, and between that sea and his warriors, spread hundreds of miles of impenetrable forest, every thicket of which harbored its hosts of implacable and sleepless enemies.

And as the details of his real condition met his ear, the gloom grew deeper upon his visage and within his soul. Very wretched was the condition of the Spaniards after the battle of Mauvila. More than two hundred of them had been slain or put *hors de combat*. Scarcely a man had escaped entirely unhurt. De Soto himself was thrice wounded, and though not, in either instance, severely, yet the hurts were of a sort to goad, to mortify his passions, and to vex his pride. We have seen, what were his personal humiliations also. But he was not allowed to brood on them. The condition of his army demanded all his thoughts. His soldiers, covered with wounds, were attended by a single surgeon, and he was at once slow and unskilful. There was neither lint, nor linen, nor liniments; neither medicines nor bandages; neither ointments nor instruments; not even clothing and shelter. The fires of the wild Mauvilians had consumed all the stores of commissary and surgeon—all the food and physic— all that was needful for the healthy, no less than the suffering and sick. The dwellings were all consumed, and but a poor shelter was found in the miserable tents of boughs and branches, which could be raised by the feeble efforts of the least wounded among the Spaniards. For bandaging wounds, they tore the shirts from their backs; to procure unguents for the hurt, the slain Indians were torn open, and the fat taken from their bodies; the slain horses were cut up and their flesh preserved, for sustenance for all. Even their devotions were interrupted, in the loss of the wine and wheaten flour which they had used in the performance of the mass; and to the superstitious, the question became one of serious importance, whether bread of Indian meal might be employed for the sacrament,—a question gravely discussed among them, and terminating in the unfavorable resolve, that it was not tolerated by the canons of the church. When to the real physical miseries of their situation, we add those of their spiritual hunger, we may conjecture the terrible gloom which overspread the encampment of the Spaniards.

This gloom of his followers was naturally of deeper and darker complexion in the soul of De Soto, than it was among his people. His had been the loftiest ambition, the most exulting hope. His pride, and station, and responsibility, were greater than all the rest. He was proportionately overwhelmed in the common catastrophe. He was utterly unmanned by his reverses. Not that he was unwilling to fight and peril himself as before; but that he was no longer able to control his passions, and hide his infirmities, and develop the strength and resources of his genius. moody irritable and savage, he was now purposeless in his aim, and utterly hopeless of favorable events in his future progress. He had no longer the heart for enterprise, or the spirit for adventure; and, for eight days, he lay in his rude and inadequate encampment, among the ruins of Mauvila, like a wounded tiger, licking his wounds in his jungle. Meanwhile, the wounded suf fered, or recovered, died or lived; without seeming to arouse his active sensibilities. The army, under his gallant cavaliers, began slowly to repair its hurts, and to recover, after a fashion, from its maims and bruises. But it was the skeleton only of its former strength, and symmetry and beauty. The despondency of their chief oppressed the spirits of all. Hope had deserted them, and they now only sighed for the opportunity to return to those distant homes which few of them were ever destined to behold again.

It was while they lay thus, and suffered, in the town of the Mauvilians,—groaning with their hurts, and dreading every moment that the red men would surround, and compel them to resume the struggle to which they felt themselves so unequal, that they received intelligence which was calculated to cheer them with the hope of escape from the perilous meshes in which their enterprise had involved them. Tidings reached them, unexpectedly, of the arrival, at Achuzi (now Pensacola) of certain ships from Cuba, under the command of Gomez Arias and Diego Maldonado. The moment this news was received, both officers and men began to calculate the distance between Mauvila and Achuzi. It was—according to their eager estimate—but eight days journey to the sea coast; and all hearts began to cheer themselves with the hope of soon reaching the ships, the succor of their comrades, and finally the pleasant country which all now were prepared to regret that they had so idly left. No one thought to remain in a region which yielded them no golden cities, and the people of which betrayed such implacable hostility, such indomitable courage, and such sanguinary fierceness of character. They discussed the matter among themselves. They encouraged each other with their new born hopes of escape from a country, in which they beheld nothing but sleepless and bloody enemies—in which they could now anticipate nothing but disaster and a gloomy fate for all. These resolves and desires were freely spoken. They were not confined to the common soldiers; and De Soto, by accident, overheard one of these discussions, in which the same opinions and wishes were expressed by his favorite cavaliers.

From that moment, his resolve was taken. *He* could not return a vagabond to Cuba. He who had gone forth in such state and splendor, could not crawl back in the sight of his people, a maimed and stricken fugitive. He must first conquer. He must win the spoils he sought. He must carry back the proofs and the trophies of the golden cities which he had promised. He still had faith in the hidden treasures of the Apalachian. He still looked to the conquest of a semi-civilized people, such as those of Mexico and Peru, the overthrow and dominion of whom would crown the close of his life with glory, and redeem and repair the hurts of character and credit which had confessedly accrued from his enterprise, up to the present moment. He resolved to confound his cowardly followers, and to baffle all their imbecile calculations. He determined that they *should* share his fortunes, in spite of all their fears. He did not suffer them to know that he was aware of their secret hopes. He simply gave his orders—to turn their backs upon his shipping, and go forward, deeper, deeper, into the wild abodes of the savage Apalachian.

His cavaliers, as soon as they heard these orders, boldly undertook to expostulate with him upon them. They spoke of the sea, of the shipping at Achuzi, of their hopes and homes in Cuba.

"Tell me not of sea, or ships, or Cuba!" was the angry reply of the Adelantado. "I will see neither, until I have conquered these savage Apalachians, and won possession of their great cities."

They would still have expostulated. "There were no great cities" was the answer. "These people are mere savages. Our people despond. They have not the heart for further adventure. Their hearts are set only on returning to the sea coast, and availing themselves of the shipping, of once more reaching Cuba. They are already discontent with the delay. They will mutiny—."

"Ha! mutiny! Tell you this to me? Then get ye ready your executioner, and prepare to do as I require, for by the Holy Cross, so long as I breathe, the Vice-Gerent here of our Royal Master, I will put to sharp justice the soldier who shall only dare to murmur. Away, Sir Knights, and let me hear no more of this."

"The habitual exercise of authority had imparted to De Soto a power of command, which was admirably seconded by a submission as habitual, as well among his cavaliers, as common soldiers. The obedience of the one, necessarily enforced that of the other. The army was put under marching orders, and, with weary footsteps and desponding hearts, the remnant of the army took its way into the great solitudes once more.

But the one purpose of progress, in De Soto's mind, was undirected by that aim and design which constitute the first true essentials of successful adventure on the part of the soldier. Disappointed hitherto in the results which followed his several enterprises, he knew not now whither to direct his footsteps,

From this moment, his only labor seemed to be to increase the distance between his people and the sea. Haunted by the dread of their desertion, he simply hurried forward, on a route that perpetually changed its direction, now east, now west, hither and thither, but always to no purpose. He knew not, nor seemed to care to know, whither he sped. Stern, silent, irritable, he scorned counsel and forbade expostulation. He wandered thus, in weary pilgrimage, day by day, passing from forest to forest, from village to village, fighting wherever the red men crossed his path—which they did perpetually—and fighting always without an object. One is forced to think, seeing how erratic was his progress, and how recklessly he incurred all perils, that his real purpose was to end a struggle which brought him vexation only, and a life which, his pride taught him, was dishonored by the defeat of all his expectations.

While our Spaniards were recreating themselves in Mauvila, what of the people of the Great King, Tuscaluza? what of the Portuguese Knight, whom we now know as Istalana, the immediate confidant of the Mauvilian Cassique, sorely wounded in the final battle with the Spaniards. Both of these chiefs were seasonably borne away by their red followers to a place of safety in the contiguous forests. As these proceedings were all transacted with the greatest secrecy, by a people practised in the utmost subtleties of savage warfare, as cunning as the serpent, and as stealthy as the cat, the Spaniards never dreamed of the vast numbers, that, more or less hurt, were carried safely from the melee; and the still greater numbers, who escaped when the conflict went too decidedly against them. The Mauvilians had lost probably three thousand warriors, and a few score of women had perished also fighting in their ranks; but a numerous army still remained to the Great King, even of those engaged at Mauvila; while others daily poured into his assistance, led by the Cassiques of tributary provinces. Had he or Istalana been able to take the field, the Spaniards had never been suffered to rest a moment in Mauvila; had never been permitted time to repair their disasters and to recruit themselves for a fresh campaign. Had their quarters been beat up daily and nightly with incessant alarm; had their foragers been cut off whenever they went forth; it is probable, that the eight days of rest at Mauvila, would have been so many days of struggle and starvation, ending in their utter annihilation. They were then in no condition to fight, and as little to endure.

But, in the wounds and incapacity of their great leaders, the red men did not dare to venture upon the enterprise for themselves. They were content to gather and prepare themselves; to provide a new armory; to lay in supplies of provisions; to guard their wounded monarch; and watch closely all the movements of the Spaniards. Tuscaluza had been severely hurt, but the red men, rarely outraging nature with the too frequently impertinent pretensions of art, were good nurses, and not bad surgeons, in that day, when they did not feel their own deficiencies and had not learned to succumb to the genius of the white man. They had considerable knowledge of pharmacy, and dealing with green wounds, which were not necessarily mortal, they were singularly successful. The conquering people have borrowed many good lessons, and much knowledge, from their skill in medicine.

Of course, Istalana shared with the Great King, in the best attentions of his people. Nay, he had probably even better attendance, for was not Coçalla his nurse, and was not Juan nigh, jealous of her cares, and watchful of every opportunity to interpose his own? Vasconselos had suffered from several wounds. He had been brought from the field in a state of utter insensibility. Borne on a litter through the forests to a place of safety, remote from the scene of action, he had undergone a long struggle with the mortal enemy of life. Youth, great vigor of constitution, fond and sleepless cares, and a loving solicitude that neglected nothing; to those he owed his recovery. During all his sufferings, through a long insensibility, fever and delirium, Coçalla never slept. Ah! the devotedness of the loving heart— the loving woman! How it galled the soul of Juan to see her officious tenderness, when he could not interpose—when he dared not. How it angered him, when Coçalla bound the fever balm to the forehead of the unconscious Knight—when she bathed his hands and arms in cooling waters; when she applied the bruised herbs to his wounded side and bosom, when she poured the cooling beverages into his burning lips, when she sate by him, and lifted his head upon her arms, and against her bosom, and murmured softly in his ears, her fond, exulting consciousness—" oh! Philip! *my* Philip."

Then would the page chafe with vexation. He betrayed his anger. He was rude to Coçalla. He complained even of her officious zeal, and sleepless attendance.

And Coçalla pleaded with him as if she had been no princess. She knew that the boy loved the cavalier, and for this she forgave him all his offences. It was quite enough with her, that the rude boy was devoted to his master. That, she saw. She was not anxious to see further. But she said to Juan, one day when he was absolutely insolent?

"Why does the page of Philip grow angry? Doth he not love his master? And loving Philip, doth he not see that Coçalla loves him too, and because she loves him, that she watches him, and tends him, and dresses his wounds, and makes his couch of suffering soft and easy? What would Juan desire but to make well and happy his master? would he have Coçalla to hate Philip? Coçalla will not hate Philip! Coçalla loves Philip with her whole heart. She loves nothing, nobody, so well as Philip."

But this was precisely what Juan did not desire. But, to this, what could he answer? He could only turn away, and conceal his tears, and curse his fate, that suffered other hands and other cares than his own, to nurse and tend, and minister to the being whom he so much loved, with a like love also. Verily, great were the tortures of the page, during that long trial, while Vasconselos lay wounded and insensible upon the fringed couch of the beautiful princess, and so long as she alone had power to watch beside him.

But gradually both Tuscaluza and Istalana grew better from their hurts, and the eyes of the Portuguese Knight opened to a knowledge of his friends; and he took the hand of Coçalla within his own,—and the hand of Juan too; as they stood on opposite sides of the couch; and he kissed the hand of Coçalla; while the princess laughed merrily with joy, and kissed his forehead in return. But as for Juan, he could only turn away, and weep. The joy of the princess was the sorrow of the page.

CHAPTER XLIX.

"Set we forward :—
Never was a war did cease,
Ere bloody hands were washed."
CYMBELINE.

THE warriors of the Apalachian had been set in motion, by the impatient Tuscaluza, before Vasconselos was able to take the field. His pride made him impatient. Advised of every step in the progress of the Spaniards, he had commanded that their steps should be followed; and, taking counsel, for awhile, from Istalana, he had pursued a cautious policy, which studiously forebore risking anything on a general battle. His present chief warrior was Chicaza, who controlled an immense district of country, and could bring at least five thousand warriors into the field. The progress of De Soto had now brought him into the territories of this Chief. To him, Tuscaluza — preparing himself to take the field — had sent instructions to harass the Spaniards, cut off detachments and supplies, whenever occasion offered, but, on no account, to engage in general action. It was the fortune of the Great King to Apalachia, to possess great Captains, who, like the ambitious Chiefs among more civilized nations, have too much self-esteem to hearken to the words of counsel, or even to obey the commands of their superiors always. Chicaza ventured battle with the enemy, and was defeated. But not till a dreadful massacre had taken place, as terribly murderous to the red men as that of Mauvila, and quite as fatal to the Spaniards.

De Soto had possessed himself of the village of Chicaza. The first act of the fierce Cassique was the destruction of his own town. He decreed it to the flames. It was a bitter cold night in February, the north wind blowing wildly, and dark clouds scudding across the sky, when the Cassique led his forces, in three separate bodies, to the attack. The Spaniards knew not of their danger, till the dwellings, in which they had sheltered themselves, were all in flames. Scouts and sentinels, officers and men, had been alike neglectful of duty. The red men stole into an unwatched camp. They gave no alarm, until they had laid their inflammable torches beneath the cottages, and until their shafts, tipped with lighted matches, had swept to the straw-roofed lodges, and fastened themselves inextricably among the reeds. Then did the war-whoop sound the signal for assault; then did the wild conchs deliver their mournful blasts, and the wooden drums, and rattles of the Chicazas resound fearfully about the beleaguered habitations. Then did the red men, three thousand in number, rush to the battle, surrounding the village on every side, and dealing their effectual arrows whenever the Spaniards sallied forth.

We must not enter into the details of this battle. We can only give results. The red men were beaten,—that is, they were driven off, for shelter, to their thickets, and several hundred of them were slain. But the victory, like that of Mauvila, was one over which the Spaniards could only groan, not exult! Fifty of their soldiers had been slain, with several hidalgos among them; as many horses had perished also, and a like number were more or less hurt. At one time, but for Nuno de Tobar and Andres de Vasconselos, the Spaniards must have been utterly destroyed. An entire company fled in panic from the scene of action, and were brought back by Tobar. The Portuguese captain and his veterans, in fact, were the true saviors of the army. When the morrow's sun shone upon the work, the hot tears, spite of himself, gushed forth from the eyes of the haughty Adelantado, who felt, with the onward progress of each day, how nearer he approached the complete annihilation of all his hopes. His gloom and vexation of spirit increased the gulph between himself and his followers. He had for them no words of patience. He was guilty of daily injustice. He mortified their pride by his haughty disregard to their sufferings and wishes; he discouraged their sympathies, by the rejection of all communion with them. His best officers, among them Nuno de Tobar and Andres de Vasconselos, approached him with entreaty and exhortation. But the presence of the latter—of both in fact—only reminded him painfully of one, to whom he ascribed the ruin of his fortunes. Though he named not Philip de Vasconselos to either—though, in their ignorance of what he knew, he offered them no clues to the secret origin of his own agonies, he yet replied to them with a bitterness that seemed to take for granted their perfect knowledge of his secret.

"Oh, ye do well to exhort and to entreat, and counsel. Why do ye not go further? Why not command. Ye know not the presence of this fiendish fate that pursues our steps. Ye know not the damnable presence that haunts our fortunes with daily terrors. Yet ye wear his aspect. Ye are innocent forsooth;

Yet why do ye go with him in your hearts, that ye may the better pluck down ruin on my head."

"What means his Excellency," demanded the confounded Nuno de Tobar. The scowling eyes of De Soto were set upon Andres de Vasconselos. The latter proudly answered, and with a calm cold sternness of manner, which made the resemblance between himself and brother much more evident than ever.

"I know not what your Excellency designs to say, for a truth all that you have spoken sounds strange and unmeaning in mine ears; but if their be any purpose to charge aught of our disasters upon my neglect of duty or want of loyalty, then do I demand that you name my accuser, and my sword shall answer to his falsehood."

"Even thus he spoke! Thus he looked! Thus he defied me ever!" cried De Soto, his memory still retaining full recollection of the reserve and self-esteem which in the case of Philip de Vasconselos had always offended the *amour propre* of the Castilian.

"Of whom speaks the Adelantado?" demanded Tobar.

"Of whom! Jesu! one would think you had slept, without hearing the cries of war, without feeling the shock of battle, without scathing in the scorching flames that swept over us by night, during the last thirty days of strife and honor."

Such was the sudden burst of seeming astonishment, with which the adelantado replied to his lieutenant. He continued, ardently and wildly—

"Of whom should I speak, but of that insolent Fate which has dogged our steps from Chiala, and which hangs over us with ruin. Oh! ye know not. Ye are blind. Ye will remain blind until the knife is at your throats, and there is no means left ye for escape. Hark ye! Ye have seen De Soto overthrown, for the first time overthrown, in single combat; man opposed to man, lance to lance steed to steed. And ye have seen all this achieved by a naked savage of the Apalachian! No mail upon his breast, no helmet upon his brow, no crest upon gleaming shield, declaring his deeds in war. Yet he had a name. Once he had crest and shield, and cuirass. Ha! Ha! A red savage! and ye thought it was a mere savage, a naked Apalachian of the hills, whose lance could foil that of Hernan De Soto, whose charge and thrust could roll the Castilian warrior into the dust. Oh! blind! Hark ye! It was no red man no Apalachian, though wearing his semblance. It was this accursed Fate, I tell you, that pursues us now, that will still pursue us, that will feed upon us all, even as the vulture and the wolf glean among our bones bleaching in the wilderness. But I will not fall in vain! There will be a bloody issue yet. His crest against mine, and so help me, Blessed Jesu, as I shall yet plant a fatal stroke of the battle-axe between his accursed eyes—that Fate of mine! He shall not overthrow me quite. In my fall, ye shall behold his also! ay, ay! but a little while. But a few days now—so gentlemen, get ye ready for march, away."

The officers stared aghast. The mind of De Soto was evidently affected. His brain was wild and fevered; and such for several days continued to be the mood which prevailed with him, and the manner of his speech. But his inflexible will was still active and commanding, and sufficed for authority. He drove his reduced regiments still forward, after a very brief delay, spent in repairing swords and armor, and giving rest to the wounded. But dreadful were the sufferings of the troops. The winter was very cold, and, dreading the torches of the red men, they could no longer venture to occupy the villages.

Tuscaluza and Istalana were now both in the field once more, and the authority of the latter prevailed with the Great King. The redmen were no longer so confident of their prowess as to risk a general action. They contented themselves with guerilla warfare. They hung upon the wings, and in the rear of the Spaniards, harrassing them at every step. They encountered them in front with sudden darts, whenever the thickets enabled them to cover themselves readily from the cavalry. De Soto, maddening with every day's experience, with fever burning high in his temples, and uncicatrized wounds scalding him beneath his armor, grew more savage in his moods, and more and more persuaded himself that a Fate hung above his banner, which should finally swoop down in vengeance, burying it in blood forever. With such a superstition working in his soul, he was no longer the great Captain, who had won eminent position in arms, with a glory second not even to that of Cortes and Pizarro. He was now moody and capricious, unstable of resolve, changeable of purpose, without purpose in fact, and wandering, like a vagrant with his army, to and fro, as the winds blew and the waters ran.

At length they told him of a red man seen on horseback, even then in sight of the army, though at a distance.

"Ha!" he cried—"It is the Fate! He seeks me; we shall meet once more! we shall meet! we shall end it soon. Ha! Ha! now shall we see!"

And he bade them help buckle on his armor, and he rode forth at the head of his army, and lo! upon a little eminence, there stood the mounted warrior of the Apalachian, as if awaiting him.

"Now," cried De Soto to his followers—"Now, do ye keep

back, while ye see me transfix this insolent enemy—this Fate that haunts my footsteps to destroy—with but a single thrust of my good spear. Ho! Sant Iago, to the rescue!"

And with the famous slogan of Spanish battle, the maddened cavalier dashed forward to the assault.

Meanwhile, as the Spaniards clearly saw, the red warrior welcomed the encounter; for he waved his long lance aloft in the sunlight, and he, too, advanced as if glad to engage in the mortal struggle with the noble Castilian. But it was no part of the policy of the Spanish knights or soldiers to suffer the Adelantado to peril himself in single combat, in his present diseased and feeble state. Besides, they had seen the wonderful and unaccountable prowess which the red warrior had shown on horseback. They naturally concluded the one before them to be the same who had already overthrown their leader, and they began to share in the superstitions which he had taught them to respect. They dashed forward in a body to the support of De Soto, and, with their approach, the strange warrior of Apalachia melted from sight, man and horse, into the dim shadows of the impenetrable forest.

"Whither went he?" demanded the Adelantado. "Did the earth swallow him? Did ye see him ride away?"

"Verily," said one, "he disappeared as suddenly as he came! We saw not how! Perhaps into the forest."

"But had he not been a fiend from hell, could he have sped from sight unseen—unheard?"

The knights crossed themselves solemnly, and each muttered to himself a prayer.

"It is the Fate—*my* Fate!" exclaimed De Soto as they led him back; "but I shall cross weapon with him yet! Sant Iago against the Fiend, my friends! I will conquer mine enemy!"

Days passed; the Spaniards still pressed forward; still harassed by their sleepless enemies, and unable, with all their arts, to bring the wily red men to a general action. But De Soto was told of a fortress into which Chicaza, the Cassique, had thrown himself, upon the very borders of his province, and where he appeared preparing to defend himself. The news seemed to concentrate all the energies and purposes of De Soto. It gave him a definite purpose. The fortress was called Alabama, and stood upon the banks of the Yazoo river. The garrison was large. The fortress was strong and built like that of Mauvila. The Adelantado at once led his army against it; clouds of the red men, under Tuscaluza and Istalana, hanging upon his wings and rear. A terrible fight ensued; the infantry of the Spaniards assailing the fortress, while their cavalry was required to defend their rear against the forest rangers that hovered on their flanks. The Spaniards were again victorious, at the usual price of victory. They lost some twenty of their bravest soldiers. The loss of the red men was more severe, but not such as the superlatively extravagant chroniclers of their people would have us believe. In fact, the defence of the fortress was only one of those modes which the policy of the Apalachians taught them to employ, by which gradually to waste and exhaust the strength of the invaders. They did not expose themselves unnecessarily; those who fought without the fortress had the woods for a convenient shelter, with a thousand avenues open to their light-heeled rangers for flight, while they were almost impenetrable to the cavalry of their enemies. The garrison, on the other hand, when closely pressed on three sides of the fortress, simply leapt the river, and swam over to the other side. In this conflict, both De Soto and Philip de Vasconselos were again wounded, but neither severely. A snare was laid by the Spanish knights for taking the mysterious horseman of the Apalachians; but the plan was badly conceived, or badly managed. It was suspected, and Istalana fought on foot, with battle-axe and macana. Once he came nearly to blows with De Soto, and, but for the sudden fluctuations of the combat, would have succeeded in his efforts to do so. A press of knights suddenly threw a wall of iron and defensive spears between him and his prey, and he was baffled. The red men melted away from before the Spaniards, even as the morning mists before the sun, satisfied with what was done, and leaving to their enemies but a barren conquest.

The event of this battle was to confirm De Soto in the bitterness of his moods, and that strange phrenzy—not, however, unnatural—which had taken possession of his brain. He was a terribly stricken man, and his mind frequently wandered, while his frame seemed no longer capable of that hardy endurance; was certainly no longer seen to exhibit that elastic energy, which had hitherto distinguished it in every progress. But still he pressed his people forward, heedless whither, except that he always religiously strove to leave the sea behind him. He dared not contemplate the sea. He dared not move the heads of his columns in that direction, lest he should so madden his followers as to be unable to control their future course. They had too fully shown him the lingering passion in their hearts to return; and this return was what his pride could not contemplate. Failing to conquer as he had promised, he preferred to bury his fortunes and his shame together in the depths of the wilderness. He was a fine example of the terrible selfishness of ambition.

The erratic progress of De Soto at length brought him to the banks of the Mississippi. His was the first European eye, according to the authentic history in our possession, which ever beheld the vast, turbid and wondrous streams of the "Father of Waters." De Soto gazed upon them with but little interest. He dreamed not of the glorious territories which they watered. He saw not, through the boundless vistas of the future, the numerous tribes who should dwell upon their prolific borders crowning them with the noblest evidences of life, and with the loveliest arts of civilization. The spirit of the Adelantado was crushed. The fires of ambition were quenched in his bosom. His heart was withered: his hope was blasted forever. He was now a dying man; not exactly a maniac, but with a mind ill at ease, disordered, vacant, capricious; striving with itself: weary, and longing only for the one blessing, which he had never suffered himself to enjoy;—Peace! His heart did not exactly crave a restoration to his home in Cuba, but the image of the noble woman, his wife, rose frequently, reproachful in his sight. He had loved her, as fervently as he could have loved any woman; but, in the ambitious soul, love is a very tributary passion. It craves love, but accords little in return. Its true passion is glory!

We have foreborne a thousand details of strife, anxiety, dread and suffering, which the Spaniards were doomed to experience before they reached the Mississippi. They were haunted by the perpetual terrors of the Apalachians. Tuscaluza and his Portuguese Lieutenant Istalana gave them no respite. They crossed the Mississippi. They penetrated the country of the Kaskaskias, and still they were under the eye and the influence of the Great King of the Apalachians. The terrors of his name met them on every side. The powers of his arm smote them in all their progresses. "The Fate! The haunting and pursuing Fate! Oh! Philip de Vasconselos!" cried De Soto to himself—"thou art terribly avenged. Would that we could meet, mine enemy! would that, alone, we stood naked, front to front, on the borders of this great heathen river, spear to spear, and none to come between. Then, then! Thy spear or mine! Thy fate or mine! I have wronged thee, Philip de Vasconselos, but I should slay thee nevertheless. Verily, thou art terribly avenged. I have wronged thee, but what had these done to thee, thy christian brethren, that thou should'st decree their destruction also? Yet thou shalt not!

Sant Iago! there shall come an hour when thou shalt be delivered nto my hands."

The griefs, the sufferings of De Soto prompted a revival of his religious enthusiasm. He commanded that a pine of gigantic height should be hewn into the form of a cross. He had it planted with solemn ceremonials upon the banks of the stream, and consecrated its inauguration with great solemnity, and with propitiatory sacrifices. His secret thought was to persuade the blessing influences to resist and defeat the terrors of that fien l,— that Fate,—with which he now believed himself to be pursued. Thus then, more than three hundred years ago, the emblem of Christian faith towered above the Father of Waters, and Christian rites consecrated his mighty billows as they hurried with glad tidings to the sea.

But these solemn ceremonials compelled no friendly auguries. The further marches of De Soto only brought him to the bloody embrace of newer enemies. How the arms and influence of the Apalachians pursued him wherever he sped—how they roused against him the warriors of Capaha, Tula and other tribes ; what were the combats, what the losses, the surprises, the fears, the sufferings of the Spaniards, in their daily progresses, may be faintly gathered from their own meagre chronicles. Incessant strifes, sleepless nights, weary marches, wounds and toil, these, with final mutiny among his own followers, utterly broke down the soul of De Soto, and took from him all his strength. Let it suffice that the noble Castilian at last consented to retrace his steps. The decision came too late for his own safety. But he despatched a small force, following the great river, with the hope to find the sea at no great distance. Meanwhile, warring at every step with new enemies, De Soto planted himself at length at a village which he had captured, called Guachoya, on the western banks of the Mississippi. Here he prepared to build brigantines, and make his way out of a country in which death hunted forever at his heels, and an angry Fate welcomed, with a constant defeat of hope, wherever he ventured to plant his footsteps

CHAPTER L.

> "Last scene of all
> That ends this strange eventful history."
> SHAKSPEARE.

Our previous narrative of events has brought us to the opening of the summer of the year 1542. We have reached the melancholy close of all those glorious prospects, and triumphant hopes, with which Hernando de Soto left the shores of Cuba, for the country of the savage Apalachian. He was a subdued and broken-hearted man; humbled in spirit, mortified in pride, ruined in fortune. He had survived all his hopes. Despair had taken possession of his soul. To crown his misery, physical suffering was superadded to his griefs of mind, and wounds, and travail, fatigue and fever, had combined to prostrate the iron frame of him, who, in the pride of muscular vigor, had never dreamed that any toil or trial should have forced him to succumb. Nothing short of this utter prostration of his physical strength and energies, would ever have compelled him to yield the point to Fate—would ever have moved him to listen to the entreaties of his followers—now urged with a stern resolution that would no longer brook denial, to turn back from the forests to the sea, and endeavor once more, to regain the shores of that beautiful island, which, even the proud spirit of De Soto himself, bemoaned in secret, with a fond and fearful anxiety. On the banks of the vast and lonely Mississippi, occupying the Indian village of Guachoya, the Adelantado gave his orders for the construction of a couple of brigantines, such as would enable him to seek the sea.

His people set themselves to this work, with the eagerness of men, to whom the fruition of all their hopes is promised. While bodies of them were engaged felling and seasoning timber, others scoured the country, seeking adventures and provisions; and above all, to prevent the too near approach of the swarming hordes of red men, by whom, ever since their approach to the territories of Tuscaluza, their fortunes had been followed. That Fate, as De Soto himself esteemed it—which had hung upon their steps and striven against them, with a bitter hostility from the moment when Vasconselos was lost to the Castilian columns, and Istalana suddenly sprang into existence, as the leader of those of the Apalachian, was still present, still a haunting terror, still making itself felt unseen, still cutting off detachments, striking at posts, beating up the bivouac, carrying off, or smiting down, the straggler, and shewing itself as resolute as before, in its evident purpose to root out and utterly destroy the invaders. Tuscaluza's power and influence were everywhere brought to serve this Fate and promote this terrible purpose. His runners traversed the whole country, passing from tribe to tribe, bringing tidings of the Spaniards where they came; of their bloody character, selfish treachery, the power of their arms, the grasping ferocity of their desires. The Captains of Tuscaluza presented themselves as volunteers in the conduct of remote tribes. His troops, as principals or auxiliaries, were to be found carrying the banner of the Great King; with its bright ground of yellow, and its three broad stripes of blue; a sign that now waved ominously in the eyes of our Adelantado, whenever it appeared. It had been to him the omen of evil always, and he trembled in his secret soul when he beheld it. He associated it ever with the aspect of that mysterious warrior of the red men—mysterious to his followers, but too well known to himself, by whom he had been overthrown in single combat! That overthrow rankled in his soul, but it also tended to disarm his spirit. De Soto was cowed by his Fate! The forest chieftains sent him insolent messages, defying his arms and challenging him to combat. Once, and such defiance would have spurred him to the most desperate achievement! Now, he suffered it to go unheeded. Like a tiger, with broken limb, he lay crouching in his lair, full of venom, but without the power to spring upon his victim. The Adelantado was sinking beneath his cares, growing daily worse and worse, more morbid of mind, more feeble of body. His ferocity subsided into melancholy. A fever preyed upon his blood, and affected without exciting his brain. His physician at length despaired. He himself had despaired some time before. But the doom was, as yet, withheld from his people.

Meanwhile, the work of the brigantines was rapidly pressing forward, under the eager anxieties of the Spaniards to leave the inhospitable territories of the Apalachian. While companies hewed timber, others gathered rosin from the trees; others again wove ropes and wrought cordage out of vines and mosses; a third division was employed for foraging; while a fourth was kept in hand, vigilant and ready, for the protection of the camp. So long as De Soto, himself, could give orders, or take any interest in the business of the garrison, its vigilance was never once permitted to relax. Guachoya was not, like Mauvila, a fortified town, and the scattered dwellings of the place, required to be well watched. De Soto, to his usual habits of precaution, had, of late, adopted others of an extreme sort, betraying a morbid apprehension of danger. His sentinels were doubled; each night his cavalry mounted guard in the suburbs of the village, bridle in hand, and ready for the sally or defence. A patrol of troops alternated, during the night, between the several stations; while, along the river, cross-bowmen in canoes kept vigilant watch upon all approaches from the opposite shores.

But this vigilance was observed only while De Soto was himself able to assert his authority. With his increasing illness, all this organization fell to pieces. The extra sentinels were dispensed with; the cavalry found it hard to mount guard during the night, when they had probably been on a foray all day; the troopers finding there were no alarms, gave up patrolling; the cross-bowmen fell asleep in the canoes. The Spaniards were now steadfast only in the labor of building their brigantines; and all duties that seemed to interfere with the prosecution of this work, were, either in part, or entirely foregone. Gradually, as the heats of summer began to prevail, all toils in the sun were relaxed. The forbearance of the red men, for several weeks, had persuaded the Spaniards that they had endured the worst of their dangers from this source. They little knew how much of this forbearance they owed to that person, who had grown into the embodied Fate of their great leader; and to whose agency, in especial, he ascribed the defeat of his enterprise and the destruction of his fortunes.

Philip de Vasconselos—the Cassique Istalana,—who had now the entire charge of the forces of Tuscaluza on the Mississippi—seeing how the Spaniards were engaged in the construction of their brigantines, readily divined their object. He had no motive to prevent their departure, and, consequently no desire to embarrass them in their progress. Still, there was one hostile feeling, the gratification of which he had not enjoyed. His revenge was incomplete. Could he have separated the Spaniards from their Captain—could he have struck at *him*—*him* and *another*—there had been nothing left him to desire! He well knew that through him De Soto had been baffled—that he was a subdued and broken-hearted man; but it must be confessed that he still yearned for the opportunity to bring the long issue between them, to the final settlement of blood! This was the black spot in the soul of the Portuguese Cavalier.

It was a warm and sunny afternoon of summer. The Spaniards might be seen in groups along the shore, strolling through the camp, or fishing along the river in canoes. They little suspected the near neighborhood of the mysterious warrior, who could manage the war horse as bravely as themselves. He occupied a close fortress of forest in the immediate proximity of the camp. A bend of the river at Guachoya, somewhat isolated the spot. It was a sort of promontory. An arm of the river penetrated, to some distance, in the rear of the village. This was thickly shrouded with canes, and the dense thickets natural to a swamp precinct.

Here Istalana found shelt... ith a select body of his warriors. Here he kept sleepless watch upon the movements of the uns ispecting Spaniards. With canoes always at hand, he crossed from side to side at pleasure; and was thus enabled to change the place of surveillance whenever he thought proper to do so. He now harbors in the shadow of great trees which have pressed closely to the banks of the river, their boughs hanging over and dipping into the mighty stream. Here, in the great shadows, Istalana lies at length along the slope; and the Princess Coçalla sits beside him; and the page Juan leans sadly against a gigantic cotton-wood tree in the rear, and looks gloomily upon the pair before him!

Vasconselos has been for some time silent,—deep in thought. He has occasionally answered, but in monosyllables only, to the questions of Coçalla. She has been very curious about that world beyond the waters, which could send for h, without feeling his loss, such a noble creature as the warrior whom she now boldly calls her own! Juan has been listening with heedful and curious ear also; but with growing sullenness of aspect. Suddenly Vasconselos rises. He approaches Juan, and, speaking rather in the manner of one who soliloquizes than asks a question, remarks:

"Verily there is one thing that troubles me. I have striven in vain to encounter one bitter enemy, one foul spirit, in that Spanish host; and always in vain! I have watched for him whenever they have been upon the march. I have sought for him through all the ranks of battle; yet never, since the fearful hour when his bitter malice wrought my disgrace, have I been able to see his accursed visage, or bring him within the stroke of my weapon! Yet are his colors still visible among yonder people. Still do I see his banneret waving aloft, when they are upon the march, and I trow he hath never left the expedition Were he to escape me now, I should feel as if nothing had been done for my own revenge;—nothing for the repair of his brutal wrong to one,—but no, I must not speak of her!"

"Of whom does the Señor speak!" demanded Juan. "What bitter enemy is this?"

"Of one, boy, of whom we have both had frequent cause of

anger and suspicion. Don Balthazar de Alvaro! Have you seen ought of *him* since we have followed the fortunes of the red men?"

"Had I known, my Lord, that such had been thy quest, in especial, I had spared thee much search and unnecessary peril. The Señor Balthazar was slain the very night upon which I fled, in search of thee, from the camp at Chiaha."

"Ha! slain! slain!—and why did'st thou tell me nothing of this?"

"The Señor will remember how little hath been said between us, safe from other ears, since that time."

And the page looked gloomily in the direction of Coçalla. Verily, the page had been suffered but few opportunities to commune with his master.

"And wherefore thy reserve of speech in the hearing of the Princess? She hath no reserves from us. She is faithful, boy: what hadst thou to fear?"

"Fear, Señor!"

The words and manner were those of one who would rather say—

"What had I *not* to fear?"

"Ay, fear! But speak, Juan, and tell me how the villain perished! Thou sayst the very night when thou hadst that perilous and maddening ride in search of me?"

"Even then Señor; that very night!"

"And how?—was it in sudden strife with the red men, that he perished?"

"No, Señor."

"Well?"

"He died of dagger stroke, Señor,—dagger stroke from some unknown hand!"

"Ha! dagger stroke, and from unknown hand! Speak, boy, tell me all that thou knowst. Where did this hap? and how knowst *thou* that he who gave the blow was unknown? tell me that!"

The lips of the page quivered. He cast his eyes upon the ground. He was silent. Thronging memories and violent emotions seem to confound his speech, and to shake his frame. Philip beheld his emotion, and a new light seemed to gather before his senses.

"What troubles thee, Juan? What hadst thou to do in this matter? Ha! the night thou fledst; that fearful flight of thine! Speak, boy, tell me *where* was the blow given; *where* did Balthazar de Alvaro fall?"

It required a great effort of the page to articulate the answer.

"It was in the chamber of thy own lodge, Señor, that Don Balthazar was slain."

"And thou wert there—present—and beheldst it all! Boy, boy! was it *thy* hand that struck the blow at the heart of mine enemy?"

The boy nodded the answer that he could not speak.

"What! then thou wast my avenger on that base and brutal wretch!"

"And mine own too!" was the half muttered sentence of the page. But Philip did not hear. He caught the boy in his embrace.

"I thank thee, boy; next to mine own, it was perhaps most proper for thy hand to do the deed! Yet would it had been mine own! Enough! I must think no more of him. Then is this no more a duty in my thought!"

He released Juan from his embrace as he felt the hand of Coçalla upon his shoulder, and heard her voice in soft murmurs in his ears.

"Philip—is Philip angry with Coçalla!"

Juan broke away from the group at this moment, and buried himself in the thicket, with a heart quite too full for speech.

"Philip! Philip!" the boy murmured ever as he fled from sight.

"One yet remains!" quoth Philip de Vasconselos to himself. "One yet remains! There is a mystery here! I see *him* not. Nuno de Tobar hath crossed the river with his lances: Andres, my brother, hath gone above with his company. Who is now in command? De Soto doth not show himself. *He* must not escape me also! No arm shall deal with him but mine! Yet have I resolved not to set upon the Spaniards again. My vengeance now must light upon the only proper head. Never must *he* return to Cuba; though well I know that it will prove to him a pang worse than any death I can give, to have the eyes of Cuba set upon him now;—now, when all his hopes are baffled, when his pride is humbled, his fortune lost, his honor gone forever. Oh! I *have* tasted of the bitter-sweet of vengeance; but it is not enough! Hernan De Soto, I tell thee, it is not enough! Thy blood or mine, I tell thee!"

He shook his hand threateningly towards the Spanish camp, then strode towards the edge of the creek which divided him from the lodges of Guachoya. Here he leapt into a canoe having a single paddle. He was seen by several of the red men as he went; Juan also saw and followed him. He rowed himself rapidly across the creek, and stood upon the opposite bank, at no great distance from the line of lodges which the Spaniards occupied.

All was quiet in the encampment. Groups of the soldiers and workmen could be seen in the distance, along the banks of the river. An occasional figure wound his way along the public thoroughfares. The approach to the cabins was partly covered by trees: but beneath them not a single sentinel could be seen. Philip eagerly pushed forward, but with the subtle stealthiness of the red man, and taking care always to cover his person from sight. How was the page, Juan, astonished, when, crossing the creek as rapidly as he could after his lord, and ascending also to the level of the high ground leading to the Spanish camp, he beheld the Knight entering one of the lodges of the enemy!

At that moment, he was called to by name from some one in the rear. He looked back. Coçalla had crossed also; bow and arrow in hand, and her face and voice equally declaring her alarm. She was followed by several well manned canoes. Very hateful was the beautiful and loving Coçalla in the eyes of the page. He never answered her call, but, as if vexed by her presence and pursuit, he too pushed forward, in the direction which his lord had taken, seeming quite reckless of the peril which he ran.

Hernan De Soto, a mere skeleton of himself, lay weak, emaciated, weary of life, upon his bed of death! He was alone—he had been left to sleep by his attendants who had withdrawn to an outer apartment. The building was one of those great odges of the red men, which were capable upon occasion of holding a thousand men. It had been divided by the Spaniards into several compartments by the employment of quilted stuffs, hides of wild beasts, and of their own horses, and mattings wrought by Indian art from native grasses and the bright yellow reeds which grew along the banks, woven together with wild oziers which were every where found in great abundance. The couch of De Soto was prepared of like materials, over which soft dry rushes were strewn in sufficient quantity. The lodges, thus divided, as we have described, afforded several capacious chambers; the best of which, fronting the south west, was occupied by De Soto, but having in front of it a verandah which had been carefully enclosed with vines and mats, in order to the exclusion of the fierce glare of the sunshine. In this verandah, lay drowsing a group of his attendants; others were wont to occupy the chamber immediately adjoining, which lay east of that of De Soto, while one upon the north, was usually confided to his body guard, a corps now reduced to half a dozen men. These, the better to prevent the disturbance of the Chieftain's slumbers, had been commanded to leave vacant this northern chamber, and retire to the verandah beyond it. Here they usually kept watch. But, after a little while, it was found that when they were not drowsing in the verandah, they were at play in the court without. Here they lay upon the long grasses, and, spreading a cloak or skin, with the smooth side upward, they rolled the dice, to the perpetual change, equally of mood and fortune. To pass from court to court, from the north to the south, was a next and natural transition; and in the languid influence of the climate, and in the utter freedom for some weeks from all alarm, the Spaniards relaxed all their vigilance, and soon—he himself totally unconscious—the dying Adelantado grew to be even less guarded than the camp itself.

Such was the condition of the scene the evening when we find Philip de Vasconselos making his entrance into it unattended—without shows or sounds of war—without followers; himself armed only with battle-axe and dagger. Nothing, of course, could take place within the Spanish encampment, which was not well known to the vigilant red men who watched it sleeplessly by day and night. The very lodgings of the several Spanish capta'ns had all been discovered by their spies. The lodge which De Soto occupied, was, from its greater size and superior structure—it having been that of the Cassique of Guachoya—necessarily indicated as the one most proper for the Spanish adelantado. Vasconselos approached it with direct aim and undeviating footstep Saving the natural caution which he observed, covering himself with tree or shrub, wherever he could employ them while making his approach,—he went not once aside from the single object. The circumstances all favored his enterprise. The guards were withdrawn. They might be seen in the shadows of the trees in the court yard, on the South and West. Some loitered in the Eastern court, others lay along the banks of the river, looking to the south-west. The north and north-west showed no sign of human being. Yet there, in the woods of the swamp opposite, lay hosts of the red men of the Apalachian. It was from this quarter that Istalana stole forward to the camp. In his course, he caught frequent glimpses of the drowsy Spaniards. There were groups at cards and dice. A score of them lay in the shadows of the brigantines which they had been working upon during the cooler portions of the day. Now they slept, or gamed, or wandered in the shady thickets—they did anything but watch. They left this duty to the foragers, who, under several of the most active knights, usually made a daily progress over a circuit of ten or fifteen miles along the higher country, and, thus scouring it daily, persuaded themselves that they kept the danger at a distance. It would have been easy to have darted in upon the camp, thus loosely guarded, destroyed the growth of the brigantines, and cut off, at one fell swoop, the entire garrison, with its once brilliant captain. But the soul of Philip de Vasconselos, even while it nursed fondly the passion for a great revenge, was not prepared to fall upon the people with whom he had so long marched as a companion. He found it easy to persuade the Great King to consent to the wiser policy of suffering the Spaniards to depart, rather than to risk the lives of thousands more of the red men, in the effort at their violent extermination by battle. Tuscaluza had lost so many of his bravest warriors already, that he listened to the counsel thus given him, and the war, thenceforth, was conducted at the discretion of Istalana.

But Philip de Vasconselos demanded his one victim. Had he been able to see Hernan de Soto, in field or camp, he might have curbed his passion until the opportunity should offer of cutting him off when but few troops should be engaged on either side. Not seeing him for so long a space, he began to apprehend that he, too, might have fallen in battle, or by disease, and had been buried secretly by his followers, who naturally dreaded lest the red men should wreak their savage fury on his remains, should they be discovered. Curious to ascertain the truth, eager to pacify his great revenge, Vasconselos could no longer forbear the inquiry, though urged at the peril of his own life and liberty.

Circumstances, as we have shown, favored his adventure. There were no guards in attendance; there was no watch about the lodge of De Soto, and though certain esquires occupied the closed verandah upon the south-west, whom Philip could not see, and whose presence he did not suspect, yet were these as little prepared for danger, or assault, as were the several groups that lay in the shadows of the trees, and brigantines, or who loitered among the broad avenues of the woods. The greater body of the Spaniards in camp, were distributed among the several lodges, either gaming, or enjoying that repose which the heats of the season began to render exceedingly grateful, after several hours of labor in the sun. A deep silence overspread the dwelling in which De Soto was sighing away his life, when Vasconselos passed between its portals. He had been utterly unseen. He paused in the ante-chamber, on the northern side of the building, and listened. Sounds, as of a slight moaning, came to him from the inner apartment. He drew aside the great bear-skin which constituted the door-way, and advanced silently within the dim shadows of the room. His moccasined footstep gave forth no sound. The moaning continued. De Soto slept imperfectly,— the sleep of exhaustion, and of approaching death.

Philip approached his bed-side, and gazed upon the bleached and bloodless features of him whom he had seen in his hour of pride and hope,—exulting in all the vigor of manhood,—and in the indulgence of the most exulting hope, and the most eagle-eyed ambition. His hand grasped the battle-axe, but the spectacle disarmed his rage. He was chilled by the survey. For several moments, he gazed in silence upon the foe, whom he had so long destined as the one victim whose death alone could pacify his rage. He now scarcely felt this emotion.

"And this then," he murmured to himself—" this is the brilliant cavalier, the haughty warrior, the proud chieftain, the insolent and ambitious Castilian. This is the man by whose decree I was dishonored—made to face and to endure a terror worse than death—destroyed in hope—degraded from position, dishonored in the sight of man forever. Verily, I would give the life that I have passed when life was a joy and every emotion promised delight and triumph,—could I once more behold thee, Hernan de Soto,—as I have seen thee so oft,—as thou look'dst on that terrible day, when thy doom gave my honor to disgrace, and left me to the horrors of a beast's death in the wilderness of the Apalachian!"

The lips of the dying man parted, even as he slept, speaking in feeble accents.

"Philip de Vasconselos," he murmured faintly, but still intelligibly, "give me back my forces. Philip de Vasconselos, thou hast robbed me of all my fame. Thou hast destroyed me forever, in hope and fortune. Oh! that I had thee here, and no arm to interpose between us, with weapon bared, and thy life and mine upon the issue!"

"Ha! he invokes me in his dream!"

"Thou art my Fate!" murmured the sleeper. "Thou hast robbed me of all! Oh! that I could have thee in mine eyes once more, and avenge upon thee the slaughter of my soldiers."

"Open thine eyes, Hernan de Soto!" cried Vasconselos. "Behold! I am with thee—The Fate thou hast summoned. Would to Heaven thou wert as fit and ready for the strife as I."

He laid his hand upon the skinny arm of the sleeper as he spoke, and the eyes of the dying chief opened upon him. Very glassy was the gaze they sent forth; for a while, very meaningless and uncertain. But, as the light of consciousness gradually dawned upon his mind, the gaze quickened with intelligence.

"Ha!" he said—"I dream! I do not see!"

"Thou dost see, Hernan de Soto! thou dost not dream. The Fate thou hast challenged is beside thee."

"Ha! then! It is true. Thou art here. Ah! wilt thou strike when I have no weapon. Let me but prepare for thee, Philip de Vasconselos, by the Holy Virgin, thou shalt see what is the prowess of a true man, against the bosom of the renegade and traitor!"

And the feeble chieftain lifted his hand and pointed to his armor hanging against the wall, and motioned as if he would have risen; but he sank back feebly and shut his eyes, murmuring—

"Be it as thou wilt! strike, if thou hast the heart for it! I have no prayer to offer to thee, traitor as thou art."

"That word alone should doom thee to sudden blow, Hernan de Soto," answered the Knight with stern emphasis, "but I will not strike thee. I will lay no hand upon thee now in anger. There is a more powerful grasp upon thee than any I can lay. Thou art in the hands of the great master of life, and I will do nothing more against thee. Yet, Heaven be my witness, de Soto, if I would not gladly help thee to thy armor, and see thee once more put on all thy strength, while I stood before thee, with battle-axe, armed as now, and thou with any weapon or armor that thou wouldst, with none to come between us, and thy life and mine decreed to hang upon the justice of our cause. Traitor! Who made me a traitor, if I be one? Who robbed me of my rights, my good name, my honors and my manhood? Who drove me into the arms of the red men,—who despoiled me of my abode, and security among a christian people? Who but thou? and it is thou that darest now, with the hand of death upon thee, and the dread of eternal judgment staring thee in the face—thou, to call me traitor! It is thou, I tell thee, Hernan de Soto, that art the traitor and the criminal! Thou that hast dishonored the noble order of knighthood by dishonest judgment; thou that didst debase thee from the rank of the gentle and the noble, in becoming the tool and the slave of the cunning criminal, who warped thee to his villanous purpose, making of thy soul a thing even fouler than his own!"

"Ha! shall I submit to this insolence!" answered De Soto in louder accents. His soul, goaded by the speech of Vasconselos, became aroused for the moment. There was a sudden lighting up of the fires in his eye and bosom. Nature, nerved by indignation, put on the appearance of sudden strength.

"Shall I listen to this foul-mouthed renegade!" he exclaimed in still louder accents; and, with the words, half rising from his couch, he stretched his arm out suddenly, and with unexpected vigor, the last fierce energetic action of expiring nature, he grasped the throat of Vasconselos, crying aloud the while—

"What, ho! without there! Guards, soldiers. Castilians, seize on the traitor. Help, that I may secure this renegade."

Vasconselos shook off his grasp with ease, and the dying Adelantado sank back upon the couch. The fire was exhausted in the single expiring blaze. The momentary ebullition was over. The effort was fatal. His eyes were suddenly glazed, the spasmodic gasping declared the agonies of death.

"A Dios!" exclaimed Vasconselos, pointing upward. De Soto lay before him a corse.

For a moment, the Portugese cavalier contemplated the rigid features of his enemy—the unconscious glare of his widely staring eyes. But, suddenly, he started, battle-axe in his grasp, and strode across the chamber. There was a noise of armor in the southern verandah. There was heard the tread of heavy and hurrying feet in the chamber which lay between. De Soto's dying summons had been heard by his drowsing attendants, and they were approaching. Vasconselos lifted the bearskin, closing the entrance from the northern chamber, and passed through, just as a couple of the squires of De Soto entered from the opposite chamber. He passed without interruption through the northern apartments, through the verandah unseen, gained the court, and sped with swift foot-steps, but only in a walk, towards the forest cover whence he emerged. Suddenly, a wild cry, a shout of mixed fury and horror, was heard to arise behind him. He looked backward: a group of Spaniards was seen to rush from the quarters of De Soto. They cried to other groups in the squares, and, as they shouted their anger and alarm, the instinctive defiance in the heart of Vasconselos, prompted the fierce war-whoop with which he replied to them in the manner of the red men.

There was pursuit; but Vasconselos did not increase his speed. His soul was at its full stature, and he disdained to have recourse for safety to the eager paces of the fugitive. He strode onward with the gait of one who would rather welcome than escape the danger. Nor did he need to hasten, unless to escape the bolt or the shot of his pursuer. He was so fairly beyond them that they could not have made him captive; could not have crossed weapon with his own; and the river swamp was nigh, on the edge of which lay his canoe.

At that moment, the voice of Juan was heard behind him, crying aloud,

"Hasten, Señor Philip—hasten my lord, they prepare to shoot."

He turned with surprise, in the direction whence the sounds arose, much wondering to perceive the boy behind him; when, even at that instant, the bolt was delivered from the cross-bow of one of the Spaniards, and he beheld the boy, as he threw himself directly upon his path. The next instant he saw Juan roll over upon the sward, with the arrow quivering in his bosom. The boy had thrown off his armour of escaupil, as most of the red men had done in that warm season, and not expecting strife; and in his jacket of thin, unquilted cotton, the deadly shaft had met with no resistance.

With a deep cry of sincere sorrow, Vasconselos darted backward to where the boy lay upon the strand. To gather him up in his powerful arms, and hurry with him down the slope, to the canoe, was the work of a few moments only. As he reached the shore, he heard the voice of Coçalla, crying—

"Hither, Philip, hither! Here is a great canoe."

He followed the sounds, and safely entered the canoe with his speechless burden. The rowers bent to their task, the boat shot through the reedy thicket, and had nearly reached the opposite shore, when a crowd of Spaniards, all armed with arquebuse and cross-bow, appeared along the margin of the shore which they had left. There were shots sent after the fugitives, bullet and arrow, but with hurried aim,—they were delivered fruitlessly; and while a thousand of the red men answered with their fearful whoops, the shouts and threats of the Spaniards, the canoe of Coçalla shot safely into cover, in a lagune hidden from all sight by the dense thickets of its reedy shore.

In a green lodge by the river side, they laid the insensible form of Juan, the page, upon a bank of rushes; and Philip de Vasconselos, with a grievous sadness at his heart—for he saw that the wound of the boy was mortal—proceeded tenderly to withdraw the deadly shaft from his bosom, where it was deeply lodged. But, at the very first effort, when it became necessary to tear open the vest of the boy, his eyes opened, and he raised his hands, and pressed down his garments, and murmured that they should desist. But in this effort he again fainted: and while he was thus unconscious, Philip de Vasconselos cut the strings which secured the jacket of the boy in front, and lo, when he had opened the garment, the white skin beneath, and the full, round, white bosom of a woman. "Ha! Philip!" cried Coçalla, who had assisted the knight in his effort; "ha! Philip! it is a daughter of the pale faces. It is one of your people. It is a woman who hath followed Philip to the battle."

And Philip greatly wondered, as much at his own blind ignorance, which had kept him so long in darkness, as at the strange revelation, the secret of which he now comprehended in a moment.

"Holy Maria!" he exclaimed. "Holy Maria!" and the eyes of the page again unclosed; and she now knew what had been done, and what had been discovered; and she sighed deeply, and the tears gathered into her eyes, and she strove to cover them with her hands. Then the knight said—

"My poor Olivia! is it thou?"

And she murmured—

"Wilt thou forgive me, Señor?"

"Forgive! what have I to forgive?"

And the child again wept, and her sobs were long and deep; and while she sobbed, the knight tenderly withdrew the barbed arrow from the wound; and though he strove to save her from pain, yet the agony was very great, and again she fainted. But the blood issued freely from the wound, and when they strove to staunch it, her eyes once more opened to the light, and she saw that it was Coçalla who was busy about her, to stay the bleeding and to bind up the wound; and with a sharp word she pushed her away, and tore off the bandages. Then Philip interposed and she lay silent, as he strove to do for her that which she had denied should be done by Coçalla. But though the knight bound up the hurt, and strove, with the help of liniments and styptics which the red men knew well how to use, yet was all his care in vain, for the wound bled inwardly, and they soon beheld that the hurt was mortal, and that the life was fast ebbing out of the sweet fountain which it had warmed with such fidelity, and made to glow with so much passion, and such feminine devotion; and the girl murmured to Philip, speaking of Coçalla—

"Let her go hence for a while, Señor. I have that to show thee, to say to thee, which should have no ears but thine own."

And Philip whispered Coçalla away, and Olivia de Alvaros said—

"It is well. Now, Philip, that I am about to lose thee, let me tell thee how much I love thee."

"Alas!" he said, "my poor Olivia, it needs not. Know I not now?"

And she answered—

"But thou knowest not that I am innocent of wrong doing, Philip, and this is what I would show thee."

She spoke but little more, but of this she was most eager to speak. And she bade him look into her jacket of escaupil, where a packet had been sewn up, which should teach him all her cruel history; how she had been wronged, but how she was innocent; how she had been dishonored, but how she was an unwilling and unconscious victim to the base and cruel arts of her brutal kinsman. In this packet thus delivered, he read the terrible history of her griefs, even as we have already delivered it. But he did not read until she was no more.

She died in the arms of Philip; but she bade that Coçalla should turn away her face, and leave the spot, ere the parting moment came. Then she bade that Philip should lift her from the rushes; and when he did so, she threw her arms about his neck, and laid her head upon his bosom, and so her pure and suffering spirit went, with a sweet sigh, and a fond embrace, the memory of which, in long years after, sweetened greatly the solitude to the heart of the knight of Portugal. They buried her, in the great solitudes of the Mississippi, under the shades of many guardian trees, and the river rolls ever along with a deep murmur near the hallowed spot, as if it sang fond anthems for the repose of a troubled soul.

Midnight, and there was a solemn stir in the Spanish encampment. There was a roll of martial music, and the wail of solemn voices, as they sang the awful dirge of death over the remains of the once mighty Adelantado, Hernan de Soto. Then, in the deepening darkness of the night, they placed the corse of the Adelantado in the core of a green pine-tree, which had been hollowed out to receive it, and, nailing over this a cover of heavy plank, they towed it from the shore, under an escort of a hundred canoes, to the centre of the river, and there, with a solemn service, they consigned it to a bed beneath the great stream, sinking it deeply lest the avenging red men should possess themselves of the corse of him who had wrought them so much evil while he lived, and wreak upon his unconscious frame the fury which possessed their souls against him.

But Philip de Vasconselos, who beheld the scene, and readily divined the nature of the solemn service, would not suffer his warriors to disturb its progress; and from the banks of the river, in the darkness of the night, his eye watched, and his soul brooded gloomily over the close of De Soto's career, and he reflected upon the strangeness of that ambitious fortune, which should have found, in all its wild career, nothing so wonderful as the river which became the burial-place of the hero. Nor, when De Soto was thus consigned to his last repose, did Philip suffer that the Spaniards should be troubled by his followers. He saw them depart in their brigantines, following the flowings of the Mississippi in its passage to the sea, and, when one of the vessels bearing the banner of his brother Andres glided down the stream, beneath the banks upon which he stood, as it went by, he cried audibly—

"Farewell to thee, my brother; fare thee well, Andres de Vasconselos; farewell for ever!"

And the Spaniards went from sight; and in due season, after many strifes and trials, did they reach their homes. But Philip, leading his warriors back to the great king, Tuscaluza, turned away once more toward the mountains of the Apalachian; and when he had left the territory of Tuscaluza, and once more got back to that of Cofachiqui—and when the warriors of Cofachiqui once more assembled with greetings and songs of welcome about their princess, the well-beloved Coçalla—then did that noble creature lay her hands upon the shoulder of the knight and say—

"Philip is now the great chief, the well-beloved of the people of Cofachiqui!"

And the knight smiled with a sweet sadness upon the dusky princess, as they passed into the great thickets leading to the ancient village, where the two first met, on the banks of the Savannah. And how the heart of the woman gladdened, when at last, in reply to her frequent murmur of the name of Philip, he answered with that of Coçalla!

www.ingramcontent.com/pod-product-compliance
Lightning Source LLC
Chambersburg PA
CBHW031947290426
44108CB00011B/715